RIGHT STAR RISING

ALSO BY LAURA KALMAN

Yale Law School and the Sixties: Revolt and Reverberations

The Strange Career of Legal Liberalism

Abe Fortas: A Biography

Legal Realism at Yale, 1927–1960

W. W. NORTON & COMPANY
NEW YORK LONDON

RIGHT STAR RISING

A NEW POLITICS,

1974–1980

LAURA KALMAN

Printed in the United States of America
First Edition

Manufacturing by RR Donnelley, Harrisonburg
Book design by Barbara Bachman
Production manager: Julia Druskin

Library of Congress Cataloging-in-Publication Data

Kalman, Laura, 1955–
Right star rising : a new politics, 1974-1980 / Laura Kalman. — 1st ed.
p. cm.
Includes bibliographical references and index.
ISBN 978-0-393-07638-7 (acid-free paper)
1. United States—Politics and government—1974–1977.
2. United States—Politics and government—1977–1981.
3. Conservatism—United States—History—20th century. I. Title.
E839.5.K35 2010
973.925—dc22
2010004814

W. W. Norton & Company, Inc.
500 Fifth Avenue, New York, N.Y. 10110
www.wwnorton.com

W. W. Norton & Company Ltd.
Castle House, 75/76 Wells Street, London W1T 3QT

1 2 3 4 5 6 7 8 9 0

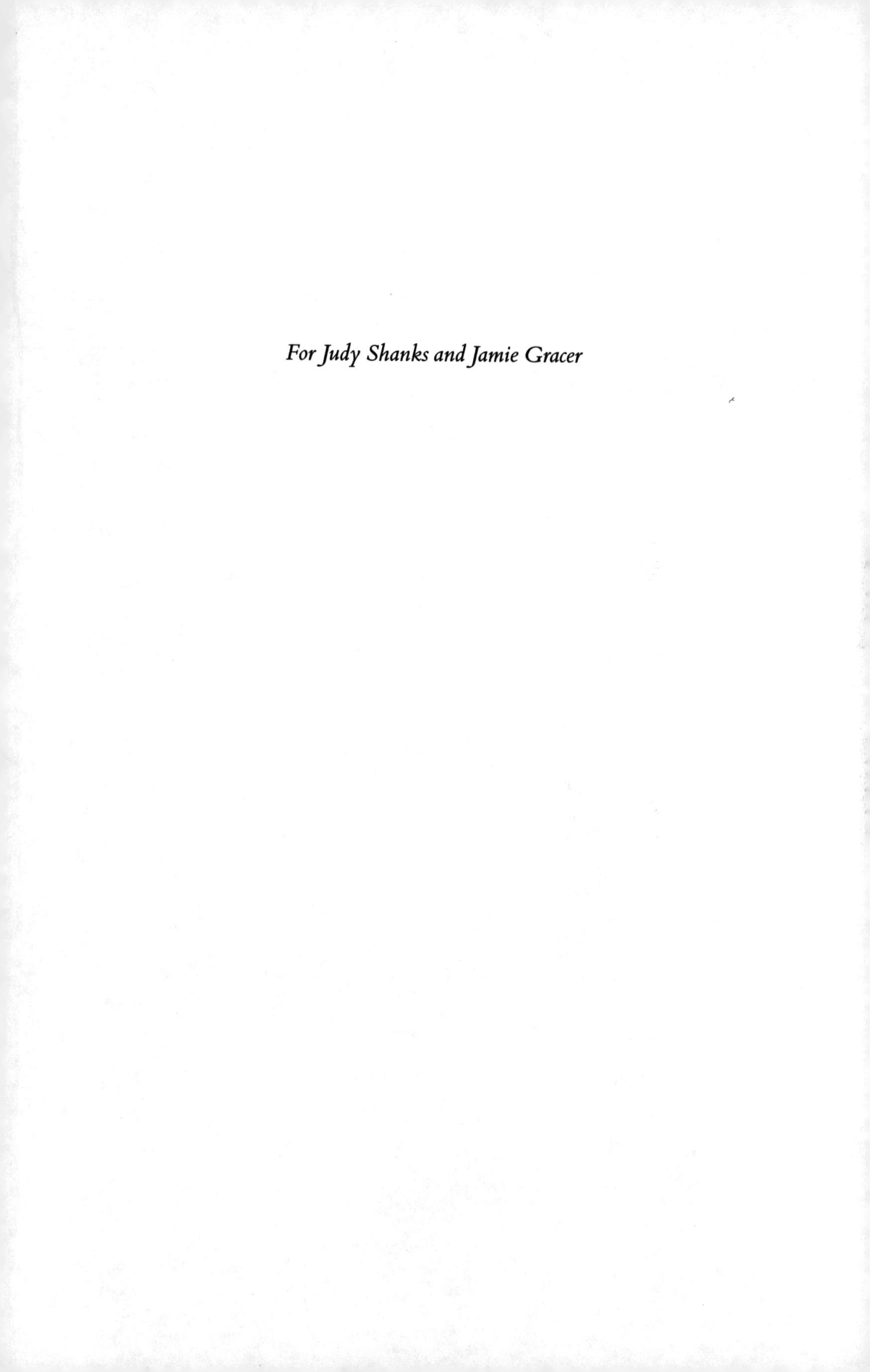

For Judy Shanks and Jamie Gracer

CONTENTS

ACKNOWLEDGMENTS

IT HAS OFTEN SEEMED AS IF I HAVE BEEN WRITING THIS BOOK SINCE the 1970s. While that is not quite accurate, I have worked on it long enough to realize again that each generation writes its own history. Time and again what brought me back to this project was some event in the present that reminded me of the past. For his friendship, understanding, patience, and tactful nagging while I took detours from it to write other books, I am most indebted to Ed Barber at W. W. Norton. When Ed finally gave up waiting and retired, he turned me over to the legendary Steve Forman, an inspired editor. I also thank Rebecca Charney, Pearl Hanig, and Nancy Palmquist at Norton; and Cohen Carruth, Inc.

The research for this project took me to the Ford, Carter, and Reagan libraries, Brigham Young University Special Collections, the Hoover Institution, the Library of Congress, the State Historical Society of Wisconsin, and Yale University Manuscripts and Archives. I am very grateful to Martin Elzy, David Horrocks, Carol Leadenham, Nancy Lyon, Jennifer Mandel, Nancy Mirshah, Albert Nason, James Yancey, and all the other archivists who aided me and to the Gerald R. Ford Presidential Foundation for the research travel grant that enabled me to make my first trip to Ann Arbor. I thank my UCSB colleagues John Woolley and Gerhard Peters for digitizing the papers of presidents in their invaluable American Presidency Project, http://www.presidency.ucsb.edu/, Lexis-Nexis, and every newspaper, periodical, and archive that have digitized their holdings.

Colleagues, friends, and family pored over the many versions of this manuscript, which was once nearly double this size. For their comments on it, I will be forever grateful to John Morton Blum, W. Elliot Brownlee, Beverly Gage, W. Randall Garr, E. Stanly Godbold, Sarah Barringer Gordon, Ariela Gross, Newton Kalman, Pnina Lahav, Nelson Lichtenstein, Serena Mayeri, Yanek Mieczkowski, William E. Nelson, James Patterson, Kim Phillips-Fein, Leo Ribuffo, Chris Sagers, John Henry Schlegel, Bruce Schulman, Eran Shalev, Judy Shanks, and Dennis Ventry. I especially thank Yanek, Stanly, and Leo for all the work they did for someone who started out as a stranger and for their informative responses to my incessant queries about Ford and Carter. Craig Shirley graciously answered a stream of unrelenting questions about Reagan and allowed me to read much of his book about the 1980 campaign, and Bethany Moreton kindly shared editions of *Wal-Mart World*. I would like too to express my great gratitude for the many helpful comments I received when I presented chapters at the American University Law School, where Lewis Grossman provided especially good advice; the Miller Center of Public Affairs, where Martha Derthick did the same; the Los Angeles Legal History Reading Group; the Cleveland-Marshall Law School, where I was the eighty-fifth Cleveland-Marshall Fund Visiting Scholar; Pomona College, to which I had the joy of returning as the Hart Lecturer; and the Stanford and University of Texas history departments.

UCSB hired me to teach twentieth-century U.S. political and legal history in 1982, and I have been very happy here, in spite of the never-ending budget crises that have plagued the University of California. Much of the narrative was first hatched in lecture courses and graduate seminars, and I so appreciate the thousands of students who helped shape it. While it seems wrong to single out any of them, since I have loved teaching and being taught by almost all of them, I would particularly like to celebrate Christine Adams and Mark Etzel for their intellectual curiosity, enthusiasm, and friendship.

Among those who have sustained me, in addition to those I mention above and discuss below, I thank Pamela Blum, Penn and Morton Borden, Cyndi Brokaw, Mary Brownlee, Jane DeHart, Alex and Nat Dennett, Lupe Diaz, Mercedes Eichholz, Celia and Steve Fassberg, Bill Felstiner, Hope Firestone, Wendy Fisher, Rena Fraden, Guy Garr, Jesus Gil, Sophya, Dan, and Patrick Gordon, Talia and Mira Gracer, Tom and Ruth Green, Denis Grunfeld, Morton Horwitz, Leslie Jacobs, Bladey Kalman, Barbara Kern, Eva and Ruthie King, Steve Kliegman, Elizabeth

Hon-Ming Li, Joy Mahalo, Harriet Mayeri, Kate and Pat Metropolis, Melissa Murray, Thasana Nivatpumin, David Rabban, Jeff Richman, Chris Runge, Kate Saltzman-Li, Harry Scheiber, Linny Smith, Ray Solomon, Dan Story, Meg Taradash, Michael Teter, Vicky Saker Woeste, Eva Yeranyak-Ktoyan, and Rosemarie Zagarri. Alice and Tremper Longman patiently answered the many naive questions about evangelicals that I unartfully posed around the dinner table. As ever, Sarah Barringer Gordon and Pnina Lahav proved indispensable friends and colleagues, and Pat Bagley, unfailingly heartening.

Like his parents, Connie and Ward Schweizer, John Schweizer has been a vital part of my life since the 1970s, and John has kept me in Post-Its and memorable Parisian holidays. My other adopted brother, W. Elliot Brownlee, has instructed me on the mysteries of academic life since I arrived at UCSB. My dean, David Marshall, has solved them for me since I was a graduate student at Yale and he joined its faculty; I am also very thankful for Candace Waid, whom I first met in Howard Lamar's seminar, and Daniel Marshall. My neighbor, IT consultant, and dear friend Daniel Richman saved this book from destruction by computer more times than I can count and provided countless hours of happy distraction from it. John Blum taught me in the 1970s that criticism before publication was an act of friendship, and he has been my best critic and cheerleader since then. My erudite and witty father, Newton Kalman, now in his ninetieth year, and I wrangled over every word here. In a fit of pique, I once told him that he could have made the Gettysburg Address twice as long. My eternally optimistic mother, Lee Kalman, soothed us, assured us we were wonderful, and reminded us how much fun we were having. My beloved mother-in-law, Celeste Garr, lights up whenever she sees me. Above all, I thank her son and my husband, W. Randall Garr.

I have known Judy Shanks since John Schweizer decided we would like each other and introduced us when we all attended Pomona. But Judy and I became best friends during the bicentennial summer, when as a law student at UCLA I worked for California Supreme Court Justice Stanley Mosk, who was very generous to me. After a long day, Judy and I would sit on the stoop of the unforgettable Russian Hill apartment that John also found for me. We had each just turned twenty-one, and we always drank Wente Grey Riesling. We felt very sophisticated as we talked about all matter of things, ranging from presidential politics, to whether Judy should become a rabbi and I should practice law (I always knew that she should, and I shouldn't), to her boyfriend, Jamie Gracer. During the decades since, our palates have changed, but our love for each other has not, and our friendship has only deepened. To Judy Shanks and her husband of thirty years, Jamie Gracer, I dedicate this book.

PROLOGUE

—

LIKE MOST HISTORIANS, I LIVE TO READ OTHER PEOPLE'S MAIL. Come the millennium, I heard about the opening of new collections at the Jimmy Carter Library in Georgia and the Gerald R. Ford Library in Michigan. Three days later I was in Atlanta.

Weekends present a challenge to the researcher on the road. Life seems pointless when the archives are closed. I fight the torpor by visiting historical sites. Franklin Roosevelt's Little White House at Warm Springs is a choice destination for political historians and Democratic politicians. From there it is a two-hour drive to Plains, Carter's hometown.

After paying a teary homage to FDR, I arrived in Plains on a Saturday afternoon. A ranger at the Jimmy Carter National Historic Site said I was in luck: Carter was teaching Sunday school that weekend. Though I had only shorts with me, I was assured I was still welcome.

It seemed too good an opportunity to miss. I had never seen Carter. Moreover, I am Jewish, and I had never been inside a Baptist church or attended Christian Sunday school. The following day I was among the first in the long line in front of Maranatha Baptist.

Like everything in Plains, the small white church bears the mark of the 1976 election. In the final days the Reverend Clennon King, an African American, applied for membership in the Carters' church. To the campaign's consternation, Plains Baptist canceled its services rather than admit him. A group left in protest and established Maranatha. But to the dissidents' surprise, King never joined them. He had simply been proving anew another King's remark that the hour starting at eleven o'clock Sunday morning remained the most segregated in America.

A friendly church member told us that she wanted no "backbench

Baptists" and settled us in the front pews. She explained that Carter taught Sunday school whenever he was in Plains and that he and his wife would gladly be photographed with every one of us after the service. We could also purchase a video of the former president's lesson. The proceeds would fund the church's mission in Nicaragua. In Carter, Maranatha had obviously stumbled upon a fund-raising tool for its good works.

Carter appeared suddenly and quietly, dressed in white jeans, a striped shirt, a checked sports coat, and a bolo tie. He looked better than that sounds, though he seemed tired. His theme was the need for risk in Christian life; his message, "Risk your routine."

The text was 1 Corinthians 9:19–23, Paul's letter beginning, "Am I not free? Am I not an apostle? Have I not seen Jesus our Lord?" Yet, Paul explained, "though I am free with respect to all, I have made myself a slave to all, so that I might win" more converts to Christ. "To the Jews I became as a Jew, in order to win the Jews"; to the weak, weak. "I have become all things to all people, that I might by all means save some. I do it all for the sake of the gospel, so that I may share in its blessings."[1]

Paul, Carter said, was the greatest theologian. Christ had come as a revolutionary, dedicated to eliminating legalism and the "more than 600 little tiny rules and regulations" that preoccupied Jerusalem's religious leaders. (I flinched, wondering whether Carter's description of Judaism missed something.) Yet niggling disagreements bogged down the early church. Paul's advice still resonated: Discard the disputes and our prejudices for the good of the kingdom of Christ. The specific question Paul addressed in Corinthians, Carter reminded us, involved the propriety of consuming meat previously offered to idols. Since Paul did not believe in idols, he could eat sacrifices, but he had decided that when he was with idol worshipers, he would not. It was not a matter of "flexible character," Carter stressed, but of relating to people in sympathy. Paul's message was to take a risk, subjugate oneself, put aside routine, and copy the life of Christ. So substantial would be the reward that "I guarantee" we would not feel deprived. We would win access to a life of expansion, exaltation, and exhilaration.

Carter taught semi-Socratically but did not seem too interested in our answers. Even so, I marveled at the sight of a former president leading us through the Bible and relating the text to his experiences. During the 1976 campaign, Carter said, when the media had been on him like—pause and smile—"Georgia gnats" (then another pause while he waited for us to laugh), reporters had scoured his pronouncements for inconsistencies and juxtaposed his statements about abortion in Des Moines and at Harvard. A quarter century later he remained incredulous at the scrutiny.

Though I stayed for church, I remember little else, other than that we sang "The Nail-Scarred Hand," which made me squeamish. Though I might have been welcome, I was severely underdressed. I was mortified to find myself standing in the pew directly across from the Carters. And there I was, decked out in Big Dogs polo shirt, Big Dogs shorts, and flip-flops. The former first lady was in suit and heels. I caught her eye at one point when I calculated that she might have difficulty seeing my body. I grinned at her and received a welcoming smile.

How to match hearing Jimmy Carter teach? The following weekend when the Carter Library closed, I drove to Virginia. That Sunday (dressed suitably), I was in Lynchburg to listen to Jerry Falwell preach.

Unlike Maranatha, Thomas Road Baptist is not a small-town church. It bustles. "I'm just a visitor," I apologetically told a volunteer, before saying I wanted to attend Sunday school. There was no such thing as *just* a visitor, I was informed. Which Sunday school did I want to attend, someone asked: Singles; Young Families—Together, Young Couples, Homebuilders, or Growing Families; Adults—Genesis, Basic Training, Choir, Logos, Faith Bible, New Hope, New Dimensions; or Pastor's Class? The guide must have seen my eyes glaze over because she added that the Pastor's Class was for everyone.

I gratefully made my way into a huge round sanctuary that reminded me of the Reform synagogue in which my bat mitzvah occurred. We recited the Twenty-third Psalm. The minister of music and Falwell joked about Falwell's tone deafness. There was an occasional shouted "amen," a twenty-piece orchestra, and Falwell told us the next president would be Republican. Then the regular service began, and thousands filled the church. The choir dipped and swayed as we sang "When We All Get to Heaven," "Amazing Grace," "What a Day That Will Be," and "I Love to Tell the Story." Everyone was smiling.

The topic of Falwell's sermon was "Prayer Explosion in These Last Days," his text Joel 2:28–32: "The sun shall be turned into darkness, and the moon into blood before the great and terrible day of the Lord comes. And it shall come to pass, that whosoever shall call on the name of the Lord shall be delivered for in Mount Zion and in Jerusalem shall be deliverance." Falwell said evangelicals had fallen short. "We are all commanded to preach the Gospel of Christ to every soul in our generation." It was time to stop talking about saving souls and to save them.[2]

Falwell seemed friendly, smart, dynamic, and dedicated. He put on a great show. Perhaps I am overly egotistical, but I sensed that had I stood and shouted, "I'm not a Christian, I'm a liberal, and I believe the Constitution forbids prayer in public schools," he would have stopped everything to convert me.

I had read that Falwell sounded more stern before his own fundamentalists than before a general audience. When the cameras recording the service for his TV show flickered off, he condemned gay rights and abortion. Then "the invitation" occurred. No one had bidden us to the altar at Maranatha, but at Thomas Road, we were all urged up to commit or recommit our souls to Jesus Christ. Falwell repeatedly told us not enough were coming.

We had a chance, he thundered. We all would leave church and get into our cars. If we were in an accident and we had been saved, we would be lifted up to heaven. If we had not, we would roast in hell. Strong stuff, this, for a Jew facing an eight-hour drive back to Atlanta. By the time the service ended, I was terrified.

The following weekend I was in Grand Rapids. As I entered the Gerald R. Ford Museum, I felt as if I had fallen into a time tunnel. The multimedia show featured popular culture circa 1975—disco, bell-bottoms, platform shoes—and exhibits re-creating the Watergate crisis and the agony of Vietnam.

I faced a vanished era. Equally striking, Ford seemed at home in it. The impression grew stronger as I watched his wife defend abortion on *Sixty Minutes* with a fervor few politicians would display today. Like the holdings in the Ford and Carter libraries, my experiences those three weekends provided vivid reminders that in the middle and late 1970s the United States moved right.

What had happened? I could see how the liberal political culture of the Age of Roosevelt—the mood and values that shaped politics between 1932 and 1974—produced Richard Nixon. But whence came Gerald Ford? And how had he yielded to someone in some ways more conservative, Jimmy Carter? And how had Carter come to be challenged by someone more conservative still, Jerry Falwell, and been replaced by that "Roosevelt of the Right" Ronald Reagan?[3]

That is the story I have tried to tell in this book. When I began graduate school in the 1970s, political historians of the recent United States were focusing on the liberal consensus. Largely left of center ourselves, we insisted that our subjects—Franklin Roosevelt, Adolf Berle, Abe Fortas, Hugo Black, Allard Lowenstein, Lyndon Johnson, Walter Mondale—personified liberalism's promise and paradoxes. Assume that liberalism is defined as "an understanding that the federal government had the responsibility, power, and ability to reduce inequality, protect historically oppressed minorities, and balance the private sector's singular focus on making money with a broad concern for the nation's long-term good," as well as a global responsibility to spread capitalism and democracy. When and why did that liberalism falter? Some contend that it unraveled at the end of the 1960s because liberal policy makers promised more reform and equality than they could deliver, and the Vietnam War undermined their global vision. Others blame Richard Nixon for polarizing the United States. Still others maintain that the racial politics and cleavages we associate with the backlash predated the decade and were rooted in the very rights consciousness supposedly at the root of postwar liberalism.[4]

Meanwhile, when conservatives write their history, they often make their "watershed year" 1964. That was when Barry Goldwater wrested the Republican presidential nomination from Nelson Rockefeller before receiving a thumping from Lyndon Johnson. Add in Nixon's victories over Hubert Humphrey in 1968 and George McGovern in 1972, and Watergate becomes a bump in the road to Ronald Reagan's inevitable 1980 victory.[5]

These interpretations are invaluable. Without a doubt, liberals felt besieged by 1968. The war in Vietnam weighed them down, Lyndon Johnson's Great Society programs and civil rights legislation were under attack from those who claimed they did too much and those who contended they did too little, and the judicial activism of the Warren Court had become unpopular. Yet these interpretations can lead readers to ignore the survival of liberalism after the 1960s, underestimate the complexity of conservatism, and overlook the extent to which liberalism and conservatism have coexisted. Consequently, I have joined the ranks of the many who have tried to make sense of Reagan's election by setting their sights on the seventies.[6]

During the 1970s many conservatives recognized that President Nixon had betrayed them, but only during the 1990s did historians routinely note the liberal nature of many policies and programs he supported. Perhaps Nixon aspired to realign American politics and create a new majority unified around "patriotism, morality, religion." But he failed. When Nixon resigned, both the Republican Party and conservatives seemed even more divided, endangered, and mired in scandal than in 2008.[7]

Everything changed during the five years after Nixon left office because of discontent with the leadership of his moderate successors and conservative entrepreneurialism. Unlike those who have argued for a "long 1970s" that lasted from 1968 to 1984 or 1975 to 1986, I present the case for a "short 1970s" from 1975 to 1979. My two themes, the problems that Ford and Carter experienced governing and the growth of conservatism, are intertwined. There have been excellent studies of conservatism at the grass roots and before the 1970s. I tell largely a Washington story and situate the explosion of conservative activity against the backdrop of the Ford and Carter presidencies. Mine is not a comprehensive history of the two administrations or conservatism. Instead I write about how events and issues that the right seized as opportunities illuminate American politics. As Republicans and conservatives seek to rebuild their party and movement in the wake of Barack Obama's 2008 election as president, they hearken back to a similar journey out of the wilderness in the 1970s. "Think the Republican Party is in bad shape today?" one conservative asked recently. "You should have seen it then. In the wake of stagflation, Watergate, and America's first lost war—all either starting or ending in ignominy in the Nixon-Ford years—early GOP recovery was far from a betting favorite."[8]

But the middle and late 1970s are not significant simply because they may provide grist for contemporary Republican and conservative playbooks. I have focused on what happened between the 1960s that sputtered out in 1974–75 and 1980. Watergate and Ford's pardon of Nixon, the energy crisis, the shattered economy, shocking revelations about individuals and institutions from John F. Kennedy to the FBI, and the loss of Vietnam, I contend, undermined confidence in politics and politicians. Between mid-1975 and 1980, those who yearned to lead fought over how to fill the vacuum as energy and economic woes, the Sunbelt, culture wars, racial tensions, the emergence of law as the arena of struggle for social issues, frustration with presidents and Congress, splits in the Democratic and Republican parties, a resurgent Russia, Middle

East and Afghan tensions, intelligence failures, terrorism, and a desire for change in national direction created our world. During this period two presidents who failed as party leaders and the growing power of the New Right, neoconservatism, market liberalism, the religious right, and anticommunism transformed American political culture.

PART ONE

THE END OF THE SIXTIES

I

THE NIGHTMARE CONTINUES

—

SUDDENLY EVERYONE WANTED TO BECOME A LAWYER. MORE THAN 135,000 Law School Admissions Tests were administered in 1973–74, up nearly 10 percent from 1972 to 1973 and more than 1.5 times as many as during any year of the 1960s. Yet the reputation of lawyers had never been lower. Watergate ensnared President Nixon and the many other attorneys in his administration in an excess of illegal events: misuse of campaign donations, the Internal Revenue Service, the FBI, and the CIA; creation of an extralegal group to carry out surveillance and burglaries, including the June 17, 1972, break-in at the Democratic National Committee headquarters in the Watergate office complex; and cover-up of White House involvement. *Time* claimed "there has been no comparable conspiracy of lawyers in history." The collapse of Nixon's presidency in August 1974 created unexpected opportunities not just for Gerald Ford but for conservatives to Ford's right.[1]

"THE SUN IS SHINING AGAIN"

On August 8, Richard Nixon's last night in Washington as chief executive, the sobbing president and Secretary of State Henry Kissinger knelt in prayer in the White House. Ironically, Nixon had destroyed himself by ordering the installation of a voice-activated tape recording system in the Oval Office. When the existence of the tapes became public in July 1973, Nixon desperately tried to keep them out of the hands of those trying to learn what the president had known about the Watergate scandals and cover-up and when he had known it.[2]

But Nixon's days were numbered after his showdown on Saturday night, October 20, 1973, with Special Prosecutor Archibald Cox of Harvard Law School, or, as Nixon referred to him, "that fucking Harvard professor." Appointed to investigate Watergate at the Senate's demand, Cox insisted that the president must comply with a court of appeals order to deliver tape recordings of Watergate-related conversations to the special prosecutor. In the "Saturday night massacre," Attorney General Elliot Richardson and Deputy Attorney General William Ruckelshaus resigned, rather than follow Nixon's directions to get rid of Cox and close down the office of special prosecutor. Solicitor General Robert Bork, who briefly became acting attorney general, dismissed Cox and abolished the office of special prosecutor. Then, on the order of Nixon's chief of staff, General Alexander Haig, the FBI sealed the offices of Richardson, Ruckelshaus, and Cox. "There was a real sense," said one of Cox's colleagues, that "a fascist takeover" could be imminent. The ensuing uproar about Nixon's disregard of the rule of law increased the likelihood of his impeachment and forced the president to name sixty-eight-year-old Leon Jaworski, a conservative Texas trial lawyer and former president of the American Bar Association, as the new special prosecutor.[3]

Aided by a force of thirty-seven young lawyers, most of them less than half his age, Jaworski pressed forward on Cox's mission while Nixon dribbled out some edited tapes and worked to block the disclosure of others. On July 24, 1974, the United States Supreme Court unanimously ruled in *U.S. v. Nixon* that the president must turn over sixty-four contested tapes to Jaworski. As he debated whether to comply, the House Judiciary Committee voted in favor of three articles of impeachment, including one that charged him with obstructing justice by blocking the investigation of the June 17, 1972, Watergate break-in. On August 5, 1974, the White House bowed to the authority of the Supreme Court and released the "smoking gun," a tape recording that proved Nixon had ordered a cover-up of the June 1972 Watergate burglary just six days after it had occurred.

On August 7, Republican members of Congress who had previously defended the president made it clear to him that the full House would impeach him. They told Nixon that he would be lucky if he could muster ten votes for acquittal in the Senate. The next day Nixon informed the nation that on August 9, he would resign the presidency and yield the office to another lawyer, Gerald R. Ford.[4]

The resemblance between the two men ended at their choice of career. Brilliant, cunning, secretive, and insecure, Nixon divided the world into enemies and friends. "Always remember," he mawkishly told his staff the day Watergate forced him to resign, "others may hate you, but those who hate you don't win, unless you hate them, and then you destroy yourself." Ford reflected that "[if] he'd followed his own advice, . . . this moment might never have come."[5]

In contrast with Nixon, Ford thrived on camaraderie, conciliation, and compromise. By the time he reached seventh grade, he had resolved to get ahead by accentuating the positive in others. The one person he exempted was his father, who had brutally abused his mother before their divorce and his disappearance. As a teenager Ford did not know of the violence when his father suddenly appeared and invited him to lunch, but he knew his father had never provided financial support. Nonetheless, the young man searched for good in his elder. When he concluded that his father was "a carefree well-to-do man who really didn't give a damn about the hopes and dreams of his son," he consoled himself with a prayer his loving mother had taught him: "Trust in the Lord with all thine heart; and lean not unto thine own understanding."[6]

His sunniness fueled Ford's rise to power. Elected to Congress from Michigan in 1948, he provided devoted service to Grand Rapids constituents. At the same time, Ford became a congressional insider. His colleagues rewarded him by making him chair of the House Republican Conference, then minority leader. "It wasn't as though everybody was wildly enthusiastic about Jerry," one supporter said, but he lacked Republican enemies.[7]

Ford paid a personal price for this lukewarm praise. He appeared only for cocktails and dessert at the rehearsal dinner before his own wedding; he missed the main course to make a speech. "I had to bring four kids up by myself," his wife said. But geniality and self-assurance cloaked her husband's ambition, and he had integrity.[8]

By 1973 Ford was contemplating life after politics. He promised his wife he would retire in 1976, practice law three days a week, and golf four. Then Vice President Spiro Agnew was charged with having accepted bribes and resigned in disgrace. Nixon reluctantly reached out to Ford, the only Republican in Congress acceptable to the Democrats who controlled it, to fill Agnew's place. In the seventeen hundred pages of Ford's FBI file, the most damning allegation was that he once tackled a player in a football game after the whistle blew. With a sure sense of place, Ford insisted he be sworn in at the Capitol, rather than the White

House, as Nixon wished. The new vice president winningly told his cheering former colleagues that he was "a Ford, not a Lincoln."[9]

To many, his modesty seemed fitting. Ford's mother, beloved stepfather, and three half brothers had clung to the lower middle class through the Depression, and he worked his way through the University of Michigan, where he became the football team's star center and linebacker. Nevertheless, he graduated in the top quarter of his class, an accomplishment he repeated at Yale Law School while working full-time coaching Yale's boxing and football teams. Even so, in the 1960s, Lyndon Johnson had made those two observations that were to dog Ford's career: "Jerry's a nice guy, but he played football without a helmet," and he "can't chew gum and fart at the same time." His staffers winced when their boss pronounced judgment as "judge-uh-ment" or toasted President Anwar el-Sadat of Egypt and "the great people of the government of Israel" Sadat led. Senate Majority Leader Michael Mansfield said that Ford has "had a remarkable career because he has been so unremarkable himself."[10]

BUT AS FORD TOOK the presidential oath on August 9, 1974, his modest virtues were welcome. Presidents had so increased the power of the office that historian Arthur Schlesinger, Jr., aptly wrote of an "imperial Presidency" claiming primacy over Congress and the Supreme Court. Ford seemed likely to reduce the presidency to the right size.[11]

In his inaugural address, President Ford stressed his own honesty, humility, and hope to heal. He pledged openness and candor. His best line confronted Watergate and promised an end to the era: "My fellow Americans, our long national nightmare is over." Ford had worried the sentence was too hard on Nixon, but his speechwriter said that the trauma of Watergate demanded it. In fact, Watergate raised a number of constitutional issues that Nixon's resignation left unanswered, but when Ford said it showed that "[o]ur Constitution works" and that "our great Republic is a Government of laws and not of men," he voiced a popular and comforting misperception. Acknowledging the "painful" and "poisonous" nature of Watergate's "internal wounds," he begged his listeners to "let brotherly love purge our hearts of suspicion and of hate." He pleaded with them to pray for the Nixons and "to confirm me as President with your prayers." He mentioned love three times, God four. No one doubted his sincerity.[12]

With Ford's acclaimed speech, relieved Americans could indeed contemplate the end to their collective Watergate nightmare. He seemed to represent real improvement, particularly in his reminders to Americans that he was one of them. Nixon had seen himself as royalty. He dreamed of outfitting his White House security as elaborately as the Buckingham Palace guards. So uncomfortable did he become at state dinners that Nixon pressed his aides to cut them down to fifty-eight minutes. As part of this effort, he banished the soup course on the ground that "[m]en don't really like soup." Ford, however, was easy, hospitable, and open, determined to "replace a national frown with a national smile." He substituted the University of Michigan fight song for "Hail to the Chief." He invited the Democrats and reporters Nixon had labeled enemies to his first state dinner, where Ford recalled staying past midnight "stomping to 'Bad, Bad Leroy Brown.'" Americans went wild when they learned that Ford was still toasting his English muffins. A *New Yorker* cartoon featured a sleepy wife reminding her irate husband that "the President of the United States of America makes his own breakfast."[13]

Americans rooted for Ford. "I do not want a honeymoon with you," he told Congress. "I want a good marriage." The honeymoon, however, was wonderful.[14]

Though generous and humane to a fault, Ford had never supported government programs for the poor. According to the liberal Americans for Democratic Action, he had voted the ADA's way just four times between 1970 and 1973. Yet he now seemed ready to rise above his conservative ideology. An aide to the chair of the liberal Congressional Black Caucus was so surprised to hear the president was telephoning her boss that she suspected someone was playing a trick on her. But it was indeed Ford, urging caucus members to come by for a chat, an invitation he repeated to the feminists in Congress, to whom he vowed to fight for the Equal Rights Amendment, and to labor leader George Meany.[15]

SEVERAL ACTIONS FORD TOOK in his second week as president highlighted his desire for national reconciliation and testified to the power liberal rhetoric retained in Washington. Key congressional Republicans urged him to sound liberal and conciliatory. The House minority leader advised Ford "to continue the healing process . . . and not in any way raise issues that could tend to divide the country"; the Senate minority leader stressed that "the President must represent *all* the people, including the poor and black" and "find some formula for amnesty for deserters and draft dodgers."[16]

Nixon's determination to mobilize support for his actions in Southeast Asia had started him down the road to Watergate, and he had fought any such formula. In one typically divisive remark, Nixon saluted the Americans who had served "in a country far away in a war that they realize had very little support among the so-called better people, in the media and the intellectual circles, and . . . among some elements of Congress—particularly the United States Senate—but which fortunately did have support among a majority of the American people, despite the fact that they were hammered night after night and day after day, with the fact that this was an immoral war, that America should not be there." The country could not forgive shirkers, he maintained, without first punishing them.[17]

In his first show of leadership, Ford decided on a different approach. He would make his position public, he courageously concluded, not before a welcoming liberal audience but before a conservative one. Standing before thousands of stunned Veterans of Foreign Wars, Ford threw "the weight of my presidency into the scales of justice on the side of leniency." The amnesty would be "conditional," and draft evaders and deserters would "earn" it through a process he would announce later.[18]

Next, Ford named his vice president. His cabinet and staff, along with Republican congressional members and governors, listed Republican National Committee chair George H. W. Bush as their first choice, and Bush lusted for the job. Still, he had recently been fingered as a beneficiary of Nixon slush funds. Further, some Ford advisers believed Bush was not "ready to handle the rough challenges of the Oval Office" and that his selection would seem partisan, a "weak and depressingly conventional act." So, after receiving the tabulation that placed Bush a strong first, former Governor Nelson Rockefeller of New York second, Senator Barry Goldwater of Arizona a distant third, and former Governor Ronald Reagan of California fourth, Ford again reached out. He chose Rockefeller, a moderate not all liberal Democrats liked, but one whom all conservative Republicans absolutely detested.[19]

A charismatic politician and the heir to a fortune so vast that Congress held up his confirmation while exploring his use of it, Rockefeller had served as governor of New York and patron to Henry Kissinger and had sought the presidency several times himself. Some on Ford's staff worried that Rockefeller would overshadow the president, but Ford himself did not; he was secure in himself. Then, as soon as he named his vice president, Ford authorized his press secretary, Jerald terHorst, to say he would "probably" seek the presidency in 1976. Here was no caretaker but a confident leader in his own right with a strong second-in-command.[20]

The national mood had not changed so quickly since Franklin Roosevelt relieved Herbert Hoover. From the Democratic side of the aisle, Senator Mansfield declared, "The sun is shining again." The mainstream media agreed. The *New Republic* compared the nation to a child who had "swallowed something nasty and thrown up and feels better. Mr. Ford is everything that Nixon wasn't, with warmth and openness and decency, and he has engendered national affection."[21]

THE GHOST OF RICHARD NIXON

In these first happy days, the fiercest hostility to Ford lay inside the White House. Criminal charges arising from Watergate had already dispatched nearly 25 of Nixon's men, but some 480 others remained. When Ford chose his friend Donald Rumsfeld to head his transition team, it looked as if their days were numbered. A former member of the House of Representatives, the Nixon administration, and Nixon's ambassador to NATO, Rumsfeld was conservative, fiscally; moderate, socially; and he had irritated Nixon by expressing his doubts about the Vietnam War. Within the Nixon administration, which was not known for its selfless or gentle men, Rumsfeld was thought ambitious and ruthless. Predictably, he urged Ford to clean house. But the new president desired continuity and disapproved of a "purge." Always considerate, Ford disliked tarring Watergate innocents "with the Nixon brush." He asked Nixon's staff to remain for the rest of the year and pleaded with cabinet members, especially Secretary of State and National Security Adviser Henry A. Kissinger, to stay on permanently. ("Reaffirm H.A.K," Ford noted to himself before his first cabinet meeting.) He also urged General Haig to continue on as chief of staff and declared himself "very grateful" when Haig agreed to do so.[22]

Ford's thankfulness was misplaced. A skilled infighter, Haig was assured or arrogant, depending on whether friend or foe described him. He remained devoted to Nixon and proved ingenious at putting down the usurpers. So closely did Haig exert control that he frustrated the new president's smallest attempts to step out of Nixon's shadow. For example, Nixon had ordered portraits of Theodore Roosevelt, Woodrow Wilson, and Dwight Eisenhower hung in the Cabinet Room. In the spirit of change and continuity, Ford decided to keep Ike and told Haig to replace Roosevelt and Wilson with Harry Truman and Abraham Lincoln. Truman's outspoken honesty would play well in post-Watergate Washington, and both Truman and Lincoln had supported postwar amnesties. The switch of portraits would have greatest symbolic impact if they occurred by the time Ford gave his amnesty speech. But Haig, who disapproved of amnesty, managed to delay the change until the day Ford named Rockefeller vice president, and the media overlooked the gesture. Later the incident became illustrative of Ford's inability to command. At the time it seemed just a minor irritant.[23]

As he assumed the presidency, Ford faced two more troubling questions about his predecessor. What should he do about the former president and his records, the 46 million pages Nixon left behind and the 950 reels of tape on which he had recorded his Oval Office conversations? Named an unindicted coconspirator by the grand jury investigating Watergate, Nixon had been subpoenaed to appear as a witness in the upcoming trials of his administration officials and feared he might yet be indicted for obstruction of justice. As Nixon settled down with a skeleton staff in his beachfront mansion in San Clemente, California, to prepare his testimony and looked ahead to writing his memoirs, he badly wanted the tapes.[24]

And the White House wanted no part of them. "Get Nixon materials out of W.H. as soon as possible," Rumsfeld advised. "Quite apart from any illegal . . . dealings" revealed on the tapes, another memorandum observed, the "hair-down discussions" of politics and expletives memorialized on them could "demean and embarrass the participants, the Republican Party, the Presidency, and perhaps government generally." Yet while presidents had traditionally treated their records as their private property, the tapes contained evidence that courts might require and Nixon might destroy. Nevertheless, White House Counsel Fred Buzhardt, a Nixon holdover, ruled that the tapes were Nixon's property. Buzhardt then shaded the truth and led Press Secretary terHorst to believe he had reached his decision after consulting with Special Prosecutor Leon Jaworski.[25]

If, in his eagerness to protect Nixon, Buzhardt had not implied that he had Jaworski's consent, the White House might have passed on the hot potato of the tapes before it burned Ford's fingers. As it was, terHorst's August 14 announcement that the decision to treat the tapes and records as Nixon's property was "collective" created the impression that the administration was working overtime to help Nixon. The public reaction compelled the White House to announce that Buzhardt had resigned and that there had been no decision on the disposition of Nixon's records.[26]

When it came to trying to persuade Ford to end his predecessor's ordeal, Haig and other Nixon loyalists proved equally zealous. Asked at his own vice presidential confirmation hearings whether a president possessed the power to prevent the criminal investigation and prosecution of his predecessor, Ford had responded: "I do not think the public would stand for it." That answer did not preclude a presidential pardon.[27]

According to Ford, on August 1, 1974, eight days before he became president, Haig first pointedly informed him "that a President does have authority to grant a pardon even before criminal action has been taken against an individual." When Ford recounted the conversation to staff members, they told him the obvious: Haig might have been proposing a deal by which Nixon would surrender the presidency in exchange for Ford's promise to pardon him, and Ford's silence implied consent. Ford then telephoned Haig in the presence of witnesses to say he could make no commitments. He did not expressly rule out a pardon.[28]

The pressure from Nixon's retainers and family for one continued after Ford became president, with a drumbeat of warnings that Nixon suffered from potentially life-threatening phlebitis and was depressed, even manic. Kissinger told Ford that Nixon would "never get through a trial or even an indictment without grave physical and psychological repercussions," and a "spectacle" would damage American credibility. On August 27, the day before Ford's first press conference, presidential assistant Leonard Garment spoke with several anti-Nixon journalists, and even they favored an early pardon. Garment then called on Abe Fortas, a liberal who had served as a Supreme Court justice until forced to resign as a result of one of Nixon's first presidential dirty tricks. Should he make the case to Ford for a pardon? Garment asked. It was "Ecclesiastes time," Fortas answered, "a time for repair and reconciliation."[29]

At Haig's urging, Garment now drafted a memorandum justifying a pardon. "Most of the country does not want Richard Nixon, hounded, perhaps literally, to death," Garment maintained. An immediate pardon would be greeted by "a national sigh of relief" and would exorcise Nixon's ghost. At 10:30 A.M., after meeting with Ford, Haig telephoned Garment to say, "It's all set."[30]

Wishful thinking as yet, but the matter was closer to resolution after the new president's first press conference four hours later. Ford had carefully prepared for questions ranging from the Soviets to the economy. The latter seemed urgent: The *New York Times* described Nixon's legacy as "the worst inflation in the country's peacetime history, the highest interest rates in a century, the consequent severe slump in housing, sinking and utterly demoralized securities markets, a stagnant economy with large-scale unemployment in prospect, and a worsening international trade and payments position." But from the initial inquiry—did Ford believe Nixon should have immunity from prosecution?—the press was primarily interested in one issue: How would he handle Nixon? And as Ford subsequently realized, his answers seemed confused and contradictory, sometimes suggesting that he would grant his predecessor early immunity from prosecution, at others that he would make no decision until Nixon had been tried and the jury reached a verdict.[31]

So Ford told his close friend and the new White House counsel Philip Buchen secretly to research the president's pardon power. Did he have the legal right to pardon someone not yet indicted or convicted? Buchen concluded that a broad constitutional pardon power existed, the president could legitimately issue a pardon before indictment, and acceptance of the pardon constituted an admission of guilt. The prospect of a pardon might solve another problem too, by encouraging Nixon to make a satisfactory disposition of those pesky records. Unless an agreement with respect to his papers and tapes was "accomplished before the granting of a pardon—or [was] . . . prescribed as a condition of the pardon—the present administration will continue to be enmeshed in burdensome aftermaths of acts and deeds which were not of its own doing," Buchen advised. If Ford intervened, he should do so quickly before Special Prosecutor Jaworski was pressured into indicting Nixon.[32]

Though virtually all the lawyers on Jaworski's staff did urge him to seek an indictment, the special prosecutor did not want to do so if Ford planned to pardon Nixon. When Buchen and Jaworski met a week later, the special prosecutor complained about Ford's press conference: "It sounded like he was saying that any action I might take against Nixon would be futile." Yet indictment, followed by trial, would consume months. The publicity around Watergate, Jaworski told Buchen the same day, ensured that at least nine months must elapse before a jury could be selected for Nixon's trial.[33]

Faced with this information, Ford reasoned that a pardon would deliver his administration from Watergate's shadow. Indictment, followed by a trial, would not. The decision was simple. He confronted pressing domestic and foreign policy issues. He did not want to be distracted by "lawyers' endless arguments" about the tapes and records and journalists' incessant questions about Nixon's legal status. At Yale, Ford had learned to see law as a tool of public policy, and while "I respected the tenet that no man should be above the law, public policy demanded that I put Nixon—and Watergate—behind us as quickly as possible." Ford's determination also reflected his long relationship with his predecessor and his compassion for Nixon's family. "I looked upon him as my personal friend," Ford acknowledged. "And I had no hesitancy about granting the pardon, because I felt that we had this relationship." Primarily, though, one adviser realized, the pardon was "a selfish act" to enable him "to get on with the business of the Ford presidency."[34]

The decision was reasonable from Ford's perspective. But having reached it, he made several mistakes. Oddly, the president chose Benton Becker, an attorney under investigation for criminal misconduct, as his envoy to draft an agreement on Nixon's records to announce with the pardon. Nixon's representatives gave little to Becker during the negotiations. Perhaps Haig had tipped them off that Ford was not making the pardon conditional on a satisfactory agreement about the records, as Buchen had recommended. Nixon stated his intention "to donate" his records to the United States "with appropriate restrictions." But he received exclusive power over access to the papers and tapes for the present, the right to withdraw papers after three years had elapsed, the right to destroy any or all tapes after five years, and the guarantee that the tapes would be destroyed at his death or in a decade, whichever came first.[35]

Nor did Ford demand an admission of guilt and repentance from Nixon. Legally, acceptance of the pardon was an admission of guilt: For years afterward Ford carried in his wallet a quotation from a 1915 Supreme Court decision declaring that a pardon "carries an imputation of guilt; acceptance a confession of it." But Becker and others also let Nixon's team know that the president welcomed, though he did not require, a statement of contrition. Twenty years later Ford blamed Haig when he did not receive one. "I assumed he was totally loyal to me," Ford said. "I'm [now] sure what Haig apparently transmitted to

Nixon convinced Nixon that he didn't have to make an outright admission of guilt." Predictably, Nixon acknowledged only having made "mistakes over Watergate," a declaration so ambiguous that it proved counterproductive.[36]

Finally Ford made the decision as if he were still in Congress, where adversaries then made peace when the battle ended. Yet the White House was not the Capitol. Moreover, the president refused to lay the groundwork for the pardon by selling it in advance to members of Congress and the cabinet, who could have helped him justify it.[37]

The "full, free and absolute pardon" that the president announced upon his return from church on Sunday, September 8, 1974, the same day daredevil biker Evel Knievel unsuccessfully attempted to rocket across Snake River, proved a public relations disaster. Evel Knievel received millions for the stunt, but there was no silver lining for Ford. It brought his honeymoon to a halt and left disillusionment and cynicism in its wake. Two weeks after the president announced the pardon, the media reported: "Outside the White House, some 250 pickets from George Washington University lofted a bedsheet with the words 'PROMISE ME PARDON AND I'LL MAKE YOU PRESIDENT.'"[38]

To be sure, the next generation was to vindicate Ford. (It is still too soon to say whether "history" has.) When Ford received the Profile in Courage award from the John F. Kennedy Library in 2001, the citation dwelled on his decision to pardon Nixon. At Ford's death five years later, journalists maintained that the pardon "spared the nation an ordeal of recrimination and allowed the healing to begin." Reasonable people can disagree on the wisdom of the pardon. Without a doubt, however, the timing of the pardon was poor, its justification, ill conceived, and the deal on Nixon's records accompanying it, unacceptable.[39]

Both Nixon's resignation and Ford's decision to pardon him were controversial, but the pardon provoked a more negative reaction. For one reason or another, Nixon's decision to quit pleased two-thirds of those polled. Yet to Ford's "immense shock," almost the same percentage thought the pardon wrong. Researchers later found that "Ford's pardon of Nixon was more highly correlated with the drop in political trust than were any of the previous events of Watergate."[40]

Reporters were even angrier than the public. In part, the pardon was their fault. The president would have thought he "could get away with it," one columnist acknowledged, because in "reading his notices for the first month in office, Ford learned that he was irresistible." Livid journalists began pounding "Ford and his lousy English muffins." They had transformed him from a frog into a prince just a month earlier, and now they made him a frog again.[41]

Ford was worse off because suspicions that he had agreed to the pardon before he became president put his decency in doubt. They were apparently groundless. Ford's conversations with Haig and Nixon probably led them to guess that a pardon was forthcoming, but no concrete evidence of a deal has ever surfaced.

Even without one, though, Ford's September 8 announcement of the pardon remained problematic. He rationalized it poorly by claiming that protracted litigation would stir "ugly passions." Other trials had aroused the public, and no one had stopped them. Moreover, if Ford wanted to defend the pardon primarily by stressing the need "to heal the wounds throughout the United States," as he insisted publicly at the time, he should have have toned down the portion of his statement declaring that "serious allegations and accusations hang like a sword over our former President's head, threatening his health as he tries to reshape his life." He also should not have said that "Richard Nixon and his loved ones have suffered enough."[42]

Further, Ford's timing was unfortunate. As Republicans realized, by acting when he did, he guaranteed that the pardon would become an issue in the upcoming congressional elections. Why not wait until after they had occurred, especially when Ford could have calmed his predecessor with a telephone call hinting a pardon was forthcoming? More important, by acting when he did, Ford had "created the impression that he would have pardoned Nixon no matter what criminal charges might have been lodged against him or what evidence might have been presented to support them. In effect, the President said that no crimes that Nixon might have committed would have precluded a pardon." Presidential pardons typically specified the acts the accused had committed, and even many who did not want to see the former president sent to the country club prisons to which so many of Nixon's colleagues were to be consigned sought a full accounting of the crimes he had allegedly committed.[43]

Had Nixon been impeached, of course, a Senate trial at which his guilt or innocence would have been adjudicated would have followed. Since he had resigned to avoid impeachment, a criminal indictment would have allowed revelation of the facts and allegations. True, Jaworski did not want to request an indictment if Ford planned a pardon. But

Jaworski knew the grand jury would indict Nixon "in a minute." He also acknowledged that some of his lawyers had "wanted to indict and signal President Ford that a pardon was in order . . . if Nixon would admit his guilt," a recommendation the special prosecutor admitted "had some merit." Alternatively, other countries were beginning to experiment with truth and reconciliation commissions to reveal their past human rights violations and heal the divisions they caused. Ford might have established a commission that would have guaranteed Nixon amnesty if he had cooperated with its investigation of his behavior.[44]

Ford also should have required his predecessor to display repentance. Though evidence of rehabilitation almost always accompanied a pardon, there was none here. One clergyman aptly described the tone of Nixon's statement acknowledging the pardon: "Get this behind me so that I can get on with writing my memoirs and tell that I was right in the first place."[45]

Even if mercy justified it, the pardon sent the message that the powerful could break the law with impunity. Like most criminals, other Watergate defendants also had families who suffered because of their imprisonment. Now Ford had placed himself in an untenable position. On the one hand, he had damaged the principle of equal justice under law. How could the trials of the Watergate minnows proceed when the whale swam free? On the other, how could he free all the fish? When a presidential spokesman suggested on September 10 that pardons were "under study" for all former and prospective Watergate defendants, the ensuing uproar forced the White House to issue an immediate retraction.[46]

Finally, no matter how they felt about the pardon, few praised the agreement that Becker had made with Nixon's representatives giving the former president control of his records. When Buchen replied to a reporter's question about "the right of history" by saying that "the historians will protest, but I think historians cannot complain if evidence for history is not perpetuated which shouldn't have been kept in the first place," he seemed to have taken leave of his senses. Congress promptly abrogated the agreement by enacting the 1974 Presidential Recordings and Materials Preservations Act, requiring delivery of the tapes to the "complete possession and control" of the archivist of the United States and ordering the archivist to give highest priority to processing those portions of the tapes and records that would "provide the public with the full truth . . . of the abuse of governmental power popularly identified under the generic term of 'Watergate.'" (Nixon then sued to recover possession of the tapes, and the ensuing litigation tied up access to most for two decades. His estate only agreed to begin releasing the tapes in 1996.)[47]

So too Congress asserted itself by creating a Judiciary Committee subcommittee that directed President Ford "to furnish to the House of Representatives the full and complete information and facts upon which was based the decision to grant a pardon to Richard M. Nixon." Prior presidents had routinely declined to testify before Congress for fear of weakening their power, but by October 1974 Ford was so frantic to defend the pardon that he agreed to appear. "The hearing presents a real opportunity for the President," an aide said beforehand, as long as the risk of "political mischief" was minimized.[48]

It was not. After hinting darkly of a deal, Representative Elizabeth Holtzman fired seven questions at Ford. How could the president explain his failure to specify the crimes for which Nixon was pardoned, his refusal to require "any acknowledgment of guilt" from Nixon, his lack of consultation with the attorney general, the haste and secrecy with which he had decided on and arranged the pardon, the accompanying agreement on the tapes, his choice of Becker as an envoy, and his failure to discuss the tapes agreement with Jaworski? The "most damaging aspects" of Ford's appearance, one staffer reflected afterward, "were the unanswered questions posed by Ms. Holtzman."[49]

Amid all the controversy over the pardon in 1974, the metaphor of Watergate as a national wound became stronger. "You can't pull a bandage off slowly," Ford had reasoned. But his press secretary, who resigned in protest over the president's decision, said "the pardon tore the scab off the Watergate wound just as it was beginning to heal." Even Ford began to wonder whether he had just rubbed salt in it.[50]

THE DAMAGE MIGHT have been reparable, some advisers believed, had Ford dismissed Haig and the other Nixon holdovers, who had pressed for the pardon, deserved the blame for so many of the missteps with respect to it, and scorned the new president and his advisers as mediocrities. Since Ford did not, there were tensions between his loyalists and Nixon's. These soon became public knowledge.[51]

At the time Ford was pondering the pardon, for example, the White House was also developing the amnesty program. Attorney General William Saxbe and Secretary of Defense James Schlesinger opposed it. The president unveiled what he now called the clemency program a week after announcing the pardon: It permitted draft resisters and military deserters to earn dismissal of their charges by performing up to two years of "alternate service [that] shall promote the national health, safety, or interest." Predictably, leaks indicated that the Justice and Defense departments had branded Ford's program as "too gentle." Nor were critics pleased to learn that the president had ensured a range of opinions on the Clemency Review Board by appointing Charles Goodell, a Nixon administration critic, as its chair. Though his selection "appeared to signal a real desire on Ford's part to make the program work," Goodell faced constant backbiting from administration aides.[52]

Meanwhile, clemency board members fought among themselves. One, civil rights activist Vernon Jordan, resigned in protest over the defective program and called for "complete, immediate, universal and unconditional amnesty" for all Vietnam veterans. "President Ford, who was compassionate enough to pardon Richard Nixon, should also be compassionate enough to pardon those who were right about an evil war and those whose service for their country has resulted in the unfair, lifelong punishment of a bad discharge," he said publicly. Fourteen board members covered their disappointment to sign a draft report declaring their pride in serving as "partners in a mission of national reconciliation, wisely conceived by the President. A less generous program would have left old wounds festering; blanket, unconditional amnesty would have opened new wounds." The minority maintained that the majority had indiscriminately excused applicants and betrayed the memory of soldiers who had risked all in Vietnam, along with the president.[53]

Regardless of which side came closer to the truth, the clemency program was not a success. The president estimated that 105,000 were eligible to participate and that about 20,000 elected to do so. "I think it was tragic that more didn't apply," Ford said. But why should they? Charges were dropped in 9 out of 10 draft evasion and desertion cases adjudicated in the courts, and deserters who turned themselves in at a military base were ten times more likely to receive a discharge that entitled them to veterans' benefits and that required no additional service than those who surrendered at a clemency processing center. Why pursue a clemency discharge that left one ineligible for veterans' benefits, required as much as two years' service at a low-paying job, and branded one cowardly or traitorous? As a draft resister said, " 'They want me to shuffle and scrape and mumble, I'm sorry, folks, I shouldn't of done it—please forgive me, all so Ford can feel good about letting Nixon off the hook. They can cram it.' "[54]

Conflict within the administration had guaranteed the clemency debacle. The president's new press secretary, Ron Nessen, aptly joked that "when the Ford White House pulled its wagons into a circle, all the guns were pointed in." Throughout Ford's presidency, the Nixon appointees battled for control.[55]

Ford showed greater independence with respect to his cabinet, to which he appointed a diverse array of respected Republicans and independents. Next to the presidency, Watergate had most tainted the Justice Department. Of Nixon's attorneys general—John Mitchell, Richard Kleindienst, Elliot Richardson, and William Saxbe—Mitchell was on trial for his role in the Watergate cover-up, and Kleindienst had pleaded guilty to a charge that he had misled Congress. Saxbe was undistinguished. When Ford heard that Saxbe wanted to become ambassador to India, he named Edward Levi attorney general. The son and grandson of rabbis, Levi had served in Franklin Roosevelt's Justice Department and as dean of the University of Chicago Law School and president of the university. Levi restored the legitimacy of the department, guaranteeing that whenever Justice was in trouble afterward, calls for "a new Edward Levi" would follow.[56]

The president also appointed William Coleman, a distinguished lawyer and the president of the NAACP Legal Defense Fund, secretary of transportation. He was the second African American ever to receive a cabinet post. Ford named Carla Hills, another outstanding attorney, secretary of housing and urban development, and the Harvard economist John Dunlop, secretary of labor. "There is no aspect of President Ford's administration that offers greater hope than the high quality of people whom he is bringing into the Cabinet," the *Washington Post* editorialized.[57]

But those appointments were the exceptions. "The tendency at the top level, except for some Cabinet posts, has been to move people around within the Administration or appoint former Nixon officials," reporters observed. When one Nixonite left the White House senior staff, another would take his place. Belatedly worried about White House friction, Ford finally eased Haig out after six weeks and installed Rumsfeld as chief of staff. So what? Rumsfeld was as high-handed as Haig, and the chaos continued. A historian of the Ford administration who interviewed staffers reported that one spoke "for many" when he said that "Rumsfeld was only for himself—I don't think he served the President well."[58]

The presence of the Nixon faces symbolized the shadow that his predecessor cast over Ford's presidency and the Republican Party. A framed quotation in Nessen's office said it all: "Watergate is harder to wash away than the spray of a skunk." Republicans knew, of course, that the incumbent president's party nearly always did poorly in the midterm elections, particularly when the economy was weak. In the halcyon days of August, however, they had hoped to limit their losses. Now Ford's offer to endorse every Republican in Congress up for reelection was disdained. Asked what the president should put in his endorsement, "one Republican snapped: 'That he's sorry he pardoned Nixon, that he just doesn't know how he could have made that blunder.' "[59]

Ford's willingness to barnstorm for Republican candidates made matters worse. The reporters who traveled with him as he jetted around the country referred to him as "Dummy" and compared him publicly to Bozo the Clown. As Ford's first hundred days ground to a depressing end, one journalist wondered whether "Richard Nixon's final revenge on the America that turned against him was to pick Gerald Ford as his successor."[60]

On November 5, 1974, voters repudiated the GOP. The Democrats won forty-three seats in the House and the two-thirds majority required to override presidential vetoes. They came five votes shy of a two-thirds majority in the Senate and swept the statehouses. Democrats won even in twenty-one traditionally Republican suburban districts. The Republicans now held only thirteen governorships and four state legislatures. Only 38 percent of eligible voters cast a ballot, the lowest percentage since 1946. Those who went to the polls overwhelmingly marked their ballots for liberal and "left-liberal" Democrats, who had gained forty congressional votes. The winners had run against Watergate, the pardon, and the economy.[61]

Indeed many believed that despite Nixon's earlier victories, the Democrats had achieved "a great *party* landslide" that might constitute "the greatest shift from one party to another . . . since the New Deal triumphs of the 1930s." Despair pervaded the GOP's ideological spectrum. The national conservative weekly *Human Events*, aimed at rousing the grass roots, had been grimly charting Ford's move left all fall. Instead of arguing for a strong defense, he had "virtually" promised "conditional amnesty for deserters and draft dodgers!" He wooed "women's libbers—

endorsing the so-called Equal Rights Amendment" and left the Black Caucus "all smiles." The Rockefeller nomination was "most galling," even as the "outrage over pardon shows liberals cannot be appeased." The future of the Republican Party seemed precarious.[62]

TWILIGHT OF THE REPUBLICAN PARTY?: FROM "OLD" RIGHT TO "NEW"

At some level, Republicans on the right nonetheless cheered these developments, which they thought might move the GOP in their direction: Things were so bad that they could only get better. During the 1930s, what later generations called the Old Right melded opposition to New Deal economic intervention with isolationism. In the memorable words of libertarian Murray Rothbard, the Old Right "said 'no!' to the welfare-warfare state." The Old Right included some businessmen who believed that Franklin Roosevelt wanted to destroy them and that his government's intervention in the marketplace endangered their liberty. It beguiled some Christians who feared the modernism some Americans then associated with Jews, who played such an important role in FDR's administration that anti-Semites spoke of his "Jew Deal," along with those who preferred tradition to modernity for other reasons. The Old Right also attracted some from the Midwest and West, who feared American imperialism. Here was a force that southern Democrats could welcome. A coalition of Republicans that included Senator Robert Taft of Ohio, who embodied Old Right values, and southern Democrats, who had emerged in opposition to perceived New Deal infringements with states' rights by 1939, blocked virtually all domestic reform and civil rights legislation for the next quarter century.[63]

The cold war divided and damaged the Old Right. While all its members wanted to root out subversion inside the United States and communism in Asia, some embraced a global crusade against communism, while some remained isolationist. Republicans on the right would be haunted by their support for the intense anticommunism within the United States that was bigger than, but became known as, McCarthyism. By 1955, a year after the Senate condemned Republican Senator Joe McCarthy of Wisconsin for saying that the U.S. Army was a Communist hotbed, the Old Right was in disarray. Publisher Robert McCormick, whose *Chicago Tribune* had spread the Old Right gospel, was dead. Taft had died in 1953, a year after losing the Republican presidential nomination, and therefore the presidency, to Eisenhower, whom the Old Right believed as culpable as FDR of statism and interventionism. The chief Old Right organizations were "anti-Semitic and neo-isolationist throwbacks." The conservative coalition remained powerful in Congress, and conservative intellectuals had published a spate of warnings about the decline of traditional values, the danger that government represented to business and the individual, and the Communist threat. But the presidency remained off-limits to conservatives in either party, and some conservatives thought their movement did not yet hang together.[64]

Enter William F. Buckley, Jr. The Catholic son of an anti-Semitic Old Right millionaire had gained notoriety early. In 1951, as a recent graduate of Yale College, Buckley had denounced his alma mater as a liberal bastion that shattered students' faith in Christianity, individualism, and free enterprise. He also embraced Joe McCarthy. When Buckley became fearful that the Eisenhower administration too blithely accepted the New Deal and would not fight an all-out battle with the Soviet Union, he resolved to found a conservative journal. First, he tried to purchase *Human Events*. Then, in 1955, businessmen provided him with the financial support he needed to found *National Review* in Manhattan. As editor in chief Buckley hoped to mobilize conservative intellectuals in much the way that the *New Republic* then galvanized liberals, and the *Nation*, the left. Some *National Review* contributors focused on communism. Others concentrated on the federal government's interference with the individual and the market. Others struck out at the civil rights movement and school desegregation and the activist Supreme Court that they claimed supported both and undermined states' rights. Still others decried godlessness and modernity and championed tradition.[65]

Oddly, the magazine's cacophony united conservatives. While Buckley sought to sanitize the 1950s New Right, it still encompassed intellectual multitudes. Though *National Review* made isolationists persona non grata, denounced libertarian Ayn Rand for her hostility to religion, and carefully distanced itself from those on the far right its staff considered "kooks" or irresponsible, the journal began to free itself of association with anti-Semites only in the late 1950s; went after Robert Welch, who claimed that Eisenhower was a Communist, in 1962; condemned the far right organization Welch founded, the John Birch Society, in 1965; and exposed the neofascism of Willis Carto's Liberty Lobby in 1971. So too *National Review* reached out to southern segregationists who spoke of states' rights and insisted that the civil rights movement was Communist infiltrated: "It was characteristic of *National Review* in the 1950s and early 1960s to be more agitated by Supreme Court activism than by racial segregation." The magazine did not relinquish talk that African Americans in the South "are, by comparison with the Whites, retarded" until the 1970s, when it adopted the rhetoric of color blindness. Still, the magazine made conservatism more genteel, respectable, and coherent. Like anticommunism itself, *National Review* enabled libertarians and traditionalists to join together against Communists (though, of course, some at *National Review* did not think others anti-Communist or libertarian enough) and the Republican establishment. (Here too some contributors considered others insufficiently pejorative.)[66]

National Review's dream candidate in 1960 was Senator Barry Goldwater of Arizona, who had been elected to the Senate in 1952 with support from Taft, McCarthy, and Eisenhower and had carefully styled himself the symbol of "cowboy conservatism" for both westerners and Americans who loved westerns. But it was the turn of Eisenhower's vice president, Richard Nixon of California, especially after he adjusted the party platform positions on foreign and domestic policy to suit the more liberal eastern wing. Though Nixon's "surrender" outraged the right, Goldwater counseled his supporters at the 1960 Republican convention against a walkout. "Let's grow up, Conservatives!" Goldwater exhorted. "We want to take this party back, and I think some day we can. Let's get to work!"[67]

Six weeks later Buckley threw open his parents' Sharon, Connecticut, estate one weekend to ninety young Goldwater conservatives who wanted to launch a national organization. By Sunday they had formed the Young Americans for Freedom. They had also approved the Sharon Statement drafted by M. Stanton Evans and declared their faith in "the individual's use of his God-given free will, whence derives his right to be free from the restrictions of arbitrary force"; "the interdependence of political and economic freedom"; the limitation of government functions to the "preservation of international order, the provision of national defense and the administration of justice"; the brilliance of the Constitution; the importance of the free market; the certainty that when government interferes with the economy by taking from one person to give to another, "it diminishes the incentive of the first, the integrity of the second, and the moral autonomy of both," while damaging the nation; "the great current threat to liberties posed by Communism"; the need for the United States to conquer, rather than coexist with, Communist countries; and the importance of judging American foreign policy "by this criterion: does it serve the just interests of the United States?"[68]

The Young Americans for Freedom included future architects of the 1970s right. Howard Phillips helped Buckley revise the Sharon Statement, and Richard Viguerie became the YAF's first executive director. So closely yoked were *National Review* and the Young Americans for Freedom that one YAF officer considered them "inseparable." The two scored a success when Goldwater won the Republican presidential nomination from Rockefeller in 1964. Despite Lyndon Johnson's landslide, Goldwater's campaign became the gateway to the future.[69]

Determined to revive conservatism after Goldwater's defeat, Buckley, *National Review* colleagues, and other conservatives formed a YAF for adults, the American Conservative Union. Intended to serve as a lobbying organization, the ACU, like *National Review* itself, was also meant to clean up conservatism by distancing it from Birchers and other "less-savory Right wing leaders." To remind those in the House and Senate that voters were watching, the ACU annually rated them on their conservatism just as the Americans for Democratic Action rated them on their liberalism. To mobilize conservatives to watch members of Congress, the American Conservative Union developed a web of state chapters.[70]

Goldwater exemplified the anticommunism, libertarianism, whiteness, traditionalism, and moralism of *National Review*, *Human Events*, the American Conservative Union, and the YAF. At the time his message seemed more limited as he hammered away at the Soviet Union, the evils of government, and the threat posed by federal civil rights legislation to property rights, law and order, and states' rights with words that enabled him to woo racists, such as Senator Strom Thurmond of South Carolina, a onetime Democrat who now declared that he was becoming a Republican, and the far right, while declaring opposition to racism. But there was more. "Why do we see riot and disorder in our cities?" Goldwater asked. "A breakdown of morals of our young people? A flood of obscene literature?" The answer was that "[t]he moral fiber of the American people is beset by rot and decay." For the first time in nearly a century, five southern states went Republican in 1964. But only Arizona joined them.[71]

What some referred to as the new New Right of the 1970s; others, the seventh New Right since the 1940s; and still others, simply the New Right offered two reasons for Goldwater's rout. The first was that "many

Republicans stabbed Barry Goldwater in the back and then used the size of his defeat to try and prove that conservatism was dead." Goldwater warmed the hearts of conservatives when he accepted support from the John Birch Society; shouted, "Extremism in the defense of liberty is no vice, and moderation in the pursuit of justice is no virtue"; fantasized about bombing the men's room of Moscow's seat of government; ran down the war on poverty in Appalachia; confided his dream of ending Social Security to the aged; and informed farmers that he disliked subsidizing them. As conservatives recognized, however, mainstream Republicans cringed. To them, the candidate seemed a shrill voice on the far right—and a tactless and stupid one. (Goldwater himself reportedly once said, "I haven't really got a first-class brain.") The second explanation for Goldwater's defeat was that he lacked ambition. Despite his vilification, Goldwater had piled up twenty-seven million votes before hanging out to dry the very conservatives he had galvanized by refusing to continue leading them. Nonetheless, Goldwater made the 1970s New Right possible, and its bright lights worked in his campaign.[72]

There they learned the importance of circumventing the media and reaching voters by mail. As the YAF's executive director Viguerie realized he could bypass soliciting demanding, wealthy donors for funds and request smaller contributions from a larger group. In 1964 he noticed that Goldwater was raising money through direct mail appeals. Viguerie copied by hand the addresses of 12,500 individuals who had donated fifty dollars or more to the Republican presidential campaign and, in 1965, founded RAVCO, Richard A. Viguerie Company, to raise money for conservative causes and candidates through computerized direct mail appeals.[73]

By the mid-1970s Viguerie had become the New Right's fund-raiser in chief. Each of his clients had to share its contributor lists with him. Contracts required a client, such as the National Right to Work Committee, to solicit donations only through RAVCO's computers and authorized Viguerie to lease its list to others, such as the National Rifle Association. Since direct mail, largely used up until that time for commercial and charitable purposes, was expensive (one of Viguerie's tricks was "to use first-class stamps instead of the commercial bulk-rate frank, which announces 'junk mail' inside"), it was crucial to target likely contributors. Viguerie centralized financial control of the New Right in his hands and copied the Democrats in reaching out to special interest groups. Intentionally shrill direct mail appeals to "Dear Friend" graphically portrayed what would happen "to you" if "liberal politicians" (always the enemy, sometimes Republican, frequently Democrat) executed whatever plot was exposed—e.g., awarded taxpayers' money to "communists, anarchists and other radical organizations" that did not respect property rights or supported busing to desegregate schools, gun control, abortion, or the elimination of school prayer.[74]

Direct mail was vital to the New Right, Viguerie contended, because liberals controlled not just "all three branches of government" but "the major universities, the three major networks, the biggest newspapers, the news weeklies, and Hollywood." Direct mail enabled the New Right to circumvent the monopoly and inform constituents that their congressman or senator was not representing them. Just as he overstated the influence of liberals, so Viguerie may have exaggerated his own value. While some of his direct mail campaigns successfully raised funds for the client, others seemed to enrich only RAVCO and to enlarge its bank of conservative names. Yet while direct mail was only sometimes a good way of raising money, it always proved an effective tool of mobilization.[75]

Elsewhere the Democrats provided additional inspiration. Paul Weyrich, the New Right's master strategist, experienced an epiphany when he unexpectedly witnessed how foundation representatives, lawyers, lobbyists, and columnists worked together to coordinate the marketing of a liberal measure. "I determined from that moment on that if I had any reason to be here at all, it was to duplicate that effort on the Right."[76]

He and others consciously did just that in 1974. To this point, *Human Events*, the American Conservative Union, and Liberty Lobby had been the right's principal Washington outposts. Now a host of institutions appeared to promote conservatism. Weyrich's new political action group, the Committee for the Survival of a Free Congress, provided the same assistance with polling and media to conservative congressional candidates that the National Committee for an Effective Congress gave liberals. Terry Dolan soon formed the National Conservative Political Action Committee to fund selected candidates. The new House Republican Study Committee and Senate Republican Steering Committee were patterned after the House Democratic Study Group, that developed strategy and did research and speechwriting for liberals. Since Washington was "the capital city of American liberalism," Howard Phillips reasoned, D.C. often ruined conservatives as they learned they had more to fear from organized liberals than from other conservatives. Immediately after the midterm elections, he used Viguerie's mailing lists to establish the Conservative Caucus. It mobilized single-issue groups throughout the nation to lobby Congress. Some four hundred registrants in 1974 attended the American Conservative Union's first Conservative Political Action Conference, where policy sessions were coupled with panels about direct mail and campaign logistics.[77]

The vision extended beyond Capitol Hill. The right viewed the Brookings Institution as the "liberal Democratic think tank," and conservatives wanted one of their own. Convinced that the American Enterprise Institute was too small, academic, and mainstream Republican, Weyrich persuaded beer magnate Joseph Coors to award the Heritage Foundation $250,000, and Weyrich became its first president.[78]

Viguerie and Weyrich symbolized the continuity between the Goldwater campaign and the New Right in terms of technique; Phyllis Schlafly, the ideological continuity and the importance to conservatism of a legion of right-wing mothers who feared the danger communism posed to "children, family and community." No one had stated the case for Goldwater in 1964 more eloquently than Schlafly. The "First Lady of American Conservatism" had detailed the chicanery of establishment Republican "kingmakers" who had repeatedly stolen the nomination from conservatives for liberal patsies. As Schlafly observed, except in the case of Eisenhower, a war hero, voters repeatedly opted for the liberal Democrat over the liberal Republican. She contended that if the Republicans presented voters with a real alternative, appreciative conservatives would ensure the candidate's victory.[79]

Schlafly became increasingly discontented with the Republican Party after 1964 and urged Americans to wake up to the Communist menace. She insisted that Soviets were plotting a surprise attack on the United States and that Washington "defeatists" were trying to stave it off through unilateral disarmament. When the Republican leadership passed her over as president of the National Federation of Republican Women for a moderate in 1967, she cried foul and that year launched a monthly newsletter, the *Phyllis Schlafly Report*, to which three thousand disillusioned Republican clubwomen on the right immediately subscribed.[80]

Like many other conservatives, Schlafly felt personally betrayed by Richard Nixon, for whom she had stumped in 1968. Nixon won over conservatives by suggesting that he had become one of them and espousing a racially tinged antigovernment populism that promised law and order to white conservatives, southerners, westerners, and suburbanites.

Then he took office. His Family Assistance Plan and attempted welfare reform, promotion of the Occupational Safety and Health Administration, and wage-price controls were bad enough. But Nixon's negotiations with the Soviets made him anathema. So did his overtures to the Communist Chinese, a recent Soviet enemy whom Nixon courted as he sought to play the Chinese and Russians against each other and to enlist Communist nations in the enterprise of containing communism. Ever since the Truman administration had deserted the Nationalist Chinese in their civil war against the Communists, relegating the Nationalists to Taiwan and leaving the Communists ensconced on the mainland, most conservatives had viewed Taiwan's protection as an article of faith. They saw Nixon's move to accommodate the Soviet Union and keep it on the defensive by triangulating foreign policy and visiting mainland China as a prelude to the abandonment of Taiwan, whose security the United States had pledged to protect by treaty in the 1950s. The board of directors of the American Conservative Union voted to "suspend our support of the Administration" in 1971. During the 1972 primary season Schlafly, Buckley, and other conservatives supported Representative John Ashbrook of Ohio in his quixotic attempt to seize the Republican nomination from Nixon, even though Ashbrook, who attacked the Nixon administration for its "presentation of liberal policies in the verbal trappings of conservatism" and extension of the New Deal, never had a chance of capturing the party machinery. By now Schlafly had a new cause: She would fight the Equal Rights Amendment to the Constitution, forbidding sex discrimination, which Nixon supported and which, after congressional approval, was sent to the states for ratification in 1972.[81]

There were real differences between Goldwater and the conservatives that Schlafly exemplified. Though Goldwater also disliked the ERA, his belief in liberty and privacy sometimes led him to speak of a woman's right to abortion, a cause his political descendants spurned. Like Buckley, Goldwater was also ultimately a party loyalist. After Nixon won the nomination in 1972, *National Review* tepidly endorsed him. Goldwater urged conservatives to stand "shoulder to shoulder" with Nixon and campaigned for him.[82]

Goldwater's intellectual "children" were mavericks. Consequently they and he reacted differently to Ford's appointment of Nelson Rockefeller. Goldwater had considered Ford just the "Mr. Clean" that the United States needed in the aftermath of Watergate. Though he voted against Rockefeller's confirmation as vice president, Goldwater remained loyal to Ford. Buckley also went so far as to maintain that Ford had chosen wisely because of Rockefeller's appeal to Democratic and independent voters. Angrier conservatives launched a campaign to replace Ford in 1976. At the American Conservative Union board of directors meeting after the president announced the Rockefeller nomination, everyone stressed the need "to discredit Rocky and show the rank and file Republicans that he and Ford are not conservatives." According to Viguerie, the selection of "the high-flying, wild-spending" Rockefeller spawned the New Right. Certainly, the reaction against the pardon also increased the sense among conservatives that Ford was vulnerable, making the pardon itself a landmark in the rise of conservatism.[83]

Pundit Kevin Phillips pushed the phrase "New Right" in 1974 to describe "the populist-conservative groups in the orbit of fund-raiser Richard Viguerie, the focus being the newness of these rightist elements emphasizing social issues, religious and cultural alienation, antielite rhetoric, lower-middle-class constituencies and plebiscitary opinion mobilization." Phillips contended that the New Right represented "a *major* cultural and tactical departure for 'conservative' politics." One did not hear New Right architects talking about the free market, Edmund Burke, and Adam Smith, he maintained, as the 1950s intellectuals did, so much as decrying "the moral and cultural tone of 1970s liberalism." They maligned abortion, the Equal Rights Amendment, busing, and the end of school prayer. They celebrated southern populists, such as Governor George Wallace of Alabama, a Democrat. In fact, Phillips was certain "the New Right is a partial heir of the Wallace movement."[84]

That was a sleight of hand, but a shrewd one. In truth, as historian Leo Ribuffo observed, the roots of "populist conservatism" stretched back even farther back than Henry Clay. Conservatives of all stripes helped explain the shape of Social Security, Medicare, and labor legislation; the lack of meaningful civil rights legislation until the 1960s; and Lyndon Johnson's Americanization of the Vietnam War "against his better judgment even at the peak of liberal power."[85]

Moreover, the New Right was the heir to the Goldwater campaign, plain and simple, and it would not have existed but for the promotion of *National Review*, *Human Events*, the Young Americans for Freedom, and the American Conservative Union by 1950s and 1960s conservatives. In an attempt to underscore the newness of the 1970s New Right and to justify its existence, its members exaggerated their differences with the Old Right, which had long cared about "moral and cultural tone." Buckley grumbled to M. Stanton Evans, by now the American Conservative Union's chair, that Phillips had gone on a "bender." Many at the ACU despised the New Right. From their perspective and that of many of their donors, the proliferation of new organizations splintered the conservative movement and overwhelmed potential contributors with too frequent demands for cash. The American Conservative Union lamented that its own former staffer Howard Phillips had established the Conservative Caucus over its objection, that the Conservative Caucus's program needlessly duplicated the ACU's, and that Viguerie's fund-raising brought in neither new prospects nor additional funds. Evans grumbled that "Viguerie, Weyrich et al. . . . claim credit for what ACU is doing," while American Enterprise Institute president William Baroody complained that the Heritage Foundation was "reinventing the wheel." Nevertheless, Phillips, "Viguerie, Weyrich et al." continued to stress the Old Right's inattentiveness to cultural conservatism, elitism, exclusiveness, secretiveness, defensiveness, fatalism, and rigidity. In fact, both factions were actively seeking to build a "counter-establishment" of their own against the "Establishment" they wrongly believed liberals controlled, and some members of the Old Right shared the New Right's interest in fusion politics with conservative Democrats and independents.[86]

Insofar as a difference existed between the Old and New Right, it was largely one of background, geography, and tone. The key figures of the New Right were more likely to come from "blue collar" families than "blue blood" ones. They were less likely to have attended Ivy League institutions, though Howard Phillips had received his B.A., Phyllis Schlafly, her M.A., from Harvard. Many members of the New Right, such as Jesse Helms, the first Republican sent by North Carolina to the Senate in the twentieth century, hailed from the South and the West, not the Northeast. While Buckley and William Rusher stressed civility, New Right leaders could be defiantly abrasive. By characterizing the GOP as "a social club where rich people go to pick their noses," they promoted the replacement of country club conservative Republicanism with a country and western conservatism more likely to bring aboard Democrats from the West and South.[87]

In 1974, Viguerie and Weyrich dreamed of realizing their goals for the New Right through a new political party. "I understand marketing, and I don't believe that in my lifetime you will ever be able successfully to market the word 'Republican,'" Viguerie often said. The party was "poisoned" by its association with Watergate and Nixon. In a decade "there won't be a dozen people in the country calling themselves Republicans."[88]

If conservatives did give birth to a new party in time for the 1976 election, who would head it? Opinions diverged. One obvious candidate was sixty-three-year-old Republican Ronald Reagan, who unsuccessfully attempted to seek the Republican nomination at the last minute in 1968. It was easy to dismiss Reagan, a onetime Democrat who had voted for Franklin Roosevelt four times, as a former actor and not a very good one at that, who was not very bright, had a cornball sense of humor and an "aw, shucks" manner, and was prone to exaggeration. Although Reagan was to rally the right and make himself rich during the 1970s with weekly radio broadcasts that he wrote himself, many politicians underestimated him. Nixon told Ford that Reagan was "a lightweight and not someone to be considered seriously or feared." In person, Reagan would deliver what his staffers called the Speech, which was full of tall tales illustrating the evils of big government and Washington and the need to liberate the American people from them. Ford said scornfully that Reagan "would talk about the New Jersey man who stopped receiving veterans benefits because the Veterans Administration had notified him that he was dead, the 'welfare queen' in Chicago who was ripping off $150,000 a year from the taxpayers, the subsidized housing project in New York City that had a doorman and parking garage." Moreover, while Reagan and his second wife were devoted to each other—the canny and comely Nancy Reagan fixed him with the same adoring look every time he delivered the Speech—the United States had never had a divorced president (just divorced first ladies).[89]

But writing off Reagan was foolish. He had rallied Goldwater's supporters in 1964. Reagan too had conservative credentials, rode a horse, and hailed from the West, and he was better-looking than Goldwater. He had grown up in a working-class family in Illinois during the Depression and spoke compellingly of simpler times. In 1966, Reagan won election as governor of California by running a strikingly modern and sophisticated campaign against Washington, the welfare state, UC Berkeley as "a rallying point for Communism and a center of sexual misconduct," and civil rights "extremists" who caused unrest in the inner cities and the breakdown of law and order. He succeeded by thinking in terms of "the category of 'white conservative Democrats'" and going after the

Democrats, a feat few but his devoted "suburban warriors" dreamed a conservative could accomplish. (The civil war between California's two leading Democrats, Governor Pat Brown and Los Angeles Mayor Sam Yorty, had not hurt.) Goldwater himself declared that Reagan's victory vindicated his own 1964 campaign. Moreover, Reagan had proved surprisingly flexible during his governorship—so moderate socially and economically, in fact, that some conservatives questioned his ideological purity. Governor Reagan had signed into law a bill liberalizing access to abortion, participated in a bipartisan effort to achieve welfare reform, realized that the withholding taxes he had vowed to oppose were essential, raised other taxes, and more than doubled government spending. Nevertheless, Reagan had always diverted attention from his pragmatic record through ideological rhetoric that stirred the faithful at the grass roots. His geniality made his message more palatable: Reagan's message was one of "Goldwater-Conservatism-with-a-Smile." For all his negativity about government, he seemed one of the most optimistic, ebullient, and hopeful politicians since Franklin Roosevelt. He was self-assured, he looked like a leader, and he possessed FDR's sense of theatricality. As Reagan ended his second term as governor in 1974, some thought he should begin a serious run for the White House straightaway. *Human Events* touted him as "Ronald Reagan: Spokesman for Conservatism," and he was a hero to *National Review*, the American Conservative Union, and the Young Americans for Freedom.[90]

Another possible candidate as head of a new party was George Wallace. The shrewd and folksy southerner had become a hero in Alabama by pledging segregation forever. He had done surprisingly well in the 1964 Democratic presidential primaries in Wisconsin, Indiana, and Maryland when he took a toned-down version of his message to the national stage. One political scientist observed that racism "both saturated and was masked" by Wallace's anticommunist, anti-Washington populism. After unsuccessfully trying to sell Goldwater on an interparty Goldwater-Wallace ticket, Wallace decided against running as an independent. Once again in 1968, some white Democrats outside the South backed Wallace, and this time he did not withdraw. It was, one reporter famously said, as if Wallace had come to a realization: "They all hate black people, all of them. They're all afraid, all of them. Great God! That's it! They're all Southern! The whole United States is Southern!" (That was a great line, and the white residents of some northern and western cities, such as Chicago, Boston, and Milwaukee, could indeed teach those in Birmingham and Selma lessons about how to hate. Yet while many white southerners adored Wallace, most did not identify with either the civil rights movement or those who fought it. They kept their heads down.) Wallace became the candidate of the American Independent Party, which he joked should be renamed the Squirrel Party because it attracted all "the nuts" on the far right. Though Strom Thurmond campaigned for Nixon and said that a vote for Wallace was a gift to the Democrats, Wallace won 13.5 percent of the vote in 1968. When he went after the Democratic nomination in 1972, he drew even larger crowds. That year, however, a would-be assassin who hated Nixon decided Wallace's loose security made him an easier target: The five bullets left Wallace a paraplegic and ended his campaign.[91]

In the next two years Wallace exercised doggedly, showed off his biceps, and made his wheelchair a boon. "I'm not trying to compare myself to Roosevelt," he told journalists, "but he couldn't walk." By the time Ford tapped Rockefeller and inflamed the New Right, Wallace had become Viguerie's client.[92]

In late 1974 Viguerie touted Wallace as "the first national candidate since Goldwater" who could appeal to conservatives, despite the fact, as Viguerie later admitted, that Wallace "never showed any interest in building a conservative movement." As Viguerie saw it, Wallace's supporters and Republican conservatives agreed on "about 80% of the important issues, social issues like busing and law and order, and the need for a strong national defense." Wallace interested other conservatives too, particularly if Ford received the 1976 Republican nomination. For his part, while Wallace said he simply wanted to ensure his reelection as governor, no one believed him, especially since as the *New York Times* said, Wallace "invariably added, 'However, if I decide to run in '76, I will, and nobody can stop me,'" and had hired Viguerie, "one of the best money men in politics." Viguerie had recently mailed out nearly two million letters asking whether recipients believed there was a need for "a third party" and would support Wallace.[93]

MEANWHILE, THE DISSONANCE that had once served *National Review* so well reduced its influence. Buckley treated the New Right as unhousebroken. As *National Review* publisher and American Conservative Union member William Rusher fumed over the selection of Rockefeller as vice president, however, he decided it represented the end of "the conservative movement's long love affair with the GOP." Rusher determined to join forces with Viguerie and the New Right to create a conservative party, a prospect in which the American Conservative Union also displayed interest.[94]

So in the second half of 1974 Rusher began urging replacement of the Republicans with a new party that brought together the majority of Americans that he claimed opposed liberalism. He sought to marry blue-collar, socially conservative Democrats to the Republican economic conservatives who made voters label the GOP the fat cats' party. Just as the nineteenth-century Republican Party had developed out of the disintegration of the Whigs and united antislavery Whigs and Democrats, so might a new party now rise like a phoenix from the ashes of the dying GOP.[95]

By Rusher's reading of the past, the heyday of modern conservatism *could* have begun in 1968. Nixon received 43.4 percent of the popular vote; Wallace, 13.5 percent; Hubert Humphrey, liberalism's champion and Lyndon Johnson's vice president, 42.7 percent. Then, in 1972, Nixon routed the junior senator from South Dakota, Democrat George McGovern. As Rusher summarized it, "The election of 1968 roughly exemplified, in the votes for Nixon and Wallace, the strength of the two components of the coalition when separated. The election of 1972, in which Nixon carried every state but Massachusetts, demonstrated the overwhelming power of the same two components when they were united." There was something else: Polls of the early 1970s indicated that "substantially more voters" identified themselves as conservative than liberal.[96]

Rusher's history was controversial. Many conservative Republicans had never liked Wallace. Buckley dismissed him as an uncouth rabble-rouser, and virtually no leading conservatives supported Wallace. While conservative Republicans backed big business, Wallace populists assailed it. While conservative Republicans opposed big government, Wallace populists supported spending on entitlements and attacked bureaucracy. While members of both groups could agree on some social issues and the menace of the Soviet Union, the Alabama farmer who shared the midwestern banker's fear of the Soviets was thankful his mom had Medicare. Rusher also ignored how close Humphrey had come to victory in the campaign's final days, even though liberals had split over his candidacy because of the Johnson administration's role in escalating the Vietnam War. In 1968 the thirty-one-year-old Americans for Democratic Action, once the very center of cold war liberalism, endorsed the antiwar candidate, Senator Eugene McCarthy of Minnesota. When it chose him over Humphrey, another Minnesotan, who was one of its own original guiding lights, it split "the liberal-labor-Negro coalition that had elected every liberal president" since 1936. Further, the 1968 convention where Humphrey received the nomination was a brawl broadcast around the world. Wallace believed his candidacy was responsible for Humphrey's loss, and some analysts also maintain that it threw the election to Nixon.[97]

Nor did Rusher fully take into account the limited appeal of McGovern, the godfather of the "left-liberal" position on the contemporary political spectrum. After 1968, McGovern had chaired a committee to democratize the party's rules. Out of the process had come the Democrats' decision to seek making the number of women, minorities, and the young in each state delegation to the national convention proportionate to their percentage in the state. That undermined party discipline. Politicos reasoned that delegates chosen by the few in state caucuses and conventions were more susceptible to challenge under the rules than those selected directly by voters, and more states than ever before held primaries in 1972. During a brilliant primary campaign, McGovern folded the remains of the 1960s left into the Democratic Party as he tried to untangle liberalism from its cold war moorings. In spite of the efforts of more centrist Democrats, such as Humphrey, Henry Jackson, and Edmund Muskie, to paint McGovern as a radical, he received a nomination he would not otherwise have won.[98]

Republicans tarred McGovern as "the Barry Goldwater of the left," who placed his faith in "acid, amnesty and abortion." That was unfair. To the dismay of feminists, who backed him anyway, abortion made McGovern uneasy, and he proposed only to spare recreational users of marijuana prison time. Still, the Republican rhetoric was effective. Further, McGovern insisted that Americans "didn't have any mission to police the world" and pledged to withdraw troops from Southeast Asia within ninety days of his inauguration, grant amnesty to draft evaders, "beg" the North Vietnamese for the release of American prisoners of war, slash defense spending, provide the poor guaranteed annual incomes, raise taxes on the rich, and protect minority, women's, and gay rights. His promises alienated more traditional labor leaders, such as the AFL-CIO's George Meany, working-class whites, ethnics, white southerners, and Democratic Party regulars at the same time that they won

McGovern support from the young, feminists, gays, African Americans, and Latinos. Moreover, McGovern ran a terrible general campaign, which caused him to seem at once sanctimonious and hypocritical.[99]

Save for the president, the Republicans still did badly. Despite Nixon's 1972 landslide and the Democrats' loss of twelve seats in the House, Democrats picked up one in the Senate. They still held enormous majorities in Congress.[100]

Rusher also sometimes equated ideology with party and treated Republicans and conservatives as synonymous. Yet conservative Republicans took a beating in the 1974 midterm elections. Not all Republicans deserved the "conservative" label either. Nixon was Exhibit A, and Rusher recognized Nixon's apostasy. Still, Rusher insisted that Nixon and Wallace voters could attain conservatism together.[101]

As the Republicans' fortunes plummeted after Watergate, Rusher went to Reagan and asked him to lead the new party. The Republican presidential nomination in 1976, even if attainable, would require compromise with GOP power brokers and prove "worthless" because there were so few Republicans, he warned. Reagan seemed intrigued. "I see the statements of disaffection of people—in both parties," he mused to the media. "Do you restore the confidence or do you change the name?" His backers reined him in, and the day after the 1974 midterm elections, Reagan denied that the GOP was dead. He maintained that "the Republican Party represents basically the thinking of the people of this country, if we can get that message across to the people. I'm going to try to do that."[102]

That was an announcement that should have created consternation in the Ford White House, particularly since Reagan constantly "bad-mouthed" the president. Rusher was certain that Reagan had not closed the door on a new party if the Republican nomination eluded him, and Reagan's kind words about George Wallace had some fantasizing about a Reagan-Wallace ticket. But from the outset of his presidency, Ford refused to take Reagan seriously. Although he telephoned George H. W. Bush to say he was passing him over as vice president, he made no effort to woo Reagan. Rumsfeld and his deputy chief of staff, Dick Cheney, neglected conservative Republicans too, despite a staffer's pointed warning that White House positions on "Rockefeller, amnesty, Goodell etc." had "cooled conservative GOP support" and "could cause severe right-wing problems in the future."[103]

Ford worried about neither Reagan nor the New Right. Why should he? New Right activities, though intense, still remained below the White House radar screen. The New Right did not score its first legislative victory until the end of 1975 and did not find "the big issue we were looking for" until 1977. Conservative Republicans were divided, and the media ignored everyone but Reagan, whom they treated as a dimwit.[104]

Consequently, as Ford faced the hostile Congress after the midterm elections, he feared his left, rather than his right. In the meantime, one conservative historian said, "the GOP was sinking into oblivion." Many of the politically powerful in 1974 still spoke the language of liberalism and left-liberalism. Conservatism was in disarray. Those who contended later that the tide had turned toward conservatism in the sixties and that Reagan was bound to win in 1980 rewrote the past. The story of the growing power and appeal of conservatism and the Republican Party—two distinct but intertwined forces—was more interesting than that. It was a story of the seventies.[105]

II

THE POVERTY OF POWER

—

THE TITLE OF BARRY COMMONER'S INFLUENTIAL 1976 BOOK SAID it all. From its first paragraph, *The Poverty of Power* stressed the crises that had brought the United States to its knees. "First there was the threat to environmental survival; then there was the apparent shortage of energy; and now there is the unexpected decline of the economy." Commoner drew attention to the interrelationship of "the three e's," the domestic problems that helped define the seventies. His title also described the impoverished state of public life as president and Congress battled each other to a standstill.[1]

STALEMATE

Nixon's high-handedness had transformed the Ninety-third Congress from lamb to lion, and it continued to roar at Ford. During the second half of 1974, Congress investigated the pardon, upset Nixon's plans for the tapes, and held up Rockefeller's confirmation. The Congress that emerged from the Democratic sweep in November outdid its predecessor in aggressiveness.

The many young, inexperienced Democratic beneficiaries of Republican misfortune became known as the Watergate Babies. These babes did not sleep; they screamed. They distanced themselves from the powerful liberal Democrats of yesteryear ("We're not a bunch of little Hubert Humphreys," Gary Hart, Colorado's new senator, said defiantly), and they had even less use for conservatives. The Watergate Babies joined forces with older reformers to democratize power in Congress, make it operate more smoothly and progressively, and boost its stature. Among other things, they stripped the legendary Representative Wilbur Mills of Arkansas of the chairmanship of the all-powerful Ways and Means Committee after he was seen cavorting with a stripper, then deprived other senior Democrats of committee chairmanships. They reduced the power of committee chairs, created more subcommittees, expanded the size of congressional staffs, promoted campaign finance restrictions, and modified the budget process. These changes lessened the power of the members of Congress who had been there longest. They also reduced efficiency, undercut party discipline, accelerated the breakdown of the party system, made it even more difficult for Congress to define, much less implement, a legislative program, and contributed to the rise of the very conservatism they were intended to circumscribe.[2]

But the president had even less of a chance. The 1974 elections, White House Deputy Chief of Staff Dick Cheney recalled, left Ford "virtually no options vis-à-vis Congress but to pursue a veto strategy." In his first year, the president who had vowed his commitment to a good political marriage turned down a staggering three dozen bills. The accusations that "Mr. Veto" attempted "minority rule" left his handlers scrambling to portray Ford's use of the veto as a statesmanlike action.[3]

They blamed the president's political spouse. Thanks to the transformation of Capitol Hill, the overwhelmingly Democratic Congress could not muster the votes to override even a fifth of Ford's vetoes. On every important issue, "Gerald Ford was on the defensive," but Congress was, too.[4]

ALICE IN WONDERLAND

Americans observed this "gridlock" while struggling with economic problems that demanded concerted solutions. The prosperity and expansion that the United States had experienced since World War II made it the envy of the world. But by August 1974, Ford said, inflation had become "public enemy number 1."[5]

The roots of double-digit inflation stretched back to the mid-1960s, when Lyndon Johnson decided to fight both the war in Vietnam and the war on domestic poverty. Understanding that Congress would demand cutbacks in his poverty program if he urged a tax increase to fund the military, he delayed asking for one until a deficit forced him to do so.

By 1968 the economy had boomed, but it had also become dangerously overheated. Worldwide hikes in commodity prices and a run on U.S. gold supplies increased the instability.[6]

Nixon tried to remedy this sad situation by fighting inflation and announcing the Nixon Doctrine: "The United States rather than sending men will send arms when we consider it in our interest to do so, arms to help other countries defend themselves." American troops returned from Vietnam, and Nixon made further points with the public by ending the draft, in place since 1940, in the mistaken gamble that he could gain "breathing space to ask Americans to support a renewed militarism without confronting middle-class fears about their sons." Defense spending diminished, but it remained significant. At home, the president first rejected demands for wage-price controls and exhorted management and labor to represent their interests, which led to a surge in prices and wages at the same time that the nation experienced high interest rates, growing unemployment, and disaster at the stock exchanges. The upshot was "stagflation," the combination of inflation and recession that wrought havoc for Republicans in the 1970 midterm elections. By 1971, with unemployment and inflation rising, confidence in the dollar falling, and the United States experiencing its first trade deficit since the nineteenth century, Nixon had concluded that the economy must "take off like hell." Preempting the beloved television show *Bonanza*, he announced the introduction of wage and price controls, the most dramatic government intervention in the economy since World War II. He also sought to recapture American leadership in trade by imposing a tax on imports, abandoning the international gold standard, and devaluing the dollar. He told every department in government "to get out and spend" and approved a large congressional hike in Social Security benefits. The Federal Reserve cut interest rates. A boom followed, along with Nixon's reelection.[7]

The boom ended in the winter of 1973. Inflation, however, rose, particularly after the president reacted to the downturn by lifting controls. Their end and worldwide food shortages pushed prices higher. Nothing government did, including the reimposition of controls, made things better. The American standard of living dropped for the first time since World War II.[8]

That hurt workers even more than employers, and not just because inflation hit hardest those with shallow pockets. Many blamed the economic woes on the unions' demands for higher wages, which business often cited to justify price increases. As a consequence, the 1970s witnessed a shift in the balance of power between labor, long a pillar of the Democrats, and business. Prosperous workers had been equated with the national interest since World War II. Wages must grow so workers could spend, even if mild inflation ensued. Now, ending runaway inflation became the patriotic act that spending had been between World War II and Watergate. Corporate America tried to restore its profits by making "the great U-turn": Instead of stressing the relatively high wages that it paid workers, business now highlighted the low prices that it provided consumers. The middle class, which had largely tolerated labor unions, divided and weakened the Democratic Party further by turning its back on them. And most controls were discredited. When Nixon left office, the only ones that remained were on oil and natural gas, and Washington's intervention in the energy field underscored for many the danger of interfering with the marketplace.[9]

The energy crisis that began to worry Americans in 1973 worsened inflation. In 1970 the global market price of crude oil was under $3 a barrel. But in 1973 oil seemed scarce and was definitely expensive. Then, in October, Egypt and Syria launched the Yom Kippur War to recapture the territories Israel had seized six years earlier in the Six-Day War. When the United States supported Israel, Iran became the only Persian Gulf country to supply Americans with oil for six months. (The United States had won the allegiance of Iran's shah twenty years earlier, when the CIA coordinated the overthrow of Iran's reform-minded prime minister and secured the shah's throne.) Further, just before Christmas, the Organization of Petroleum Exporting Countries (OPEC) quadrupled the price of oil to $11.65 a barrel. The "Great Oil Shock Horror Show" had begun.[10]

The oil shock pushed gas prices at American pumps from 40 cents to 55 cents a gallon. The higher price was cheap by contemporary standards, the equivalent of about $2.39 thirty-five years later. But the average American car during the mid-1970s could travel less than fourteen miles on one gallon of gas, and there were long gas lines. Auto sales were down 35 percent. "We sell more cars than Ford, Chrysler, Chevrolet, and Buick combined," Matchbox toy cars facetiously advertised. Layoffs in the airline and automobile industries, home construction and energy-related businesses became commonplace in 1973–74. To help, the Federal Reserve System reduced interest rates. That miscalculation, when combined with the end of price controls on everything but oil and gas, set off a new round of inflation. Further, just as food shortages seemed to be coming under control, drought struck the American farm belt. The stock market crashed too. By the time Nixon resigned, inflation was at 10 percent, unemployment at 5 percent and rising.[11]

AS FORD TOOK OFFICE, his advisers were obsessed with inflation. Council of Economic Advisers chair Alan Greenspan, a Juilliard dropout who had earned a living playing clarinet and tenor sax in a swing band during World War II before he discovered economics, was the most conservative individual ever to be appointed to that position. Greenspan frequently jogged to work "in full business dress," but he knelt at the altar of libertarian Ayn Rand, who stood by him as he was sworn into office. Greenspan championed the traditional Republican medicine of budget cutting, and Ford revered him. Federal Reserve System chair Arthur Burns, Greenspan's amiably autocratic graduate school mentor, and Secretary of the Treasury William Simon, an abrasive former bond trader who had made a fortune on Wall Street, sang from Greenspan's songbook. Burns, who had ensured Nixon's triumph in 1972 by expanding monetary supply and contributing to inflation, described President Ford as "truly angelic," perhaps because Ford gave him more of a free rein than Nixon had. Despite widespread complaints that monetary policy, which had turned tight, was strangling the economy, Ford cheered the Fed's refusal to loosen the money spigot in 1974 and 1975. Simon urged Americans to throw off the shackles of government regulation and counseled Ford to fight inflation by raising taxes.[12]

These men found President Ford more sympathetic than his predecessor. Nixon's heterodoxy and budget allocations sometimes qualified him for the label "liberal" as his economic policy zigzagged in different directions. Ford, however, associated liberalism with the Democrats and defined himself as a conservative, budget-balancing believer in the market. Consequently, the $305 billion budget Nixon had submitted for 1975, an increase of almost 5 percent over 1974, with its $3.5 billion projected deficit, worried Ford. Defense spending had declined from 40 percent of the budget during Eisenhower's presidency to 24 percent during Nixon's, while federal payments to individuals had climbed from 24 to 44 percent, Ford grumbled. He hated "[a]ll these entitlement programs," such as Social Security and food stamps, for redistributing income and sapping American freedom and solvency.[13]

Ford's economic advisers made sure he fretted about inflation as "the prime problem," not about unemployment and recession. The blindness to the approaching recession was understandable for many reasons. First, the old macroeconomic solutions had stopped working. Economists influenced by John Maynard Keynes had long preached that government should steady the economy through fiscal and monetary policy—the adjustment of taxing and spending, along with money and credit. Keynesians had also promised a trade-off. At worst, higher unemployment and its partner, falling wages, carried the silver lining of less inflation; higher inflation, the bonus of lower unemployment and rising wages. All government need do was decide its priorities and choose its poison for regulating demand. The Republicans, with their rhetoric of austerity, could concentrate on battling inflation and anticipate greater unemployment. The Democrats, with their emphasis on jobs, could focus on fighting unemployment and expect high prices. The soaring inflation and unemployment of the 1970s and the economy's unresponsiveness to governmental solutions proved mystifying. Second, Ford's focus on inflation made sense from his perspective because historically inflation was a Republican issue. Third, higher costs, especially for energy and food, bothered many Americans more than unemployment. Fourth, Ford believed that a declaration of war on inflation would build business confidence and create additional jobs. Finally, he considered inflation an easier opponent than unemployment. He knew he risked increasing unemployment by raising taxes and slashing the budget. But if he supported a tax cut and more government spending to jump-start the economy, he feared increased inflation and more unemployment. Soaring prices might cause consumers to stop buying and workers to lose jobs—unless, perhaps, the president reimposed controls, as the liberal Americans for Democratic Action called upon him to do.[14]

But even most congressional Democrats now opposed additional controls. So did AFL-CIO president George Meany, who realized that during the Nixon administration wages had been more strictly regulated than prices and profits. Moreover, controls were anathema to Republican traditionalists. At his first press conference, President Ford announced that "wage and price controls are out, period."[15]

In September 1974, Ford held a televised conference on inflation with economists from left, center, and right, the first of a series around the country. But his economic advisers viewed them as window dressing. The culmination came at month's end, with a Washington summit where Ford made the participants a strange promise: "All of you will be the Founding Fathers—if we succeed." In any case, none of the economists in attendance predicted how bad the downturn would be, and the president was distracted during it by his wife's unexpected mastectomy. After the Washington summit, however, with the situation worsening, some economists warned that the country was heading into recession, with one predicting that it would be the worst since the Depression. Yet Ford continued to focus on the deficit and inflation.[16]

THE ADMINISTRATION'S INITIAL PROGRAM, however, provided little hope of accomplishing those goals. Ford wanted to impose a 5 percent surtax on corporations and on the incomes of most individuals above the lower-middle-class level. Ostensibly designed to fund unemployment insurance benefits and new public service jobs, should unemployment increase, the surtax was in fact intended to cut consumer spending. On October 8, 1974, the president presented the surtax to Congress as "the acid test" of his resolve to whip inflation. He outlined other proposals in his package too: tight money, a five-billion-dollar budget cut, increased investment tax credits to stimulate capital investment and offset the surtax, tax relief for the poor, the appointment of a National Energy Board to develop a national energy policy, and reduced reliance on foreign oil.[17]

Inspired by the ballyhoo of the New Deal and World War II, Ford added a chorus of exhortation. When the president went before Congress to call for cutting the budget and raising taxes, he invoked the metaphor of war. Ford announced the creation of a nonpartisan Citizens' Action Committee to Fight Inflation, which would promote citizens' groups to "whip inflation now." The president sported the committee's symbol on his lapel, a WIN button, and promised one to everyone who enlisted "as an Inflation Fighter and Energy Saver for the duration." Created by a Madison Avenue ad agency, WIN was more appealing than that agency's 1968 slogan for battling inflation, "Let's all be a little less piggy." It was still just a slogan.[18]

Ford promised to elaborate on inflation fighters and energy savers' contributions in his forthcoming speech to the Future Farmers of America. But when his press secretary unveiled the text, the networks declined to broadcast it and reversed themselves only when the White House formally requested time. "For the first time in our history, to the best of our recollection, we broadcast live a Presidential speech which in our serious, careful, professional news judgment did not warrant such coverage," the president of CBS scolded Ford. It was difficult to quarrel with that evaluation. Ford's speech was a collection of chestnuts. "Clean up your plate before you get up from the table," he urged.[19]

His appeal to the voluntarism of times past, undertaken with so much hoopla and so little planning, was a public relations disaster. Six months after the announcement of the Citizens' Action Committee, only one local committee had been formed. "The Citizens Action Committee has not made a perceptible contribution or performance in the past and I am unaware of any reason to expect it to do so in the future," Greenspan wrote the president. Treasury Secretary Simon publicly mocked the WIN program. Ford himself later conceded that the WIN symbol and, by implication, the anti-inflation campaign were "too gimmicky."[20]

Few liked his proposed governmental program either. Polls showed that Americans opposed the surtax by two to one. Democrats called for raising the rates on the income and estate taxes of the wealthy instead. Charging that the president must want "to shoot us completely out of the saddle" as midterm elections neared, one congressional Republican characterized the surcharge as "politically revolting."[21]

The media damned the president's program. Cartoonists depicted hungry African American children eating WIN buttons. Like *National Review* and *Human Events*, *Newsweek* denounced Ford's "placebo to ease the pain of stagflation." The *Nation* dismissed Ford as a "cheerleader" and characterized his appeal to memories of Franklin Roosevelt as "grotesque."[22]

Ford actually identified with Herbert Hoover, Roosevelt's unfortunate predecessor. But liberals soon wore BATH buttons: "Back Again to Hoover." The *New Republic* blamed the president's advisers. "Poor old Herbert Hoover was his own economist and dug his own pit; Gerald Ford, somehow, still seems like innocent Alice, surrounded by Red Queens, Tweedledums and Mad Hatters in an economic wonderland."[23]

Depending on whether the speaker was crony or critic, Ford remained positive or in denial as the economy worsened in the fall of 1974. He believed it would improve and thought it unwise "for me as President to stand up and say, 'Yes, we're in a recession.'" After voters punished Republicans in November, he acknowledged that the country was moving toward one. By now the Dow was down nearly four hundred points from 1972. The unemployment rate was 6.5 percent, the highest since 1961. Greenspan warned that unemployment would reach 7 or 7.5 percent during the first half of 1975, at which point the economy might or might not hit bottom. At Thanksgiving, the *Washington Post* reported that lines for food stamps in Detroit had "grown so long that some are closed off at 8:30 or 9:00 a.m. so that those already waiting will have a chance to be processed by closing time in the late afternoon." Ford insisted, though, that "our country is not in an economic crisis." Those who pressed him to make a "180 degree turn" from fighting inflation to attacking unemployment by priming the pump would "be disappointed."[24]

"ENERGY VERSUS ENVIRONMENT"

The nation's energy problems contributed to its economic disarray. In 1950 the United States produced most of its oil. By 1960 foreign oil was satisfying 16 percent of its needs; by 1973, 35 percent. After the Arab world made oil a political weapon in 1973–74, the public feared the Organization of Petroleum Exporting Countries' power and prices. Like OPEC, American oil companies were feeling their oats. Even with controls, they had posted record-high profits in early 1974. At the same time, the U.S. energy industry warned of an oil and natural gas shortage, which it blamed on the Arab oil embargo and OPEC price hike.

Scarcity and expense were two worries; environmental damage, another. As the demand for energy grew after 1960, it became obvious that production and use of oil, natural gas, coal, and nuclear power endangered the environment. In the West the automobiles that clogged the Los Angeles freeways destroyed air quality. In the East the pollution that fouled the waters and beaches of Lake Erie led biologists to proclaim its "death." But only an enormous oil spill in 1969 off Santa Barbara spurred the growth of a national environmental movement that was to flourish during the Nixon-Ford-Carter years alongside the antinuclear, feminist, and gay rights movements. The National Environmental Policy Act of 1969 charged the federal government with environmental protection, and in the Clean Air Act of 1970, the government enlisted in the battle against air pollution. Many said that environmental protection was an individual responsibility too. The first Earth Day was held in 1970 amid fears of ecological catastrophe. But whether environmentalism would prove a fad or wave of the future remained unclear.

Environmentalists favored the development of solar energy and, more important, conservation. They pointed out that Americans, just 6 percent of the world's population, consumed more than a third of its energy. Though conservation did not necessarily limit economic growth and employment, if it did, so be it.

From the environmentalist perspective, the "shortage" claimed by the U.S. energy industry represented a mixed blessing. On the one hand, it provided new reason for conservation. On the other, industry assertions about dwindling domestic oil and natural gas reserves fueled demands to develop coal and nuclear power. The public's doubts about industry truthfulness complicated matters. It did sometimes seem as if American reserves of the most accessible oil and natural gas were being depleted. Yet oil companies and natural gas producers could have worked more aggressively to get the rest out, and they might have done so if Middle East opportunities had not beckoned or if, conservatives stressed, they had sufficient profit incentives.[25]

As it was, those who urged conservation were unsure that a domestic shortage existed. The sudden transition from abundance to scarcity seemed bizarre. Many surmised that American oil companies were feeding the inflationary spiral by conspiring with one another, their government, and OPEC to keep prices high. Washington's use of industry data to justify claims of shortfall was well known, and many regulators had ties to those they regulated. The many congressional investigations of the energy crisis between 1973 and 1975 provided no straight answers. The uncertainty lent an air of unreality to the debate about energy policy.[26]

It also made following Europe's example and imposing prohibitive taxes on gasoline difficult. True, astronomical gas taxes forced Europeans to build smaller and more efficient cars and to promote mass transportation. But most Europeans had long lived in town; they went home for lunch. And since the United States once had a great deal of oil, policy makers, oil producers, and popular culture had aggressively championed Americans' love affair with big cars and the suburbs. Mass transportation in the United States was inadequate. Under the circumstances, pursuit of a tax policy that would cause the accelerator to be abruptly yanked out from underneath American feet did not seem entirely fair—or, more to the point, politically feasible. Some increase in gas taxes made sense. But how much was too much?[27]

ONE THING WAS CERTAIN. Republicans were more eager to reduce dependence on Arab countries than energy use. "Conservation is not in the Republican ethic," one snorted. When Nixon urged Americans to save energy, he did not sound sincere. Convinced that energy=economic growth=jobs, he launched Project Independence to make the United

States self-sufficient in energy by 1980. Although vast oil reserves had recently been found in Alaska's North Sea, the discovery counted for little as long as there was no way to transport oil through the tundra. The quest for independence guaranteed billions in government funding for the Trans-Alaska pipeline. Completed in 1977, the pipeline was soon carrying millions of barrels of black gold daily eight hundred miles across Alaska from Prudhoe Bay to Valdez, though overall production remained below 1970 levels, when American oil production peaked. Nixon also promoted natural gas, nuclear power, and increased coal production.[28]

Entering office, Ford spoke of conservation. In October 1974, however, he fired Federal Energy Administrator John Sawhill for advocating an increase in the gasoline excise tax that even the chairman of Ford Motor Company thought wise. Refusing to accept energy scarcity, Ford also announced his commitment to Project Independence, with its focus on nuclear power and coal.[29]

For environmentalists, nuclear power was a chimera. In 1971 it provided less than 2.5 percent of the nation's energy supply. The United States housed fifty-one nuclear power plants in the mid-1970s; Ford envisioned two hundred by 1985. (As it turned out, there were just over one hundred by 2000.) But economic and technical difficulties dogged the nuclear industry, and like other nuclear power advocates, Ford downplayed the risks of waste disposal and radiation exposure to workers and nearby residents. The Atomic Energy Commission chair insisted nuclear power was safe, while her critics charged that the commission had suppressed studies by its own scientists challenging her conclusions. In November 1974 Karen Silkwood, a worker and union activist at Oklahoma's Kerr-McGee plutonium processing plant, died in a mysterious car crash, apparently on her way to meet a reporter to discuss safety issues at the plant. When plutonium was found in her apartment, environmentalists said her story showed that safe nuclear power plants could not be built.[30]

Nuclear experts had been wrangling about safety for years. The specialists had deliberately hidden their disagreements and stressed the benefits of nuclear power to allay public anxieties. In the mid-1970s the old order collapsed as experts' fears became public knowledge. Antinuclear activism surged. Even so, in all the United States, just Madison, Wisconsin, officially opposed the construction of a nuclear power plant near its environs.[31]

In 1974–75 most environmentalists brooded even more about coal than nuclear power. Though cheap and abundant, burning coal destroyed air and water quality by releasing toxic sulfur oxide and other pollutants, including massive amounts of carbon dioxide that some warned would produce climate change. But few then took global warming seriously. In fact, some worried about global cooling.[32]

Without a doubt, however, surface or strip mining for coal, which had largely replaced underground mining, did scar the environment by causing soil erosion and stream pollution. Anxiety about strip mining led Congress in 1974 to approve a bill requiring mining companies to mitigate the damage. Some of Ford's advisers thought he should sign it. "The environmental damage from strip mining is excessive and should be subject to effective control," his Environmental Protection Agency administrator told him. But Pat Buchanan, who was about to leave his post as a White House aide to join the ranks of Ford's conservative critics, disagreed and said a veto would better position the president "in the energy versus environment quarrel which is developing nationally." Ford vetoed the strip mining bill while spending the Christmas holiday in the Vail chalet of a friend who reportedly would have lost a hundred million dollars had it become law. The president contended that the bill and a second strip mining bill, which he also vetoed, would mean loss of jobs and increased dependence on foreign oil.[33]

Some wondered whether Ford dreamed of increasing Americans' energy supply by more dramatic means. In a Christmas interview, Secretary of State Kissinger hinted darkly that oil shortages might prompt an American invasion of the oil nations of the Middle East. With magazines asking, "Will Araby Bankrupt the World?" and rumors rampant that the Arabs had bought up all the real estate in Beverly Hills and other tony spots, Kissinger's talk probably helped Ford's image. But promotion of the troubled nuclear power industry, championship of the nation's dirtiest energy source, and insinuations about seizing foreign oil wells did not constitute a credible energy program. Meanwhile, rising fuel prices aggravated inflation and unemployment, made it expensive to heat houses, and caused Detroit's inefficient new models to be christened gas-guzzlers.[34]

THE "179-DEGREE SHIFT"

Sensing that the intertwined issues of the economy and energy placed his presidency at risk, Ford changed course during a break from the ski slopes. Soon after Christmas, his advisers gathered to warn him that the looming recession would most likely prove the worst since the Great Depression and to urge him to acknowledge that. His advisers recognized that the January 15, 1975, State of the Union address would represent "perhaps the last opportunity to blow away the rising public doubts about Ford."[35]

The president used the speech to reverse himself. "The state of the Union is not good," he said. "Millions of Americans are out of work. Recession and inflation are eroding the money of millions more." Abandoning the surtax, he asked Congress for a temporary tax cut to fight the recession, a move his press secretary joked represented only a "179-degree shift" from his October anti-inflation program. Congressional Democrats wanted to fight the worsening economy by enacting a tax cut, and if he did not move quickly, they would beat him to the punch and get the glory.[36]

As it was, the president received some of it. To jump-start the economy, he proposed creating a $16 billion increase in purchasing power. He asked Congress quickly to enact a tax rebate of $12 billion for individual consumers on their 1974 income taxes and $4 billion for corporations. All told, he proposed putting as much as $1,000 ($3,975 in 2009 dollars) in American families' pockets by that summer.

Announcing that the United States must come to grips with the energy crisis, Ford also called for reducing consumption and increasing production, with emphasis on the latter. Along with additional nuclear power plants and better home insulation, he urged greater production of coal, oil, synthetic fuels, and fuel-efficient motor vehicles. He proposed experimenting with a cause dear to free market advocates—deregulation—and urged decontrol of energy prices to swell the supply of domestic crude oil and newly discovered, or "new," natural gas, along with higher taxes on oil imports. To prevent American oil companies from benefiting too much, the president called for enactment of a windfall profits tax. He also asked for a new phased-in tax, or tariff, of up to three dollars a barrel on imported crude that he said would reduce oil imports by a million barrels a day. Ford estimated that the new energy taxes would yield thirty billion dollars, which could be given back to the public through the tax cut.[37]

Enactment of his energy and economy plan, Ford recognized, would increase both the federal budget and national debt, since he also wanted to increase defense spending. If Congress went along with him, the deficit would climb to $52 billion, even though the president called for a moratorium on most new federal programs, cuts in many existing ones, and temporary limits on Social Security increases. All told, the president's bicentennial budget ran to a record $349 billion.[38]

"THE FORD PRESIDENCY has begun," a White House staffer crowed after the State of the Union address. "We know he is not home free, but we think he has taken a long step away from Bozo the clown," another White House aide said more tellingly. The media were reporting that the proposed tax cut was decided upon against the advice of Greenspan, Simon, and Burns, who warned it would increase inflation, the deficit, and unemployment and who criticized the president for flip-flopping from a 5 percent tax surcharge to a 12 percent tax cut. Thus the proposed tax reduction was either courageous or foolhardy. The president's own economists admitted that killing inflation—11.03 percent for 1974 and 11.8 percent for January 1975—would continue to plague the economy and predicted an unemployment rate of 7.9 percent for 1976.[39]

Economists and critics outside the administration were scathing. Why was the administration so worried about the deficit? asked Brookings senior fellow Arthur Okun, who was to coin the term " 'Discomfort Index'—a simple addition of the unemployment and inflation numbers—that enabled anyone to measure the relative extent of trouble in the economy." (Democratic politicians called it the misery index.) The deficit simply dramatized the awful state of the economy. Most Democratic economists favored a larger tax cut, though some liberal ones said that government should instead stimulate the economy by spending more on public services and jobs. The Americans for Democratic Action and the AFL-CIO branded Ford's program inflationary and inequitable. Their remedies included a larger tax cut targeted at low- and middle-income families and programs that would create more housing, increase federal jobs, and establish revenue sharing in distressed communities.[40]

No one but hard-core conservatives liked energy decontrol. Given the suspicion of American oil companies, *Newsweek* described "the President's proposal to save oil by jacking up its price" by an average of ten cents per gallon (the equivalent of thirty-five cents in 2009) as "almost universally unpopular." Granted, decontrol might promote conservation by forcing people to drive less, but that argument would annoy so many Americans that the White House could not use it. Privately, the administration acknowledged that even the domestic oil industry did not support its decontrol proposal because of the fear that it would make a windfall profits tax inevitable. Democrats doubted that Ford seriously contemplated a windfall profits tax, and they were certain big oil needed no profit incentives. Though the Federal Energy Administration, a creation of Richard Nixon, estimated that the president's program would cost the average family of four an additional $171 in energy bills annually, another study projected the cost at more than quadruple that. Polls indicated that nearly 80 percent of Americans, like many congressional Democrats, favored federal fuel rationing over immediate decontrol. The administration's response equating federal rationing with socialism proved ineffective.[41]

Ford was soon complaining that "the opposition has tried to nit pick" his program "to death." The president imposed a tariff of a dollar a barrel on imported oil by proclamation in February and threatened to increase it unless legislators moved quickly. On Capitol Hill, his action seemed as arbitrary a use of presidential power as the Nixon pardon. Yet the public also proved skeptical of congressional attempts to develop an energy program.[42]

In that, the Ford administration took comfort. As members of Congress assailed the administration with criticisms of his program, speechwriter John Casserly noted in his diary, they said Ford had "a low IQ" and taunted the president "with the remark that they were elected and he wasn't." After the president took to the hustings to press for his policies, Casserly attended a gathering at a Topeka motel. "I marveled as Greenspan, Nessen, Cheney and many of the top White House aides stood around a television set and actually cheered as both CBS and NBC News carried stories attacking the Congress' inability to act on either energy or the economy" and "roasted" Congress, he recorded in his diary. "I had witnessed no scene at the White House so vividly partisan. Nessen concluded: 'Maybe *they* (the Congress) are the dumb bastards.' "[43]

PERHAPS. STILL, "THEY" won on energy and the economy, and Ford lost. After northeastern governors brought suit to block the oil import tariff, the D.C. Circuit Court of Appeals ruled in August 1975 that Congress had correctly claimed the president had no power to impose the tariff on oil imports without legislative approval. And Congress gutted the decontrol program. The fight dragged on until year's end, when Ford had to decide whether to sign the energy policy and conservation bill. Congress had extended controls on domestic crude oil and natural gas for forty months until the spring of 1979. The president would then have a two-and-a-half-year window in which he would have the discretion to continue, phase out, or end controls. All controls would automatically expire in October 1981 unless Congress extended them. Further, in the legislation, Congress initially *cut* the price of domestic crude by some 12 percent a barrel. The bill left Ford's market-based strategy in tatters.[44]

In part, the legislation was the president's fault. Ford had pressed hard publicly for oil decontrol while privately encouraging Federal Energy Administrator Frank Zarb to make a deal with Congress. At a meeting with GOP leaders, Zarb's insistence that the White House had gotten the best possible result was not selling. "The bill is an absolute and total disaster," one senator told Ford, "180 degrees away from your earlier position" and a Democratic victory. Simon and Greenspan wanted him to veto it.[45]

But Zarb and others advised approval. "With every step in the forty-month process," Ford recalled his FEA administrator saying, "prices would rise, and the oil companies would have new incentives to produce. Phased deregulation over a long period was far better than no deregulation at all." Deregulation would also, most believed, mean higher fuel prices in an election year. So at Christmas 1975 the president finally signed a bill that would remove controls—eventually. "Given the frequency with which such deadlines were extended, the outcome was viewed more as a loss than a victory for Ford."[46]

The Democrats had put together the Energy Policy and Conservation Act so poorly, however, that the legislation haunted Americans in the short and long terms. It did provide for the establishment of a Strategic Petroleum Reserve, a federally owned reserve of crude oil, which could be drawn upon in the event of a disruption in commercial oil supply, that proved invaluable after Iraq's invasion of Kuwait in 1990–91 and Hurricane Katrina in 2005. Moreover, the new corporate average fuel economy (CAFE) standards in the act required U.S. automobile manufacturers to raise the average miles their fleets of passenger cars could travel on a gallon of gas from the current 13 to 18 by 1978 and 27.5 by 1984 and, along with Jimmy Carter's energy policies, restored the United States to energy independence by 1982—briefly. But CAFE standards had unintended results. Unwilling to make big cars more efficient,

American manufacturers expedited production of dangerous, tiny lemons that enabled manufacturers to meet CAFE standards. When Detroit won lower fuel economy standards for light trucks that allowed "trucks" to be dirtier and less efficient than automobiles in the legislation, one dubious achievement of the Energy Policy and Conservation Act was to spark the sports utility vehicle craze. Ford's collapse on oil deregulation also greatly alienated his party.[47]

Signed earlier, on March 29, 1975, the tax bill was another political loss for Ford. Once again, the president was a victim of his willingness to negotiate. In Congress, Al Ullman of Oregon had replaced Wilbur Mills as chair of Ways and Means. Committee Democrats thought Ullman weak. The House "disarray is working in our favor," one Republican initially exulted. Not for long. Where Ford had spoken of a $16 billion tax cut, the committee reported out a $21.3 billion tax reduction bill that increased aid to low-income families.[48]

Then the bill went to the Senate, whose Finance Committee was chaired by the wily Russell Long of Louisiana, a "cleaned-up version" of his father, the flamboyant governor Huey Long. In the hands of "Mr. Tax," relief and reform flourished: Long's Senate bill provided for a tax cut of $29.2 billion. Long also seized the chance to slip in one of his pet projects, the earned income credit (EIC), to provide the underemployed with a credit of up to 10 percent on earnings up to $8,000 to offset Social Security taxes and encourage them to seek work. The measure enabled Long to court antiwelfare sentiment and provide the working poor with tax relief that would stimulate the economy. Like the tax cut, the EIC was also intended as a temporary measure, though it became a permanent part of the Internal Revenue Code in 1978 as the earned income tax credit (EITC).[49]

Even after the tax cut had been whittled back to $22.8 billion in conference because of White House pressure, and Congress had approved the bill, complete with EIC, Ford was furious. His "responsible tax cut" had become "something different" and would increase the deficit by about $100 billion, he raged. The president now confronted "one of the most difficult decisions I ever had to make: should I veto the bill, or should I swallow my pride and sign it into law?"[50]

Ford's economic advisers hated the tax cut. Treasury Secretary Simon urged a veto, as did Federal Reserve Chairman Burns. Greenspan recommended that Ford sign it and "simultaneously come down very hard on the expenditure increases." The White House also found the bill's individual provisions undesirable. No one from the president on down liked the EIC, for example. Ford's congressional allies agreed, and one warned that "if I did not do something for conservatives soon, I would risk a party polarization that would damage my attempts to win the GOP nomination in 1976."[51]

Indeed Ford would. In February 1975 conservative activists from around the country had met at Washington's Mayflower Hotel for their second annual Conservative Political Action conference sponsored by *Human Events*, *National Review*, Young Americans for Freedom, and the American Conservative Union. Ronald Reagan proved the star of the show. "What side can be taken in a debate over whether the deficit should be $50 billion or $70 billion or $80 billion preferred by the profligate Congress[?]," he inquired of his "nearly 1000 admirers." The pleas that Reagan make a presidential run were growing louder. So were the calls for a new party that would bring together Republicans on the right with their Democrat counterparts. Out of the conference came the Committee on Conservative Alternatives, charged with mastering the arcana necessary to field a third party candidate. In addition to *National Review*'s William Rusher and Senator Jesse Helms, its members included the chairs of the American Conservative Union and Young Americans for Freedom, Phyllis Schlafly, the editor of *Human Events*, one former assistant of George Wallace's, and one of Reagan's.[52]

Reagan, however, remained unwilling to say he would run, much less that he would become a third party standard-bearer. He seemed anxious to distinguish himself from Wallace too, and he stressed the difficulty of launching a new party. "Is it a third party that we need or is it a new and revitalized second party, raising a banner of no pale pastels, but bold colors which make it unmistakably clear where we stand?" he asked his Mayflower audience. Many left speculating that Reagan might make a second charge at the presidency but were unsure how.[53]

There could be no doubt, however, about conservatives' opinion of the Ford White House. Save for a few exceptions, and despite Nixon's lack of loyalty to them, conservatives had been the last to abandon Nixon. According to *Human Events*, "to observers who had attended last year's gathering and witnessed the profound sense of pain with which many conservatives then viewed the growing entanglement of former President Nixon in the Watergate web that ultimately destroyed his Administration, one of the most striking differences this year was the almost total antipathy of U.S. conservatives toward the new Ford Administration." With only 18 percent of voters now calling themselves Republicans, a significant portion of that tiny percentage seemed determined to destroy Ford. Here was another reason for the president to veto the tax bill.[54]

Nevertheless, Ford's political advisers agreed with Greenspan that he should both sign and condemn the bill. The president summed up their counsel as he heard it: The bill might be "shaped like a Christmas tree with expensive gifts for everyone," but it would "give the economy a shot in the arm," and it was impossible to "please the right wing anyway." It was unclear that Congress would sustain the veto, and an override would prove embarrassing. And there was Ford's credibility to consider. For three months, the president had called for a quick tax cut, one staffer stressed. "You have won—but only if you sign the bill and proclaim your victory."[55]

That scenario stretched credulity, but Ford decided to follow the advice. In a dramatic television address on March 29, 1975, the president told the public that the tax cut would raise the 1976 deficit to sixty billion dollars and charged that Congress was scheming to raise the deficit higher. But Ford drew the line at sixty billion dollars before millions of viewers: "I will resist every attempt by the Congress to add another dollar to this deficit by new spending programs."[56]

HARD TIMES

Meanwhile, "the Ford recession" worsened. Productivity, measured by output per worker, was plummeting. The U.S. gross national product dropped 9.2 percent during the first quarter of 1975. Mass production industries were particularly hard hit. Workers tried to stop the exodus of jobs abroad with appeals to economic nationalism. Advertisers for the International Ladies' Garment Workers Union created a hit song in 1975. Incredibly, Americans were singing the last verse of "Look for the Union Label":

> Look for the union label
> When you are buying that coat, dress or blouse.
>
> Remember somewhere our union's sewing,
> Our wages going to feed the kids, and run the house.

We work hard, but who's complaining?
Thanks to the I.L.G. we're paying our way!

So always look for the union label,
It says we're able to make it in the U.S.A.[57]

Incredible, but so what? Textiles—like unions, for that matter—were still in trouble. At 11:00 P.M. on March 7, 1975, while Ford and Congress clashed over the tax cut, one of New England's last mills, the Chicopee Manufacturing Company at Amoskeag Falls in Manchester, New Hampshire, shut down after nearly 140 years in operation. "People don't say very much when they're leaving," one factory hand observed. "They're very sad, and a lot of them cry. It's a bad thing when there are no jobs to be had." No one could then foresee that a twenty-first-century New Hampshire governor would boast that old textile mill buildings housed software designers. No one other than a few geeks even knew what computer hardware and software were. Bill Gates was still a student at Harvard. He dropped out to launch Microsoft in the summer of 1975, and Apple computers was not founded until 1976. New England, the cradle of American history, seemed headed for decline.[58]

So too, the once-thriving Manufacturing Belt between Chicago and Manhattan was becoming a Rust Belt as capital moved to Mexico, overseas, or the "cheap labor South," where unions were weak. "Deindustrialization," a word that became popular later to describe "the closing, downsizing, and relocation of plants and sometimes whole industries," had been under way since the 1950s. But as shutdowns increased in steel, textiles, automobiles, and other manufacturing, more Americans noticed it. As workers fled the Northeast to find work in a Southeast and Southwest transformed by World War II and cold war defense spending, it was difficult to miss the distressed towns and cities in Illinois, Indiana, Michigan, Ohio, and Pennsylvania. So too, it was hard to overlook the crowds that flocked to the Sunbelt, which stretched from Virginia to Southern California, and shopped at one of the 244 ostentatiously friendly (at least, by northeastern standards) Wal-Marts that opened during the 1970s. Indeed one big story of the decade was the migration from the Northeast and North-Central states in the Frost Belt to the Sunbelt.[59]

As industry continued to decline, there were fears that the United States would become "a nation of 'fast-food servers'" and clerks. The good factory jobs that had enabled union men to buy houses, perhaps even lakeside cabins, and send their children to college had disappeared. "Rather," historian Bethany Moreton said, "under the stress of deindustrialization, men's jobs came to look more like women's work. Casualization, 'flexibility,' part-time or temp work, and the erosion of benefits, seniority and tenure—the conditions that had once best described most women's work in an industrial economy became generalized to the work force as a whole." Yet in 1975 it was hard to find any kind of job, period. Unemployment was rising to 9.1 percent; 13.9 percent, for minorities. The numbers in the Sunbelt looked good only next to those of the Rust Belt. Ultimately, in 1975, for example, the unemployment rate in Florida was 11.4 percent; in California, 9.9 percent. But it was 13.8 percent in Michigan.[60]

Ford's home state was in extremis. The end of cheap gas turned those who could afford new cars to smaller imports. Inflation made Motor City models more expensive than the new Volkswagen Rabbits or Honda Civics, both of which drove more than thirty-seven miles on one gallon of gas. In the first third of 1975, foreign car purchases in the United States ran more than 20 percent ahead of 1974, while sales of American cars were down nearly 13 percent. For the Japanese, especially, 1975 was a banner year. Within the United States, Datsun sold more cars and trucks than any import; Toyota, more cars than Volkswagen; and Honda, ten thousand Civics monthly. Some feared a backlash. One Datsun executive "nervously" noted that "we really don't want to sell less, but we sure wish Detroit would sell more."[61]

United Auto Workers president Leonard Woodcock was hearkening back to the past. At a February 1975 Washington rally of ten thousand jobless workers, he articulated the bewilderment. "What the hell is going on?" he shouted. Woodcock's threat to return with 190,000 more of the unemployed awakened memories of the Bonus March of 1932, when World War I veterans marched on Washington to demand relief from Congress and President Hoover.[62]

Hoover had tried to lift morale during the Depression with a nightly seven-course White House dinner at which trumpeters heralded his arrival, and Ford followed his example. To be sure, the White House was cutting back and making do with less expensive items, substituting soup for fish as a starter, and chicken for beef. But some still found the meals overly elaborate.[63]

Economically the recession touched everyone from blue-collar workers, historically the principal victims of a bad economy, to corporate managers. Except for repairmen, junkmen, and bankruptcy attorneys, few prospered. It was chic to be bleak. Humor was black and edgy. Bruce Springsteen sang about "tramps like us" in a town that "rips the bones from your back," and in a scene that might have come straight from Clifford Odets, joblessness caused two characters in the *Mary Worth* comic strip to postpone marriage.[64]

As in the Depression, many went to the movies. But whereas in the thirties Americans escaped reality with Busby Berkeley extravaganzas, they now preferred violence and disaster. Steven Spielberg's 1975 film *Jaws*, starring a killer shark that laid waste to swimmers, grossed a record fourteen million dollars in its first week. *The Towering Inferno* featured a monster fire in a multistory high-rise that claimed the lives of many innocents and of the evil builder who had constructed it on the cheap.[65]

Reported homicides, kidnappings, rapes, robberies, and arson were rising. Among novels, a surprise bestseller told the story of a schoolteacher who trolled bars in search of rough sex until a trick bludgeoned her to death. The "Slasher" roamed the streets of Los Angeles, randomly cutting victims' throats from ear to ear on Wednesdays and weekends (and helping make popular "slasher" movies about murderous psychotics).[66]

Americans during the 1970s became fixated on another form of violence, terrorism, which was sometimes defined as the use of illegitimate force on innocents to achieve a political goal. That definition was too broad. In 1975, when Ford was the target of two botched assassination attempts—one by a jailed mass murderer's disciple, the other by a radical once associated with the Symbionese Liberation Army—the president did not call them acts of terrorism. He downplayed them, and the nation did too. The assassinations of NAACP field secretary Medgar Evers and President John Kennedy in 1963, black nationalist Malcolm X in 1965, Reverend Martin Luther King, Jr., and Senator Robert Kennedy in 1968, and Black Panther Party deputy chairman Fred Hampton in 1969 had already brought home the vulnerability of American leaders. When the Symbionese Liberation Army kidnapped twenty-year-old heiress Patricia "Patty" Hearst in February 1974 and demanded that her parents distribute two million dollars of food to the poor, however, its selection of a random target did focus attention on terrorism. The abduction convinced the rich, at least, that no one was safe—especially after Hearst threw in her lot with her abductors, changed her name to Tania, and robbed a bank two months later. Apprehended in September 1975, she became an example of changing attitudes toward crime since the 1960s and a warning to criminals. Beginning in the mid-1970s, criminologists and the legal system were less likely to treat perpetrators as victims of forces beyond their control who could be rehabilitated than as persons responsible for their actions who must be punished. When Hearst stood trial for armed robbery, and her attorney argued that she had been brainwashed or acted under duress, a disbelieving jury sentenced her to six years in prison.[67]

Meanwhile, in New York, fanatic Puerto Rican nationalists claimed responsibility for the bombing of the Financial District's historic Fraunces Tavern in January 1975 that killed four. And at year's end a bomb rocked the baggage claim area of La Guardia Airport. It killed eleven and injured at least fifty. Though no group took credit, the media assumed that "what has come to seem a worldwide epidemic of political terrorism had brought its contagion to America's greatest city."[68]

Terrorism was indeed a global phenomenon on view in Britain, continental Europe, Africa, and the Middle East. Americans blamed it on the Arab world. In 1972, Palestinians in the group Black September massacred Israeli athletes at the Munich Olympics. Three years later a Popular Front for the Liberation of Palestine sympathizer, believed to have been the mastermind behind Munich, seized hostages at OPEC headquarters. Then in 1976, the Popular Front for the Liberation of Palestine and the German Baader-Meinhof Gang commandeered an Air France airliner and its 258 passengers en route from Tel Aviv to Paris and forced it to land at Uganda's Entebbe Airport. When the hijackers released the non-Jewish and non-Israeli hostages and announced that executions of the remaining 105 would begin in forty-eight hours unless Israel met their demands for prisoner releases, Israeli Defense Forces soldiers flew twenty-five hundred miles, stormed the aircraft, rescued all but 3 hostages, and were lionized throughout the United States. "This is what Americans used to do," Ronald Reagan said.[69]

While only Hollywood seemed capable of turning the mission that "reads like a movie script" into a movie, and at least six film companies vied to do so, no one seemed sure that the U.S. government could successfully execute a comparable job. In the 1975 novel *Black Sunday*, the FBI did not stop Palestinian terrorists and a crazed Vietnam vet from mounting an attack by blimp on thousands at a Super Bowl game. An Israeli Mossad agent did.[70]

At one level, Americans' concern with terrorism reflected their anxiety about their declining role in the world. That feeling of powerlessness reflected and was related to their sense of economic impotence. Later the primary scapegoat for America's problems became Japan; in the 1970s it was the Arab Middle East. Instead of books about the Wild West, a spate of "Wild Easterns" appeared in 1975. In one, the Palestinians plotted to kill the secretary of state; in another, Arabs violently prevented an inventor from developing a solar-powered car. In the hit movie *Network*, anchorman Howard Beal told his audience that "the Arabs have screwed us out of enough American dollars" to enable them to purchase the entire United States. "They're buying all our land, our whole economy, the press, the factories, financial institutions, the government! They're going to own us! A handful of agas, shahs and emirs who despise this country and everything it stands for—democracy, freedom, the right for me to get up on television and tell you about it—a couple of dozen medieval fanatics are going to own where you work, where you live, what you read, what you see, . . . your whole life!" Only the American people could stop them. "Get up! Right now! And send President Ford a telegram saying: 'I'm mad as hell and I'm not going to take this any more! I don't want the banks selling my country to the Arabs!' "[71]

"PRESIDENTIAL PIETY"

Though the 1975 tax cut and energy bill could not calm the nation's psyche, they did help mend the economy. Once the administration correctly identified the economic problem of recession and changed strategy, Congress quickly enacted the tax cut and provided a stimulus for the faltering economy. Thanks to the rollback of prices provided by the Energy Policy and Conservation Act, gas prices fell. Food prices did too. The administration's war against double-digit inflation bore fruit: The inflation rate sank from an average of 9.2 percent in 1975 to 5.75 percent in 1976. But the unemployment rate for 1976 was still 7.7 percent, and the president showed little interest in creating more public sector jobs.[72]

Ford did not always even seem interested in increasing the number of private sector jobs. Congressman Jack Kemp scolded the White House: "We Republicans have done a lousy job in recent years in showing how the private sector can create and sustain jobs and productivity, if government's shackles are taken off its backs and its hands out of its pockets." Ford was "losing the rhetorical war" to the Democrats with an approach one presidential aide characterized as "passive and negative."[73]

All the while Republicans groused about the deficit. But in October 1975 the president stunned his economic advisers, conservatives, and congressional Republicans by requesting another twenty-eight-billion-dollar tax cut—this one permanent, to be accompanied by a twenty-eight-billion-dollar drop in the budget that would take effect nine months later. It was a good political decision, he insisted. But it was also transparent. "Ford decided that by playing louder tax-cut music, he could drown out the Democrats who merely wanted to extend the 1975 tax cuts," one reporter explained. "Then by sounding elaborate cut-spending 'knock out big government' themes, he could please the Republican right wing." The tax cuts would take effect in January 1976, the budget reduction in October, "too late to have an impact by Election Day."[74]

As Ford anticipated, Congress moved to extend the temporary tax cut in effect on December 17 and said nothing about limiting spending. When the House surprised the president by sustaining his veto, Ford held out the olive branch. "All Congress had to do for me to sign the bill, I said, was to commit itself to adopt spending cuts." Before Christmas, the lawmakers committed themselves "to trim spending simultaneously with any further extensions of the tax cut after next June 30." At least that was the way the president told the story. In fact, his press secretary conceded, Ford received only "a vaguely worded" pledge from Congress to hold down spending. Once again, conservatives castigated him for caving in to the Democrats.[75]

CONSERVATIVES DISLIKED THE president's urban policy too. In 1975 the nation's largest city teetered on the brink of bankruptcy. Ford and Treasury Secretary Simon believed they knew why. "In New York people won elections by using the word 'more': more public services of all kinds for the working and middle classes; ever greater salaries and pensions for the hundreds of thousands who worked for the New York City government; more extensive social programs for the less fortunate."[76]

In May the Democratic mayor and governor asked the president to support legislation enabling the federal government to guarantee the city's debt. Ford's domestic policy adviser recommended that he "deny the request, but leave a slight loophole which would enable the Federal Government to assist the City if disruption of the financial markets did occur as a result of a default; and/or subject to certain conditions and restrictions." The president opted for a flat denial.[77]

"Every family which makes up a budget has to make painful choices," the president proclaimed, and politicians must too. Ford's action, one aide warned, just encouraged "the average citizen" to believe "that you have all turned your backs on the city." Supported by Simon and Burns, and over the objection of Vice President Rockefeller, who publicly lobbied for federal support, Ford continued to cultivate that impression as the city's situation deteriorated.[78]

Determined to make New York an example, Ford insisted that the "contagion" could not spread and vowed to veto any bill bailing out the city. The president's harsh rhetoric earned him a spate of embarrassing headlines, with the *New York Daily News* famously observing that he had, in effect, told the city to "drop dead." In condemning "presidential piety," the *New York Times* became snotty: "For once, he read a speech as though he really believed it." What would happen if city officials had no salary or welfare checks to distribute?[79]

Under pressure, Ford changed course. At Thanksgiving, he asked Congress to approve a three-year loan to the city if it defaulted "in all but name on its obligation to redeem its notes on time" and agreed to terms that pared back public services and intensified the effects of the recession on all New Yorkers, especially the poor and working class. "The short-term loan granted by the Treasury under these conditions was hailed by politicians and press as a victory for 'New York' and a capitulation by the Treasury," Simon grumbled. The crisis was covered to the end "as though it had been a boxing match between good guys ('New York') and bad guys (Ford, Burns, and Simon)."[80]

IRRESPECTIVE OF THE MEDIA'S fairness, the president's initial position on New York reflected his moralistic stance toward the economy. He proved capable, however, of transcending it. Though his administration bore some of the blame for the worst recession since the Great Depression, Ford had fought inflation and recession in 1974–75 and demonstrated a willingness to negotiate with Congress. Instead of saluting his flexibility and pragmatism, however, many, including conservatives, considered him inconsistent and maladroit. The story proved similar as the administration made its way through the minefield of the family.

III

BETWEEN PUBLIC AND PRIVATE: FAMILY MATTERS

—

IN 1975 THE THIRD DIVORCED AMERICAN FIRST LADY SAT FOR A television interview on *Sixty Minutes*. After volunteering that her psychiatrist had warned her that she was "not taking any time out for Betty," Mrs. Ford was on a roll. "I'm not the type that's going to burn my bra," she told Morley Safer, but "nothing could be greater" than passage of the Equal Rights Amendment. On to abortion: *Roe v. Wade* was "a great, great decision." She was sure her children had smoked marijuana. Now that more young people were "living together," the divorce rate would drop. No surprises here. She might have used "shock words," her press secretary reflected, but Betty Ford had voiced these sentiments before, and these were "shock times." During the first half of the 1970s it sometimes seemed as if sex, drugs, rock and roll, and denim had become universally cool.[1]

There was one bombshell. "What if Susan Ford came to you and said, 'Mother, I'm having an affair?' " Safer asked, referring to the Fords' eighteen-year-old daughter. "I wouldn't be surprised," Mrs. Ford answered. Conservatives flooded the White House with protests. The president joked weakly that when he first heard of the first lady's remarks, he estimated that he had lost ten million votes; then, when he learned more, he doubled the figure. Now her supporters assured the first lady that they loved her, and soon her approval rating surpassed her husband's.[2]

Betty Ford's interview—with her reference to herself in the third person, her frankness about women's rights, drugs, and sex—typified the mid-1970s in its renegotiation of private and public, personal and political. In the words of another feminist, "[T]here is no private domain of a person's life that is not political and there is no political issue that is not ultimately personal. The old barriers have fallen." The changing definitions of "personal" and "political" affected everyone's sense of what should remain private and in the closet. As feminists sought to reshape the relationship between public and private, information about the past misbehavior of the CIA, the FBI, and American heroes that had long remained secret became media fodder.[3]

THE PERSONAL IS POLITICAL

Instead of selecting a "man of the year," *Time* chose twelve women in 1975, International Women's Year. "They have arrived like a new immigrant wave in male America," it gushed of the women who streamed into the workplace and earned only fifty-nine cents for every dollar paid men. More single, divorced, and widowed women worked outside the home than ever before, but the jawdropper was that nearly 45 percent of married women did too. Though most women still chose jobs out of necessity, careers were opening up: Less than 10 percent of the students in professional schools were women in 1970, compared with 20 percent five years later. The number of women lawyers quintupled during the 1970s, and women became eligible for ordination as rabbis and Episcopalian priests. *Time* maintained that "feminism has transcended the feminist movement. In 1975 the women's drive penetrated every layer of society, matured beyond ideology to a new status of general—and sometimes unconscious—acceptance."[4]

There were many feminisms. Some activists worked to win women equal rights in the public sphere; others, to transform gender relations by challenging male supremacy; still others, to celebrate women. The diversity of feminism strengthened it. And many feminists now subscribed to its watchword, "The personal is political." When women exchanged their most personal stories of rape, abortion, sexual harassment, and abuse and saw the similarities, they considered the broader implications. Shared private tribulations moved feminists to public action. What had once seemed individual, personal problems stood exposed as common, shaped by the social, political, economic, and cultural institutions that kept women subordinate to men.[5]

Take rape, for example. Susan Brownmiller's *Against Our Will: Men, Women and Rape*, became famous before its 1975 publication because of its thesis that rape was no random act of lust. Rather, it was "a conscious process of intimidation by which *all* men keep *all* women in a state of fear." Rape also went largely unpunished. Men raped because they could. Most states did not prosecute husbands for raping their wives. Like domestic violence (one 1974 book was entitled *Scream Quietly or the Neighbours Will Hear*), marital rape was considered a private matter. "If you can't rape your wife, who can you rape?" a politician snickered. Women raped by strangers fared little better than those raped by husbands or acquaintances. After Susan Estrich, a white Harvard law student, was attacked in 1975 by a man who "held an ice pick to my throat and said: 'Push over, shut up, or I'll kill you,'" and she had to convince policemen that hers was a case of "real," or stranger, rape. Then they told her how difficult prosecution was. A woman raped at gunpoint might well face "a corroboration requirement [for example, proof of penetration], a cautionary instruction [from the judge directing the jury to evaluate the victim's testimony especially carefully because of her emotional involvement and the diffculty of determining the truth about private sexual activities], a fresh complaint rule [requiring the victim's complaint to be filed within three months], and a searing cross-examination about her sexual past to determine whether she had nonetheless consented to sex." The race and class of accused and accuser might create further difficulties. In 1974, Joan Little, a poor African American prisoner in North Carolina's Beaufort County Jail, stabbed Clarence Alligood, her white jailer, to death in her cell with his ice pick after he had raped her, and the state charged her with murder. Though the civil rights activists and feminists of all colors brought together by her case insisted that Little had acted in self-defense, the prosecution claimed at her 1975 trial that she had promised Alligood sex, then killed him in the hope of breaking out of prison. "It took the six white and six black jurors only 1 hr. and 25 min. to reach the obvious decision: not guilty," *Time* reported. But justice did not always prevail. By one estimate, just 2 percent of accused rapists were convicted.[6]

To many feminists, no issue illustrated the political nature of the personal more than laws that limited reproductive freedom. There were no reliable statistics on the number of abortions, many of them illegal, performed. But feminist Gloria Steinem, who had had one after college without telling anyone, estimated that "one in three or four adult women" had had one, and she asked, "[W]hy should each of us be made to feel criminal or alone?" Reproductive freedom was essential to women's autonomy.[7]

Associating the 1960s with that autonomy was folly. Premarital sex had always been a fact of life, and the sixties proved noteworthy only because that became apparent. As long as heterosexual partners risked a "back-alley" illegal abortion to avoid creating a child, "free love" could not exist. The price remained high throughout the sixties. The U.S. Supreme Court did not even declare that married couples had a right to use contraceptives until 1965. As late as 1969, William Baird, a medical school dropout who became an abortion rights activist in 1963 after he saw "a woman screaming in the hall, with a coat hanger protruding from her uterus" at Harlem Hospital, received a jail sentence for distributing spermicide to singles. No American judge recognized a right to abortion until 1970.[8]

Nor were sixties feminists the first crusaders for legal abortion. Rather, the roots of the movement stretched back to an 1879 Connecticut statute proposed by circus man P. T. Barnum. It criminalized the prescription or use of contraceptives by doctors or their female patients, and other states enacted similar legislation. Many courts read a "medical exception" into laws outlawing contraceptives that permitted physicians to prescribe them for married women. But in 1940 the Connecticut Supreme Court ruled that Barnum's law included no implied medical exception. Physicians continued to distribute contraceptives to married women who could afford their services, but Connecticut birth control clinics shut down. The power of the Catholic Church doomed efforts to amend Barnum's statute, and litigation challenging the legislation foundered too. In 1961 the U.S. Supreme Court reasoned that the statute had been rarely enforced, and where "no realistic fear of prosecution existed," the Court could not "be umpire to debates concerning harmless, empty shadows."[9]

Did that mean that Planned Parenthood's Estelle Griswold could at last open a birth control clinic in Connecticut? Apparently not. When she did, police raided it.

In *Griswold v. Connecticut* (1965), the Court finally invalidated Barnum's statute. Justice William O. Douglas's majority opinion declared a constitutionally protected right to privacy. He derived it from the "emanations" and "penumbras" of the First, Third, Fourth, Fifth, and Ninth Amendments. That right, Douglas said, enabled couples to use contraceptives in "the sacred precincts of marital bedrooms." Justice John Harlan sided with the result, but for different reasons. He called attention to the Constitution's Fourteenth Amendment, which said a state could not "deprive any person of life, liberty or property, without due process of the law." Harlan developed an alternative rationale for a constitutional right to privacy based on substantive due process, the notion that the Court could hold state legislation unconstitutional because justices deemed it an unfair infringement of individual liberty.[10]

Griswold ushered in a new constitutional era. The next step was *Eisenstadt v. Baird* (1972), declaring unconstitutional the Massachusetts ban on distribution of spermicide and other contraceptives to unmarried individuals. "If the right of privacy means anything, it is the right of the *individual*, married or single, to be free from unwarranted governmental intrusion into matters so fundamentally affecting a person as the decision whether to bear or beget a child," Justice William Brennan declared. That remark signaled the future killing of more sacred cows.[11]

Some physicians, public health officials, and attorneys had long battled for liberalization of abortion laws. These elites scorned the typical legislation criminalizing abortions except when the woman's life was "directly at risk." They advocated legislative reform out of the conviction that physicians required the right to decide when abortion was necessary for "therapeutic," or "justifiable," reasons, such as avoidance of fetal injury, protection of the mother's health, or termination of a pregnancy that resulted from rape or incest. Yet despite widespread sympathy for pregnant women who sought abortions because of fetal disability, only three state legislatures had liberalized abortion laws by early 1967. Even those victories were largely hollow. The new laws approving therapeutic abortions proved restrictive; hospitals and doctors, conservative about implementing them because of the vagueness of key terms, such as "health." The pressure for reforming the legislation turned into advocacy for its repeal.[12]

At this point, feminists entered the debate. "A group of women who valued motherhood, but *valued it on their own timetable*, began to make a new claim, one that had never surfaced in the abortion debate before this, that abortion was a woman's *right*," sociologist Kristin Luker wrote, and "was essential to their right to equality—the right to be treated as individuals rather than as potential mothers." In the banner year of 1970, legislatures repealed abortion restrictions in Hawaii, New York, and Alaska. Yet "pro-choice" activists soon saw the window of opportunity for repeal slam shut as "pro-life" forces gained ground. Elected officials were not reliable allies.[13]

There was no reason they should be. Abortion was vital to its enthusiastic supporters and vociferous opponents. Most Americans were neither. During the 1960s a majority had opposed a right to abortion. In the early 1970s public opinion changed. But support for abortion was soft; the majority cared little about it. Under these circumstances, politicians obfuscated.[14]

Consequently, eyes turned to the federal courts. The first abortion rights case was filed there in 1969. Soon more than twenty cases were on their way to the Supreme Court.

The 1973 decision of *Roe v. Wade* was just one of them. Justice Harry Blackmun's majority opinion struck down a Texas statute making it criminal to procure or attempt abortion for any purpose other than saving the life of the mother. Blackmun blended the Douglas-Harlan approach in *Griswold* and embedded a privacy right in substantive due process. He found a right of privacy "in the Fourteenth Amendment's concept of personal liberty and restrictions upon state action." It was not, he stressed, an unqualified right, except during the first trimester of the pregnancy, when "mortality in abortion may be less than mortality in normal childbirth," and "the attending physician, in consultation with his patient," was "free" to decide on termination. During the second trimester, when abortion became riskier for the mother, the state could "regulate the abortion procedure in ways that are reasonably related to maternal health." During the final trimester, after experts agreed the fetus had become "viable" and able to live outside the mother's womb, the interest in safeguarding "the potentiality of human life" became important. "We need not resolve the difficult question of when life begins," Blackmun added. For the purposes of abortion, the crucial question was viability, and the Court announced it occurred at six months. A companion case, *Doe v. Bolton*, struck down restrictions on where abortions could be performed. Together, *Roe* and *Doe* declared abortion laws in forty-six states unconstitutional.[15]

Despite the Court's reputation as pacesetter, Blackmun's opinion confirmed, rather than led, most of the public's. For its time *Roe* was hardly revolutionary. Blackmun spoke for seven justices, and he stressed doctors' rights to perform abortions without fear of prosecution more than women's rights to them.[16]

Nevertheless, *Roe* was divisive. It bred complacency in pro-choice activists, while rallying pro-life forces. Divided, as Luker said, by "different definitions of motherhood," they were united by the certainty that abortion should become their battleground. Pro-life advocates contended that the embryo was a human life and motherhood was women's duty. Pro-choice proponents maintained that an embryo was a fetus and women had many roles.[17]

Pro-life activists, most of them Catholic, were awakening by the time Betty Ford appeared on *Sixty Minutes*. Beginning in 1974, they poured into Washington on *Roe*'s anniversary each year to demand a constitutional amendment overturning it. State legislative sessions now featured acrimonious debates over bills designed to fetter *Roe* by, for example, allowing a minor to have an abortion only after parental notification.[18]

Even many who liked the result in *Roe* were troubled by the Court's reasoning. Constitutional theorist John Hart Ely attacked *Roe* not because it was "bad constitutional law" but because it was "*not* constitutional law and gives almost no sense of an obligation to try to be." Ely conceded that were he a legislator, "I would have voted for a statute very much like the one the Court ended up drafting." But of course, neither he nor the justices were elected. To him and others, *Roe*, like *Griswold*, represented "the classic example of judicial usurpation and fiat without reason."[19]

As a clerk to Chief Justice Warren when *Griswold* was decided, Ely had suggested a different constitutional route to a right to abortion. He derided Harlan's reliance on substantive due process and Douglas's creation of the right to privacy as dangerous judicial activism. Rather, Ely pointed to the Fourteenth Amendment's guarantee of equal protection of the laws and recommended that his boss apply the nineteenth-century case of *Yick Wo v. Hopkins* to strike down Barnum's statute, which effectively allowed physicians to provide the well-off with contraceptives and restrained birth control clinics from making them available to the poor. There, the Court had announced, "Though the law itself be fair on its face, and impartial in appearance, yet if it is applied and administered by public authority with an evil eye and an unequal hand, so as to practically make unjust and illegal discrimination between persons in similar circumstances, material to their rights, the denial of equal justice is still within the prohibition of the Constitution." But Warren ignored Ely, and *Griswold*'s concept of privacy became a stepping-stone to *Roe*.[20]

Thus the constitutionality of abortion did not ensure availability. To Betty Ford, it was all part of "the same old story: the helpless are the ones who will suffer, poor people and twelve-year-old girls who aren't old enough to assume responsibility for bringing babies into the world," while the wealthy acquired a new right. (Her husband personally opposed *Roe* but did little to make the case an issue.) Beyond that, resting *Roe* on privacy, instead of equality, reinforced "the public/private distinction" at the core of liberal thought and American law. According to tradition, law correctly operated largely in the "public" sphere with respect to "public" issues. Legal interference was kept out of the "private" sphere to minimize state intervention in family matters and to protect individual choice.[21]

Feminist scholar Catherine MacKinnon and other feminist critics of the public/private distinction observed, however, that the home too often operated as a zone of oppression. The home could become a place where women might be abused with impunity because of society's rationalization that they could leave, though they might be too terrorized to do so. By assuming women's equality at home, where they might experience abuse and exploitation, privacy as a legal concept preserved the very institution, the family, that deprived women of autonomy. "This is why feminism has had to explode the private. The private is public for those for whom the personal is political." Consequently, the privacy rationale articulated in *Roe* constituted "an injury presented as a gift." Nevertheless, constitutional history had led Blackmun down the privacy road.[22]

In 1975 most feminists nevertheless treated the decision as a victory, and the Court seemed inclined to make abortion more, not less, available. The Court had not challenged the distinction between public and private in *Roe*. But it had made the private the basis for more rights and had given women new options.[23]

FOR MANY FEMINISTS by 1975, adoption of the Equal Rights Amendment to the Constitution to prevent the federal government or the states from denying or abridging equality of rights under the law on account of sex was as important as the right to abortion. Victory by the nation's bicentennial had once seemed preordained. Approved by enormous majorities in both houses of Congress by 1972, the ERA had already been ratified by thirty of the necessary thirty-eight states in 1973. Though three additional states approved the ERA in 1974, the year public support for it peaked at 74 percent, two states had rescinded ratification by then. In 1975 only one state legislature ratified the ERA.[24]

One person slowed the juggernaut. Conservative Phyllis Schlafly had originally lacked interest in the Equal Rights Amendment to the Constitution, which she considered somewhere "between innocuous and mildly helpful." But as she learned about it, Schlafly's apathy turned to anger. Feminists, she decided, sought "to remake our laws, revise the marriage contract, restructure society, remold our children to conform to lib[erationist] values instead of God's values, and replace the image of woman as virtue and mother with the image of prostitute, swinger, and lesbian."[25]

The ERA appealed to Schlafly as an issue for many reasons. First, though Catholic, she was a fundamentalist who believed equality between the sexes violated the authority God gave husbands over wives. Had not Paul advised in Ephesians 5:22, "Wives, submit yourselves unto your own husbands, as unto the Lord?" Second, she maintained that the ERA would destroy the institution of marriage. Third, as a conservative who mistrusted Washington, she feared the ERA would increase federal power. Fourth, she maintained that its supporters opposed capitalism. The "American free enterprise system," not feminist whiners, had produced the automatic washers and inventions that "lifted the drudgery of housekeeping from women's shoulders." Finally, she saw the ERA as a way to rally grassroots conservatives, especially women. In sum, this battle against "the unkempt, the lesbians, the radicals, the socialists, and the government employees who are trying to amend the United States to force us to conform to their demands" was waged "to keep America good."[26]

Schlafly understood that to have any chance of success, her "heavenly cause" must itself mobilize women warriors. She folded her supporters into STOP (Stop Taking Our Privileges) ERA in 1972. Later she launched the Eagle Forum, and it too joined the battle. (The happily married mother of six had taken the eagle as her symbol because "the eagle is almost the only creature that keeps one mate for a lifetime.")[27]

A brilliant polemicist, Schlafly insisted that the very simplicity of the ERA's language made it sinister. She argued that the ERA would blend the sexes together and destroy traditional gender roles and the sacredness of the family by making men and women the same. According to Schlafly, the amendment would give gay and lesbian "perverts" the right to marry. "ERA bans discrimination on account of sex, and it is precisely on account of sex that a state now denies a marriage license to a man and a man." The words "on account of sex" came to mean "on account of sexual orientation."[28]

But that was not all. Schlafly made feminism a threat to women as well as to the family. God had meant men to win the bread and women to make it, and according to Schlafly, "the most basic and precious legal right that wives now enjoy" was "the right to be a full-time homemaker." The "Extra Responsibilities Amendment," she warned, would wipe out that right and impose on wives and mothers the "*legal* obligation to go out to work to provide half the family income." The ERA would also legalize rape and other violence against women because to enforce the law with no reference to sex would require eradicating sex crimes. It would also, Schlafly contended, require women to participate in state-sponsored violence by subjecting them to a military draft and combat duties. That would damage morale because women would "get out of heavy work by throwing tantrums or crying" and make for a weaker military to pit against Soviet males. And in war and peace, the ERA would require women to use the same public bathrooms as men, since "the only reason that this nation has separate restrooms for men and women and boys and girls is sex. Consequently, being a distinction based on sex, the ERA would abolish the power of the Federal Government and the power of the 50 states to require separate facilities of this nature for persons of different sexes." (Manipulating racial fears that the ERA would bring black boys into contact with white girls in public bathrooms, some ERA opponents stressed it would "desexregate" the United States.)[29]

Moreover, a 1974 headline in the *Phyllis Schlafly Report* proclaimed ERA MEANS ABORTION. Schlafly was sure that activist federal judges would interpret the ERA to say that "women must be made equal to men in their ability *not* to become pregnant." Further, the ERA would mean sticking the American people with the bill for "abortion on demand, financed by the government and made socially acceptable any time, any place."[30]

Schlafly's parade of horribles imbued the ERA with far more authority than most academics or feminists believed it would possess. Paradoxically, she offered "a more robust reading of the feminist movement's claims than the movement itself felt able publicly to own." To be sure, some lawyers thought judges might interpret the ERA to send women into combat, though most did not. But unisex potties? The legislative history of the amendment "clearly preserved an exception for privacy-related regulation," and ERA opponents already used single-sex bathrooms on airplanes. Since the Court had grounded its decision in *Roe* on privacy, not equality, how could the ERA affect abortion? Nor did the language of the ERA make legalization of gay marriage a possibility: Courts had not taken advantage of the laws that already prohibited gender discrimination to strike a blow for gay rights. And the legal obligation to support the wife during marriage that Schlafly labeled imperiled did not exist. When marriages ended, legal protections for former financial dependents would survive—for all the good they did. Statistics suggested that judges already awarded alimony and child support in relatively few cases where the divorcing parties were well off and that most ex-husbands shirked their obligations. In short, most knowledgeable individuals thought the ERA would not bring about any major changes in the relations between men and women beyond those already taking place.[31]

Indeed, in retrospect, it seems mysterious that 1970s feminists would have hitched their wagon to the ERA's star. Scholars often suggested that for all practical purposes, the Supreme Court was already creating a "de facto ERA" by striking down sex discrimination as a violation of the Constitution's equal protection clause. The most that could be said for the ERA, one concluded, was that its passage "gradually would have promoted legal uniformity in the treatment of females in state and federal statutes in a way that no previous acts of Congress, executive orders, or Supreme Court decisions could."[32]

For both sides, the ERA's importance was ultimately symbolic—no more, no less. To proponents, the ERA meant treatment of women and men as equals; to opponents, it signified treatment of women and men as the same. Thus, like abortion, the ERA came to represent an assault on marriage, morality, and motherhood.[33]

In this debate, Schlafly had an advantage. The word that admirers and detractors most often used to describe her was "poised," and Schlafly thought it strange indeed that feminists lacked "self-discipline." Though she herself was wealthy, employed a housekeeper, and had run unsuccessfully for Congress, she could speak to "average" women who did not work outside the home better than feminists could. Was she for real? Feminists snorted when Schlafly informed reporters that "I think of my marriage and family as my No. 1 career," said she would prefer to "scrub bathroom floors" than write her newsletter, and bragged about her fruit cobblers. But the antiratificationists who read the *Phyllis Schlafly Report* adored her as much as feminists abhorred her.[34]

Since polls showed a majority of Americans supported the ERA, its opponents faced an uphill battle. When New York and New Jersey voters rejected state equal rights amendments in 1975, ERA activists could blame complacency and treat the defeats as a blessing in disguise. "The troops are there," one sympathetic reporter announced. "Next time, they'll be fighting." They had ammunition in Betty Ford, who lobbied lawmakers for the amendment. Her husband appointed a feminist, Mary Louise Smith, the first woman chair of the Republican National Committee, and the president also declared that he "wholeheartedly" supported the ERA. Together, the ERA and *Roe* seemed to symbolize new possibilities in the public and private spheres. Of course, that terrified some. But in 1975 traditionalists still seemed very much on the defensive.[35]

THE EMPHASIS ON expanded options that underlay *Roe* and the ERA seemed all-pervasive. Where "counterculture" had been the phrase of the 1960s, "alternative" had become one for the 1970s. Instead of espousing a rhetoric of opposition to the dominant culture, many explored alternatives to it. Put "alternative" together with other buzzwords of the 1970s—"lifestyle" and "self-fulfillment"—and an explosion of liberating experimentation aimed at "getting loose" followed.[36]

Of all social institutions, the family was most dramatically affected. By 1976–77, when approval of cohabitation peaked, polls of college freshmen showed that 43 percent of women and 55 percent of men believed that couples should live together before they married. Divorce became more acceptable and available during the decade. The trend began in 1970, when California tried to make marriage dissolution less acrimonious by sweeping away the fault-based requirement for divorce (such as adultery, cruelty, or desertion). With the establishment of the first no-fault divorce law in all the Western world, rights consciousness spread to divorce. Within a decade forty-seven other states had adopted no-fault divorce, which required simply that one spouse declare that "irreconcilable differences" had caused the marital breakdown. The divorce rate, on the rise since the mid-sixties, nearly doubled between 1965 and 1975. Perhaps two in five marriages made in the 1970s ended in divorce.[37]

Later in the decade the unintended consequences of "the divorce revolution" became clear. Because the new laws made fault irrelevant and financial settlements were difficult to enforce, women and children were hit hard. When a divorcing couple had children, the father typically became single; the mother, a single parent. By the late 1970s many were stressing the relationship between poverty and divorce. According to the sociologist who invented the term "feminization of poverty," a "double trend" characterized the decade: "More of the poor were women, and more women, especially those heading families with minor children, became poor." Almost two-thirds of the poor over the age of sixteen in 1976 were women, and one out of every three families headed by women (compared with one in eighteen families headed by both parents) lived below the poverty line.[38]

At mid-decade, however, many thought the proliferation of "non-married statuses" a positive development. Soon after the *Sixty Minutes* interview, Susan Ford informed her mother she *did* intend to have an affair. By that time the word "affair" seemed curiously old-fashioned.[39]

"Everybody got laid in the Seventies, the high-water mark of the one-night stand"; many, on wall-to-wall shag carpeting. And why not? No one had heard of AIDS. At most, the careless would have thought they risked venereal disease or herpes, neither of which received much attention, or unwanted pregnancy, which, with the money and inclination, could be made to go away. Consequently, in Erica Jong's celebrated 1973 book *Fear of Flying*, the heroine lauded the brief and anonymous "zipless fuck." Some wedded couples experimented with "open marriages." Some unmarried individuals "slept around," while others engaged in "serial monogamy" with one partner at a time. Obviously, not everyone was heterosexual. The mainstream, counterculture, and much of the feminist movement had been antigay in the 1960s, but lesbians and gays now shunned the closet. They too could pursue the "zipless fuck," open and serial relationships, and alternative lifestyles, as Rita Mae Brown's 1973 book *Rubyfruit Jungle* and the 1975 film *Saturday Night at the Baths* made clear.[40]

The apparent change in social attitudes toward gays and lesbians was remarkable. In 1973 the American Psychiatric Association ceased classifying homosexuality as a mental illness. By 1975 eleven states had repealed laws criminalizing sodomy. Washington Redskins linebacker Dave Kopay became the first professional athlete to come out publicly.[41]

No place seemed a more vibrant center of gay and lesbian life than San Francisco. There a coalition of gays, lesbians, and liberals had elected George Moscone mayor in 1975. "Hey, Michelle," Moscone shouted jovially to a drag queen at one event. "How come you didn't wear a gown at the swearing-in ceremony like you promised?" There were signs of an impending backlash here too. Despite San Francisco's progressive reputation, Moscone's margin of victory was very slim. And when a disabled gay veteran saved President Ford from an assassination attempt that fall, the president had to be pressured to write him a note of thanks. Perhaps gay rights activists, like feminists, should have read the handwriting on the wall. But what stood out in 1975 was the heightened openness.[42]

THE POLITICAL IS PERSONAL

Even the Central Intelligence Agency and the Federal Bureau of Investigation seemed to be coming out of the closet and into the sunlight. As the International Women's Year Conference was about to begin in Mexico City, Gloria Steinem was accused of past involvement with a Central Intelligence Agency front organization. The charges were true, but Steinem herself had made the facts public long before, and there was no evidence to support the insinuation that *Ms.*, the magazine she cofounded, "was part of a CIA strategy" to water down feminism. Still, allegations that an individual and an organization possessed CIA connections during "the intelligence wars" of 1975 damaged them as much as accusations that they had had Communist affiliations during the 1950s, which was surely why Steinem's rivals in the women's movement did so much to keep the charges alive.[43]

The CIA's ordeal began in 1972 with the revelation that one director of the Watergate burglary had once been a CIA operative. After the Nixon administration unsuccessfully sought to blackmail the CIA director Richard Helms, a "gentlemanly planner of assassinations," into paying hush money to the Watergate burglars, the president got rid of Helms by naming him ambassador to Iran in 1973. Nixon replaced Helms with James Schlesinger, a temperamental systems analyst with no prior connection to the agency, who sought to "demythologize" it and got rid of hundreds of employees. When the Senate Foreign Relations Committee quizzed Helms about the CIA's past covert operations at a hearing about his nomination as ambassador, he lied. He swore that the CIA had not tried to overthrow the government of Salvador Allende, the Marxist president of Chile. Then, in 1974, the agency was tainted anew by Watergate revelations and damaged by investigative reporter Seymour Hersh's exposure of the millions that the CIA had spent to undermine the Allende government.[44]

But the real public relations nightmare began at Christmas 1974, with the publication of Hersh's front page *New York Times* story "Huge CIA Operation Reported in U.S. Against Anti-War Forces, Other Dissidents." According to Hersh, who lay most of the blame on Helms, during the Johnson and Nixon administrations, the CIA had orchestrated Operation Chaos, "a massive illegal domestic intelligence operation" against antiwar protesters and other dissidents, in violation of its charter, which restricted its capacity for domestic spying. By Hersh's account, the agency had engaged in illegal wiretaps, break-ins, burglaries, and mail openings and had kept files on some ten thousand suspicious American citizens. In the words of William Colby, a thirty-year CIA veteran who had become the agency's director in 1973, when Nixon made Schlesinger secretary of defense, Hersh's story "triggered a firestorm" that gave "all the dreadful fears and suspicions about the CIA" that essential touch of credibility.[45]

Colby may have exaggerated. Still reeling from their role in bringing down Richard Nixon, mainstream reporters were loath to embark on another crusade that might altogether destroy trust in government and/or cause a backlash against the media. Further, many journalists disliked Hersh. And reporters had long protected the agency: They shared CIA spooks' faith in the agency's importance and, often, relationships to them that dated back to prep school. Consequently, one perceptive historian concluded, Hersh's "determination to carry the Watergate mentality into the post-Watergate era" discomfited his colleagues. Still, Colby felt cornered.[46]

Once he would have denied Hersh's story. But in a futile attempt at damage control Colby had given Hersh a lengthy interview before the story broke. Instead Colby urged the White House to pick apart Hersh's article and to make the case that the journalist had exaggerated the massiveness of the CIA's domestic snooping.[47]

The president, en route to Colorado for his skiing holiday, had a different theory of damage control. After waiting vainly for a call to join Ford, Colby realized that "the White House planned to 'distance' itself from the CIA." Though Colby "felt very lonely," he could understand "the Ford Administration's determination not to take on almost thirty years of CIA's sins."[48]

Those sins the CIA had itself documented for internal purposes. On January 3, 1975, when Ford summoned him to the White House, Colby disclosed the existence of the "family jewels," the 693-page document that Schlesinger and Colby had amassed when Schlesinger ordered all current and former CIA employees to fill him in on past agency activities that definitely or possibly violated its legislative charter. They included

Operation Chaos, another mail intercept program, the bugging of journalists, the links to the Watergate burglars, experiments on subjects with mind control drugs, questionable involvement in the activities of other agencies, and the agency's attempts to plan the assassination of or to assassinate Cuba's Fidel Castro, the Congo's Patrice Lumumba, and the Dominican Republic's Rafael Trujillo.[49]

Colby at first considered the compendium more encouraging than alarming. For him, "the most remarkable thing" was that the list "did not include more widespread dangers to the lives and liberties of our citizens." But Colby soon realized he was deluding himself. Since the CIA's creation in 1947, its officials had maintained that the less Congress, the media, and the public knew about its activities, the better. If the agency claimed something "secret," on the ground of its importance to "national security," it remained private. How else would the United States win the cold war? The Soviets were no choirboys, and no one held KGB practices up to a mirror. But as Colby came to understand, "the era of trust" had ended. Hersh's reporting rang in "the era of skepticism."[50]

The White House appeared oblivious. Ford determined to accept the advice of Deputy Chief of Staff Dick Cheney and others. The White House would try to head off a congressional inquiry by appointing a blue-ribbon committee to investigate Hersh's allegations. Such a scheme might have worked in 1963, when Ford had served on the Warren Commission, a joint executive and congressional body established by President Johnson to study the Kennedy assassination. Now no congressional leaders wanted to participate in Ford's project. A bipartisan commission chaired by Vice President Rockefeller was the best the president could do. (For once, the Republican right was on Ford's side: *Human Events* repeatedly warned that the CIA might "be wrecked by 'People's Right to Know' Zealots" and characterized the eight-member Rockefeller Commission as "top-flight.") No sooner did Ford announce the creation of the Rockefeller Commission than the Senate and House said that they were establishing committees to investigate the intelligence community. Like the media, Congress treated the president's blue-ribbon commission, which included Ronald Reagan and various individuals linked to the national security establishment, as a joke.[51]

When the Rockefeller Commission came up at a luncheon the president hosted for Tom Wicker and others from the *New York Times* later in January 1975, Ford launched into an astonishing monologue. It had been essential, Ford contended, to appoint "responsible" people and limit the scope of the investigation. As president Ford "had learned enough about the CIA to know that there were things on its record that would 'blacken the name of every president back to Harry Truman'—the phrase rings as clearly in my ear now as it did then," Wicker wrote years later. Ford left no doubt he was referring to the agency's assassination plots. Allegations about them had long swirled around the CIA, and Lyndon Johnson had privately confirmed their truth to Wicker in 1964. "Then, it had not occurred to me that we should print such things," and Wicker could not recall whether he had even found Johnson's revelations outrageous. In the wake of Watergate, however, Ford's candor confounded the reporter. Had the president placed the entire luncheon discussion off the record? Wicker asked himself as it continued. He thought not. Returning to the office, he and other guests wrangled over how to handle Ford's remarks. By 1975 Wicker had come to think it "intolerable" that the American government should try to assassinate foreign leaders, and he saw no reason to protect Ford. (In fact, since the evidence implicated Democratic presidents more than Republicans, Ford may have been trying to "blacken" the names of his political opponents.) But his colleagues remained under the spell of the old "national security mystique" that had once gripped Wicker and helped explain the media's initially cool reaction to Hersh's story. "National security—the phrase rings with masculinity, patriotism and heroism." And so the *Times* did not publish Ford's "monumental leak."[52]

Someone else did. Ford's disclosure was passed along to CBS news reporter Daniel Schorr, who questioned Colby about it. Had the CIA ever killed anyone within the United States? Schorr asked. "I was so stunned at the President's opening up this topic that I retreated to the long-time practice of answering only the specific question asked," Colby recalled. "Not in this country," he told Schorr. Of course, that reply, a negative pregnant, suggested that the CIA had engaged in assassination attempts on foreign officials abroad. Schorr announced on television that "President Ford has reportedly warned associates that if current investigations go too far they could uncover several assassinations of foreign officials involving the CIA." The media began to chase the story.[53]

Yet though "the national security mystique" seemed to be crumbling before Colby's very eyes—with a bizarre push from the president—it had not disappeared. The Rockefeller Commission embodied it. Rockefeller himself took Colby aside during the closed hearings "and said in his most charming manner, 'Bill do you really have to present all this material to us? We realize that there are secrets that you fellows need to keep.'" Now that news about political assassination attempts was flowing out, however, even the Rockefeller Commission felt compelled to explore them and, Colby complained, ordered him to give it "all relevant documents—unsanitized, without even the excision of names of the individual agents involved." The commission's report, especially after the White House had rewritten it, represented a coup for Colby. Rockefeller summarized its findings for the media: "There are things that have been done in contradiction to the statutes, but in comparison to the total [CIA] effort, they are not major," and the CIA had cleaned house.[54]

Possibly, the commission's revelations might even help the president. The media focused on the sad story of Frank Olson, a civilian biochemist in the employ of the U.S. Army, who had become an unwitting participant in the CIA's 1953 mind control experiments when agency operatives dosed him with LSD. When he died soon afterward, the agency informed his family that Olson had suffered a breakdown. "We have agonized over the question of what kind of horrid 'nightmare' or 'event' could have driven him to hurl himself at a full run out of a 10th story window, and how this 'suicidal nervous breakdown'—the terms we have always used—could have developed so suddenly, so inexplicably," his wife and children said publicly. Thanks to the Rockefeller Commission report, they knew they had been deceived. Olson's death, his survivors said, had meaning "only when it is placed in the context of a family story on the one hand and in the context of global CIA misconduct and immorality on the other." Perhaps, but the commission disclosures enabled Ford to do what he did best: demonstrate his personal decency. He apologized to the Olsons and promised that the government would look kindly on their wrongful death action, and they were soon declaring themselves "heartened" by the presidential response. Most of the other illegalities the Rockefeller Commission exposed likewise seemed comfortably in the past.[55]

Just as important, the commission deleted its chapter on assassinations from the final report. The excision was made at the insistence of Rockefeller, over the protest of the commission's executive director. The report simply included a statement that allegations about assassination plots had surfaced after the commission began its work, and since "time did not permit a full investigation before this report was due," it had given all relevant materials to the president.[56]

As Colby had feared, and over his protest again, the White House passed along to the Senate committee the unsanitized documents he had given the commission. That committee did delve into assassinations. Nor was it headed by the Senate titans who had faithfully protected the CIA's privacy and budgets. Rather, beginning in the spring of 1975, Frank Church of Idaho, a handsome liberal with his eye on the 1976 Democratic presidential nomination, chaired the Senate Select Committee to Study Governmental Operations with Respect to Intelligence Activities. Testifying before the Church Committee in 1975 "was like being a prisoner in the dock," Colby told the president. "All the questions were on assassination and it was like 'when did you stop beating your wife?' " So perhaps because he was a devout Catholic who considered confession the route to salvation, perhaps because he hoped to purify the CIA, Colby did not stonewall. He sang. At least, many of his agents and the White House thought so. Among other things, Colby's revelations about the CIA's Chilean activities, many believed, led to Helms's indictment for perjury. Though the Church Committee did not always find the CIA director cooperative, Colby said enough to stun.[57]

By the time the Church Committee completed its work, it had learned that the agency had "actually instigated" plans to murder foreign leaders Lumumba and Castro. In neither case had it been successful. Rival assassins had beaten the agency's men to the punch to kill Lumumba. Castro still reigned in Cuba, though he had been the target of at least eight agency assassination plots, and the CIA had enlisted the Mob to help with some. In other instances, the depth of agency involvement was less clear. By the Church Committee's interpretation, between 1961 and 1970, local dissidents over whom the CIA lacked control had murdered Rafael Trujillo in the Dominican Republic, Ngo Dinh Diem in Vietnam, and General René Schneider in Chile. The evidence, however, unquestionably indicated that CIA agents had befriended the assassins and given them weapons. This much detective work was remarkable, given the memory loss that affected most witnesses except Colby.[58]

Who was responsible for the agency's transgressions, the White House or the CIA? Had presidents ordered the killing of Castro and Lumumba, for example, or had the agency acted on its own? At one point Church wondered aloud if the CIA was a "rogue elephant on a rampage." At other times it seemed the White House had kept the agency on a strict leash; at still others, that the CIA had misread presidential desires. Was the agency "out of control," operating on a "wink-and-a-nod" from chief executives who needed "plausible deniability," or had the CIA misinterpreted their wishes? The Church Committee's answer here was fuzzy too: "The most that could be said against the agency and its senior officers was that they had misunderstood presidential instructions, but in all cases there was good ground for their misunderstanding—just not quite good enough to blame the President concerned."[59]

Whereas the Church Committee demonstrated that the agency had behaved unlawfully, the concurrent CIA probe undertaken by the House Select Committee on Intelligence and chaired by Representative Otis Pike revealed that the CIA had operated incompetently. Among agency bloopers were its failures to foresee the Soviets' 1968 invasion of Czechoslovakia, the 1973 Yom Kippur War, the 1974 coups in Cyprus and Portugal, and India's 1974 explosion of an atomic bomb.[60]

Yet none of the 1975 investigations significantly improved congressional oversight. Nor, with the exception of the annoying new executive order prohibiting political assassinations ("It is an act of insanity and national humiliation to have a law prohibiting the President from ordering assassination," Kissinger fumed), did the hearings result in rules that dramatically changed the agency's operations. The hearings also did not undercut the assumption that information about "enemies" must sometimes be acquired through undemocratic, immoral, and illegal means. As Colby's successor, George H. W. Bush, said in his confirmation hearings late in the year, "Some people today are driven to wantonly disclose sensitive information—not talking here about the Congress—to friend and foe alike around the world." Thirty years later Bush publicly complained, less diplomatically, that Congress had "unleashed a bunch of untutored little jerks" to hamstring the CIA. But the impact of the "jerks" was limited and temporary; the eagerness to clip the agency's wings had disappeared even before the hearings' end. Though Jimmy Carter initially seemed suspicious of the agency, by the end of his presidency its relieved boosters were acknowledging that he leaned "more and more heavily on CIA and covert action as the action arm of his efforts to cope with Soviet and Cuban aggressiveness around the world," a trend that continued under Ronald Reagan.[61]

TO LIBERALS' CHAGRIN, the National Security Agency and the Federal Bureau of Investigation also emerged relatively unscathed from the 1975 congressional investigations. As the Church Committee hearings revealed, the NSA's twenty thousand employees had monitored the international telephone calls and telegrams of more than fifteen hundred American citizens and groups suspected of subversive activity and of nearly six thousand foreign nationals or organizations. Thanks to the cooperation of Western Union, the NSA also had access to all incoming and outgoing telegrams to the United States. Committee members questioned the legality and propriety of these operations.[62]

Thus the hearings created the impetus for the passage of the Foreign Intelligence Surveillance Act of 1978. FISA required the NSA and other intelligence agencies to obtain warrants for electronic and physical surveillance of U.S. citizens suspected of contact with foreign powers and terrorist organizations from a specially constituted Foreign Intelligence Surveillance Court that met secretly "in a sealed, secure room in Washington, D.C., received on average about 750 warrant applications per year, and before 2001, . . . never rejected an application." Some supervision. When it was disclosed that President George W. Bush had nonetheless circumvented the FISA courts after the September 11, 2001, attack on the World Trade Center and the Pentagon, in the interest of collecting information on terrorists, Washington old-timers recalled the 1970s. "For those of us who went through it all back then, there's disappointment and even anger that we're back where we started from," one said.[63]

The Federal Bureau of Investigation also had little to fear. The Church Committee's hearings documented the systematic campaign of harassment and intimidation ordered by Director J. Edgar Hoover. The bureau had undertaken nearly twenty-five hundred domestic intelligence operations and had files on millions of Americans, many of them produced as part of its counterintelligence program, COINTELPRO. Launched in 1956 to destroy the nearly moribund American Communist Party, COINTELPRO had soon mushroomed into operations to harass any organization Hoover thought threatened the government. COINTELPRO operatives had the authority to disrupt targeted groups by using subterfuge and agents provocateurs, leaking derogatory information to the media, and rumormongering. Their quarry between the 1950s and 1970s included the civil rights, women's, and antiwar movements; the New Left; black nationalist groups; the Ku Klux Klan; and the Socialist Workers Party. Chaos, an FBI-directed CIA operation, was part of COINTELPRO.

COINTELPRO's targets included the famous and the average. Its most well-known was the Reverend Martin Luther King, Jr., whom it tried to drive to suicide. But Senator Philip Hart of Michigan, a liberal Democrat, said during the hearings that the FBI had investigated many ordinary people too. Hart, whose children had been active in the antiwar movement, said that his family had told him for years that the FBI was out of control. He had scoffed. Now he knew that the bureau had undertaken "a series of illegal actions intended to deny certain citizens their First Amendment rights—just like my children said."[64]

Yet by this time Hoover was out of the picture. And having directed the bureau for forty years, he was supposedly a special case. "He's got files on everybody, God damn it," Nixon had said. In 1975 it was easy to believe that no one would ever again possess Hoover's power. After all, the new director was saying, falsely, that the FBI's worst abuses took place "chiefly during the twilight of Mr. Hoover's administration" and, reassuringly, that no one should direct the bureau for more than a decade. Because Congress enacted no legislative charter for the FBI, the way was still wide open for Ronald Reagan to "unleash" the bureau, along with the CIA, during his presidency.[65]

WHAT, THEN, WAS the significance of the congressional hearings? At one level they dramatized the executive branch's loss of power over the ship of state. The Church and Pike committee hearings symbolized the continuing stalemate between Congress and the executive. Ford publicly accused the Church Committee of taking "reckless . . . action to cripple the effectiveness of our intelligence services." That was mild, compared with what members of his administration and those of the Pike Committee said about each other. The return to the status quo after the hearings demonstrated the difficulty of grasping the helm. At another level, the hearings suggested that the passengers, the American public, no longer cared about the ship.[66]

For if the Church and Pike committee revelations were unsettling, so was the public reaction. The president opted to oppose publication of the Church Committee's assassination report, even though he knew he would not prevail. He told Kissinger that "[t]he country is not behind the committee." After the full Senate met in a rare secret session and declined to vote on publication, Church simply released the report in November. When the House voted against releasing the Pike Committee report in February 1976, it was given to Daniel Schorr, who leaked it to the alternative weekly the *Village Voice*, which published it under the headline THE REPORT ON THE CIA THAT PRESIDENT FORD DOESN'T WANT YOU TO READ. Outside Washington no one cared. There never had been much angry mail to the White House or Congress about the CIA, and there was not much interest in any of the FBI's activities, other than its pursuit of King. Just a year earlier Watergate had consumed Americans. By 1975 their faith in public institutions had sunk so low that the revelations during "the year of intelligence" engendered less shock than they merited.[67]

THE CONGRESSIONAL COMMITTEES' disclosures about John Kennedy did fascinate the public. His presidency had come to symbolize the idealism of the sixties. Now, in 1975, thanks to the Church Committee, the media reported that Judith Campbell Exner, whom the committee euphemistically called a "close friend" of Kennedy's, was also the girlfriend of Sam Giancana, a mafioso connected to CIA assassination plots against Castro. Exner held a press conference to deny she had been a go-between for Kennedy and the Mob (a story she later changed), but to confirm her "close personal" association with JFK. Though she initially refused to comment on whether the relationship was sexual, she was soon comparing Kennedy's skill as a lover with Giancana's. The president came out poorly. (That story changed too.)[68]

A drumroll of reports revealed that Exner had been one of Kennedy's many conquests. Of course, the White House press corps had always known that Kennedy played around. Exner's press conference broke the "code of silence." *Time* showcased "Jack Kennedy's Other Women," while *Newsweek* opened the "Closets of Camelot." Republican columnists suggested that the Church Committee's taciturnity about the Kennedy and Exner relationship reflected a cover-up by Democrats to protect their favorite icon. An angry Church responded that committee members had concluded they should not "wade into the personal life of the president."[69]

That was a decision with which many agreed. The political was becoming personal. Just as Americans were making once-private matters, such as abortion, political, so too they were moving toward "a politics of personality." Yet the curtain going up on the private lives of public figures was rising slowly. During Ford's presidency the media wrote about his wife's candor, not about her alcoholism or addiction to painkillers, though there was plenty of evidence of both. The curtain was also rising with considerable hand-wringing. *Time*'s story about Kennedy's other women generated a flood of letters, most of them critical. The magazine had proved, one reader grieved, that it was "possible to assassinate someone twice."[70]

The hearings also reignited interest in the "first" Kennedy assassination. Conspiracy theorists had long suspected that neither the FBI nor the CIA had been candid with the Warren Commission, which had concluded that Kennedy's assassin, Lee Harvey Oswald, acted alone. New Orleans District Attorney Jim Garrison's 1967 inept and unsuccessful prosecution of Clay Shaw, a businessman with CIA ties, for conspiracy in the assassination had relegated conspiracy buffs to supermarket tabloids. In 1975 the buffs returned to the mainstream. The Church and Pike committee hearings revealed that the CIA had withheld information about the assassination plots against Castro and that the FBI had destroyed a letter that Oswald delivered to the bureau ten days before JFK's assassination. The famous Zapruder footage of the assassination, which suggested that Kennedy had been killed in crossfire, was shown on television for the first time. Journalists attacked the Warren Commission. They found consumers aplenty. Bantam published 250,000 copies in its first printing of Robert Anson's book *"They've Killed the President!,"* which portrayed Kennedy's murder as the result of a CIA-Mob conspiracy. Nearly two-thirds of the public thought the Kennedy assassination was the result of a conspiracy.[71]

The intelligence investigations had confirmed for the public the disturbing lessons of Watergate and of the pardon: There was no reason to trust the government or those who governed. Watergate had indicated the corruptibility of the president. The lesson many drew from the Church and Pike hearings—with their revelations about Kennedy, the CIA, and the FBI—was that the corruption stretched back far beyond Richard Nixon. According to one poll, 70 percent of Americans believed that during the last decade "this country's leaders have consistently lied to the people." It was no coincidence that just as 1974 witnessed the brief lionization of Gerald Ford as presidential everyman, so 1975 saw the frank and feisty "Give 'Em Hell Harry" Truman become a cult figure. As the country turned toward a politics of personality, few Americans had use for politicians. The fall of Vietnam only increased the doubts.[72]

IV

THE FADING OF AMERICA

—

IN MARCH 1965, AMERICAN MARINES STORMED THE BEACHES OF Da Nang. Lyndon Johnson had Americanized the Vietnam War in a misguided attempt to realize John F. Kennedy's inaugural promise that the United States would "pay any price, bear any burden, meet any hardship, support any friend, oppose any foe to assure the survival and success of liberty." A decade later Ford was in Palm Desert, California, vacationing on a friend's estate. Though the president's men warned that the March holiday "would sit badly with a country in the grip of hard times," Ford insisted that he needed a break. The spotlight rarely left him as he relaxed. Vietnam was falling. The nightly news juxtaposed pictures of the end game with those of Ford golfing. To date, one magazine said, the 1970s had been "the hangover of the '60s." But in the spring of 1975 the sixties finally ended. As those on the right and left combined to challenge the president's power to make foreign policy, the loss of Vietnam exposed the myth of American will.[1]

DÉTENTE AND ITS NEOCONSERVATIVE CRITICS

Nowhere was Ford's reliance on a Nixon holdover more pronounced than in the realm of foreign policy. In 1968 Nixon had tapped Henry Kissinger, a forty-five-year-old professor of government at Harvard, to become his national security adviser. By the time Nixon resigned, Kissinger was national security adviser and secretary of state. Hailed as "Super K," Kissinger was shown on a 1974 *Newsweek* cover in Superman costume, circling the globe. Kissinger never shared Superman's becoming modesty. Despite a deep sense of marginalization that may have been fostered by the need both to flee Hitler as an Orthodox Jewish teenager and to return to Germany as one of the American military intelligence members to occupy it at war's end, Kissinger seemed pregnant with an inflated sense of himself. Even so, Nixon thought Kissinger indispensable, and Ford depended on him even more, which must have been draining at times. When Kissinger was low about his public standing, which waned and waxed, he could be pathetically needy and paranoid. When he was high, he could be insufferable. "I got a great reception in Laramie," he once exulted to Ford when the president himself was having a rough time politically. "The biggest crowd they'd ever had except for rock groups!"[2]

Kissinger symbolized continuity, not change, in U.S.-Soviet relations. Particularly since the Cuban missile crisis had brought the United States and Soviet Union to the brink of nuclear war in 1962, Americans and Soviets had made mutual assured destruction (MAD) their guiding philosophy. Each side held the other's population hostage. If one power launched a nuclear attack, it did so with the certainty the other would destroy its major cities in retaliation. Since nuclear war represented mutual suicide, both must prevent it. The MAD logic lay behind all strategies the United States pursued to "contain" the Soviet Union, including the Nixon-Kissinger notion of détente.

The seven letters of détente, a French word meaning both "calm, relaxation, easing" and "trigger of a gun," held the entire history of the cold war within their boundaries. Because détente implied conciliation between the great powers, as well as confrontation, it seemed to promise one of the periodic thaws. Yet the cold war continued. No one, least of all the Nixon administration, expected to beat swords into plowshares. It resisted Soviet expansion in the third world at the same time it made overtures to Moscow and to Communist Party General Secretary Leonid Brezhnev, a realist with romantic hopes of making relations between the United States and the Soviet Union friendlier. American practitioners of détente sought to modify Soviet behavior through negotiation. The SALT I Treaty in 1972, the first between the United States and the Soviet Union to set ceilings on different categories of offensive nuclear weapons each could build, fitted the bill. Though SALT applied to a fraction of the Soviet and American arsenals, it possessed symbolic significance. When the Soviets and Americans signed the Antiballistic Missile Treaty that year, which prohibited each side from building a defense system against the other's nuclear weapons, they codified MAD. Détente also required linkage; Americans told the Soviets that all important issues were intertwined. Détente was supposed to create a peaceful world order, and not so coincidentally, it was also supposed to enable its promoters to clamp a lid on the revolutionary unrest within their borders and to win elections in the name of maintaining international stability.[3]

With SALT I due to expire in 1977, Ford wanted to get started on negotiating SALT II right away. "Anything that would bring the arms race under control would be a plus for the entire world," he reasoned. To his dismay, some in Congress resisted. SALT I had left the Soviet Union with more missiles than the United States. The Nixon administration had justified that imbalance by stressing that the United States retained a qualitative, if not quantitative, advantage, and counteracted it by reaching out to China. Some doubted that the Chinese and détente were sufficient to keep the Soviets in line. They knew that the Soviets were building up their military while American defense spending declined. Tellingly, when Congress approved SALT I, it added an amendment urging the president to seek a future arms agreement based on numerical equality.[4]

ANOTHER DÉTENTE-RELATED Nixon legacy, the Middle East peace process, also troubled some. Linkage had proved its effectiveness when Kissinger persuaded the Soviet Union to join the United States in compelling Arabs and Israelis to end the 1973 Yom Kippur War. Israel's American supporters believed that the United States and Soviet Union had helped the Arabs politically by depriving Israel of the victory it would have won had the fighting continued. Kissinger then barred the Soviets from the peacemaking process after the cease-fire because they simply "parrot Arab proposals." His "step-by-step diplomacy" with Arabs and Israelis was designed to manage, rather than resolve, the Arab-Israeli conflict by deferring the most difficult issues while age-old enemies took baby steps toward peace.[5]

What were those issues? The first entailed the return by Israel to Egypt of the Sinai Peninsula, which Israel had captured during the 1967 Six-Day War. In the aftermath of that war, the world viewed Egypt, Israel's most feared enemy, as vulnerable. Only another war, Egypt's Anwar el-Sadat understood, could alter the strategic balance of power and pave the way for Israeli withdrawal from the Sinai. While Egypt lost the Yom Kippur War, its initial successes shattered the idea of Israeli invulnerability.[6]

The second issue related to the other territories Israel occupied as a result of the Six-Day and Yom Kippur wars. The strategically significant Golan Heights overlooked Syria. The captured land also included the Gaza Strip, where hundreds of thousands of Palestinian refugees, displaced when Israel had become independent in 1948, lived in squalor, as well as two other centers of Palestinian life, the West Bank and East Jerusalem. Since Israel had been repeatedly attacked from Gaza, the Golan, and the West Bank, Israelis feared that the return of the territories to the Syrians, Palestinians, or Jordanians would threaten their country's existence. Moreover, East Jerusalem, a holy city for Christians and Muslims, housed the Western Wall of the ancient Temple, Jews' most sacred site. In biblical times Israel included Jerusalem and the West Bank, which some Israelis liked to say they had "liberated" in 1967. Like the territories themselves, the Israelis who lived in the territories proved controversial. As soon as Israel had acquired its "accidental empire" in 1967, the government had begun quietly approving settlements of Israeli civilians there, despite a warning from the legal counsel of its Foreign Ministry that the Geneva Convention prevented civilian colonization of occupied territories. As Israeli Jews, many of them members of the religious right, moved near vanquished foes, the territories became a powder keg.[7]

The third issue involved Palestinian self-government and sovereignty in the West Bank and Gaza. Palestinian Liberation Organization Chairman Yasser Arafat, selected by Arab nations as the Palestinians' "sole legitimate spokesman" over the more moderate King Hussein of Jordan, sought autonomy. But the Israeli government considered Arafat and the PLO terrorists and refused to negotiate with them.[8]

Step-by-step diplomacy enhanced not just American importance in the peace process but Kissinger's. That alarmed his foes, who already considered him too friendly to the Soviet Union and too acceptant of its restrictions on the emigration of Soviet Jews to Israel. Many pro-Israel Americans had become disillusioned with the larger policy of détente, which then foundered on the rock of Israel. As Israel's American friends studied the aftermath of the Yom Kippur War, they concluded that détente was dangerous. Perhaps the United States would give Israel more latitude if cold war tensions reminded Americans that Israel was their indispensable regional ally.[9]

—

AMERICAN JEWS WERE SENSITIVE about the accusation that they denounced détente simply because of their commitment to Israel. Norman Podhoretz, who edited the American Jewish Committee journal *Commentary*, considered communism at least "as great an evil as Nazism" and maintained that the survival of both the United States and Israel demanded resistance. He represented a segment of intellectuals (many, though not all, Jewish), who were turning against the radicalism and liberalism with which many intellectuals and American Jews had historically been linked. By the time Ford took office, this group had a name, neoconservative. The socialist who popularized the term meant it as an epithet. But the label "neoconservative" was appropriated by those formerly left of center it mocked. The "neo" worked: It demarcated them from the traditional conservatives they still considered adversaries, despite the fact that William F. Buckley had been reaching out to neoconservatives since the late 1960s.[10]

None of the neoconservatives was a Republican when Ford became president. For New York intellectual Irving Kristol, cofounder and editor of the *Public Interest*, who had been a Trotskyist in the 1930s before becoming a liberal, the Republicans were the "stupid party." But the Democrats' nomination of McGovern in 1972 revolted "neocons." They sought to win control of the Democrats from the "upper middle-class rabble" of left-liberal academics, activists, lawyers, journalists, and bureaucrats who had backed McGovern. Neocons believed that the McGovernites had destroyed the party by pursuing egalitarianism and "the new isolationism," as Nixon referred to it, which he characterized as "the temptation," following a "long and unpopular war . . . to withdraw from the world, to back away from our commitments." (Others called it neoisolationism.) It was the neocons who were to take the party away from the McGovernites and "back to the good old days of Harry S Truman" when Democrats won presidential elections by embracing anticommunism and moderate domestic reform. After McGovern's defeat, neocons formed the Coalition for a Democratic Majority to rescue their party.[11]

Over time their focus shifted. At the *Public Interest*, Kristol initially maintained that liberal elites' efforts to "throw money" at social problems at home produced unintended, negative consequences, while Podhoretz used *Commentary* to campaign against the New Left. Then neocons began devoting more attention to foreign than domestic policy. Many of the heavyweights at the Coalition for a Democratic Majority decried the menace of the Soviet Union. By 1975 Kissinger was the neocons' favorite whipping boy; détente and the decline of U.S. military power, their obsessions.[12]

Among politicians, neoconservatives possessed two mouthpieces. In New York, they relied on Daniel Patrick Moynihan, a "bow-tied, erudite and ebullient" sociologist, who had served in the Kennedy, Johnson, and Nixon administrations and who was to become Ford's ambassador to the United Nations. In the nation's capital, the neoconservatives' champion was Senator Henry Jackson of Washington, accurately described by his sympathetic biographer as "[a] formidable legislator, but man of little charism." The Soviets, however, did not care how wooden Jackson seemed on television: Jackson was so feared in Moscow that the KGB tried to discredit him by fabricating evidence that he was gay. A New Deal liberal on domestic policy and founding member of the Coalition for a Democratic Majority, Jackson had sought the presidency in 1972 and obviously had his eye on the Democratic presidential nomination in 1976. Violently anti-Soviet, he was virulently pro-Israel. Jackson blamed Kissinger for failing to require Moscow to allow more Soviet Jews to emigrate to Israel. Jackson also considered the Soviet Union, to use a phrase Ronald Reagan later made popular, "an evil empire" with economic problems that made it vulnerable to collapse. He thought in terms of winning, rather than managing, the cold war. Consequently, Jackson found the White House response that the Democratic Congress would refuse to spend more on defense unduly pessimistic.[13]

It was Jackson who had introduced the resolution recommending that SALT I's successors enshrine numerical equality on the ground that "in the long run, 'superior' technology cannot be relied on to offset inferior numbers." According to Kissinger, Jackson thereby created a problem. Assuming the "equal ceilings were established at the American level, the Soviet Union would have to undertake an essentially unilateral reduction of its forces. If they were set at the Soviet level, we would acquire the right to a buildup for which we had no program or strategic theory."[14]

Ironically, the domestic campaign against détente gathered force in 1974–75 just as the Soviets were ready to make concessions on SALT II negotiations. In part, Kissinger understood, the olive branch indicated anxiety about Jackson and détente's American skeptics. But the Soviets may also have sought a dramatic breakthrough. Indeed, as Kissinger acknowledged after the cold war ended, perhaps he and Ford should have taken more seriously Brezhnev's repeated proposals for a larger gesture than SALT II, such as a joint resolution to take action against any country that used nuclear weapons. Kissinger always brushed aside such discussion, as did Ford. And despite the rejections, Brezhnev always still proved willing to deal.[15]

VLADIVOSTOK AND ITS AFTERMATH

Brezhnev's flexibility was on display when he and Ford met in November 1974 at a tired resort near Vladivostok in the Soviet Far East. "Without mentioning any names—and you can imagine whom I am talking about—if the United States Government were to accept an agreement on the basis of disparity, that would be extremely difficult to sell to the American people, and in the political environment in Washington such an agreement would be severely criticized," Ford told Brezhnev soon after the two had vented about Jackson. Ford and Brezhnev went on to agree that SALT II would restrict each country to 2,400 strategic nuclear delivery vehicles (bombers, intercontinental ballistic missiles, and submarine-based missiles) and that no more than 1,320 of the missiles would be equipped with multiple warheads, or MIRVed. This was "equality" in name only. In addition to requiring cutbacks from the Soviets, who were then at the 2,600 level in strategic nuclear delivery vehicles, the Vladivostok agreement gave an advantage to the Americans because they had the edge in MIRV technology, as the Soviets well knew.[16]

As Ford and his staffers celebrated reaching agreement on SALT II on Air Force One, vodka lifted their spirits higher. Press secretary Ron Nessen effused to reporters that while "Richard Nixon could not achieve this in five years, President Ford achieved it in three months." An elated Ford believed that with the resolution of a few technical issues, SALT II would be ready for signature and the congressional ratification process.[17]

Wishful thinking. Next to the deepening recession, the president's most pressing problem related to his lack of control over foreign policy. Ford had scarcely cemented Soviet-American unity by literally giving Brezhnev the coat off his back when Congress began to undercut détente and SALT II. To Kissinger and Ford, Congress seemed determined to transform Vladivostok into a symbol that the United States was losing the cold war and abandoning Israel. Senator Jackson's aide Richard Perle joked darkly that Ford had been drinking vodka during the negotiations. To Jackson, Perle, and other neoconservatives, the agreement did not represent arms control but placed the American stamp of approval on the Soviet arms buildup. Though it was he who had insisted on equality, Jackson now complained that the SALT II ceilings of twenty-four hundred should have been set at seventeen hundred and called for reductions.[18]

Within a month of Vladivostok, Jackson and Representative Charles Vanik, a Democrat from Ohio, had persuaded an overwhelming majority of legislators to enact an amendment to the pending Trade Reform Act. Jackson-Vanik sought to reflect a commitment to human rights by prohibiting extension of most-favored-nation status to nations with nonmarket economies that restricted their citizens' right to emigrate. The target of course was the Soviet Union. Though he went along with it, Ford was furious. Soviet Ambassador to the United States Anatoly Dobrynin had orally promised him that the Soviets would permit fifty-five thousand Jews to emigrate to Israel from Russia annually, and the president believed that "quiet diplomacy" should work its magic. The Soviets were angry too. "Probably no other single question did more to sour the atmosphere of détente than the question of Jewish emigration from the Soviet Union," Dobrynin said. At the same time, Senator Adlai Stevenson III, an Illinois Democrat, successfully sponsored an amendment to the Export-Import Bank bill, restricting extension of credits to the Soviet Union.

In retaliation, in January 1975, the Soviets canceled the trade agreement with the United States that they had eagerly negotiated in 1972. They informed Americans that they would not seek most-favored-nation status, and they suspended payments on a World War II debt. They also sharply reduced the number of exit visas they issued to Jews. U.S. relations with the Soviet Union, recently so good at Vladivostok, had deteriorated anew.[19]

Congressional Democrats had the AFL-CIO, a longtime pillar of their party, on their side. George Meany had always hated communism. The union leader complained to Ford that "SALT I bugged me—it looked like we were swindled."[20]

THE AFL-CIO AND neoconservative Democrats were not the only ones to enlist in the battle against détente. Republicans to the president's right did also. William F. Buckley remained on friendly terms with Ford's secretary of state, even once offering to dedicate a novel about détente to Kissinger. Yet Buckley maintained publicly that détente produced too many empty toasts exchanged with Communist dictators. Conservative publications, such as *Human Events*, regularly trumpeted "the menace of Henry Kissinger." The *Phyllis Schlafly Report* combined agitation against the ERA with discussions of "the fraud called détente." Détente's critics on the Republican right also included other members of the New Right, the American Conservative Union, and Secretary of Defense James Schlesinger.[21]

The Chinese despised détente too. They used Vladivostok to manipulate Kissinger and the United States. When Kissinger went from Vladivostok to Beijing to discuss normalization of relations between the United States and China, the Chinese repeatedly raised "their favorite subject—the Soviet Union" and declared their desire to invite Schlesinger for a visit. That alarmed Kissinger, who cabled home that Schlesinger's trip would alienate the Soviets and that he would try to discourage it by offering the Chinese any other cabinet member or Ford himself. Of course the Chinese snatched at Ford. Nonetheless, Kissinger boasted to the National Security Council that "nothing helped [with the Chinese] as much as having made the agreement in Vladivostok." And, he continued, addressing Ford, "[T]he fact that you are going to China will help tremendously with the Soviets. We have this triangular game going again as a result of Vladivostok."[22]

The Soviets did view the American climate with alarm. Soon after Ford became president, Moscow let Washington know that it considered the United States "politically dominated by George Meany, the military-industrial complex, the Zionists who control the media and Senator Henry Jackson and his bloc." All those forces opposed détente, as did part of the Republican Party. The convergence against détente of Republicans on the right, neoconservatives, labor leaders, Jews, and a growing number of human rights activists on the left seemed utterly bizarre to the Soviets and Ford Administration alike.[23]

IMPERIAL CONGRESS

In early 1975 Ford did not focus on Republicans to his right in the anti-détente coalition. Conservatives still seemed unthreatening to him, and congressional liberals still bothered him more. That became apparent in the debate between president and Congress over Cyprus.[24]

Just before Ford became president, the military government in Greece staged a coup in Cyprus, where the majority Greek and minority Turk population uneasily coexisted. The Turks promptly invaded and occupied part of Cyprus, so outraging mainland Greeks that they overthrew their own government. Many in Washington, particularly Greek Americans who supported the new Greek democracy, were angry that the invading Turks used American weapons. Aided by the Greek American lobby, congressional liberals tried to force the Turks to withdraw from Cyprus by demanding that the United States end military aid to Turkey. Though the president considered legislation banning further military aid to Turkey counterproductive and twice vetoed it, Congress overrode him.

From Ford's perspective, "Congress was determined to interfere with the President's traditional right to manage foreign policy." Instilled with the conviction that politics ended at the water's edge, Congressman Ford had often conceded that right to presidents. Congressional reassertion in the realm of foreign policy during his own presidency left Ford fuming. The embargo on military aid to Turkey took effect in February 1975.[25]

In March 1975 there was another disaster that Kissinger and Ford laid at the feet of Congress. Since 1972 the United States had given millions in covert aid to Kurdish rebels, who battled for independence from Iraq's Saddam Hussein. Americans reasoned that the Kurdish resistance in Iraq, a Soviet and Arab ally, helped the shah of Iran, friend of the United States and Israel. But suddenly and surprisingly, the shah agreed to close Iran's border to the Kurds and to end his own assistance to them in exchange for Iraqi concessions. It was a fatal misstep. The shah's deal with Saddam Hussein enabled Iranian Shia Muslims to make pilgrimages to Iraq, where they fell further under the sway of the shah's enemy, Iranian exile Ayatollah Khomeini, then living in the holy city of Najaf. But at the time many Americans worried about the consequences for the Kurds, whose rebellion Saddam Hussein now crushed. Some accused the shah, the Ford administration, and Kissinger of abandoning the Kurds.

Kissinger, however, rationalized that covert action was not "missionary work," and he attributed the shah's switch to the "steadily declining executive authority" that made the United States an unreliable ally.[26]

March 1975 also saw one of the few foreign policy setbacks Ford and Kissinger did not immediately blame on Congress. The collapse of Kissinger's latest round of shuttle diplomacy because of Israel's "lack of flexibility" and the secretary of state's departure from Tel Aviv in tears made the president "mad as hell." Egged on by Kissinger, Ford ordered a "reassessment" of U.S. policy toward Israel. While it occurred, the president told the National Security Council, the United States would maintain a "businesslike but arms-length and aloof" relationship with Israel, and there "must be a suspension of certain deliveries and contacts." That made Israel and its congressional allies mad as hell.[27]

At the same time, the international strength of communism grew. Portugal had decided to launch the decolonization process after the bloodless 1974 "carnation revolution" toppled its authoritarian regime and gave the left a voice in the new government. The failure of a military coup in Portugal in March 1975 left Kissinger concerned that Portugal would become Communist. The political situations in Italy and Spain seemed precarious too. That same fateful month, a staffer also warned Kissinger that because the Indonesian government feared that the Portuguese departure from Timor would strengthen the left there, Indonesia might attack Timor. Kissinger embraced "a policy of silence," and he and Ford later gave the green light to an Indonesian invasion of Timor that led to the slaughter of more than two hundred thousand Timorese by Indonesian troops using American-supplied weapons.[28]

During this month of crises, Ford and Kissinger went to Palm Desert. By this time the secretary of state seemed less like Superman than "Gulliver in Lilliput." The *Economist* announced "The Fading of America."[29]

GAMESMANSHIP

No problems were as serious as those involving Indochina. The Paris Peace Accords that Kissinger and the North Vietnamese negotiated in 1973 did not bring the honorable peace that he and Nixon promised. True, the accords provided for a cease-fire in South Vietnam, but they included no mechanism for enforcement. And although the whole war revolved around the question of South Vietnam's political future, the accords did not resolve that issue. One hundred and fifty thousand North Vietnamese troops remained inside South Vietnam, and their presence and the accords gave political legitimacy to their communist allies in South Vietnam's Provisional Revolutionary Government who fought the U.S.-backed government of South Vietnam. At the same time, the accords permitted the president of South Vietnam, Nguyen Van Thieu, who accepted them only because Nixon threatened that otherwise Thieu would go it alone, to remain in power.[30]

Since the North Vietnamese and the Provisional Revolutionary Government hated Thieu, it was understood that the war would continue—for everyone but American ground troops. Under the two provisions of the Paris accords that came closest to being implemented, the United States promised to withdraw its forces from Vietnam over the next sixty days in exchange for North Vietnam's return of American prisoners of war. Yet the Pentagon did not believe it got back all American prisoners of war, and twenty-eight hundred Americans, many of them former military, stayed on in Vietnam as privately employed technicians to service South Vietnamese hardware, one facet of what *New York Times* reporter David Shipler called "a vast program of American aid that continues to set the course of the war more than a year after the Paris peace agreements and the final withdrawal of American ground troops." In addition to rushing financial aid to Thieu, the president interpreted a section that gave Thieu and the Provisional Revolutionary Government the right to replace used-up military equipment to confer upon the United States the duty to replace the weapons that Thieu's forces lost in combat. Moreover, the president and his secretary of state anticipated that the North Vietnamese would violate the terms of the accords and had every expectation of then resuming the bombing of the Communists, though Nixon and Kissinger also understood that South Vietnam was doomed to defeat. In Cambodia, a country not covered by the accords, Nixon directed American B-52s to continue bombing.[31]

But Nixon did not reckon with a Congress moved by war and Watergate to challenge him. President Johnson liked to complain that he had to depend on Republicans and conservative Democrats to support his Vietnam policies while "I'm getting kicked around by my own party in the Senate." But even though nothing divided liberals more than the Vietnam War and many liberals had early misgivings about Johnson's decision to escalate American involvement, congressional liberals were scared to inject themselves forcefully into the debate about the war during the Johnson years. Given a Democrat in the White House who forcefully insisted through 1967 that the United States and South Vietnam were winning, one historian wrote, "many in Congress swallowed their reservations and chose to accept the claim—or at least to keep their mouths shut." The Communists' apparent advances in the surprise Tet Offensive in 1968, however, suggested to many that despite Pentagon claims of enemy defeat, victory was not imminent. Nixon faced a bolder, bipartisan liberal antiwar coalition in Congress that included Senate Democrats, such as Frank Church of Idaho, George McGovern of South Dakota, Thomas Eagleton of Missouri, Mike Mansfield of Montana, and Ted Kennedy of Massachusetts, and Senate Republicans, such as John Sherman Cooper of Kentucky, Clifford Case of New Jersey, George Aiken of Vermont, Jacob Javits of New York, and Mark Hatfield of Oregon.[32]

The group did not march in lockstep or achieve everything that all its members wanted. On June 29, 1973, as the noose of Watergate began to strangle Nixon, Congress enacted legislation sponsored by Church and Case that prohibited the use of all American military forces in Southeast Asia without its permission. The legislation had been designed to force the president to end the bombing in Cambodia, but when Nixon indicated that he would go along only if it allowed the bombing to continue for another six weeks, Church and Case agreed to an August 15 deadline, which Congress approved, despite vehement criticism from Kennedy and others that "this cruel and calculated pact" gave the president "a license for six more weeks of slaughter in Cambodia." Congress also enacted the War Powers Act over Nixon's veto in 1973. Though it too was watered down, the final legislation nevertheless required presidents who sent troops overseas to notify Congress within forty-eight hours of their decision to do so and to withdraw them within sixty days unless Congress approved.[33]

In 1974 and 1975, Congress also tightened the purse strings. "I want to reassure you we will support President Thieu in every way—economically, politically, and diplomatically," Ford told South Vietnamese officials soon after he became president. "Our problem is not us, but on the Hill."[34]

In Hanoi, the North Vietnamese observed war-weariness in Washington with delight. The withdrawal of American financial support and troops destroyed the economy of South Vietnam. When Thieu tried to prop up his corrupt regime by cracking down on his critics, morale in

South Vietnam hit bottom. Judging it their moment, the North Vietnamese worried that an offensive might bring back the Americans. At the end of 1974 the North Vietnamese decided upon a trial invasion of Phuoc Long, about eighty miles north of the South Vietnamese capital of Saigon. None of the American B-52s appeared, and in just three weeks the North Vietnamese won their first South Vietnamese province in fifteen years. Now the North Vietnamese resolved to begin an all-out invasion of South Vietnam. In neighboring Cambodia, the revolutionary Khmer Rouge, its membership swollen by hatred of American bombing, launched a new assault against President Lon Nol's right-wing pro-American government.[35]

These developments spurred Ford and Congress to battle each other. Although his advisers agreed that Congress would reject more aid for South Vietnam and Cambodia, the president determined to request it. He followed his 1975 State of the Union address urging a tax cut with a speech pleading for a supplemental military appropriation of $300 million for South Vietnam and $222 million for Cambodia that he said would enable them to "hold their own." But even congressional cold warriors had given up on South Vietnam and Cambodia. And the president guaranteed that Congress would turn him down by linking his supplemental request to a three-year multibillion-dollar aid program for South Vietnam.[36]

Events belied Ford's assurances that each country could hold its own. The Cambodian capital of Phnom Penh had remained an island of serenity during the country's five-year civil war. Now the Khmer Rouge encircled and besieged it. By April 1, 1975, Lon Nol had fled.[37]

But the real shock was in South Vietnam. There the North Vietnamese were succeeding beyond their wildest hopes. On March 10 they overran the city of Ban Me Thuot in the central highlands. Frightened, Thieu decided upon retreat. Surprising the United States and his own commanders, he abandoned the central highlands to Saigon's west. Thieu's forces and South Vietnamese civilians jammed the roads to the sea. The North Vietnamese began pounding away at coastal cities and provinces. On March 19, the North Vietnamese captured the strategically important city of Quang Tri; one week later the South Vietnamese abandoned the historic city of Hue. Hundreds of thousands of refugees streamed toward Da Nang, South Vietnam's second-largest city.

In Da Nang, deserters from Thieu's army rampaged the city in an orgy of looting. Then they pushed aside women and children to force their way onto the last American flight out. It lifted off while outsiders clung to it. On March 30, Da Nang fell to North Vietnam. In his desperate gamble to save half of South Vietnam, Thieu had given up the other half in one month.[38]

MEANWHILE, THE FORD ADMINISTRATION requested aid from Congress. North Vietnam had violated the Paris Accords, the president contended, and the United States must help its allies. The accords created an American obligation to replace arms the South Vietnamese lost in combat. The congressional refusal to make good was wreaking disaster. Echoing Thieu, Ford claimed that the president of South Vietnam had decided to withdraw from the central highlands because of his uncertainty about continued congressional assistance. Financial aid would sustain the South Vietnamese and Cambodian military, the president promised, and make likely a victory or negotiated settlement. The fact that the South Vietnamese were fleeing the North Vietnamese indicated their commitment to freedom. While the United States might have no commitment to Cambodia, the president claimed that American policy since World War II had been "to help those nations with military hardware . . . where the government and the people of a country want to protect their country from foreign aggression or foreign invasion."[39]

If the United States abandoned Cambodia and South Vietnam to the Communists, Ford predicted a "bloodbath" in both countries. Reviving the domino theory, he also warned that if Cambodia and South Vietnam fell to communism, they might take all Southeast Asia with them. The Soviets and Chinese would believe that the United States had lost its will, Ford said, and allies the world over would question American credibility. Further, the fall of Cambodia and Vietnam would leave Americans with "a deep sense of shame."[40]

Few found Ford's arguments persuasive. Like North Vietnam, South Vietnam had violated the Paris accords. On their face, at least, the accords did not oblige the United States to replace arms lost in combat. In any event, the accords neither required nor received congressional ratification. "Poor generalship and a breakdown in morale—not an immediate shortage of equipment and ammunition—caused the rout," the *New York Times* declared. There was reason to believe that military assistance for South Vietnam would only benefit the North Vietnamese: Thieu's army was estimated to have abandoned seven hundred million dollars of military equipment in its recent retreat. "We might just as well send the stuff directly to Hanoi—then it wouldn't get damaged," a Pentagon official joked. The South Vietnamese were fleeing, most agreed, because they had panicked, not because of their faith in democracy, which Thieu had never provided. Having spurned negotiated settlements when Thieu and Lon Nol were stronger, why would North Vietnam and the Khmer Rouge agree to them now? Moreover, the United States had not always provided military hardware to nations resisting external aggression.[41]

Ford's predictions about the future fell on equally deaf ears. The congressional investigations of 1975 did not foster confidence in American intelligence, and not everyone was convinced that a new "bloodbath" would follow Communist takeovers. The prediction was "founded in propaganda purposes and, as such, it was clever," one American journalist observed in the *Nation*. "No one could prove there would be no blood bath—it is always impossible to disprove a prediction."[42]

As it turned out, there were bloodbaths. After North Vietnam won the war, it cruelly expelled the ethnic Chinese, opponents of communism, and thousands of others, prompting an orgy of second-guessing of the pullout on the American left and "we told you sos" on the right. By the spring of 1979 sixty-five thousand were fleeing South Vietnam in leaky boats monthly. Many never saw shore again: An estimated three hundred thousand had died at sea since 1975.[43]

Cambodia became a charnel house. Yet few anticipated the subsequent slaughter in the spring of 1975, and despite his warning, it is not clear that the president was among them. Indeed, wrote one reporter who had stayed behind, those who remained in Phnom Penh believed that "when the Communists came and the war finally ended, at least the suffering would largely be over. All of us were wrong." Even after the Khmer Rouge released that reporter from captivity, he dismissed as exaggerations predictions that thousands of Cambodians would be executed. Wrong again. As he and others on the left subsequently documented, the Khmer Rouge under Pol Pot inaugurated an utterly brutal program of murder, forced relocation, and reeducation that left 1.7 million dead over the next three years—more than 20 percent of the population. American conservatives called attention to the Khmer Rouge atrocities and additionally complained that "American leftists cheered, justified and denied as the communists plunged Cambodia into a nightmare." While the response of Americans left of center to the Pol Pot regime was indeed uneven, it was more significant that Ford, Kissinger, and Carter too tolerated the Khmer Rouge and turned a blind eye to the Cambodian genocide, which the American government did not even condemn until April 1978. The United States wanted to placate China, a Cambodian ally, and thought Cambodia's independence under Pol Pot and the Khmer Rouge served American interests.[44]

Nor did American allies view the survival of Vietnam and Cambodia as tests of American credibility. If anything, the CIA's William Colby hinted to Ford, allies were relieved the United States was cutting its losses. Without a doubt, the Soviets would rejoice at American defeat, but the victory belonged to North Vietnam, not the Soviet Union. The United States should never have assumed that North Vietnam was Moscow directed. And clearly the United States was not relinquishing its role in the world.[45]

Above all, Ford was wrong to say Americans would feel shame if Vietnam and Cambodia fell. One reporter branded him "completely out of touch with the mood of the country." Americans approved an airlift of Vietnamese orphans and clamored to adopt the children. (The crash of the first flight seemed a metaphor for the whole American misadventure in Southeast Asia.) But according to 1975 polls, more than 75 percent opposed further military aid.[46]

Some Americans were going to see the Vietnam documentary *Hearts and Minds*. Reviewer Penelope Gilliatt described the film as "a complex tale about possessing apparently infallible power and then finding that it doesn't work." She watched one matinee with a passerby who had wandered in to escape the rain. "She took in everything, looked startled, cried." Then she told Gilliatt: "I liked what the American woman said about a mature person's being able to make a mistake so why can't a government?"[47]

If anyone should feel ashamed and mistaken, some thought, it was Ford. He was golfing and jovially jogging away from reporters who asked about South Vietnam and Cambodia. In a column that stung the White House, William F. Buckley contended that "the world has a right, in the face of our staggering diplomatic and military ineptitudes, to expect from the President a sense of decorum."[48]

NONE OF THE REASONS Ford gave for supplemental military aid were compelling, and all were bogus. The real reason for the president's request, magazines as diverse as the *Nation* on the left and *National Review* on the right correctly alleged, lay in his determination to make the Democratic Congress a scapegoat for the Southeast Asian debacle. If it denied him money, as Ford had every indication it would, he and Kissinger could attribute the defeat of South Vietnam and Cambodia to congressional interference with the president's formulation of foreign policy.[49]

Though Ford publicly insisted he was not "assessing blame on anyone," internal White House memorandums showed otherwise. At a National Security Council meeting on April 9, the day before the president was to address Congress, Defense Secretary Schlesinger urged Ford to admit that the situation in Vietnam was hopeless (privately, so as to avoid chaos in Saigon) and to ask for $300 million to get out the Americans and the Vietnamese who had provided them with special help. Ford, Schlesinger said, should look beyond Vietnam in his speech, inspire Americans to sacrifice, as Winston Churchill had roused the British during World War II, and stress that détente "cannot be a one way street." Kissinger, however, urged the president to ask for $722 million in military aid alone and to challenge Congress, not the Soviet Union. Ford sided with Kissinger. One of his congressional liaisons reasoned that "the President should come out strong now requesting additional military assistance." The plea would "probably" fail to carry Congress, but "the President must be on record strongly in support of an ally about to go under. I don't see that it would hurt him politically that much if he made the request and then were turned down by the Congress."[50]

On April 10, 1975, the President gave his State of the World speech to Congress, defending détente and demanding additional aid for Southeast Asia. With words Kissinger wrote, Ford reiterated the litany. Congress had hamstrung the president by cutting off aid to Turkey, enacting Jackson-Vanik, and reneging on the Paris Peace Accords. Because it could not count on Americans, South Vietnam had sounded retreat. In jeopardy were six thousand Americans and thousands of South Vietnamese. Ford asked his former colleagues to "put an end to self-inflicted wounds." While he knew that U.S. military forces in Southeast Asia were authorized to protect "American lives by ensuring their evacuation, if this should be necessary," he wanted Congress to spell it out for him. Further, he hoped Congress would amend existing law in the next nine days to enable the same troops to evacuate high-risk South Vietnamese.

Ford also wanted money fast—again, by April 19. He did not repeat his call for aid to Cambodia, which he conceded was gone. He requested nearly $1 billion for South Vietnam, $722 million in military aid, the remainder in economic and humanitarian support. The funds, he argued, "might enable the South Vietnamese to stem the onrushing aggression, to stabilize the military situation, permit the chance of a negotiated political settlement between the North and South Vietnamese, and if the very worst were to happen, at least allow the orderly evacuation of Americans and endangered South Vietnamese to places of safety."[51]

Even administration officials acknowledged that the president's public rationales were flimsy. One unstated reason Ford had appealed for funds, they told reporters, was to demonstrate a commitment to South Vietnam. Otherwise, the president worried that bitter South Vietnamese soldiers crying betrayal might join Vietnamese Communists in turning their guns on the Americans. But if that was Ford's fear, he should have followed Schlesinger's advice and immediately begun to evacuate the Americans. The predominant reason for his request was to implicate Congress by forcing it to turn him down again. He was making an argument for history: Congress must bear responsibility for the "loss of Vietnam" and restore the president's power to make foreign policy.[52]

Congress too was creating its own record. After Ford finished his address, members competed to express their outrage that the president continued the failed policy of Kissinger and Nixon. As members of Congress told the story, the executive branch was responsible for the loss of Vietnam, and the legislative branch deserved a stronger voice to avoid future presidential errors. Senator Jackson announced that he had been "reliably informed" that "secret agreements" between Nixon and Thieu at the time of the Paris accords contemplated "fateful American decisions." The White House insisted that Nixon's and Thieu's letters simply echoed their public declarations, but when an assistant to Thieu distributed copies of Nixon's correspondence, many concluded otherwise.[53]

Whatever their politics, outsiders who observed the riot of finger-pointing realized "an air of gamesmanship" infected the final Vietnam debate. Ford had started it. His home state newspaper had stood by him to date, but now the *Detroit Free Press* condemned Ford's "sleazy attempt to create a scapegoat." But for all that, Congress too bore responsibility for missteps in Vietnam. "Of course there may well have been 'secret agreements'," the *Nation* editorialized. "Does that really surprise Senator Jackson?" The powerful wanted to put the war behind the United States in 1973, and few cared how.[54]

MEANWHILE, THE SITUATION in Southeast Asia worsened. Evacuation of American embassy personnel from Cambodia began the day after Ford addressed Congress. By this time the North Vietnamese were pressing toward Saigon.

On April 17, 1975, the Senate Armed Services Committee announced its rejection of Ford's military aid package. Kissinger declared that the Vietnam debate had ended. But he sent a mixed message as he adjured all to "abide by the verdict of Congress—without recrimination or vindictiveness." Thieu resigned on April 21 and fled Vietnam, reportedly with ten tons of baggage.[55]

And in an uplifting address as sharply at odds with his glum State of the World speech to Congress as Ford's move from tax hike to cut, the president told Tulane students on April 23 that "America can regain the sense of pride that existed before Vietnam. But it cannot be achieved by refighting a war that is finished as far as America is concerned." As Ford said the word "finished," his audience whooped enthusiastically. The secretary of state was annoyed, especially after anonymous White House officials characterized the speech as "a presidential 'declaration of independence' " from Kissinger.[56]

But when Ford's press secretary announced the next day that the president was still asking for the $722 million that Congress would obviously refuse, administration speechwriter John Casserly was perplexed. He decided that "the end of the war statement at Tulane was not planned or placed in the speech by any logical design" and "was, to some extent, an accidental remark." Casserly had a "favorite question" about the Ford White House: "What the hell is going on here?"[57]

DEFEAT

While the administration turned rhetorical somersaults, many remained stranded in Saigon. Evacuation had begun. But it was proceeding altogether too slowly for Pentagon officials, who publicly complained that the planes sent to carry it out were coming back empty.[58]

Graham Martin, the American ambassador to South Vietnam, was most responsible for that sorry state of affairs, though Kissinger and Ford were also at fault. Martin joined the Ford administration in holding Congress responsible for Thieu's reverses. The night Ford gave his State of the World speech, Martin cabled Kissinger that "it is, as of today, one hell of a mistake to write South Vietnam off as finished, despite what your so-called experts tell you." Analysts were just covering their asses, Martin said, while he risked his on the ground. Ford's nine-day deadline to Congress of April 19 placed "us on a very short fuse" in Saigon and increased the risk that the South Vietnamese military would join the North Vietnamese in attacking fleeing Americans.[59]

Martin adopted that scenario for a reason. More fully than Ford and Kissinger, and for even longer, he clung to the hope of saving the Thieu regime through a congressional appropriation. "Essentially, this policy meant gambling the lives of the 6,000 Americans in Vietnam on the promise of a last-minute miracle, and because of the hazards it implied, Martin knew he would need a powerful rationale for it," the CIA's chief strategic analyst in Vietnam recalled later. "The recent reports indicating that the army might turn against us in the event of an American evacuation served nicely" and gave Martin an excuse to proceed at snail's place in executing it.[60]

Even after Thieu left, Martin apparently thought he could pull a rabbit out of the hat and negotiate a settlement with the North Vietnamese that would allow the United States to exit with honor. (Martin possessed a large ego, and some thought he had become delusional.) So far, he told Kissinger, everything was on track. "The most calming influence in Saigon is my wife who goes about her regular way, makes appointments for weeks in advance, and who has refused to pack anything at all."[61]

Reports of Mrs. Martin's behavior did not soothe the Senate Foreign Relations Committee. On April 14 it took the unusual step of calling on the president to tell him that all Americans must leave immediately. "It was apparent from that meeting that their full concern is with evacuation of Americans and that the Senate wants to make sure that it's the President who gets stuck in the event any American gets hurt or killed," Kissinger told Martin. The president insisted, however, that "we just couldn't cut and run." He wanted no talk of evacuation, Ford told the cabinet on April 16. "It is my hope that we can get the dollars and the authority, to stabilize the situation and hopefully get negotiations started."[62]

But by the following day Ford and Kissinger had to admit that Congress would not provide the money. Officially, the final vote on Ford's military aid package was still pending. Meanwhile, many Americans in Vietnam were trying to save the South Vietnamese by marrying them.

The War Powers Act authorized U.S. military personnel to get Americans out, and probably Vietnamese dependents. Congress was stalling on approving the use of American troops to aid with nondependent high-risk Vietnamese. If a large number of high-risk Vietnamese were going to leave, Ford still wanted Congress to give him authority—and share the responsibility. "How do we signal we don't want a vote and still get the legal authority to evacuate them?" Chief of Staff Rumsfeld asked. That was indeed the intractable problem.[63]

At the request of the United States, the Soviets helpfully extracted a promise from the North Vietnamese to delay the occupation of Saigon until Americans left and made the presidential solution obvious. By "front channel," Kissinger and Ford would exhort Martin to hasten the evacuation and create a record to protect the president. By "back channel," they would sing a different tune, one that sounded much more like Martin's than that of Congress or the Pentagon. The president, Kissinger advised Martin, "recognizing his moral obligations to those who for so long have worked with us, is determined to do all he can to help the Vietnamese as well as the Americans."[64]

All three men understood that they needed Americans in Saigon to continue bringing out the South Vietnamese who had helped them. Yet since Martin also still fantasized about negotiating a settlement between the United States and both halves of Vietnam and believed that the North Vietnamese would interpret evacuation as a sign of weakness, his policies were at cross-purposes. At one point, Kissinger told Martin he and the president were "amazed at the small number of Vietnamese being evacuated, considering the substantial amount of aircraft available" and urged him "to redouble your efforts."[65]

So Americans stayed on in Saigon. In the words of one reporter, they "served as hostages for the withdrawal of South Vietnamese marked for death by the Communists." By the last week of April, Saigon was a cauldron of desperation. As diplomats destroyed their secret files, those who would be left behind realized that Americans and other foreigners were bailing out. "The ashes were flying all over," one Vietnamese said later. "We knew that the British were not burning incense for their ancestors."[66]

Still, Ford, Kissinger, and Martin waited until April 29, when North Vietnamese rockets hit Saigon's Tan Son Nhut airport. At last, the administration was ready to order the final pullout—too late to use fixed wing aircraft. Americans had previously been told how to identify the last phase of the evacuation. At noon on April 29 they heard the signal. First, the radio broadcast a weather report of "105 degrees and rising." Then Bing Crosby sang "White Christmas." When he crooned, they ran to the helicopters. But the South Vietnamese knew the code too. The poor planning by Americans ensured that when the evacuation finally moved into high gear, one Vietnamese served as well as another. Cooks and bar girls received seats that should have gone to those most endangered by the North Vietnamese arrival.[67]

During the night of April 29 thousands of South Vietnamese broke into the American Embassy. Undaunted by the tear gas grenades the marines fired, they made their way toward the helicopter pad on the roof. By the time the final flights carried off the last marines soon after dawn on April 30, the U.S. troops were shooting at the South Vietnamese they left behind.[68]

When the evacuation ended, the United States could report it had gotten out 6,500 South Vietnamese and Americans in the last sixteen hours alone. Of course, the president complained, the "Monday-morning quarterbacks" in the United States second-guessed him. So did many who had borne witness. "The big numbers [of evacuees] are irrelevant," one diplomat complained. "The rest of our lives we will be haunted by how we betrayed the people." But the big numbers of South Vietnamese—some 120,000 extricated in April—created difficulties. What was the United States to do with the refugees?[69]

Ford hoped to take them in, just as the United States had provided a new life for nearly 1.5 million displaced persons after World War II. When the president asked Congress to approve the expenditure of one billion dollars for the care and transportation of the Vietnamese, however, the House turned him down. "Despite the House vote, I believe that in this tragic situation the American people want their country to be guided by the inscription on the Statue of Liberty," Ford scolded Congress.[70]

But the president was mistaken. Many Americans had long been dubious about admitting large numbers of immigrants, particularly those of color. Immigrants were, after all, characterized as "wretched refuse" in that Statue of Liberty inscription. Unemployment in the United States was at nearly 9 percent in May 1975. When Ford insisted that "we could afford to be generous to the refugees" because "it was a matter of principle," the mayor of Chicago said that "charity begins at home."[71]

THERE WAS MORE at stake in the debate over the fate of the refugees than Americans' economic woes and racism. Americans' reaction also reflected their attitude toward the war. More than fifty-eight thousand Americans and three million Vietnamese had died in the conflict since 1960, and the United States had still lost. "Probably the only people who have the historical sense of inevitable victory are Americans," the British historian D. W. Brogan had once written. The sense of destiny was gone now. The war emerged as a critical reference point and made the public, military, media, and government ever anxious that any future military intervention might become "another Vietnam"—a sinkhole. Americans had emerged from World War II confident that they could spread freedom and capitalism around the globe. After Vietnam, they became less certain of their mission. In that sense, the United States did seem to be fading and becoming a superpower in decline.[72]

In addition to destroying faith in American omnipotence, defeat in Vietnam affected the way politicians thought about reporters. Future presidents blamed the loss of South Vietnam on the media, which had revealed, rather than caused, defeat. In fact, American journalists largely parroted Washington's line through 1968. Afterward reporters became more suspicious of presidential promises that there was light at the end of the tunnel. The fall of Cambodia and Vietnam received especially compelling coverage. It was impossible to open a newspaper or magazine, turn on a television or radio, in the winter and spring of 1975 without hearing about, or seeing, the gruesome images that were the legacy of America's longest war.[73]

Defeat in Vietnam increased cynicism about the government and the presidency, in particular. Presidents since James Polk had lied to bring the United States into war and keep it there. But never, it seemed, had so much of the American public and media suspected their government of lying at the very moment it did so. The hopefulness and optimism that had made the sixties exciting disappeared. By 1975 the executive branch and its legislative challengers seemed a menace to society, rather than a panacea. And politics had become a dirty business, in which means and ends lacked integrity and nobility.

Coupled with the draft, these by-products of the Vietnam War made the United States a battleground. "This goddamn war was the American Civil War of the twentieth century fought twelve thousand miles away," one policy maker remembered. Vietnam divided the United States along the lines of race, region, religion, and, above all, class. Though a broad cross section had served in the armed forces during World War II and Korea, a disproportionate number of Vietnam draftees were from poor or working-class backgrounds, inner cities, and rural areas. Because college students were generally deferred until 1971, and graduate students until 1968, guilt permeated higher education. Vietnam was a poor person's war, which also exposed how many minorities the dream of upward mobility had failed.[74]

Almost all American society had an interest in forgetting all this in 1975. Few were the parades to welcome home Vietnam veterans. The White House did not proclaim a Vietnam Veterans Week until 1979, and fittingly, at his reception for the veterans that year, President Carter read aloud Philip Caputo's eulogy for a friend in his brilliant 1977 memoir *A Rumor of War*: "As I write this 11 years after your death, the country for which you died wishes to forget the war in which you died. Its very name is a curse. There are no monuments to its heroes, for memorials are reminders and they would make it hard for our country to sink into the amnesia for which it longs." As the Vietnam War had divided the country, so amnesia might unify it. In 1975 most of the public immediately buried the questions of why the war had lasted so long and had resulted in defeat.[75]

There was one important exception. Many antiestablishment conservatives associated with the New Right delighted in "recriminations." Defeat in Vietnam galvanized them. Above all, these conservatives blamed liberals. They had taken the United States into the war. "Then, after the majority of the sacrifices had been made and the job of saving South Vietnam was nearing completion," as conservatives recounted the story, liberals lost their nerve. "That was their hideous crime, and it should not be casually forgotten." Then there were the antiwar demonstrators, who had participated in "orgies of affection for the enemy." Then there were the intellectuals, who had acted as "cheerleaders" for North Vietnam, and "Hollywood," which was "lost to liberalism" and where "pro-Communist propaganda," such as *Hearts and Minds*, won an Oscar. Then there was the Department of Defense, which "sent its soldiers into battle, bound and gagged" by restrictions that forced them to fight with one hand tied behind their backs. Finally, there were détente's apostles, Ford and Kissinger, who followed Nixon in confusing the American people by telling them "we were supposed to fight the

Communists in Vietnam" while Washington supplied equipment and technology to North Vietnam's Soviet "masters." No wonder, conservatives said, Americans came to ask: "If Communism is something we can cheerfully live with in Peking and Moscow, why should we keep spending billions to prevent its triumph in Saigon?"[76]

In May 1975, "at almost the exact moment of America's greatest military defeat," Richard Viguerie launched *Conservative Digest: A Magazine for the New Majority*, designed to unite the followers of George Wallace and Ronald Reagan. "Our country, which badly needs a strong Winston Churchill, is stuck with a weak Gerald Ford," Viguerie proclaimed. The American Conservative Union had preordered five thousand copies of William Rusher's call for a marriage between followers of Ronald Reagan and George Wallace, *The Making of the New Majority Party*, as a fund-raising premium, and it was the talk of conservatives.[77]

While conservatives awaited their man on horseback, most Washington politicians encouraged the memory lapse about Vietnam. The debate about who lost the war ended as abruptly as it began. With blood on the hands of Democrats and Republicans, presidents and members of Congress, Ford belatedly realized that further discussion of the war was fruitless. Asked about "the lessons of Vietnam" at his first press conference after the final flight out of Saigon, he insisted that "[w]e ought to look ahead." To what? The sixties had ended, but the contours of the seventies remained unclear.[78]

PART TWO

MODERATION AND ITS DISCONTENTS

V

THE DEATH OF DÉTENTE

—

"DÉTENTE" HAD BECOME A BUZZWORD IN THE UNITED STATES DURing the early 1970s. In an era that made *I'm OK—You're OK* a best seller, the concept took flight. But the second half of 1975 witnessed the death of détente—and not just as a cold war strategy by which the United States sought to contain the Soviet Union. Peaceful coexistence within the Republican Party and between whites and African Americans was threatened too.[1]

"TOO TOUGH TO TACKLE"

While Ford preached forgetfulness at home after the fall of Vietnam, he seized the chance to prove that the United States was still a player. On May 12, 1975, Khmer Rouge troops captured the *Mayaguez*, a rusty U.S. merchant ship making its way through what were, by American definition, international waters. Kissinger presented the capture of the *Mayaguez* as an opportunity. "You must establish a reputation for being too tough to tackle," he told the president. "If you use force, it should be ferociously." That way the Soviet Union, Asian allies, and even Congress would realize that defeat in Vietnam represented an aberration, rather than an abdication, of American global responsibility.[2]

Believing that the *Mayaguez* and its crew members had been taken to the island of Koh Tang and anxious to avert their removal to mainland Cambodia, the president directed airmen to attack Cambodian boats headed to or from the island. He also sent more than one thousand marines to invade Koh Tang and ordered the bombing of the mainland to show "we meant business."[3]

When the mission ended two days later, the forty crew members had been saved. But thirty-eight American servicemen had died, and three marines had been left in Cambodia alive (a fact the Ford administration went to great lengths to conceal). Nonetheless, Ford believed he had rescued the crew, American credibility, and his own reputation. "Many people's faith in their country was restored and my standing in the polls shot up 11 points," he recounted in his autobiography. Liberal Democrats and conservative Republicans alike hailed the rescue of the *Mayaguez*.[4]

The euphoria faded amid questions. Why bomb Khmer Rouge boats leaving Koh Tang? "If they weren't carrying *Mayaguez* crew members, their exodus from the island only weakened the defensive forces there and made it more vulnerable to attack," one critic observed. If they were, bombing them could hurt the *Mayaguez* crew. In fact, the Cambodians had removed the crew from Koh Tang by the time the marines landed on the island, and one Khmer Rouge boat escaped bombardment only because a pilot happened to notice some "Caucasian faces." Why had the attack begun after the Khmer Rouge announced the release of the *Mayaguez*? Ford had an answer for that: The Khmer Rouge had said nothing about the crew. Then why had the bombing continued after the president knew the crew was safe and the *Mayaguez* captain reported his men had been well treated? Would American behavior awe the world? Or was the victory over a new regime that had no air force unimpressive?[5]

Of the many damning findings in the General Accounting Office's contemporary study of the *Mayaguez* incident, two stood out. With undue haste and poor intelligence, the United States had eschewed diplomacy for force. While "certain U.S. actions probably" contributed to the Cambodians' decision to free the crew, "the final Marine assault and the bombing of the Cambodian mainland did not." That meant, said one of the few reporters to read the study, "41 American lives were lost unnecessarily" in a "futile" raid. Deputy Chief of Staff Dick Cheney accurately described the *Mayaguez* crisis as "only a footnote in history."[6]

Ford himself sometimes seemed a footnote after he fell down a few steps of an airplane ramp in Salzburg two weeks later. Ever thereafter, he remembered, the media focused on his every slip and stumble "to the exclusion of almost everything else." Although he was surely correct in saying that "all those reporters who are reporting how clumsy I am" got "most of their exercise sitting on bar stools," he still seemed like a joke. In the new television show *Saturday Night Live*, comedian

Chevy Chase lampooned the president's awkwardness. Ford's own staff mourned his transformation from "a goodhearted, not-very-bright jock" to "a klutz."[7]

FROM HELSINKI TO THE UNITED NATIONS

After the *Mayaguez* had been rescued, Ford exulted that "the American people are getting out from under the trauma of our problems in Vietnam" and expressed the hope that "we may be entering a new era." But in this new era the prospects for détente were bleak. Whereas early in 1975, Ford worried about the congressional Democrats in the anti-détente coalition, such as Senator Jackson, by summer the president's attention was shifting to its Republican members on his right. As the "Solzhenitsyn affair" showed, they were the ones who could now make his life miserable.[8]

The author of chilling books and novels about the penal labor camps in which the Soviet Union enslaved tens of millions of prisoners, exiled Russian dissident Aleksandr Solzhenitsyn had become the symbol of Soviet denial of human rights. At the end of June he arrived in Washington. So great was his following that the Senate unanimously voted to make him (as it had Winston Churchill) an honorary American citizen. Solzhenitsyn was expected to blast détente at an AFL-CIO banquet that George Meany was hosting in his honor. The State Department said that presidential attendance would insult the Soviets, and on Kissinger's recommendation, Ford did not go.[9]

He was not to avoid Solzhenitsyn so easily. Republican Senators Jesse Helms and Strom Thurmond asked if they could bring Solzhenitsyn by the White House. Ford was preparing for the Conference on Security and Cooperation in Europe (CSCE) with Brezhnev, and he knew that he might boost his ratings with conservatives by seeing Solzhenitsyn. "With all due deference to Dr. Kissinger, I believe that if détente is so fragile that it cannot stand a meeting with Solzhenitsyn, it will fall on some other account," wrote one aide, who stressed the importance the "right wing" on Capitol Hill attached to the meeting. Yet Ford might anger Brezhnev and sabotage the CSCE talks by greeting the famous dissident. The decision proved easy for Ford, who privately labeled the difficult Solzhenitsyn "a goddamn horse's ass." He told aides to say he could not see Solzhenitsyn because he was swamped by trip preparations. Ronald Reagan condemned Ford's "snub"; Senator Jackson declared that Kissinger and Ford should have "met with Solzhenitsyn, rather than cowering with fear of the Soviet reaction." Jackson and Helms brought Solzhenitsyn to the Capitol, where the Russian again condemned détente.[10]

When Ford realized how much he had angered Solzhenitsyn's admirers, he reconsidered. He offered to see the writer when he returned from the CSCE in Helsinki. But the Russian was no longer interested. As a final insult, Solzhenitsyn announced that the conference represented "the betrayal of Eastern Europe" and warned that "an amicable agreement of diplomatic shovels will bury and pack down still-breathing bodies in a common grave."[11]

SOLZHENITSYN HAD LOTS of less eloquent company. The Helsinki Accords, which Ford, Brezhnev, and representatives of thirty-three other nations planned to sign at the CSCE on August 1, 1975, just a week after astronauts on the U.S. *Apollo* and Soviet *Soyuz* achieved "détente in space" by linking ships and dining together, proved controversial. The accords formally recognized the boundary settlements in Eastern Europe that the United States and the Soviet Union had agreed to at Yalta in 1945 as "legitimate" and inviolable. The signatories promised to respect human rights and pledged not to change the boundaries by force.[12]

By Ford's calculus, the accords gave the United States something for nothing. Even in the 1950s, when Eisenhower spoke of "liberating" countries from communism, the United States did not use military power to challenge Eastern European boundaries, and to conservatives' chagrin, it had no intention of doing so now. Nevertheless, the Soviet Union renounced force in Eastern Europe and vowed support for human rights. Years later, after the cold war ended, it seemed clear that in the 1970s and 1980s, the CSCE and the accords provided the rhetorical underpinnings that dissident leaders, such as Václav Havel and Lech Wałesa, used to challenge communism in Eastern Europe. At century's end Ford proudly told one historian that the Helsinki Accords were his "greatest foreign policy achievement" and Kissinger characterized the CSCE as "a political and moral landmark."[13]

But in 1974 and 1975 Kissinger took a different line. "We are just going along" with the CSCE, though "we never wanted it," he informed Ford. At bottom the CSCE and the Helsinki Accords just conferred respectability on the Soviet Union, the reason why so many thought them a sellout. Ignoring the accords' emphasis on human rights, Ford's critics accused him of ratifying Franklin Roosevelt's Yalta "surrender" of Eastern Europe to the Soviets.[14]

Yet Ford decided to go to Helsinki, a symbolic triumph for Kissinger. Just before the president departed for the CSCE, Congress refused to lift its embargo on the sale of military arms to Turkey. Then, when Ford and Kissinger sat down with the Soviets in Helsinki, Brezhnev and Soviet Foreign Minister Andrei Gromyko lambasted the Americans for acting contrary "to the spirit of détente" by shutting the Soviets out of Middle East peace negotiations. Then the two powers deadlocked on SALT II.[15]

Kissinger put the best face on the CSCE and on rumors that the hosannas Ford heard when he stopped in Poland, Romania, and Yugoslavia afterward had not been heartfelt. Though critics were "bitching now about the borders we did nothing to change when we had a nuclear monopoly," those borders had been "legally established long ago," and "the new things in the document are in our favor," he told the cabinet. Ford had "dominated the conference," and the West had been "on the offensive. It was not Brezhnev who took a triumphal tour through Eastern Europe—it was the President. And even if every spectator was paid—which I don't believe—the leadership in those countries felt strongly enough about demonstrating their independence [from the Soviet Union] to put out so much money."[16]

Ford too thought the trip had been "a great success." Doubtless he was happy to be out of Washington for ten days during the furor over Solzhenitsyn, his wife's *Sixty Minutes* interview, and the New York City fiscal crisis: The *New York Times* reported that the president informed the Belgrade City Council that Gotham leaders "don't know how to handle money—all they know how to do is spend it." He had taken saunas in Finland, visited the Nazi crematoriums at Auschwitz in Poland, eaten cake with American troops in West Germany, planted a tree in Yugoslavia, and enjoyed picnics and boat rides. But he had so angered conservatives by this time, he recognized later, that he should have known a primary challenge "was inevitable" and prepared for it. He did not: "I expected to win the Republican nomination for President in a breeze."[17]

Republicans on the right used the summer of 1975 to seize possession of the anticommunism issue for the first time since the 1950s. Because most mainstream politicians since World War II hewed to the anti-Communist line, neither political party had owned it. Consequently, the issue had been whether anticommunism was "responsible" or "extreme." When Republicans tried to make points by declaring, as Barry Goldwater had in 1964, that they hated communism more than the Democrats did, they risked being called warmongers. Both parties opposed communism, and in early 1975 cold war Democrats headed the antidétente coalition, with conservative Republicans acting as junior partners.

Now Senator Jackson, George Meany, and other cold war liberals were reduced to saying "me too." Within the Democratic Party, they were on the defensive. The neoconservative intellectuals Jackson attracted constituted only a small group, and Meany complained that workers did not understand the importance of defense spending. In contrast, conservative Republicans seized every chance to declare that despite repeated American concessions, the Soviets used "détente as a Russian one-way street."[18]

Why was the domestic challenge to détente so successful in 1975? In part, of course, it was because of Soviet aggressiveness. The Soviets interpreted the American defeat in Vietnam, U.S. attempts to control Middle East diplomacy, the legitimacy conferred on them by SALT I, and their growing military might as reasons to adopt a more confrontational attitude toward the United States and to flex their muscles in the third world. Ironically, the Soviet Union thus began to overextend itself, a process that ultimately led to its collapse in 1991. No one, least of all Ford or Kissinger, foresaw that outcome in 1975.[19]

In part, the domestic challenge to détente had legs because Americans had Kissinger fatigue. Those to Kissinger's left viewed his foreign policy as amoral; those to his right, as naive. Both factions complained that Kissinger cared nothing about human rights. In part, the doubts about détente reflected concern about the Soviet military buildup under way despite SALT I and II. The Ford administration shared that anxiety.[20]

But Kissinger insisted that the Soviet buildup showed the importance of keeping a lid on the arms race. Brezhnev was old and ill. "With him will go the entire age group that has such a morbid fear of war, based on their World War II experiences," Kissinger reasoned. Brezhnev's successor, State and the CIA believed, would prove less supportive of limiting the arms race and less capable of selling it to the Soviet military. And what was the alternative? It would be no easier to increase defense appropriations if SALT II were scrapped, Kissinger argued. "We'll end up further behind." Yet his critics now viewed the détente he personified as "a fancy French word for appeasement." In the wake of Helsinki, Kissinger had become a liability.[21]

THE CLOSEST KISSINGER came to a last hurrah was his negotiation of the Sinai II Accord between Israel and Egypt in August 1975. Israel's American allies had attacked the secretary of state and the president since the United States had begun its "reassessment" of Israel in March. In May more than three-quarters of the Senate wrote a letter to Ford urging him to "be responsive" to Israel's plea for $2.5 billion in military and economic aid. Although the president professed to welcome the correspondence, it "really bugged me," and he was sure it was Israel inspired. "For me that kind of pressure has always been counterproductive. I was not going to capitulate to it."[22]

But capitulate he and Kissinger did. Sinai II provided for Israeli evacuation of strategically important passes and oil fields in the Sinai in exchange for Egyptian commitments to keep the peace. It also required Israel and Egypt to permit United Nations and U.S. peacekeeping forces and technicians to be stationed in the Sinai. In a memorandum of understanding that accompanied the accord, the United States guaranteed some two billion dollars annually in military aid to Israel for five years and oil, if necessary. "If this agreement is implemented in good faith," Kissinger exulted to congressional leaders, "it will be the largest single step [apparently toward peace in the Middle East] since the creation of the State of Israel." Although members of Congress went along with it, they carped about the expense and complained that the United States was paying "a pretty stiff price for a small first step."[23]

Sinai II angered the excluded Soviets. It irritated Arab nations, which joined together to condemn and isolate Egypt. It indulged the Israelis, who got the better end of the bargain, and not just because they received American dollars. The United States ensured continued stalemate over the West Bank and Gaza when it gave Israel the power to veto Palestinian Liberation Organization participation in the peace process. Annoyed by Kissinger's pressure, Israelis made Americans pay a stiff price to vindicate his step-by-step diplomacy.[24]

There were repercussions for Israel and détente. In the fall of 1975, under Soviet and Arab pressure, the United Nations approved a resolution characterizing Zionism as "a form of racism or racial discrimination." Since Egypt had to vote for the "Zionism as racism" resolution or lose all credibility among Arab nations, it undermined whatever cooperative spirit Sinai II fostered. Israelis would have understood why Egypt behaved as it did. Nevertheless, the passage of the "Zionism as racism" resolution by a two to one margin convinced the Israelis of what they had always feared: that the rest of the world wanted to drive them into the sea. To be sure, the resolution partially backfired by rousing Americans' protective instincts. Passionately objecting on behalf of the United States, Ambassador Daniel Patrick Moynihan declared the resolution an "obscenity" that put the United Nations "at the point of officially endorsing anti-Semitism." But two days after his speech, a State Department official enraged Israel and its friends by implying that Washington now viewed the PLO sympathetically. Moreover, Kissinger complained that Moynihan had gone "wild about the Israeli issues."[25]

Within the United States, the prospects for SALT II dimmed as Israel's friends agonized about its survival, accentuated its geopolitical importance, and attacked Soviet unwillingness to allow more Jews to emigrate there. Middle East expert William Quandt saw the connection. "All these opponents of détente proved to be ardent supporters of Israel: Israel was anti-Soviet; Israel was in the forefront of defending the human rights of Soviet Jews; Israel was democratic." Jewish Defense League members protested the *Apollo-Soyuz* mission by burning a cardboard rocket outside the Soviet Mission to the United Nations. "Dump détente, dump Kissinger, let my people go," they shouted. Moynihan himself soon resigned as UN ambassador and became another critic of Kissinger and détente.[26]

All the while, SALT II hung fire. Ford and Kissinger had submitted a revised proposal for SALT II to the Soviets to resolve issues that had arisen since Vladivostok. The Americans wanted to count the new Soviet Backfire bombers toward the Soviet ceilings; the Soviets, the new American cruise missiles against the American ceilings. The Soviets condemned the American position as "cynical." In Helsinki, they contended that though the Backfire could operate as an intercontinental weapon, the United States must know that they intended Backfire to be used at a shorter range (i.e., against China and Europe). Since that was true and Kissinger and Ford sought a deal, they wanted to "find where we can make some modification in the cruise missile and Backfire areas." But Secretary of Defense Schlesinger disagreed, and the Pentagon leaked his opinion in late August that "we were willing to give up too much," Ford recalled. "That upset conservatives."[27]

THE COLLAPSE OF AMERICAN FOREIGN POLICY

Ford soon increased their ire. To the president's bewilderment that fall, his approval rating remained well under 50 percent. An adviser explained to him that "the growing feud" between Kissinger and Schlesinger was "creating the impression that I was not fully in command." On Halloween, the president made his move and announced that several administration officials would be trading places or leaving. He had already privately pressured Rockefeller to remove himself from the 1976 ticket in what he later described as "one of the few cowardly things I did in my life." As a sop to conservatives, the president now publicly announced that Rockefeller would not be his running mate.[28]

Moreover, Ford fired bloodied CIA Director William Colby and replaced him with former Republican National Committee chair George H. W. Bush. "I do not have politics out of my system entirely and I see this as the total end of any political future," Bush cabled Kissinger. But Bush valued the agency, as he wrote his children, and "the ugliness and turmoil swirling" around it made him "feel I must try to help." Democrats were as unhappy as Bush and agreed to his appointment only after Bush had pledged that he would not become Ford's running mate.[29]

Announcing he was depriving the secretary of state of his national security adviser's hat, Ford also made Kissinger's deputy Brent Scowcroft the new national security adviser. Although Kissinger was humiliated, Scowcroft strongly supported détente: According to one senator, the headline should read KISSINGER REPLACES KISSINGER AS NATIONAL SECURITY ADVISER. That was not fair. Scowcroft, who was called Babycakes by his secretaries, was much nicer than Kissinger. Yet the replacement of Kissinger by Scowcroft signaled continuity in foreign policy.[30]

Consequently, the president's actions did nothing to make up for his biggest blow to conservatives and neoconservatives, the firing of the secretary of defense. As part of the "Halloween Massacre," the president replaced Schlesinger with his chief of staff, Donald Rumsfeld, who became, at forty-three, the nation's youngest secretary of defense. Ford was right to fire the ill-tempered Schlesinger, who was in cahoots with neoconservatives, such as Jackson, and conservatives to undermine détente. Schlesinger and Kissinger also detested each other. Schlesinger spoke openly of the need for "détente without illusions" and confided to journalists that "Henry is always tough with everyone but the Russians." Yet at Kissinger's urging, Ford disingenuously insisted that neither personal nor policy differences between Kissinger and Schlesinger caused the change.[31]

By the time the president was ready to concede publicly that "a growing tension" between the two men contributed to his decision, it was too late. His Halloween Massacre had awakened memories of the Watergate Saturday Night Massacre. As *Newsweek* said, "Ford's great shuffle was hastily planned, badly timed and clumsily executed, and in the end, it only inflamed the doubts it was intended to settle: whether he really is in control of his unelected Presidency and his uncertain political future." *Newsweek* itself bore part of the blame for the faulty implementation. Originally, Ford had intended to give conservatives the good news and announce Rockefeller's withdrawal of his candidacy before he displeased them by firing Schlesinger some days later. But when *Newsweek* pieced together what was afoot before Schlesinger had any inkling that his days were numbered, the White House had to announce all the impending personnel changes immediately at Halloween, lest it be scooped.[32]

The media portrayed the White House as panicked, and conservatives focused on Schlesinger's dismissal. Rumsfeld may have been the only real "winner" in the musical chairs game that many believed he had engineered. He had received one of the most powerful cabinet slots and preserved his White House influence, since Ford moved Rumsfeld's thirty-four-year-old deputy, Dick Cheney, into Rumsfeld's old job. Cheney, who had flunked out of Yale College and sought four student deferments to avoid serving in Vietnam, was considered a better manager by White House staffers and was more popular with the press than Rumsfeld. According to *Newsweek*, "While Rumsfeld is abrasive, severe and brusque, Cheney is amiable and even-tempered; while Rumsfeld has transparent personal political ambitions, Cheney, so far, seems to have no interest in holding elective office." Neither Rumsfeld's victory nor Cheney's low-key style, however, helped Ford with conservatives. *Human Events* maintained that the Rumsfeld appointment "has only fueled the concern of those who fear that Secretary of State Henry Kissinger can now pursue his détente policies unchecked."[33]

Even so, Ford still considered himself safe from a Reagan challenge. By November's end the president finally knew better. "I am not appeased," Reagan announced after the Halloween Massacre, and he officially declared his candidacy for the Republican nomination. At this point Reagan was running against big government and business as usual in Washington. But the critique of détente that became such an important part of Reagan's campaign was always implicit. While he promised to honor the "Eleventh Commandment"—"Thou shalt not speak ill of any fellow Republican"—Reagan said that the Soviet Union, "a nation that has never made any effort to hide its hostility to everything we stand for," threatened to surpass the United States.[34]

IN ADDITION TO UNDERMINING Republican Party unity, the Halloween Massacre sounded the death knell for détente, SALT II, and the Ford administration's efforts to normalize relations with China. For his part, Kissinger blamed the collapse of American foreign policy on the congressional denial of funds to the CIA to operate in Angola. Even as the administration defended itself from slurs of softness on the Soviets in 1975, it had tried to reduce the risk of takeover of the former Portuguese colony of Angola by the pro-Cuban and pro-Soviet Popular Movement for the Liberation of Angola (MPLA). The United States had to provide aid secretly to the anti-MPLA forces, lest it embarrass those it wanted to help. So in January 1975 Ford authorized the CIA to fund the leader of one anti-MPLA contingent that was also backed by China. When the Soviets and Cubans increased their aid to the MPLA, the White House decided it must do more to help the MPLA's opponents. It was not that the Ford administration had any sympathy for the anti-MPLA forces. It was not even that Angola seemed important for strategic or economic reasons. It was that Ford, prodded by Kissinger, was determined to give the Soviets no additional reason to crow. "I push détente in order to be able to be tough," Kissinger explained to Ford in July 1975. "If we were publicly tough the Soviet Union would have no incentive. Now, so long as they think we are pushing détente, they will keep their heads down. Call the Agencies and give them the decision." Without congressional consultation, Ford then authorized a multimillion-dollar covert operation against the MPLA. Despite leaks about the CIA's activities, Congress did nothing.[35]

In October, with the secret encouragement of the Ford administration, the white minority that controlled South Africa launched an invasion of Angola. In response, and without first consulting the Soviet Union, Castro poured in thousands of troops. Angola was Castro's adventure, his chance to present himself as a leader of international revolution, though the Soviets, for reasons of their own, provided essential aid. Brezhnev himself at first showed little interest in Angola and apparently followed Castro only because the Cubans insisted and Brezhnev feared the blow to Soviet prestige if Angola was lost to the West. As Kissinger later acknowledged, however, the United States mistakenly viewed Castro as the puppet of the Soviet Union. When Kissinger, Ford, and Scowcroft gathered in the Oval Office on November 13, 1975, Kissinger kept up the pressure: "The Soviets are pouring in equipment in Angola. Brent, I hope you will be tough." Without saying anything about prior American behavior in Angola, Ford announced at a news conference two weeks later that "the Soviet actions in Angola were not helpful in the continuation of détente."[36]

Then, in December, the Senate Foreign Relations Committee chief of staff remembered, "the shit hit the fan." Administration nemesis Seymour Hersh got hold of the Angola story and reported in the *New York Times* that CIA involvement preceded the Soviet buildup. He also wrote that the former assistant secretary of state of African affairs, who had resigned in protest over Kissinger's refusal to seek a diplomatic solution, had warned that the United States was backing the "losers" in Angola, that their inevitable failure would weaken moderate African governments, and that "the United States would end up with racist South Africa as its only African ally." Engaged in its intelligence investigations and emphatic that there must be "no more Vietnams," Congress decided that Angola might become another "quagmire" that could ultimately swallow American troops. Senator John Tunney of California sponsored an amendment to the Defense Appropriations Act denying funds to the CIA for its Angola program. Unwilling to maintain the uneasy silence of the *Mayaguez* crisis, liberals and left-liberal Democrats easily won the votes for the Tunney amendment. For the first time ever, despite intense lobbying from the president and Kissinger, and to the shock of South Africa, which promptly withdrew from Angola, the legislative branch stopped an American covert operation. It was a low moment for the CIA and the Ford administration. "We are living in a nihilistic nightmare," Kissinger complained. "We would have had Angola settled by January if these bastards had not been in town." Ford groused that "Congress has lost its guts."[37]

By 1976 the new People's Republic of Angola had signed a treaty of friendship with the Soviet Union. Some powerful Russians had also decided that the way was clear for third world interventions. According to cold war historian Odd Arne Westad, Brezhnev himself came to view Angola as "a benchmark for 'active solidarity with the peoples of Africa and Asia' and evidence that the Soviet Union could advance socialism in the Third World during a period of *détente* with the United States."[38]

Angola became Kissinger's favorite scapegoat. "I am deeply worried about our position in the world resulting from Angola," he told the president. "It is opening the Vietnam wounds again." Once Congress had enacted the Tunney amendment, "the geopolitical context for SALT was gone" and "the psychological environment" for negotiation with the Soviets had evaporated, the secretary of state lamented. He also insisted that the Tunney amendment thwarted American cooperation with China. In fact, it had taken a combination of Helsinki, Israel, the Halloween Massacre, the Soviet Union, and the Tunney amendment to undercut détente, SALT II, and American cultivation of China.[39]

Ironically, by trying to bolster détente with the Halloween Massacre, Ford had put the nail in its coffin and damaged the already wobbly SALT II negotiations. For all the right's fear of Rumsfeld, the new secretary of defense nit-picked to death the very agreement Schlesinger had gone after with hammer and tongs. Kissinger later acknowledged that he knew Rumsfeld's cautiousness guaranteed American stalling on SALT II. Within the reshuffled administration, Rumsfeld and the Joint Chiefs of Staff successfully spearheaded the opposition to SALT II. Ford soon realized that no agreement would be possible unless he won the election.[40]

Ford's decision to fire Schlesinger also hurt Chinese-American relations. True, the top Chinese official in Washington did cite the Tunney amendment when he reminded the White House that "appeasement will whet the Soviet appetite for expansionism." But the Chinese had been saying that for a while. And when Kissinger went to China just before the Halloween Massacre to prepare for Ford's December visit, the Chinese continued complaining. The Chinese also attacked the European "Insecurity" Conference in Helsinki, analogized American propitiation of the Soviet Union with European conciliation of Hitler, and all but anointed Schlesinger.[41]

The strained atmosphere during Kissinger's trip could have led Ford to cancel his visit to China. The Chinese were clearly in no mood to bargain about normalization of their relationship with the United States, and the president's trip would hurt him at home. One of Reagan's "main themes will be anti-Communism, anti-détente, anti-Red China, anti-Helsinki, and anti-disarmament," lamented a presidential adviser. Was it really advisable for Ford to "be on TV nightly smiling at Chinese Communists?" But Kissinger warned that cancellation "would lose us all our leverage with the Soviet Union" and "give the Chinese a chance to invite all the Democratic candidates over to say you screwed up the Chinese policy." Ford decided to make the trip and "get the word out that we don't expect anything of substance but that it is important to exchange views." That was a lame justification.[42]

Triangulation had come a cropper. "Without Congress, we would have the Soviet-Chinese triangle working again," Kissinger contended. Though the Chinese received Ford politely and Ford was granted a rare audience with their ailing leader, Mao Zedong, Kissinger concluded that normalization of the relationship between China and the United States was a chimera. *Human Events* summed up the trip harshly but accurately: The Americans resisted Chinese calls to "stand up to the Russians" but reassured the Chinese that the United States would not stand up to the Chinese. The Soviets rejected the administration's new SALT II proposal, and in December a controversy about whether the Soviets had violated SALT I and whether Kissinger had intentionally kept Ford in the dark about it further damaged the prospects for SALT II. Schlesinger came before the Senate Foreign Relations Committee to rescue Kissinger from the charge of deliberate deception. There the former secretary of defense also stressed that the Soviets had "clearly stretched" interpretations of the agreement, exploited its "ambiguities," violated the letter of SALT I in one instance and its spirit in another, and repeated that the "swiftly growing military power" of the Soviet Union jeopardized the United States.[43]

By now even Kissinger seemed uncertain whether he should make the trip to Moscow he had been scheduled to make in December and had postponed until January. "The conservatives will scream that we are protesting Angola and still toady up to them [the Soviets]," he told Ford. "If I don't go, the liberals will scream that we are jeopardizing everything for Angola when we shouldn't be there in the first place." But Kissinger wanted to go, and the president encouraged him to do so. Ford maintained that SALT II was "in the best interests of the United States and the world" and that while there might be political arguments against the trip, there were substantive ones in its favor. So Kissinger went, and nothing happened. As he summarized it, by "publicly rubbing our noses in our defeat in Angola, however self-inflicted, Brezhnev destroyed whatever sentiment was left in the United States for agreement with the Kremlin."[44]

SALT II by now did have little appeal in Washington. In 1976, Cheney and Rumsfeld pressed for the appointment of a panel of outside experts, Team B, to analyze Soviet intentions and to compare its findings with those of Team A, the relatively inexperienced CIA team. Neoconservative critics of American foreign policy and SALT, such as Paul Nitze, Richard Pipes, and Paul Wolfowitz, dominated Team B. Of course, Team B found that Team A had underestimated Soviet capabilities and ambitions and concluded that the Soviets did not seek parity in nuclear weapons with the United States but superiority. That should not have been newsworthy, since Team B had been charged with developing a pessimistic scenario. But when Team B's findings were leaked at Christmas, the Ford administration looked complacent about Soviet expansionism, and neoconservatism acquired greater legitimacy. "The competitive analysis idea seemed good at the time and I certainly did not think it would go public," Bush told the National Security Council. "But now I feel I have been had."[45]

Détente was on the ropes long before Bush's embarrassment. As the presidential primary season swung into high gear in February 1976, Ford repeatedly alluded to the American foreign policy of "peace through strength." In March, as conservative Republicans hammered him and as Kissinger and Nitze and other neoconservatives began to organize the nonpartisan Committee on the Present Danger to awaken the United States to the Soviets' "unparalleled military buildup" and the folly of "an illusory détente," Ford went so far as to announce that "we are going to forget the use of the word détente" and replace it with the phrase "peace through strength." That sop to his detractors did nothing to make him look more presidential. Nor did it please Kissinger. "I think we are undermining détente," he told the president. "Except for Angola, I think the Soviets are getting a bum rap." After the Halloween Massacre, Ford's foreign policy died on the vine.[46]

BUSING

In domestic policy too, leadership proved difficult, and détente—this time between white and African Americans—was threatened. Here, however, the Congress that lashed out with respect to foreign policy could not rouse itself to fill the vacuum. What Congress proposed, Ford disposed of, and Capitol Hill could rarely muster the votes to override his veto.

Nothing illustrated the unmet need for leadership more than the busing crisis. Ever since the Supreme Court had held public primary and secondary school segregation unconstitutional in the 1954 decision of *Brown v. Board of Education*, many liberals had viewed the Court as a great engine of social change. True, the Court, led by Chief Justice Earl Warren, had declared a constitutional right to attend desegregated schools and deferred its exercise. In issuing the decree implementing *Brown*, the Court had said desegregation need only occur with "all deliberate speed." Nevertheless, *Brown* became the "paradigmatic" event for liberals.[47]

Justices appointed for life, it developed, were less timid than elected officials about extending rights to racial minorities, criminal defendants, prisoners, workers, women, children, the poor, the disabled, the mentally ill, and the press. As Americans liked to say, "I've got my rights." It was the Court, beginning with *Brown*, that gave bite to rights talk and wings to the rights revolution. While conservatives spoke angrily of the "war against democracy" waged by "an imperial judiciary," reformers made "legal liberalism" their article of faith. The concept implied trust in the potential of federal courts, particularly the Supreme Court, to bring about "those specific social reforms that affect large groups of people such as blacks, or workers, or women, or partisans of a particular persuasion; in other words, policy change with nationwide impact."[48]

In time, scholars were to question both the depth of opposition to Warren Court opinions and the ability of federal courts to transform society. They were to demonstrate, for example, the broad public support for much of the Warren Court's work, as well as the failure of its decisions to reconstruct the landscape. But in the 1960s and 1970s the Warren Court remained larger than life to both its fans and its detractors.[49]

President Nixon set the Republicans' strategy for playing race politics. *Brown* was "correct," he liked to say, but "forced integration" was wrong. He stressed the importance of color blindness and of making it on one's own, and he wrapped racialized messages in the language of pocketbook politics. He reassured white voters that "there is no reason to feel guilty about wanting to enjoy what you get and get what you earn, about wanting your children in good schools close to home, or about wanting to be judged fairly on your ability." Nixon never mentioned that since the New Deal the federal government had created predominantly white neighborhoods, suburbs, and schools by directing a disproportionate share of funds to white families. Nor did he acknowledge that until 1968, when the practice was finally made illegal, lenders routinely redlined areas where low-income minorities lived and refused to make loans on mortgages there, freeing slumlords to jack up rents. Nixon's rhetoric proved powerful because white Americans wanted to protect their "homeowner, taxpayer, and school parent status" and the dream of "middle-class entitlement" that they harbored between the end of World War II and the onset of "stagflation." While he certainly understood the political advantage of "sealing off white suburbanites from the city," many other politicians did too.[50]

But despite Nixon's attempts to make the Court conservative through judicial appointments, the law marched forward. In *Green v. County School Board of New Kent County* (1968), the Court declared its impatience with the token desegregation that so many southern officials had used to comply with the letter of *Brown*. Then in *Swann v. Charlotte-Mecklenburg Board of Education* (1971), a unanimous Court declared district-wide busing a permissible means of achieving racial balance in school systems where de jure segregation—intentional separation of the races written into law—prevailed. Ironically, the focus on de jure segregation was to render southern schools more desegregated than those in the North and West. Outside the South, the de facto segregation that arose as a matter of practice because of residential patterns continued to keep minorities and whites apart. In some places, though, the Court's stand against de jure segregation came too late. So many whites had already fled from Atlanta to the suburbs even before *Swann* that African American civil rights leaders successfully sought a way to avoid full compliance with the decision, lest there be "no white kids to bus." (Doubtless, busing to achieve racial balance contributed to white flight but was not its only cause.) *Swann*, complained Governor Jimmy Carter of Georgia, was "clearly a one-sided decision; the Court is still talking about the South; the North is still going free."[51]

Carter's adjective, "free," was telling. It was also inaccurate since parts of the South avoided desegregation. Anxious that wealthy whites in southeastern Charlotte would flee the district or enroll their children in private schools, the Charlotte-Mecklenburg School Board developed a plan that reinforced class inequalities and resentments by putting the burden of two-way busing on less affluent black and white neighborhoods.[52]

In any event, neither the North nor the West remained "free" for long. Traditionally, the Court had stayed away from de facto segregation, despite civil rights activists' protests that it was indistinct from de jure segregation. Now it belatedly began to find that school districts outside the South had also been intentionally segregated, even if segregation did not exist as a matter of law. The gerrymandering of school attendance zones to separate whites and African Americans, for example, became evidence of intent.[53]

In *Keyes v. School District No. 1* (1973), the Court held that Denver public schools must be desegregated. It also held that a finding of intentional segregation in one part of a school district justified a district-wide busing order. If "purposefully segregative actions" were employed in one place, Justice William Brennan said, "common sense" suggested they were used elsewhere too. In such situations, the school board had "the affirmative duty to desegregate the entire system 'root and branch.' " It remained more difficult to prove intent to segregate in school districts outside the South. But busing to achieve racial balance moved beyond the South.[54]

Yet despite *Keyes*, legal liberals worried that the Nixon Court was withdrawing from *Brown*. In the spring of 1973, just two months after it had enshrined personal autonomy and the right to abortion in *Roe*, and three months before it decided *Keyes*, the Court handed down *San Antonio v. Rodriguez*. Demetrio Rodriguez and other parents of minority and/or poor schoolchildren had challenged the way Texas financed public education. Historically, the state had approved minimal funds to provide children with a "basic" education. School districts then used proceeds from locally levied property taxes to supplement the state grant. The amount schools had for their students thus depended upon the level of wealth—or poverty—of a neighborhood. The parents charged that this system of financing violated the right of children in areas with low property tax bases to the equal protection of the laws guaranteed by the Constitution's Fourteenth Amendment. The district court agreed and ruled that Texas's system of financing public education operated to the disadvantage of the poor, whom it characterized as a suspect class, and also impinged on the right to education, which it declared a fundamental constitutional right. Because a three-judge panel had heard the case, it was appealed directly to the U.S. Supreme Court. Here was a case of potentially far-reaching importance: If the Supreme Court agreed with the district court that poverty was a suspect classification under the Constitution, all wealth-based classifications would be subject to "strict scrutiny" by judges, just as all race-based classifications were. Courts would be able to invalidate discrimination against the poor far more easily, for such legislation would withstand scrutiny only if it advanced a compelling state interest. And if education were a fundamental right, all legislation involving education would be subject to strict scrutiny too.

But the Supreme Court reversed. Though the Court itself had recently seemed on the verge of finding poverty a suspect classification, it now declined to do so. Nor did it declare education a fundamental right. In dissent, Justices Thurgood Marshall and William O. Douglas mourned the Court's "retreat from our historic commitment to equality of educational opportunity."[55]

In 1974 the Court stepped farther back. If intentional segregation in one part of a district justified district-wide busing, as *Keyes* maintained, should not intentional segregation in one district justify multidistrict busing throughout a metropolitan area? That was the only way to achieve racial balance in Detroit, the federal judge in *Milliken v. Bradley* reasoned. After concluding that the Detroit school district had intentionally employed segregative practices, he prepared a busing order that applied not only to Detroit but to some of its suburbs. True, he did not find that the suburban school districts had engaged in intentional segregation. But they had white students. The court ordered multidistrict busing between the predominantly black center city and the surrounding suburbs, and the court of appeals affirmed. To decide otherwise, it said, would "nullify *Brown v. Board of Education*." Once again, the Supreme Court reversed. Accepting "suburban secessionism," it rejected a multidistrict busing order when there was proof that just one district had engaged in intentional segregation. In dissent, Justice Douglas objected: "The inner core of Detroit is now rather solidly black; and the blacks, we know, in many instances are likely to be poorer, just as were the Chicanos" in San Antonio. The majority was saying that "the poor must pay their own way" even when they were sent to segregated and inferior schools.[56]

Milliken was Douglas's swan song. He had joined the Court in 1939 and come to personify the legal liberalism, or judicial activism, associated with the Warren Court. Congressman Ford had unsuccessfully sought to drive him off the Court. In 1975 poor health forced Douglas, the longest-serving U.S. Supreme Court justice in all history, to submit his resignation to his old enemy. To avoid a confirmation battle, Ford and Attorney General Levi passed over ideological conservatives in favor of the distinguished Seventh Circuit judge and centrist John Paul Stevens. The president announced the appointment just before he left for China. Democrats and the left could have hoped for no better choice. The *Nation* ungraciously saluted Ford for making "a decent appointment—for a change." Yet while Pat Buchanan and other conservatives were sure "Judge Stevens will be a decided improvement upon the judicial Jacobin he replaces, William Douglas," they wondered, What might "a judicial moderate do to bring an end to the disaster the federal courts have made of America's public school systems?"[57]

Douglas's departure left two liberals on the Court, Marshall and Brennan. To Marshall, who had argued *Brown* for the National Association for the Advancement of Colored People (NAACP) and become the first African American Supreme Court justice, *Milliken* represented an "emasculation of our constitutional guarantee of equal protection of the laws." With polls suggesting that whites overwhelmingly opposed busing to achieve racial balance, he saw *Milliken* as "a reflection of a perceived public mood that we have gone far enough." During the Ford years the president lost charge of foreign policy, and liberals lost control of the Court.[58]

YET AS LONG AS *Keyes* was on the books, federal judges had a duty to order city-wide busing in the North and West in some cases. For a quarter century, African American mothers in Boston like Ruth Batson protested the educational inequity there with boycotts, sit-ins, and picketing. Nothing changed. "We were told our kids were stupid and this was why they didn't learn," she remembered. Then they sued. In 1974, Judge Arthur Garrity found that "the Boston School Committee knowingly carried out a systematic program of segregation affecting all of the city's students, teachers, and school facilities." Garrity paired white neighborhoods with black ones and ordered busing between them.[59]

Though many schools remained peaceful when they opened that fall, a number did not. In the white middle-class neighborhood of Hyde Park, the high school was the scene of a race riot. But the media focused on working-class resistance in Boston. Garrity had paired working-class

Irish Catholic South Boston and Roxbury, the heart of Boston's inner city, and South Boston High exploded. Whites greeted the buses that transported African Americans from Roxbury with rocks and bottles. As the violence continued, African Americans retaliated. When one stabbed a white student at Southie in December 1974, all hell broke loose. More than a thousand people sympathetic to ROAR, an antibusing organization pledged to "restore our alienated rights," fought off police and surrounded the school, imprisoning more than 130 African American students. After a police decoy operation freed them, Southie closed for a month. Boston, the *New York Times* reported, had become "a city divided by fear and violence."[60]

All the while Ford temporized. The president resisted Boston Mayor Kevin White's pleas to send in federal marshals. And although he declared the violence "most unfortunate," Ford stressed that Garrity's decision, "in my judgment, was not the best solution to quality education in Boston" and described busing as a "problem . . . forced on the country" by the Supreme Court. Like civil rights activists, White complained that Ford "fanned the flames of resistance."[61]

The resistance did continue. In 1975, Garrity ordered busing between Roxbury and Charlestown, another working-class Irish Catholic stronghold. Members of the Charlestown ROAR chapter, Powder Keg, attacked police and screamed at Senator Ted Kennedy to "[l]et your daughter get bused . . . so she can get raped."[62]

Violence roiled school districts elsewhere in the country that employed busing to bring about desegregation. Busing to achieve racial balance seemed "the most unpopular institution imposed on Americans since Prohibition." Justice Marshall had been right about the polls. Neoconservatives, conservatives, and working-class whites liked to point out that those to their left who promoted busing often enrolled their own children in private schools, like Kennedy, or moved outside city limits to the suburbs, like Garrity. While some liberals worried about the Court's apostasy in *Milliken*, others condemned them of hypocrisy. But in fact, busing, like Vietnam, pitted liberal Democrats against one another. While Senator Joe Biden of Delaware described busing as "a bankrupt concept," Senator George McGovern of South Dakota supported it as "one way to pay the bill for the ancient regime of racism."[63]

What was the alternative? Ford liked to insist that there was "a better way to achieve quality education in America than by forced busing." But as one of his staffers privately admitted, the federal courts ordered busing to achieve not "quality education," but school desegregation. As long as the president missed the point by focusing on "quality education," an adviser warned, "the question arises: Do we, in fact, oppose desegregation?"[64]

MANY AFRICAN AMERICAN PARENTS also lamented that the pursuit of desegregation crowded out the quest for "quality education." Indeed the Boston busing crisis spawned Critical Race Theory, a movement on the legal left that examined the relationship among law, society, and racial subordination. Law Professor Derrick Bell, perhaps the first Critical Race Theorist, opened an important 1970s article by reprinting a petition that Roxbury parents submitted to Judge Garrity seeking "dramatic improvement in the quality of education available to our children." It made no sense, the parents said, "to endure the dislocation of desegregation without reasonable assurances that our children will instructionally profit." When the parents met with the civil rights attorneys assigned to the Boston case, however, they were told that the goals of desegregation and racial balance must trump educational improvement.[65]

Bell, a former NAACP attorney himself, understood the lawyers' position. Liberal middle-class African Americans had made integration their watchword since *Brown* and had opposed majority black schools. Though divided about busing to remedy educational injustice, white liberals also continued to lionize *Brown*: Richard Kluger's magisterial 1976 book about the case, *Simple Justice*, presented it as a matter of just that. Within the liberal community, the goal of integration remained preeminent, despite the calls of black power advocates for cultural autonomy. Bell himself celebrated the achievements of integrationist civil rights activists and the heroism of lawyers and judges like Marshall.[66]

But in the context of the seventies, Bell asked, were the civil rights groups still correct? Inflation made desegregation more costly. A growing number of studies questioned the benefits of desegregation for students, and the federal courts' "once-vigorous support" was vanishing. Was it still appropriate to make integrated schools the "symbol of the nation's commitment to equal opportunity?" Perhaps there were better alternatives. Sometimes it might prove useful to accept, say, limited desegregation, in exchange for, say, greater parental control. In any event, did the focus on integration represent good lawyering? Civil rights lawyers, Bell observed, behaved as if African American parents had awarded them a lifelong contract to fight for racial balance.[67]

If polls were any indication, many African Americans agreed with Bell. Though African Americans were more inclined to advocate busing than whites, in some surveys, fewer than 40 percent supported it. Most black power groups disliked busing to achieve racial balance: The Black Panthers said it would enable white educators to brainwash African Americans. The violence daunted other African Americans. Even many who thought the end result of desegregation worth the struggle felt ambivalent. "You're going to be spat at, maybe pushed around," one Boston mother told her daughters. "It's something we have to go through—something *you* have to go through—if this city is ever going to get integrated." Privately, however, she admitted wondering, "[W]hat good . . . could possibly come from all this?"[68]

DREAM'S END

What good, indeed, and for whom? Both white and black student soldiers in the busing battles tended to be working class or poor, and few of the schools involved were excellent or even above average. The disparate responses between middle-class NAACP lawyers and African American inner-city parents that Bell identified found an echo in the 1975 TV sitcom *The Jeffersons*, which made its debut as Boston erupted. Leaving behind the working-class bigots who had bedeviled him in Queens, black entrepreneur George Jefferson moved his family to a deluxe Manhattan high-rise. After investigating the new digs, Jefferson's African American maid, Florence, was incredulous. "How come we overcame and nobody told me anything about it?" she asked.[69]

Florence rightfully remained caustic. The 1970s had witnessed a dramatic growth in the black middle class: According to the publisher of *Black Enterprise* magazine, which targeted that group, by 1977 almost 20 percent of the nation's black families had a household income of fifteen thousand dollars (fifty-three thousand in 2009 dollars) or higher, an increase of 216 percent since 1969. There had also been a substantial increase in black political power as African Americans were elected mayors of big cities, especially ones decimated by white flight. African Americans had achieved greater prominence in sports, and shows such as *The Jeffersons* and that blockbuster docudrama *Roots* became wildly popular. Yet in 1975, 31.3 percent of African Americans lived in poverty in the inner cities, where there were too few legitimate jobs. Despite all the divorces, 83.5 percent of whites under the age of eighteen were living with both parents by 1979, compared with 43.4 percent of African Americans.[70]

And as was so often the case in American history, race prevented the less fortunate from uniting around class. In the wake of the country's Vietnam defeat, white supremacy groups flourished. "The real issue is *nigger*!" one speaker informed an enthusiastic white working-class Boston audience. "It's not the distance, it's the niggers," the NAACP bitterly agreed. Why else would the parents and students of Southie protest the admission of a small number of people of color with exhortations to "KEEP SOUTHIE WHITE"? When demagogue Louise Hicks of ROAR spoke of defending the "neighborhood school as long as I have a breath left in my body," she was alluding to an idea of community with deep historical roots. But it was a fantasy. By the 1960s "school buses were linked to quality education across the North," and white Boston children did not routinely walk to school even before Garrity handed down his decision. Hicks was using "neighborhood school" as a code word for "white school."[71]

Because she and so many South Boston whites were Irish Catholic, Hicks might also have said she was talking about ethnicity when she spoke of the neighborhood school. And in fact, during the 1970s, interest in "ethnic consciousness," "roots," and preservation were faddish. Few still believed the United States operated as a "melting pot," where new arrivals and their children blended with others to become "American." The new metaphor was that of the "salad bowl" (which seemed appropriate, since the popularity of lettuce was skyrocketing).

One melting pot skeptic, Michael Novak, a Catholic of Slovakian descent, devoted his 1972 book *The Rise of the Unmeltable Ethnics* to blue-collar ethnics he called PIGS, "those Poles, Italians, Greeks, and Slavs, those non-English speaking immigrants numbered so heavily among the workingmen of this nation." He suggested that they were waking up to the fact that "the liberal wing of the Democratic party" had little respect for their culture and hopes. Many other Americans were also rejecting liberalism, however, and it was unclear how strong the PIGS' dedication had ever been anyway. Moreover, in northern and midwestern cities, Catholics played crucial roles in supporting, as well as opposing, civil rights.[72]

The suggestion that white ethnic consciousness was a defining characteristic of the 1970s did prove misleading sometimes. It often just obscured the facts that a portion of whites, some of them ethnics, had resolved to fight for the little they believed they had left as inflation and recession victimized them; that they used the language of race and ethnicity in doing so when that of class might possibly have served them better; and that they overlooked the chance to combine with similarly situated minorities. When at mid-decade, sociologist Jonathan Rieder studied the Jews and Italians precariously perched in the middle-class New York City community of Canarsie, he found that a "key source of opposition to busing lay in the apprehensions of white parents about exposing their children to tough lower-class kids." Canarsians frequently used the metaphor of "squeeze" to describe their position between the poor and wealthy. But the whites Rieder interviewed seemed confused and shifted among the idioms of race, class, and ethnicity to describe their situations. Whatever the idiom, though, the problem was that working-class whites and minorities were "both competing for a very limited piece of pie," instead of joining forces to fight for a larger slice. As Demetrio Rodriguez might have said, "The poor people have lost again."[73]

THE FOCUS ON IDENTITY in the 1970s, which was hardly unique to white ethnics, was not significant simply because it enabled its proponents to fudge the division of the United States along class lines. Americans had always found a way to conceal class distinctions and to preserve the dream of their country as a land of "equal opportunity." As Hispanics, American Indians, African Americans, Asian Americans, "PIGS," Jews, and others trumpeted their ethnicities, the idea of a unitary American identity fell by the wayside and was replaced by an ideal of American identities.

Recent history made the resurgent sense of ethnicity understandable. By abolishing the old national origins quota system and encouraging the close relatives of American citizens to settle in the United States, the Immigration Act of 1965 transformed the face of the country. Immigration from Latin America, the Caribbean, and Asia exploded as an average of nearly four hundred thousand individuals flowed into the United States annually during the next decade. The new immigrants had little connection to even the recent American past. During the 1960s black power advocates produced a model for cultural autonomy that helped inspire demands for "brown," "red," and "yellow power." Moreover, the largely white political left stressed the need "for identities that might rescue individuality (and meaning) from the dreaded anonymity of mass society." Then Vietnam, the failed economy, and Watergate tarnished faith in American institutions and in an American identity grounded on the inspiration of one nation indivisible, with liberty and justice for all. As *The Harvard Encyclopedia of American Ethnic Groups*, itself a product of the 1970s, observed, it was therefore "highly functional for people to remember that they were really ethnic, simultaneously disassociating themselves from responsibility for the defects of the American system and establishing a claim against those who were responsible—the WASP establishment." National crises made a search for new identities possible and gave groups a chance to substitute their own particular for the universal. Even WASPs had the option of redefining themselves as a beleaguered minority.[74]

But this was a risky business. One could hope that the surge in ethnic consciousness that marked the seventies might ultimately lead to "true" détente between groups, with genuine appreciation for their separate contributions. And one could fear, particularly after the busing crisis, that balkanization might prevail. Americans resolved to redesign what it was to be American at just the moment when, in the aftermath of the collapse of Vietnam and détente, they questioned their role in the world. Perhaps the sheer ambitiousness of these concurrent projects helped explain why so many proceeded to turn the bicentennial presidential elections into an escape from reality.

VI

INTANGIBLES

—

IN THE SUMMER OF 1976, AUTHOR AND JOURNALIST TOM WOLFE announced that the United States had entered "the me decade." *New York* magazine featured his story, complete with cover photograph of twenty-eight young adults in yellow T-shirts emblazoned "ME" pointing at themselves. According to Wolfe, narcissism and "ecstatic, non-rational, holy-rolling religion" were sweeping the United States and changing its politics. "The new alchemical dream is: changing one's personality—remaking, remodeling, elevating, and polishing one's very *self* . . . and observing, studying, and doting on it. (Me!)" Wolfe's mockery, which suggested that nothing good could come of introspection and individualism, was unfair. True, thousands of Americans were wearing a bizarre piece of jewelry, the mood ring, which changed colors to reflect their shifting frames of mind. But in the aftermath of Watergate, the Vietnam War, and the sixties, it seemed only appropriate to look inward. The first presidential election of the new era reflected the concern with character, self, and God. It focused on "style" and "spirit," more than on issues. As the winner said, the election was about "intangibles."[1]

THE DEMOCRATS PREPARE

The Democrats had reason for optimism in 1976. Their opponents remained a tiny minority party: *Newsweek* reported that "ominously, only one in five voters seemed to be stepping forward to be counted as a Republican," while 40 to 45 percent identified themselves as Democratic. Moreover, for the first time, thanks to the 1974 revisions of the Federal Election Campaign Act (FECA) of 1971, presidential candidates could receive federal funds. FECA set $1,000 as the maximum contribution an individual or group could give any one congressional or presidential candidate in the primary and general elections; $5,000 as the maximum any political committee could donate. The act also provided that no individual could give more than $25,000 in total to various candidates in an election cycle. Moreover, it forced candidates to report how they spent and raised their money. In addition to limiting contributions, FECA established ceilings on expenditures. It provided that no candidate could spend more than $50,000 of personal funds on a campaign and prevented expenditures of more than $10 million on the primary campaign and $20 million on the general election, excluding fund-raising costs. In an attempt to exorcise some of Watergate's worst demons, FECA also promised that the federal government would grant as much as $5 million to each presidential candidate in the two major political parties who raised a total of $100,000 in twenty states by matching individual donations, up to $250. Once a candidate had won the nomination of either the Democrats or Republicans, he would receive just over $20 million in governmental funds for the general election. (Third party presidential candidates were eligible for something, but considerably less, based on the support they could demonstrate, and congressional candidates got nothing.) Had these contribution and expenditure restrictions been in place in previous elections, Nixon could not have accepted millions from one executive, and Rockefeller could not have spent millions of his family fortune on his presidential quest.[2]

In January 1976 the Supreme Court ruled on FECA in a convoluted 227-page opinion handed down in a rush because of the approaching presidential election. *Buckley v. Valeo* was a suit brought by a broad coalition of those on the ideological fringes, ranging from Senator James Buckley of New York, William F. Buckley's conservative brother, to former Senator Eugene McCarthy. The Court ruled the restrictions on contributions in FECA constitutional; those on expenditures, unconstitutional. The Court upheld the key contribution, disclosure, and public financing sections against contentions that they violated the First Amendment protection of political speech. But the Court invalidated the limitation of expenditures for presidential and congressional candidates as violations of the First Amendment, except for presidential candidates who chose to accept public subsidies. It also said that an individual or group could spend unlimited amounts on media advertising to support or undercut a candidate as long as the expenditures were "independent" of the candidate, the candidate's campaign, or any other candidate or campaign in a particular race.[3]

With large contributions restricted for those presidential candidates who accepted matching funds, small donors became more important. FECA increased the significance of television and direct mail, each of which provided effective ways of reaching small donors before the arrival of the Internet. FECA also heightened the influence of multicandidate political action committees (PACs) and contributed to partisan dealignment by reducing the influence of the national parties and political machines that had traditionally provided crucial funding. Contributions from unions and corporate treasuries to candidates in federal elections were illegal before FECA. Business and labor circumvented the restrictions in two ways. They illegally gave favored candidates cash. Alternatively, or additionally, they created PACs that drew on separate segregated funds raised from shareholders or union members. FECA spurred the growth of PACs by setting guidelines for them and making their legality unquestionable. The 1970s became the PAC decade. The number of PACs increased by more than tenfold between 1972 and 1976, and they provided candidates with more money than ever before. Between 1972 and 1976, for example, the amount of PAC contributions to candidates grew from $8.5 million to $20.5 million. Here too, direct mail was important; PACs relied on direct mail solicitations more than any other type of fund-raising.[4]

Historically, PACs were notable for the influence they gave labor over the Democratic Party, but that changed in the 1970s. In 1974 labor PACs still outnumbered corporate PACs by more than two to one, and corporate PACs often hedged their bets by donating to liberal, as well as conservative, candidates. In 1975 the New Right established the National Conservative Political Action Committee (NCPAC), a pioneer in the "independent" expenditures realm. By 1976 corporate PACs were outnumbering labor PACs by more than two to one and were shifting their contributions to conservatives. Businessmen could cite Ronald Reagan's friend Justin Dart, who became the cheerleader for the corporate PAC movement: "Talking to politicians is fine, but with a little money they hear you better." Ideologically conservative PACs also grew far more quickly than liberal ones. Of the top ten PACs, the National Congressional Club, founded by the New Right's Jesse Helms, and NCPAC together raised more money than all the others combined.[5]

Nonetheless, FECA generally helped Democrats. Nonideological PACs funneled most of their contributions to incumbents, and Democrats dominated Congress. Contributions to congressional candidates from PACs totaled $8.5 million in 1972 and $20.5 million in 1976. Moreover, *Buckley v. Valeo* denied Ford some of the advantages of incumbency by approving the public campaign financing system for presidential candidates. In 1976, in contrast with previous presidential elections, the Democratic and Republican presidential candidates were to receive virtually all their funding from public subsidies and compete with each other on a level financial playing field. (Presidential candidates who accepted matching funds did not figure out how to undermine the campaign finance system by taking advantage of "soft money" contributions to their parties until the 1979 FECA amendments created new loopholes.)[6]

Yet revisions in the Democrats' rules made their presidential nomination more difficult to win. The changes in the delegate selection rules that catapulted McGovern to the nomination in 1972 cast almost as long a shadow as the magnitude of his defeat, which made him "a whipping-boy for everybody on the center-right of the Democratic Party" who said no liberal could win the presidency. Whereas a record twenty-two states had held primaries in 1972, twenty-nine were holding them in 1976. The preconvention campaign season was to be long and brutal.[7]

As it approached, some Democrats hoped that Senator Ted Kennedy would enter the race. As a freshman at Harvard College in the 1950s he had cheated on a Spanish exam and been caught and expelled. He joined the army, was readmitted to Harvard after his tour of duty, and graduated, then went to University of Virginia Law School and entered politics. A charismatic liberal, he possessed the most famous name in American politics and a share in the family fortune. Had he run, the senator might well have won the nomination and, perhaps, the presidency. But Kennedy's wife had a drinking problem, his son had cancer, he was surrogate father to the thirteen children of his two slain brothers, and he worried about assassination. Questions about his character and extramarital activities also plagued him. His college expulsion seemed slight next to the fact that in 1969 Kennedy unconscionably delayed for hours before reporting the death of a female passenger who drowned when he drove an automobile off the bridge between Chappaquiddick Island and Martha's Vineyard. Even so, when Kennedy declared he would not run in September 1974, many suspected he planned to emerge as the candidate from a brokered convention. One magazine cover asked: "Is Teddy Running? Do Birds Sing in the Morning?"[8]

Coming as it did on the heels of Ford's pardon of Nixon and the disastrous WIN program, Kennedy's announcement opened the floodgates. Fifteen Democrats declared that they sought the presidency. McGovern wisely decided against another presidential race, while Senator Eugene McCarthy ran in 1976 as an independent. Of those who early declared their aspirations for the 1976 Democratic nomination, the most visible were Representative Morris Udall of Arizona, Senator Walter Mondale of Minnesota, former Senator Fred Harris of Oklahoma, Governor Milton Shapp of Pennsylvania, Senator Birch Bayh of Indiana, former U.S. Ambassador to France Sargent Shriver of Maryland, Senator Henry Jackson of Washington, Senator Lloyd Bentsen of Texas, former Governor Terry Sanford of North Carolina, former Governor George Wallace of Alabama, and former Governor Jimmy Carter of Georgia.[9]

The candidacy of most was problematic. Mondale soon bowed out; he said he wanted to avoid a year of "sleeping in Holiday Inns." Sanford withdrew after his weak showing in the first caucus. Harris was so unpopular in his home state that he fretted about carrying Oklahoma. Shapp, one of the first Jews to seek the presidency, had no charisma. Bayh, with his annoying tendency to refer to himself in the third person, was too bombastic. Though Shriver had married a Kennedy and held important posts in the Kennedy and Johnson administrations, he was often dismissed as a "lightweight." Bentsen looked presidential but had little political experience.[10]

Three contenders stood out as more formidable prospects, and each occupied a different place on the Democratic spectrum. Udall, a respected member of the House from Arizona, was farthest left of center. He shunned the word "liberal" and described himself as "progressive," but the liberal Americans for Democratic Action, which endorsed him, regarded him as one of its own. He was decent, smart, and funny. Reporters loved him but doubted his toughness.[11]

Senator Jackson liked to point out that he was "the only Presidential candidate who is willing to call myself a liberal." Though the Americans for Democratic Action refused to call him one, Jackson had a point: One political scientist stressed that Democratic candidates had "been running away from liberalism, the New Deal, the welfare state, and labor unions for a long time"—since the 1950s. Jackson's record on economic policy made him popular with the right wing of the labor movement led by George Meany. He was also a ferocious opponent of busing to achieve racial balance, which endeared him to neoconservatives and many whites. So too, neoconservatives liked his anti-Soviet, pro-Israel stance. Yet while Jackson enthusiasts agreed on foreign affairs, their views on domestic policy made for a different story. Neoconservatives contended that governmental activism hurt the very individuals it was intended to help, while unions pressed for more of it. Further, Jackson himself was antiseptic.[12]

Wallace of course was on the extreme right of the Democratic spectrum and seemed less animated than in years past. He no longer put on such a good show, and he was provincial. When he tried to compensate for his ignorance of foreign policy by taking his first trip abroad in 1975, he praised Belgium as "this fine small country, which has sent a number of people to Alabama." Still, he terrified Democrats to his left. He had name recognition, and thanks to his employment of the New Right direct mail king Richard Viguerie, his campaign coffers were larger than those of any other Democratic candidate by early 1976.[13]

THE CARTER PHENOMENON

Of the early Democratic front-runners, only Carter's ideological position was unclear. That fuzziness was characteristic of the candidate. Raised in South Georgia outside the sleepy town of Plains, Carter had attended the U.S. Naval Academy at Annapolis and served in the navy. Then he followed in his father's footsteps and became "a prosperous New South agribusinessman" as a peanut farmer and warehouser. But he was much more. In his own words, he was "a farmer, an engineer, a father and husband, a Christian, a politician and former governor, a planner, a businessman, a nuclear physicist, a naval officer, a canoeist, and, among other things, a lover of Bob Dylan's songs and Dylan Thomas'[s] poetry." He was also, he often said, an admirer of the theologian Reinhold Niebuhr. It was all technically truthful, but some of it was a bit of a stretch, as were his claims that he had "voluntarily 'served in two wars'" and his insistence that his parents had been poor. In fact, Carter had spent World War II at Annapolis; though he had received practical training in nuclear physics as an engineer on a nuclear submarine, his formal education was limited to less than a year of graduate study, and his family was wealthy.

Despite appearances, Carter, like many politicians, was a master of the expedient.[14]

His political success was mixed. In 1962 he had become a state senator when he successfully challenged the election fraud and stuffed ballot box that purported to sweep his "good old boy" opponent into office. After four years in the Georgia legislature, Carter mounted a centrist campaign for the governorship in 1966. He lost the Democratic primary and therefore the election to archsegregationist Lester Maddox, a "hard-scrabble tenth grade drop out who sold fried chicken for a living" and who had become notorious when he distributed ax handles to his supporters to fight integration of his restaurant. His loss devastated Carter; religion saved him. Carter recommitted himself to Jesus Christ. He then spent the next four years campaigning for governor as a born-again George Wallace, even exhorting voters to support Maddox as lieutenant governor. (Georgia law prohibited governors from serving more than one consecutive term.) At Carter's gubernatorial inauguration in 1970, however, as he stood in front of a portrait of himself made out of more than two thousand camellias, he made an about-face and bravely declared: "I say to you quite frankly that the time for racial discrimination is over." Suddenly Carter had established himself as the voice of the racially tolerant "new South." At least, so it seemed to the media. The *New York Times* provided front-page coverage of his speech. Several weeks later he was on the cover of *Time*, its star example that Dixie was whistling "a different tune."[15]

As governor Carter mastered symbolic politics. He hung Martin Luther King, Jr.'s portrait in the State Capitol. He invited the Allman Brothers to perform at the governor's mansion and feted stock car drivers. Through it all, he found time for religion. "I spend much time in prayer on my knees in the back room of the Governor's office," he said. Carter estimated that he prayed "about 25 times a day, maybe more" and reported that he read the Bible in Spanish every night before retiring. He cited his experience in Georgia politics as proof that "government at all levels can be competent, economical and efficient" and boasted of reorganizing state government by eliminating 278 of the state's 300 agencies. (Skeptics said that few had been sufficiently important to warrant funding.) But, Carter hastened to add, not the Declaration of Independence, not the Constitution, not the Bible mentioned words like "competence" and "efficiency." "[Y]ou discover other words like *honesty, integrity, fair-*

ness, liberty, justice, courage, patriotism, compassion, love—and many others which describe what a human being ought to be. These are the same words which describe what a government of human beings ought to be." He sometimes seemed like a born-again, loving, and hip version of another engineer, Herbert Hoover.[16]

Like Hoover, Carter had problems with other politicians. Though "he could charm the lard off the hog when he wanted to," he was a mean adversary whose own mother hinted that he was ruthless. He was "[a]lways so goddamned right, and righteous," one antagonist complained. Carter and Maddox feuded viciously and publicly, and Carter also had problems with the Georgia legislature. By the end of his gubernatorial term in 1974, it was unclear that Carter could have won reelection. But he had long ago ceased to display interest in his job. In 1972, Carter had helped lead the " 'ABM' (Anyone but McGovern Movement)" and nominated Jackson for president at the Democratic National Convention. Why not seek the presidency himself?[17]

In 1972, Carter's advisers had begun talking with one another about the presidency. To create a national image, Peter Bourne thought Carter should write a book, embark on a national speaking tour to raise money for Democrats, and build a constituency by capitalizing on his "greatest asset," his "personal charm." Gerald Rafshoon reassured Hamilton Jordan that Carter had the "Kennedy smile" (in fact, though he was often compared with JFK, Carter may have had the widest and toothiest smile of any candidate ever) and simply needed to add some "depth to his image." The conspirators worried that Carter might think their presidential aspirations absurd, but he and his wife enlisted enthusiastically.[18]

Jordan then wrote a memorandum setting out the strategy for winning the nomination. Carter should learn foreign policy. He should develop a national image as someone who would satisfy the nation's "thirst for strong moral leadership" after the agonies of Vietnam and Watergate. He should encompass and expand on "the Wallace constituency and populist philosophy" by posing as a "better qualified and more responsible alternative to George Wallace." Since Wallace might be annoyed that Carter had courted Wallace supporters in 1970, then declared segregation a relic of the past, Carter should be sure to woo Wallace too. Carter should also follow the example of McGovern, who had emerged as a front-runner by concentrating on selected states, doing unexpectedly well in the New Hampshire primary, and achieving victory in Florida. He should prove that he was more than a regional candidate by triumphing in a medium-size state outside the South, such as Wisconsin, and he should win in either Pennsylvania or Ohio, two industrial states with early primaries. And in what became a standard election tactic, Jordan counseled Carter to run against Washington, D.C., and as the antipolitician. Later, with Jordan's support, Carter amended the plan by competing seriously in all caucuses and primaries. That move, which successful candidates were to copy in the future, altered the course of American history by making presidential campaigns interminable.[19]

In all other respects, Carter followed his adviser's blueprint. He became the first governor to serve on the Trilateral Commission. Founded in 1973 by banker David Rockefeller and directed by Columbia University Professor Zbigniew Brzezinski, the commission sought to move foreign policy away from excessive concentration on cold war tensions toward a greater focus on relations among the United States, Western Europe, and Japan. (Despite its prestige, both the Soviets and the American right mistrusted the commission. Conservatives subsequently seized upon the news that seventeen top Carter administration officials had Trilateral connections as proof that the commission had groomed Carter for leadership as part of its plan to seize control of the government of the United States or even to establish a one world government.) Carter traveled around the country, urging Americans to vote Democratic in 1974. He also wrote *Why Not the Best?*, a campaign autobiography that displayed such dazzling self-assurance that "it might just as well have been titled, 'I'm the Best, You're O.K.' "[20]

The presidential candidate was blessed with a tight-knit organization comprised largely of Georgians. Carter's casual, jocular campaign manager, thirty-two-year-old Hamilton Jordan, a University of Georgia graduate, had also managed Carter's 1970 campaign for governor. Some called the stocky Jordan a boor; others preferred to describe him as unpolished. Carter's more obviously sophisticated press secretary, thirty-one-year-old Jody Powell, was quick and sarcastic and could even joke about his own expulsion from the Air Force Academy in his senior year in a cheating scandal. Powell graduated from Georgia Southern and began writing a dissertation on populism at Emory, which he interrupted to become Carter's gofer and driver for the 1970 campaign. Carter said Powell, a Baptist chain-smoker who enjoyed drinking with reporters, knew him better than anyone else, except his wife. Gerald Rafshoon, a Jewish New Yorker in his early forties who had grown up in Texas, then opened an advertising agency in Atlanta, had been creating commercials for Carter since the 1960s. Another Jewish Atlantan, Stuart Eizenstat, a thirty-three-year-old graduate of Harvard Law School who had worked in the Johnson administration, was the Carter campaign's policy expert and resident worrier. Peter Bourne, a young British psychiatrist who had gone to college and medical school in Atlanta, advised the Carters on health issues. Bert Lance, a hulking, shrewd, gregarious, and fiscally conservative Atlanta banker, and Charles Kirbo, a partner at the distinguished Atlanta law firm of King & Spalding, were the campaign's two more mature presences.[21]

What united these individuals more than anything was their devotion to Carter. In 1972, for example, Bourne recalled, he himself had backed McGovern; Kirbo, Jackson; and Powell had hoped Carter would nominate Wallace. But as Bourne put it, "all of us saw qualities in Carter that were compatible with our own views." For his part, Carter liked being surrounded by people with different perspectives and did not even care "if they were compatible with each other. He was the unifying force." But as Rosalynn Carter said, as late as the summer of 1975, "[i]t seemed that no one had ever heard of him."[22]

LUCK, PLUCK, AND PLENTY OF COVERAGE

In the fall what Udall called "[t]hat silly poll in Iowa" changed everything. A Carter worker guessed correctly that the Des Moines newspapers would canvas guests at a Democratic fund-raiser about the upcoming Iowa caucus. Surmising that the evening would become a media event and realizing that "politics is theatre," the staffer arranged to bus in supporters, plaster cars in the parking lot with Carter bumper stickers, and pack the audience with people sporting Carter buttons. Carter won 23 percent of the votes cast at the event, far more than any other Democratic candidate.[23]

Enter the media. Writing in the *New York Times*, R. W. Apple announced that the former governor "appears to have taken a surprising but solid lead" in the Iowa race. Suddenly Carter seemed viable. Donors hastily contributed to his presidential campaign, while reporters scrambled to cover him. "I prefer Harris on most things," one Iowan told a reporter, but "I like Carter's sincerity, and maybe I sense there's support for the man here." Did he mean he just wanted to choose a winner for a change? "Yes," he answered, "a response that would be heard from many a Carter voter."[24]

Though "uncommitted" won the most votes in the Iowa caucus on January 19, 1976, Carter received more than those cast for any other Democrat. His breakthrough there ensured Iowa's subsequent preeminence in presidential politics. Carter sat out caucus night in New York City so that he could appear on the morning network news shows the following day.[25]

Then it was on to New Hampshire, where nearly one hundred Georgians in his "Peanut Brigade" had already given Carter a lead by chatting up Democrats. Now Carter and his family tried to meet "almost every Democrat in the state." He hoped simply to do respectably. But because of his outstanding organization and Jackson's decision to stay out of the state, Carter won the New Hampshire primary in February.[26]

The dark horse now became the front-runner. Udall, who had placed second, received 96 lines in *Time* and *Newsweek*; Carter, 2,630 and both covers. Though Jackson won in Massachusetts the next week, Carter got lucky. Reporters thought Jackson ugly and boring.[27]

The bottom line was that Carter made good copy. Reporter James Reston might ridicule him as "wee Jimmy," and Elizabeth Drew might declare him the "automatic candidate—automatic answers, automatic lines, automatic smiles." But everyone acknowledged that Carter used television brilliantly and that he understood the rules of the media. Younger reporters took special interest in him. In 1976 it was big news when a politician dressed in blue jeans instead of a suit and talked about Dylan. And while most journalists did not have the same affection for Carter that they had for Udall, some admired Carter's shag haircut and willingness to carry his own luggage.[28]

Part of Carter's appeal lay in his realization that Americans had tired of traditional politics. Patrick Caddell, who had made a name for himself as a Harvard College senior in 1972, when he was put in charge of George McGovern's polling, joined Carter's campaign in 1975. When Caddell became Carter's pollster, he found that Americans wanted change—backward. *Happy Days*, *American Graffiti*, *Grease*, and other popular television shows and movies created an aesthetic of nostalgia by glorifying the 1950s family. Americans in the mid-1970s were in the throes of "a major psychological crisis" and sought a return to the values of yesteryear, Caddell told one reporter. After the Vietnam War and Watergate, they feared, but yearned, to trust their leaders again. When an interviewer asked what he thought of being labeled a "wishy-washy candidate," Carter replied that liberals, moderates, and conservatives could all project their views onto him. "So I think this is a kind of image that's a good one." While other candidates who sought to identify with voters of all inclinations came off as opportunists, Carter seemed to have a feel for the "post-ideological leadership" Americans found appealing.[29]

And Carter offered more. He insisted that as an outsider, a "fresh face, not one associated with a long series of mistakes made at the White House and Capitol Hill," he could restore love, trust, and morality to government. He absolved Americans of responsibility for their recent history and assured them that they remained the world's greatest people.[30]

It was the people and his personal relationship with them that invigorated him, Carter said constantly. When he shook the hands of factory workers, he told an interviewer, "for that instant, I really care about them in a genuine way." So what if the feeling was fleeting or if Carter once carried his desire to touch the people so far that he shook the hand of a department store mannequin? So what if he unerringly repeated the same message?: "What we want in this country is a government, once again, that's as good [pause] and honest [pause] and decent [pause] and truthful [and the pauses continue] and fair, and competent, as idealistic, and compassionate [and then dropping his voice and placing his hand, palm out, in front of him exactly the way he does it every other time he says this], and as filled with love [pause] as are the American people." Since when did presidential candidates talk about love? When he ended his speech at one school, he lifted his arms. "As if on cue, the children sprang to their feet and swarmed up to him," and Carter hugged them all. "Suffer the little children to come unto me," said one witness.[31]

Carter obviously relished the fact that his initials were "J. C." He seemed more preacher than politician. His staff occasionally worried that Americans would recoil from his moralism and religiosity. But in 1976 nearly 40 percent of Americans, including Carter and Ford, had found salvation by accepting Jesus Christ as their personal savior, and some were saying that a "Fourth Great Awakening" had been under way for some time. While *Christianity Today* remained skeptical about whether "we are [even] on the threshold of a great awakening," it acknowledged that "1976 seems to be the year of the evangelical." And no matter how "mushy" Carter's words about his relationship with Jesus and the need for love, compassion, and trust looked on paper, they had a different sound when he uttered them. "Perhaps because behind his words there is the faint rattle of steel."[32]

Sometimes it was not so faint. Fond of the old adage "Show me a good loser, and I will show you a loser," Carter regularly announced that he did not "intend to lose." His campaign symbol, a fourteen-foot-high, 450-pound "monster peanut" built of hoops, chicken wire, tinfoil, and foam, "had a sort of humble quality to it, and this became convenient to a campaign in which, as an aide put it, smiling, 'humility was not our long suit.' "[33]

CARTER'S CANDIDACY TESTIFIED to what historian Bruce Schulman has called the Southernization of American life during the 1970s. Once the media began to pay attention to Carter, journalists could not get enough of stories about the migration to the Sunbelt. Now that southern racists' worst excesses had been moderated (or at least it had become clear that whites elsewhere behaved no better), the *New York Times* displayed concern about how much the Sunbelt had to offer: good climate most of the time, space, cheap housing, weak unions, ports, postmodern architecture. Though federal money had been pouring into the Sunbelt since World War II, northerners had continued to dominate American culture. Now Sunbelt culture went national. Southern rock, country music, and the National Association for Stock Car Auto Racing boomed. Wal-Mart trumpeted the magic of the down-home Ozarks, and big business spoke "with a southern twang." Hollywood produced "redneck cinema," "hick flicks," such as *Smokey and the Bandit*. As the distinguished historian of the South C. Vann Woodward would have pointed out, irony abounded. At just the moment that defeat in Vietnam meant that "Southerners were no longer the only Americans who had experienced collective failure, lost innocence, and military defeat," southerners themselves no longer seemed defeated.[34]

"How Southern is he?" *Time* asked about Jimmy Carter. Plenty. He was "a Southern farm boy at heart who still knows how to turn sweet-potato vines, chop cotton and pull peanuts, and who looks homeward to a hamlet so archetypically Southern that it is almost parody." His cousin owned a worm farm. His wife, Rosalynn, "a marine disguised as Scarlett O'Hara," was so clearly his alter ego that he and she were labeled "the two Jimmy Carters." One of his sisters was a farmer and motorcyclist; the other, a famous evangelist.[35]

Her southern accent, shrewdness, folksiness, wit, and liberalism made seventy-eight-year-old "Miz Lillian," who bore a strange resemblance to pop artist Andy Warhol, a candidate's dream mother. One Republican was awestruck as he listened to "the nation's grandmother" discuss her favorite wrestlers for a Boston sports talk radio show. "One little phone call and 100,000 avid Boston sports fans had undoubtedly fallen in love with Jimmy Carter's mother. I pictured her hanging up the phone and dialing city after city, talk show after talk show, a smiling campaign worker at her shoulder, sliding typewritten notes under her elbow." She also advocated integration and identified with the civil rights movement.[36]

To balance her out and to attract Wallace admirers, Carter had redneck brother Billy, who operated a Plains gas station and rode around in pickup trucks while drinking beer. "The best compliment I got in the whole campaign," Billy said, "was when they asked George Wallace what he thought of Jimmy Carter and he said Jimmy was his third choice for President. His first choice was himself. Then they asked him who his second choice was and he said Billy Carter."[37]

Carter made shrewd use of his southern roots. Through Billy and parts of his own record, he appealed to the old Confederate South and Wallace supporters. Yet Carter also persuaded some of his more liberal competitors to stay out of Florida on the ground that only another southerner could defeat Wallace there. Carter's mother helped him with African Americans, as did his own gubernatorial record as a racial moderate. Carter understood that the Voting Rights Act of 1965, which made it easier for African Americans in the South to register to vote, had transformed the region. "It used to be Southern politics was just 'nigger' politics—a question of which candidate could 'outnigger' the other," Carter supporter Andrew Young, the first African American to be elected to Congress from Georgia since Reconstruction, wryly told *Time*, but "now that we've got 50%, 60%, 70% of the black votes registered in the South, everybody's proud to be associated with their black brothers and sisters." As one Republican observed, "Carter is playing upon two essentially conflicting myths—the 'good ole boy' rural South and the 'black and white together' new South." He expertly used "the three Rs": race, religion, and region.[38]

Victory upon victory followed. In March, Carter won in Florida, the next crucial primary, then again in North Carolina, and knocked Wallace out of the running. Thanks to the support of Mayor Richard Daley, longtime "boss" of Chicago, Carter triumphed in Illinois too.[39]

Later Caddell attributed Carter's accomplishment to "skill and luck."

Horatio Alger would have renamed skill "pluck," but the Carter story was following Alger's formula: The lucky and plucky succeeded. The pluck had been evident in the decision of an unknown to run and to run everywhere. But as Carter's finance director admitted, "We had no structure after Florida; we had planned only for the short haul." As he also pointed out, however, that did not matter. "After Florida, it was all NBC, CBS, and the *New York Times*." And after Illinois, it was a matter of luck.[40]

The next important primaries were to take place in New York and Wisconsin at the beginning of April. In New York, Jews, many labor leaders, and party officials favored Jackson. When Carter donned a yarmulke, he looked as out of place as "grits at a seder." He came in third after Jackson and Udall. The media might have begun to speculate about Carter's electability, for he had now been humiliated in two key industrial states to which Jackson devoted attention, Massachusetts and New York. But the senator had raised expectations for a stronger first-place showing, and he was still boring. One Jackson adviser was astonished to hear reporters declare that "it was still Carter versus the pack, . . . [i]nstead of it finally being a head to head clash between Jackson and Carter." Meanwhile, the networks mistakenly called Wisconsin for Udall, and the *Milwaukee Sentinel* jumped the gun with the headline on its morning edition: CARTER UPSET BY UDALL. Carter was photographed smilingly holding the paper aloft. "The next day, thousands of newspapers across the country featured the picture—an updated version of the famous Harry Truman photo displaying the Chicago *Tribune* headline on the night of the 1948 election reading: 'Dewey Wins,' " a reporter remembered. It was another media coup.[41]

Carter's luck continued to hold in Pennsylvania, where his Wisconsin victory momentarily eclipsed his attempt to appeal to Wallace supporters by reassuring them that there was nothing wrong with maintaining "ethnic purity" and that he would never "force" racial integration of a neighborhood. When the comment caught up with him, and reporters began asking if he understood its "Hitlerian" overtones, Carter arranged a massive rally of his African American supporters in Atlanta. In turn, the rally and Carter's apology overshadowed the dangerous resignation of speechwriter Robert Shrum from his campaign.[42]

In the first months of his campaign, Carter's nebulousness proved appealing because it enabled Americans to fit him to their fancies. But by the spring of 1976 more voters were complaining that Carter either said nothing specific or too frequently changed positions. As the Pennsylvania showdown between Jackson and Carter loomed, Caddell persuaded Carter to hire Robert Shrum, who had written speeches for McGovern and others, to sharpen his image. But Shrum resigned in disgust nine days later. Carter was vague, Shrum charged, and worse, he was vague deliberately. He spoke sympathetically about miners publicly but did not seek increased health benefits for them because "it would offend operators." The candidate's supporters said Carter had dropped the section about health benefits from his speech because Shrum had given it to the candidate "less than an hour before he was to descend into a mine in Mathias, Pennsylvania," could not satisfactorily respond to Carter's "questions about it," and applauded "Carter's inclination to master personally the principles of his program." Still, Shrum's observations possessed the power to damage Carter. Shrum saw a "dichotomy" between the public and private Carter: "public compassion, private callousness; public indignation over tax loop holes, private concern to mollify special interests; public allegiance to new priorities, private sympathy for the military-industrial complex; public smiles, but no private smiles." The candidate who promised truthfulness was so manipulative and deceptive that "I really believe it would be bad for this person to be President." Those strong words could well have destroyed Carter had Shrum uttered them a month later. But because the story followed so closely on the heels of the "ethnic purity" episode, "the press and public had already been drained by press crises," political scientist Betty Glad explained. The media largely buried Shrum's cri de coeur. Carter won a huge victory in Pennsylvania on April 27 and ended Jackson's candidacy.[43]

ABC

For a moment it seemed as if only Hubert Humphrey stood between Carter and the nomination. The ebullient, loquacious liberal had refused to declare his candidacy earlier in the hope that he might be drafted at the convention. Thanks to Carter's early victories, however, the prospect of a brokered convention was disappearing, and many in Washington were urging Humphrey to jump into some remaining primaries. "How can he be nominated?" Democratic Party elder statesman Averell Harriman reportedly said of Carter. "I don't know him, and neither do any of my friends." As another insider observed, "The problem is that no one in Washington owns a piece of Jimmy Carter." Almost every Democrat who counted, though, owned a piece of the sixty-five-year-old Humphrey, who had been a fixture in national politics since 1948. But common sense prevailed, and on April 29 the old pol tearfully declared at a press conference that "one thing I don't need at my stage of life is to be ridiculous." Humphrey left the door open a crack, saying of the presidential nomination, "I shall not seek it; I shall not compete for it; I shall not search for it; I shall not scramble for it. But I'm around." As the ABC ("Anybody but Carter") movement gathered momentum, he lurked in the wings while two new contenders scrambled for the nomination.[44]

One was California Governor Jerry Brown. The son of a governor and a graduate of Yale Law School, the thirty-eight-year-old Brown managed to portray himself as an outsider. Like Carter, he refused to identify himself as liberal or conservative. While Carter preached the politics of love, Brown said that the United States had entered an era of "limits" to what government could do for people and spoke of a "politics of lowered expectations." Having spent four years in a Jesuit seminary, then become a Buddhist, Brown was "California hip." He shunned the new governor's mansion and limousine for an ascetic apartment and a blue Plymouth, appointed an acupuncturist to the California Medical Quality Assurance Board, and spoke of the "inner meaning" of garbage dumps. Californians affectionately referred to him as "Governor Moonbeam," but they had a reputation for liking weirdos. That he did so well outside the state indicated the intensity of the national desire for change. Brown was "the new me," Carter remarked tellingly. "Jimmy Carter made us important," Brown's campaign manager observed later. "If he had said Jerry Brown was a nice young man and let it go at that, we would have fallen flat." On May 18, Brown whipped Carter in Maryland.[45]

Between May 11 and June 1 a second latecomer with excellent liberal credentials, Senator Frank Church of Idaho, won the Nebraska, Idaho, Oregon, and Montana primaries. But those were his only victories, and Carter was still gathering delegates. Further, Carter's run-everywhere strategy meant that for every primary he lost, he could point to a victory elsewhere.[46]

Nevertheless, the losses hurt. In the last week of May even the media noticed that Carter lost five of nine primaries. The bloom was off the rose. At least one audience groaned when Carter said, "God bless you." In 1972 the United Auto Workers had endorsed George McGovern. But Carter wooed United Auto Workers president Leonard Woodcock, and Woodcock and a number of UAW leaders were supporting Carter in the hope he could unite minorities, moderates, liberals, and blue-collar Wallace fans. Nevertheless, Carter had barely eked out a victory over Udall in the UAW's stronghold, Michigan. With Kennedy publicly criticizing Carter for vagueness and Humphrey reconsidering his options, eyes focused on the last major round of primaries on June 8. The three states involved—California, New Jersey, and Ohio—possessed a third of the delegates required for the nomination. Brown was a sure winner in California, as was the "uncommitted" slate in New Jersey, clearly a front for either Brown or Humphrey.[47]

In desperation, Carter turned to a power broker and telephoned Chicago's Mayor Daley to say he would win in Ohio but lose in California and New Jersey. Obligingly, Daley held a press conference and made the startling announcement that Ohio was the day's only important race. The mayor's words carried weight with the media: If Daley said Ohio was important, it became important. Though he did poorly in California and New Jersey, Carter won big in Ohio.[48]

The next day most of the politicians who had once dismissed Carter as a nobody scurried toward his side. Udall congratulated Carter, Humphrey bowed out for good, Jackson "glumly" said, "We can all add," and Wallace endorsed the Georgian. Though Kennedy remained silent and Brown accused the "Nervous Nellies" who had jumped aboard the Carter train of misreading public opinion, all possibility of a brokered convention vanished. Ever protective of his image, Carter took off his suit and put on his blue jeans and denim jacket before going out to announce to the press that he had sewn up the nomination.[49]

JULY 1976: NEW YORK

The next month the United States celebrated its bicentennial. Two years in the making, the commemoration of the nation's two hundredth birthday encouraged the crassest commercialism. Consumers could buy bicentennial bikinis, teddy bears that declaimed the Declaration of Independence, even bicentennial caskets. But when 212 tall ships of thirty-four nations sailed into Manhattan's harbor, they captured imaginations, and July 4 proved inspiring. Americans seemed to realize that they had survived Watergate and Vietnam.[50]

The Democratic National Convention began on the same hopeful note in Madison Square Garden on July 12. The first Democratic convention to be held in Manhattan since Al Smith and William G. McAdoo's supporters deadlocked there in 1924, it displayed New York City and the party at their best. No one fought. "This is the convention where the Deep South is welcomed back to the party" it had abandoned in presidential elections beginning in 1964, a journalist said, after it had "captured" the Democrats. "It is also the convention where the Democratic liberals and conservatives decided to stand together and cheer together." But their cheers were acquiescent, rather than ardent, and though some reported the convention as a "love-in," it was not. Many delegates saw Carter as "some hillbilly who had blundered into the nomination." The equally suspicious Carter operatives purchased equipment that would enable them to bug powerful Democrats and the networks and decided against using it only because they feared "their own Watergate."[51]

The convention crawled. Carter did delight the delegates by naming liberal insider Walter Mondale as his running mate. But only on the final night, during the rousing speeches of Mondale and Carter, did the mood really lift. Martin Luther King, Jr.'s father delivered the benediction. "We must close ranks now," he thundered. "Surely *the Lord* sent Jimmy to come on out and bring America back where she belongs." At that one moment, at least, Democrats seemed united. Peter Duchin's orchestra swung into the civil rights movement's anthem, and TV viewers witnessed everyone in Madison Square Garden, from George Wallace supporters to civil rights movement veterans, clasp hands and sing "We Shall Overcome."[52]

Good feeling between the candidate and media, however, evaporated. The next day, as Carter returned to Plains for a vacation, a reporter aboard his airplane, *Peanut One*, inquired whether his convention address had been liberal or conservative. Carter, who was unknowingly leaning against a poster featuring him with a beard, long hair, and in biblical dress, captioned, "J. C. can save America," replied that "the speech not inadvertently shifted back and forth between the liberal and the conservative." After reporters laughed at him, he characterized it as "populist." Asked to explain populism, he snapped, "I don't want to be in a position where I have to define it." For the next month journalists preparing nightly news stories photographed Carter teaching Sunday school or draining his fishpond. "If Carter becomes president, within eighteen months 62% of the White House press corps will have become hopeless alcoholics," one said. There was little to do "but drink" at the Best

Western motel to which they retired between events. Favored younger reporters, at least, could escape to the house of one Carter adviser to smoke pot and listen to Fleetwood Mac.[53]

The bored reporters anticipated that Carter would win. Polls showed him thirty-three points ahead after the convention. Some thought he might carry all fifty states.[54]

REPUBLICAN CHAOS

In addition to Watergate fallout, Republican fratricide helped explain the Democrats' apparent strength. Three forces loomed large over the Republican Party in 1975–76. They were the New Right, Ronald Reagan, and Gerald Ford.

After Ford's selection of Nelson Rockefeller in 1974 infuriated Richard Viguerie and other members of his circle into making themselves a movement, the New Right first displayed its political clout on the national scene in 1975 in a surprising way. It forced Ford to renege on his pledge to support legislation that would have enlarged the right of unions to picket construction sites. The president had not known what hit him when nearly three-quarters of a million letters and postcards deluged the White House demanding a veto of the common situs picketing bill. At first, only the construction industry lobbied against the bill, but then Ford's staff noticed that a broad spectrum of opponents had mobilized. Antiunion businessmen had been brought aboard by the appeals of the National Right to Work Committee, a client of Viguerie's. Reagan opposed the bill too, and the *New York Times* reported that Ford had developed the "fear that if he lost any more of his conservative Republican support, he might not get his party's Presidential nomination." Trapped, Ford caved at the end of 1975 and vetoed legislation that the AFL-CIO had sought for more than twenty years, that he had pledged to support, and that his own secretary of labor, Harvard economist John Dunlop, had drafted. Dunlop resigned in protest, and George Meany called Ford a weakling who "ran out" on his promises.[55]

Most considered the National Right to Work Committee a businessmen's front and the defeat of the common situs legislation bad for workers, but the New Right contended otherwise. Refusing to concede workers to the Democrats, it insisted that labor leaders did not represent workers' interests. "Most of our fathers belonged to unions," New Right strategist Paul Weyrich said. Unions themselves were not evil, but "big union leadership" ignored its members' issues, and "big union bosses" siphoned off their "hard-earned contributions." The National Right to Work Committee wanted to "help" workers.[56]

Here was the first widely noticed victory for Viguerie, the New Right, and direct mail. The "fund-raiser extraordinaire" was beginning to attract breathless media coverage. According to one profile, an elaborate security system at Richard A. Viguerie Company protected his "3000 rolls of magnetic tape," on which were "encoded the names of 15 million people and vital information about them. Richard Viguerie points to the round cans holding the tapes and grins. 'If you're a conservative, your name should be in there somewhere,' he says." After a session with Viguerie, one reporter explained to readers that a member of Congress would find a poll saying that three-quarters of his constituents favored common situs legislation of only limited value. The two hundred messages urging a vote against it (often on pre-addressed postcards Viguerie provided in the original mailing) left a stronger impression. The politician would reason that most of those polled cared little about this particular issue. "But the two hundred people who have been prompted by a computer letter to write him of their opposition are very real." They might come together to defeat him at the next election.[57]

Although the New Right was beginning to score legislative victories by 1976, it still lacked a presidential candidate. To its disgust, Barry Goldwater supported Ford after Dick Cheney urged the president to let Goldwater "know that the bottom line is that you need him now, not later, and that you need him publicly, not just privately." Ford was of course anathema; his record, "a trail of broken promises."[58]

Grassroots conservatives and the moving forces behind the American Conservative Union, Young Americans for Freedom, *Human Events*, and *National Review* still wanted Reagan. When Ford announced that "I say with emphasis and conviction that homemaking is good for America" and told teenagers "never be ashamed to say, 'I am an American homemaker,'" he seemed ridiculous. Reagan roused cheers from the right with equally odd statements, as when he said he was angry because "a housewife can't buy a box of breakfast cereal without being cheated unless there's a government agency there to protect her."[59]

Viguerie and New Right organizers in Viguerie's orbit, however, remained unsure of Reagan. His flexibility as governor of California still raised questions about the sincerity of his conservatism for them, as it did for many on the far right. In May 1975, when the talk of a

Reagan-Wallace partnership was loudest, Viguerie had told the *New York Times* of his "fervent hope . . . that George Wallace and Ronald Reagan will team up as the ticket of a new party next year" and said that he didn't "know who should run for what." But Reagan's employment of another direct mail expert grated on Viguerie. Moreover, the New Right leaders hated Reagan's campaign manager, John Sears, a traditional Republican professional who had once worked for Nixon. (In a strange turn of events, Stu Spencer, a longtime Reagan consultant, had jumped ship to become Ford's campaign manager.) "If he gets in, we're out," Paul Weyrich reportedly said of Reagan. "We'd have no input in that administration."[60]

Consequently, although many on Viguerie's mailing lists held Reagan close to their hearts in 1975 and 1976, not all New Right leaders did. The Ford administration did not seem to understand that they were almost as suspicious of Reagan as they were of Ford. Instead the White House blamed the president's problems on Viguerie and a "small number of highly motivated right-wing nuts." And the New Right carefully obscured its stance toward Reagan.[61]

Thus Viguerie, Weyrich, Howard Phillips, and other New Right chieftains continued working with *National Review* publisher William Rusher, the American Conservative Union, and Young Americans for Freedom to form a new party. The plan was to put conservatives on the ballot in every state if the Democrats denied the nomination to Wallace and the Republicans refused it to Reagan. Generally, the most promising strategy for accomplishing this goal was to work with the remnants of Wallace's American Independent Party, particularly if the extremist "kooks" at its fringes could be purged. The intention was to remake the AIP, whose nominee had been Wallace in 1968 and John Schmitz, a John Bircher, in 1972. Rusher's pledge to produce a big name that would garner the necessary percentage of the November vote to qualify the AIP for federal election campaign funds in 1980 intrigued some of its leaders. Many conservative Republicans, however, were wary. In the eyes of William F. Buckley and most at *National Review*, for example, everyone in the AIP was a "kook," and Rusher tainted himself by working with it.[62]

Nonetheless, the drive for a new party went forward, with Rusher keeping Reagan apprised of its progress. In the cases of Rusher, the American Conservative Union, and the Young Americans for Freedom, the work for a new party partially reflected a wish to keep a seat warm for

Reagan, should the Republicans disappoint him. In the case of Viguerie and others more closely identified with the New Right, however, the effort to form a new party surely reflected their own ambivalence toward Reagan. When Wallace decided against running in New Hampshire, Viguerie organized a last-minute thirty-five-thousand-dollar write-in campaign in New Hampshire for "Big John" Connally. A tall Texan who favored elegant suits and cowboy boots, Connally was inevitably described as a larger-than-life wheeler-dealer. He was even more swaggering and ruthless than his mentor, Lyndon Johnson, and more suave. As Texas's Democratic governor from 1963 to 1969 Connally had been shot and wounded in Dallas as he rode in the car with John F. Kennedy. In 1972 he chaired Democrats for Nixon. When his candidate won, Connally became secretary of the Treasury and a Republican. Connally, who received just forty-two votes in New Hampshire (thirty-three from Democrats, nine from Republicans), decided not to throw his Stetson in the ring and ultimately endorsed Ford.[63]

Later, after Reagan had won the Republican nomination and presidency in 1980, Viguerie and his New Right associates understandably concealed their earlier lack of enthusiasm for him. The way they told the story, the New Right had launched "a bloodless revolution" to topple Goldwater as the head of the conservative movement in 1975 and "turned to Ronald Reagan for energetic leadership." Had the New Right actually thrown its full support to Ronald Reagan as Republican candidate, Reagan might have received the 1976 nomination.[64]

THEN AGAIN, HE MIGHT not have. Like the Democrats, the Republicans were holding more primaries than ever, in more than half the states. For all his appeal, candidate Reagan had a number of problems as primary season began. Early wins, stressed journalist Jules Witcover, were "critical for Reagan because his campaign had contended that Ford was not a bona fide incumbent, being unelected; that as soon as the voters could, they would make clear they did not consider he had the assumed right of the usual incumbent to another term." Early primary victories were also important because the Ford campaign painted Reagan as an extremist whose candidacy would ensure a Democratic triumph, and the media had no use for Reagan. Witcover viewed travels with him as "a never-ending excursion into fantasy," and the media painted Reagan's entire campaign that way. And early wins were important because many dismissed Reagan as the mouthpiece of his handlers and public relations executives.[65]

So the New Hampshire primary on February 24 was crucial for Reagan, as well as for Ford. Reagan blew it. John Sears planned to present Reagan as a moderate. Nevertheless, Reagan delivered a speech written by conservative Jeffrey Bell that said the federal budget could be cut by ninety billion dollars. Control of federal housing, welfare, education, and Medicaid could be transferred to states and localities that could kill or fund them. The savings would make it possible to balance the budget, pay off the national debt, and slash taxes. Aside from conservative Republicans, who were overjoyed to hear the anti-Washington message from someone other than Carter, everyone challenged the basis for Reagan's projections. Then Reagan appeared to muse aloud about investing the Social Security trust fund in the stock market. "Reagan slips every time he opens his mouth because he has no background," Chief of Staff Cheney reassured the president. Yet Ford was still in trouble. Nixon undercut him by making a very public February trip to China, where reporters thought the former president derided the Helsinki conference as naive, which Ford and Kissinger believed reflected Nixon's desire for a "stalemate" between Ford and Reagan "so Connally will get in." As Reagan recouped, it began to look as if Ford would become the first incumbent president ever to lose the New Hampshire primary. Then, however, Reagan abandoned New Hampshire for Illinois on the Sunday before the vote. Ford won New Hampshire—by just 1,317 votes. The victory made him credible. "We did especially well in the Keene area where I campaigned," and Ford spoke about his foreign policy of "peace through strength," he told a White House caller. "They can't say I've never won any place outside Grand Rapids," he gloated.[66]

Obviously, Reagan needed to change strategies. While Ford waged a "savage" campaign against Reagan as a right-wing extremist, Reagan criticized détente "without ever mentioning President Ford or Secretary of State Kissinger by name," worried *Human Events*. Now Reagan's campaign manager belatedly advised him to "to go after Ford" on foreign policy. "You could talk to Reagan," Sears said. "For one thing, he knows more about acting than politics, and he knew it." (Like many Democrats and Ford Republicans, Sears underestimated his candidate's intelligence.) In Sunbelt states, Reagan now waged an "ideological holy war" against the president. "Under Kissinger and Ford, this nation has become Number Two in a world where it is dangerous—if not fatal—

to be second best," he charged. He also brought to the fore the Panama Canal, whose return to the Panamanians Ford and Kissinger were quietly planning. "We built it, we paid for it, and we're going to keep it," Reagan shouted in the closing days of the Florida primary. Elections rarely turn on foreign policy, but Reagan's frustrated nationalism proved popular. "The Panama Canal issue had nothing to do with the canal," one Reagan adviser said. "It said more about the American people's feelings about where the country was and what it was powerless to do, and their frustration about the incomprehensibility of foreign policy."[67]

But Ford could still use the presidency. Despite the popularity of Reagan's critique of bloated bureaucracy, many Republicans wanted "more, not less, from the federal government." The promise of a new hospital here, the award of a defense contract there, and "Santa Claus Ford" barely carried Florida on March 9. The Reagan campaign was broke, and many Republicans were pressing Reagan to withdraw from the race. "We must give some sort of lead to our readers," one *National Review* editor wrote Buckley. "They are going to want to know, What Now? Stay in plugging for Reagan until the end? Ease over to Ford? Follow Rusher in whatever of a third party will o' the wisp he comes up with?"[68]

Having predicted that conservatives could not win the Republican or Democratic nomination, Rusher observed the tottering of Reagan's candidacy with a gloomy satisfaction. He still hoped to show Reagan and Wallace "a better way," running together on the new party ticket. Rusher thought Wallace might well agree to the venture, but that Reagan lacked the "stomach" for it. "Republicans are so fussy about the company we keep!" But perhaps Reagan might agree to run with someone else if he lost the Republican nomination to Ford. And if Reagan refused to do even that, perhaps someone else, such as Jesse Helms, though he was just a first-term senator, might answer Rusher's call. Another possibility was to offer Wallace the top slot. Despite the difficulties posed by the Alabamian's "reputation as a primitive," Rusher thought that his candidacy made some sense "since it has always been more or less clear that Wallace could have the third-line nomination if he wanted it, assuming Reagan didn't."[69]

Reagan's surprise victory over Ford in North Carolina on March 23 brought him back from the dead. Engineered by Helms, whom the win confirmed as a conservative leader, it was also made possible by a $250,000 "independent expenditure" from the American Conservative

Union. For the third time in all American history, an incumbent had lost a primary. Without a doubt, Reagan's denunciations of big government, Kissinger, détente, and the Panama Canal "giveaway" were touching a nerve.[70]

Then, on May 1, Reagan won all the delegates in Texas, a state Ford had expected to take, by hammering away at the president for breaking his vow to decontrol oil prices. The next five primaries yielded four more Reagan victories. As National Republican Committee chairman Rogers Morton sat behind a row of empty liquor bottles after the fifth, he said that the president had to win in Michigan "to prove he is viable" and seemed to compare the campaign to a sinking ship. Reagan now had more delegates, and Ford's press secretary was scheming to run the president as a third party candidate if he lost the Republican nomination. Only Ford's May 18 win in his home state put the president on track.[71]

EVEN SO, AND DESPITE the Ford campaign's efforts to paint Reagan as both too far to the right to win election and a menace whose presidency would mean nuclear war, when the primaries, caucuses, and state conventions were over, neither president nor challenger possessed the required 1,130 delegates. Counts varied, but it appeared that Reagan had the commitments of at least 1,050 delegates, Ford of at least 1,100. If the first ballot at the convention beginning on August 16 in Kansas City did not produce a winner, some "committed" delegates might well switch camps. Perhaps 100 had not yet pledged themselves to either candidate.[72]

No matter who triumphed, according to *Newsweek*, "more than a few Republicans were beginning to wonder out loud whether their party had any long-term future." *Time*'s cover story featured "the plight of the GOP." It had been more than twenty years since the Republicans controlled Congress, sixteen since they controlled the White House.[73]

Despite his party's diminished status, Ford rejected the urging of Robert Teeter and Dick Cheney to reach out to Reagan by making him his running mate, and the Republican civil war continued. Each side tried to raid the other's delegates and courted "uncommitted" ones. One joke had Ford telephoning a delegate to invite him to a White House party for Queen Elizabeth. After a long silence the delegate asked, "What's for dinner?" Ford had boodle to hand out, an effective delegate stalker in his own former undersecretary of commerce, the "handsome, well groomed, and exceedingly smooth" James Baker III of Texas, and control of the Republican National Committee machinery. Nevertheless, Reagan was still coming on strong as he showered undecided delegates with autographed photos and personal notes. Still, as the Republicans moved toward their first convention floor fight since 1952, Sears sensed that his candidate was slipping.[74]

So Sears persuaded Reagan to tap a liberal Republican as his running mate, Senator Richard Schweiker of Pennsylvania, and to break with tradition by revealing his choice before the convention. In some ways, it was a smart move: Sears had created enough uncertainty to keep the media from concluding that Ford had wrapped up the nomination and to keep Reagan in the news until the convention. Ultimately, Schweiker did little to help Reagan with liberals, however, and the Schweiker choice gave the leader of the Mississippi delegation the excuse he had sought to switch his state from the Reagan to the Ford column. While some disappointed conservatives, such as Helms and the American Conservative Union, reaffirmed their support for Reagan, Helms's admirers, with his encouragement, nominated him as vice president. Helms received 103 votes and pulled out when he was promised he could address the convention during prime time. Schweiker's selection infuriated most of the New Right and increased its suspicion of Sears and Reagan. Richard Viguerie complained publicly that Reagan was building "a coalition on expediency and hypocrisy," and Howard Phillips said he had "betrayed" his followers.[75]

Yet Reagan hung on, and he insisted that Ford follow his example. So it was that the great fight at the Republican convention was over Rule 16-C, a proposed procedural change in party rules that would force Ford to disclose his running mate before the delegates cast their votes. If the Reagan forces prevailed on 16-C, which Ford's people called the misery-loves-company provision, some Ford delegates who disliked the president's choice might switch to the Reagan camp. But the delegates narrowly voted down 16-C on August 17.[76]

Relieved, Ford bowed to his strategists' advice that he accept the convention's overwhelming endorsement of the morality in foreign policy plank that Helms and other Reaganites demanded be part of the party platform. Ford realized that the plank, which condemned the Helsinki Accords and "secret agreements" over the future of the Panama Canal while celebrating Solzhenitsyn for his "human courage and morality," impugned administration foreign policy. Yet as James Baker, who was soon to replace the hapless Morton as campaign chairman, said gratefully, at least the challenge was veiled. "I could see a two-word plank: 'Fire Kissinger,' and we would have had to fight it. And if we had been beaten, we could have lost the whole thing." The Reaganites then rammed through a plank demanding a constitutional amendment to "restore the protection of the right to life for unborn children." Republican feminists just barely beat back the attempt by Phyllis Schlafly and others to delete a platform plank supporting the ERA. When the roll call of delegates began, Ford received 1,178 votes on the first ballot to Reagan's 1,070.[77]

But it was still not Ford's convention. The president absolutely refused to choose Reagan as his running mate, and by this point Reagan disliked Ford so much he did not want the job anyway. In an effort to placate conservatives that was almost as transparent as Reagan's selection of Schweiker, the president chose Senator Robert Dole of Kansas as his running mate. Nonetheless, Reagan's staff deliberately kept the emotional demonstration for Reagan going forty-five minutes over schedule on August 19. As a result, it was nearly midnight in the East before Ford gave his acceptance speech challenging Carter to debates.[78]

Ford turned in a strong performance, but Reagan stole the show. When Ford insisted that "my good friend Ron Reagan . . . come down and bring Nancy," Reagan claimed an ideological triumph. "I believe the Republican Party has a platform that is a banner of bold, unmistakable colors with no pastel shades," he said, and Ford had issued "a call to arms based on that platform." As delegates wept, Reagan cited Douglas MacArthur: "We must go forth from here united, determined, that what a great general said a few years ago is true: 'There is no substitute for victory.' "[79]

Reagan had done spectacularly well, and his platform victory testified to his skill in moving the GOP to the right. Moreover, ultimately Reagan won in losing. His campaign had lost its steam by the convention. His nomination would have outraged the Ford wing, and he almost certainly would have lost the general election in 1976. Further, his defeat in 1976, most intimates believed, hurt his pride, made him want the presidency more than ever, and taught him that he could win in 1980 only by stressing his ideological differences from Jimmy Carter, while sounding more optimistic. Yet in 1976 no one, with the possible exception of Ronald and Nancy Reagan, was thinking ahead to 1980. Reagan was sixty-five, then an advanced age in political life. To journalist Murray

"All the News That's Fit to Print"

The New York Times

LATE CITY EDITION

Weather: Partly cloudy today; cool tonight. Fair, pleasant tomorrow. Temp. range: today 65-78; Thursday 64-85. Highest Temp.-Hum. Index yesterday: 75. Details on Page 66.

VOL. CXXIII . . No. 42,566 — NEW YORK, FRIDAY, AUGUST 9, 1974 — 15 CENTS

NIXON RESIGNS

HE URGES A TIME OF 'HEALING'; FORD WILL TAKE OFFICE TODAY

'Sacrifice' Is Praised; Kissinger to Remain

By ANTHONY RIPLEY

Special to The New York Times

WASHINGTON, Aug. 8—Vice President Ford praised President Nixon tonight for "one of the greatest personal sacrifices for the country and one of the finest personal decisions on behalf of all of us as Americans."

Mr. Ford, who will take office as the 38th President at noon tomorrow, vowed to continue Mr. Nixon's foreign policy and announced that Secretary of State Kissinger had agreed to stay on in the new Administration.

"I pledge to you tonight, as I will pledge to you tomorrow and in the future, my best efforts in cooperation, leadership and dedication to what's good for America and good for the world," he said.

The Vice President, who never sought the nation's highest office and disclaimed any intention of seeking it after Mr. Nixon's term, will take the oath of office in a private ceremony at the White House.

Thus will he become the first man to serve as President without being chosen by the American people in an election. Tomorrow night he will address the nation on radio and television. It is expected that he will speak at 6 P.M.

All day today the signs of the historic change were in the air, sensed by the crowds that gathered along Pennsylvania Avenue near the White House. Applause rang out from the crowds when Mr. Ford appeared briefly.

Text of Mr. Ford's remarks appears on Page 2.

After watching Mr. Nixon on television tonight with his family, the Vice President stepped outside into a slight drizzle at his suburban split-level home

SPECULATION RIFE ON VICE PRESIDENT

Some Ford Associates Say Selecting a Successor Could Take Weeks

By CHRISTOPHER LYDON

Special to The New York Times

WASHINGTON, Aug. 8 — Potentially the most revealing and most important decision of Gerald R. Ford's Presidential

Vice President Ford meeting with newsmen last night

President Nixon on TV as he announced his resignation

POLITICAL SCENE SHARPLY ALTERED

G.O.P. Prospects Improved, Ford in Good Spot for '76 and Watergate Fades

Rise and Fall
Appraisal of Nixon Career

By ROBERT B. SEMPLE Jr.

The central question is how a man who won so much could have lost so much. How could a public figure who so well perceived the instincts of the majority and who, on reaching his destination, was not always certain what to do when he got there—except, perhaps, to keep going.

JAWORSKI ASSERTS NO DEAL WAS MADE

Says Nixon Did Not Ask for and Was Not Given a Way to Avoid Prosecution

The 37th President Is First to Quit Post

By JOHN HERBERS

Special to The New York Times

WASHINGTON, Aug. 8—Richard Milhous Nixon, the 37th President of the United States, announced tonight that he had given up his long and arduous fight to remain in office and would resign, effective at noon tomorrow.

At that hour, Gerald Rudolph Ford, whom Mr. Nixon nominated for Vice President last Oct. 12, will be sworn in as the 38th President, to serve out the 895 days remaining in Mr. Nixon's second term.

Less that two years after his landslide re-election victory, Mr. Nixon, in a conciliatory address on national television, said that he was leaving not with a sense of bitterness but with a hope that his departure would start a "process of healing that is so desperately needed in America."

Text of the address will be found on Page 2.

He spoke of regret for any "injuries" done "in the course of the events that led to this decision." He acknowledged that some of his judgments had been wrong.

The 61-year-old Mr. Nixon, appearing calm and resigned to his fate as a victim of the Watergate scandal, became the first President in the history of the Republic to resign from office. Only 10 months earlier Spiro Agnew resigned the Vice-Presidency.

Speaks of Pain at Yielding Post

Mr. Nixon, speaking from the Oval Office, where his successor will be sworn in tomorrow, may well have delivered his most effective speech since the Watergate scandals began to swamp his Administration in early 1973.

In tone and content, the 15-minute address was in sharp contrast to his frequently combative language of the past, especially his first "farewell" appearance—that of 1962, when

The culmination of the Watergate affair. *From the* New York Times, *August 9, 1974.* New York Times.

President Ford toasts and butters an English muffin for his breakfast for the benefit of the media, September 5, 1974. *White House Photograph by David Hume Kennerly. Courtesy, Gerald R. Ford Library.*

Secretary of State Henry A. Kissinger plays Pass the Straw with a geisha while having dinner in Kyoto, Japan, November 21, 1974. *White House Photograph by David Hume Kennerly. Courtesy, Gerald R. Ford Library.*

President Ford and General Secretary Leonid Brezhnev during the president's arrival at Vozdvizhenka Airport in Vladivostok, USSR, November 23, 1974. *White House Photograph by David Hume Kennerly. Courtesy, Gerald R. Ford Library.*

Secretary of State Henry Kissinger interrupts a senior staff meeting to relay the latest information on the U.S. evacuation of Saigon, April 29, 1975. Clockwise: President Gerald R. Ford, Richard Cheney, Alan Greenspan, Vice President Nelson Rockefeller, Donald Rumsfeld, Kissinger, Frank Zarb, Max Friedersdorf, and John Marsh. *White House Photograph by David Hume Kennerly. Courtesy, Gerald R. Ford Library.*

Americans evacuate Saigon. A CIA employee (probably O. B. Harnage) helps Vietnamese evacuees onto an Air America helicopter at the U.S. Embassy, April 29, 1975. *Photograph by Buffon-Darquennes. Buffon-Darquennes/Sygma/Corbis. Courtesy, Corbis.*

President Carter carries his bags as he boards Marine One, March 16, 1977. *White House Staff Photographers. Courtesy, Jimmy Carter Library.*

Hamilton Jordan, Zbigniew Brzezinski, William Quandt, Cyrus Vance, and Jimmy Carter at Camp David, September 17, 1978. *Courtesy, Jimmy Carter Library.*

Anwar el-Sadat, Jimmy Carter, and Menahem Begin meet on the Aspen Cabin Patio at Camp David, September 16, 1978. *Courtesy, Jimmy Carter Library.*

Concerned parents and teachers protest the passage of Proposition 13 in Los Angeles, June 19, 1978. *Bettmann. Courtesy, Corbis.*

Gas shortage, Las Vegas, May 11, 1979. *Bettmann/Corbis. Courtesy, Corbis.*

U.S. Embassy hostages in Iran. Iranian students who occupied the U.S. Embassy in Tehran on November 11, 1979, and took staff members hostage for 444 days gather around a blindfolded American hostage who was brought out to the compound in front of the international media. The profile of a man holding the hostage's hand and carrying a briefcase is suspected by some former American hostages and U.S. government authorities of being Iran's current president, Mahmoud Ahmadinejad. This information has not been officially verified. *Photograph by Kaveh Kazemi. Courtesy, Corbis.*

New Right leaders portrayed on the cover of Richard Viguerie's *Conservative Digest*. Left to right: Phyllis Schlafly, Jerry Falwell, Howard Phillips, Viguerie, Senator Jesse Helms, John T. Dolan, Morton Blackwell, and Paul Weyrich. *Courtesy, Richard Viguerie.*

Four presidents (Ford, Reagan, Carter, and Nixon), Vice President and future President George H. W. Bush, and former First Lady Rosalynn Carter meet in the White House Blue Room prior to leaving for President Anwar el-Sadat's funeral in Egypt. *Courtesy, Ronald Reagan Library.*

President Reagan gives a campaign speech in Austin, Texas, July 26, 1984. *Courtesy, Ronald Reagan Library.*

Kempton, Reagan deserved "to be counted as one of the great candidates in our memory, perhaps the greatest who never got his chance."[80]

Predictably, William Rusher, Richard Viguerie, Howard Phillips, Paul Weyrich, and others decided to throw their support to the American Independent Party. Equally predictably, Reagan declined Rusher's invitation to become its candidate, which guaranteed that the American Conservative Union, Young Americans for Freedom, and *Human Events* would lose interest in the venture. Every other prominent conservative, including John Connally and Jesse Helms, also turned Rusher down. Wallace continued to support Carter. The best candidates Rusher could muster were Richard Morris, president of the University of Dallas, as president, and Viguerie, as vice president. Though Viguerie promised to raise a war chest for Morris and to turn over his mailing lists to the American Independent Party, party members resolved "to choose some standard-bearer closer to their hearts' desire if no bigger name was available."[81]

After the keynote speaker at its September 1976 convention incoherently denounced "atheistical political Zionism," the American Independent Party nominated Carter's enemy, segregationist Lester Maddox, for president. Maddox's running mate, William Dyke, was a Republican unknown. "Against us," Rusher told Joseph Coors in accounting for the defeat of Morris and Viguerie, "were not only the crazies (who unquestionably exist in the AIP, but were *not* in control of this convention), but ultimately also those AIP leaders who had worked with the Committee for the New Majority." So much, it seemed, for the marriage on the right between populists and conservatives.[82]

Surprised and disappointed, Rusher and the New Right bolted once more. "We're conservative," observed one Viguerie associate, "but these people are something else." The New Right's effort to co-opt the AIP and create a new majority party had proved a disaster, as Viguerie acknowledged. The American Conservative Union's political director maintained that Maddox, who received fewer than 175,000 votes in November, was an "unrealistic and ineffective spokesman for the conservative philosophy" and that conservatives lacked a candidate. While *Human Events* editors proclaimed their "Reluctant Vote for Gerald Ford" over "Carter-as-collectivist-liberal," Viguerie announced that some of his colleagues were voting for Carter "because they feel we need a new conservative party and it won't happen until the Republican Party dies." Though Viguerie himself tentatively planned to write in Ronald Reagan's name, he had "no strong recommendation" because conservatives lacked "much stake" in the presidential election.[83]

Oddly, despite conservatives' lukewarm support of Ford, or outright opposition to him, and his humiliation over the platform forced on him by Reagan, the president was gaining. In a pessimistic memorandum, Ford's strategists had warned the president, "If past is indeed prologue, you will lose on November 2—because to win you must do what has never been done: close a gap of about 20 points in 73 days from the base of a minority party while spending approximately the same amount of money as your opponent." Polls showed voters considered Ford a "loser" because he had been unable to dispose of Reagan easily and generally thought him "befuddled" and incompetent.[84]

Nevertheless, a week after the Republican convention, Caddell's ashen-faced assistant reported that Carter was only eight or nine points ahead of Ford.[85] When Carter began campaigning on Labor Day, the gap narrowed further.

DOWNHILL

"Carter's career peaked with the primaries," two writers said. "From the moment his nomination was assured to the last day of his administration, the entire nation seemed to be wondering 'Who is this guy, and how did we get stuck with him?' "[86]

Insofar as it was about anything, the election seemed to be about "leadership" and "trust." Carter's television advertisements characterized him as "a leader, for a change," while Ford's trumpeted his "lifetime of leadership." Carter told voters to "trust me," while Ford spoke of the need to earn trust. But where did that leave the candidates on the issues?[87]

"In 1976," many agreed, issues "were no more important than the price of hoopskirts." The candidates did talk about them, but no one was listening, and Carter tried to be on all sides of them. Consider busing, for example. The Carter campaign tried to seem more liberal than its Republican counterpart. It charged that Ford "failed to do anything about the problems and concerns raised by busing, other than to repeatedly attack the concept of busing." Nevertheless, Carter followed Ford in opposing busing to realize racial balance whenever there was an alternative, and he made sure that the Democratic platform dodged busing altogether. Or consider abortion. Unlike the Republican platform, the

Democratic one opposed a constitutional amendment banning abortion. But Carter also sought out Democrat Joe Califano and asked him, as "a good Catholic," to pass the word to Catholic leaders of his "unyielding opposition to abortion and his determination to stop federal funding of abortions."[88]

To one observer, it was as if prospective voters and candidates alike were engaged in a "flight from thought." That should have helped Carter. He had planned it that way.[89]

In his first week, as during most of the general campaign, however, Carter lurched between disasters. He kept stepping on his lines. So, for example, he went to New York to attack Ford's stinginess during its financial crisis and to demonstrate his concern with urban problems. The Democrat received attention that day, though, because of his casual remark that Ford should fire the FBI director, Clarence Kelley, for ordering the bureau's carpenters to install new window treatments in Kelley's Washington home. At a press conference, a maudlin Ford complained that Carter had heartlessly ignored the fact that Kelley's wife was dying at the time. Carter had his rejoinder ready: Implicitly questioning the depth of Kelley's grief, he told reporters he had heard the director was remarrying. "And with that," one reporter said, "the Kelley affair hit rock bottom."[90]

But the Carter campaign did not. It proceeded to Scranton, Pennsylvania. No one wanted to shake Carter's hand at the plant gate, and the sound system broke down at a panel discussion between the candidate and the unemployed. Reporters who could not hear the event staged for the media also learned that the "unemployed" included a Carter volunteer and several with jobs.[91]

Bad organization and advance work continued to plague Carter. He and his advisers had put all their energy into the primaries and had lost their focus. Worse, he had become the issue. Ford had not changed, and he was well known to the American public. The numbers were moving toward the president because of the loss of support for Carter, which had always been tentative. Carter needed to sell himself to the American people.[92]

Thus the three debates, the first between presidential candidates since 1960, were crucial. The media had given them the buildup reserved for major sports playoffs. At the first, in September, "the atmosphere was electric—a feeling that we were about to witness some momentous historic event."[93]

To reporters' surprise, Carter lost his cool. His hair was too short, and so was he. With his crooked tie, "[h]e looked like Howdy Doody," while Ford towered over him. Carter licked his lips repeatedly, spoke too quickly, and gave disjointed answers. The media gave him "B-" for substance and "F" for delivery.[94]

The same week Carter's press secretary, Jody Powell, received an advance copy of his candidate's *Playboy* interview with journalist Robert Scheer. As soon as Powell read Carter's musings about religions, politics, and sex, he knew "we were going to catch some shit." In his interview, Carter reassured nonbelievers that his religion would not make him a rigid president. Though Christians did their best to live by the laws of Jesus, he stressed that they understood there was forgiveness for those who could not. "Christ set some almost impossible standards for us," Carter admitted. "Christ said, 'I tell you that anyone who looks on a woman with lust has in his heart already committed adultery.' I've committed adultery in my heart many times. . . . God forgives me for it." That did not make him a better person than "someone who not only looks on a woman with lust but leaves his wife and shacks up with somebody," Carter added. "Christ says don't consider yourself better than someone else because one guy screws a whole bunch of women while the other guy is loyal to his wife."

Having said his religion did not make him superior, Carter then contradicted himself. He told Scheer: "I don't think I would *ever* take on the same frame of mind that Nixon or Johnson did, lying, cheating, and distorting the truth. Not taking into consideration my hope for strength of character, I think that my religious beliefs alone would prevent that from happening to me."[95]

"*Playboy* killed us," a Carter staffer said later. The interview showcased Carter's certainty that he had "a straight line to God" and proved anew that he would do anything to win over voters. Why else was he talking with *Playboy* readers about screwing? Some newspapers even refused to quote Carter: The *New York Times* said he used "a common if mild vulgarism for sexual intercourse." At one campaign stop, demonstrators held a sign advising Carter to "Smile if You're Horny," while bumper stickers proclaimed, "In his heart he knows your wife."[96]

Carter's suggestion that Johnson and Nixon were equally evil was also unpopular in Johnson's native Texas, a crucial state. Carter only sharpened doubts about his credibility when he subsequently implied that he had not equated the two presidents and that *Playboy* had done so in a postinterview "summary" of his remarks. In the words of Carter's speechwriter, the man "who promised never to tell a lie had told a whopper"—as journalists made clear. "Everything Jimmy does is examined under a microscope," Powell complained, "while Ford sits there hiding in the White House and gets off scot-free."[97]

REPUBLICANS ACKNOWLEDGED THAT Powell was right. "[W]e would go out in the Rose Garden and say nothing," Dick Cheney later recalled, and network news would feature Ford looking presidential. That beat sending him on the road. "Mr. President," his campaign manager said, "as a campaigner, you're no fucking good!" The assessment stung Ford, but he obligingly remained in Washington. The "Rose Garden strategy" went according to plan through the first debate.[98]

After that, it all began to unravel for the president. In the vice presidential debate, Mondale trumped Dole, who came off as Ford's hatchet man. In a rare campaign swing, Ford referred to Ohio State University as "Iowa State," claimed that he was in Indiana when he was in Illinois, and called a "flyswatter" a "flyspotter." Charges that Ford had once accepted illegal campaign contributions also surfaced. At the same time, *Rolling Stone* reported a comment by Secretary of Agriculture Earl Butz. Asked why African Americans showed so little interest in the GOP, Butz announced that "coloreds only want three things . . . first, a tight pussy; second, loose shoes; and third, a warm place to shit." The Ford campaign clung to the hope that Butz's attempt at humor might not receive publicity because "the language in the Butz quote was so vile that we doubted the newspapers and networks could use it." It was wrong, and Ford waited too long before firing Butz.[99]

These troubles paled next to Ford's misstatement in the second debate. First, Carter said that "[w]e've got a chance tonight to talk about, first of all, leadership, the character of our country, and a vision of the future. In every one of these instances, the Ford administration has failed." Then he charged, "As far as foreign policy goes, Mr. Kissinger has been the president of this country." (In another echo of Reagan, Carter promised that "I would never give up complete control or practical control of the Panama Canal Zone.") Then, when an interlocutor asked whether "we virtually signed, in Helsinki, an agreement that the Russians have dominance in Eastern Europe," Ford meant to answer that the United States recognized, but would never condone, Soviet domination. He said instead that "there is no Soviet domination of Eastern Europe, and there never will be under the Ford Administration." Carter replied that he "would like to see Mr. Ford convince the Polish-Americans and the Czech-Americans and the Hungarian-Americans that those countries don't live under the domination and supervision of the Soviet Union behind the Iron Curtain." Ford's response in the debate, historian Leo Ribuffo observed, "stands out as one of the great presidential gaffes of the past century."[100]

The media was responsible for that. Ford's performance in the second debate had initially pleased his chief of staff. "I was aware that his response to the question on the Soviet role in Eastern Europe had not been accurate, but I also knew what he meant and hoped that the public would also," Dick Cheney recalled. When Robert Teeter polled voters afterwards, 54 percent intended to vote for Ford, as compared with 36 percent for Carter. But when Ford's advisers met with reporters, the first question they received was sarcastic: "Are there Soviet troops in Poland?" A day later, when Teeter sampled voter response, the numbers were reversed. Clearly, "the general public did *not* know that Ford had made an error until they were told it was an error by the news media."[101]

Yet Ford delayed five days before admitting to outraged Americans of Eastern European descent that he had misspoken. In the meantime, reporters and Democrats alike renewed doubts about his competence. "It was the 'dumb' issue all over again," an aide said. By the anticlimactic third debate, Ford seemed so pathetic to the media that as the president took notes, one reporter loudly whispered: "He's not writing, he's coloring!" Still, the presidential race was tightening.[102]

FOR CARTER DID NOT seem to know what to say, and he kept changing the way he said it. The candidate of love and compassion now stridently attacked the president. Like Ford, Carter was a moderate. But when he talked foreign policy, Carter sounded like Reagan. He was courting neoconservatives in the Jackson wing. When he talked domestic policy, Carter was suddenly using the language of Franklin Delano Roosevelt. In an attempt to appeal to liberals and traditional Democrats, his media adviser, Gerald Rafshoon, complained later, "you tried to out-Humphrey Humphrey," extolled FDR, "and you looked silly." Carter had also fallen into a habit associated with Roosevelt: He was promising too many groups too much. When his aides compiled his campaign pledges, the document was 111 pages long. As he changed course and floundered, Carter seemed a riskier choice.[103]

Encouraged by Carter's missteps, Ford took to the hustings for what Dick Cheney called "a ten day orgasm." Certainly Ford seemed to be having a good time. His campaign had reserved millions for a last-minute advertising blitz, and Ford enlisted radio personality and former Major League Baseball catcher Joe Garagiola, to throw him softball questions that the president answered masterfully. The "Joe and Jerry Shows" were broadcast in key states.[104]

The Ford campaign also unveiled a campaign song. Americans wanted "to 'feel good' about things," Carter's pollster said. "The Ford people caught on later than we did." In fact, the Ford people had seen that early but feared emphasizing the issue. They knew their campaign slogan, "He's making us proud again," was "a gamble" and had "secret visions of people hooting and laughing all over America." When Americans accepted it, the campaign gambled further, with a song, "Feelin' Good:"

> There's a change that's come over America
> A change that's great to see
> We're livin' here in peace again, we're goin' back to work again
> It's better than it used to be
>
> I'm feelin' good about America
> And I feel it everywhere I go
> I'm feelin' good about America
> And I feel you ought to know
> That I'm feelin' good about America
> It's something great to see
> I'm feelin' good about America
> I'm feelin' good about me[105]

Ford had reason to feel good. In the presidential campaign's last forty-eight hours, Gallup declared the race virtually tied. Harris gave the president a one-point lead.[106]

ELECTION

But when Americans went to the polls on November 2, voters elected Carter. Not that many of them went. Of those eligible to vote, only 53.6 percent did, the lowest turnout in a national election since 1948. They gave Carter 40.8 million popular votes, a scant 2 percent more than Ford. Carter received the smallest edge in the electoral college since Woodrow Wilson's reelection in 1916: He took 297 electors to Ford's 241. Ford carried Iowa and every state west of it except Texas. He won Illinois, Indiana, Virginia, Maryland, New Jersey, and all of New England save Massachusetts. Ford carried four more states, but his opponent won larger ones. (Though Eugene McCarthy won none, the 1976 race left the Carter camp with a deep fear of third party challengers. According to its calculations, but for McCarthy's run, Carter would have carried Iowa, Maine, Oregon, and Oklahoma.) African Americans went for Carter, as did Jews and neoconservatives. The AFL-CIO also saved Carter: Asked about his role in the new administration soon after the election, a grinning George Meany said he expected to become its "[e]lder statesman." Rural voters and many Christians helped. The South came home. Carter won almost the entire Confederacy. For the moment the Democrats retained a hold on George Wallace's followers. The Americans for Democratic Action swung behind Carter, though many liberals did not warm up to him. The old New Deal Democratic coalition remained largely intact.[107]

The meaning of the vote was unclear. When Ford died in 2007, Vice President Cheney and others who paid tribute to him described the pardon as a major factor in his defeat, as he himself had recently done. In the 1990s, however, Ford attributed his loss to Reagan. Ford stressed the drain of the primary challenge and Reagan's failure to work for him more wholeheartedly. (The charge that Reagan had not vigorously supported Ford circulated frequently in GOP circles during the late 1970s, and Reagan, whose form letter on the subject stressed that he had campaigned for the president in half the nation's states and helped deliver California, always bridled at it.) And during the campaign the president's pollster made a puzzling finding: Ford was "to the left of the voters on every issue except one." But what did that mean, exactly?[108]

In 1976, Republicans were even more pessimistic about their future than they had been in 1974. Despite a general election campaign that his own advisers thought miserable, Carter won. Republicans lost another seat in the House. There was a 62–38 Democratic majority in the Senate. The campaign had left Reagan and Ford with a deep animosity for each other. The GOP was more divided than ever: Neither Ford's nor Reagan's candidates to chair the Republican National Committee could muster enough support to win election. The only bright spot for conservative Republicans was the election of Senator Orrin Hatch of Utah. The GOP seemed to be making no headway in the South, where Nixon had staked its future when he sought to make the Republicans the new majority party by developing the "Southern strategy" to capture Wallace voters: A mere 30 percent of southern conservatives in 1976 were Republicans, and only three Republican senators from the South in recent memory—John Tower of Texas, Strom Thurmond of South Carolina, and Howard Baker of Tennessee—had won more than one term. William Rusher dismissed the Republicans as "the party of business." By 1978, he observed, they would "have held simultaneous control of Congress and the White House for exactly two of the past 46 years," which hardly qualified them as "a genuine opposition." Indeed the GOP seemed on the verge of "extinction." Though Reagan said on election day that "he wouldn't rule out and wouldn't rule in" another run, he would be sixty-nine in 1980, and Ford was dead set against him. But the first half of the Carter presidency became a crucial turning point, and by the end of 1978 Republicans and conservatives had experienced a reversal of fortune.[109]

VII

FROM BUSING TO *BAKKE*

—

WAS THERE EVER A LIBERAL CONSENSUS ON CIVIL RIGHTS? PERhaps not. Still, it was even harder to tell what liberals thought about racial equality in the 1970s than it had been in the 1960s. Civil rights policy divided liberals, Democrats, and the Supreme Court and possessed the potential to make or break Carter's presidency and party. As the *New York Times* editorialized soon after the election, "If President-elect Carter can turn his personal triumph in the South into a viable biracial coalition, the Republican Southern strategy will stay wrecked for a long time to come."[1]

STRANGE BEDFELLOWS

"As a white Southerner, the Governor is probably more able to do something about harmony between the races than any recent President," Patrick Caddell said before Carter's inauguration. Yet while the Democrats could hold on to voters of color "as long as the party fulfills the easy task of being more sensitive to their concerns than the Republicans," Caddell, who continued polling for Carter throughout his presidency, brooded about whites "at odds" with minorities. How could the new president keep both groups aboard?[2]

Carter used symbols. He astonished many, for example, by naming Griffin Bell attorney general. In some ways, the appointment was not surprising. Charles Kirbo, who filled the role of the new president's "gray eminence" and who would accept no administration position himself, wanted the job to go to Bell, his law partner, and Bell was one of a number of Georgia campaign veterans rewarded. The new president refused to appoint a chief of staff, but he tapped Hamilton Jordan, who had bested another of Kirbo's law partners in a transition power struggle, to function as first among equals in the White House and to develop political strategy. Predictably, Jody Powell became press secretary; Bert Lance, Office of Management and Budget director; attorney Stuart Eizenstat, executive director of the Domestic Policy Staff, which was to coordinate White House strategy on domestic issues. But the appointment of Bell was controversial because running for office in the shadow of Watergate, Carter had promised to depoliticize Justice. Moreover, as a federal judge Bell had not moved with dispatch to integrate the schools, and he also belonged to clubs restricted to white men. "You're a Southern gentleman—just what we need," Carter told Bell. Carter also sent civil rights activists a reassuring signal and made Drew Days, a former attorney for the NAACP Legal Defense Fund, the first African American to head the Justice Department's Civil Rights Division.[3]

All the while, the Supreme Court's busing jurisprudence seemed increasingly incoherent. In 1976 the Court ruled that busing to achieve desegregation in Pasadena, California, need not produce racially balanced schools "in perpetuity." If "the quite normal pattern of human migration" resulted in resegregation, so be it. In 1977, Days recalled, the Court appeared to turn its earlier decision requiring busing in Denver "on its head" when it hinted that if the Dayton, Ohio, School Board had engaged in "isolated" instances of illegal segregation or "minor indiscretions," it need not fear city-wide busing. With evident relief Bell informed Carter: "The recent decisions of the Supreme Court should reduce the chances that excessive busing will be required by the Federal Courts." As it turned out, though, the Court reaffirmed its earlier busing decisions and ordered desegregation of the Dayton and Columbus school systems in two murky 1979 squeakers that nonetheless had the effect of constraining the use of the busing remedy. The opinions revealed ominous fault lines: Writing in dissent, Nixon appointee William Rehnquist likened the majority to Pontius Pilate. Affirmative action brought whites, rather than minorities, to the Court for relief and raised new questions about its solicitude for civil rights.[4]

THE CONSTITUTION ITSELF enshrined affirmative action. It provided special privileges for white elites and permitted black slavery. After the Civil War, Union army veterans received pensions, and the Freedmen's

Bureau and Civil Rights Acts provided former slaves with assistance. Generally, "federal help often gave the freedman 'preferential treatment' in an attempt to make up for over two centuries of slavery; yet that aid was of short duration and was not particularly successful." As World War II approached, civil rights activists pressured Roosevelt into creating the Fair Employment Practices Committee to prevent discrimination in government hiring and the defense industries. It became another failure.[5]

Never having actually moved too close toward African Americans, the pendulum swung back toward whites when Congress enacted the 1944 Selective Service Readjustment Act. The GI Bill provided nearly one hundred billion dollars of federal funds to educate, house, and otherwise subsidize veterans by 1971, and so much of the money was directed toward white male beneficiaries that veterans of color complained the legislation was "'For White Veterans Only.'" This was the period, one historian said later, "when affirmative action was white." But the GI Bill did not refer to "affirmative action." That phrase first appeared when Kennedy issued Executive Order 10925 in 1961 and directed that federal contractors "take affirmative action to ensure that applicants are employed, and that employees are treated during employment, without regard to their race, creed, color, or national origin." The order was weak. White male veterans still had the better deal.[6]

Minorities received a boost with the passage of the Civil Rights Act of 1964. Title VI barred discrimination on the basis of race, color, religion, or national origin in educational institutions and other programs that received federal funds, grants, and contracts. Title VII, which was extended to educational institutions in 1972, prohibited discrimination in employment on the basis of race, color, religion, national origin, or sex. Despite their repeated assurances that the legislation promoted color blindness, civil rights activists and white liberals who worked for it understood that color blindness would not ensure equal opportunity. As Lyndon Johnson famously said, "Freedom is not enough. . . . You do not take a person who, for years, has been hobbled by chains and liberate him, bring him up to the starting line of a race and then say, 'you are free to compete with all the others,' and still justly believe that you have been completely fair."[7]

As the limitations of color blindness became clearer, and inner cities in the United States erupted during the middle and late 1960s, the federal agencies that administered the Civil Rights Act replaced the ideal of color blindness with one of color consciousness. Enforcement remained problematic until the early 1970s, when the Supreme Court and Congress began to give teeth to the Civil Rights Act. The Nixon administration took giant strides to promote affirmative action in the workplace in part because the president perceived it as a beautiful wedge issue for dividing the white ethnic workers and African Americans at the heart of the Democratic Party. But even the Nixon administration reportedly feared that affirmative action in higher education was a "hot potato."[8]

It was. The affirmative action plans adopted by colleges and universities, beginning in the 1960s, to increase the presence of minorities and women as students and professors had arisen principally because of the demands of activist students and, to a lesser extent, because of white guilt. In the early 1970s the Department of Health, Education, and Welfare added its voice to those urging colleges and universities to hire and enroll more women and minorities. As affirmative action programs multiplied amid reminders that continued federal funding might be at stake, white males now began to see themselves as the victims of discrimination.[9]

One of the most disgruntled was Yale Law School's Alexander Bickel. Like many other Jewish neoconservatives, Bickel had once considered himself a strong liberal. In the aftermath of Nixon's resignation, Bickel observed that the Watergate conspirators, the Warren Court, and left-wing students of the 1960s had equated law with morality. For Bickel, the moral was that "the highest morality almost always is the morality of process." Law must be divorced from politics, advocacy from ideology, and ends subordinated to means.[10]

Yet at the time Bickel wrote about the morality of process in *Commentary*, he had just put the finishing touches on his brief for the leading organization fighting anti-Semitism in the first case involving affirmative action and higher education to reach the Supreme Court. Rarely has a legal document mixed ideology, politics, and morality more than Bickel's 1973 brief for the Anti-Defamation League in *DeFunis v. Odegaard* on behalf of Marco DeFunis, a Jew rejected from the University of Washington Law School. Bickel charged that the school's minority admissions program favored the "less qualified" over DeFunis because of their race. "To reject an applicant who meets established, realistic and unchanged qualifications in favor of a less qualified candidate is morally wrong, . . . practically disastrous," and bore a suspicious resemblance to the quotas once used by Harvard and elite institutions to restrict Jewish admittees, Bickel wrote. Only "merit" must determine admissions.[11]

He had an unexpected ally. When the Supreme Court declined to decide the constitutionality of special admissions programs in 1974, Justice William O. Douglas set out his own attitudes toward affirmative action. "There is no constitutional right for any race to be preferred," Douglas said. Every applicant "had a constitutional right to have his application considered on its individual merits in a *racially neutral* manner." In the past, that focus on individual rights had led Douglas toward the liberal judicial activism of the Warren Court that Bickel scorned as result oriented. Now, in *DeFunis*, it brought Douglas into an alliance with Bickel, the protégé of Douglas's great rival Justice Felix Frankfurter.[12]

Racial preferences in higher education made for the proverbial strange bedfellows and made politicians nervous. The Nixon administration did not take a stand in *DeFunis*. The Carter administration could not dodge the issue.[13]

ALLAN BAKKE WAS THE blond, blue-eyed son of a mailman and schoolteacher, with a 3.51 undergraduate grade point average from the University of Minnesota. After his marine tour of duty, he received his M.A. in engineering from Stanford and joined NASA. While researching the impact of flight on the body, Bakke became convinced he must study medicine. Yet despite his good Medical College Admission Test score, the dozen schools to which he applied turned him down. The most likely reason was that they considered him, at thirty-three, too old to become a doctor.[14]

But to Bakke, the reason for his rejection was more sinister. He felt particularly victimized by UC Davis Medical School, which twice refused to admit him, in 1973 and 1974. Davis, he was told, possessed an affirmative action program that saved sixteen of one hundred places in its entering class for "disadvantaged" applicants in order to integrate the medical school and profession, counter the effects of societal discrimination, increase the number of physicians in disadvantaged communities, and achieve a diverse student body. Though it had accepted African Americans, Mexican Americans, and Asian Americans, Davis had never included Caucasians in its group of "disadvantaged" admittees. Bakke learned this information about the program from an assistant dean, who also confided that Bakke's grades and scores were higher than those accepted through the special admissions program, which, the administrator suggested, might possess "the overtones of a quota." After the dean explained *DeFunis*, he gave Bakke the names of two legal experts on affirmative action. Bakke decided to file a lawsuit alleging that Davis's special admissions program unconstitutionally made race a factor in medical school admissions.[15]

To defenders of affirmative action, his was a nightmare test case. Then, as now, affirmative action took many forms, ranging from outreach to mentoring and coaching; to treating race and/or sex as positive factors in selection and using goals and timetables to gauge progress; to set-asides, or "quotas" that might be filled by one admissions committee, evaluating all candidates together and in relation to each other, or by two separate admissions committees, one concentrating on affirmative action candidates and one on others. *Bakke* seemed to involve affirmative action in its most rigid and least popular form.[16]

Further, although the regents of the University of California said that they wanted the constitutionality of affirmative action upheld, the university's mistakes, omissions, and sloppy presentation of the case suggested otherwise. When the case reached the California Supreme Court, UC relegated to a footnote the information that every medical school had rejected Bakke. The worst evidence against UC was that Davis had never admitted white applicants under the special admissions plan, though more than two hundred had labeled themselves "disadvantaged." Nowhere did the university show that the special admissions committee had interviewed a number of them and determined that they did not meet its criteria. UC also neglected to say that the dean of its medical school had his own special admissions program: In the mid-1970s he routinely set aside an average of four slots annually for the well connected. Nor did the university explore whether the MCAT was culturally biased against minorities, though judges had said in other lawsuits that such evidence might justify affirmative action programs. So too, UC conceded that Bakke had received higher MCAT scores than those accepted under its affirmative action program without mentioning that Davis Medical School had admitted thirty-six white applicants with worse grades than Bakke's.[17]

In short, UC hardly tried to prove its claim that Bakke would not have been admitted even if Davis had no special admissions program. The accusation by one civil rights lawyer that the university colluded with Bakke to seek a holding that affirmative action was unconstitutional may have been unfair. But the university made the case for the Davis program so poorly that it was just as unfair for a regent to dismiss the charge as "paranoid rantings and ravings."[18]

In a startling September 1976 opinion, the California Supreme Court, one of the most progressive state supreme courts, ruled against the university and for Bakke. The majority ordered Bakke's admission to Davis, declared that Davis's special admissions program violated the Fourteenth Amendment rights of "better qualified" white applicants to equal protection of the laws, and banned the use of race in admissions. The majority opinion was written by Justice Stanley Mosk, one of the court's two most liberal members.

Mosk's opinion denied that the majority was resorting to reliance on the "objective" criteria of test scores and grades. It emphasized that the court instead promoted class-based affirmative action: "[T]he standards for admission employed by the University are not constitutionally infirm except to the extent that they are utilized in a racially discriminatory manner. Disadvantaged applicants of all races must be eligible for sympathetic consideration." The California Supreme Court would uphold race-based affirmative action only if the institution offered proof that the program was needed to compensate for its own prior wrongs. Mosk conceded that the university had no interest in pointing out its own past discrimination. Nonetheless, the court adopted a "sin-based paradigm" and approved race-based affirmative action only as "penance" for specific past acts of racism.[19]

The lone dissent in *Bakke* was delivered by the court's most liberal member, Matthew Tobriner. It defended the constitutionality of "benign" racial "discrimination" as a necessary remedy to correct "[t]wo centuries of slavery and racial discrimination [which] have left our nation . . . a largely separated society" and "all of society's benefits" in the hands "of the white-Anglo majority." Tobriner insisted that making class a proxy for race was disingenuous and would not take the medical school where it wanted to go, since Davis sought "a racially and ethnically integrated, rather than an economically diverse student body." According to Tobriner, the search for a "racially neutral criterion" represented a "retreat into obfuscating terminology."[20]

Mosk had ordered the case returned to superior court to determine whether Davis would have accepted Bakke in the absence of an affirmative action program. But in an effort to gain quick review of the California Supreme Court opinion by the United States Supreme Court, the university abandoned its earlier claim that Bakke did not meet its admissions standards and stipulated that he was a "highly qualified applicant." The California Supreme Court directed Davis to admit Bakke but agreed to delay enforcement of its decision if the U.S. Supreme Court heard the case. UC regents decided to appeal. The U.S. Supreme Court took the case soon after Carter's inauguration.[21]

IN THE COURT OF PUBLIC OPINION

The extent of public interest in *Bakke* was unprecedented. The UC regents resolved to appeal over the protests of most civil rights activists, who contended that the record in *Bakke* contained too many omissions and errors to make the case a good vehicle for testing the constitutionality of affirmative action in higher education. After the U.S. Supreme Court accepted the regents' appeal, the National Conference of Black Lawyers continued to argue that the case should be returned to the lower courts to flesh out the record. Most minority groups, however, concentrated on mounting the best possible defense of affirmative action in higher education. They filed briefs on the side of UC, as did many universities and professional associations. White ethnics, business interests, neoconservatives, and conservatives, however, lined up behind Bakke. In all, a record fifty-eight friend of the court briefs were filed with the United States Supreme Court.[22]

Since the U.S. Supreme Court had never dealt directly with the constitutionality of affirmative action programs in higher education, the *New York Times* correctly observed that the Court could legitimately strike them down or uphold them. One could argue that the Constitution envisioned racial justice that was either "color-blind" and prohibited affirmative action, or "color-conscious," to remedy the legacy of a discriminatory past. There were a number of relevant legal precedents, none precisely on point, that could be invoked. Despite the weak record, numerous intellectually respectable constitutional arguments supported each side. The stakes were high, because affirmance of Mosk's opinion might mean every affirmative action program in higher education became unlawful. Yet the law was so indeterminate it almost seemed irrelevant.[23]

THE POLITICAL, SOCIAL, and economic climate had changed since affirmative action programs sprouted in the late 1960s and early 1970s. In part because of affirmative action, by 1976, 14 percent of those entering University of California medical schools were African American or Latino. Yet while African Americans and Latinos constituted almost a quarter of California's population, they constituted just 3 percent of its doctors. Nonetheless, minority advances made white men edgy.

Many white men were already anxious. One reason rednecks may have become chic was that straight white men were on the defensive. Where the rock music of the sixties had placed them at its center, for example, the disco forever associated with the seventies was gay, black, and female. Even after John Travolta moved disco to the mainstream in *Saturday Night Fever*, the music still made white men uneasy. "Now is the summer of our discotheques," a journalist observed in 1977. The white man who called himself Son of Sam cut it short: After he shot a woman and man as they left a disco in Queens, New York, discos emptied. (One popular theory was that Son of Sam had taken his name in homage to rock legend Jimi Hendrix, whose "Purple Haze" included the words, "Help me, help me, son of Sam, son of Sam.") But after the killer was caught in August, disco business boomed anew, to the disgust of rock aficionados. Some suburban white male teens became victims of a "discophobia" that was "as much racist and homophobic as it was musical," had them screaming, "DISCO SUCKS," and, later, storming Comiskey Park in Chicago to burn thousands of disco records. Were straight white men to be condemned to learn the hustle and be denied places in colleges and professional schools?[24]

Far more white women than men and women of color were following the example of Joanie Caucus in the *Doonesbury* comic strip and entering professional school. (Like Bakke, Caucus was much older than the average applicant and was rejected repeatedly before UC Berkeley's law school admitted her.) Of the students in medical schools, 5.7 percent were women in 1969; 22.5 percent, in 1977. But some white men seemed to blame the increasing competition on minorities more than on their female counterparts. To the *Atlantic Monthly*, whose cover on *Bakke* depicted a white hand wrestling a black one for a diploma, the case raised one supremely important question: "[W]ho gets ahead in America? Should we reduce opportunity for some whites, in some ways, in order to enhance opportunity for some blacks and other victims of long-standing discrimination?"[25]

Neoconservatives thought not. They were disillusioned. One defined a neoconservative as "a liberal who has been mugged by reality." They pointed to July 13, 1977, when lightning struck Westchester County power lines at 8:37 P.M. and left New York City in the grip of its first blackout since 1965. The earlier blackout had almost been fun. In many of the more affluent parts of New York, the 1977 blackout was too: High atop the World Trade Center, at its Windows on the World restaurant, and at Shea Stadium, where the Mets and Chicago Cubs were in the sixth inning, with the Cubs actually leading, there were sing-alongs. But in the mean streets of Harlem, the South Bronx, Queens, and Brooklyn, there were looting, vandalism, arson, and more than three thousand arrests in one long night of violence and terror. Neighborhoods into which African Americans and Hispanics were crowded were hit hardest by the carnage; African Americans and Hispanics also constituted a disproportionate percentage of the miscreants. In a *Commentary* article, "Looting and Liberal Racism," one neocon blamed the outbreak of lawlessness on white liberals. For the past decade, she maintained, they had sent African Americans the message that "they are inherently and by virtue of their race, inferior, . . . and that they are not fully enough human to be held morally responsible for their own behavior. They are children, as the Southerners used to say." White liberals had spread the "racist idea that being black is a condition for a special moral allowance."[26]

The question of who should get ahead came at a difficult moment in American history. Economic growth, rather than redistribution of wealth and income, had funded domestic reform and reduced class conflict since World War II. In the 1960s an expanding economy had helped increase support for the civil rights movement and the "minority rights revolution" that stopped short of protecting white ethnics and gays. By the mid-1970s economic growth seemed but a memory. At the same time, more baby boomers were finishing college, and thanks to stagflation, universities lacked the funds to expand to meet the growing demand for graduate training. Both trends caused professional schools to become more selective: In 1973, Davis Medical School received 2,464 applications for each of its 100 seats; in 1974, 3,737. The explosion of interest in professional education amid an atmosphere of scarcity helped make affirmative action unpopular in some circles by 1977.[27]

By this time at least four arguments were commonly heard against

Davis-type special admissions programs at the undergraduate and graduate levels. First, according to a *New Republic* symposium on *Bakke* entitled "Meritocracy and Its Discontents," affirmative action programs threatened the ideal of the United States as a meritocracy prevalent since the New Deal. Meritocracy supposedly ensured that the best academic credentials, not political connections or social status, determined advancement. Second, affirmative action programs favored groups at the expense of individual rights by penalizing persons, such as Bakke, and groups, such as Polish Americans, who might never have engaged in discriminatory behavior and might even have suffered discrimination themselves. Polish Americans maintained that the ethnic slur "Polack" was as bad as any racial epithet and that if minorities deserved protection, so did they and other white ethnics, who once had not even been considered white. Opponents of affirmative action stressed the difficulty of defining group membership and warned that "the logical next step" would be "race certification" and "balkanization." Third, affirmative action programs institutionalized preferential treatment and reflected "reverse discrimination" against whites, rather than help for the economically disadvantaged. And fourth, the programs stigmatized minorities by suggesting they could not succeed on merit.[28]

Of course, the supporters of affirmative action had their own counterarguments. They dismissed as patronizing the suggestion that affirmative action stigmatized its recipients: A 1978 Harris Poll revealed that 68 percent of whites and 91 percent of African Americans favored "affirmative action in higher education for blacks provided there are no rigid quotas." Defenders maintained that special admissions programs represented necessary, temporary attempts to redress past discrimination and increase the infinitesimal number of minorities in higher education and the professions. Class-based affirmative action would not suffice because of the disparities between minority and white test scores. A racial problem required a racial solution. Bakke and other white individuals might suffer when minorities were preferred as a group, but minorities had been disadvantaged because of their color as a group. Moreover, it was unclear that the United States had ever been a meritocracy; college applicants with high grades and test scores had often lost out to athletes and to children of alumni and the wealthy. Nor was it apparent that standardized tests evaluated merit fairly. Who was to say that a white who could identify the meaning of "audacious" was more intelligent than an African American who knew the meaning of "handkerchief head"?[29]

Almost as an afterthought, some affirmative action supporters mentioned that it would create a more diverse university that would benefit all students. Whites and minorities could learn from each other. So long as race remained the crucial fault line in American society, it did not much matter whether minorities came from middle-class or rich families or from inner cities. Soon after the United States Supreme Court agreed to hear *Bakke*, photographer Stanley Forman won a Pulitzer Prize for his bicentennial-year photograph *The Soiling of Old Glory*, which shows a white high school student at a Boston City Hall antibusing rally using the American flag as a spear against an African American in a three-piece suit on his way to an affirmative action meeting. The victim, Ted Landsmark, had grown up in public housing in Harlem, attended St. Paul's on a scholarship, been one of the first African Americans to graduate from that elite prep school, and received degrees from Yale College and Yale Law School. "I couldn't put my Yale degree in front of me to protect myself," he said. "I was just a nigger they were trying to kill."[30]

But just 22 percent of whites and 47 percent of African Americans favored quotas in higher education. And one did not need a pollster to see that most white Americans were on Bakke's side. When the *New York Times* editorialized that "the national interest would be best served if Mr. Bakke lost," correspondents disagreed by "a ratio of about 15 to 1."[31]

THE IMPLOSION OF LIBERALISM

As the U.S. Supreme Court prepared to hear *Bakke* in 1977, the cracks within the liberal alliance struck some as more significant than the arguments for or against affirmative action. The split between Justices Mosk and Tobriner, the most liberal members of the California Supreme Court and its only two Jewish ones, crystallized and reflected the fragmentation of liberalism as well as divisions in the Jewish community. Once Jews, African Americans, and workers had viewed one another as fellow outsiders and had worked together for equality and social justice. Their alliance had hit rocky spots before, but disagreements over affirmative action threatened to destroy it.[32]

Jewish neoconservatives were the strongest opponents of affirmative action. Bickel and other Jewish neoconservative intellectuals, some of whom also became active in the antidétente coalition, had formed the Committee on Academic Nondiscrimination and Integrity in 1972. The antiaffirmative chorus also grew to include the New Right and traditional conservatives. The American Conservative Union presented Bakke with its Conservative of the Year Award at its 1978 convention. But Jewish neocons led the charge against affirmative action and provided vital support for conservatism in the process by linking it to a rhetoric of color blindness and antidiscrimination.[33]

Jews had split over *DeFunis*. While Bickel had filed the lead brief supporting DeFunis for the Anti-Defamation League, the National Organization of Jewish Women had joined with the Commission on Social Action of the Union of American Hebrew Congregations, to file a brief against DeFunis and on behalf of affirmative action. But a number of Commission on Social Action members believed that *Bakke* involved a quota and declined to support Davis. Anxious, one recalled, because the Anti-Defamation League was siding with Bakke, some nevertheless argued for filing a friend of the court brief in support of the University of California "because they felt that for the sake of community relations, there needed to be a Jewish balance to the ADL's visible role as the leading opponent of affirmative action." They did not prevail. Thus the Jewish groups filing briefs sided with Bakke and against the University of California, which created the impression that all Jews had turned against affirmative action.[34]

In an article entitled "The War Inside the Jews: A Painful Breakdown of the Liberal Consensus," Brandeis political scientist Leonard Fein suggested two reasons for the apparent collapse of the "once proud and productive alliance between Jews and blacks." Jews were threatened by the possibility that affirmative action would shade into quotas. They constituted only 2.7 percent of the American population and were "extravagantly overrepresented in certain sectors of the economy." Would "the logic of numbers" mandate that they could have only "2.7% of the places in any sector of the society"? Fein insisted, though, that affirmative action also threatened "fundamental perceptions of equity." Because the American Jewish story was one of "a society forced by law and sometimes by enlightenment to ignore Jewishness," Jews had developed "a special affinity for the merit system." Fein asked: "How then, shall Jews be expected to feel now that they may be forced to say, 'my son, the doctor'—except that there were one hundred places in the medical school, and he was 85th?" Perhaps Jews would feel differently if affirmative action plans affected only "bricklayers and plumbers." But *Bakke* involved the professions, and "the combination of an assault on merit and a battleground for that assault that is so dear to Jews, challenges both Jewish principles and the Jewish self."[35]

Many bricklayers and plumbers felt no more enthusiastic about affirmative action. Unions split over *Bakke*. The United Auto Workers filed a brief on the side of the University of California, as did the United Mine Workers, the Electrical Workers, the American Federation of State, County and Municipal Employees, and the United Farm Workers. Predictably, the American Federation of Teachers, which had been responsible for persuading the AFL-CIO to file a brief opposing minority preference programs in *DeFunis*, sided with Bakke. But the AFL-CIO did nothing.

George Meany may have stayed silent to avoid straining the tense relationship between minorities and labor to the breaking point. By the time *Bakke* reached the Supreme Court, unions had seen Title VII of the Civil Rights Act, with its ban against employment discrimination, interpreted to upset sacred principles, such as seniority and "last hired, first fired," and one lawyer thought that unions had lost their zeal for equality when it became apparent civil rights applied to them. Trade unionists had a clearer notion of their rights because they were used to bargaining for them and "a more concrete reaction" against "the notion of special treatment than most people." That was probably true: According to one study, minority unionists during the 1970s supported seniority "even if it meant curtailing affirmative action." Still, and despite Meany's studied neutrality, obviously a large number of rank-and-file workers, many of them white ethnics, and the AFL-CIO hierarchy supported Bakke.[36]

For Carter, the first elected president from the Deep South since Zachary Taylor and the first Democratic president since Lyndon Johnson, the questions *Bakke* raised proved especially unsettling. Candidate Carter had routinely tried to make the issue of racial preferences go away by saying that he supported affirmative action but opposed quotas. Since 82 percent of the African American vote in 1976 had gone to him, President Carter had deep obligations to African Americans, which civil rights groups early on decided that he was ignoring. They saw his talk of a "balanced budget" as "'anti-black, anti-poor, anti-city.'" Carter might appease minorities by supporting the University of California and its affirmative action program. But the president had already disappointed Meany on the minimum wage, and, Hamilton Jordan stressed, Jews had "extraordinary voting habits." Though they constituted less than 3 percent of the population, Jews in 1976 had "cast almost 5% of the total vote," of which Carter had received about 75 percent.[37]

THE POLITICS OF JUSTICE

Some hints of the administration's affirmative action position appeared when Griffin Bell rebutted contentions of racism during his confirmation hearing. Senator Strom Thurmond applauded Bell as someone who favored "justice for all," an endorsement that made Bell more suspect. Another conservative senator, William Scott of Virginia, tried a different approach. "Have you reached any decision as to whom you may recommend for Solicitor General of the United States?" When Bell replied only that he had chosen a federal judge to argue the government's cases before the Supreme Court, an exasperated Scott asked: "Well, can you tell us what color he is?" Bell then announced he had chosen Wade McCree, an African American judge, as solicitor general. To Senator Scott, the fact that "you have already selected one of your chief assistants who happens to be a black man" meant Bell could not be a racist. Bell volunteered that he planned to hire African Americans, women, and Mexican Americans, and "I am searching for an Indian." And, he added, there would be no double standard: "The people I have will be excellent people. I think it denigrates groups to say that you have to lower the standards."[38]

Bell's caginess about *Bakke* made Carter's Domestic Policy Staff (DPS) nervous. "We have had problems in getting information from the Justice Department," one attorney complained to DPS executive director Eizenstat. "Bell is very skiddish [*sic*] about White House 'interference at Justice' " and had directed its litigators "not to talk to us because it might appear to others that the White House is trying to influence litigation. Bell's words are reported to be: 'Shucks, those folks should come to me.' " But DPS attorneys were unable to get to Bell to discuss *Bakke*. Since "the legal issue is somewhat fuzzy," and the law enabled the government to defend or oppose affirmative action, "this is really a serious and volatile policy decision which I think that we and even the President should be involved in."[39]

From the Justice Department's Civil Rights Division, Assistant Attorney General Drew Days urged Justice to file a brief supporting affirmative action. That did not mean it would do so. By Justice Department tradition, Solicitor General McCree was independent. Obligated to represent the United States before the U.S. Supreme Court, the solicitor general was also required to help the Court reach the right result. When Days's recommendation was forwarded to McCree's office, its fate suggested "the illusion of presidential government" and the challenge facing any chief executive who tried to reshape the federal bureaucracy in his own image. It landed on the desk of Frank Easterbrook, a conservative lawyer who had worked in the solicitor general's office since the Nixon administration. Easterbrook apparently was the first in the Carter administration to say the government's brief should support Bakke and oppose UC.[40]

As a result, the draft brief prepared by the Justice Department declared that "racial classifications favorable to minority groups are presumptively unconstitutional" and that the University of California's special admissions program used a quota in violation of the equal protection clause of the Fourteenth Amendment. The brief backed Bakke's admission to Davis and stressed the need to inspect the considerations underlying "race-conscious decisionmaking . . . in a dispassionate way." Then it contended that affirmative action programs demeaned minorities, expressed doubt that "it is advantageous for white students to attend school with a more diverse group of fellow students," and maintained that only minorities and white "altruists" supported affirmative action programs. But just as it appeared that the draft brief was about to recommend the invalidation of all affirmative action programs, it supported some. It proposed that "color-conscious admissions program[s]" be limited "to black applicants, who have been subjected to unparalleled discrimination." Almost as an afterthought, it argued that the California Supreme Court's judgment must be reversed "to the extent that it bars all color-conscious decisions."[41]

Left to his own devices, Carter would have approved Justice's draft brief. Though he was generally a vigorous proponent of affirmative action in the White House, cabinet, and judiciary, like everyone else, he had an opinion about the case. "Hate to see Bakke excluded from Med[ical] School," he wrote in the margin of a memorandum to him from Eizenstat about the case. But when the *New York Times* reported in September 1977 that the brief attacked the Davis program and recommended Bakke's admission, the civil rights community became alarmed. One Congressional Black Caucus member saw the draft when he received a call saying that there was a taxicab with a copy of the brief outside his office. "Anxiety over Bakke is at fever pitch" at the NAACP board meeting, the White House was warned. According to one activist, *Bakke* was "the most important civil rights case in over 20 years," and "[f]iling the present brief would be a breach of faith with those who thought you were on our side."[42]

Attorney General Bell now made what he later called his "greatest mistake." He took the draft to Carter, who circulated it to appalled members of the executive branch. "Neither you nor I have been able to understand the legalisms in this case," Hamilton Jordan told the president. "How can we expect illiterate and disadvantaged people to understand when they are told by their leaders and the media that, 'Carter has ruled against the blacks and Hispanics of the country.' Judge Bell—who I love and respect—takes comfort in the fact that . . . two blacks [were involved in the brief-writing process and thinks that] will make our official involvement on behalf of Bakke more palatable." According to Jordan, however, the brief would only "discredit" Assistant Attorney General Days and Solicitor General McCree "in their own community." DPS executive director Stuart Eizenstat thought the Justice Department right on the law, but he feared that African Americans and liberals would "treat our position as a retreat" and "Mex[ican]-Amer[icans] will go bananas" at the idea of restricting affirmative action to African Americans. He told Carter that the draft brief was "too 'dispassionate,'" even "offensive."[43]

Eizenstat proffered a solution. The brief should be revised to claim more positively that a university might constitutionally take race into account to remedy societal discrimination, strongly endorse affirmative action, and clearly differentiate affirmative action from quotas. Then, Eizenstat thought, it could duck by expressing no opinion about the constitutionality of the University of California's program or Bakke's admission. Like the National Conference of Black Lawyers, but for different reasons, he wanted to recommend the return, or remand, of the case to California courts to gather the facts necessary to determine whether the Davis program represented a legitimate exercise of affirmative action or a quota. Remand meant "the Administration would not have to take a formal position against or for Bakke." It was "the simplest and least explosive way to deal with the lawfulness of the University's program" and "a responsible legal position . . . given the sorry state of the record." While Carter still hoped that Bakke would soon be admitted to Davis Medical School, he liked Eizenstat's remedy. The president told White House lawyers to "jump into the drafting process."[44]

But the lawyers at Justice did not want White House aid. To accommodate Carter and insulate McCree and, perhaps, to keep alive the draft brief, Bell ordered White House officials to send their arguments to one of his assistants, who would transmit them to the solicitor general. Stationery without White House letterhead must be used so that positions would succeed or fail on merit.[45]

Bell's maneuvers resulted in a mixed victory for the White House. McCree ultimately decided to do everything Eizenstat wanted except clearly distinguish affirmative action from quotas. The solicitor general's final brief defended affirmative action and recommended remand to gather more information about the Davis plan. Yet although Eizenstat and Carter had urged denunciation of racial quotas as unconstitutional, McCree demurred. The brief contained only one sentence deep within opposing "rigid exclusionary quotas" and differentiating them from "reasonable goals or targets." Some suspected that McCree dodged the issue because he thought that if the government inveighed against quotas, logic would compel it to claim that the Davis program was unconstitutional.[46]

Thus the solicitor general's final brief took only some political realities into account. The draft had originally argued that because quotas were unconstitutional, Davis's program was unconstitutional and Bakke deserved admission. It conceded the constitutionality of limited forms of affirmative action. The final version contended that affirmative action was constitutional, barely expressed opposition to quotas, and recommended remand. "Although it is not the brief the civil rights movement would have written, it is a lot better than the draft circulated ten days ago," said one civil rights lawyer. "We can live with it." But Eizenstat realized that since Justice only "added one relatively mild anti-quota statement, . . . many Jewish groups were disappointed." And while the brief saved Carter with minorities, the administration raised expectations among African Americans that it did not fulfill.[47]

Nor had Bell's bizarre attempt to protect the solicitor general preserved the integrity of the rule of law. During the two weeks the White House and the Justice Department tussled over the contents of the brief, their disagreements were leaked daily. The chief justice reportedly told McCree "that the entire Court was offended and displeased by the numerous news leaks of early drafts of the brief."[48]

In prior cases, the White House had sometimes worried about a Justice Department brief. But in *Bakke*, the president's staff developed a position for Justice. The unprecedented degree of White House intervention reflected a sense that law was too important to politics to be left to the lawyers. During the late 1970s, law came to be seen as *the* arena of struggle for social issues. Affirmative action became a proxy for race, just as it became clear that the Court must settle many polarizing issues. Thus *Bakke* came to stand for the principle that the White House could "dictate the government's legal positions in the Supreme Court."[49]

THE POLITICS OF THE SUPREME COURT

That did not of course guarantee that the Court would accept those positions. In June 1978 the U.S. Supreme Court affirmed the California Supreme Court decision ordering Bakke's admission and invalidating the Davis program. Yet it reversed the decision of the California Supreme Court insofar as it prohibited all race-conscious admissions programs.

The Court's tortured deliberations resulted in six separate opinions. Four justices, led by Ford appointee John Stevens, wanted UC to admit Bakke and to find the Davis plan invalid, because, they believed, on the basis of race and in violation of Title VI of the 1964 Civil Rights Act, the Davis special admissions program unlawfully barred whites from competing for its sixteen slots. Four others, led by William Brennan, wanted to keep Bakke out of medical school and to hold that the Davis affirmative action program was a permissible means of remedying past societal discrimination against minorities under the Fourteenth Amendment's equal protection clause.[50]

Though no one else signed the opinion of Justice Lewis Powell, it was treated as the Court's opinion because he broke the logjam. As a corporate lawyer the courtly Virginian had written a memorandum for the United States Chamber of Commerce just before Nixon appointed him to the Court that some in the twenty-first century "routinely"—and wrongly—credited with creating "the blueprint for virtually all of the conservative intellectual infrastructure built in the 1970s and 1980s." There Powell declared that the American free enterprise system was "under broad attack" and urged businessmen to mount a counterrevolution. Above all, he blamed the crisis on the liberal and left professors he said dominated campus life, but Powell explained that the principle of academic freedom was "sanctified." Among the remedies he pressed the chamber to consider was the establishment of "a staff of highly qualified scholars in the social sciences who do believe in the system" and who could restore "balance" to campus life by presenting "diverse views." In

Bakke, Powell restated his commitment to diversity. With the Stevens camp, Powell agreed that Bakke must be admitted and the Davis program invalidated, as the original Justice Department brief had suggested. With Brennan's group, Powell acknowledged that race might constitutionally be used as one factor in admissions, as Frank Easterbrook and the Justice Department had also initially hesitantly recommended.[51]

But Powell found more value in diversity than Easterbrook had. He approved the use of affirmative action to attain a diverse student body, but only if race was one aspect of an admissions program that was "flexible enough to consider all pertinent elements of diversity in light of the particular qualifications of each applicant." Powell singled out for praise the Harvard College special admissions program, which treated "each applicant as an individual in the admissions process" and awarded extra points for race, ethnicity, musical ability, athletic prowess, geographic background, and "a life spent on a farm." Davis, Powell said, focused *solely* on "ethnic diversity" and hindered the attainment of "genuine diversity" in its student body. According to Powell, the Davis admissions program also employed a two-track system that impermissibly insulated minorities from competition with all other applicants, while at Harvard everyone competed for the same seats.[52]

Proponents of affirmative action had been in a stronger position before *Bakke*. Powell's rhetoric left diversity the principal justification for affirmative action. Gone from the supporters' quiver were the arrows justifying race-conscious affirmative action to compensate for prior injustice, increase minority representation in higher education and the professions, and provide better services to minority communities. The rhetoric against affirmative action has stayed the same since the 1970s. Thanks to *Bakke*, the rhetoric in its favor had to change.[53]

Even in 1978, Powell's opinion had little value as precedent. "This is a landmark case, but we don't know what it marks," one constitutional scholar observed. Although Powell laid out his view that racial preference plans had to serve a compelling interest to withstand strict scrutiny clearly enough, he did not indicate the criteria for recognizing compelling interests. Nor did he explain why the goal of diversity, the only goal he did identify as compelling, had achieved that status. Nor did Powell set out a principled distinction between the operation of the constitutionally prohibited Davis program and the constitutionally permissible Harvard program.[54]

In fact, Justice Brennan said, the Harvard program had the advantage of intentional vagueness. Beyond saying that it awarded bonus points for certain criteria, Harvard did not make its selection standards public. But even on the basis of the limited information available, it was clear that Harvard, like Davis, gave an advantage to "marginal" minorities, and if applicants of color received extra points, some white ones suffered. What was the difference between the Davis plan, which Powell condemned for segregating minorities from comparison with white candidates, and the Harvard program, which he celebrated? Both plans produced similar levels of minority enrollments. The gist of Powell's opinion was that if universities did not say too much about how their affirmative action programs operated, the Court would tolerate them. Consequently, neoconservatives mourned *Bakke* as a lost opportunity to eviscerate affirmative action.[55]

As a political statement for the late 1970s, however, the Court's "Solomonic" opinion was far more successful than the Carter administration's final brief. Bakke and affirmative action both won: "That was the comforting paradox communicated to the world." Paradoxically too Powell's opinion ultimately helped affirmative action in higher education to survive. In the quarter century after *Bakke*, his handicraft came under such attack that when the Fifth Circuit struck down the University of Texas Law School's affirmative action program in 1996, it questioned whether Powell's "lonely" opinion even deserved to be considered the opinion of the Court. But just as it seemed that the Supreme Court was about to inter the Powell opinion in the 2003 University of Michigan cases, Justice Sandra Day O'Connor resurrected *Bakke* and justified affirmative action on the ground that it promoted diversity. As big business and the armed services joined educators in rallying around the diversity flag, O'Connor and her colleagues "embraced not only Powell's result, but also all his reasoning [about diversity], in all its logic-chopping contradiction." Powell might have cut away the strongest arguments for affirmative action, but he had ensured its survival.[56]

Bakke's ambiguous legacy had been evident long before the millennium arrived. "[E]very time a showdown over the issue [of affirmative action] has seemed inevitable in the Supreme Court, both sides have been left standing when the shooting has stopped," one constitutional scholar wrote. The Carter administration was a fair-weather friend. It supported civil rights groups on potentially significant, inexpensive, low-profile issues, but the attorney general continued to feud publicly with the White House about affirmative action.[57]

In 1978, Congress enacted the Omnibus Judgeship Act, which created 35 new judgeships in the federal courts of appeal and 117 in the federal district courts. White House officials told Carter he had a chance to rectify "an injustice: of the 525 active Federal Judges, only twenty are black or Hispanic and only six are women." Although ultimately Carter reshaped the federal bench by infusing it with women and minorities, some in his administration fought diversification. Bell delegated his authority to "white male establishment lawyers" and delayed the appointment of the NAACP's general counsel for months while he pressed the president to name a Greek American, instead of the African American, to the Sixth Circuit. White House lawyers groused that "the Attorney General does not adequately represent either the President's views or his interests," and Bell grumbled that his adversaries "set themselves up as the keepers of morality."[58]

Because of such skirmishes, the administration alienated white ethnics and appeared a reluctant and ungracious supporter of the civil rights groups it took for granted As it vainly sought to please all its constituencies, it seemed at war with itself. Democrats had assumed that a pluralistic, interest group–oriented liberalism would benefit all society. New issues, Carter's convictions, and new times made old liberal allies uneasy with one another and created openings for conservatives and Republicans alike.

VIII
LIMITS

"WE HAVE LEARNED THAT 'MORE' IS NOT NECESSARILY 'BETTER,' that even our great nation has its recognized limits," Carter had said in his 1977 Inaugural Address. He meant to allude, he explained later, to "the potential shortage of energy supplies and the need for our people to stop looking to the federal government as a bottomless cornucopia." The president had appropriated Jerry Brown's message. While Carter did not yet realize that "dealing with limits would become the subliminal theme" of his presidency, he recalled watching "the sea of approving faces" and wondering how many would agree with his message if they carefully analyzed it. Carter soon learned the answer. Energy, the economy, and the environment retained their importance, and his solutions often diverged from those advocated by his party. The president's understanding of "limits" to governmental capabilities determined his approach to what historian Steven Gillon has referred to as the "Democratic dilemma" in the "post-liberal" age that began in the 1970s: "How does a party, whose coalition was forged during depression and sustained by decades of economic growth, face the threat posed by slower growth and rising inflation?" The energy issue exposed both the existence of limits and Carter's unevenness as a politician.[1]

"MY ONE-WEEK HONEYMOON WITH CONGRESS"

For much of the country the winter of 1977 was as bad as the winter of 1934. An arctic blast and blizzard wrought cold without mercy. A natural gas shortage left houses frigid and forced businesses and schools to shut down. Together, the cold and natural gas shortage temporarily put well over a million out of work.

Where Roosevelt had concentrated on creating jobs for the unemployed in 1934, Carter focused on the most severe energy crisis since the 1973–74 Arab oil embargo. The United States had imported 35 percent of its oil when Ford became president. When Carter became president, it imported 50 percent and paid twice as much for each barrel of foreign oil as it had before the 1973 Yom Kippur War. The task, Carter perceived, was to persuade Americans to conserve energy. The United States must cut consumption of oil and natural gas, generate more of both at home, develop other sources of fuel, and distribute its energy resources more equitably. Regulators, for example, had set the price of natural gas transported across interstate lines well below oil and far below that of natural gas sold in states where it was produced. Thus sellers marketed natural gas in the South and West, where it was drilled, and the East got it last.[2]

Within just two weeks of his inauguration, Carter had steered the Emergency Natural Gas Act of 1977 through Congress and won temporary power to lift price ceilings on interstate gas. Inspired by Roosevelt's fireside chats, Carter made the signing of the act the occasion for a talk to the American people. Seated in front of burning logs, the sweater-clad "Jimmy Cardigan" said that the energy shortage was here to stay. The president announced he would have a comprehensive energy bill for Congress just after Easter.[3]

It was too much too soon. Carter placed a premium on efficiency. Sometimes that was good politics. Like Ford, for example, he launched his presidency with an embrace of reconciliation. "For myself and for our Nation, I want to thank my predecessor for all he has done to heal our land," Carter graciously declared in his Inaugural Address. A day later he issued a "full, complete and unconditional pardon" to all Vietnam-era draft evaders—except those who had forcefully resisted the draft or deserted the armed forces. The right thought this action disgraceful. The left said it unfairly benefited white draft dodgers with the money to flee the country. (As one journalist recognized, despite the facts that battlefield desertion was extremely rare and "nearly seventeen million draft-age men, often through scams as well as legal measures, never served in the military at all," deserters had become "tailor-made victims for the nation's pent-up venom about this class war.") If Carter were to make any gesture of forgiveness, the president wisely did so by executive order during his honeymoon. Yet Hamilton Jordan complained that Carter's need for speed led him to set "too many arbitrary deadlines" that the White House and cabinet scrambled to meet. It also moved the president to send all his proposals to Congress at once without prioritizing them.[4]

That did not bother Carter. "Everybody has warned me not to take on too many projects so early in the administration, but it's almost impossible for me to delay something I see needs to be done," he wrote in a diary excerpt reprinted in a chapter of his memoir he titled "My One-Week Honeymoon with Congress." That left him with little time to use his office to educate the public. Scholars have pointed to "the rise of a 'plebiscitary presidency'" during the mid-1970s and the tendency of presidents to lead by asking for public support. But energy had played only a small role in the campaign, and Americans still doubted the need for conservation.[5]

Consequently, legislative cooperation became especially important. Yet bringing the program in on time required its preparation in secret, or so believed the president and his energy czar, James Schlesinger, creator of the notorious CIA "family jewels" and Ford's in-house critic of détente. Carter put Schlesinger, who had been chairman of the Atomic Energy Commission before Nixon moved him to the CIA, to work on energy and subsequently named him the first secretary of the new Department of Energy. The president and Schlesinger made virtually no attempt to consult legislators and left even administration officials in the dark. Worse, by the time the president sent his energy plan to Congress, he had already alienated key legislators.

BREACHES

"I had several serious disagreements with Congress, but the issue of water projects was the one that caused the deepest breach between me and the Democratic leadership," Carter said. To stress the need for economy and environmentalism, the new president tried to save five billion dollars by deleting funding for nineteen dams and other water projects in seventeen states in the budget he sent to Congress on February 22, 1977. He also announced that another fourteen in an additional six were under review. He had good reason for the decision: Many of the projects were unnecessary, environmentally questionable, or unsafe. But fifteen of the thirty-five congressional members affected were among the "most powerful" in the House, and the Senate Finance Committee chair Russell Long stood to lose too. Carter himself conceded that the projects "represented major political plums."[6]

Members of Congress rightly perceived the president's move as an attack on politics as usual, and it angered them. For that reason, Office of Management and Budget Director Bert Lance, one of the president's best political advisers, considered cancellation of the water projects Carter's "worst political mistake." Vice President Mondale, a former senator himself, told the president that thriftiness and democracy were incompatible; one person's waste was another's treasure. But Carter signaled the press that he was determined to "hang tough."[7]

Then the president capitulated to legislators' lobbying. When the final "hit list" was announced on April 18, 1977, it turned out the administration had agreed to fund almost half the threatened projects. Buckling further, Carter subsequently approved funding more. As he later said, his surrender proved an egregious error that was "accurately interpreted as a sign of weakness on my part."[8]

He also seemed unprincipled. As he wooed environmentalists, candidate Carter had declared that "we have built enough dams in this country." Instead of talking in terms of energy and the economy versus environment, as Ford sometimes did, Carter maintained that environmentalism strengthened economic and energy policy. During his presidency he was to issue executive orders protecting wetlands and other endangered environments, successfully support the reauthorization of the Clean Air and Clean Water Acts, ensure the passage of legislation that controlled strip mining, create a superfund that would require and enable the Environmental Protection Agency to clean up abandoned hazardous waste sites, and protect millions of acres of Alaska wilderness from exploitation. "The Carter Administration, under determined prodding from environmentalists, is trying to lock up hundreds of millions of acres of public land in Wilderness areas—an effort that, however, has met unexpectedly fierce resistance," *Conservative Digest* proclaimed in 1978, as the Sagebrush Rebellion, which sought the return of public land to state control, heated up in the mountain states. There developers, oil and mining interests, ranchers, and loggers recognized Carter as the enemy. But environmentalists did not always count him a friend. The president's change on the water projects at the outset alarmed them. (He upset them further on water projects by signing a congressional appropriation for the Tellico Dam on the Little Tennessee River in 1979, despite the fact that the Little Tennessee was the "only known habitat" of a tiny fish protected by the Endangered Species Act.)[9]

Carter may have surrendered on the water projects at the outset of his presidency partially to win Senate approval of his unpopular tax policy. He had proposed giving each taxpayer a $50 rebate (the equivalent of about $176 in 2009 dollars) as part of his economic recovery package. Intended to prod quick consumption among working-and middle-class families, the rebate alarmed Secretary of Treasury Michael Blumenthal and Lance, both of whom said it would alienate business, and Federal Reserve chair Arthur Burns, who campaigned to kill it. Council of Economic Advisers chair Charles Schultze, one of the few fans of the rebate, realized that Congress also despised it. While the House nevertheless approved it, the rebate stalled in the Senate. Long compared it with "throwing bushels of $50 bills off the top of the Washington Monument," liberals called for a substantial job creation program, and Republicans denounced the rebate as a gimmick. "The concern around the Senate is that you are naïve or selfish or stubborn, perhaps all three," one congressional liaison informed Carter. "As a result, the rebate is in deep trouble." Under the circumstances, the new Senate majority leader, Robert Byrd of West Virginia, told the president his water project hit list was "stupid."[10]

But Carter surprised everyone and announced he would abandon the rebate on April 14, 1977. Insisting that he had not acted out of fear of defeat, the president pointed out that the unemployment rate had dropped from above 8 percent in December 1976 to 7.3 percent and claimed that a rebounding economy made the rebate unnecessary and inflationary. The economy did seem to be improving, in part because the Fed was, surprisingly, expanding the supply of money and cutting the discount rate. (One theory was that Burns hoped to win presidential approval for another term as Fed chairman by pursuing a policy of easy money in late 1976 and early 1977. The White House, however, was reportedly put off by Burns's open opposition to the $50 rebate in the spring and by his efforts to fight inflation by pushing up short-term interest rates in the summer and fall. A spate of embarrassing stories about the feud between the president and the Federal Reserve chief dampened business confidence, which was never high where Carter was concerned, and led the president to replace Burns with G. William Miller, who was considered more of a "team player," in 1978.) The inflation rate in April was 6.95 percent, up from 5.2 percent. The president reversed himself on "the $50 folly" without taking the time to warn his treasury secretary, who had just delivered a speech loyally defending the rebate.[11]

Like Ford's 1974 shift from tax hike to cut, Carter's turnaround hurt his early credibility. "In one quick and regrettably memorable act," the president had changed focus. His own advisers told him his economic policy "has too often zigged and zagged." Worse, his administration was already showing a tendency to fight inflation with hot air. In 1977, comic Ben Stein and his father, economist Herbert Stein, published a novel about inflation, complete with steamy sex scenes between a presidential adviser and a Madeira School junior. As their story began, OPEC doubled the price of oil and the president fell in line with a Federal Reserve Board chair who believed in easy money. Within days, a twelve-mile cab ride cost six thousand dollars. Like Jimmy Carter, the Steins' fictional president had blue eyes.[12]

Carter also withdrew the rebate ineptly. House Ways and Means Committee chair Al Ullman, who was taken by surprise, labeled the decision "a little less than fair to those of us who supported the rebate against our better judgment." The president was viewed as an untrustworthy ally and a weak adversary. During the energy fight Ullman pointed to the withdrawal of the rebate as reason to be "very cautious about the strength of Administration support." At the same time, and as energy politics confirmed, Carter's turnaround convinced the Democratic Congress it was worth facing him down.[13]

"VINTAGE JIMMY CARTER": "THE MORAL EQUIVALENT OF WAR"

Whereas Ford originally hoped to make energy deregulation his first priority and increase supply, Carter considered conservation the primary goal and sought to compel it through government controls. Carter wanted Americans to reduce oil imports by one-eighth by 1985, gas use by one-tenth. He also wanted them to triple coal production, relax licensing procedures for nuclear power plants, develop synthetic fuels, insulate virtually all buildings, and use solar energy in more than 2.5 million homes. To show his enthusiasm for solar energy, which had never interested Nixon or Ford, Carter proclaimed May 3, 1978, Sun Day and called upon Americans to observe it "with activities and ceremonies that will demonstrate the potential of solar energy." He bestrode the White House roof to dedicate the solar collectors that he had ordered installed there.[14]

The president proposed to accomplish these aims through a combination of carrots and sticks. His program included a stiff tax on newly purchased "gas-guzzling" cars that got less than ten miles to the gallon. Where energy legislation during the Ford years had set fuel economy levels for manufacturers, the government would now also tax consumers who purchased wasteful cars and provide rebates for those who bought efficient ones. Carter's plan also provided for a standby tax on gasoline; federal taxes could rise by as much as ten cents a gallon annually if consumption exceeded targeted goals. Homeowners and businesses would receive tax credits for installing insulation and solar energy. To encourage factories and utility plants to rely on coal and to stop them from generating electricity by burning oil and natural gas, they would be given tax incentives to convert to coal, and user taxes would be imposed if they did not.

Producers too would be prodded with incentives and penalties. A multitiered system of price controls for natural gas already in production would be retained. "Old" gas would be earmarked for residential use. Controls on newly discovered natural gas, which would be targeted for industrial use, would stay in effect too, though the administration would promote its exploration by permitting producers to raise its price. That would make "new gas" as expensive as domestic crude oil. Developers of gasohol, or ethanol, would receive tax breaks.

These proposals represented a dramatic change in course for Carter. As a candidate he had pleased oil and gas interests by sending letters to the governors of Texas, Oklahoma, and Arkansas in which he promised to deregulate prices for new gas. (He carried Texas but lost Oklahoma and Arkansas.) Now, recalled Domestic Policy Staff executive director Stuart Eizenstat, "as part of our rushed and poorly conceived energy proposal," the president followed Schlesinger's advice and reneged on his promise to support deregulation of oil and gas. The oil and gas interests "thought they'd been lied to right off the bat," and they did not appreciate the president's harsh rhetoric against them either. Carter's decision to press for continued regulatory controls on new gas also confused legislators and, according to Eizenstat, "led to the impasse that derailed his entire energy program for 18 months and did more than anything else to contribute to the notion that he could not effectively lead the Congress." At least, however, natural gas would be priced the same, whether sold intra- or interstate.[15]

With oil too, Carter and Schlesinger opposed decontrol and contended that lifting price ceilings on domestic oil would prove economically disastrous. The task, as Schlesinger saw it, was to spur conservation by raising the price of domestic oil to world market levels while denying oil companies the chance to make a killing. His crude oil equalization tax would permit the price of existing supplies of domestic crude to climb gradually to world levels, a popular step with American allies. American buyers would pay more for gas and heating oil, but producers would not profit. They would pay the government what was essentially a windfall profits tax equal to the difference between the current controlled price of oil and the world market price. The government would return the tax revenues to consumers through tax credits or payments to prevent recession. Thus prices would annoy consumers by rising, without benefiting producers. To encourage exploration and production, however, "new" oil discovered after 1975 would be taxed at a lower rate than old oil, and no tax would be imposed on oil discovered after April 20, 1977, which could then be sold at world market prices.

Carter described his energy program for the nation in a televised speech on April 18. "I know that some of you may doubt that we face a real energy shortage," he said. "The 1973 gas lines are gone, and with this springtime weather, our homes are warm again." But the shortage was worse than in 1973 or during the recent natural gas crisis. At the present rate, the world would run out of oil and natural gas by the 1980s. "I know that many of you have suspected that some supplies of oil and gas are being withheld," he added. But even if producers were playing games, the United States was "the most wasteful nation on earth." It relied on foreign countries for more than 50 percent of its oil, and Americans used twice the energy per capita as citizens in other industrialized countries. Sounding "like Winston Churchill on the eve of the Battle of Britain" to some and Henny Penny to others, the president called for "changes in every life." He faced an uphill battle in Congress, he said, for the special interests—the oil and gas producers and automobile manufacturers—would say, "Sacrifice is fine, as long as other people do it." Characterizing the energy crisis as "the greatest challenge that our country will face in our lifetime" except averting war, Carter proclaimed that the decisions ahead would "test the character of the American people and the ability of the President and Congress to govern this nation."

He staked the credibility of his administration on the enactment of his energy program in 1977 and likened the crusade ahead to the " 'moral equivalent of war.' "[16]

THE NEW SPEAKER of the House, Tip O'Neill of Massachusetts, was more impressed by the speech than what happened afterward. At sixty-four, the Irish Catholic O'Neill was a "big, overweight, cigar-smoking, whiskey-drinking, back-pounding Boston politician." An inveterate liberal, he championed blue-collar workers and he had made headlines when he "desert[ed] LBJ on Vietnam" in the summer of 1967. A master arm-twister, O'Neill urged the president to target certain members of Congress for special attention. "No," he recalled Carter replying. "I described the problem to the American people in a rational way. I'm sure they'll realize that I'm right." A preinauguration encounter in which Carter had said he need not cooperate with Congress because he could take his causes to the voters had already left the Speaker bemused. Now, O'Neill said, "I could have slugged him." Trying to contain his frustration, the Speaker answered that "this is politics," and Congress needed the president "to push this bill through." Carter was unimpressed. "It's *not* politics," the Speaker recorded that the president answered. "Not to me. It's simply the right thing."[17]

This was "vintage Jimmy Carter," one aide said. He had won election by running as an outsider, and he disliked slapping insiders' backs now. "It's the damndest thing," his devoted press secretary, Jody Powell, admitted. "He went all over the country for two years asking everybody he saw to vote for him for President, but he doesn't like to call up a Congressman and ask for his support." Carter saw himself not as party leader but as the people's trustee. In energy, as in so much else, his "rhetorical flourishes" were reserved for the public; his efforts to reach Congress, often lackluster. When the president went before legislators to present his plan two days later on April 20, *Time* reported, "Carter rushed through its main proposals in low-key style, putting a number of members of Congress to sleep."[18]

Had Carter consulted legislators beforehand, they could have pointed out the problem with his energy plan. It was not its radicalism. Though the left, consumer groups, and environmentalists spoke of breaking up big U.S. oil companies, for example, Carter stayed away from divestiture. Instead he opted for a program that required sacrifice from everyone, imposed tens of billions of dollars of new taxes on Americans, and contributed to inflation. Energy policy set Sunbelt against Frost Belt. Price controls repulsed conservatives, producers, and southwesterners who believed that they kept entrepreneurs from enlarging energy reserves. Price increases angered liberals, consumers, and northeasterners.[19]

So instead of focusing on sacrifice, as he had done in his speech to the nation, Carter told Congress that his program would protect jobs and the environment. That claim made the energy crisis seem less real, opened the president up to new charges of inconsistency, and undercut the credibility of administration statistics. By his press conference at week's end, the president was sounding positively cheerful as he suggested that his program might create "several hundred thousand" new jobs. "Energy Plan Now Featured as Consumer Boom," the *Washington Post* reported. Journalist Russell Baker observed that the acronym for "Moral Equivalent of War" was MEOW.[20]

However frequently Carter changed his tune, the new Speaker wanted to show the president he could deliver. When the White House sent over its energy package, O'Neill "leafed through the five volumes of legislation" and "groaned." House procedure required that the bill be "taken up by as many as *seventeen* different committees and subcommittees," which would pick it to death. The Speaker changed procedure. In a masterstroke, he created an Ad Hoc Select Committee on Energy in May and rammed the bill through that committee and the House by August—with little help from Carter, who fell strangely silent about energy. Miraculously, the presidential plan remained virtually intact, though the standby gas tax had disappeared. *Human Events* warned that "the fate of the non-Socialists and those who favor energy growth in this country now hangs by a slender hope in the Senate."[21]

"AN UNMITIGATED DISASTER"

The Senate dismantled Carter's energy program and turned it into an oil and gas producer's dream, but the president bore much of the blame. He could have devoted the summer to capitalizing on his victory in the House and preparing for Senate consideration of the bill. But he did not. Whereas 61 percent of the American public had approved of the way Carter was dealing with the energy situation in February, only 44 percent did by August, and only 38 percent of Americans thought the energy crisis "very serious."[22]

Understandably, the president was distracted by allegations that his friend and Office of Management and Budget director Bert Lance had engaged in illegal practices when he had been a Georgia banker. The scandal consumed the administration in June, July, and August, tarnished its reputation for honesty, and further cut into Carter's congressional support. (Lance resigned on September 21, 1977, one month after the president had publicly declared, "Bert, I'm proud of you.") But at the high tide of Carter's inattentiveness, Congress neared its summer recess. A poll reported that "too few people believe the nation's problems are serious enough—and even fewer understand them well enough—to provide broad support" for the administration's energy program, and business opposition became more apparent. It was incumbent on the president to keep his eye on the Senate battle ahead—especially since few thought he handled the Lance imbroglio skillfully anyway.[23]

Yet Carter did not even seem to recognize that a fight loomed. By summer Russell Long, the canny senator from oil- and gas-rich Louisiana, was describing the plan as "an unmitigated disaster on the production side" and declaring that oil companies, not government, should receive the revenues from the increase in prices. Obviously, Long's remarks signaled that the crude oil equalization tax would face tough going when it came before his Senate Finance Committee, particularly since he was seconded by the oil and gas interests and "free market" fans. The close relationship among OPEC, major American oil companies, and the independent oil and natural gas producers made a free market impossible. Yet conservatives and southwesterners, along with Republicans who saw Carter's energy plan as their ticket out of oblivion, contended that Carter's energy program would swell bureaucracy, stall economic growth and energy production, and hurt workers and consumers by raising gas prices.[24]

Liberal Democrats from districts with harsh winters were unhappy too. They complained that the poor would bear a disproportionate burden of higher energy costs. Yet energy policy continued to create strange alliances: The National Association for the Advancement of Colored People decided that "[w]e can't through conservation get any more jobs for blacks" and teamed up with the Chamber of Commerce to support decontrol. ("NAACP Discovers the Enemy," *Human Events* crowed.) Clearly, the Senate would provide lobbyists with fertile ground.[25]

Standing above the fray was the new Senate majority leader, Robert Byrd, a conservative southerner who had once belonged to the Ku Klux

Klan and who thought "three things were sacred—God, my family, and the United States Senate." Byrd treasured the Senate's independence, had less control over the Senate than the Speaker had over the House, and lacked O'Neill's desire to please the president. These developments, all of which were foreseeable, seemed to surprise Carter.[26]

As the Senate gutted the administration program in September, Carter reaffirmed his commitment to the House bill and threatened to veto a Senate version that would deregulate newly discovered natural gas, which Carter warned would "add about $20 billion to the price of natural gas already discovered in Alaska alone." That emboldened a band of liberal Democratic senators, led by James Abourezk of South Dakota and Howard Metzenbaum of Ohio, to launch a filibuster, the first in almost a decade, to prevent a vote on the deregulation of new gas and provide the president with more time to lobby their colleagues. After two weeks Byrd had enough and ordered Vice President Mondale, as the Senate's presiding officer, to end the filibuster. The liberals believed that the vice president was following a White House script, and Abourezk called the president a double-crosser. "The initial suspicion that Mondale was acting with Carter's blessing—encouraged by Byrd in the heat of debate—was denied all around," *Newsweek* reported, and "gave way to the unflattering revisionist view that Carter wasn't dealt in because his counsel was considered superfluous. His lobbying, according to several lobbyees, was diffident to a fault." Then, when the Senate voted to decontrol newly discovered natural gas in October, Carter came out swinging and called the bill "unacceptable" and "an injustice to the working people of this country."[27]

With attention focused on the conference committee that would broker a compromise, the president blundered. Schlesinger and Eizenstat had advised him that it was "critical" that he take a "strong public stance in favor of the entire House bill at the outset of the conference." Carter, who noted in the margin of their memorandum, "not only at the outset," overdid it. He listened to Hamilton Jordan, who recommended that he postpone a scheduled trip overseas. If the administration could "resurrect" the House version, Jordan reasoned, "we will be given credit not only for having a good year, but also given credit for working well with Congress." So in November 1977, Carter announced he had delayed his travels because of the urgency of obtaining his energy bill before Christmas. As one Washingtonian said, "No savvy leader would dramatically cancel a trip, causing the public, Congress and the press to take notice before arranging for a breakthrough to be imminent." None was forthcoming. The Ninety-fifth Congress adjourned at the end of its first session without making an energy bill law.[28]

When Carter finally did depart Washington at year's end for a nine-day tour of seven countries, his New Year's Eve destination demonstrated that energy warped foreign, as well as domestic, policy. Liberals had long criticized Mohammed Reza Pahlavi, shah of Iran, for brutalizing Iranians, and as a candidate Carter had denounced the shah. Iranians studying in the United States had demonstrated against the shah and his wife when the Carters greeted them on the White House lawn. The tear gas that police fired at the demonstrators left the two couples weeping. But Carter put on a happy face. Iran was vital to U.S. security in the Persian Gulf: Armed to the gills with American military technology, it shared a fifteen-hundred-mile border with the Soviet Union, was the site of American radar and listening posts, and exported more oil than any other country, except Saudi Arabia. Further, in Washington, the shah, traditionally an "OPEC price hawk," promised "a grateful Jimmy Carter" that he would not press for a hike in oil prices.[29]

As Carter told the story, when he asked the first lady where she wanted to spend New Year's Eve, she said she wanted to ring it in with the shah and the empress because she had so enjoyed their company in Washington. (This was, one journalist dryly and skeptically observed, "a surprising reply for a populist first Lady" who had shunned the presidential limousine on inauguration day to walk with Carter down Pennsylvania Avenue.) So, on December 31, 1977, Carter uttered words in Tehran that were to haunt him. Holding high a flute of Dom Pérignon, the president declared that "Iran, because of the great leadership of the Shah, is an island of stability in one of the more troubled areas of the world. This is a great tribute to you, Your Majesty, and to your leadership and to the respect and the admiration and love which your people give you." He also saluted the shah's devotion to human rights, despite his awareness that a violent crackdown against dissidents was under way. The immensity of Carter's gaffe became clear when the Iranian Revolution swung into high gear in 1978.[30]

For the present, the Carters' decision to ring in the New Year in Iran underscored the importance the president attached to energy policy. Because he had staked his presidency on energy, the media judged his first year a failure. His press secretary lamented that "your take-charge, decisive, executive manner has not come through to the public or to opinion molders here in Washington." Carter said he was undiscouraged. "At least," he rationalized, "I had confronted an issue which had been postponed too long—I could now understand why—and the energy issues had become clearly defined."[31]

MEOW

The better defined energy issues became, the more the president had to surrender to the bargaining he despised. The crude oil equalization tax was a lost cause. All now hinged on natural gas: whether to deregulate it, and if so, how. Schlesinger now understood "what hell is. Hell is endless and eternal sessions of the natural gas conference." While Carter was in the thick of the negotiations, he received little credit for flexibility or pragmatism. "President Carter wiped out a year of history yesterday, saying that of course he would accept gradual deregulation of new natural gas, he had campaigned for it," the *Washington Post* sardonically reported on March 10, 1978.[32]

The president was listening to public relations executive Gerald Rafshoon, who became his new assistant for communications in July 1978. With press coverage stressing that Carter's presidency was in trouble, Carter brought in Rafshoon to remake his image. Rafshoon, who had warned Carter soon after the presidency began that "[y]ou are running the risk of *boring* the people and you have 3½ years to go," was eager to come aboard. Though the stories about "Rafshoonery" damaged the battered president further, Rafshoon provided wise counsel on energy. As Rafshoon's staff realized, the shortage argument was going nowhere: "There is significant disagreement among experts about this point; the public sees no tangible evidence—like gas lines or rationing—to support the position; we tried this approach before to mixed reviews; the public likes to think that technology will bail us out—and it might well; and at the very time we hope to have public concern peak . . . there will probably be a glut of oil on the market," as there was. Since Carter's speaking trips around the country to highlight the need for an energy bill also accomplished little, Rafshoon urged him to take his case to Congress, engage in the necessary bargaining, and contend that his energy package was vital to the achievement of every one of his goals, from guaranteeing national security to rescuing the declining dollar.[33]

Consequently, Carter made energy a top priority in 1978. He even won Senator Byrd over to the cause. Nonetheless, the bill was still tied up in conference in August. Virtually every administration proposal "turns to ashes," the *New Republic* editorialized. "The energy program has spent 15 months being launched and is still in danger of going under." In the end, the program survived, just barely—as a faint "meow," rather than a rousing "moral equivalent of war." The national energy bill that Congress approved at dawn on October 15, 1978, just before it adjourned, bore little resemblance to the plan the president had presented a year and a half earlier. Had Carter displayed a willingness to bargain sooner, he might even have won it at the end of 1977.[34]

So many of the original provisions of the act that the administration touted as its "major legislative accomplishment for the 95th Congress" were gone or transformed. The gas guzzler tax had been tempered, and the standby gas tax, crude oil equalization tax, and tax on the industrial use of gas and oil had disappeared. Oil prices on domestically produced oil, including the one million barrels beginning to flow in daily via the Alaska pipeline that "more than offset" the decline in oil production elsewhere in the United States, remained "artificially low." Consumption of course stayed high. In an administration setback and partial victory for southwestern governors, the act placed new gas under a program of phased-in deregulation, with its price increasing by 15 percent immediately and rising each year until controls ended altogether in 1985. The environment had definitely taken a backseat to energy, and Carter was warned that "environmentalists feel 'seduced and abandoned,' with no friends and many enemies in the White House." Nevertheless, the president had assured more equitable distribution of interstate and intrastate natural gas. Many of his other proposals encouraging conservation, such as tax credits for insulation and solar energy, tax breaks for synthetic fuel production, and the tightening of restrictions on the use of gas or oil to generate electricity, had survived, although often in diluted form.[35]

Above all, Carter had confronted the energy crisis. In an editorial titled "At Last, the Energy Bill," the *Washington Post* speculated that although the legislation was "battered and dented and stripped not only of its hubcaps but also some of the parts that the designers originally considered essential," it might become "a turning point in the way that Americans think about fuel and energy." Yet while the president and his staff had demonstrated courage in telling Congress and the American people what they did not want to hear and had bargained with Congress relatively skillfully as they gained experience, the legislation did not become a turning point. The administration failed to convince Americans and their representatives that the energy crisis required conservation or recognition of the nation's limits.[36]

IS IT FAIR to take the 1977–78 energy program as the case study by which to judge the Carter administration's domestic policy record? Over the same twenty months that the White House battled with legislators over energy, Carter and his staff mounted what the president rightly called a "massive campaign" to steer a civil service reform bill through Congress that was enacted, as Carter put it, "relatively intact." It overhauled civil service law for the first time in nearly a century, made it possible to reward and discipline government employees on the basis of merit, protected those who blew the whistle on government fraud and scandal, and was a partial success. Why not choose civil service reform instead of energy?[37]

The president himself made energy a test of his effectiveness. Further, the energy story exemplified his problems with respect to domestic policy and suggested that the very factors which had enabled Carter to win the presidency made it nearly impossible for him to govern. The administration was constrained by Carter's idea of himself as an outsider and trustee, the fractious nature of the Democratic Party, the resurgence of Congress after Watergate, and the public's refusal to sacrifice. Carter's initial insistence on secrecy and speed, his refusal to consult, and his self-righteousness, inconsistency, and unpersuasiveness proved typical. One Senate Democrat grumbled that the president would be incapable of selling "a prostitute's services on a troop train." But such complaints did not particularly bother Carter. As historian E. Stanly Godbold has observed, his experiences in Georgia had conditioned him to expect "his most bitter rivals to be within his own party."[38]

The president's difficulties with Congress were certainly not entirely his fault. *Time* judged the Congress that served with him, which was rocked by sex and influence-peddling scandals, "one of the most quarrelsome and rebellious ever faced by a President." One *Time* 1978 cover story highlighted "a dramatic new development in Washington: the startling increase in the influence of special-interest lobbyists," who killed or gutted labor law reform, hospital cost containment, a consumer protection agency, and tax reform and made Congress hard to manage. Further, as Carter's congressional liaison, Frank Moore, stressed, "many of the tensions have a Congressional ancestry rather than a Presidential one. The growing institutional independence of Congress, the 'democratization' of the House and the reduced power of committee chairmen, the evaporation of party loyalty, and the growing political independence of individual members have all contributed to the current situation." Nevertheless, Moore acknowledged, many problems were "of our own making." Members of Congress had interpreted the appointment of Moore, who had been Governor Carter's liaison to an unhappy Georgia legislature, "as a sign that Carter did not want to work with them" and complained about his office's inattentiveness. Congress found the White House staff inept and disrespectful. As far as Hamilton Jordan, its de facto head, "was concerned, a House Speaker was something you bought on sale at Radio Shack," O'Neill groused. For their part, Carter administration members made it abundantly clear that they considered O'Neill "a horse's ass." As Moore informed Carter, "perhaps a majority in Congress do not feel they share common goals with you or the Administration generally."[39]

THE PARTY FAITHFUL

Traditional Democratic constituencies became especially disaffected. The Americans for Democratic Action had endorsed Carter in 1976. In domestic and particularly in economic and energy policy, Carter profoundly disappointed the ADA and other liberals within one hundred days of his inauguration. ADA president George McGovern's "slashing attack on Administration priorities" in the summer of 1977 "was reported in virtually every newspaper in the nation," the ADA happily told its members, and by fall the ADA was talking of working to deny the president renomination in 1980. "In many cases I feel more at home with the conservative Democratic and Republican members of Congress than I do with the others," Carter wrote in his diary. On energy policy in 1978, he clashed repeatedly with liberals, who resented the inducements to oil and natural gas producers Carter made to win passage of the energy bill. Denouncing the administration's "Herculean lobbying effort," Senator Metzenbaum complained that the White House now "put anything on the table to get votes." Though O'Neill kept them in line, House liberals were angry too. It seemed "a fitting irony" that when the House split 206–206 on the final version of the energy bill, a Republican broke the tie in the administration's favor.[40]

Symbolic and ironic, perhaps, but also common. Carter constantly irritated traditional Democrats. It always seemed to come down to money. Without even notifying labor leaders in advance, for example, as a new president he proposed increasing the minimum wage from $2.30 to $2.50, instead of $3. Though Carter had campaigned hard for farmers' votes, the program he sent Congress also would have cut their subsidies. "You are making major domestic policy decisions with tremendous political implications in a political vacuum," Hamilton Jordan stressed at the time. "These decisions are also being made at the 11th hour with no opportunity for political give and take." Congress would not take administration proposals seriously and would "come up with a more expensive program than would have been originally acceptable to the various interests if we had come in with a politically credible proposal." The result was to reduce party regulars' confidence in Carter.[41]

Jordan exploded with frustration in 1978 when he learned about the administration's urban policy program. Carter endorsed a plan that transferred "the burden of urban problems to the private sector and to community groups" and led toward "small-scale, gradualist, locally administered programs." That direction seemed reasonable, given the president's repeated warnings that Washington and government could not "eliminate poverty." It seemed especially sound in the realm of urban policy, where everyone from local activists to neoconservatives lauded the virtues of community. But the president's "New Partnership to Conserve America's Communities" contained just six hundred million additional federal dollars for cities. Sending it forward would constitute "the single biggest political mistake we have made since being elected," Jordan warned. "Mr. President, I do not see how we can continue to alienate key groups of people who were responsible for your election and still maintain our political base," he wrote plaintively. "The groups that make up the urban coalition—blacks, Hispanics, labor, Democratic mayors, etc.—have been waiting all year for the 'comprehensive, major program' we promised them." Carter added only $142 million. When he unveiled the New Partnership, it received little applause.[42]

EVEN THE VICTORIES liberals achieved during Carter's presidency with his help seemed like defeats. During the 1976 campaign, the old coalition of liberals, minorities, and labor had pressed Democratic candidates to support Humphrey-Hawkins. Developed in 1974, as the postwar boom ground to a halt and unemployment began to climb, by Senator

Humphrey and Representative Gus Hawkins of California, a member of the Congressional Black Caucus, the bill aimed at full employment and would require national economic planning to achieve it. As originally proposed, Humphrey-Hawkins would reduce the maximum unemployment rate for adults over the age of twenty to 3 percent and for all workers to 4 percent within five years and would guarantee that the government would become employer "of last resort," if necessary, to achieve these joblessness rates. Candidate Carter had worried Humphrey-Hawkins was inflationary, but soon after his "ethnic purity" slip, he came out in favor of the bill. (Ford, who opposed the bill, accused his opponent of flip-flopping to placate minorities.) Once Carter became president, his economic advisers attacked the bill as expensive and inflationary and warned him, correctly, that it would alienate business. By the fall of 1977, with the unemployment rate still above 7 percent and the black unemployment rate 14.5 percent, the president and his White House were seeking to dilute Humphrey-Hawkins. For example, achievement of the overall 4 percent unemployment rate became a "goal," rather than a "commitment"; the proviso pledging the government to be employer of last resort was dropped, along with discussion of national economic planning; and a "commitment" to reducing inflation to 3 percent was added. Eizenstat warned Carter that the changes would only make "the distance between the Administration's economic views and those of the Black Caucus and other Congressional liberals" obvious, while another aide said that the White House was changing "everything about Humphrey-Hawkins except the name."[43]

That Senate conservatives then shredded Humphrey-Hawkins reflected two trends: Labor was losing power, and business interests openly hostile to labor were acquiring it. The Democratic Congress also narrowly defeated the common situs picketing legislation enlarging the right of unions to picket construction sites that candidate Carter had pledged to sign. (That President Carter did not press for it spoke volumes.) Eleven Democrats who had voted for the common situs legislation in 1975, when Ford vetoed it, now opposed it. Labor law reform became another casualty when big business interests mobilized against a bill to increase protections for union members that Carter supported in principle but that some thought he could have done more to promote. Irate about "this so-called 'Labor Reform' Act" that "could wreck our company," Wal-Mart founder Sam Walton took to the pages of his employee newsletter to plead for "everyone's help to put down this labor law that is now being debated by the Senate." New Right senators from the Sunbelt mounted a successful filibuster against the bill. The administration poisoned its relationship with organized labor by allowing consumer protection, welfare reform, hospital cost containment, and a diluted version of a national health insurance system that the president had promised to back in 1976 to fall by the wayside too.[44]

Yet Eizenstat understood that Humphrey-Hawkins was special, "one of the few bills in which we are clearly aligned with our major constituencies—labor and the minority community." Disappointing them would be "a dramatic mistake," given their disillusionment with the administration. Even George Meany, no radical, had condemned the president as "a conservative" who cared only about balancing the budget, and Black Caucus members openly and angrily questioned the depth of Carter's commitment to Humphrey-Hawkins. Thus in October 1978, as Humphrey-Hawkins hung fire in the Senate, the president successfully called for passage of the toothless bill that had acquired so much symbolic importance. But Carter was not upbeat at the signing ceremony. He lectured the liberals, civil rights workers, and labor leaders who had come together to celebrate Humphrey-Hawkins, the last gasp of the New Deal, "that our fight against inflation must succeed" in order to attain the full employment goals of the legislation. The budget proposal he submitted several weeks later did not even allude to full employment goals.[45]

LIKE FORD, CARTER had the misfortune to become president when the postwar economic boom ground to a halt, and the economy and energy emerged as the two most pressing domestic problems. At the beginning of 1978 the economy was booming by 1970s standards, with the gross national product growing more than 7 percent, real per capita income rising, and unemployment falling to 6 percent. Then, in April, came the news that wages and prices had unexpectedly increased. Food prices had risen at an annual rate of more than 20 percent since January, and meat prices were astronomical. The dollar promptly fell to record lows against the German mark, the Japanese yen, and the Swiss franc. The federal debt, which had doubled between 1965 and 1975, was in the process of doubling yet again between 1975 and 1980. State and local government debts were soaring too, along with mortgage and consumer debts. The administration generally received no credit for the reduction in unemployment figures, a staffer complained, and even when "we do, it is wiped out by increasing apprehension over inflation, the dollar, huge trade and budget deficits, and sagging stock market. All of this together, plus the lack of any high presidential profile in recent months on economic concerns, has, I'm afraid, led many people to conclude that a) we don't share their deep concerns about the economy, b) we have no policies to deal with them, or c) if we do have such policies, we're somehow unable to make them effective." Carter's mid-April 1978 acknowledgment that inflation, then at a rate of 6.5 percent, had "become embedded in the very tissue of our economy" did not quell the anxiety, particularly since he just asked labor and business to keep a lid on wage and price increases. Inflation became the most pressing economic problem.[46]

With inflation now at a rate of 8.9 percent, the president announced Phase II of his anti-inflation drive on October 24, 1978, just three days before he signed Humphrey-Hawkins into law. In the past Carter had often denied that deficits significantly contributed to inflation. He blamed inflation instead on "a cycle" of wage and price increases that "kind of grow on one another." Now he became a deficit hawk and joined ranks with those who insisted deficits caused inflation and had to be reduced. Like economic growth, the reasoning went, inflation swelled federal coffers by moving taxpayers into higher tax brackets at the same time that it reduced purchasing power by forcing up interest rates and prices. Government borrowing drove interest rates higher and spurred the Fed to expand monetary supply. That led to a new round of higher prices, which set everything off again, and led to dire predictions that it would soon require a wheelbarrow full of dollars to purchase a loaf of bread. So with Phase II, Carter called for voluntary wage and price guidelines aimed at deceleration and holding wage increases to 7 percent, price hikes to 5.75 percent, and the budgetary deficit for 1979 to thirty billion dollars.[47]

Americans were not heartened. At Halloween 1978, the *Washington Post* reported: "The dollar plunged to record lows throughout the world yesterday while U.S. investors sold off stocks in near panic amounts in apparent uneasiness over President Carter's new anti-inflation program." As dollars accumulated abroad, Arabs, Europeans, and Japanese flaunted their wealth. "Foreigners are buying America," *Newsweek* said in November. American industrialists continued looking for cheap labor in less developed countries, which accelerated the pace of deindustrialization. The outlook for employment in the United States remained bleak outside service, retail, and white-collar sectors, where unions were relatively weak. The price of imports, on which Americans were becoming more dependent as their own productivity lessened, skyrocketed.[48]

On November 1, a week before the midterm elections, Carter announced that the administration would rescue the dollar as part of his anti-inflation program. Only by taking a number of steps away from easy money, including raising the discount rate by a full point to 9.5 percent, the steepest climb in nearly a half century, did the Fed save the dollar from collapse. Even so, by year's end in 1978 the inflation rate was above 9 percent. The prime interest rate that banks charged their best corporate customers was 11.75 percent, up from 8 percent in January. The Steins' nightmare scenario of six-thousand-dollar cab rides was coming closer to reality.[49]

Neither liberals nor conservatives liked Phase II. Carter's economists thought stringency more necessary than did his political strategists. Vice President Mondale did not believe that cutting the deficit was worth Carter's "killing himself" with the old Democratic coalition. When Ted Kennedy suggested that Carter's austerity penalized the poor, reporters spoke of "a widening schism in the Democratic Party between yourself and Senator Kennedy," which Carter denied existed. Characterizing Carter "the most conservative chief executive since Calvin Coolidge," George Meany now urged mandatory wage and price controls, and 1978 polls repeatedly showed that a majority of Americans favored them. Most business leaders, conservatives, and Republicans of course resisted them. They warned that the president's guidelines, though technically voluntary, represented a step toward mandatory controls and questioned his commitment to the inflation fight. At bottom, though, they agreed with Meany that Phase II would not rescue the economy. The problem with voluntary wage and price guidelines was just that: They were voluntary. They did not curb inflation.[50]

LIKE THE ENERGY CRISIS, inflation undermined Carter's presidency. The annual average inflation rate of 7.6 percent in 1978 looked good next to that of 11.2 percent in 1979 and 13.6 percent in 1980; the prime interest rate of 11.75 percent in December 1978 looked good next to that of 15.25 percent in December 1979 and 21.5 percent in December 1980. Later, however, reflecting on the administration's failure to negotiate more effectively with congressional Democrats, Hamilton Jordan said,

"Probably most importantly [*sic*]—and here this is no one's fault but our own, we did not arrive in Washington with a unifying philosophy to pull the political considerations, problems, needs, hopes, and aspirations of the American people together." That was not quite right, for the president had set out a philosophy in his Inaugural Address.[51]

In truth, the administration's domestic legacy was a question. Perhaps no president, no matter how adroit, could have succeeded in the 1970s. Perhaps no president, particularly not a Democrat who came to power by running against the troubled post–New Deal liberal order, could have prospered. Yet what if Carter had set out his vision of president as trustee and his theme that America possessed "limits" more persuasively?[52] Perhaps he might not have lost liberals at just the point that conservatives set out to persuade more Americans of the magic of the free market.

PART THREE

READY FOR THE EIGHTIES: MOBILIZATION ON THE RIGHT

IX

THE MARKET AS MAGNET

IN ONE OF THE MOST MISTAKEN PREDICTIONS EVER, JIMMY CARTER'S pollster dismissed the Republicans. They "are bent on self-destruction" and "in deep trouble," Patrick Caddell informed the president-elect. "Their ideology is restrictive; they have few bright lights to offer the public." During the late 1970s, however, Republicans trumpeted the market as an alternative to acceptance of "limits."[1]

CALIFORNIA: FREE LUNCH?

It seemed so simple and satisfying. The Keynesians' Phillips Curve suggested that higher unemployment meant lower inflation; higher inflation, lower unemployment. But the simultaneous high inflation and high unemployment of the 1970s undermined the Keynesian consensus. "Is Keynes dead?" pundits asked.[2]

Not quite, but his hegemony and that of the Phillips Curve were teetering. In place of the Phillips Curve, some were touting the bullet-shaped Laffer Curve on which two tax rates produced identical revenue. A high tax rate on a small dollar value yielded the same revenue as a low rate on a large dollar value; both a 0 percent and 100 percent tax rate would bring in nothing. Tax people beyond the equilibrium point, and productivity slowed.

It followed, according to the Laffer Curve, that beyond the equilibrium point, lower tax rates would actually bring in greater revenues than higher ones. By giving Americans the incentive to awaken their ingenuity, the right tax cut would enlarge the tax base and the supply side of the economy, to the government's profit. Republicans who

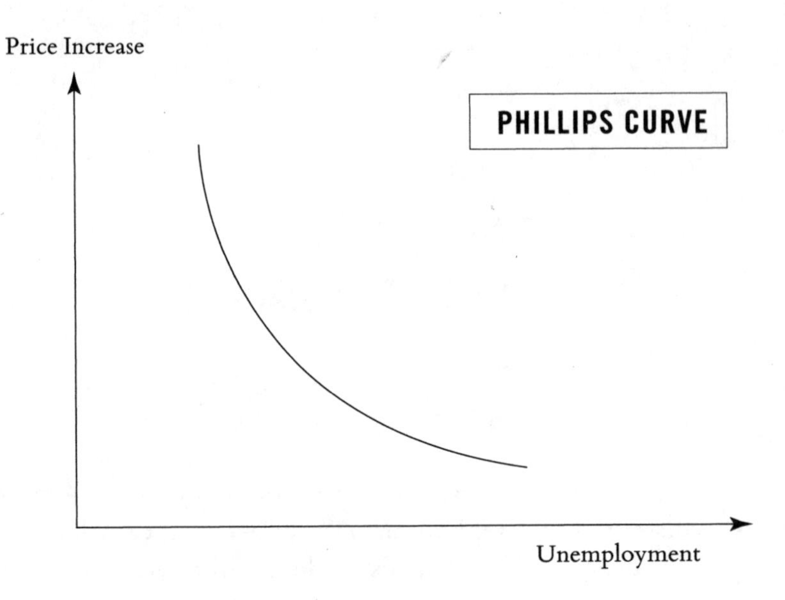
Price Increase
PHILLIPS CURVE
Unemployment

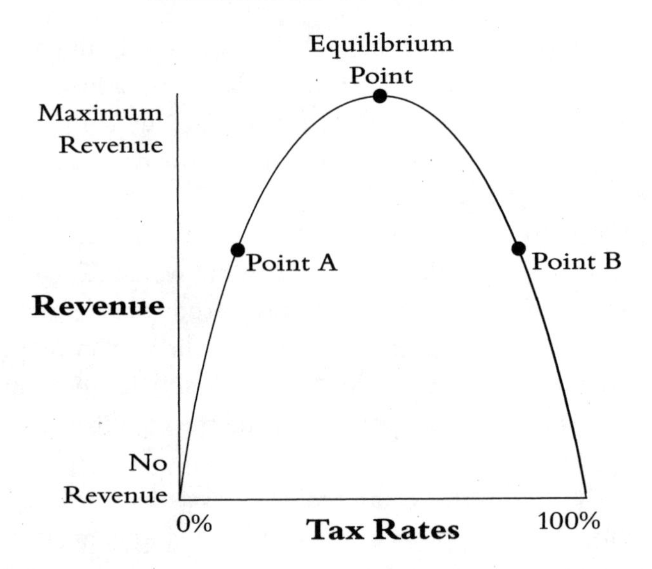
LAFFER CURVE
Equilibrium
Point
Maximum
Revenue
Point A
Point B
Revenue
No
Revenue
0%
Tax Rates
100%

had divided over whether to reduce the deficit or taxes no longer need anguish between priorities: Tax cuts would ensure a balanced budget and prosperity. And less reliance on deficit spending, along with lower taxes, when combined with prudent monetary policy and free trade, would end inflation. Those who stopped worrying about wealth confiscation would work harder and invest more responsibly. They would, for example, shun tax shelters—those unproductive investments that provided taxpayers with deductions, losses, and other tax benefits—and put their money in projects that would increase productivity.[5]

Voilà! Lower tax rates and tight money would generate greater governmental revenues and reduce deficit and inflation. In the late 1970s, supply-side economics promised "the proverbial 'free lunch,'" economist Arthur Laffer said, for it transformed lower taxes from a bonanza for the rich into increased revenues that would benefit the public interest. All the while, it preserved the safety net, a cause dear to Laffer, who had only recently switched from the Democrats to Republicans and thought it "immoral" to "cut Social Security or unemployment insurance in a down economy."[6]

The emphasis on compassion may have seemed new, but everything else was recycled. As Laffer stressed, "supply-side economics is little more than a new label for standard neoclassical economics" that concentrated on modifying behavior by changing economic incentives. Urged by Adam Smith, it had been popularized by economist Jean-Baptiste Say in the nineteenth century, then remade into Say's law of markets by Keynes, who then reduced it to five simple words he could easily disprove during the Great Depression of the 1930s: Supply creates its own demand.

Now Say's law ascended again. One of the first to rediscover it was Columbia University economist Robert Mundell, who won the Nobel Prize in 1999. Twenty-five years earlier Mundell had proposed attacking stagflation by combining two policies the Keynesians thought at odds: tight money to check inflation and a tax cut to stimulate production. "It just set me off," Laffer said. Laffer focused on determining how to structure the tax cut. *Wall Street Journal* reporter Jude Wanniski spread the gospel according to Mundell-Laffer.[7]

Irving Kristol was another Laffer enthusiast. Most neoconservatives had remained Keynsians. Kristol, the first to become a Republican, did not. Uncertain that the theories of Mundell and Laffer's work were good economics, he understood that they were good politics. "Republican economics was then in truth a dismal science, explaining to the populace, parent-like, why the good things in life that they wanted were all too expensive." Kristol was to move Mundell and Laffer from the GOP fringes to the center of popular culture.[8]

It was tough going. Wanniski remembered meeting with Dick Cheney for cocktails after the 1974 Republican midterm election disaster so that Laffer might explain how cutting taxes might turn around the economy and GOP fortunes. When Cheney seemed mystified by the idea that two taxes could yield the same revenue, Laffer grabbed a napkin and drew his curve.[9]

Neither Laffer nor Cheney later recalled anything about curve or napkin, but the story made good copy. So did Laffer, a "bubbly" economist who had abandoned tenure at Chicago for USC; shared the good life in California with pet terrapin, ferret, macaw, and five parrots; and wore alligator cowboy boots, listened to Waylon Jennings, and collected rare crystal. Just as important, Wanniski said, the Laffer Curve "saved us years. You could, in drawing the curve, persuade someone." Wanniski provided historical examples, such as the Kennedy-Johnson tax cut of 1964, that he claimed demonstrated the wisdom of the Laffer Curve.[10]

But the salesmen needed a catchier title for their wares than "Mundell-Laffer Hypothesis." They found one in 1976, after Republican economist Herbert Stein had lampooned them as "supply-side fiscalists" in an allusion to their obsession with tax cuts, production, and increased supply. Like neoconservatives, "supply-siders" appropriated the derogatory reference.[11]

Cheney and other policy makers shared Stein's scorn. The tax reduction that Ford signed into law represented no victory for supply-siders. "That wasn't what we wanted at all," Mundell said. It did not cut taxes sufficiently, and it aimed at stimulating demand and consumption, instead of supply and production.[12]

Whatever their politics, prominent economists of the Kennedy to Ford era initially condemned supply-side economics too. As the architect of the Kennedy-Johnson tax cut Walter Heller mocked the reliance of supply-siders on it as precedent: The 1964 tax cut was intended to increase demand when inflation and the deficit were low. Of course, lower tax rates would increase revenues at some point in the long run, others observed. But where was the equilibrium point, and when would the long run arrive, and how much would short-term revenue losses raise deficits in the meantime? "Laffer is no longer a very serious scholar," said

George Stigler, a conservative University of Chicago economist, of his former colleague. "The Laffer curve is more or less a tautology."[13]

Laffer concurred that his curve was "almost a tautology," confessed he could not identify the equilibrium point, and conceded that he had no proof that before that point on his curve, lower tax rates would deliver higher revenues. "There's more than a reasonable probability that I'm wrong," he admitted. "But the system is not working, so why not try something new?"[14]

What supply-siders needed was a politician to tout their program. They found their man in Jack Kemp, a former pro football quarterback who represented Buffalo in Congress. Wanniski first wrote him off as "a right-wing football player," then reconsidered after a dinner with Kemp at which the main course was supply-side economics. Kemp brought more to the cause than his passion, persuasiveness, and elected status. As a representative of a working-class district he was ideally situated to argue that supply-side economics was not traditional trickle-down economics aimed at aiding the rich and leaving crumbs for the poor. Rather, Kemp made the case that the "rising tide" of lower taxes would "lift all boats." Lower taxes, Kemp said, would encourage the steelworker who refused overtime because taxes left him just fifty cents of each dollar to put in more hours to enlarge the economic pie. And if the worker did lose his job, Kemp continued, a Republican government must show compassion. Anything else was bad policy and politics. The Democrats picked up votes for spending while the Republicans played the heavy and insisted on balancing the budget. He no longer thought of government and Democrats as "the enemy," Kemp said. "I have come to realize that the real enemy is my own party, which hasn't been offering a real choice to the electorate. We're the ones who have said to the people, 'Don't come to our table for dinner. All we're going to do is tighten your belt.'"[15]

Those words from that source gave supply-side economics credibility and enticed Ronald Reagan. When Wanniski told one Reagan strategist in 1976 that Kemp, a Ford delegate, might switch to Reagan if the Republican challenger endorsed supply-side economics, he was brushed off. But after Ford won the nomination, Reagan examined supply-side economics and began to laud it, though whether he believed that a tax cut would generate increased revenue immediately or "would not lose as much revenue as one might expect" remained obscure. The New Right, *Human Events*, and *Wall Street Journal* were supply-side converts too.[16]

In October 1977, Kemp and another Republican, Senator William Roth of Delaware, called for a 30 percent cut in federal income tax rates over the next three years and a reduction in corporate taxes that they said would inject $43.4 billion into the economy and create 1.2 million new jobs that would substantially reduce the unemployment rate below 7.1 percent. It remained only for Wanniski to gather together the supply-siders' program in a best seller, *The Way the World Works*, an entertaining paean to the contribution of tax cuts to civilization that Laffer described as "the best book on economics ever written."[17]

In the fall of 1977, when the Senate was beginning to destroy Carter's energy bill, Robert Livingston rode Kemp-Roth to victory in a special New Orleans election and became the first Republican to represent his district in the House since Reconstruction. Though Republicans constituted less than 6 percent of the voters in his district, Livingston sold Kemp-Roth's promises to blue-collar whites and African Americans. For supply-siders, the significance was clear: If Republicans realized that their misfortunes resulted from their "failure to understand the nature of the Laffer Curve" and rammed Kemp-Roth into law, a GOP "renaissance" would follow.[18]

Strong stuff, this, and best demonstrated in a laboratory. California was an obvious proving ground. To supply-siders, Proposition 13 offered "a dramatic test" of their theory.[19]

"DEATH AND TAXES may be inevitable, but being taxed to death is not!" So Howard Jarvis, a Republican who had worked for Herbert Hoover and whose own Holy Grail was lower taxes and less spending, shouted during his Proposition 13 campaign. He seized upon the misery of working- and middle-class homeowners in California, where the legislature routinely defused property tax rebellions by approving modest cuts before elections.[20]

Inflation made a new constituency angry and hardened the old one's resolve. As late as 1973 Southern California housing prices remained below the national average. But between 1974 and 1978 the average price of a single-family house in Los Angeles jumped from $37,800 to $83,200, while the national average price rose less than 50 percent. Given California's formula for computing property taxes—assessed valuation (25 percent of property market value) multiplied by a tax rate that ran as high as 10 percent in some places—tax bills soared. The less fortunate homeowners were hit especially hard; Jarvis maintained that some elderly Californians saved money for taxes by eating pet food. So what if their houses were increasing in value? Where would they go if they sold them? Beginning in 1976, the prosperous screamed too. At a time when inflation caused bracket creep by forcing them into higher income tax brackets, the rich took larger property tax bills personally. According to one historian, the participation of the upper-middle class in the tax revolt distinguished it from earlier protests. The haves had tempers too hot to ignore.[21]

Yet government did. And it rankled, especially when everyone knew that larger property tax revenues meant California was operating in the black. Lawmakers could not agree on the size of the projected budgetary surplus or how much tax relief the state could afford. A 1977 bill that would have provided a break for lower-income homeowners foundered. While politicians were posturing, California homeowners were receiving their 1977 tax bills. Something strange was happening too: They had stopped complaining to legislators. They had lost faith in them.[22]

And Jarvis, who had teamed up with Paul Gann to put a tax reduction initiative on the ballot, was now collecting signatures "by the truckload." By the end of 1977 they had one million more than they needed to qualify their initiative, a proposed amendment to California's constitution, for a vote in June 1978. The Jarvis-Gann amendment, soon referred to nationwide as Proposition 13 or 13, would provide a cure. First, it cut the property tax rate, which averaged about 2.6 percent of current market value, to a flat 1 percent. Second, it froze the "current" market value of property at what it had been on the 1975–76 tax bill or its most recent sale, whichever was later. Third, at a time when assessed market values were rising by 20 percent a year, it limited the annual increase in market value to 2 percent, as long as the same owner held the property. It added up to a two-thirds cut in property taxes and a loss in local property tax revenues of seven to eight billion dollars.[23]

The impact of Proposition 13 on individual lives was even more striking. An accountant who owned a house assessed at $110,000 (about $360,000 in 2009 dollars) would no longer pay $3,400 in property taxes. Rather, he would owe $1,100 and could rest assured that assessed value would rise at a rate well below inflation. (Since 13 also required a two-thirds vote of the legislature to enact new revenue-raising taxes, he need not fear the enactment of most other new taxes either.)[24]

Panicked, legislators scrambled for a horse of their own with which to beat Jarvis-Gann. Their solution provided half the tax relief offered by Proposition 13 to homeowners and enabled the state to tax commercial property at a higher rate than residences. It too required an amendment to the California Constitution and appeared on the June 1978 ballot as Proposition 8. The foes of Proposition 13 also launched a negative campaign. They said Jarvis was "the paid director of an association of apartment house owners" and contended that 13 would benefit owners of apartment houses and commercial real estate, which were sold less frequently than houses. Homeowners would receive just a third of its relief. (They overestimated: Homeowners ultimately received less than a quarter of the Proposition 13 savings, while the rest went to owners of businesses, apartment houses, and commercial property.)[25]

Opponents warned that 13 would make winners out of those grandfathered in at the 1975–76 rates and losers out of the subsequent buyers. Was it fair that the accountant's property tax bill would still hover around eleven hundred dollars in thirty years while that of his neighbor might be many times that? They painted scenarios of crippled local institutions and massive layoffs of teachers, librarians, and government employees for lack of state funds. There was "no sugar daddy in Sacramento who will bail you out if Proposition 13 passes," Governor Jerry Brown threatened.[26]

Elected politicians, however, were no match for the roguish Jarvis. "Mr. Proposition 13" portrayed politicians as "dummies, goons, cannibals or big-mouths" and said those who called him the front man for apartment landlords were "liars" spouting "manure." Every residential and commercial property owner would receive the same tax reduction as apartment owners. Further, how could he be a corporate pawn when big business, labor, bureaucrats, the press, and establishment politicians all were opposed to him? (Business executives feared that legislators would make up for the loss in revenue by increasing corporate taxes.)[27]

All he had "against that lineup were the people," Jarvis liked to say, and two economists. University of Chicago economics professor Milton Friedman, a veteran of the Goldwater brain trust and an engaging spokesperson for the free market in his own regular *Newsweek* column, pushed Proposition 13 on the assumption that it would force government to cut spending. Laffer contended that like Kemp-Roth, reduced taxes would attract new capital to California. Under either scenario, Jarvis said, "everyone's a winner." So what if neither occurred right away?

No matter what politicians said, the state would have to bail out local government. And "if a library here and there has to close Wednesday mornings from 9 to 11, life will go on. Who the hell goes to the library in the morning anyway?"[28]

Though Jarvis clearly struck a chord, support for Proposition 8 grew. Then, in mid-May 1978 came the coup de grâce. With a bullfighter's skill, Jarvis taunted the Los Angeles Country assessor into releasing the latest assessments, and Angelenos realized that average tax bills were scheduled to increase by 125 percent. No official backpedaling reduced the shock. Then the state finance director announced that California's 1978 surplus would approach five billion dollars, rather than the three billion projected.[29]

That did it. The astronomical tax bills and huge state surplus led two-thirds of voting Californians to support 13. His movement had "put a fence between the hogs and the swill bucket," Jarvis rejoiced. He would "go big league" and national. "We have a new revolution," he told reporters. "We are telling the government, 'Screw you!' "[30]

While Jarvis was sending that message, most of his supporters were not. Statistics showed that most homeowners simply sought a tax break. And why not? Predictably, legislators did approve the use of the surplus to bail out municipalities. (In an irony lost on Jarvis, that heightened the dependence of local governments on the state.) True, pollsters reported that "very strong majorities, in California and throughout the nation, felt 'the government' was getting too big and too powerful and was spending too much." Yet except for the predictable scapegoat of welfare, polls also showed that most of 13's backers wanted more spending on services they found useful.[31]

Nor did the success of Proposition 13 necessarily herald a shift to the right. As one journalist said, "California voters' supposed conservative allegiance proved utterly empty when the next political expression of economic outrage turned out to be—of all things—a successful rent control drive." But Californians' contradictory attitudes ("Taxes, No! Big Government, No! Services, Yes!") helped explain the appeal of supply-side economics.[32]

CHICAGO: RECLAIMING LIBERALISM

Among those who chose to misinterpret the meaning of Proposition 13 was Milton Friedman. "The populace is coming to recognize that throwing government at problems has a way of making them worse," he cheered. His desire to cut government spending also led him to support what he called the Kemp-Roth free lunch. By increasing the deficit and pushing government closer to bankruptcy, Friedman reasoned, Kemp-Roth would ultimately inhibit spending.[33]

This was hardly a ringing endorsement of supply-side economics. Yet to Friedman, what united him with supply-siders was more significant than what divided them. Though they differed about the desirability of big, beneficent government, they shared a faith in the market.

Along with others at Chicago, Friedman preached "true" neoclassical economics. To be sure, as he would have stressed, many differences divided Chicago economists. Still, Stigler acknowledged, "the public and much of the economics profession now take to be the central position of the Chicago School—a devotion to private (competitive) markets to organize the production and consumption of goods, with only limited economic functions for the state."[34]

Friedman and Stigler had begun publicizing Chicago School economics in 1946, just two years after Friedrich von Hayek, a student of Ludwig von Mises and a sometime Chicagoan, had published his polemic against the welfare state, *The Road to Serfdom*. According to Friedman and Stigler, by artificially setting price ceilings, wartime and postwar rent controls discouraged the construction of new buildings that would have provided sorely needed roofs and perpetuated the demand for rent controls. Government price controls inevitably backfired. The long gas lines in 1973–74, they argued, emerged because government bureaucracy interfered with the price system that otherwise would have efficiently brought together buyers and sellers.[35]

A second message accompanied Friedman and Stigler's praise of the price system: Regulatory agencies were neutralized by those they regulated. Not always. Small businessmen in the 1970s, for example, who joined the STOP OSHA campaign spearheaded by the American Conservative Union, claimed that the welter of regulations issued by the Occupational Safety and Health Administration, which *Human Events* labeled "the chief federal harassment agency," made it nearly impossible for them to function. Yet regulatory capture often occurred. As Woodrow Wilson had warned, "If the government is to tell big business men how to run their business, then don't you see that big business men have to get closer to the government even than they are now?" Stigler provided empirical evidence supporting Wilson's rhetoric, which Friedman publicized.[36]

Rich, conservative businessmen had promoted Hayek, Friedman, and Stigler and had funded a number of think tanks, organizations, and other institutions to promote the free market since the 1930s. Moreover, Hayek, Friedman, and Stigler each won the Nobel Prize in Economics between 1974 and 1982, a period when business was becoming the nation's most popular undergraduate major and Students in Free Enterprise chapters were springing up on college campuses. Nevertheless, in the early 1970s neoclassical economists felt marginalized. As *Human Events* complained, the media gave "disproportionate attention to the interventionist views" of Keynesians, among them Gunnar Myrdal, the socialist who shared the 1974 Nobel Prize with Hayek. Stigler once remarked that "[a] few people believe that almost all regulation is bad, and by a singular coincidence a significant fraction of the academic part of this group resides within a radius of one mile of my university." That was an overstatement: As they became more aggressive lobbyists in the 1970s, businessmen, large and small, repeatedly cited the warning of Washington University's Murray Weidenbaum that Americans would spend more than one hundred billion dollars annually on regulation by 1979. Market liberalism also flourished at the University of Virginia and at think tanks on other campuses. But Stigler did not exaggerate that much about the hold of the Keynesian consensus on the elite scholars.[37]

The task, Friedman believed, was not simply to celebrate the price system and expose the regulatory process but to reclaim the mantle of liberalism for Republicans. He believed that the Democrats were deficient on two counts: They did not protect liberty, and they limited economic freedom. Contemporary liberals championed free speech for pornographers, for example, while encouraging government to rein in cigarette manufacturers.[38]

Realizing his vision of market liberalism, or neoliberalism, Friedman believed, required revising the standard understanding of America's history. By the conventional account, the late nineteenth century was "an era of rugged, unrestrained individualism . . . with the closest approximation to pure economic laissez-faire in American history" when greedy robber barons exploited farmers and workers. Only governmental intervention in the twentieth century through minimum wages and other social welfare legislation relieved the oppressed. When the Great

Depression exposed the limitations of the free market, the story continued, Franklin Roosevelt and the New Deal saved capitalism and paved the way for a larger governmental role in the economy. In the decades that followed, government kept the economy running smoothly by following the gospel according to Keynes and adjusting taxing, spending, and interest rates and providing a safety net for prosperity's orphans.[39]

The story was true, Friedman maintained, only insofar as the nineteenth century was the heyday of individualism and laissez-faire. Beyond that, the conventional understanding was a tissue paper of lies. The wealthy had not been robber barons, but philanthropists. During the late nineteenth century the "ordinary" American had not been downtrodden but had experienced an unparalleled "increase in his standard of living." If life had been so tough for the poor, why had so many immigrants come to the United States? Friedman's mother had arrived as a teenager and worked in a sweatshop. Had a minimum wage existed then, sweatshops would have proved unprofitable, and she might not have found her way station to a better life. Nor had a crisis of capitalism and unregulated private enterprise caused the Depression. On the contrary, "government mismanagement" and the Fed's constriction of money were the culprit.[40]

Beyond regulating the growth of the quantity of money, government should do as little as possible and should become the "policeman and umpire" the Founding Fathers envisioned, Friedman maintained. He devoted his 1976 Nobel Prize lecture to demonstrating that the tradeoff between inflation and unemployment portrayed in the Phillips Curve was wrong, and he soon wrote a best seller that stressed the interdependence of capitalism and freedom. As Keynes's star fell, Friedman's rose. Abroad his admirers and advisees included Augusto Pinochet, the brutal dictator of Chile brought to power by the Nixon administration, and Margaret Thatcher, who would launch Britain in a neoliberal direction after her 1979 election as its prime minister.[41]

AS FRIEDMAN PERSONIFIED the Chicago School of Economics, so Richard Posner symbolized Chicago law and economics. In his 1972 book *Economic Analysis of Law*, Posner, a law professor at Chicago, set out his key proposition. In the legal system, as in the economic world, "man is a rational maximizer of his self-interest" and would "respond to incentives" aimed at changing his behavior. Like the market, "law should be efficient."[42]

Yet was not law about "justice" and "fairness"? If X, while out hunting, shot a careless Y, Y's attorney might insist that it was "just" or "fair" that X compensate Y. But the judge had to look to the future when his or her decision would become precedent. Y's victory, Posner maintained, would encourage carelessness. If the judge ruled for X, Y would suffer, but the decision might make others behave more responsibly. "The legal and economic approaches are not so divergent after all."[43]

The increasing prominence of law and economics scholars during the 1970s attested to the rise of a conservative legal movement bankrolled by the Olin Foundation and other conservative philanthropies. That movement was to challenge and undermine legal liberalism and the liberal consensus in elite law schools, but its influence was not fully felt until the 1980s. Even in the 1970s, though, Posner and other Chicago lawyer-economists were spreading a similar message to Friedman and Stigler's. Governmental compassion for the individual backfired against the many. Further, judges were less likely to display that compassion than legislators.[44]

Not always, again. Sometimes judges were at fault. In his 1978 book, *The Antitrust Paradox*, former solicitor general Robert Bork, now a Yale law professor steeped in University of Chicago law and economics, argued that judges had misinterpreted the Sherman Antitrust Act. According to Bork, legislators had sought to promote "consumer welfare" by fostering economic efficiency and "free markets with minimal government involvement." The Supreme Court had perverted the legislative vision and the market by introducing "conflicting goals, the primary one being the survival or comfort of small business." Judges should return to first principles and cease threatening the most efficient corporations. Though historians ridiculed Bork's attempt to dress the framers of the Sherman Act in the garb of neoclassical economists, *The Antitrust Paradox* immediately became the "symbol of the Chicago School approach to antitrust."[45]

Just as important, the book may have spurred Posner to speak with greater candor. "Bork called his theory 'maximization of consumer welfare,' but that is just a reassuring term for wealth maximization," Posner said. Soon afterward Posner embraced wealth maximization as the highest policy goal. If a "Nazi Germany wanted to get rid of the Jews," it would "buy them out" and maximize Jews' worth. The wealth maximization principle worked because everything had its price.[46]

All society would benefit because everything, including body parts, would be for sale. In a famous 1978 article about the scarcity of adoptable infants, "The Economics of the Baby Shortage," Posner and Elizabeth Landes spoke of partially deregulating adoption and permitting adoption agencies to pay pregnant women considering abortion to carry babies to term. After all, there could be "no immorality in the idea of a baby market, when morality is derived from economic principle itself."[47]

Predictably, Posner's proposals proved controversial. Though the guideline of wealth maximization was clear, one skeptic said, Posner did not explain why society should adopt it, and "hardly anyone since King Midas has really believed that wealth is an ultimate goal." Further, the wealth maximization criterion reinforced the status quo: The richest could pay the prices that would most increase society's wealth. Nonetheless, together with Chicago economics and antitrust, law and economics ensured a reconsideration of the relationship between government and the market.[48]

WASHINGTON: TOWARD A NEW RELATIONSHIP BETWEEN GOVERNMENT AND MARKET

More and more individuals in the nation's capital became interested in rethinking that relationship in the mid-1970s. The deregulation movement began to gain momentum in 1975. After an explosion of regulatory activity between 1969 and 1974, Senator Ted Kennedy held hearings on the airline industry. They revealed that the Civil Aeronautics Board (CAB) stopped new aviation companies from entering the business, doled out lucrative and unprofitable routes so each carrier received a combination of "plums and dogs," and ensured that much travel was expensive. Small wonder carriers did not favor deregulation. The Kennedy hearings vindicated Stigler's thesis of regulatory capture. Although Ford declared that "[f]ederal regulatory commissions have actually thwarted competition," opposition from the regulated stalled deregulation.[49]

What to do? President Carter made Alfred Kahn, a wisecracking Cornell economist, the CAB chair. Deregulation bills were stacked up in Congress, and Kennedy had introduced one the White House favored. But as Mary Schuman, a twenty-seven-year-old lawyer on the Domestic Policy Staff, reported, "[t]he industry pressure on Capitol Hill is *intense*." For their part, airline executives scorned "Typhoid Mary" and scared labor unions into joining the antagonists.[50]

Kahn and the White House mobilized a diverse and unlikely array of allies in favor of deregulation, including Milton Friedman, the American Conservative Union, consumer advocates, and liberal Democrats. The result was the Airline Deregulation Act of 1978. It allowed airline carriers to set their fares on a competitive basis, enabled them to choose their own routes, permitted new carriers to enter the market, and provided for the CAB's phase-out. Carter considered airline deregulation one of his administration's "great success stories" and used it to promote and achieve full or partial deregulation of trucking, railroads, banking, cable TV, and natural gas. Yet it was difficult to position Carter as an opponent of bureaucracy since, for example, as conservatives delighted in pointing out, he had actively supported the creation of two new cabinet-level departments, Energy and Education. Most associated deregulation with the Chicago School of economists and Carter's successor. "These were genuine accomplishments of the Carter administration, and I find it absolutely infuriating that the public ignorantly gives principal credit instead to President Reagan," Kahn lamented.[51]

DEREGULATION WAS A BIPARTISAN effort, but the Republicans owned supply-side economics and Kemp-Roth. "In 1978 there was a revolution in the Republican Party," recalled Kemp staffer Bruce Bartlett. "Led by proponents of the Kemp-Roth Bill and its later variations, the Steiger Amendment to slash capital gains taxes, and Proposition 13, the Republicans established a new antithesis to the dominant thesis of New Deal liberalism." The observation was inaccurate insofar as it gave supply-siders credit for the passage of Proposition 13. In fact, they co-opted it. (So did everyone else, including Carter, who used 13 as an excuse to back away from a costly national health insurance bill that Kennedy and labor held dear and to bury a welfare reform bill.) In other respects, Bartlett was on point. Since 1976 the GOP had developed supply-side economics and Kemp-Roth and had joined in the celebration of the market.[52]

Yet with the temporary tax cuts enacted during the Ford administration due to expire in 1979, President Carter stuck to the old Democratic standby of tax reform. Characterizing the tax system as a "disgrace" during his campaign, Carter promised to make it simpler, fairer, more efficient and progressive. He spoke of ending the preferential treatment of capital gains and taxing the profit on the sale of capital assets, such as stock and real estate, at the same rate as ordinary income. Since the wealthiest cut their taxable income through shelters or by deducting "three-martini lunches" and other luxuries as business expenses, he also vowed to go after shelters and deductions. The tax burden would be moved from the shoulders of those who could least afford it to the rich and corporations.

From the standpoint of conservatives, business and the wealthy, the $25 billion tax reform and reduction package Carter sent to Congress in January 1978 could have been worse. It did show government cracking down on tax shelters, deductions, and other loopholes. It also effectively raised the capital gains tax rate for the wealthiest. Yet although $17 billion was earmarked for relief for low- and middle-income taxpayers, Carter proposed corporate tax cuts of $6 billion. By now, however, Carter had violated another tax-related campaign pledge. As a candidate he had promised that Social Security payroll taxes would not rise. But when he learned in 1977 that Social Security faced financial problems, the president presented a plan to Congress that resulted, in December, in the approval of additional payroll taxes of $227 billion during the next decade, the largest peacetime tax increase in American history.[53]

Carter's tax reform package was a bust. His staff found that many dismissed the proposed cuts "as little more than a wash for the Social Security tax increases." At a time when the president was becoming more concerned about inflation, the business community produced study after study showing that his tax cut would raise prices. Like Ford before him, the president was vulnerable to charges that he had structured the cut to increase consumption (in Carter's case, particularly among lower-income Americans), rather than the productivity that supply-siders considered all important.[54]

REPRESENTATIVE WILLIAM STEIGER, a "baby-faced" Wisconsin Republican, sensed that the political winds were shifting and that Congress was ready to cut, rather than raise, capital gains. The administration had judged Steiger one of the Republicans on the House Ways and Means Committee most likely to support its tax bill. Instead, as Ways and Means began to consider Carter's tax proposals in April 1978, Steiger moved to cut top capital gains taxes for individuals and corporations, which Congreess and the Nixon administration had raised from 28 to

49 percent. He and Senator Clifford Hansen, a conservative Wyoming Republican, introduced the Investment Incentive Act of 1978, also known as Steiger-Hansen and the Steiger Amendment, as an amendment to Carter's tax bill. For the first time since Democrats won control of Congress in 1955, Steiger and Hansen openly sought to structure a tax cut in favor of the wealthy. They would roll back the maximum capital gains tax rate to 25 percent. Supply-siders loved Steiger-Hansen, which Laffer promised would inspire investment, increase capital mobility, and boost revenues.[55]

There were two additional reasons for Steiger-Hansen's fame. One was the mobilization of a sophisticated campaign mounted by Charls Walker, Nixon's deputy secretary of the treasury. After leaving government, Walker had followed an old and profitable path and become a lobbyist for the regulated. Among his clients was the Business Roundtable, an organization of leading corporate executives formed in 1972 that, according to *Business Week*, "has emerged as the nation's most influential group of business leaders." In the old days Walker would have sought to block a presidential reform package by concentrating on House Ways and Means Committee chair Al Ullman. Since the chair had less power after the 1974 changes in congressional operations, every committee member also heard from Walker's troops. Abner Mikva, a liberal Democrat from Chicago, remembered being contacted by progressive brokers and bankers who "had their facts. We have to do something for the economy; look at the low rate of savings." Although Mikva understood that "obviously, somebody back in Washington was masterminding this," the letters, calls, and luncheons still packed a wallop by capturing "members one at a time." So did the message. Walker said that Steiger-Hansen would create national prosperity, jobs, and greater income for ordinary taxpayers. Pressed, Walker acknowledged that was not true. "In this game," however, as he "cheerfully" acknowledged to the *Washington Post*, "it's the perception that counts." In fact, the immediate beneficiaries would be the rich: By Secretary of the Treasury Blumenthal's estimate, the bill's enactment would reduce government revenues by over two billion dollars annually, cut the tax bills of those with incomes of over two hundred thousand by an average of fourteen thousand, and save those in the fifteen- to twenty-thousand-dollar range twenty-six cents. But the lobbying proved so effective that Walker soon informed an astounded Ullman that he had the votes to have the Steiger Amendment reported out of committee. After Walker, the second reason for Steiger-Hansen's success was the Proposition 13 "roar from California" and the increased credibility of tax reduction.[56]

The Steiger Amendment stopped the momentum for Carter's tax package. "The numbers and the mood are against us," Blumenthal warned. Yet as it had done in a critical moment on energy, the administration remained curiously mum in April 1978.[57]

Consequently, negotiations did not go well. "I think the story may well be that not only did we send up a tax package which misread the mood of Congress," Domestic Policy Staffer Bob Ginsburg privately told Stuart Eizenstat, "but upon being rebuffed, we retired from the field and became eunuchs." Ullman had suspended work on the Carter tax reform package and was now backing the attempt of Ways and Means member Jim Jones, a conservative Oklahoma Democrat, "to tone down Steiger's capital gains tax bill and see whether the Democrats could get a bit of credit for it." Jones proposed to leave intact almost all the loopholes the president had originally wanted to plug and to cut the maximum capital gains tax to 35 percent, instead of the 25 percent urged by Steiger. For Ullman, the compromise was a godsend.[58]

But Carter disagreed and, during the summer, reentered the fray. The media characterized his opposition as "loud but late," while Ways and Means staffers leaked their frustration that he had remained quiet for so long. He could live without tax reform, Carter hinted, but he had concluded that capital gains tax cuts would unfairly benefit the rich, "add more than $2 billion to the Federal budget deficit," and fuel inflation. In an allusion to Proposition 13, he acknowledged that Americans demanded tax relief. Nevertheless, "neither they nor I will tolerate a plan that provides huge windfalls for millionaires and two bits for the average American." Unimpressed, Steiger declared that the president was bluffing.[59]

The administration belatedly developed an alternative to the Steiger Amendment and Jones compromise. And Speaker O'Neill judged that the House would have approved the administration version five months earlier. Now it had no chance.[60]

On July 20, 1978, Carter repeated his veto threat at a news conference. "The President had a golden opportunity last night before a prime time audience to (1) contrast the American people's support for tax reform with the failure of the Ways and Means Committee to face up to the issue and (2) distance his own decent proposals from what Congress is doing," Ginsburg mourned. He had wasted it with "that flat wooden statement."[61]

As expected, Ways and Means approved the Jones bill. In August the House did too, by a vote of 362–2. Ullman said it would "look good" to Congress after he saw the Senate revisions to it.[62]

It was a stunning moment. *Human Events* maintained that the Jones compromise indicated that liberals were on the defensive for the first time since FDR took office. That was ridiculous. Liberals had often been on the defensive since 1933. Nevertheless, in election years, Congress had long sought tax relief for "regular" middle-income families, and as recently as 1976, Charls Walker had insisted that "[b]usiness feels misunderstood and unloved." The Jones compromise served the wealthy and business. Nor did it remain compromised long. As Ullman predicted, the Senate increased the size of the capital gains cut. "Carter Ignored During Senate Romp," *Tax Notes* proclaimed.[63]

In the end, the Revenue Act of 1978 dissatisfied liberals and conservatives. It provided for some twenty billion dollars in tax cuts for 1979, including a reduction in the maximum capital gains tax rate for individuals to 28 percent, almost what Steiger had proposed. The bottom half of the population received just over a fifth of the tax relief, the top half, just less than four-fifths. The act included some minimal concessions to Carter: Though executives could still write off those three-martini lunches, they could no longer claim yachts and hunting lodges as business expenses. Kennedy and other liberals condemned it as "a Wall Street dream." The equally irate *Wall Street Journal* claimed that the package did not offset increased Social Security and other taxes and that "[t]he taxpayers have been had again."[64]

Nevertheless, Carter signed the bill. With congressional elections approaching, Democrats had to take home something they could call tax reduction. The president rationalized that he was fortunate the revenue act had not been worse.[65]

THAT WAS TRUE. Like the *Wall Street Journal*, Jack Kemp had wanted more. Congress had applied the Kemp-Roth approach to capital gains. But what about Kemp-Roth?

With the victory of Proposition 13 and capital gains tax reduction, Republicans were contemplating making Kemp-Roth, the Laffer Curve, and supply-side economics a centerpiece of the 1978 midterm elections. Uncertain whether the tax revolt was a "bandwagon issue or hot potato," they divided among themselves about the wisdom of embracing tax reduction or the traditional theme of austerity.[66]

But Kemp-Roth was seductive. And on the day of 13's victory, conservative Jeffrey Bell upset Senator Clifford Case, a liberal Republican, in the New Jersey primary. Bell, who had written the speech that created trouble for Reagan in the New Hampshire primary, ran on a supply-side platform against Case. Maybe Kemp was on to something.[67]

So the Republicans decided to gamble. "The issue to be decided this year is whether the people get the tax cut they deserve, or whether they cut down those officials who stand in the way," the Republican National Committee chair Bill Brock announced. Kemp and Roth used the debate over the capital gains tax cut to force both houses of Congress to consider their proposal.[68]

In August, as the House approved the Jones compromise and prepared to send it to the Senate, Kemp launched Kemp-Roth as the "No. 1 offensive play in the country." He urged the committee to cut individual income tax rates by 12 percent, or $32 billion, in 1979; 23 percent, or $79 billion, in 1980; and 35 percent, or $121 billion, in 1981. The familiar debate ensued, with Kemp forecasting that his tax cut would reduce the deficit and inflation and opponents warning that it would cause both to skyrocket. In the House, liberal Democrats became "born again budget balancers" and defeated Kemp's amendment, 240–177. On September 18, Senate Finance Committee members narrowly rejected Senator Roth's attempt to attach a Kemp-Roth proposal to the revenue bill before it went to the Senate floor.[69]

Undeterred, Kemp, Roth, and the minority leaders of the House and Senate clambered into a plane they dubbed the *Republican Tax Clipper* and launched a three-day blitz in September to promote Kemp-Roth and the GOP in the midterm elections. In California, Ford joined them to shout his enthusiasm for the "Republican tax attack of '78." As early as March 1977 Ford had told reporters he might enter the presidential race in 1980. A May 1978 Gallup poll showed him leading Ronald Reagan and all other comers, and by July, Ford was saying he might run without entering state primaries. In Chicago, Reagan climbed aboard. He had used the surplus from his 1976 campaign to establish a multicandidate political action committee, Citizens for the Republic, to contribute to conservative Republican candidates. Reagan himself had been ubiquitous since early 1977, when he electrified conservatives at the Conservative Political Action Conference by insisting that "most Americans are basically conservative" and calling for the creation of a "New Republican Party" that drew its principles from the 1976 Republican platform he had forced on Ford and that combined economic and cultural conservatism. "The New Republican Party I envision will not be, and cannot be, one limited to the country-club big business image that, for reasons both fair and unfair, it is burdened with today," Reagan said, but would welcome the "social conservatives" on whom the "Democratican Party turned its back" during the 1960s: the factory worker, farmer, the "cop on the beat and the millions of Americans who may never have thought of joining our party before, but whose interests coincide with those represented by principled Republicanism." Now Reagan was saying that there was "a distinct possibility" that he would run for president in 1980 on a Kemp-Roth tax-cutting platform. Whereas Goldwater had stressed the need for liberty from government and President Ford had behaved as a scold, Reagan embraced a cheerful market liberalism. He had decided to launch a "rhetorical revolution": He would make it clear that balanced budgets were "for chumps" and that government could benefit all Americans by lowering taxes on individuals and businesses.[70]

Democrats had a field day, attacking Kemp-Roth as another "free lunch" for the rich that would double the deficit and contribute to inflation. But they protested too much. As the revenue bill was about to leave the Senate, Georgia Democrat Sam Nunn sponsored an amendment that would cut taxes by about 25 percent over the next five years if Congress reduced spending enough to ensure a balanced budget. Two-thirds of the Senate voted for it. "The Nunn Amendment was such an election year ploy that Republican leaders dubbed it 'Son of Kemp-Roth.'" It did not survive. Carter could rejoice that there was no trace of it or Kemp-Roth in the Revenue Act of 1978.[71]

TO SOME, IT SEEMED as if neither the defeated Kemp-Roth proposal nor the victorious Proposition 13 were likely to outlast midterm elections. "Proposition 13 had ragged coattails," *Tax Notes* proclaimed on Tuesday, November 7, one day after Carter, without ceremony, had quietly signed the Revenue Act of 1978. Nevada adopted a measure like 13; Oregon defeated one. The Democrats retained large congressional majorities, and Jeffrey Bell lost to liberal Democrat Bill Bradley. Though the *Wall Street Journal* kept the faith, it reported a consensus that Kemp-Roth had been " 'a political blunder of the first magnitude.' " Wanniski recalled that "[t]he political establishment, Republican and Democratic, . . . [was] quick to blame us for preventing greater GOP gains, which would have come about on a Republican platform of austerity and spending cuts." Most politicians concluded that the tax revolt was a mistake.[72]

Hardly. The movement of the market from margin to mainstream was crucial to the rise of conservatism. "The only thing the elections proved to us was that the issue would have to be decided in a Presidential race, with a single leader carrying the revolutionary banner," Wanniski insisted. In 1978, supply-siders saw their proposals had struck a chord, even among Democrats. At the same time, the New Right and the Christian right were drawing closer together.[73]

X

GENDER, GOD, AND GOVERNMENT

—

On November 27, 1978, disgruntled office seeker Dan White assassinated San Francisco mayor George Moscone and Harvey Milk, the first openly gay member of the Board of Supervisors, at San Francisco City Hall. Just three weeks before White opened fire, Californians had reassured the gay community by rejecting an initiative sponsored by fundamentalist John Briggs that would have barred gays and "anyone advocating, imposing, encouraging or promoting . . . a homosexual lifestyle" from teaching in the public schools. Nine days earlier 909 members of the Peoples Temple, a San Francisco–based cult in Jonestown, Guyana, that included hundreds of children, had committed "revolutionary suicide" by drinking a toxic punch distributed by their crazed leader, Jim Jones. San Francisco seemed to be unraveling. The evening of November 27, tens of thousands of San Franciscans marched in protest against the murders of Moscone and Milk. But the following May a jury acquitted White of the murders and convicted him of just two counts of voluntary manslaughter. It bought the defense argument that White, "the voice of the family," was "supremely frustrated" when he saw the city become Sodom, even that his compulsive Twinkie consumption caused variations in his blood sugar level and aggravated his manic depression. One juror described the verdict as "God's will," and the Reverend Jerry Falwell agreed. The remedy, as he saw it, lay in the return of God to government, a goal that united the Christian right and the New Right.[1]

THE CHRISTIAN RIGHT

Evangelicals had long been involved in American politics. They had spearheaded the antislavery and Prohibition movements. The Reverend Martin Luther King, Jr., was an evangelical, as were many African Americans and whites involved in, or supportive of, the civil rights movement. Many evangelicals followed the Reverend Billy Graham, who routinely desegregated his church services throughout the nation, beginning in the mid-1950s, toward the Republican Party. As Lyndon Johnson's friend Graham refused to endorse Barry Goldwater in 1964, but as a Nixon partisan in 1968 and 1972 he helped shape Nixon's racial overtures to southern whites and white evangelicals. (In 1972, however, some younger evangelicals supported Methodist George McGovern.)[2]

Anticommunism and opposition to desegregation had politicized fundamentalists, a more theologically rigorous subset of evangelicals, well before the 1970s. Beginning in the 1930s, southern Baptists, Pentecostalists, and other white Protestants who were to exhibit skepticism about liberal civil rights legislation and fierce opposition to communism deserted Oklahoma, Texas, Arkansas, and Louisiana for Southern California. By the 1950s Christian mothers were laying the foundation for a later conservative takeover of Sunbelt politics as they struggled to control what their children were taught in Southern California's public schools.[3]

Thus, while leaders of the Christian right during the 1970s sometimes talked as if they had awakened the sleeping giant of evangelicalism, it had never dozed. The change was that more evangelicals and fundamentalists embraced political involvement. They also became willing to contemplate alliances with other religious and political groups.[4]

That became evident in 1974, when the Kanawha County, West Virginia, School Board approved new textbooks, and some Christian parents threw themselves into the culture war that erupted. The "dirty" textbooks included selections from Alice Walker, James Baldwin, John Irving, and a number of other writers whose books were attacked as anti-Christian, anticapitalist, depressing, profane, and loaded with teen sex. The board's decision spurred those who objected to engage in school boycotts, strikes, even shootings. One fundamentalist clergyman was sent to prison for conspiring to blow up two elementary schools. Though the new textbooks remained part of the curriculum, few Kanawha schools used them, and sales languished elsewhere. Publishers became more cautious about the textbooks they accepted, and parents realized that others shared their concerns. The Heritage Foundation provided the protesters with legal counsel and financial support. "In the past, parents' groups were not aware of each other's existence because we did not have access to the media," a National Congress for Educational Excellence officer told *Conservative Digest*, which helpfully printed its address and that of the Kanawha County Mothers Organized for Moral Stability. "Today we are becoming unified."[5]

The Kanawha controversy cemented the long relationship of "right-wing religion and right-wing politics," recalled an Episcopalian minister who sided with the school board, and, by speaking to "the fear people had," increased it. "They took so much language away from us," he lamented. "We were 'for pornography,' we were 'anti-God' and 'anti-Christian.' We were all sorts of things. They claimed the titles."[6]

THERE WERE MANY fundamentalist leaders of the Christian right in the South and West during the 1970s to claim those titles, each with a different style. Jerry Falwell's was one of plump joviality; Jim Bakker, weepy or smiling emotionalism; Jimmy Swaggart, fiery honky-tonk; Pat Robertson, saccharine canniness; James Robison, sexy anger; Oral Roberts, expansive egotism. Tammy Faye Bakker was chirpy; Anita Bryant, a prudish coquette. Then there was Marabel Morgan, who preached an upbeat gospel of domestic submissiveness and told of happy Baptists greeted at day's end by devout wives clad only in black stockings, heels, and apron. Two college sweethearts from Detroit also played prominent roles: Beverly LaHaye created the Concerned Women for America, an organization of conservative women that fought feminism, and, with her husband, Tim, instructed evangelicals on how to improve their sex lives.[7]

What catapulted most of these individuals to prominence was their command of what Ben Armstrong, the executive director of the National Religious Broadcasters, called the electric church. Like Billy Graham and other predecessors who understood mass culture and new technology, 1970s "televangelists" used electricity and were "electrifying." Armstrong estimated that 130 million tuned in weekly to Bakker's

PTL Club, Falwell's *Old-Time Gospel Hour*, or the other television shows that generated more than a billion dollars in profits annually. Even those who thought that Armstrong inflated his figures were impressed.[8]

As televangelists cultivated the electric church and built their own megachurches with thousands of members attracted to the southern-style evangelicalism, the mainline churches were emptying. The Methodist Church lost more than 750,000 members between 1970 and 1977; the United Presbyterians and Episcopalians, about 500,000 each. Where did they go? Some probably renounced organized religion, while others joined the Asian religions or the many cults that flourished in the United States during the decade. Without a doubt, though, the search for spiritual guidance that marked the period drew many toward evangelicalism. Here, as elsewhere, Wal-Mart was a bellwether. Its founder, Sam Walton, was a liberal Presbyterian, and his wife championed a woman's right to choose abortion. But the people who worked at and shopped at Wal-Mart in the 1970s, historian Bethany Moreton realized, "were in the midst of a religious realignment, and it was their values that Wal-Mart came to represent."[9]

Those values were based on lessons that televangelists and others in the Christian right could simply summarize. Positive thinking and permitting God to "be in command of your life" worked miracles. "Only the Devil can mess up God's glorious plan for your life," and the devil could not triumph "if Christians would just stick together." Moreover, "it's all right to look after yourself." Indeed, as Moreton said, prime-time preachers and others in the Christian right promoted "Christian free enterprise" by yoking religious faith to faith in the market and a "procorporate populism." Like 1920s businessmen, they made money the measure of man and he who made the most of it the best servant of God, Christianity, and public.[10]

Beneath these lessons there was a darker subtext. At bottom, televangelists and other leaders of the Christian right were saying that Americans were depraved. The enemy was the "secular humanism" that made the individual, not God, the center of the universe, and denied Jesus's divinity, salvation, traditional gender roles, and patriotism. It promoted evolution, immorality, abortion, wealth redistribution, energy conservation, and disarmament. Since the Supreme Court had declared secular humanism a "religion" in an aside in a 1961 opinion, when Christians made secular humanism the foe, they could argue that "the same First

Amendment that bars pro-God religious teaching" barred the teaching of secular humanism too. In their hands, secular humanism became "liberalism" by another name.[11]

FALWELL WAS THE Christian right's most visible political activist. He believed that the Bible was the final authority, but he changed his interpretations of it over time to fit his politics. Falwell had once adjured his congregation at Thomas Road Baptist Church in Lynchburg, Virginia, to steer clear of secular life. When he preached on "Ministers and Marches" at his all-white church in 1965, Falwell had challenged "the sincerity and nonviolent intentions of some civil rights leaders such as Dr. Martin Luther King, Jr., . . . who are known to have left-wing associations." The Bible said nothing about fighting evils such as prostitution or prejudice, Falwell maintained. "The gospel does not clean up the outside but rather regenerates the inside." The preacher's calling was to win souls, the fundamentalist stressed. "Believing the Bible as I do, I would find it impossible to stop preaching the pure saving gospel of Jesus Christ, and begin doing anything else—including fighting communism or participating in civil-rights reforms." Subsequently, Falwell rejected "Ministers and Marches" as "false prophecy" and admitted that "as a segregationist I naturally wanted to uphold the status quo." When he came to understand that segregation was evil, "I realized it was not taught in the Bible."[12]

Often Falwell attributed his own involvement in politics to the legalization by the Supreme Court of "biological holocaust" in *Roe v. Wade*. But the first antiabortion activists were Catholics, who were then anathema to fundamentalists. Many evangelicals, including those in the Southern Baptist Convention, tolerated or even seemed supportive of abortion in 1973, and some said Falwell did not preach against abortion until 1978. At other times Falwell attributed his political engagement to homosexuality, the exploding divorce rate, erosion of family values, sex education in the public schools, the Supreme Court decision banning school prayer, liberal judges, or Soviet military and political successes. Many were the forces that this warrior said spurred him to battle.[13]

Most likely, his troops guided him. "Christian family women, galvanized to public action by issues like school prayer, gay liberation, and *Roe v. Wade*," proved to be "the foot soldiers" of the "political counterrevolution," Moreton made clear. "Rather than absorbing a family-values agenda from their male pastors," conservative women taught Falwell, other pastors, and politicians "which issues would send them door to door in the precincts."[14]

Without a doubt, Falwell's army included many soldiers. In the quarter century after the founding of Thomas Road Baptist Church, he built his congregation from thirty-five to more than ten thousand. By 1971 his Sunday services and the sermons he delivered in a commanding baritone were being broadcast nationwide. The Jesus its pastor pictured there was neither "pacifist" nor "sissy," but a "he-man" who demanded militancy. Falwell viewed his congregants as "Marines who have been called by God" to take "bayonets in hand, encounter the enemy face to face," and convert them.[15]

Yet somehow Falwell did not make this religious war frightening. His followers could. An observer recorded the "icy detachment" and aggressiveness of seventh-grade girls from Thomas Road Baptist Church as they cornered a potential convert. " 'Are you now ready to accept Christ into your life?,' one asked in a tone appropriate to the question 'Are you ready to be blindfolded and shot?' " But Falwell was genial. He explained God's position on gay rights by referring to the divine creation of "Adam and Eve, not Adam and Steve." The idea was not original: James Robison said that "God didn't create Adam and Edward." But Falwell's phrasing was more playful. His good cheer only made him seem more dangerous to nonbelievers.[16]

To the emerging equation of piety and politics, Falwell added patriotism lest Satan's troops triumph. The notion that "religion and politics don't mix" had been "invented by the Devil to keep Christians from running their own country." Falwell spoke of his experiences during World War II, when everyone pledged allegiance to the flag and awaited news of soldiers, instead of demonstrating against them. "We were praying for them and thanking God for them and buying war bonds." And what had happened since? Stalemate in Korea, disaster in Vietnam. Falwell's solution in the bicentennial year was "to take a musical ministry team" of seventy students from Liberty University, which he had founded, "across America for daily and nightly *America, Back to God*" or "I love America" rallies. The crowds they attracted were treated to religious and patriotic spectacles exhorting them to vote for candidates who opposed communism.[17]

AT THE TIME it looked as if that candidate would be Jimmy Carter. Even *Christianity Today* seemed bemused by the proliferation of Christian contenders for the presidential nomination in 1976. "One wonders whether evangelicals have adequately prepared themselves for such a time," its editor said. While Ford hosted evangelical hero Francis Schaeffer and addressed the Southern Baptist Convention, the president was uncomfortable giving testimony, and the Christian right had little use for him. Had Reagan, who subscribed to many evangelical precepts while declining to categorize himself as "born again," won the Republican nomination, many fundamentalists and some evangelicals might have supported him. But he did not. So Carter looked attractive.[18]

Then came Carter's infamous *Playboy* admission that he had looked upon many women "with lust" and his reminder that "Christ says don't consider yourself better than someone else because one guy screws a whole bunch of women while the other guy is loyal to his wife." Many of his Christian supporters were horrified; as one said plaintively, "[S]crew is just not a good Baptist word." Falwell declared himself "disillusioned" and endorsed Ford. "Four months ago the majority of the people I knew were pro-Carter," he said. "Today that has totally reversed."[19]

Not quite. "A majority of evangelicals voted Republican, as was usually the case, but Carter won by cutting the margin from 7.2 million in 1968 to 3.2 million," historian Leo Ribuffo explained. Carter also carried the southern Baptists, something no Democrat had done since Truman.[20]

But Carter was riding a tiger. Like many Progressives of the early twentieth century with whom he was often compared, he embodied efficiency and moralism. "I think it's very important that all of us in Government not forget that no matter how dedicated we might be and how eager to perform well, . . . we need a stable family life to make us better servants of the people," he informed government employees at the Department of Housing and Urban Development soon after his inauguration. "So, those of you who are living in sin, I hope you'll get married." Betty Ford told the *New York Times* that the president was venturing into a realm that she believed was none of his business. "He obviously interprets the Bible literally," she added, and "sounds like a very good evangelist." Not all evangelists agreed. Increasingly, some

Christians turned away from Carter to the New Right, which was also inserting religion, patriotism, and the family into politics.[21]

"FAMILY" ISSUES

"Dear Mikey," Michael Tolliver's mother wrote, "It all started when the Dade County Commission passed a law in favor of homosexuals. It said you can't refuse to hire homosexuals or rent to them, and Anita Bryant spoke out against this, being a Christian mother of four and Miss America runner-up and all, and the normal God-fearing people in Miami backed her up 100%." Since Bryant, a spokesperson for the Florida Citrus Commission, hawked oranges, gays boycotted Florida orange juice. As a Christian and an orange grower, Mrs. Tolliver thought that "we should all get down on our knees and thank the Lord that someone as famous as Anita Bryant had stepped forward to battle the forces of Sodom and Gomorrah." Unbeknownst to Mrs. Tolliver, her only child was "as queer as a three-dollar bill." He lived in a San Francisco apartment house owned by an elderly pot-smoking transsexual and frequented bars with names like The Endup and The Stud.[22]

The Tollivers were fictional characters in *Tales of the City*, a *San Francisco Chronicle* serial launched in 1976. But Anita Bryant was real; the anxiety in 1977–78 about children, epidemic. Along with worrying about whether their progeny would fall prey to cults or gangs, snort PCP and cocaine, or develop eating disorders, parents were frantic about child pornography, molestation, and abuse. They also feared serial murderers, people like John Wayne Gacy, who dressed up as a clown to fete neighborhood children, was photographed with a smiling Rosalynn Carter, and raped and murdered more than thirty boys, and Ted Bundy, the child of an unwed mother, who became addicted to pornography as a boy and eventually raped and murdered at least twenty-nine young women. As more and more mothers who worked outside the home turned to child care providers, Bryant and others made sure that they were anxious about doing so. Bryant portrayed homosexuality as a cult in which depravity and pedophilia flourished. "Why do you think the homosexuals are called fruits?" Bryant asked. "It's because they eat the forbidden fruit of the tree of life." The Bible referred to men as trees, she explained, and homosexuals consumed sperm. (Assured that women did too, she acknowledged that the "abomination" had spread.) Inspired by her pastor, Bryant launched a crusade to repeal the Dade County antidiscrimination ordinance and prevent gays from becoming teachers. "Dear Friend"—her direct mail appeals warned—"Do you realize what they want? *They want to recruit our school children under the protection of the laws of our land!*" Gay couples who could not bear children could only broaden their ranks through "recruits."[23]

Because Congress had repeatedly voted down attempts to amend the Civil Rights Act of 1964 to ban discrimination on the basis of sexual orientation, a number of college towns and liberal cities had amended their antidiscrimination ordinances to make discrimination against gays and lesbians illegal. In a few places the threat of amendment had spurred conservative religious groups and other antigay advocates to mobilize, but none of the earlier fights heralded a backlash against gay rights. When religious fundamentalists and conservatives combined to repeal a gay rights amendment by a two to one majority in Boulder, Colorado, in 1974, for example, the *Nation* dismissed the amendment as "[s]loppily drafted, ill-timed and poorly presented." Then, in 1977, Dade County, Florida, adopted an ordinance barring discrimination against individuals in housing, public accommodations, and employment "based on their affectional or sexual preference."[24]

As a beauty queen, television personage, and popular singer Bryant attracted attention in her fight to repeal the ordinance. "Who wants to discriminate?" she asked. "It's a no-no." But if homosexuals were "a legitimate minority group, then so are nail biters, dieters, fat people, short people, and murderers." Allow them to teach children, and "the depravity" would engulf "your kids and your grandchildren." Where gays argued that homosexuality was a matter of sexual orientation, Bryant portrayed it as a matter of sexual preference: "Homosexuals, unlike Jews and blacks, choose their status, have not been persecuted or enslaved, and are set apart by their behavior rather than their ethnic heritage."[25]

In fact, gays and lesbians had suffered persecution for years. That was one reason for the gay rights movement. In 1977, four men attacked Robert Hillsborough, a gay gardener, outside his San Francisco apartment and stabbed him fifteen times while shouting, "Faggot!" "Faggot!" His mother filed suit against Bryant and her husband, alleging that their "campaign of hate, bigotry, ignorance, fear, intimidation and prejudice" had caused his death. But when Bryant's opponents presented gay rights as human rights, her supporters asked what right there was "to corrupt our children."[26]

Bryant's campaign brought together those who shared her belief in Americans' decadence. Ronald Reagan came to Florida to present Bryant with California oranges, Jesse Helms saluted her, and Jerry Falwell staged a rally for her. Though Dade County was a liberal Democratic stronghold, residents of all religions voted overwhelmingly to repeal the antidiscrimination ordinance. "The people of Dade County—the normal majority—have said, 'Enough! enough! enough!' " Bryant rejoiced. After her victory, she said, "[W]e could have gotten such a momentum going that we could have wiped the homosexual out."[27]

That ambition ultimately eluded her. Bryant galvanized the mobilization of homosexuals as well as homophobes. She had the same impact on the gay rights movement that *Roe* had on the right to life movement. But around the country, people like the Tollivers and Christian moms, especially, also mobilized to defeat or repeal ordinances prohibiting discrimination against gays. And they were successful, except in Seattle and California, where the Briggs initiative cracking down on gay rights in the schools would have so severely limited teachers' rights to free speech that Reagan and Carter both spoke out against it.[28]

Carter proved a disappointment to Bryant. She had supported him even after his *Playboy* interview. "I really looked at Jimmy Carter as a hero," she herself told *Playboy*. But when senior White House staffer Midge Costanza, Carter's liaison to women's and other groups, opposed Bryant's battle and received gays and lesbians in the White House, Bryant lost hope. She joined "the majority of Christians," she announced, in deciding that Carter's first term must be his last.[29]

Though Bryant soon faded from view, the victim of marital and financial woes, homosexuality remained. As fundamentalists and conservatives embraced the rhetoric of color blindness, they attacked gays and feminists. Richard Viguerie and the New Right portrayed the Dade County victory as proof that "conservatives can win when they're fighting for traditional family values."[30]

ANTI–EQUAL RIGHTS AMENDMENT and antigay politics went hand in hand. Bryant's communications director boasted that Bryant deserved as much credit as Phyllis Schlafly for defeating the ERA in Florida in 1977 but said Bryant had the better issue. The ERA was "an abstract concept while ours is simple: you're either going to encourage a homosexual lifestyle or you're going to discourage it."[31]

However "abstract" the Equal Rights Amendment was, Schlafly was undaunted. She was expanding her base beyond Republican women and older homemakers to include age-old adversaries: fundamentalist Jews, Mormons, Baptists, and Catholics. ERA supporters needed four states to ratify the ERA, and they focused on Illinois, the only northern industrial state that had not approved it. Ratificationists reasoned that victory in Schlafly's home state would break the logjam. They held their largest pro-ERA demonstration yet in May 1976, and that fall Carter lobbied for the amendment's passage in Illinois. As the ERA made its way through the Illinois legislature, Schlafly's forces showered lawmakers with apple pies and poetry: "My heart and my hand went into this dough, For the sake of the family please vote no." On December 16, 1976, the ERA went down to defeat in Illinois.[32]

AT THE TIME ERA ratification was the centerpiece of the feminist agenda. In contrast, abortion induced apathy. It was assumed safe. Medicaid had routinely funded abortions for indigent women since the Court handed down *Roe*. In 1976, however, freshman Congressman Henry Hyde of Illinois, a Catholic Republican identified with the New Right, and Robert Bauman, a Maryland congressman and American Conservative Union activist, introduced a rider to an appropriations bill. It banned all Medicaid abortions, though when Congress enacted the Hyde Amendment, it made an exception for those in which the ongoing pregnancy would endanger the woman's life. Senate liberals counted on the United States Supreme Court, which had recently invalidated state efforts to limit the right to abortion by requiring spousal or parental consent, to strike down the Hyde Amendment. Nevertheless, in 1977, in *Maher v. Roe*, the Court upheld a Connecticut law limiting Medicaid funding to "medically necessary" abortions. The unexpected *Maher* decision suggested that the Court might sustain the Hyde Amendment, as it did in 1980.[33]

Maher pleased President Carter. At a press conference, he said states should not have to finance abortions and that federal funds should not be used for that purpose unless the mother's life was threatened or the pregnancy was the result of rape or incest. But he saved the zinger for the follow-up: "Mr. President, how fair do you believe it is then, that women who can afford to get an abortion can go ahead and have one and women who cannot afford to are precluded?" Carter replied, "Well, as you know, there are many things in life that are not fair, that wealthy people can afford and poor people can't. But I don't believe that the Federal Government should take action to try to make these opportunities exactly equal, particularly when there is a moral factor involved."[34]

The president's position reflected public opinion. By one poll, 64 percent of Americans believed in the right to abortion, but 58 percent agreed that the government should not pay for it. Yet Carter still came across as callous.[35]

Liberals and pro-choice proponents now attacked the President. The Americans for Democratic Action said his remark reflected the "defeatist" attitude that pervaded his administration's economic and social policies. Midge Costanza told the president that she had received "an overwhelming number of phone calls from public interest groups, individuals *and* White House staff members expressing concern and even anger over your remarks," particularly "your comments emphasizing the differences in opportunities available to the rich and to the poor." When Costanza organized a meeting for disapproving administration women and the media heard of it, Carter was furious. Hamilton Jordan accused her of disloyalty and of listening only "to persons espousing liberal positions."[36]

Costanza's subsequent relocation to the White House basement and resignation should have come as no surprise. At a time when it was fashionable for hip men to pretend enthusiasm for feminism, Carter's Georgians rarely did. The media portrayed Jordan as an uncouth playboy who had spit amaretto and cream at a woman who spurned his advances in a singles bar and who had groped the wife of the Egyptian ambassador while telling her that he had always wanted to "see the pyramids." Though Carter loyalists protested that such stories were false, feminists believed, perhaps unfairly, that the administration had little interest in women's issues. "I could cry for all the women throughout the country who depended so heavily on Carter," one woman in his administration said publicly.[37]

Equally unsurprisingly, right-to-lifers did not believe Carter was doing enough. To Falwell, Carter was an "abortionist run wild." In 1977 debates over abortion funding nearly paralyzed Congress. When the battle ended, Hyde had sacrificed some ground. His 1977 legislation came out where Carter did on *Maher* and provided for federal funding of abortion in the case of threats to the mother's life, rape, or incest.

Even so, grieved one pro-choice activist, "We lost, no matter how you look at it."[38]

As pro-life ranks swelled, some activists in them turned violent. The first bombing and burning of abortion clinics occurred in 1977. According to one Carter staffer, "the Hyde Amendment has strengthened rather than weakened the drive of antiabortion forces to remove abortion in all of its forms."[39]

ABORTION, THE ERA, and gay rights featured prominently in the 1977 National Women's Conference, the "high point of the women's movement of the 1970s." A product of the 1975 International Women's Year Conference, the four-day conference in Houston in December 1977 received five million dollars in congressional funding, was preceded by a year of state conventions, attracted nearly twenty thousand, and was intended to challenge the stereotype that feminism was for privileged white women only. It was chaired by the famously feisty feminist Bella Abzug, the first Jewish woman in Congress, whom Carter had appointed cochair of the National Advisory Committee for Women. Among others, the conference attracted first ladies Lady Bird Johnson, Betty Ford, and Rosalynn Carter. Two of their husbands were on record as supporting the ERA, and Lady Bird Johnson was sure that had Lyndon Johnson been alive, he "would be welcoming all this." The delegates included a large percentage of women of color and working-class women. About a fifth of them, mostly from the South and West, were conservatives.[40]

Conservatives claimed that the delegate selection process had been stacked against them. "This conference is loaded with lesbians," one reporter wrote in *Human Events*, which was increasing its coverage of social issues in 1977. Instead of the *Valley of the Dolls*, the novel about the descent of three women into drug addiction, it was the "Valley of the Dykes."[41]

It was true that conservatives had no chance at the National Women's Conference. By a five to one majority, the delegates voted for the resolution supporting the ERA. Its passage before midnight produced "a roar which the chair, Mary Anne Krupsak, Lieutenant Governor of New York, could not silence, even though the gavel she pounded was one used by Susan B. Anthony," the *New York Times* reported. By the same margin, the delegates endorsed a resolution to restore Medicaid funding for abortions. By nearly as large a majority, they approved a resolution in favor of lesbian rights. Dramatically, after years of warning that support for lesbianism would frighten the mainstream away from feminism, the recently divorced Betty Friedan announced a change of heart. "As someone who grew up in middle America, as someone who grew up in Peoria and who has loved men perhaps too well," she declared, "I believe we must help the women who are lesbians to be protected in their own civil rights."[42]

Across town, the alternative National Pro-Family Rally brought in an estimated twenty thousand demonstrators. Anita Bryant sent greetings, and the president of the Right to Life Federation and Phyllis Schlafly decried abortion and the ERA. Congressman Robert Dornan, a Republican member of the New Right from Southern California, gave the final speech, "Let Your Voice Be Heard in Washington." Schlafly said, "[T]hat's when 'pro-family' came into common usage as a term to describe our movement." The national media began to pay still more attention to the New Right and its successes too.[43]

Ultimately, Schlafly's forces used the National Conference on Women to tar the ERA with the brush of lesbianism and abortion. Rosalynn Carter declared herself dismayed that its supporters "appeared to be demanding, strident and man haters." The Republicans wanted no part of the feminist agenda of the Houston delegates, and neither did the Carters. White House lobbying on behalf of the ERA, which went down to defeat in 1982 after the ratification deadline had been extended, was considered weak. The National Advisory Committee for Women voted to cancel a meeting with the president in 1978 after the White House allocated only fifteen minutes for it, and Carter subsequently enraged feminists by firing Abzug as its cochair in 1979. But Schlafly had no use for Carter either: When the White House held a conference on the family in 1980, she and other conservatives claimed that the deck of representatives had been stacked in favor of "the same pre-selected group of left-wing, feminist, pro-abortion and homosexual activists that took over the National Women's Conference in Houston in 1977" and that "the White House Conference is IWY revisited."[44]

Schlafly foresaw that "the Battle of Houston" would prove "the decisive turning point in the war between Women's Lib and those who are Pro-Family." As recently as 1975, feminism and gay rights, like liberalism and the Democratic Party, had seemed to many almost as American as the apple pies STOP ERA women baked for legislators. By 1977, however, the New Right and religious fundamentalists had redefined feminists, the ERA, gays, and Democrats as enemies of the family. In their hands, the GOP was not "a party of big business and the wealthy, but . . . a party of the little guy, the regular American Joe and his wife, while the Democratic party belonged to elitists who imposed schemes of social engineering, social privilege and special interest" on the little guy.[45]

AS EVER, THE New Right was searching for more exciting issues that traditional Republicans ignored and that could mobilize conservatives. Even though it scorned business interests for cowering before union bosses and for behaving like "political prostitutes" who shelled out for "an incumbent no matter what he stands for," the New Right supported Kemp-Roth, along with Proposition 13 and deregulation, on the ground that they would benefit not just business interests but the family as well. At Houston, in 1977, the New Right saw issues it had previously defined as "social" become defined as ones of the "family." Paul Weyrich claimed that just as opposition to the Vietnam War in the 1960s had galvanized the left, so "family issues" could unite a religious right larger than the Christian right with the political right behind a populist conservatism.[46]

But to define the right's issues as ones of "family" was imprecise. Carter and gay rights proponents also made the family their priorities. Above all, the right's concern related to "gender bending," the blurring of roles and expectations for men and women and threats to the ideals of masculinity and femininity. That was one reason, in addition to its fear for children, why the right harped so on homosexuality and abortion—"crimes against reproduction." It was easy to make fun of Falwell when he said the largely gay Village People were destroying values with "Macho Man" and other camp disco hits and decried abortion. But the right's fears were not entirely irrational. American women's childbearing declined dramatically—from 3.7 births in 1955–1959 to 1.8 births in 1975–1980. The Center for Disease Control reported an annual increase in the abortion rate of 4 to 15 percent each year during the 1970s and 359 abortions for every 1,000 births in 1980. The first National March on Washington for Lesbian and Gay Rights in 1979 drew seventy-five thousand marchers. It was becoming clear that homosexuality tempted even supposedly respectable married people. In 1979 the media were announcing that Eleanor Roosevelt and Lorena Hickok "exchanged 3,000 letters, cards and telegrams, some of which reveal an intimacy that suggests to modern readers that the relationship may have been a lesbian love affair," and in 1980, Republican Congressman Robert Bauman of Maryland, a founding member of the Young Americans for Freedom and the American Conservative Union, was arrested for having sex with a male prostitute. Traditional gender roles were blurring, though not as dramatically as the right imagined.[47]

The media highlighted that. *Conservative Digest* readers said their two favorite television series were *Little House on the Prairie*, based on the Laura Ingalls Wilder novels about a nineteenth-century farm family, and *The Waltons*, a tearjerker about a Virginia family during the Great Depression. Despite the popularity of those shows and ones that hearkened back to the 1950s, television in the 1970s was "wallowing in sex." The debut of *Soap* in 1977 featured the first openly gay character in a TV series, Jodie Dallas, played by Billy Crystal. When Jodie learned that the quarterback he was seeing was also maintaining his masculine image by dating women, Jodie decided to eliminate the competition by having a sex change. "He looks better in that dress than I do," lamented his mother (who, like her daughter, was sleeping with the tennis pro). *Conservative Digest* lambasted *Soap* as "a tangle of immoral and perverted sex relationships" and touted the efforts of church groups to get it off the air. Though the 1977 blockbuster *Star Wars* was "drenched in Christian imagery and apocalyptic battles between good and evil," many of the era's popular films featured child prostitution and "pornochic," and the American institution of Times Square had become the site of sex shops and shows.[48]

The right's worries also reflected an anxiety about "liberal" attempts to expand government and its spending. Activist judges were a particular source of irritation. The increasing popularity of religious fundamentalism in 1977 and 1978 coincided with the growth of fundamentalist approaches to constitutional interpretation. In 1977, in *Government by Judiciary*, constitutional scholar Raoul Berger contended that the Warren Court's decisions on school segregation "revised the Fourteenth Amendment to mean exactly the opposite of what its framers designed it to mean." If liberal judicial activists had turned the equal protection clause upside down, what had they done to the rest of the Constitution? The Constitution said nothing about the right to privacy, the cornerstone of the right to abortion in *Roe*, and conservatives were certain its framers had not intended to outlaw school prayer. Berger's book, which was widely reviewed, made its many readers sure that the Supreme Court "has jumped the bounds of legitimate government review."[49]

Jimmy Carter was also in the right's crosshairs. Tough the president was. Macho he was not. A quintessential 1970s guy, Carter jogged, hugged other men, and generally preferred wine to spirits (which his wife refused to serve at White House functions anyway). The *Washington Post* reported that he was the first president since Eisenhower to serve "his first 12 months in the White House without firing a single shot in anger at a foreign country." That it seemed to assume his predecessors had personally done so was telling: The *Post* said Carter had not tried to "demonstrate his manhood as president." Though he was the last Democratic presidential candidate in the twentieth century to receive a significant percentage of the white male vote (47 percent), he did not seem *manly*.[50]

COALITIONS AGAINST CARTER

To the New Right, nothing illustrated Carter's "softness" more than his willingness to "surrender" the Panama Canal, which the virile Theodore Roosevelt had gloriously acquired in 1903. TR sent forces to support a French company that wanted to build the canal in its rebellion against Colombia, of which Panama was then a part. Then he recognized the new Republic of Panama. The United States and a company representative signed a treaty that allowed Americans to build the canal and cut the distance between New York and San Francisco by ship by some eight thousand miles. Neither negotiated nor signed by Panamanians, the treaty had long been unpopular in Panama.[51]

Soon after Lyndon Johnson became president, a riot in the American-controlled Canal Zone left more than twenty dead. Because of the difficulty of defending the canal, Johnson began negotiations to replace the 1903 treaty. In 1974, Kissinger and Panamanian Foreign Minister Juan Tack finally agreed that Americans would renounce sovereignty in the Canal Zone. But first Secretary of Defense James Schlesinger undercut Kissinger-Tack, and then Ronald Reagan made the canal an issue. During the 1976 campaign, Carter himself said that he did not favor relinquishing control of the canal.[52]

Carter was not just pandering to Reaganites. Kissinger misspoke when he told Panamanian General Omar Torrijos Herrera: "The basic problem is that most Americans don't give a damn" and that while "[a] small minority" was "violently opposed" to Kissinger-Tack, "no group is really for it." It was true that no group was "really for" it. But many gave "a damn." In response to Kissinger-Tack, Strom Thurmond and thirty-four cosponsors approved a Senate resolution proclaiming that "the government of the United States should maintain and protect its sovereign rights and jurisdiction over the Canal and Zone."[53]

Courageously—and as he himself later admitted, perhaps foolishly—Carter ignored the Senate hint. Though his shrewd wife urged him to hold off Panama Canal negotiations until his second term, the new president changed course in the names of morality and national interest. As he saw it, he needed to correct the "injustice" of the original treaty and show the world that the United States had renounced colonialism. An early "win" on the Panama Canal could also provide momentum for the administration on SALT II and other tough foreign policy issues. Further, the president had every indication that Panamanians might fire on Americans and attack the canal if he did not revise the treaty. Soon after Carter's election as president, Torrijos had declared that "Panama's patience machine only has fuel for six more months." Asked by *Newsweek* in the summer of 1977 whether violence against the United States might develop in the absence of a treaty, Torrijos responded, "[V]ery definitely. Tension is a product of the situation because the U.S. has lied to us for so long." He cited those to his left who said, "[W]e can't decolonize ourselves just by screaming," and himself made secret arrangements to blow up the locks of the canal and close it down if the United States did not scrap the old treaty for a new arrangement.[54]

By summer 1977 the president's negotiators had prepared two treaties that embodied the principles of Kissinger-Tack. The Panama Canal Treaty set out the provisions for increasing Panamanian participation in the operation of the Canal Zone until the end of the century and provided that Panama would gain control of the canal in 2000. The Treaty Concerning the Permanent Neutrality and Operation of the Panama Canal spelled out the obligation of the United States and Panama to defend the canal against any threat to its status as a neutral waterway. His national security adviser recalled that the president " glowed" as he and Torrijos signed the treaties in September.[55]

Carter recognized that many glowered. The polls indicated that "the American public strongly opposed relinquishing control of the Canal." Its fate fed anxiety about "vanished mastery." Americans not yet prepared to refight Vietnam used the debate about the Panama Canal treaties as a proxy.[56]

"Don't Let Carter Surrender Our Canal," conservatives urged. They insisted that the United States owned the canal. If the United States relinquished it, they said, General Torrijos, a Marxist dictator with a terrible human rights record and, the right insinuated, a drug trafficker to boot, would prevent the U.S. Navy from using the canal. The neutrality treaty did not give the United States the right to defend the canal from Panamanian violence. The Soviets might seize it. Conservative activist Pat Buchanan pointed out that the United States had grown large through questionable land grabs. What was next? The return of Texas, New Mexico, Arizona, and California by the "Chablis-and-cheese set?"[57]

The administration could not make its case for the treaties without opening itself up to counterarguments that perpetuated the debate on conservative terms. If the White House cited the taking of the Panama Canal as evidence of past American colonialism, the right would reply that the revolution against Colombia had been bloodless and that but for "Teddy," Panama "would be nothing today but a malaria-infested backwater province of Colombia." If Carter said that sabotage would occur absent ratification of the treaties, conservatives would condemn the administration for employing "blackmail" to win their passage. If the administration observed that the United States had never owned the Canal Zone, the right would ask why the 1903 treaty explicitly permitted the United States to behave "as if it were sovereign." If the administration boasted that the Joint Chiefs of Staff supported the treaties, Reagan would maintain that he had "seen a figure" that 324 "top-ranking military officers who are retired and thus free to speak their minds" opposed the treaties. If the White House stressed that the treaties provided for the defense of the canal if its neutrality was jeopardized, the right would ask what would happen if the threat came from the Panamanians. If the administration said there was no evidence the Soviets would seize the canal, the right would query how it could be certain. If the White House maintained that the significance of the canal had declined, the right would say that the canal had been used to send supplies overseas during the Vietnam War. If the administration said Torrijos was not a Marxist but a populist, the right would say that was a distinction without a difference. If the administration portrayed Torrijos as a lovable rogue, the right would focus on his vicious chief of intelligence, Manuel Noriega. If the White House maintained that Torrijos did not traffic in drugs, the right would ask why the Senate had held closed hearings about allegations that his brother smuggled heroin. In fact, when the United States decided it had no more use for Noriega in 1989, it trumpeted long-standing Panamanian drug trafficking, corruption, and abuses of human rights aplenty.[58]

There was no percentage in picking apart the right's case. The treaty fight revealed that by 1977 conservatives had created an effective alternative to the mainstream media. When the American Conservative Union, *Conservative Digest*, *Human Events*, and the *Phyllis Schlafly Report* all were sending the same message that Ronald Reagan broadcast, Carter would not be able to win over conservatives.

The Panama Canal treaty battle was another milestone in the development of conservatism. Although the New Right claimed that the Old Right supported the treaties, that was untrue. Barry Goldwater voted against them. The American Conservative Union spent $500,000, the equivalent of $1.65 million in 2009 dollars, to fight passage of the treaty. In fact, its dapper new chairman, Representative Philip Crane of Illinois, a Viguerie client and Reagan enthusiast until the Schweiker selection, opposed the Equal Rights Amendment and abortion rights, along with the Panama Canal treaties, and hoped to wrest the Republican standard in 1980 from Reagan. ("Phil is a cinch to get nominated because every woman who sees him will want to sleep with him," said one GOP state chairman.) Crane used the treaty fight to paper over the long-standing friction between the ACU and the Viguerie circle. Further, almost everyone at *National Review* opposed the treaties. But the voice of William F. Buckley was the one that counted, and Buckley backed them. So did U.S. multinationals and their PACs and organizations, such as the Business Roundtable and the AFL-CIO. The treaties did not interest neoconservatives. Opposition to the treaties became identified with the New Right.[59]

Though the issue did not separate New from Old Right in the way that the New Right implied, it did drive a wedge between Republicans. Ronald Reagan, whose relations with the Republican National Committee were strained, charged that chairman Bill Brock had used him to raise money from treaty opponents, then refused to fight the treaties. Carter knew he was not going to win over Reagan or the "nuts like Strom Thurmond and Jesse Helms." Realizing the importance of bipartisanship, the president therefore relied "very heavily on some of the Republican leaders who had been involved in the negotiations," a group that included Ford, Kissinger, and Senate Minority Leader Howard Baker. Consequently, treaty opponents said that the Panama Canal battle demonstrated anew the folly of relying on "mainstream" Republicans at the same time that it provided a chance to seize control of the GOP. Pat Buchanan was convinced that a battle "could realign American politics, reinvigorate a weakened spirit of nationalism, and[,] if lost," come back to bite those who voted for the treaties. That was the point, said Viguerie, who considered the canal conservatives' best issue ever. So it was, according to Viguerie, that "the New Right picked up the flag and set out to do battle with the American establishment."[60]

As the president tried to mobilize Americans behind his energy package in 1977–78, millions of postcards and letters urged them to tell the White House and the Senate that they opposed the treaties. Crane, who possessed a doctorate in American history, wrote *Surrender in Panama: The Case Against the Treaty*. The American Conservative Union experimented with using the infomercial for political purposes, rather than to sell exercise machines. Sitting atop a desk, Crane opened the broadcast with the remark "This may be the most important TV program you have ever watched. I can make that statement because at this very moment, the President of the United States and a majority of U.S. senators in Washington are preparing to ignore your expressed wishes—and the wishes of perhaps eighty percent of the American people." A voice-over announced, "There is *no* Panama Canal! There is an American Canal at Panama." The thirty-minute program, which included appearances by conservative Republican senators Jesse Helms of North Carolina, Jake Garn of Utah, Paul Laxalt of Nevada, and Strom Thurmond of South Carolina, was broadcast 209 times and watched by an estimated nine million Americans. A "truth squad" that included Crane and other congressional conservatives toured the states of uncommitted senators. Reagan and Schlafly debated the treaties with Buckley. Reagan, who was trying to woo New Right leaders and white ethnics with a rhetoric of home, family, tax cuts, neighborhood, and national strength in 1978, also contributed an introduction to *Surrender in Panama* and made the case against the treaties in newspaper columns and radio broadcasts. (New Right chieftains who had wondered whether Reagan was a true conservative in 1976, however, noticed now that he did not denounce the treaties with the same vehemence he had displayed earlier. His pollster saw that opposition to the treaties did not appeal to the moderates Reagan needed to win in 1980. Reagan's inconstancy gave the New Right another excuse to defect to Crane.)[61]

The Panama Canal treaty fight became a "family" or gender issue about American "impotence." According to the *New York Times*, the media covered the treaty debate as if it were "about Jimmy Carter's manhood," and Buckley complained that the opposition was obsessed with "our national masculinity." The politics of testosterone aroused not just the New Right but the religious right as well. Asked to explain her opposition to Carter, Anita Bryant responded, "I can't dismiss the straddling of the fence he's done so far on all the important issues like E.R.A., homosexuality, the Panama Canal," and Falwell maintained that the Bible required him to oppose the treaties. Senator Mark Hatfield of Oregon, an evangelical member of the dwindling breed of liberal Republicans and supporter of the treaties, was appalled by the letters from his evangelical constituents telling him that God wanted them voted down. "Now that's what I call apostasy," Hatfield told a reporter, "that is politicizing the gospel."[62]

For all the attempts to manipulate it, public opinion about the treaties did not budge. Between June 1976 and January 1978, Americans opposed their enactment by a five to three majority. Though the White House convinced the media that public opinion then turned in the administration's favor, it did not.[63]

But in the end the Senate did not follow public opinion. The treaties sparked the longest debate over foreign policy since the 1919 fight over the Treaty of Versailles, the first carried live on radio. When the shouting stopped in April 1978, the Senate had approved each treaty by a one-vote margin. Carter labeled the win one of his "proudest moments."[64]

As Vice President Mondale observed, however, Carter had scored "a Pyrrhic victory because we spent so much of our early good will and trust." Elderly and in poor health, Senate Foreign Relations Committee chair John Sparkman of Alabama had tapped Frank Church of Idaho and Paul Sarbanes of Maryland to lead the floor fight for the treaties. Church performed the assignment ably, despite the treaties' unpopularity in his state. But in a press conference called to celebrate the treaties' passage, Carter irked liberals by thanking Sparkman, instead of Church and Sarbanes. Some Republicans who bowed to the president's appeal to put patriotism above politics refused to follow his lead on other foreign policy issues. Howard Baker of Tennessee, who voted Carter's way on Panama, despite the fact that he received twenty-two thousand letters about the canal in one month, "not 500 of which supported the treaties," wanted the Republican presidential nomination in 1980 and became one of the stars of the American Conservative Union's anti-SALT II infomercial, *Soviet Might/American Myth: The United States in Retreat*. Instead of gaining momentum for SALT II through the Panama battle, the administration used up its chips. Much of the media, the Senate majority leader, and the American ambassador to Panama considered the president's selling of the Panama Canal treaties ineffective.[65]

In Panama, the reaction to the treaties should have been positive. Two-thirds of Panamanians had approved them in a 1977 plebiscite. But as Torrijos would have said, "Panama's patience machine" no longer had gas. The long delay that occurred while the White House won the vote of a junior senator by permitting him to attach a "reservation" spelling out the American right to use force to keep open the canal proved humiliating. Panamanians worried about manhood too.[66]

In losing the treaty fight, the right made significant advances. After the final vote, Carter had been "particularly eager to see reelected this year Senators who voted for the Treaties." But Viguerie thought "the New Right really came of age" by making Carter and the Panama Canal treaties dirty words and described 1978 as "our critical year" in shifting "the entire spectrum of politics . . . to the right." Ford's chief of staff, Dick Cheney of Wyoming, won his first congressional election by campaigning against the Panama Canal treaties that his former boss supported. Of the fourteen senators who voted for the treaties and sought reelection, seven did not survive the fall contests. And as the battle over implementation legislation for the treaties dragged on in the House, the "giveaway" remained a sensitive issue. As Carter later said, "Eleven more of the senators who supported the treaties were defeated in 1980—plus one President of the United States." Among them was Frank Church. In contrast, only one senator who had voted against the treaties went down to defeat in the elections of 1978 and 1980. Though both Carter and the New Right overstated the importance of the canal to most of these elections, the Panama Canal treaties proved a better rallying point for the right than Kemp-Roth in 1978.[67]

AS GOOD AN ISSUE as the canal was, a threat closer to home and family was necessary fully to galvanize the Christian right. It came with the debate about Christian schools. Enrollments had tripled since 1965. No thanks to the government. "In some states it is easier to open a massage parlor," Falwell grumbled. During the summer of 1978, Carter's Internal Revenue Service commissioner announced guidelines for revoking the tax-exempt status of private schools. Any school that "was formed or substantially expanded at or about the time of desegregation of the public schools, and . . . has an insignificant number of minority students" must "clearly and convincingly" rebut the presumption it was engaged in racial discrimination "by showing that it has undertaken affirmative steps to secure minority students."[68]

The guidelines had been in the works since 1970, when the IRS revoked the tax-exempt status of Bob Jones University in South Carolina because that Christian institution prohibited interracial dating and marriage. At the same time, the IRS also denied tax-exempt status to Mississippi's Goldsboro Christian School, which had never admitted a child of two African American parents. Christian schools had begun to appear around the time of desegregation, and they were most prevalent in the South. Defenders of Christian schools countered that they also flourished outside the South and in all-white communities, that some enrolled significant numbers of African Americans, that they did not teach racist doctrines (though Christian schools often prohibited interracial dating), and that racism did not explain their emergence. Even those who depicted desegregation as "the fear that built the schools" acknowledged that whatever the motivation for their establishment, the schools were intended to provide a distinctively Christian education.[69]

Christian schools created a "total world" in which pupils learned of "the single path to salvation—by accepting Jesus as their personal savior." They taught the "Christian view of sex roles." Boys focused on "craft skills, work habits, gardening, manners, economics, leadership, music, and rhetoric," and girls studied "cooking, housekeeping, household management, manners, sewing, growing and arranging flowers, interior decoration, literary skills, and child care." Only manners, apparently, were gender neutral. They stressed absolute truths, rather than the contemporary materials of public and prep schools, which allegedly reinforced the "secular humanist" youth culture of sex, drugs, and rock and roll. (Just as some rock enthusiasts burned disco records in the 1970s, so some Christians burned or smashed rock albums, while others argued that "the devil" should not have "all the good music" and promoted Christian rock.) Teachers steeped their students in patriotism and piety, celebrated the free market, attacked communism, questioned evolution, and explained that "sexual equality denies God's word; abortion is murder; and homosexuality is a sin."[70]

Aided by Paul Weyrich and Falwell, a conservative coalition spearheaded by Phil Crane and the Reverend Robert Billings sounded the alarm. "IRS SAYS: GUILTY UNTIL PROVEN INNOCENT," the American Conservative Union warned. Christian parents flooded the IRS with more than 120,000 protests. Insulted by the implication that they were racists, they feared higher tuition if the schools lost their tax-exempt status. The IRS guidelines proved particularly useful in mobilizing Christians behind Sunbelt Republicans, who were conservative on race, such as Senator Jesse Helms of North Carolina and Representatives Trent Lott of Mississippi and Robert Dornan of California. Helms ensured that Congress enacted legislation blocking implementation of the IRS guidelines in 1979. "The Stamp Act of the Religious Right was the interference of the federal government in the Christian school movement," *Christianity Today* said.[71]

FOR WEYRICH, THE crucial moment had come. "We are a novelty and getting enormously good coverage, and it's relatively accurate," he had observed in the summer of 1978. "But I think if we are viewed as a genuine political force in 1980, the media will take a different view." Governmental disruption of Christians' lives had "suddenly" convinced them "that they were not going to be able to be left alone." There were other promising portents. When John Paul II became pope in 1978, the Catholic Church moved in a more conservative direction. As 1979 began, Southern Baptists launched a successful campaign to install a fundamentalist at their helm and Brooklyn's Borough Park and other neighborhoods in some big cities teemed with Orthodox Jews drawn to a conservative lifestyle. In January 1979, Robert Grant also founded Christian Voice, "the nation's first successful, comprehensive, Christian Right political action group," to work "for a Christian majority in a Christian democracy," topple liberals, and install "Christian statesmen." In six months Christian Voice had one hundred thousand members, including many conservative Catholics. At the same time, a Dallas network yanked James Robison's television show off the air after the preacher said gays sought to use schools as recruiting grounds. When Jews, Catholics, and other Christians jammed a meeting to protest that freedom of speech included "the right to preach" and advertisers threatened to pull commercials, the network reversed itself. Howard Phillips, who was Jewish before he became an evangelical Christian, and Weyrich, a Catholic, told Robison that the Dallas rally was "the beginning."[72]

But the real coup came with the enlistment of the Christian right's most visible agitator. Viguerie salivated when he contemplated the "2 million names" on Jerry Falwell's mailing list. In the spring of 1979, Weyrich, Phillips, and Viguerie went to Virginia with lay leader Ed McAteer and Billings to see Falwell.[73]

As Falwell liked to tell the story, Weyrich said, "Jerry, there is in America a moral majority that agrees about the basic issues" but was disorganized, lacked a platform, and was overlooked by the media. "Somebody's got to get that moral majority together. Suddenly, a bell went off in my head," Falwell recalled. Though Weyrich had been "thinking lower case *m*," Falwell had "the perfect name for a new organization that would bring together the people who believed in this nation," Anita Bryant's "normal majority." Falwell would surrender his mailing list to mobilize Christians, Catholics, and Jews, and Republicans, Democrats, and independents who were "pro-life, pro-traditional family, pro-moral, and pro-American (that included favoring a strong national defense and support for the state of Israel," where some evangelicals believed Jesus would return). The Christian right would be transformed into the religious right.[74]

And so Falwell announced the formation of Moral Majority, Inc. in May 1979. His proclamation merged the religious right and the New Right—two institutions essential to the growth of conservatism and two that as recently as 1975 few Americans had even known existed. The New Right and the religious right would offer an alternative to the civil religion of the United States embodied in the Constitution. *Conservative Digest* publicized the Moral Majority and "Jimmy Carter's Betrayal of the Christian Voter." The Christians who had assured Carter's rise had become partners in a coalition devoted to "family values" and to his destruction. Anticommunism and the Middle East cemented the bonds among the New Right, the religious right, conservatives, and neoconservatives.[75]

XI

RETURN TO THE COLD WAR: THE UNITED STATES, THE SOVIET UNION, AND THE MIDDLE EAST

—

"WHO IS ALLEN WEINSTEIN AND WHAT HAS HE GOT ON ALGER Hiss?" *Human Events* asked in 1978. After Hiss, a former State Department official who had accompanied Franklin Roosevelt to Yalta, denied the 1948 charges of Whittaker Chambers and Congressman Richard Nixon that he had been a Communist spy during the 1930s, he was convicted of perjury. Hiss's supporters maintained that he was a victim of cold war hysteria and launched a new campaign to exonerate him after Watergate destroyed Nixon's reputation. But Weinstein, a historian who was originally part of that effort, unearthed a wealth of evidence pointing toward Hiss's guilt, which he set out in *Perjury*. His book challenged "those intent on resuscitating Hiss as a method of showing the Cold War was and is a myth," a conservative said happily. The right viewed Carter as one of those who did not take the cold war seriously.[1]

Some revisionist accounts of Carter's foreign policy challenge the image of him "as weak, indecisive, inconsistent, and the victim of conflicts among his advisers." Yet the right portrayed him that way during his presidency. Alarmed Ford and Reagan Republicans, conservatives, neoconservatives, the New Right, and religious fundamentalists united in condemnation of his foreign policy. When Carter tried to improve upon the SALT II accord and initiated, then backed away from steps to involve the Soviets in the Middle East peace process, his behavior also caused consternation in Moscow. As it turned out, said one CIA insider, "relations between the Soviet Union and the United States were more consistently sour and antagonistic during the Carter administration than was (or would be) the case under any other President of the Cold War except for Harry Truman—including Ronald Reagan." Middle Eastern policy and Carter's relationship with American Jews suffered too.[2]

MCGOVERNISM WITHOUT MCGOVERN?

In 1976, Carter criticized Kissinger and détente from the right and the left. Sometimes he sounded like Reagan. At other times he pledged to make foreign policy more openly and to recapture the country's moral leadership by protecting human rights, an increasingly popular and visible cause. (The 168,000 individuals in 107 countries who belonged to the leading human rights organization Amnesty International were to win the Nobel Peace Prize in 1977.)[3]

As Carter settled on a foreign policy during the transition between his election and inauguration, he resolved to work for nuclear disarmament and normalization of relations with China. He would reduce use of the military abroad and spending by withdrawing U.S. troops from Korea. He would urge allies to shoulder more of the burden and to solve regional conflict through diplomacy. Here was the Nixon-Ford foreign policy, updated to ensure austerity. But Carter also wanted to abolish all nuclear weapons from the earth and to patch together an alliance of neoconservatives, Jews, liberals, and left-liberals. Along with announcing that the United States must recognize "limits," he declared in his Inaugural Address that its commitment to human rights must be "absolute." Where Ford, critics charged, had hidden from Solzhenitsyn to please the Soviets, Carter would not accommodate anyone who abridged human rights.[4]

The presidential candidate who had said he would appoint "a new generation of leaders" also named establishment pillars to his cabinet. Cyrus Vance became secretary of state; Zbigniew Brzezinski, national security adviser. Those appointments ensured administrative cacophony. For though the two men agreed on much, their diverging concerns by 1978 caused the administration to sound inconsistent. As befitted a decent gray Wall Street lawyer, Vance sought to reduce conflict quietly. He insisted that it was crucial to obtain an arms control agreement and that progress on SALT II could not be "linked" to other issues. In contrast, the flamboyant and flirtatious Brzezinski espoused a philosophy of confrontation and "linkage." A Catholic whose family had fled Poland before the Nazis, then the Russians overran it, Columbia University's Brzezinski lived in two shadows. Henry Kissinger cast one. One reporter said that Brzezinski "has always been the other European-accented professor of foreign policy." The Soviet Union provided the other. Within a year of Carter's inauguration, Brzezinski, a master infighter and courtier, had become, as Betty Glad has shown, the president's "gatekeeper, policy advisor, and teacher," the "chief of staff for American foreign policy." In Carter's eyes, he could do very little wrong.[5]

Meanwhile, neoconservatives presented the president-elect with a list of fifty-three candidates for administration jobs. Many on it, such as Paul Nitze, a founder of the Committee on the Present Danger, had vigorously supported candidate Carter. "We were completely frozen out," one Henry Jackson aide recalled. "The Carter administration turned out to be ideological, a New Left administration."[6]

While Vance and Brzezinski were hardly New Left exemplars, it was easy to understand how some would think the administration's foreign policy tilted toward the left. In addition to Carter's pardon of draft evaders, there was his attempted appointment of Theodore Sorensen as director of the Central Intelligence Agency. Sorensen's critics included the American Conservative Union, the New Right, Senate Minority Leader Howard Baker, Ronald Reagan, and CIA officials. Sorensen had burnished his cold warrior credentials in the Kennedy White House, but his opponents focused on his registration for military service as a noncombatant in the late 1940s and asked whether a "conscientious objector" should head the CIA. They became more irate when Sorensen admitted he had removed cartons of classified documents from the White House without authorization when he wrote his memoir of Kennedy. By the time Sorensen withdrew his name for the CIA directorship in January 1977, it seemed clear that had it gone forward, he would have been the first presidential nominee since the 1920s to be rejected by a Congress controlled by the president's party.[7]

Carter also appointed civil rights activist Andrew Young his United Nations ambassador. When Young told newsman Dan Rather that Cuban mercenaries "bring a certain stability and order" to Angola, conservatives and neoconservatives branded him an "apologist for Marxist Repression." Largely with Carter's support, Young advocated black majority rule in Rhodesia and Namibia. The administration recognized that civil rights activists saw the region as "our Israel" and wanted to hold on to the votes of African Americans. Further, for better or worse,

Carter and Young saw the fight for majority rule and human rights in southern Africa (except in South Africa) through the prism of the civil rights struggle in the American South: They more easily set aside cold war considerations than they did elsewhere in Africa and the world. Thus Carter and Young pressed the white minority in Rhodesia, for example, to reach a settlement with the black nationalist leader Robert Mugabe, who became notorious for brutalizing his subjects after Rhodesia achieved independence and became Zimbabwe in 1980. During the 1970s many Rhodesian whites viewed Mugabe as "a murderer and a Communist," and the Carterites' pressures infuriated Jesse Helms and others on the American right, who pointed out that white minorities proved more reliably anti-Communist than black majorities.[8]

Further, Carter named civil rights activist Patt Derian the State Department's coordinator for human rights and humanitarian affairs. Opponents faulted her for focusing on the human rights abuses of American allies, such as the Philippines and Argentina, in addition to those of Communists. Arriving in Buenos Aires in 1977, where the military dictatorship, with Kissinger's go-ahead, had launched a crusade against the left, she warned that American aid might dry up unless the disappearances and murders stopped. Argentina's "dirty war" nonetheless continued, and the administration rarely went far enough in making good on its threats to withhold aid from friendly dictators to suit Derian or congressional liberals. So too, despite an unprecedented American attempt under Carter to address the British occupation of Northern Ireland and to promote "a solution that the people in Northern Ireland, as well as the Governments of Great Britain and Ireland can support," some complained that State Department sensitivity to British interests made human rights in Northern Ireland "an expendable consideration."[9]

Carter also nominated Paul Warnke as chief SALT negotiator and head of the Arms Control and Disarmament Agency. The Senate, led by Jackson, almost rejected Warnke, a McGovern adviser, who urged the United States to be "first off the treadmill" of the nuclear arms race and pursue "a policy of restraint while calling for matching restraint from the Soviet Union." Neoconservatives, convinced that the United States underestimated the Soviet threat, had publicly announced the establishment of the Committee on the Present Danger only a week after Carter's election. The Committee on the Present Danger joined with conservatives and the New Right to form the Emergency Coalition

Against Unilateral Disarmament in order to fight Warnke's nomination. He was confirmed in March 1977 by just 60 percent of the Democratic Senate.[10]

McGovern and other liberals liked Carter's early foreign policy far more than his domestic policy. But to the president's critics on the right, the Warnke, Young, and Derian appointments, like the failed Sorensen nomination, proved his "McGovernism." Rarely defined, "McGovernism" was an epithet. Neoconservatives alleged that Carter was trying to create a "*new* foreign policy establishment" of Warnke, Young, and "younger government officials of the 'Vietnam generation' such as Leslie Gelb, Richard Holbrooke, and Anthony Lake." (Just as the Nixon-Ford administration served as the "incubator" for the George H. W. and George W. Bush's administrations, so Carter's became one for Bill Clinton's and Barack Obama's.)[11]

SALT I was due to expire on October 3, 1977. Two-thirds of the Senate would have to ratify SALT II, and only fifty-eight Senators had voted for Warnke as SALT negotiator (though seventy had voted for him as Arms Control and Disarmament Agency director). "When the SALT I treaty was ratified," one of Carter's congressional liaisons explained to another that fall, "everything was going in its favor: it was an historic breakthrough—the first of such agreements; it was negotiated by Nixon and Kissinger—two hardliners whom no one suspected of being soft on the Soviets or in favor of weakening our national defense; the country was in the midst of a war and this was an initiative against future wars." Then the antidétente coalition emerged, and many came to believe Nixon and Kissinger "sold us down the river in SALT I—which they probably did." (Whether the liaison spoke for himself or Carter was unclear.) If the Russians could outmaneuver Nixon, how could Carter succeed, especially when Warnke was negotiating for him? As a result, "before we even know" the details of SALT II, "we are in trouble." The administration needed "a ramrod" who could sell SALT II on the Hill with the same kind of expertise as Senator Jackson's thirty-five-year-old staffer Richard Perle, described by journalists as possibly "one of the dozen most important people in Washington in the area of strategic arms policy," and devoted to fighting both SALT II and Warnke. "In short, we need our own Richard Perle." Otherwise SALT II would be dead on arrival.[12]

WHILE THE PRESIDENT'S appointments sent one message to domestic critics, Carter sent another to the Soviet Union. Brezhnev had delivered a major speech in January 1977 before Carter's inauguration saluting détente. The Soviets wanted to cut defense spending and move quickly to an agreement based on the Vladivostok Accord.[13]

Carter disregarded their signals. Instead he decided to pursue "deep cuts" of more than 20 percent in the ceilings set at Vladivostok and to change the focus of the SALT process from arms limitation to reduction. Vance and Warnke recognized that the Soviets viewed Vladivostok as "politically sacrosanct" and understood that the reductions Carter urged would impose a disproportionate burden on the Soviet Union. On Vance's recommendation, the administration also developed a backup proposal, based on Vladivostok. But that proposal deferred agreement on some of the issues about which the Soviets most wanted resolution until SALT III, and Carter made his personal preference for deep cuts very clear.[14]

From a domestic political perspective, deep cuts made some sense. But if the president really wanted them, he might have been better off walking away from SALT II altogether in 1977, as he did after the Soviets invaded Afghanistan in 1979. For there was no chance the Soviets would agree to them. Brezhnev privately accused Carter of "putting forward deliberately unacceptable proposals."[15]

That was one possibility. When Ronald Reagan tried a similar gambit early in his administration, many on the left accused him and Richard Perle, by now a Reaganite, of promoting arms reduction to undercut arms control. Given the depth of dissatisfaction with détente by the time Carter took office, what better way to torpedo arms control than by saying it did not go far enough and pressing for something the Soviets would reject? American hard-liners welcomed deep cuts. Perhaps at some level, the president hoped to sabotage SALT II, or he was duped by its opponents into proposing unacceptable terms.[16]

Yet the president seemed surprised and disappointed by the Soviets' negative response. More likely, he hoped to prove he was his own man, his a new administration. With characteristic self-confidence that was particularly high during those first days when he tried to bring Congress to heel by canceling construction of dams and other water projects, Carter probably also believed he could achieve an agreement that would go farther in heading off nuclear war than the nearly completed SALT II negotiations. But no matter what moved him—cynicism, naiveté, arrogance, grandiosity, or idealism—the deep cuts proposal proved as unsuccessful as his crusade against water projects.[17]

To make matters worse, Carter broke with the tradition of confidentiality in SALT negotiations and made the details of the administration's deep cuts proposals public before Vance left for Moscow in March 1977 to present them. Soviet policy makers concluded that "the Carter Administration was weaseling out of the SALT process." Just as bad, the administration made Andrei Sakharov, a Soviet dissident who championed Jewish emigration, the symbol of its human rights campaign.[18]

The president disavowed any linkage between SALT and Sakharov and insisted his human rights campaign did not single out the Soviet Union and would not affect American-Soviet relations. Press Secretary Jody Powell reasoned that the Soviets were "surely . . . sophisticated enough" to understand that the American public would reject SALT unless the president gained "domestic political flexibility" by defending human rights. Yet Soviet Foreign Minister Gromyko told Carter that whenever any American "talked about human rights, the Soviet leadership reacted with a conditioned reflex, as it were, waiting for the arrow that would be launched in the direction of the Soviet Union."[19]

Given the administration's focus on human rights, the Soviets were likely to reject Carter's call for deep cuts. After angrily turning down Vance's proposals, Brezhnev ended the meeting abruptly without even presenting a counteroffer. Gromyko publicly decried deep cuts as a "cheap and shady maneuver."[20]

The Carter administration had gotten off on the wrong foot with the Soviet Union. Equally important, the new president had, as he frequently would do, played into American hard-liners' hands. His first SALT II package came back to haunt the administration. Any subsequent proposal that did not go as far would not measure up. When the administration unveiled a new SALT II proposal in May that did not cut so deep, neoconservatives condemned it. After Carter upbraided them, they treated him as the enemy.[21]

The deep cuts initiative hurt the president. Only the left applauded it. The *Nation* editorialized defensively that the evidence suggested that "Carter knew exactly what he was doing." Yet the editors admitted that the rest of the media concluded that the "Moscow confrontation ended in a knockout" because the Americans had misread the Soviet mood.

Those to Carter's right were now certain that as a negotiator he was incompetent.[22]

NOR WERE THEY IMPRESSED by his May 1977 Notre Dame speech calling for a new foreign policy of human rights. Appealing to an image of America as a force for good older than the Republic, the president urged "constant decency in our values and optimism in our historical vision." Democracy was prevailing throughout the globe, Carter maintained. "Being confident of our future," he continued, "we are now free of that inordinate fear of Communism which once led us to embrace any dictator who joined us in that fear." For decades the United States had embraced the "flawed principles" of its adversaries and fought "fire with fire," instead of water. "This approach failed, with Vietnam the best example of its intellectual and moral poverty. But through failure we have found our way back to our own principles and values, and we have regained our lost confidence." Exactly how his country had discovered its way back Carter did not say. Presumably it was by putting him in charge. But his speech suggested that in the future a new kind of intervention, not isolation, was the answer. With decolonialization nearly complete and the creation of nearly one hundred new nations, it was time to seek "justice, equity, and human rights." The United States must pursue a policy of "constructive global involvement," based on collaboration with industrial democracies, watchful cooperation with the Soviet Union and China, elimination of the gap between rich and poor nations, and transcendence of self-interest.[23]

Carter sometimes behaved as if he were "free of that inordinate fear of communism" that had led the United States to dance with dictators. That was one reason he wanted to withdraw American troops from South Korea, where the Park regime tortured and jailed hundreds of dissidents. The same day the president spoke at Notre Dame, the White House released the news that Carter had relieved General John Singlaub as U.S. chief of staff in South Korea for telling a reporter that troop withdrawal would prompt a North Korean invasion. "Who did President Carter think he was—Harry Truman?" editorialized the *Washington Post*. "And who did he think Maj. Gen. John K. Singlaub was—General of the Army Douglas MacArthur?" Unlike MacArthur, who had repeatedly undercut Truman during the Korean War, Singlaub had simply made "some irresponsible remarks." Many American officers in South Korea opposed the removal of American troops as long as Kim Il Sung remained the Communist dictator of North Korea. Carter wisely suspended withdrawals after U.S. intelligence at the end of 1977 belatedly revealed that North Korea had nearly tripled its ground forces and doubled its inventory of tanks and artillery since 1970.[24]

Within the United States, many had not freed themselves of "that inordinate fear of communism" either. Singlaub instantly became a martyr to both Ford and Reagan. Conservatives also condemned the president's Notre Dame speech for unilaterally declaring the end of the cold war. They did not share Carter's optimism about democracy aborning. Since "the most important reality facing us today is the shrinking global influence of the West," Ronald Reagan contended, the United States must cling to dictatorships "which, despite not always behaving precisely as we might like, have nevertheless been our friends."[25]

Neoconservatives also distinguished between totalitarianism and authoritarianism. Like Reagan, who soon began to court them, neocons declared it necessary to cooperate with the latter to confront the former. That was the point Jeane Kirkpatrick famously made in her essay "Dictatorships and Double Standards," which scorned the Carter administration for abandoning the Somoza regime in Nicaragua and the shah in Iran. Neoconservatives did not become the global champions of democracy until the 1980s.[26]

THE RIGHT REMAINED OUTRAGED when Carter declared in June 1977 that he would discontinue production of the B-1 manned strategic bomber. Representative Phil Crane, the American Conservative Union's chair, decried "one of the most dangerously foolish, short-sighted decisions I have ever seen." Neoconservatives maintained that the president was pandering to post-Vietnam neoisolationists. Ford and Kissinger were angry too. So were many congressional Democrats. Indeed Carter reached the decision he did partly to show them who was boss. "We'd better defy Congress once and get the test case over with," he told Mondale. Even those who agreed with Carter that the B-1 was expensive and inefficient, as the president had argued some of the time during the campaign, thought he should have used "cancellation as a bargaining chip with the Soviets."[27]

With the Soviets signaling they were ready to negotiate on SALT II, Carter may have been moved in part by a desire to use the B-1 as a bargaining chip. Over vodka and caviar the week before Carter announced his B-1 decision, Dobrynin told Brzezinski "that the Soviet leaders are very perplexed about what it is that the Carter Administration is trying to do." At his press conference announcing the B-1's cancellation, Carter hinted that his decision might signal to the Soviets that he hoped for quick progress on SALT II and a summit meeting soon.[28]

But the gesture, if intended as one, backfired. For Carter also suggested in June that the United States would proceed with the cruise missile system. That pleased Senator Jackson. Where Rockwell would have built the B-1 in California, Boeing would develop the cruise missile system in Washington State, and Jackson was so attentive to the aerospace industry in his home state that he was nicknamed the Senator from Boeing. The announcement riled the Soviets, particularly since during the same week the administration declared that it might develop the enhanced radiation weapon (ERW). Ignoring the B-1 news, the Soviet press warned that Carter's "militaristic plans" "seriously complicated" progress on SALT II.[29]

While Soviet and American foreign policy leaders sparred, Carter's critics on the right beat the drum about the Soviet threat. Divided by the Panama Canal, they were united by anticommunism and their certainty that the United States was "becoming Number 2." When Major General George Keegan said that the United States had fallen behind the Soviet Union, the Joint Chiefs of Staff disagreed. Yet as the *Washington Post* said, that did not mean much. "How Do We Know Who's Ahead?" its editorial page asked plaintively. It was not just that so much of the information was classified but that the experts disagreed about how to measure it. In retrospect, it appeared that the new Carter administration correctly claimed that the Soviet Union had achieved parity rather than superiority. But at the time many on the American right believed that the Soviets possessed or sought superiority, and the very idea of parity was alarming.[30]

Given the fear, both the Ford administration and the right had had high hopes for the manned B-1 bomber as a replacement for the B-52s developed in the 1950s. And while candidate Carter had reached out to members of a grassroots coalition of anti–B-1 peace groups by sometimes denouncing the B-1 as a waste of money in 1976, most signs had pointed to presidential authorization of its development in 1977. Thus Carter shocked the media and the military when he said he wanted to modernize the aging B-52s and to consider developing the unproved cruise missile system and ERW instead. The recently retired intelligence officer General Keegan spoke for Ford Republicans, Reagan Republicans, the New Right, and neoconservatives in the summer of 1977: "Are we once again to tempt fate through a return to the evangelical didacticism of the Wilsonian era or the isolationism of the 1930's?"[31]

As that rhetorical question indicated, Carter's opponents found him both overly and insufficiently ambitious. To them, he sounded like Woodrow Wilson, who idealistically spoke of making the world safe for democracy when he brought the United States into World War I. But he behaved like British Prime Minister Neville Chamberlain in the 1930s by promoting a "culture of appeasement," which encouraged dictators. The president's positions also alarmed neoconservatives, because they worried that as in the 1930s, Jews would be the losers. Neoconservatives still feared that the United States would abandon Israel to curry favor with the Soviets.[32]

CARTER'S JEWISH PROBLEM

As Carter dealt with fallout over his cancellation of the B-1, Hamilton Jordan gave him a memorandum on the domestic implications of foreign policy. Jordan wrote about what he alternately called "the Jewish lobby" and "the American Jewish community." Jews voted, and they also bankrolled political campaigns. Jordan thought they cared only about Israel and that the American Israel Political Action Committee (AIPAC) could count on sixty-five to seventy-five votes in the Senate on any issue. While Jews "know and instinctively trust" Jackson, they feared Carter. Jordan included an appendix listing twenty-one administration actions since the inauguration that had alienated American Jews.[33]

As it was with SALT II, so it was with the Middle East. The new president did not want to duplicate Ford's foreign policy. Just as he urged deep cuts, so Carter called for a comprehensive Middle Eastern settlement. He would abandon the step-by-step diplomacy that had excluded the Soviet Union. Like Nixon in 1973, Carter spoke of convening another Geneva conference, chaired by the United States and the Soviet Union under the auspices of the United Nations, to bring together Israelis, Arabs, and Palestinians. As he envisioned it, the conferees could work to ensure Israeli security, provide the Palestinians with new rights, and resolve control of the disputed territories.[34]

This was an ambitious undertaking. The Arab states emphasized, with varying degrees of intensity, the creation of a Palestinian state and the importance of Palestinian Liberation Organization participation in the peace process, but the Israelis refused to consider a PLO role. Both Israelis and Egyptians mistrusted the Soviets, who mistrusted the United States after the deep cuts debacle. President Sadat thought Geneva the spot at which to sign, not negotiate, an agreement, while the Israelis felt they had been burned there in 1973. Nonetheless, the new administration embarked on a whirlwind of meetings with Israeli and Arab leaders, during which Carter proved "an unguided missile."[35]

As he welcomed Israeli Prime Minister Yitzhak Rabin to Washington on March 7, 1977, for example, Carter expressed his commitment to achieving "defensible borders" for Israel, "a code phrase" for the Israeli argument that it should retain the land it had occupied since 1967. The Arabs were distressed. Then, in the spirit of his desire to formulate foreign policy openly, Carter made his peace plan public and announced that Israel must return to its 1967 borders, with only "minor adjustments." Now the Israelis were alarmed, by both Carter's words and the fact that he had not first consulted Rabin. On March 16, 1977, at a town meeting in Clinton, Massachusetts, the president bravely, and apparently spontaneously, declared in answering a question that there could be no Middle East settlement without "a homeland for the Palestinian refugees who have suffered for many, many years." Here was another loaded phrase. While the United States had previously declared its support for a Palestinian state or self-governing entity in the territories, no American president had ever spoken of a "homeland" for Palestinians. "This helped to create the impression that the new Administration was tilting away from Israel," Brzezinski said.[36]

So did Carter's obvious preference for Sadat over Rabin. While forging an intimate bond with Sadat in 1977, he compared his discussions with Rabin to talking "with a dead fish." The Arab visits went better too. Rabin was forced to depart Washington without ceremony because a tiny group of armed Hanafi Muslims had seized 132 hostages at three different D.C. sites. In contrast, "Tutmania" was sweeping the United States when Sadat visited Carter. Crowds mobbed "Treasures of Tutankhamun," a National Gallery exhibit of artifacts found in a pharaoh's tomb, and Carter touted the show when he toasted Sadat, his "very close, personal" friend. (Outside the United States, Carter also made his affections clear. He hailed President Hafiz al-Assad of Syria, whom the Israelis particularly hated, as "brilliant" and "very enjoyable.")[37]

With Israel's Labor Party weakened by a financial scandal and the Israeli economy floundering, Carter's foreign policy became yet another factor that created an opening for the Likud Party, which pledged to annex the territories. Its upset victory in June 1977 ended nearly thirty years of Labor hegemony and made Menachem Begin prime minister. As a fighter for Israeli independence in the 1940s Begin had authorized acts of terrorism against Arab and British civilians, and he remained a superpatriot or fanatic, depending on one's point of view. American conservatives hailed Begin as "Israel's Ronald Reagan," said that his promises to cut taxes and spending made his victory "a taxpayer's revolt in the Holy Land," and thrilled to his "thoroughgoing" anticommunism. The Carter administration thought Begin "a total disaster."[38]

At a news conference one reporter observed that the Soviets had rejected Carter's deep cuts proposal after the president announced it publicly, and "your public statements with respect to a Palestinian homeland are being credited as being a factor in the election of a conservative, hard-line political group in Israel. Do you think you are going to be able to continue your policy of open discussions of foreign policy issues and at the same time achieve agreements?" When Carter answered affirmatively and went on to hint that American Jews could press Begin to show "moderation," he made another faux pas.[39]

Nor could Begin be moderated. He would not consider either a Palestinian homeland or inclusion of the Palestine Liberation Organization in peace talks. He maintained that "Palestine is a foreign translation of the historic word Israel" and that Palestinians will "live here with us in peace." He refused to curtail Israeli West Bank settlements. Return of the "liberated" territories, he told an American newscaster, would simply help the Soviet Union. "It was frightening to watch his adamant position," Carter said.[40]

Begin's visit to the United States that summer only briefly alleviated the president's concerns. "I found him to be quite congenial, dedicated, sincere, deeply religious," Carter wrote in his diary. American Jews distressed by the media portrayal of Begin as a terrorist and by Washington's move away from Israel liked him too. But as soon as Begin returned to Israel, he reneged on the spirit, if not the letter, of an agreement

Carter thought they had reached and authorized new West Bank settlements. Begin, who had decided to build on Sinai II and seek a separate peace with Egypt, had also begun negotiations with Sadat about which the United States was not fully apprised. Obviously, Washington was losing control.[41]

So Carter tried to recapture the American initiative. He negotiated secretly, for a change, with the Soviets. In October 1977, he announced that the United States and the Soviet Union would devote their efforts to overcoming the differences of the regional players and to cochairing a United Nations meeting in Geneva by year's end. He alluded to the "legitimate rights of the Palestinian people" but said nothing at the time about Israel's right to secure borders.[42]

Carter's critics had one explanation: Having recently backed away from deep cuts to woo the Soviets, the president was also now sacrificing Israel on the altar of détente. The Soviet-American joint communiqué brought together Soviet foes and Israeli friends. When the United States and the Soviet Union also announced that despite the expiration of SALT I, they would continue to live by its restrictions while they worked toward SALT II, Israel's friends were certain that Israel had been subordinated to SALT II. The White House liaison for Jewish affairs said that the joint communiqué had driven "Jimmy Carter's stock in the American Jewish community substantially below any U.S. President since the creation of the State of Israel."[43]

So Carter reconsidered when he met with Israeli Foreign Minister Moshe Dayan later in the month. Brzezinski recalled that "Dayan intimidated Carter" by threatening to denounce the president to American Jews. Carter tried to be "reassuring," but at least to Brzezinski, the president seemed weak. The United States and Israel issued a "working paper" in which the United States seemed to retreat from the joint communiqué.[44]

Whenever the door to Middle East negotiations at Geneva opened, it slammed shut. The Palestinian representation issue was hardest to fudge. Sadat informed Carter that Arafat agreed that Edward Said would head the Palestinian delegation. No one told Said, the Columbia professor who was about to launch the field of postcolonial studies with his critique of orientalism. When the press learned of Said's designation in November 1977, the Israelis objected, and Said himself seemed unenthusiastic. "I think what's lacking," he told a reporter, "is any kind of full invitation to the Palestinians and their representatives, who in this case are the Palestine Liberation Organization."[45]

SEEING THAT THE Geneva initiative, about which he had always been ambivalent, was going nowhere, Sadat dropped his own bombshell. He declared that he would go to Jerusalem to seek peace. Though Carter had privately appealed for the Egyptian's support in breaking the impasse, the White House was understandably displeased at "the wide currency given to the idea that Sadat's move had come out of desperation and disappointment in American diplomacy." Surprised Israelis, however, waved homemade Egyptian flags and greeted Sadat enthusiastically on November 19, 1977. The Egyptian talked tough to the Israelis. Declaring that he had not come "for a separate agreement between Egypt and Israel," he made "the Palestinian cause . . . the crux of the entire problem" and demanded "[c]omplete withdrawal from the Arab territories occupied after 1967." But Sadat had recognized Israel's right to exist, so Israelis warmly applauded him.[46]

Few Arab nations did. Only Morocco, Tunisia, and Sudan approved of Sadat's mission, and the Saudis were ambivalent, at best. Syria, the PLO, the Popular Front for the Liberation of Palestine, Iraq, Libya, and Algeria congregated in Tripoli to denounce him. "It is no longer secret that many organizations are aiming to finish Sadat," one participant told a reporter. Obviously, Sadat needed concessions from Israel on the Palestinian issue. Though Begin spent Christmas with Sadat, these he would not give. Negotiations had broken down by year's end, and the American-Soviet relationship had deteriorated further.[47]

The Geneva Conference that never happened became a club with which the Soviets beat the Americans. The Soviets and the Americans had both "invested not a small political capital" in the joint communiqué, Brezhnev told Carter. Then the United States had undermined the communiqué, and the Egyptians and Israelis had created "great anxiety" in the Arab world by meeting away from Geneva. "The question is: either the green light will be given to the attempts to blow up the Geneva Conference even before it is convened, or through joint efforts we shall bring the matter back to the track of a genuine settlement in the Middle East." The Soviets blamed the United States for giving "the green light" to the Egyptians and Israelis "to blow up" the conference. The KGB was certain that the Americans had known of Sadat's impending trip to Jerusalem when they had "treacherously" signed the Geneva communiqué. Brezhnev repeatedly reaffirmed that "it is the United States and not the Soviet Union that has departed from the Statement jointly adopted on October 1, 1977, has embarked upon the path of encouraging separate negotiations between Egypt and Israel," and had excluded the Soviets, whom it no longer needed as Geneva cochair, from the peace process.[48]

"RETURN TO THE COLD WAR"

While the Soviets complained about the American betrayal of Geneva, they and the Cubans were moving forward in Africa, the Middle East, Asia, and Europe. The Soviets increased their presence in the Horn of Africa by supporting Cuban and Ethiopian troops who successfully fought off Somali invaders in the Ethiopian province of Ogaden in March 1978. In their most ambitious imperial venture outside Eastern Europe in decades, the Soviets provided more than one billion dollars of military equipment and nearly one thousand military personnel to the violent Marxist ruler of Ethiopia. The Soviets backed a coup that installed a friendly government in South Yemen, which they supported against North Yemen. They gave their blessing to a bloody Communist coup against Afghanistan's left-wing government that they apparently learned of only after it had occurred. The Soviets decided to replace their aging intermediate-range weapons in Europe with new SS-20s and to build up the military forces of their Warsaw Pact allies. Carter also maintained that the Cubans had encouraged rebel forces to invade the Shaba province of Zaire and that there and elsewhere they acted "as a surrogate for the Soviet Union."[49]

These actions were probably not intended to send the cold war into a deep freeze, though Brezhnev had apparently lost his passion for détente. The recent evidence from Soviet archives and players suggests that the Soviet and Cuban success in Angola in the mid-1970s, together with the perception that Americans had lost confidence after Vietnam, "gave rise to unprecedented optimism in Soviet Third World policy—'the world,' according to one of their high officials, 'was turning in our direction.'" In Angola, the Soviets believed they had just gotten "lucky." The coup in Afghanistan apparently came as a surprise, and they simply moved to exploit it. Moreover, the evidence indicated that the Cubans were not directly involved in the Shaba invasion and that if anything, Castro might have tried to prevent it. And the Ethiopian-Somali controversy originally involved a dispute between two Soviet clients. But the Soviets apparently viewed the victory in Ethiopia at Ogaden as proof they had "become a complete superpower—a global alternative to the United States." Soviet prowess in Africa helped compensate for the loss of Egypt and might even impress China. Détente, KGB chairman Yuri Andropov apparently concluded, rather than provide for the management of the Soviets with carrots and sticks, as Nixon, Kissinger, and Ford had intended, was a Soviet boon. Though the third world spending spree ultimately helped destroy the Soviet Union, Russia's fortunes seemed to be rising during Carter's presidency.[50]

One theory in Washington had the Soviets behaving as they did out of unhappiness over the Carter administration's abandonment of the Geneva communiqué. Another was that they had decided that the Carter administration wanted SALT II too much to retaliate.[51]

In any event, the United States sat by and watched in 1978 as the new leaders in Afghanistan tried to beat off challenges from Islamic fundamentalists and drew closer to Moscow. Americans had a harder time ignoring Communist successes in Africa. At the 1978 Conservative Political Action Conference, Reagan warned that the Communists' success at Ogaden raised "the prospect of a Soviet empire of protégés and dependencies stretching from Addis Ababa to Capetown." Neoconservatives described the African stakes in equally heated terms, and even Gerald Ford said that if the Soviet "adventurism" in Africa continued, "we may well have to say to the Soviet Union 'SALT II is not a possibility.'"[52]

But the president's advisers divided in 1978. For Vance, whose priority was SALT II, African developments were a sideshow. The administration, he insisted, should not create a "political linkage between SALT and worsening U.S.-Soviet relations." Echoing administration critics, however, Brzezinski maintained that Vance had been "badly bitten by the Vietnam bug" and was "fearful of taking the kind of action which is necessary."[53]

Carter delayed choosing between the two poles Brzezinski and Vance represented to the public: confrontation/conciliation, linkage/nonlinkage. The media highlighted the "Tug of War over Foreign Policy" between his national security adviser and secretary of state. Ultimately, the president moved haltingly toward confrontation.[54]

On the Horn of Africa, Carter tried to play it both ways. On the one hand, he pleased Vance by calling for Somali withdrawal from Ogaden and by refusing the aid to Somalia that Brzezinski promoted. On the other, he sided with Brzezinski in insisting that the Soviets and Cubans leave Ethiopia. They stayed, and the president never went far enough for Brzezinski, who wanted him to send warships to Ethiopia. Carter did nothing more, one NSC staffer complained, than "harp and carp" about the Soviet and Cuban presence. The national security adviser contended in 1980 that because of Carter's failure "to stand up to the Soviet drive by proxy" in Africa, the Soviets had invaded Afghanistan, and the chance for cooperation on SALT II had been lost: "SALT lies buried in the sands of Ogaden."[55]

Yet Carter increasingly indicated that he was tired of "babying" the Soviets (as President Truman would have put it). In a March 1978 speech at Wake Forest University drafted by the National Security Council staff, Carter swore that "before I sign any SALT agreement on behalf of the United States, I will make sure that it preserves the strategic balance, that we can independently verify Soviet compliance, and that we will be at least as strong, relative to the Soviet Union, as we would be without any agreement." He condemned the "excessive Soviet buildup" in Europe and warned that if the Soviets failed "to demonstrate restraint in missile programs and other force levels or in the projection of Soviet or proxy forces into other lands and continents," popular American support for cooperation with the Soviet Union would "certainly erode." Alarmed, Soviets wondered whether the speech heralded a policy change.[56]

Not so fast. The State Department let the Russian Embassy know that the president's speech was designed to quiet domestic discontent. And on April 7, 1978, Carter suddenly declared his decision to defer production of the enhanced radiation weapon and publicly said that his decision about whether to proceed would "be influenced by the degree to which the Soviet Union shows restraints in its conventional and nuclear arms programs and force deployments affecting the security of the United States and Western Europe."[57]

The development of the ERW, or "neutron bomb," had been controversial. The Soviets professed to abhor this new weapon, intended to deter their invasion of Western Europe by killing people and saving property. (Its novelty was exaggerated; it also would destroy property.) The caustic tone Brezhnev usually employed was absent when he implored Carter to cancel the "unhuman" project *and* promised that the Soviets also would develop the ERW if Americans did. Carter thought the Soviets' threat to build a neutron bomb idle and insisted that "they are unlikely to fear ERW and only want the propaganda issue." But the ERW nonetheless gave him a "queasy feeling:" He did not want to be remembered as the president who "introduced bombs that kill people and leave buildings intact."[58]

Many others disliked the ERW too. The American left opposed it, and it was unpopular in Europe, where a strong antinuclear movement had emerged. West German Chancellor Helmut Schmidt, who detested Carter as "a man who never stopped searching his soul and tended repeatedly to change his mind," had long displayed ambivalence about the ERW, and Germany was the most likely site for its deployment. Privately, Schmidt worried that the Soviet Union was overtaking the West militarily and that Carter was less concerned than Ford with European security; publicly, that a SALT II Treaty would increase Western Europe's vulnerability. Sometimes Schmidt treated the ERW as a counterweight to the SS-20s. At others, he feared that development of the neutron bomb would hurt him at home.[59]

Nevertheless, Carter's advisers had pulled together a fragile Western European consensus in favor of development of the ERW, accompanied by an offer to forgo deployment if the Soviets agreed to do something about the SS-20s. Since the Americans knew that the Soviets would not agree to take out missiles already deployed in exchange for the promise not to construct a new weapon, it appeared that the United States would build the neutron bomb, and Carter's advisers had stressed to European leaders that "the president had personally decided" on production and deployment of the ERW. Then the president rethought the plan. Why spend billions on a weapon no European leader would publicly embrace, however much willingness he privately demonstrated to have it foisted upon him?[60]

That was a good question, but Carter should have asked it sooner. When his advisers realized that the president was wavering, they fought back. Brzezinski's opposition to the president's change in position was leaked to one of his favorite *New York Times* reporters, Richard Burt, and Bonn announced that it would support the ERW. But despite warnings that he would damage his reputation by reversing course, the president decided against it. Privately, he let the European allies know that his talk about awaiting Soviet responses was just that. But that was unnecessary, since everyone knew he was blowing smoke. The deferral of ERW production was "widely seen as merely a facesaving substitute for outright cancellation."[61]

Once again Carter was excoriated. The president's pollster reported that an "astounding 28%" of Americans contacted, "without any mentioning by us, brought up the neutron bomb decision," which was "nothing short of incredible for just a passing amorphous issue. Overwhelmingly, the reaction to Carter's decision was negative, often quite vehement."[62]

By now it was clear that SALT II had become a lightning rod for American anxiety about national decline. One White House official said that while polls always showed Americans favored arms control in the abstract, "the current public atmosphere could hardly be less conducive" to winning congressional approval of a SALT II Treaty. Administration foreign policy created "an impression that we are 'retreating.'" During the first week of May 1978, all thirty-eight Senate Republicans issued a manifesto. After "15 short months of incoherence, inconsistency and ineptitude," they charged, "our foreign policy and national security objectives are confused, and we are challenged around the globe by Soviet arrogance." The Republicans claimed bipartisan support, with one boasting that had they offered it to the entire chamber, three-quarters of the Senate would have signed it.[63]

After meeting with two English diplomats, Ambassador Kingman Brewster wired home: "Even discounting British manners and understatement, both underscored the disastrous impact" of the cancellation of the ERW on Carter's credibility and leadership. "It was apparent that with European governments and opinion the problem is the uncertain trumpet, the backing and filing." Like many Americans in 1978, Western European governments wanted Carter to develop a more coherent and consistent approach to the Soviet Union.[64]

AND HE DID. In one week in late May 1978 the president made headlines by taking steps to remilitarize NATO and to normalize relations with China. Vance had reported that NATO's theater nuclear forces were outdated, limiting its ability to engage in nuclear retaliation in Europe. Meanwhile, the Soviets trained those new SS-20s on Western Europe and possessed superior tank forces. The president took advantage of a May Washington summit meeting to signal that the United States was moving to strengthen NATO's long-range theater nuclear forces (LRTNF) against the SS-20s. In view of the ERW disaster, some advisers acknowledged that he had no other alternative. But the United States turned "from uncommitted and even reluctant readiness to consider LRTNF deployments to ardent advocacy" in the second half of 1978 without taking into account how the Soviets would perceive its shift.[65]

At the same time, the White House courted China. By the time Carter became president, the power struggle that had begun after Mao's 1976 death was ending. Deng Xiaoping, a man twice purged as a right-wing "capitalist-roader," was to guide China toward a socialist market economy. Almost as soon as Carter became president, Soviet Foreign Minister Gromyko had warned him against "playing a 'Chinese card'" and said that "it would be a great mistake if some sort of dirty game were played here in terms of collusion, covert or overt, against the interests of the Soviet Union." The president had replied that he would prefer "not to change present relations at all" with China, rather than to promote "collusion."[66]

Now, in May 1978, Carter changed those relations on the advice of Brzezinski, the administration official most responsible for the American flirtation with the Chinese. Brzezinski later remembered the president's warning "that we should be careful how we went about normalization and that we 'should not ass-kiss them the way Nixon and Kissinger did, and also be careful not to antagonize domestic constituencies.'" Brzezinski responded that Moscow's abuse of détente made it essential to proceed rapidly toward normalization by sending him to China. As Brzezinski admitted, he "badgered the President" until Carter authorized his national security adviser to go.[67]

Having reached the decision to send Brzezinski to China over Vance's objection, Carter enlarged its significance. The president viewed his overture to China as a way of both intimidating the Soviet Union and improving "the lives of ordinary Chinese," whose lives had been getting better since Nixon's trip there in 1972. The tilt toward China would of course prove unpopular with Reagan, who made a widely publicized trip to Taiwan in 1978, and many others on the right who feared for the security of Taiwan. But despite China's appalling human rights record, some Senate liberals, such as Kennedy, and neoconservatives, such as Jackson, wanted to normalize relations with China. Jackson was almost as solicitous of China's leaders as he was of Israel's. Indeed, after meeting with Jackson, Brzezinski informed the president that Jackson had told him that "the Chinese feel slighted by this Administration." While the Brzezinski trip was "a good corrective," Jackson thought it crucial that "the Chinese clearly understand" that Brzezinski was "going as your personal representative" and that Carter was prepared to "move boldly on normalization." That "would help the prospects for dealing with SALT." Was Jackson signaling he might play ball with the White House on SALT II? If so, he was just toying with the administration. Carter proceeded to expand Brzezinski's Chinese mission. "You should state that the United States has made up its mind," he told his national security adviser, and was prepared to negotiate away roadblocks to normalization, such as insistence on the American right to protect Taiwan. With those words, Brzezinski explained, Carter transformed "a consultative, low-key mission . . . into a genuinely major undertaking."[68]

With his penchant for the theatrical, the NSC adviser ensured that his trip would receive even more attention. Brzezinski made real progress toward normalization on the visit. He also worsened tensions with the Soviet Union. In Beijing, Vance complained, Brzezinski "made provocative remarks in public about Soviet international actions" and presented his trip as an American "countermove" to Soviet aggressiveness. When Brzezinski, while climbing the Great Wall, issued a challenge to his aides—"whoever reached the top second would be sent off to Ethiopia to confront the Cubans"—the press got wind of it. Upon returning to Washington, Brzezinski capped everything off by appearing on *Meet the Press* and condemning the Soviets for engaging in "a pattern of behavior" incompatible with "the code of détente." *Newsweek* speculated about "a new Cold War." Carter crossly told Brzezinski that the Chinese had "seduced" him, all the while, Brzezinski recalled, "smiling one of his 'I like you but I'm really burning inside' smiles."[69]

In conjunction with America's increased interest in LRTNF, the Soviets may have found Brzezinski's China trip menacing. Interestingly, Gromyko did not mention China when he consulted with Carter and Vance in May 1978. But in a speech to the Politburo, Brezhnev decried "the growing aggression of the Carter government, the continually anti-Soviet character of the statements of the President himself and of his closest colleague—in the first instance those of Brzezinski"—and declared that Carter was "intent upon struggling for his election to a new term as President of the USA under the banner of anti-Soviet policy and a return to the 'cold war.' " In retrospect, historian Thomas McCormick concluded, "the seven days in May that produced the 1978 NATO summit, as well as Brzezinski's China initiative, constituted the watershed break between the era of détente and that of the renewed Cold War."[70]

For his part, Vance sent the president a letter warning that the Soviets "seemed to be increasingly disturbed" by their relationship with the United States, particularly "what they saw as our inconsistency and unwillingness to deal with them as equals." He recommended that Carter deliver "a major speech on U.S.-Soviet relations," continue strengthening NATO, conclude the SALT II Treaty, stop nagging Brezhnev about human rights since "our public pressure was causing the Soviets to crack down harder on Soviet dissidents," cease playing the Chinese off against the Soviets, and resist linking progress on SALT II to Soviet behavior in the Third World, while working to prevent more incursions there.[71]

Vance thought he caught Carter's ear when the president agreed to deliver an address about the United States and the Soviet Union at the U.S. Naval Academy. Exactly who wrote the president's June 7, 1978, Annapolis commencement speech was widely debated. Vance claimed he prepared one draft; Brzezinski, a more aggressive version. A speechwriter said that Carter stapled the two versions together. Brzezinski, however, maintained that the address was "largely Carter's own handiwork," as the archival records also suggest. Nonetheless, the speech read as if the president had taken the first half from his secretary of state and the second from his national security adviser. The crescendo was pure Brzezinski. "The Soviet Union can choose either confrontation or cooperation," Carter said. "The United States is adequately prepared to meet either choice."[72]

Americans and the Soviets reacted differently to the Annapolis address. A series of entries in *Time* suggested the domestic confusion about its significance. According to the first, "the speech not only represented a major policy change (from conciliation to confrontation)" but also meant that "Carter had elevated Brzezinski over Vance." A month later the magazine declared Vance the dominant administration voice, and three weeks after that it said that "U.S.-Soviet relations have sunk to the lowest point in years." The Soviet media heard the message that *Time* did the first and third times. Charging that the speech marked the end of détente, the Soviet press announced that the White House had given Brzezinski "the upper hand," a decision "fraught with a return to the cold war."[73]

Carter had traveled some rhetorical distance since Notre Dame. At times, the *New Republic* complained, he now sounded like the Richard Nixon who had insisted that the United States must not become a "'pitiful, helpless giant.'" While Nixon himself publicly implied that the Soviets might consider Carter a "pantywaist," they thought him a dangerous adversary.[74]

Carter had taken steps designed to prevent his domestic critics from viewing him as a "pantywaist" and to bolster SALT II. In the aftermath of Annapolis, as Reagan's chief foreign policy adviser, Richard Allen, warned him in counseling him to hammer at "the growing public concern with Carter's weakness and mismanagement," rather than yammer about "declining U.S. military might" and wondrous weapons systems that Carter spurned, there was still great enthusiasm for SALT II. "In essence, the public seems to want to conclude arms limitation agreements with a rival power of which it is becoming increasingly distrustful and suspicious." Moreover, while "the movement of the country has clearly been toward RR positions" since 1976, "this does not address the problem of how you are perceived by a wide stratum of the public: for many, you come across as a 'saber-rattler,' a 'button pusher' or as 'too willing to send in the Marines.' This false image is happily amplified by the media, which prays for you to enunciate a dream formula for them to report—one in which you suggest the first use of nuclear weapons to support reactionary and fascist dictatorships against hapless subjugated nonwhite majorities."[75]

While Reagan and his team pondered his "packaging," other conservatives and neoconservatives pounced on the administration. At Harvard's June 1978 Class Day exercises, Aleksandr Solzhenitsyn made the case that Americans had lost their nerve. Just as the United States had brought Nazi Germany to heel by cultivating the Soviet Union, ultimately "a worse and more powerful" enemy, he warned, so some now cozied up to China and another "doomed alliance with Evil." Neoconservatives initially rejoiced that they were no longer dismissed as "paranoid" when they spoke of the Soviet threat. But then, in July, when SALT II negotiations resumed, they again labeled the administration "irresolute."[76]

CAMP DAVID

Against this backdrop, neoconservatives urged assistance for democracy in Israel. Ford had agreed to sell state-of-the-art F-15 planes to the Saudis, who feared Soviet advances in the Middle East and who threatened to back higher oil prices and to stop supporting the beleaguered dollar otherwise. When the Israelis and their American friends protested that the Saudis would use the planes against Israel, the Carter administration developed a package deal in February 1978: The United States would sell Saudi Arabia sixty F-15s; Israel, fifteen F-15s and seventy-five of the less fearsome F-16s; and Egypt, fifty antiquated F-5s. Carter sought to tie the hands of the "Israeli lobby" by ensuring that Israel would receive aircraft only if Egypt and Saudi Arabia did.[77]

The package deal possessed symbolic, as well as substantive, significance for both Israel and American Jews. Israel cherished its status as "an only child when it came to the flow of American weapons to the Middle East." More important, the Israelis believed that the administration wrongly viewed the anti-Communist and economically helpful Saudis as moderates. The Israelis were certain that the Saudis hated Israel almost as much as the Syrians did and were trying to sabotage the peace process by their insistence on a strong PLO role. Further, as a presidential candidate Carter had courted American Jews by opposing aircraft sales to Saudi Arabia and Egypt.[78]

Since a majority vote in both the House and Senate was necessary to block the deal, Israel's American supporters swung into action to defeat the sales. In March, Carter's Jewish affairs liaison, Mark Siegel, defended the deal in a speech to the United Jewish Appeal. His audience booed and jeered. It was not that all in it approved of Begin; Jewish liberals were more likely to sympathize with the many secular Israelis who questioned Begin's hawkishness and to support the Israeli military members who founded Peace Now that month and inveighed against the establishment of new West Bank settlements. It was that American Jews feared that Washington's solicitude for Israel was slipping. Siegel joined his listeners, he said afterward, in "feeling betrayed," and he resigned.[79]

Then, just before Begin was due in Washington for tough talks intended to bring him back to the table with Sadat, eleven Palestinian members of the PLO group Fatah threw a wrench in the stalled peace process. They hijacked two buses near Tel Aviv, murdered thirty-seven Israelis, and wounded more than twice as many. The Syrian press celebrated the operation, while the Saudi state radio hailed the Palestinians' "courageous action." Begin stressed that the terrorists, whom he called Nazis, carried "Soviet-made and Soviet-supplied weapons." He used the episode to justify his refusal to give up the West Bank and Gaza and to launch an invasion of Lebanon that used American military hardware to destroy PLO sanctuaries, kill more than a thousand noncombatants, and leave tens of thousands of Lebanese homeless.[80]

Israel's backers had used the Holocaust to rally support for Israel since the mid-1970s, but most Americans did not actually know much about it. That was about to change. In 1978, Willis Carto and other white supremacists on the far right founded the Institute for Historical Review to spread the message of Holocaust denial, or, as they preferred to call it, revisionism: The institute claimed that conventional accounts wildly exaggerated the number of Jews murdered by Hitler. In April 1978, just as it also seemed as if "American Nazis clothed in brown shirts and the First Amendment" would march in Skokie, Illinois, a town populated by Jewish Holocaust survivors, nearly one hundred million Americans watched NBC's *Holocaust*. The docudrama followed two fictional German families, Jewish and Nazi, from Hitler's promulgation of the Nuremberg Laws to the Auschwitz crematoriums. Like other 1970s historical accounts of the Holocaust and of slavery, it carefully stressed the theme of resistance, along with that of victimization, and its most powerful moments celebrated the Warsaw Ghetto uprising. AIPAC sent a copy of the novel on which the miniseries was based to every member of Congress and cited the Holocaust as yet another reason why the United States should deny Saudi Arabia aircraft. When the British ambassador asked Brzezinski about the Saudi arms sales, the NSC adviser replied that "we don't know what impact the TV program, the Holocaust, has had. Also Begin will be here for a week, barnstorming."[81]

Neither the educational, though cheesy, TV miniseries nor Begin carried the day for Israel. "I described the presumptions that Sadat and I had worked out for a possible peace settlement," Carter said of his meeting with Begin. In what became known as the six noes, Begin rejected every one. Israeli negotiators later told William Quandt, the historian of the negotiations, who participated in them as an NSC staffer, that the visit "was the low point in the entire negotiating process," particularly since Carter summoned congressional leaders and blamed the impasse on Begin.[82]

Begin's intransigence, coupled with frustration about the Israeli invasion of Lebanon and Americans' need for oil, helped the White House with the plane sales. Three years earlier more than three-quarters of the Senate had ended Ford's "reassessment" by signing a letter to him supporting Israel. Now, although the House voted against the package deal, just forty-four senators did in May. The debate, one journalist said, "generated an intensity of feeling in Washington and a degree of personal bitterness and strain not evident here since the most ragged days of the Vietnam debate." Hamilton Jordan warned the president that the administration's win represented "the first time the Israeli lobby has been defeated in Congress" and the media would search "for signs that the White House is gloating." But gloat it did, according to a story that had Jordan and Powell boasting "to selected newsmen they had broken the back of the Israeli lobby."[83]

American Jews were ready to walk away from Carter. Liberals liked Ted Kennedy and Frank Church, who were more compatible on domestic policy and voted against the planes sales. Neoconservatives stayed with Jackson or became interested in Reagan and repeatedly characterized Carter as "bad for the Jews." In 1978, *Commentary* featured symposia on "Why *Bakke* Won't End Reverse Discrimination" and asking, "Is Peace Still Possible in the Middle East?" The consensus was gloomy; the anger toward the administration, palpable.[84]

ONCE AGAIN CARTER REVERSED course. As a Christian he had a special stake in the Middle East. Moreover, he was beleaguered. The energy and tax legislation still hung fire in the summer of 1978. Press coverage since spring stressed his presidential failures. Even his wins—the congressional failure to block the package deal, the Panama Canal treaties, the lifting of the Turkish arms embargo that had so annoyed his predecessor—became occasions for the media to say how poorly Carter led his party. The president must have realized, Quandt thought, that a Middle East peace treaty would "be a big plus, even though the process of achieving it might often be painful and time consuming. But the American electorate would not care much about the details of the agreement."[85]

Many of his own advisers and fellow Democrats, however, thought Carter had already done enough damage to himself, the party, and American-Israeli relations. They begged him to back off. Nonetheless, in July 1978, Carter boldly and desperately decided to bring Sadat and Begin together. And what site was better than Camp David? It was beautiful, space constraints limited the number of attendees, and its remoteness made a news blackout feasible. Vance extended the invitation to a delighted, albeit apprehensive, Begin and Sadat. On September 5, they and their delegations gathered with the Carters at Camp David.[86]

In the past the administration had sometimes dared hope that the peace process would produce one treaty that brought peace between Israel and Egypt and resolved the Palestinian issue. That had come to seem unlikely. But what exactly, then, was the relationship, if any, between an Egyptian-Israeli accord and the Palestinian question? On the one hand, Sadat could only rebuild his image in the Arab world by forcing Begin to make concessions with respect to the Palestinians. On the other, Carter reasoned—correctly, it turned out—that Sadat was so eager to move Israel out of the Sinai that he would give on the Palestinian issue. That suggested the United States should try to negotiate two agreements at Camp David. The easier would cover an Israeli withdrawal from Egypt; the more difficult, the Palestinian issue.[87]

Yet at times it appeared that all parties would leave Camp David empty-handed. Carter thought Begin behaved like "a psycho" there. Though the president and Sadat adored each other, the Egyptian arrived in high dudgeon. For his part, Begin was hurt that both Sadat and Carter disliked him.[88]

Consequently, the first three days—and the president had expected the meeting to last only that long—went poorly. Carter's diplomats had advised him to keep Sadat and Begin apart until the negotiations' final stage. But the president, who possessed "an almost mystical belief in face-to-face contact with other leaders," insisted on meeting with them together.[89]

It was a mistake. Carter reported that by day three little had been accomplished, and Sadat and Begin had argued incessantly. That afternoon Sadat said the negotiations were "over." Carter persuaded Sadat to give him another day. By nightfall everyone at Camp David was sure that "the talks had broken down."[90]

Now Carter did what he should have done from the beginning. He and his aides shuttled back and forth between Begin and Sadat to negotiate the two agreements that the Americans, and especially Carter, took charge of drafting. By the fifth day Carter had informed aides that "it was clear that the Egyptian-Israeli one took priority, and if nothing happened in the West Bank for ten years he would not really care very much."[91]

But even an Egyptian-Israeli accord seemed elusive. Begin was willing to return sovereignty of the Sinai to Egypt, provided Israel need not withdraw from its settlements. By day twelve Sadat had again nearly packed up. He stayed only after Carter warned that his departure would destroy U.S.-Egyptian relations, their friendship, and Carter's presidency.[92]

Only then did the pivotal moment arrive. Begin had once said to Brzezinski: "My right eye will fall out, my right hand will fall off before I ever agree to the dismantling of a single Jewish settlement." But Begin now told Carter he would "remove the requirements of party loyalty and let each member of the Knesset vote as an individual" on withdrawal from the Sinai settlements if an agreement could be reached on all other issues. Carter knew that the concession would satisfy Sadat. "Breakthrough!"[93]

Despite loopholes, the Framework for the Conclusion of a Peace Treaty Between Egypt and Israel, covering Israel's phased withdrawal from the Sinai, was a model of clarity, compared with the Framework for Peace in the Middle East Agreed at Camp David. Negotiated hastily, it set out a "transitional period" of up to five years during which "Egypt, Israel, Jordan and representatives of the Palestinian people" would achieve "the resolution of the Palestinian problem." They would negotiate "the autonomy" of, and an "elected self-governing authority" for the West Bank and Gaza, in addition to the "final status" of those occupied territories. At all times every step would be taken to protect "the security of Israel and its neighbors," along with "the legitimate rights of the Palestinian people and their just requirements."[94]

What did this mean? The Framework for Peace in the Middle East said nothing about Israeli withdrawal from the West Bank and Gaza and included no discussion of Jerusalem. Ironically, Sadat, who had initially seen the Camp David meeting as a chance to join forces with Carter against Begin on the Palestinian issue, was now vulnerable to Arab charges that he had sold out the Palestinians for the Sinai and its rich oil fields.[95]

How could Sadat afford that perception? Though the frameworks did not tie Israeli withdrawal from the Sinai to Palestinian autonomy, would he not have to suggest that progress on the two issues was linked to interest other Arabs in peace? And once Sadat did that, how would Begin respond? What did the frameworks do besides raise hopes they provided no means of satisfying? Carter did not see "how far we still had to go" until later.[96]

One Israeli delegation member did. Attorney General Aharon Barak voiced dissatisfaction with the language in the Framework for Peace in the Middle East. On the penultimate day at Camp David, Barak said that finding the right language would take at least another week. "There would never be a better time to try to devise a serious formula for addressing the Palestinian issue and the question of withdrawal." Finessing those issues would be a "mistake, which would come back to haunt us." But if all the time the negotiators would be given was another twenty-four hours, there was no choice but "to fuzz over" things.[97]

No one else was willing to stay at Camp David with Barak. Perhaps Begin's delegates could have worked him over, had he remained, as they had done for the previous thirteen days, but Begin was comparing Camp David with a concentration camp and wanted only to leave. The hard-liners who dominated Sadat's advisers would grow more antagonistic if they had to continue butting heads with Begin. The Egyptians would put on a game face because they needed a victory. As for Carter, his primary concern was, understandably, "to keep Begin and Sadat apart until after everything had been put into final form." Camp David ended abruptly amid uncertainty over the Palestinian issue.[98]

Nonetheless, the atmosphere at the White House ceremony celebrating the Camp David meeting on September 17, 1978, was triumphant. The president tactfully turned the spotlight on Begin and Sadat. Yet as his wife said, he deserved the credit, and when Carter received the Nobel Prize in 2002, Camp David featured prominently in his citation. As Carter's sharpest American Jewish critics shed happy tears, Begin and Sadat vied to see who could heap more praise on him.[99]

So did members of the press. "Jimmy Parts the Red Sea," said the *New Republic* of the man it had recently called "Blubber Lips." As incomplete and ambiguous as the frameworks were—and few yet saw with Barak and the Egyptians how incomplete and ambiguous they were—they seemed a turning point toward peace in the Middle East. The consensus was that Carter's "hideaway summitry" had resulted in a "spectacular success" and proved that his "relish for immersing himself in minutiae" was neither "eccentric" nor "misplaced." As a result, both his presidency and "the image of the United States as a commanding world power" had been "born again"![100]

ALAS, NOT FOR LONG. "What we had after Camp David was a framework for a peace treaty and a great deal of good will, plus extremely high expectations," Carter's press secretary recalled. "By November of 1978, the good will had largely dissipated, the framework itself appeared to be in danger, and the high expectations were beginning to create political problems." Carter blamed the Israelis. The president originally hoped for an Israeli-Egyptian treaty by the midterm congressional elections. But the ink on the frameworks was barely dry before Carter was complaining in his diary that Begin was "completely irresponsible." Begin announced that he might move his office to the Palestinian outpost of East Jerusalem. He also reneged on an eleventh-hour Camp David agreement the president thought they had reached: While Carter said Begin had promised to build no new settlements on the West Bank in the future, the Israeli maintained that he had only agreed to a three-month suspension. Apparently, the Israelis had decided to run down the clock. The longer they could postpone negotiations on the Palestinian issue, the less likely they were to occur. Once Carter turned his attention to running for reelection, he would realize the pointlessness of a fight with Israel.[101]

Meanwhile, at its Baghdad summit in early November 1978, the Arab League denounced Camp David. Sadat publicly dismissed its participants as "cowards and dwarfs" and insisted that the "snakes" did not bother him. Nonetheless, "within days the Egyptian position seemed to harden." Seconded by the United States, Egypt stressed that the Israeli-Egyptian treaty was connected to progress on the Palestinian issue. Israel of course repudiated linkage. When Begin telephoned Carter on November 21 to say that the Israeli cabinet would accept a draft treaty with Egypt, he refused to set a timetable for completion of negotiations on the future of the West Bank and Gaza or territorial elections. The Egyptians could "take it or leave it." When Sadat threatened the latter, he was accused of renegotiating the deal. In December 1978 leading American Jews alleged that Carter had ceased acting as the "mediator" he had been at Camp David and become "the advocate of Egypt's new demands." At just this moment the Iranian Revolution hit high tide.[102]

POPULAR DISCONTENT IN IRAN with the economic policies of the shah's regime, along with its corruption, human rights abuses, pro-Americanism, and hostility to Islamic traditionalism were coming to a head. As the Americans, Egyptians, and Israelis gathered at Camp David, the shah had declared martial law. Then his troops opened fire on demonstrators in Tehran's Jaleh Square. If ever there were an incident that called out for response from an administration committed to human rights, the Jaleh Square massacre of Black Friday in September 1978 was it. But Carter telephoned the shah to voice support.[103]

The slaughter might have alerted the White House that the shah's days were numbered. Just a month before, however, the CIA had reported that "Iran is not even in a revolutionary or even a 'prerevolutionary' situation." CIA director Stansfield Turner acknowledged later that "we were just plain asleep." Burying their heads in the sand, the CIA and administration officials remained in denial about the popular revolution that had been launched by a broad coalition of Iranians, ranging from "Muslims to Marxists." Americans refused to open a significant dialogue either with Ayatollah Ruhollah Khomeini, the seventy-eight-year-old leader of Iran's Shiite Muslims, or with moderates trying to find a middle way between Khomeini and the shah. Like the Soviets, Americans did not even seem to realize that the principal challenge to the shah came from religious fundamentalists. Told by the shah that his opponents were Communists, Americans assumed that the resistance came mostly from the left.[104]

The administration's ostrichlike behavior was not just a function of CIA incompetence but of Americans' historical attachment to the shah and internal disagreements. Brzezinski wanted the shah to crack down on dissent; Vance, to democratize. As the situation worsened, the atmosphere in Washington turned so poisonous that communication between the NSC and State Department about Iran had become virtually nonexistent by late fall. By then a general strike had begun in Iran, and hundreds of thousands were demanding the shah's ouster. Unknown to all but a few, the shah had cancer; quite obviously, he was depressed about the future of his country and did not know what to do. Carter did not telephone the shah now. The president refused to take direct action to keep him in power, as the United States had done in 1953 and as the NSC recommended. But Carter was also reluctant to negotiate with Khomeini's representatives, as State urged. The confusing presidential response reflected and revealed Washington's lack of alternatives to the shah. Indeed, according to the NSC staff member charged with handling Iran, "even a carefully reasoned doubt" about the shah's survival—expressed in late 1978—"was regarded as a heresy that could destroy a career." When Ambassador William Sullivan abandoned his position as the shah's "cheerleader" and sent home a memorandum in November analyzing scenarios in the event of the shah's fall, Carter was furious.

The White House took the "impossible situation" it had inherited in Iran and worsened it.[105]

All the while, the shah's political position was deteriorating. In January 1979, after summoning a stream of visitors to ask, "Where did it all go wrong?," he fled the country. Though the Carter administration had invited him to the United States, the shah elected to take his "vacation" in Egypt and Morocco in the event that the situation changed and he could return to power. Though the shah had been Washington's strongest ally in the Persian Gulf, the American press "cheered his fall." But soon Kissinger; Kissinger's friend David Rockefeller, one of Iran's bankers; neoconservatives; conservatives; and the shah's other American supporters blamed the Carter administration for losing Iran and deserting a friend. The Soviet Union exploited Iranian anti-American sentiment by declaring that the United States planned another coup to restore the shah to his throne, a charge Khomeini also circulated. As he planned his return to Iran, Khomeini carefully hid his commitment to the establishment of a militant Islamic republic. Billed by handlers as the Gandhi of Islam who would unite all Iranians, he arrived in Tehran on February 1, 1979, to a tumultuous reception. Proceeding to the cemetery where the shah's victims were buried, Khomeini condemned the shah, the United States and Jimmy Carter, and the Soviet Union. No one in Washington understood what was happening. The following day, Brzezinski warned Carter against overgeneralizing on the basis of Iran. "Islamic revivalist movements are not sweeping the Middle East and are not likely to be the wave of the future."[106]

ONE LONGTIME AMERICAN BULWARK against the Soviet Union in the Middle East, Iran, was imploding. The other, Israel, was refusing to play ball with the United States by converting the Framework for the Conclusion of a Peace Treaty Between Egypt and Israel into a signed peace treaty. The issues were interrelated. The Iranian Revolution frightened Israel and Egypt. Because Iran was Israel's major source of oil and Islamic fundamentalism was growing stronger, Israel became more anxious about relinquishing the Sinai oil fields and about Sadat's survival. Sadat believed that to steady the Middle East, he needed to be more careful than ever about seeming pro-American or pro-Israeli. And because oil production had halted in Iran, American energy prices were zooming.

Moreover, Carter "needed a political success to offset the enormous failure in Iran."[107]

So the president shuttled between Egypt and Israel. In Israel he seemed to come unhinged at one point: "He grasped his head with his hands, as if he were in pain, and began to rock back and forth" and cursed Begin. Realizing that Israel would barely budge, the president again turned to Sadat and told him that they would have to "settle for a thinly disguised bilateral peace" between Egypt and Israel ending their state of war and requiring Israeli withdrawal from the Sinai. Carter would have to dispense promises of aid and guarantees of oil for Israel too.[108]

The Egyptian-Israel Peace Treaty signing ceremony at the White House in March 1979 underlined the lack of a comprehensive settlement. In his prepared remarks, Sadat "called for action 'without delay or procrastination' on Palestinian autonomy to set the Palestinians 'on the road to self-determination and statehood,'" while Begin, "with President Sadat sitting in stony, uncomfortable silence nearby, warmly recalled the day when Israeli troops took over East Jerusalem." Sadat told reporters he had gambled on greater Israeli flexibility "as the peace process took hold" and on Carter's continued deep involvement in negotiations. That was a bad bet. By now Carter knew he had to turn his attention to reelection and to cease acting as "postman" for Begin and Sadat.[109]

And what had he accomplished? Had Carter been willing to settle for the separate peace that Begin and Sadat wanted sooner, he might have won it by sidestepping the Soviet-American Geneva communiqué. Further, despite the president's success at Camp David, the domestic reaction to the 1979 Egyptian-Israeli Treaty was, Carter realized, hardly positive. At best, on a personal level, the president had "shored-up his very shaky basis of political support among pro-Israel American Jewish voters, an important factor in the election campaign if he is challenged for renomination," a Republican operative told Ronald Reagan.[110]

Predictably, as Israel and the PLO prepared to sign the Oslo Accords at the Clinton White House in 1993, neocons raised the specter of Camp David. Israel had "not only sacrificed the strategically important territory, oil independence, and settlements, but paved the way for the rearming of Egypt by the United States" during the Carter years, one complained. And what did Israel receive in return? he asked. A cold peace, particularly after extremists assassinated Sadat in 1981. Israelis who visited Cairo would find it a "world center for the publication and dissemination of both original and 'classic' anti-Semitic literature." So what if Camp David resulted in "nonbelligerency"? Though Israel had never signed a treaty with Syria, there had been no war with Syria. When Oslo failed, and Carter characterized Israel as an apartheid regime, he demonstrated the low opinion of Israel that many American Jews during the 1970s believed he held. Oddly, however, Carter's critics portrayed him as a changed man who had become hostile to Israel since he left the presidency. They had forgotten how skeptical they had been of his Middle East achievements when he was in office.[111]

XII

TO THE MOUNTAINTOP AND BACK

—

JULY 4, 1979, 4:00 A.M.: THE CARTERS WERE AT CAMP DAVID, THE rustic mountaintop in Maryland's Catoctins. Inflation, gas shortages, and the proverbial sea of troubles had driven the president's approval rating below 25 percent. The first lady flipped through the address on energy her husband was scheduled to deliver the following day. "Nobody wants to hear it," she said. He agreed, Carter answered, and would cancel the speech. The Carters decided to seclude themselves at Camp David. Though they went there almost every other weekend in search of peace, the president and first lady always seemed to find themselves there in times of stress. Those were plentiful in 1979 and the winter of 1980, as one event after another derailed Carter's presidency.[1]

"THE SENSE OF AMERICAN IMPOTENCE"

Just ten months before Independence Day the President had left Camp David with Begin and Sadat in triumph. The 1978 midterm elections had gone well enough for the Democrats. Although Republicans gained three seats in the Senate, twelve in the House, six governorships, and eight state legislatures, pundits agreed that the GOP remained tiny. While "the baggage that any candidate carries around by virtue of being a Republican has been reduced substantially" since Watergate, one strategist told Reagan, "We're not totally out of the woods." To be sure, Republicans were gaining ground in the South, where a white middle class was proving receptive to a racialized conservative populism, with its promises of lower taxes and colorblindness. John Warner of Virginia and Thad Cochran of Mississippi had won Senate elections. Though

Cochran portrayed himself as as a moderate, the New Right was confident of him. "Don't worry, he'll vote like a right-wing extremist when we need him," a conservative said. In Georgia, Newt Gingrich had won his first House election by campaigning as a conservative Republican who opposed taxes and welfare and embraced family values. In Austin, the victory of William Clements in the gubernatorial race marked "the twilight of the Texas Democrats." Yet Republicans did not win "Dixie's heart" until the 1990s.[2]

The 1978 congressional election results did obviously spell trouble for liberalism. Most significantly, perhaps, they pushed foreign policy to the right. Though Frank Church replaced the ineffectual John Sparkman as chair of the Senate Foreign Relations Committee, liberals no longer dominated the committee, which was transformed by the arrival of new member Jesse Helms. Power over foreign policy increasingly shifted toward the conservative Armed Services Committee. Five Democrats who had voted the president's way on the Panama Canal and were expected to do so on SALT II lost their Senate seats: Dick Clark of Iowa, Floyd Haskell of Colorado, William Hathaway of Maine, Thomas McIntyre of New Hampshire, and Wendell Anderson of Minnesota. Despite Minnesota's proud history of left and liberal insurgency, Republicans won both its Senate seats and the governorship. In addition to Thad Cochran, new conservative Senate Republicans included Bill Armstrong of Colorado, Roger Jepsen of Iowa, and Gordon Humphrey of New Hampshire. The National Right to Life Committee announced its intent to defeat one well-known Republican, Bob Packwood of Oregon, and four liberal Senate Democrats—Birch Bayh of Indiana, John Culver of Iowa, George McGovern of South Dakota, and Frank Church of Idaho—who supported public funds for abortion in 1980. The committee's plan "would have been dismissed as ludicrous" as recently as 1976. Labor leaders were disconsolate after the 1978 elections. Inflation made the prospects for welfare reform and national health insurance dim. "You're going to have a skittish Congress, a more fiscally stingy Congress," said one Democratic strategist. "All my senses tell me there's a slide to the right." Yet Carter himself was "fiscally stingy," and he had an approval rating of 52 percent before and after the midterm elections.[3]

THEN HE WENT INTO free fall. By December the Camp David agreements had broken down. Liberals hit the roof when the president announced his austerity budget for his anti-inflation program and urged increased defense spending because of the Soviet threat. They turned the Democrats' December 1978 midterm conference into a referendum on the president and attacked his budget for cutting social services and raising military spending. According to the Americans for Democratic Action, "if we had had a mid-term conference in '66, the debate over Vietnam would have resembled the 1978 debate over the federal budget." Ted Kennedy roused cheers when he insisted that the party must return to its roots and work for national health insurance, along with the hopes of liberals, labor, and minorities that he would challenge the president for the 1980 Democratic nomination.[4]

For the second time, the president played the China card. He and the secretary of state had agreed to announce normalization of relations between the United States and China on New Year's Day. That would give Vance, who had scheduled a meeting with the Russians on December 21, time to iron out the last SALT II details, perhaps even arrange a summit at which the treaty could be signed. But because he feared that the normalization deal might otherwise collapse, Carter decided to upstage Kennedy and to take advantage of a congressional recess by announcing it in mid-December. Vance urged the president to wait until January 1 because the news that the United States was abrogating its mutual defense treaty with Taiwan, breaking off diplomatic relations with Taiwan at China's insistence, and establishing full diplomatic relations with China would anger the Soviets, along with congressional conservatives. But Carter insisted on moving up the date.[5]

Brzezinski took pains to spring the normalization news on the Soviets provocatively. When Ambassador Dobrynin came by on December 15, the two made cheerful small talk, "and then out of the blue I informed him that we are announcing tonight initiation of diplomatic, full-scale relations with the People's Republic of China." After the astonished Dobrynin recovered, Brzezinski said "that it wasn't directed against anyone" and that the American relationship with the Chinese "would now have as normal a character as Soviet relations with China. Formally, a correct observation; but substantively, a touch of irony."[6]

More like a dollop. The Americans followed the normalization announcement, with its accompanying news that Vice Premier Deng Xiaoping would soon visit Washington, by toughening their position on SALT II. The Soviets followed suit. They were angry that the Americans and Chinese had declared their shared aversion to "hegemony," a Chinese reference to Soviet ambitions, and resented that the Chinese had received the first invitation to Washington. The secretary of state blamed "[t]he sudden surge of Soviet inflexibility" on "the manner and timing" of the normalization announcement.[7]

The Taiwanese and their American friends were irritated too. The Taiwanese pelted with eggs, tomatoes, and rocks the American delegation that had come to break the news of normalization. Reagan and conservatives decried normalization. Insisting that the "defense of small countries and threatened peoples has never counted much for Jimmy Carter," the *New Republic* sounded almost as horrified as *National Review* when it declared, "In what he clearly takes to be a major coup," the president "has now just about told the Chinese government in Peking that Taiwan is theirs for the taking." So normalization of American relations with China was simply another of "Carter's foreign policy spectacular flops," only this one had aroused "a melange of hawks and liberals against the dumping of Taiwan."[8]

But the President could count on his predecessors to back his China policy. Ford publicly supported him. Richard Nixon wistfully watched the harvest of his own foreign policy and wrote Carter a long, private letter. He stressed the importance of protecting Taiwan, preserving American "credibility," and perceiving the dangerous implications of normalization for SALT II. The United States, the former president said, should publicly warn the Chinese off using force against Taiwan and should approve legislation providing for the sale of arms to Taiwan for defensive purposes. The Chinese would tolerate the legislation "because they need us far more than we need them" and because they knew Taiwan's best friends in Congress were the Soviets' worst enemies. Carter must conciliate the Taiwan lobby to avoid future battles that "will make the Panama Canal controversy look like a Sunday school picnic." The United States should also let its allies know that "Taiwan was a special case" and that it would honor its commitments to other regimes, no matter how dictatorial. "It would be ironical to qualify our support to any country which allows some human rights at a time when we have dramatically moved toward normalization with full cooperation with a nation which allows none," Nixon added slyly. Carter's Senate detractors could not block normalization "because it is a fait accompli," but they "might well take out their frustration on SALT." So Carter, Nixon concluded, was at one of those junctures "when you cannot afford any moves which justifiably or not are considered soft or weak, vis-à-vis the Communist powers."[9]

Normalization was indeed a fait accompli, despite congressional insistence on language in the Taiwan Relations Act that spelled out the importance of a peaceful resolution of the Taiwan issue and provided for the sale of defensive weapons to Taiwan. At most, the legislation just represented "a small step towards Taiwan." When Deng came to Washington at the end of January for a festive spectacular, Nixon returned to the White House for his first state dinner since his departure in disgrace. (The White House omitted Kennedy from the guest list and invited him only after Vance protested.) To date, January 1979 had been a bad month for the president. The film version of Hal Lindsey's 1970 best seller *The Late Great Planet Earth* hit American theaters. The book used biblical prophecy to predict the energy crisis, war in the Middle East, and the second coming of Jesus Christ; by the film's account, *New York Times* reviewer Janet Maslin said, "Armageddon may just possibly be right around the corner." Maslin thought that "the most memorable sequence shows a computer conducting a numerological analysis of various politicians' names, to figure out if Jimmy Carter, Ronald Reagan or Ted Kennedy is the Antichrist." The shah fled Iran. While escorting a Libyan delegation around Georgia, Billy Carter had urinated on the tarmac of the Atlanta airport, commented that "[t]here's a hell of a lot more Arabians than there is Jews," complained that "the Jewish media tears up the Arab countries full-time," and justified his support of Colonel Muammar Gadhafi and others in the Libyan government with the remark that "[a] heap of governments support terrorists, and they at least admit it." And the president's State of the Union had been a "dud": Having avoided a slogan for his program, such as New Deal or New Frontier during his first two years in office, Carter spoke repeatedly—and, most judged, unimpressively—of his "New Foundation." The hoopla that accompanied Deng's visit helped.[10]

The visit also showcased hostility toward the Soviets. Deng derided SALT II and made repeated reference to the "polar bear." The announcement of normalization delayed the conclusion of SALT II negotiations by four to six months. During that time Carter's popularity dropped dramatically and the American relationship with the Soviet Union worsened.[11]

DURING THREE DAYS in February the United States seemed timid to many Americans. On February 14, 1979, the same day that the United States bestowed diplomatic recognition on what was often called the Khomeini regime, though Khomeini did not officially belong to the government, one hundred militant Iranians stormed the American Embassy in Tehran. They took seventy Americans prisoner, injured two marines, killed one Iranian employee, and destroyed classified files. "Hey, Yankee, we've come to do you in," they shouted. The story had a happy ending when Khomeini sent troops to the embassy to free the hostages. The incident led the administration to believe it might work with Khomeini when it should have alerted the White House to the possibility that he might prove unwilling and unable to control the anti-Americanism he symbolized.[12]

The Iranian Revolution gave conservatives one new reason to suspect the Soviet Union. The fall of the shah deprived the United States of the radar and signal monitoring devices that would enable it to verify the Soviets' compliance with SALT II. Though the administration said it could move its listening posts to Turkey, détente critic and former Defense Intelligence Agency chief Daniel Graham labeled the claim "essentially fraudulent" because the mountains separating Turkey from the Soviet Union interfered with transmission. (Unbeknownst to Graham, during Deng Xiaoping's visit, Carter, Brzezinski, and Deng had agreed to establish a listening post in western China.) Graham pronounced SALT II unverifiable.[13]

Afghanistan provided yet another reason for mistrust. Islamic fundamentalists opposed to the pro-Soviet government of Afghanistan abducted American Ambassador Adolph "Spike" Dubs in Kabul on the same day that the U.S. Embassy in Tehran was seized. The Carter administration blamed the death of Dubs during a rescue mission the next day on the Afghans' trigger-happy Soviet advisers, who disregarded the American plea for restraint. The Soviets privately acknowledged the advisers had blown it but publicly denied responsibility for the death of the American ambassador.[14]

Exhausted by his all-night vigil monitoring the twin 1979 Valentine's Day crises in Iran and Afghanistan, Carter nevertheless made a scheduled trip to Mexico for meetings with President José López Portillo. In his opening toast, López Portillo roasted the United States for too often treating Mexico "with a mixture of interest, disdain, and fear." Ignoring (or, perhaps, responding to) López Portillo's criticism, Carter stressed in his reply that he and the Mexican president each had "beautiful and interesting wives" and reminiscenced about his own diarrhea on an earlier trip. According to one reporter, Mrs. Carter was "literally covering her face with her hands in embarrassment as Jimmy started talking about 'running' and concluded with his tale of Montezuma's revenge."[15]

By the time the president returned to Washington on February 16, Chinese forces had massed at the Vietnamese border. That came as no surprise to Carter, though when China invaded Vietnam the following day, administration officials agreed that "[o]ne of the first press questions will be 'Did Deng raise the issue of an attack of Vietnam while he was in the United States?' " and "[o]ur answer to the press is no." In fact, Deng had privately told Carter in Washington that he planned to attack Vietnam, a Soviet ally, in retaliation for its recent conquest of the genocidal Pol Pot regime that the Vietnamese had supported until border disputes between Vietnam and Cambodia got out of hand. Carter had tried to dissuade him, but Deng insisted. Brzezinski, who considered border hostilities between Vietnam and Cambodia "the first case of a proxy war between China and the Soviet Union," used the right words to condemn the invasion but could barely conceal his admiration for Deng's "appreciation of the uses of power." With Dobrynin telling Vance that many Soviet officials were certain that America's " 'anti-Soviet, pro-China attitude' had encouraged Peking to attack" and hinting that the Soviets might provide the Vietnamese with military assistance, Brzezinski reported that he, Vance, and Carter were "frozen stiff." Suddenly, alarmed Americans were speculating about the possibility of World War III.[16]

Dubs was to be buried on February 20, the day Carter was scheduled to receive an honorary degree and speak on SALT II at Georgia Tech. His advisers begged him not to go. Dubs was the first American ambassador to be killed during his presidency, "many of the vocal critics of our policies and actions" would attend the funeral, and the media would juxtapose photos of the service with those of Carter receiving his honorary degree. A speech defending SALT II now would have "little positive impact," and the funeral gave Carter a good reason to postpone it. "In terms of the events in Iran, Vietnam and China, your remarks at Georgia Tech could be inappropriate and could be undermined by events that we cannot control or foresee."[17]

But Carter chose to send Vice President Mondale and Mrs. Carter to the funeral and to go to Georgia Tech. His speech there defended American noninvolvement in the Sino-Vietnamese War and the Iranian Revolution, promised that the United States would intervene in both places if its interests were endangered, and contended that world "turbulence" made SALT II more vital than ever. Republicans of course were unimpressed. "[T]here is a growing view that America is a patsy," Senator Howard Baker said. "[W]e do more with someone who shoots a cop than someone who assassinates an ambassador."[18]

The media also maintained that it was "Time for a Leader." The *New Republic* observed that Americans had lost their disdain for "that detested 'Imperial Presidency' that we used to distrust in the aftermath of Watergate" and sought a protective "Papa." The press reported that Carter's handlers fantasized about a *Mayaguez*-type episode that would enable him to show his machismo. The president's advisers also anonymously complained to reporters that Carter would not react as Ford had done, could not rise above his "monotonic cadences," leached "the emotional appeal out of even the most crowd-stirring address," and refused "to strike dramatic postures."[19]

Media adviser Gerald Rafshoon hammered Carter. "No journalist I know has questioned the wisdom of restraint in the handling of the siege of our embassy in Tehran," Rafshoon wrote. "Yet, many of them have cited that event as if it were further evidence of a failure of leadership." The problem was not that Carter did not lead but that his leadership did not "project well." Inflation, the end of oil from Iran, Dubs's murder, the López Portillo toast, and the Chinese invasion of Vietnam had reinforced "the sense of American impotence. As President, you are the person who is expected to 'do something!'" Unless the president started "*looking, talking and acting more like a leader—even if it's artificial*," Rafshoon stressed, the "national experiment with quiet, secure, non-macho leadership" would end. As it was, when someone "stands up and raises his voice and says, goddamit, we're going to *do* something about this problem," Americans cheered. "They don't even listen to what he's saying. Nor do they listen to what you say; they only know that you say it slower and softer." Rafshoon advised the president to look for opportunities to "act quickly, firmly and responsibly in foreign policy." He should get rid of some advisers. "As far as I can tell there is only one issue on which this country is totally united: the need for you to fire some people." Carter should take lessons to improve his speaking style, "the single greatest reason (under our control) why your Presidency has not been more successful." And he should combat "the impression of softness, gentleness" by exchanging his light clothes for the "dark suits, white shirts and striped ties" that Ronald Reagan favored.[20]

Standard wisdom had the administration, and Rafshoon especially, prioritizing style over substance. But Rafshoon was on to something in 1979. Carter's persona, so alluring to Americans reacting against Watergate in 1976, had completely lost its appeal.

THAT SPRING CALAMITY struck soon after Hollywood released *The China Syndrome*, a thriller starring Jane Fonda about the near meltdown of a nuclear reactor. On March 28, 1979, the reactor core at Three Mile Island nuclear power plant near Harrisburg overheated. Radioactive steam seeped twenty miles into the Pennsylvania countryside, where some six hundred thousand people lived. Pregnant women, infants, and toddlers within five miles of the plant were urged to evacuate the area, and everyone else within ten miles was told to remain indoors. For the next six days it seemed quite possible that a nuclear meltdown would occur, and the media made matters worse by misleadingly suggesting that a nuclear meltdown and explosion were one and the same. On March 29, ABC also broadcast *The Killing Ground*, a documentary about the Love Canal residents in Buffalo who lived above ten thousand-plus tons of leaking hazardous waste and were unduly prone to miscarriages, birth defects, and cancer. With a nuclear accident and toxic waste dump in the news, attention turned again to the energy crisis and dangers to the enrivonment.[21]

Nuclear power generated about 12 percent of American electricity, OPEC announced it would raise oil prices by 9 percent, and oil was just trickling in from Iran. At the beginning of April, Carter broke into prime-time TV and delivered a brisk "summons to the Age of Limits." While the Three Mile Island accident was "of immediate concern" and he would appoint a commission to study the incident, "the fundamental cause of our Nation's energy crisis is petroleum—oil and gas." Americans wasted too much petroleum, bought too much from other countries, and did not produce enough. "This is a painful step, and I'll give it to you straight: Each of us will have to use less oil and pay more for it."[22]

The president's solution was a return to the market, phased-in decontrol over the next twenty-eight months. The legislation enacted during the Ford years gave Carter discretion over price controls on oil, beginning in June 1979 and prior to their expiration in 1981. Decontrol, Carter maintained, would permit the price of domestic oil to rise to world levels, promote production, and reduce consumption. Whereas Ford wanted to threaten a windfall profits tax if oil companies did too well, his successor wanted to impose the tax immediately. Carter also asked Congress to enact a standby plan for gas rationing in the event of an acute petroleum shortage. Nor could the nation "abandon" nuclear power, he and Energy Secretary Schlesinger agreed. The administration moved forward with a bill to streamline the process of licensing and siting nuclear plants.[23]

Despite polls demonstrating that Americans overwhelmingly considered the energy crisis a fabrication of the oil companies, Carter courageously insisted that it was real. But he inveighed against those who he insisted must ride to the rescue. "[A]s surely as the Sun will rise tomorrow, the oil companies can be expected to fight to keep the profits that they have not earned," he warned. "Unless you speak out, they will have more influence on the Congress than you do."[24]

The president's populist pose alienated everyone. Consumers protested rising energy prices. Liberal Democrats argued against decontrol, contended that the windfall profits tax should be higher, and urged Carter to fire Schlesinger. According to Senator Kennedy, the oil companies had "intimidated" the president into agreeing to decontrol, and the proposed windfall profits tax was "a transparent fig leaf." (Carter said that was "just a lot of baloney.") From his Domestic Policy Staff office, Eizenstat equated the president's "harsh and biting" attacks on the oil companies and their congressional supporters with demagoguery and reminded Carter that "we need to work with many of those . . . you are bitterly attacking in public." The antinuclear movement bloomed from California to New Hampshire.[25]

Carter had won support from many of its members in 1976, when he said he would rely on nuclear power only as a last resort. Now they called him a liar and Schlesinger a stooge for the nuclear power industry. A coalition led by Ralph Nader, Barry Commoner, and Jane Fonda organized a march on Washington to ensure "No More Harrisburgs." Aides informed the president that the protesters were concerned with "Secretary Schlesinger's perceived strong bias in favor of nuclear power and . . . our nuclear siting and licensing bill (and most recently the decision to proceed with it only a few days after Three Mile Island). To the anti-nuclear groups, the Administration is viewed as entirely pro-nuclear, having virtually no concern about nuclear plant safety or the health and environmental effects of nuclear plants." Invited to speak at the May event, which drew at least sixty-five thousand young, mostly white, middle-class protesters, Carter prudently declined. The speakers excoriated nuclear power and vowed that if the president did not replace Schlesinger, "he himself will be replaced."[26]

Energy politics again consumed Washington. In May, over a hundred House Democrats joined with Republicans to vote down gas rationing in what the media predictably referred to as a "stunning defeat for Carter." As Congress bickered over and blocked his program, gas edged over one dollar a gallon, an increase of twelve cents since December.[27]

Even then, fuel was scarce. California was the first and worst hit state. The endless gas lines, some with four-hour waits, featured slugfests and created "gas-line syndrome—the depressive sense that if cars won't work, nothing else will." On Memorial Day, waits averaged only twenty minutes, which just fed suspicions that the gas crisis was a big oil hoax. But the gas shortages had spread across the country.[28]

So had high prices. Despite the anti-inflation program, the cost of beef had jumped by more than 100 percent in the first three months of 1979. At its annual meeting, the Americans for Democratic Action resolved: "Only adoption of mandatory controls can bring inflation under control." The administration refused to consider them.[29]

As prices rose, the economy slowed down. So far, in 1979, it had been hot—too hot, complained administration officials, who wanted the Fed to tighten monetary supply. Now, as inflation continued to spiral out of control, real personal income started dropping at an average annual rate of 6.3 percent. Given the "price surge, output slump and energy crunch," economists predicted unemployment would rise to 8 percent. Clearly, inflation would continue and a recession would occur—if it had not already begun.[30]

Americans were not just anxious about prices and jobs. April 1978 had been a tense time that featured disagreements over inflation, the Panama Canal, and the neutron bomb. Yet 51 percent of those polled had said that "U.S. Problems Are No Worse than Usual." A year later nearly two-thirds believed that the United States was in deep trouble, and they blamed its woes on Carter.[31]

They had company within the administration. By May 1979 Vice President Mondale was so frustrated that some say he considered resigning. The disillusionment of another official was clear when the *Atlantic* published "The Passionless Presidency." According to the devastating account by Carter's twenty-nine-year-old former speechwriter James Fallows, the president was marked "by a combination of arrogance, complacency, and—dread thought—insecurity at the core of his mind and soul." Fallows portrayed Carter as a micromanaging control freak. He contended that the during the first six months of the administration, the president personally reviewed every request to use the White House tennis court, a charge Carter publicly denied. At the same time, Fallows maintained, the president never learned or cared how Congress worked. Carter was a bureaucrat who could not set priorities because he "believes fifty things but no one thing." (Fallows insisted to the *Washington Post* in 1979 that "20 years from now I will be gladder to have written it than not." Older, he seemed less certain. "I'm not in retrospect making the clear case this was the right thing to do," he told the *Post* in 1997. "I'm saying that at the time it seemed to be the right thing to do, and probably if I had complete foresight I would not have gone to work for Carter.")[32]

And a May 1979 poll for the Democratic National Committee revealed that Kennedy, who had just unveiled a plan for national health insurance that he knew the president would reject, held a two to one lead over Carter in a hypothetical race for the Democratic nomination. During the Memorial Day weekend one journalist said that the administration was "suffering its worst malaise since taking office."[33]

FROM RUIN TO REDEMPTION?

The word "malaise" had not yet become shorthand for the Carter presidency. And Carter sounded anything but passionless as he assured congressional members in June that "if Kennedy runs in '80, I'll whip his ass," a remark he repeated for those unsure they had heard him correctly. Yet despite his assurance, his presidency seemed to be on the rocks.[34]

SALT II showed that. The June meeting between Carter and Brezhnev in Vienna was anticlimactic. From the American perspective, SALT II represented some improvement over the agreement Ford and Brezhnev had reached at Vladivostok five years earlier, but not enough of one to justify the extra years of negotiation. Further, just before Carter left for Vienna, he and Chancellor Schmidt announced their commitment to realizing theater nuclear force modernization "expeditiously." Carter also made public the American decision to proceed with development and production of the new 190,000-pound thirty-billion-dollar MX, a mobile intercontinental ballistic missile system that would be shuttled between launching sites in the United States to frustrate Soviet discovery and "would also enable the United States for the first time, to carry out pinpoint attacks on Russian military targets."[35]

In the context of SALT II, theater and strategic nuclear modernization were signs, but of what? SALT II probably did not *cause* the administration to make the decisions it did; its behavior reflected its fear of growing Soviet power. Yet the White House also obviously hoped that modernization would improve the chances of SALT II for ratification. To be sure, the MX made Senator McGovern and Senator William Proxmire, a Democrat from Wisconsin famed for fighting wasteful government spending, so irate that they threatened to vote against the treaty in protest. Liberals despised the MX, and environmentalists were "not cheered by the idea of having nuclear-armed missiles traveling around the countryside on trucks" either. Nonetheless, SALT II was one issue where the president could count on liberal support. In contrast, before Carter departed for Vienna, Senator Jackson had attacked SALT II as "appeasement." Obviously, the MX would not "appease" him. Indeed, at the Jerusalem Conference on International Terrorism in July, Jackson accused the Soviets of trying to weaken the West by sponsoring terrorism. Nor would the MX convince Paul Nitze and other highly vocal, neoconservative fellow travelers at the Committee on the Present Danger to swing behind the treaty. But like theater nuclear modernization, the MX was supposed to bring others aboard the SALT II bandwagon. Senate Majority Leader Robert Byrd and Senator Sam Nunn, whose support the White House considered all important, would not back SALT II without a defense buildup, and White House officials acknowledged that had Carter not approved the MX, the Pentagon would have rebelled.[36]

Carter's announcement of theater and strategic nuclear modernization was one more indication of high cold war tensions. After he left the presidency, Carter revealed that he had proposed a freeze on the production and deployment of nuclear weapons at Vienna and a "mutual pledge of nonfirst use of military force in Europe." Brezhnev turned him down. The final June 1979 summit communiqué was the first since 1972 that did not specifically refer to the principle of peaceful coexistence, and the Soviets rejected an American statement that nuclear war was unwinnable. Theater and strategic nuclear modernization, along with Carter's August 1980 Presidential Directive 59, which stressed that the United States had to be able to make pinpoint nuclear strikes against Soviet military installations, seemed to suggest, despite the administration's emphasis that deterrence remained its goal, a shift away from the time-honored principle of mutual assured destruction toward "flexible response" in the event of a "limited nuclear war."[37]

The obstacles SALT II faced in the Senate made American perceptions of Vienna crucial. Informed critics focused on the facts that the treaty would leave the Soviets in possession of 326 all-powerful SS-18s with which they could wipe out American cities, did not count the Soviets' Backfire bomber as an intercontinental weapon, and did nothing about the SS-20s menacing Europe. They also questioned how Soviet compliance with the treaty would be verified. But as Rafshoon told the president, the treaty particulars would elude most Americans. Consequently, "their opinions will depend largely on their confidence in you," and the president should avoid looking "like a good-hearted dreamer or a peace-at-any-price idealist" in Vienna. He should not even smile. "Don't act as if you and Brezhnev are friends. (Above all, don't say that you are.)" Rafshoon must have winced when the *New York Times* reported on June 19, 1979, that after signing SALT II, "Jimmy Carter, 54-year-old President of the United States, clasped to his breast Leonid I. Brezhnev, 72-year old leader of the Soviet Union, and they kissed on both cheeks." *Human Events* wondered whether Carter would have "hugged Hitler."[38]

The SALT II Treaty had less chance of passage than when Carter had taken office and had barely managed to have Warnke confirmed as its negotiator. (Warnke was now history. He had resigned after two years in office.) General Edward Rowny, the Joint Chiefs of Staff representative to the SALT II meetings and a military man close to Senator Jackson, "respectfully declined" the invitation to the Vienna signing ceremony and publicly said the treaty did not serve American interests. The Soviets seemed doubtful that Carter could win Senate ratification.[39]

Carter then attended an economic summit in Tokyo with the leaders of Germany, France, Italy, the United Kingdom, and Japan. Thanks to another OPEC price hike, gas had risen 60 percent since the beginning of the year, and 1,000 percent since the beginning of the decade. The Saudi oil minister told *Newsweek* that further OPEC decisions about prices would depend in part on the achievement of "a comprehensive, overall solution for the Middle East crisis, which must—repeat must—first and foremost, mean a solution for the increasingly desperate Palestinian people." Summit participants blamed Carter for provoking OPEC by supporting Israel and for failing to persuade Americans to conserve oil. According to Carter, Chancellor Schmidt "got personally abusive" and claimed that "American interference in the Middle East . . . had caused the problems with oil all over the world," and President Valéry Giscard d'Estaing of France complained that Americans "haven't started" saving energy.[40]

American allies saw Carter, the doomsaying conservationist, as the symbol of profligate wastefulness. The United States was OPEC's largest client. To the disapproval of the European participants in the Tokyo summit (who, the United States observed, had plenty of oil in the North Sea), the leaders gathered there could only pledge to keep OPEC imports at current levels. Like OPEC's price hike, the policy of inaction just aggravated the possibility of global hyperinflation.[41]

As he left Tokyo for Korea, Carter said that OPEC had made an American recession "much more likely." By administration estimates, higher oil prices would perpetuate double-digit inflation, cut economic growth by a 1 percent point in 1979 and 1980, and result in unemployment for an additional eight hundred thousand Americans in 1980. In Pennsylvania, a truckers' strike protesting the rising price of diesel fuel had caused an energy riot, three days of violence and injuries to a hundred people. And everywhere, as the Fourth of July approached, the gas lines no longer seemed temporary. They grew, and prices rose. In a memorandum leaked to the *Washington Post*, Eizenstat suggested that the gas crisis might prove the Carter administration's "Vietnam." Interviewed by reporters, motorists in the long gas lines "typically responded 'what in the hell is Carter doing in Japan and Korea when all the problems are here?' "[42]

Carter had planned to stop in Hawaii on his way home, but his advisers summoned him back to Washington. The president then departed for Camp David on July 3. On July 4, Press Secretary Jody Powell released what the *New York Times* characterized as "a terse statement: 'The President has asked me to say he has decided to cancel the speech for Thursday night. I have nothing to add to that announcement.' " During the next ten days Carter called in 130 political leaders, academics, business and labor representatives, clergy, and journalists to ask them what was wrong with his leadership and the country. The White House gave no explanation for Carter's need for guidance. There was universal mystification.[43]

"I spent 90% of my time listening," the president wrote in his diary. He did so graciously, and he took careful notes on repeated complaints about his weak leadership and his administration. But the diagnoses conflicted. While most of his guests "indicated there was a mood of despair and alienation among the people which I needed to address," some attributed the sour mood to concrete problems, such as gas shortages.[44]

The disagreement among Carter's Camp David visitors echoed a disagreement among his advisers. Patrick Caddell thought Carter should make "our 'America is going to hell speech' " before he even broached the subject of energy. In a seventy-five-page overwrought memorandum to the president, the pollster portrayed "a nation deep in crisis" undone by assassinations, Vietnam, Watergate, the energy crisis, the economy, and the realization that the certainty "we were 'God's chosen people' " was "a myth." Americans had stopped voting and surrendered to self-gratification. The crisis was "not your fault," but it did provide "the greatest opportunity for you as President to become a great President on the order of a Lincoln, a Wilson, a Franklin Roosevelt" and to "reshape" American purpose. "Psychological more than material, it is a crisis of confidence marked by a dwindling faith in the future."[45]

The idea of a "crisis of confidence, a crisis of the spirit" was in the air, so much so that Gerald Ford had given a speech about it in 1977. But Caddell was not cribbing from Carter's predecessor. He had been influenced by *The Culture of Narcissism: American Life in an Age of Diminishing Expectations*, Christopher Lasch's devastating critique of a self-obsessed citizenry, a book that Carter too admired without, in the author's view, entirely understanding. Other scholars were also tilling the field. They included Daniel Bell of Harvard, whose work heaped scorn on Americans' hedonistic greed, and Robert Bellah of Berkeley, who called for a revival of republican values. Unlike the liberalism of John Locke, which centered on rights, self-interest, and constraints on government, republicanism bespoke a commitment to responsibilities, civic virtue, and community.[46]

Caddell had been talking about a "crisis in confidence" since 1974 and especially since Christmas 1978. He had urged Carter to devote his 1979 State of the Union speech to the topic. His 1978 polling revealed that "long term pessimism" exceeded "the previous high of 1974." Since the dissatisfaction preceded 1979, Caddell believed that gas lines and inflation had deepened, rather than caused, the "frustration born out of a continued sense of drift in purpose and goals—a stage of angst that follows the heat and fury of the last 15 years of cataclysmic events."[47]

Well, maybe. But it was at least as possible that any "crisis of confidence" reflected doubt about Carter and/or the economy. As Rafshoon's deputy, Greg Schneiders, said privately, the major complaints about Carter "are that he has no clear idea of where he is leading the country" and had "failed to inspire our people." In any event, Carter had decided on a more upbeat theme and the unfortunate New Foundation slogan for his State of the Union. The president had tried Caddell's "crisis" theme when he addressed the Democratic National Committee on American hopelessness in May, and the response had been positive.[48]

Moreover, the circumstances turned the spotlight on Carter's address, which, the White House announced on July 12, he was to deliver on Sunday, July 15 at 10:00 P.M. Carter's odd behavior beginning July 3 may even have been scripted. "I still don't know for sure to this day whether the speech was cancelled on impulse or whether it was scheduled and cancelled for dramatic purposes," Eizenstat reflected in 1982. In fact, Caddell had prepared a July 2 memorandum for the president stressing the need for a "breakthrough." According to the pollster, the American people "almost entirely tuned out" the president. "Therefore, in order to have the people follow they must first listen, and to listen, something dramatic must take place to cause a desire in them to listen."[49]

So Caddell recommended that the Carters leave Washington, ostensibly for Camp David, on Friday afternoon, July 13, then disappear. When the White House leaked word that the president had departed for "an unknown destination," he reasoned, the press would go "absolutely bonkers." Powell could then guarantee "pandemonium" by reading "a statement to the effect that (a) the President is gone, (b) that there is no national crisis, etc., (c) that the President is doing something that he views as crucial and has wanted to do for awhile, (d) and, no questions will be answered." Reporters would saturate the press and airwaves with "Where is the President?" stories and "build our audience for us." Meanwhile, Carter would be holding the first of several meetings with small groups of citizens in Pennsylvania, Ohio, and Florida "to help you recapture your 'ear' for America." Though he would request the participants to keep the meetings secret, they would talk, enabling the media to locate Carter. Then, on Saturday, Powell would request and receive time for the networks on Sunday night "for a speech of 'grave national importance.'" By Sunday "rumors will be flying of all sorts; that you are going to resign, that you are going to announce you are not going to seek reelection, that you have gone crazy." And many who would not have done so otherwise would tune in to Carter's speech about the crisis of confidence.[50]

Perhaps, in desperation, Carter seized on Caddell's scenario, moved the schedule forward, changed the venue to Camp David, and expanded the "listening" meetings. Whether or not the president had acted impulsively, as Hamilton Jordan said, Carter now had captured public attention. Jordan himself questioned Caddell's approach, and he credited Carter with seeing its potential.[51]

Others remained skeptical. In an eight-hour meeting on July 5 at Camp David, "Eizenstat, Powell, Jordan, Rafshoon, Caddell, and Mondale duked it out in the Laurel Lodge, with Rosalynn shuffling in and out," while Carter observed. Mondale and Eizenstat said that gas lines and inflation, not lack of confidence, had caused the country's woes. Shown a draft of Caddell's speech about America's loss of spirit and Carter's lack of leadership, they condemned it as "mumbly mush." The vice president advised his boss to focus on the energy crisis instead of playing "scold." From Washington, Schneiders predicted that the public reaction "would be 'bullshit.' He kept us waiting and watching for ten days to produce this?" What would the president accomplish by self-criticism, except to provide his opponents with fodder? Americans did not want to hear Carter "whine about" problems but to see him fix them.[52]

Carter decided to split the difference. On July 15 he addressed the nation about its "malaise," a word he never explicitly spoke. As in 1976, he sounded like a preacher as he preempted an episode of the TV show *Moses—The Lawgiver*. "[A]ll the legislation in the world can't fix what's wrong with America," the president declared. "It is a crisis of confidence. It is a crisis that strikes at the very heart and soul and spirit of our national will," one that threatens "to destroy the social and political fabric of America." Carter lamented that "a nation that was proud of hard work, strong families, close-knit communities, and our faith in God" had come to worship "self-indulgence and consumption" (though strangely, he also announced that his meetings at Camp David over the past ten days had "confirmed my belief in the decency and the strength and the wisdom of the American people"). As Caddell had suggested, he situated America's crisis of confidence in the assassinations of the 1960s, the loss in Vietnam, the bankruptcy of Watergate, the curse of inflation, and the realization that the nation did not possess unlimited energy. As he had done in 1976, Carter blamed Washington, which he said was "an island. The gap between our citizens and our Government has never been so wide." He castigated "a Congress twisted and pulled in every direction by hundreds of well-financed and powerful special interests." He faulted himself too and cited a visitor who had informed him that "you are not leading this nation, you're just managing the government." The answer, Carter maintained, lay in confronting "the truth" and changing "our course. We simply must have faith in each other, faith in our ability to govern ourselves, and faith in the future of this Nation."[53]

Then, shifting toward the less ephemeral, he announced a program to liberate the United States from OPEC: "Energy will be the immediate test of our ability to unite this Nation and it can also be the standard around which we rally. On the battlefield of energy we can win for our Nation a new confidence, and we can seize control again of our common destiny." The nation must never again use more foreign oil than it did in 1977, Carter maintained. He announced that he would use executive authority to reduce imports. He requested "the most massive peacetime commitment of funds and resources in our Nation's history" to develop synthetic fuels and other alternative energy sources. He asked Congress to establish "this Nation's first solar bank," enact a windfall profits tax for oil companies, force the nation's utility companies to halve their use of oil in a decade, create an energy mobilization board that could remove obstacles blocking energy projects, and "give me authority for mandatory conservation and for standby gas rationing." He proposed spending an extra ten billion dollars over the next ten years on public transportation and asked Americans to avoid unnecessary car trips, carpool, use public transportation, avoid speeding, and lower their thermostats. "Every act of energy conservation like this is more than just common sense—I tell you it is an act of patriotism." Then he promised to "do my best" and asked for help. "Whenever you have a chance, say something good about our country. With God's help and for the sake of our Nation, it is time to join hands" and bring about "a rebirth of the American spirit."[54]

The president's sermon left unimpressed the cultural critics who supposedly had inspired it. "How come all these wonderful people have all these bad characteristics?" Bellah asked. "No analysis!" Lasch mourned that his book had "played right into Carter's hands" and had enabled the president to shift the blame away from his own flawed leadership and the poor economy "to a nation of 'narcissists.'"[55]

Nevertheless, Carter was pleased with his address. "It was one of my best speeches, and the response to it was overwhelmingly positive," he rightly recalled. Thousands of Americans obviously shared his anxiety over the crisis of spirit and welcomed his Lincolnian summons to embrace the better angels of their nature. The theatrics of the previous week assured him an audience estimated at a hundred million, perhaps his largest ever. He delivered the speech unusually well. The following day Carter delightedly realized that at last "the main interest was in energy!" And he had some success. A year after his "crisis of confidence" speech, Congress authorized most of what he called for there, including a less ambitious windfall profits tax and standby gas rationing. Oil imports had also declined considerably—in part because the price of oil continued to rise and the dollar was weak. The *Washington Post* credited Carter's "dogged insistence that the oil shortage is real, serious and continuing" with creating "a widening acknowledgment that Americans have to do more with less oil" and making gas lines a thing of the past. Carter's political future appeared brighter after his speech. The media was as focused on his "rebirth" as it had been after the Camp David summit the previous September.[56]

Then Carter ruined his own revival. He had belatedly realized he needed a chief of staff. The job went to Hamilton Jordan, who told the president the obvious: Americans believed that Carter was neither "tough" nor "leading the country." They thought he had "lost touch with the average people who elected him." The White House staff and cabinet did not get along. A whole Camp David meeting in April 1978 had been devoted to the lack of trust between them, so often reflected in leaks to the media. Jordan and other Georgians considered the behavior of Treasury's Michael Blumenthal and Transportation's Brock Adams egregious. Secretary of Health, Education, and Welfare Joe Califano was another offender. His antismoking campaign, which White House officials complained to reporters he had not cleared with them, created political problems for Carter in the tobacco states, where cars were seen sporting bumper stickers saying, "Keep the Canal, Give Away Califano." Since the tough Califano, a Washington superlawyer before he joined Carter's cabinet, had once represented the *Washington Post*, he was also blamed for *Post* editorials questioning the wisdom of White House efforts to carve a separate Department of Education out of Health, Education, and Welfare, which Califano opposed. Yet as Jordan recognized, nothing much had changed after the 1978 meeting at Camp David. Now Jordan and Jody Powell advised the president to ask for the resignations of all cabinet members and White House senior staff as "[a] clear signal that you mean to get tough and do business differently."[57]

So just after the crisis of confidence speech, Carter ordered all his cabinet and senior staff members to offer their resignations and said he would decide which to accept. Within five days, the president had fired Califano, Blumenthal, and Adams. He had taken up one of Schlesinger's periodic offers to leave and accepted the resignation of Attorney General Griffin Bell, who wanted to return to Atlanta. "It went from sugar to shit right there," Mondale recalled.[58]

Certainly Carter had reason to make changes, and his wife recalled that "[w]e thought what he had done was positive until we read the newspapers." *Newsweek* reflected the typical view when it variously characterized the dismissals in the course of one story as "the Great Carter Purge of 1979"; "a purge as complete and bloody as any in recent Presidential history"; a "midsummer massacre"; and a "bloodletting" that deprived the president's "domestic policy team of some of its strongest players, signaled survivors that political loyalty has priority over professional competence and sent a seism of anxiety around the world about the stability of his reign." And that was without quoting anyone.[59]

The tactic of demanding everyone's resignations seemed excessive to many—with the notable exception of Richard Nixon, who had demanded mass resignations at the beginning of his second term and who sent Carter an encouraging letter that concluded with the odd benediction "Win or lose [in 1980]—God bless you—and I know He will." The press also faulted Carter for making more changes in the cabinet than in the White House staff. His timing was bad too. By firing his cabinet members when he did, he diverted attention from a spate of embarrassing stories for Kennedy about the tenth anniversary of Chappaquiddick and "upstaged his own rebirth." Further, some of his victims possessed strong constituencies. Next to Mondale, for example, Califano was the administration's strongest link to liberals, who protested his ouster; he was also a quintessential "Washington insider" with many friends on the Hill and in the media. Further, the president ignored some obvious problems in the cabinet. For months, the *New York Times* observed, Washington had watched Carter's "three secretaries of state—

Vance, Brzezinski and Young"—engage in "unseemly debate" with one another through the media. Yet Carter continued to do nothing about the conflict between Brzezinski and Vance and left Young alone. Only after Young shaded the truth about his private meeting with representatives of the Palestinian Liberation Organization in August 1979 did Carter accept his resignation.[60]

Some of the president's new choices to manage the economy also hurt him politically. During Carter's Camp David seclusion, his economic advisers had declared the country officially in a recession. Unlike Blumenthal, the new secretary of the treasury, former Fed chairman G. William Miller followed orders. Yet while Miller presided over the government bailout of Chrysler from bankruptcy, which saved auto workers' jobs at the same time that it required huge concessions of them, he could not fight inflation effectively. To steady financial markets, Carter bravely asked Paul Volcker, president of the New York Fed, to replace Miller at the Fed, despite a warning that "[i]f he appoints Volcker, he will be mortgaging his reelection to the Federal Reserve." Within a month, the new Fed chair had launched "the Volcker shock" by dramatically raising the discount rate to a record high of 10.5 percent and creating a credit crisis that accelerated the slide into hard times. "The standard of living of the average American has to decline" for the United States to contain inflation, Volcker told Congress.[61]

Carter's choice of Jordan as his chief of staff in July 1979 was mystifying. To be sure, Jordan understood the president well. But he had often operated as de facto chief of staff since 1978, and White House operations had not improved. Jordan himself acknowledged that he was neither a detail person nor an able administrator. Further, "I embody a lot of the criticisms that people direct at you and your staff: that we are all from Georgia, that we don't go out socially enough, that we have disdain for the Congress." By the summer of 1979 too Jordan was damaged goods, "Washington's most unreconstructed bad old boy."[62]

That reputation led the media to take seriously August 1979 charges that Jordan had snorted cocaine when he visited Manhattan's celebrated Studio 54 discotheque the previous year. Because Nixon had fired Special Prosecutor Archibald Cox, Watergate created the impetus for the Ethics in Government Act. It provided that in the case of allegations of misconduct involving the executive branch, a special panel of the District of Columbia Circuit Court of Appeals would appoint a special prosecutor to conduct investigations and prosecutions. That special prosecutor could be dismissed only by the attorney general or a three-judge panel. With his reputation for rectitude, Attorney General Edward Levi had been able to stave off enactment of the legislation during Ford's tenure, but the Carter administration did not fully appreciate its threat. Thus the first special prosecutor named under the 1978 Ethics in Government Act was appointed to investigate Jordan for allegedly snorting two lines of cocaine. Yet everyone, including the special prosecutor, agreed that had the accusation been lodged against an ordinary citizen, it would not have been sufficiently serious or credible to justify prosecution by a U.S. attorney.[63]

Jordan was ultimately cleared, but the charges against him damaged the administration. The public interest in his alleged private drug use showed that Americans were moving toward a politics of personality as they chipped away at barriers between private and public. The president himself had encouraged that shift by making character the issue in 1976 and psychoanalyzing his constituents in his crisis of confidence speech.

That Carter's own private life was irreproachable did him no political good. The *Washington Post* editorialized in July, "However much the president may have done in the past two weeks to corner the malaise vote, you have to concede that he has also done wonders in uniting his party." Its right and left wings were coming together—against him. Carter's chances of renomination "are now very, very difficult," Senator Jackson stressed. Both he and Senator McGovern spoke hopefully of a Kennedy candidacy, and the Americans for Democratic Action sought to draft Kennedy.[64]

Republicans of course also made ready for 1980. Reagan's pollster, Richard Wirthlin, an optimistic Mormon with a Ph.D. in economics, informed him soon after the crisis of confidence speech, "Never before has the battle for the Republican presidential nomination been joined by so many, so early." Along with Reagan, Representatives Phil Crane and John Anderson, John Connally, George H. W. Bush, and Senator Robert Dole all had been campaigning since the beginning of 1979, and Senator Howard Baker planned to use his opposition to SALT II to prove himself presidential timber. It was becoming ever more apparent too that Ford, whose poll numbers were almost as high as Reagan's among Republicans, wanted to become the candidate without entering the primaries and caucuses. "Truthfully, I do better in the polls when I'm not a candidate, so why become one?" Ford joked at the Washington Press Club, "as the audience roared with laughter." But for the moment, at least, Reagan remained the Republican front-runner, with the media focused on the drama and discord on the Democratic side.[65]

BESET AS HE WAS, a sham foreign policy crisis was the last thing Carter needed. But rumors now swirled that the Soviets had stationed forces in Cuba in violation of agreements with the United States concluded after the Cuban missile crisis. On July 17, two days after Carter had made his "crisis of confidence" speech and descended from Camp David, Senator Richard Stone, during Foreign Relations Committee hearings on SALT II, asked about reports that there was "a fully armed Soviet combat brigade on Cuba."[66]

The query came at a sensitive moment, not only because SALT II was under consideration but also because President Anastasio Somoza, the Nicaraguan dictator, had fled Managua for Miami. Somoza's relinquishment of power to the Sandinistas, a coalition of his opponents that included Marxists, raised Soviet and Cuban hopes for revolution throughout Central America. Conservatives criticized Carter for saying that the United States had "a good relationship" with the new Nicaraguan government (which the White House tried to establish only when it became clear that Somoza could not survive) and mocked him for insisting that "I do not attribute at all the change in Nicaragua to Cuba." Carter deserved the sarcasm: Though his point that the Soviet Union and Cuba were not inevitably the puppet masters behind left-leaning nationalist movements was as refreshing as his belief that the United States should respect them, he knew Cuba had aided the Sandinistas, of whom he was deeply suspicious. In fact, the president's desire to prevent a repetition of Nicaragua led him to request congressional approval for $5.7 million of military aid in 1980 for a new regime in El Salvador, which the American ambassador characterized as a "right-wing Murder Incorporated," because El Salvador also faced political violence from guerrillas linked to the Sandinistas and Cubans.[67]

The White House understood that Stone, a conservative Florida Democrat, had trouble with his constituents because he had voted for the Panama Canal treaties. Vance and Senate Foreign Relations Committee chair Frank Church unsuccessfully tried to placate Stone. Then, on August 30, a reporter learned of a reference in the CIA's daily intelligence report to an armed Soviet "combat" brigade in Cuba of two to three thousand men, information Church predicted would "sink SALT."

Like Stone, the liberal Church, who was under attack from the New Right, was worried about his future. According to Carter political operatives, Church "would do anything for re-election. His wife is a better campaigner than he." Vance tried to silence Church, who nevertheless publicly and dramatically called on Carter that evening to require "the immediate withdrawal of Russian combat troops from Cuba," a demand Stone echoed from the Democrats' right wing.[68]

The following day Carter met with reporters in Plains. Between queries about Cuba and the resignation of Andrew Young, he was asked about his fishing. Chatting with Press Secretary Jody Powell after a spring vacation, the president had mentioned that a swamp rabbit had swum toward his canoe and nearly scrambled aboard. Carter had foiled it with a paddle. Several months later Powell foolishly repeated the story to a journalist, and the *New York Times* published "A Tale of Carter and the 'Killer Rabbit'" on August 30. "The President was swinging for his life," one aide was quoted as saying. Whether or not the staffer was facetious was unclear. As reporters teased him, Carter insisted that "I never did hit the rabbit." News of the "Banzai Bunny" spread.[69]

In Washington, Church ratcheted up his rhetoric and substituted hearings on the Soviet brigade for those on SALT II. "I see no likelihood that the Senate would ratify the SALT II treaty as long as Soviet combat troops remain stationed in Cuba," he informed reporters. When Secretary of State Vance saw that the SALT II Treaty was jeopardized, he told reporters that the brigade was "a matter of serious concern" to the United States and "I will not be satisfied with maintenance of the status quo." On September 7, after the president had lunched with Senator Kennedy, who told Carter he would seek the Democratic nomination, the president attempted to show leadership by advising Americans against "panic." He said that although "a Soviet combat unit" was stationed in Cuba, it could not attack the United States, and its "purpose" was "not yet clear. However, the Secretary of State spoke for me and for our Nation on Wednesday when he said that we consider the presence of a Soviet combat brigade in Cuba to be a very serious matter and that this status quo is not acceptable."[70]

Incredibly, as the administration dug deeper into the matter in September, it learned that the Soviet force had been there since 1962, the Russians had never promised to remove it, and it was merely a training unit that taught Cuban troops. American intelligence officials had simply forgotten about its existence. The Soviets showed no interest in negotiating a compromise that would save face for the White House. The Soviet Union had embarked on its military buildup to avoid that kind of humiliation, and Brezhnev had come to power by criticizing his predecessor's capitulation to the United States during the Cuban missile crisis. Soviet concessions would also infuriate Castro. Further, the United States stationed twenty-two hundred American troops in Cuba at Guantánamo, and its troops encircled the Soviet Union. Finally, while some Russians believed the Carter administration had mistakenly referred to the Soviet force as a combat brigade, others speculated that the White House had concluded that SALT II was a liability and had "concocted" a "pretext" for delaying the ratification debate until after the 1980 presidential election—especially since the Russians believed that Vice President Mondale had made "anti-Soviet remarks" when he had recently been in Beijing chatting up the Chinese.[71]

Senator Jackson accused the White House of trying to resolve the crisis without ensuring the removal of the brigade. "That will go over like a lead balloon," he warned. On Thursday, September 13, 1979, a new poll placed the president's approval rating at 19 percent.[72]

Carter now went to Camp David for the weekend. Along with a thousand others, he had decided to participate in a Sunday steep 10k race. He collapsed in the heat before completing it. Although a hundred other runners did not finish the race, the media singled out the president for attention. "I suppose this will replace the rabbit stories," one White House aide said. Another joked hollowly: "Are you going to headline it, 'Carter Drops Out of Race'?" The media attributed Carter's fatigue to stress. Even the president's doctor did not "dismiss speculation that the most recent set of worries—dismal ratings in the polls, Soviet troops in Cuba, allegations of cocaine use by Hamilton Jordan, the challenge of Senator Edward Kennedy for his party's nomination—might have undermined Carter's strength."[73]

At the same time, the combat brigade crisis spun out of control. On September 23, the *New York Times* reported that Brzezinski had said that the brigade's presence reflected the Soviets' "disregard" for American interests and suggested possible retaliation. Brzezinski was summoned to a meeting with Senate Majority Leader Byrd, Vance, and Carter. Byrd reported that he had warned Ambassador Dobrynin that "SALT would be jeopardized unless the Soviets are in some fashion accommodating," Brzezinski recorded in his diary. Dobrynin replied that "the issue is a phony one," a point with which Byrd agreed. As Brzezinski summarized it for his diary, Byrd had advised Carter "to find some way to get off it in order to save SALT. He said that we have to cool our rhetoric, and he expressed disagreement with what the *New York Times* cited me as saying and also with what earlier the President and Vance had said about the status quo not being acceptable." Byrd had impressed Carter, who was now "deeply concerned that he was about to lose SALT."[74]

Yet on September 25, after Kennedy had questioned Carter's leadership and Soviet Foreign Minister Gromyko had declared the crisis "artificial," the president made an extraordinary set of statements at a town meeting. First, he took what he subsequently denied was a veiled dig at Kennedy by saying he did not "panic in a crisis," as the senator presumably had at Chappaquiddick. Next, Carter repudiated Castro as a Soviet "puppet," referred to the Soviet force in Cuba as a "combat brigade," and repeated that "the status quo is not acceptable." The United States was "now trying, through diplomacy, to get the Soviets to eliminate the combat nature of this unit," and if it was unsuccessful, "we will take appropriate action to change the status quo."[75]

Then Carter received a stern letter from Brezhnev. "We regret that you still maintain the contrived story about a Soviet combat unit allegedly located in Cuba. My advice to you: discard this story." The unit had preexisted the missile crisis, and its status had not and would not change. "We are reporting this to you in order to display good will." And in his first official statement on the matter on September 29, Castro branded Carter "dishonest, insincere and immoral."[76]

Carter decided to back down. His writers began work on a speech announcing that "the brigade issue is certainly no reason for a return to the cold war" and that "the greatest danger to American security tonight is certainly not the two or three thousand Soviet troops in Cuba" but the possibility the Senate would not ratify SALT II. Brzezinski demurred. "Every poll shows that the country wants you to be tougher," he told the president. "Unless you convey credibly the message that you will not let the Russians push us around (in addition to blasting Castro personally) you will lose SALT." When Carter gave the speech anyway on October 1, Brzezinski considered resigning. Instead, the national security adviser blew up at the president for threatening the Soviets with "consequences" and then caving in to them. Most Republicans, many Democrats, and many Europeans likewise excoriated Carter's handling of the crisis.[77]

The Soviet brigade incident was a "self-inflicted wound," concluded Deputy Secretary of State Warren Christopher. It strengthened the hand of those favoring a tilt toward China and, according to one State Department expert, "dealt a near-fatal blow to a strategic arms limitation treaty already in trouble." In mid-September, Senator Russell Long used the existence of the brigade to declare that he would oppose the treaty. The Soviet brigade crisis pushed a vote by the full Senate into 1980, when the politics of an election year made senators less likely to support it.[78]

IF THE COMBAT BRIGADE crisis of September and October demonstrated that a pseudocrisis could hurt Carter, November disclosed that a real one could help him. After the Iranians had seized the American Embassy in Tehran on Valentine's Day, Carter had retracted his invitation to the shah. The president wanted to develop a relationship with the new regime in Tehran and protect the Americans there. The shah and his entourage had to find refuge in Mexico. "Fuck the Shah," Carter reportedly said. "I'm not going to welcome him when he has other places where he'll be safe."[79]

In October, however, the president was told that the shah required cancer treatment in the United States. (Whether the shah might have received comparable treatment in Mexico City remained controversial for years to come.) Vance, who had previously opposed admission, now joined Brzezinski to support it on humanitarian grounds. Hamilton Jordan asked Carter to "imagine the field day Kissinger will have" if the shah was denied entrance to the United States and died: "He'll say that first you caused the Shah's downfall and now you've killed him." Kissinger might be so angry that he would desert the administration in the SALT II Treaty ratification fight. But Carter argued against admission, asking, "What are you guys going to advise me to do if they overrun our embassy and take our people hostage?" The White House directed American Embassy officials in Tehran to consult the relatively secular and reform-minded provisional government. The Iranian prime minister and foreign minister urged against admission. They doubted that the shah even had cancer and warned that most Iranians would assume that the Americans were simply bringing the shah to the United States before they restored him to his Iranian throne. Though they would try to protect the embassy, they predicted that the Iranian public might erupt in fury: "You are playing with fire." Carter nevertheless approved the shah's admission, and the shah arrived in New York for treatment on October 22, 1979.[80]

The president was at Camp David when he learned that his prediction had come true. On November 4, Iranian students, chanting "Death to America" and "Death to the Shah and Carter," overran the American Embassy in Tehran. They took the Americans hostage and threatened to hold them until the United States returned the shah to Iran. This time Khomeini did not aid the besieged Americans. The provisional government was powerless to intervene. It had fallen within two days of the embassy takeover, and Iran had now officially become an Islamic theocracy. These developments suggested that there would be no speedy end to the crisis, though no one expected it to continue 444 days. Now the embarrassing images of the Banzai Bunny and Ham and Coke were replaced by humiliating photos of captors parading fifty-three forlorn blindfolded Americans before a jeering Iranian mob as Khomeini demanded the shah's return.[81]

At Thanksgiving, thousands of enraged Pakistanis attacked the American Consulate in Karachi. They set the American Embassy in Islamabad afire. They trapped about a hundred individuals in its vault for hours as the floors underneath them burned. They killed U.S. Marine Corporal Steven Crowley, who was just nineteen, and Army Warrant Officer Brian Ellis. The United States blamed Khomeini, who had spread a false rumor implicating the United States and "its stooge, Israel" in the recent seizure of the Great Shrine in Mecca. (In contrast, the United States faulted Khomeini for the attack on the Great Shrine. In fact, the Islamic fundamentalists who occupied the holy shrine for two weeks were Sunnis, whom the Saudi royals tried to pass off as Soviet patsies, not Iranian Shiites.) Hamilton Jordan told Carter that in addition to causing the "national humiliation of our country," Khomeini was "responsible for the deaths of the two Americans in Pakistan; it was certainly the example of the Iranian Embassy that stimulated the Paks to overrun our embassy at Islamabad." It seemed obvious to Jordan that "a measured punitive act" against the Iranian captors "is absolutely essential to your own re-election and to America's image in the world."[82]

But Carter proceeded cautiously. He urged all Americans to "make a special prayer at churches and synagogues and places of public meeting" on Thanksgiving Day for the safety of the hostages in Tehran. He refused to return the shah to Iran. He condemned the seizure of the U.S. Embassy in Tehran as an act of terrorism and froze Iranian assets in the United States. He avoided public speculation about retaliation, lest he further endanger the hostages, and he launched secret negotiations for their release. He characterized the hostage crisis as a matter that transcended politics and prevented him from campaigning outside the White House. His administration accused Khomeini of making " 'false and irresponsible' statements that helped 'create the climate' for the attacks" in Pakistan. He went to Corporal Crowley's funeral.[83]

And his fellow citizens appeared to think his behavior was just right, even though they observed an epidemic of anti-Americanism sweeping the Islamic world, with Muslim demonstrators marching on the U.S. embassies in Kuwait City and Manila, burning Carter in effigy in front of the U.S. Consulate in Calcutta, bombing the U.S. Embassy in Bangkok, and setting fire to the American Embassy in Tripoli. When the *Washington Post* reported that the president looked "haggard" as he accompanied Crowley's mother to the funeral service and that he spent much of the time "with his eyes closed, his face conveying an attitude of intense prayer," few doubted that his grief was real. The skepticism about American politicians and the divisiveness that had characterized so much of the seventies had briefly lifted.[84]

November 1979 had been a busy month in presidential politics. Ted Kennedy declared that he would seek the nomination. So did Jerry Brown and Howard Baker, though their candidacies went nowhere. Ronald Reagan finally formally announced that he was running too, in an inspirational speech about the unique American experience. "We who are privileged to be Americans have had a rendezvous with destiny since the moment in 1630 when John Winthrop, standing on the deck of the tiny Arbella off the coast of Massachusetts, told the little band of Pilgrims, 'We shall be a city upon a hill,' " Reagan said. "A troubled and afflicted mankind looks to us, pleading for us to keep that rendezvous with destiny."[85]

Yet with the Iranian hostage crisis, Carter was suddenly considered "presidential." His "leadership" and even his staff were applauded. A year to the day before the 1980 election, the president had been handed a heartache that might just become the instrument of his redemption.[86]

THE HOSTAGE CRISIS did not help SALT II. Only nine of the fifteen Senate Foreign Relations Committee members voted to approve the treaty in November. When Carter said he would support a 5.7 percent increase in defense spending for fiscal 1981 that he had previously opposed, Senate Armed Services Committee hawks suspected that he was trolling for votes. On December 20, 1979, ten of that committee's seventeen members adopted a report written by Senator Jackson and Richard Perle declaring that the planned spending increase would not enable the United States to keep pace with the Soviet Union and that approval of the SALT II Treaty was not in the national interest. Reporters asked Jackson if the treaty was dead. "It's in a sort of state of repose," he replied.[87]

Four days later the treaty died, and Carter's second honeymoon began to fizzle too. On Christmas Eve 1979 thousands of Soviet troops invaded Afghanistan while the president was at Camp David. Brzezinski acknowledged in 1998 that Carter had "knowingly increased the probability" of Soviet intervention in Afghanistan. After the death of Ambassador Dubs, the president secretly directed the CIA to aid the mujahideen, the Muslim guerrilla fighters in Afghanistan who rebelled against the Communist regime of Hafizullah Amin. "That secret operation was an excellent idea," Brzezinski insisted later, because the mujahideen insurgency and the Soviets' loss of faith in Amin drew them into "the Afghan trap" that sapped their economic and military strength and ultimately helped to cause their collapse in 1991. The Soviets did decide to replace Amin with someone of unquestioned loyalty and to send in soldiers to put down the Muslim uprising.[88]

Although the president and Brzezinski understood they had taken steps that might well lead to Soviet intervention, the CIA may not have. Although it reported on Soviet troop deployments around Afghanistan, its "Soviet analysts just couldn't believe that the Soviets actually would invade in order to play a major part in ground combat operations." In contrast, by the time of the combat brigade crisis, Brzezinski had informed Carter that a Soviet invasion of Afghanistan had become "more probable." When it happened, Brzezinski portrayed the invasion as "a vindication of my concern that the Soviets would be emboldened by our lack of concern over Ethiopia."[89]

But there was nothing bold about the invasion. It was a last-ditch defensive effort to shore up the security of the Soviet Union. An Islamic theocracy in Afghanistan, which shared a border with the Soviet Union, would be bad news. "[I]n contrast to the claims of the most stubborn American opponents of the Soviet Union, including those in the Carter White House itself, there was no grand strategic plan designed by Moscow" to win Middle Eastern oil and access to the Indian Ocean, Dobrynin wrote later. Angry that NATO had made the final decision to deploy new missiles in Europe earlier that day, the Soviets agreed to the invasion at a late-night meeting on December 12. Because the Americans had taken in stride the 1978 Communist coup in Afghanistan, there was reason to believe they would remain calm about the invasion. Further, the American-Soviet relationship had deteriorated so much, and the Carter administration's behavior, "most notably with respect to the Soviet brigade in Cuba," was so odd that the Russians believed by Christmas 1979 that "there was nothing left to lose."[90]

They had miscalculated. Brezhnev had been misled: The KGB had assured him that a small number of troops could quickly establish a friendly government in Afghanistan and eliminate mujahideen resistance within a month. Instead, after the deaths of some fifteen thousand Soviets and a million Afghans, the Soviet forces withdrew in defeat a decade later. The invasion also proved a turning point in U.S.-Soviet relations. When Brezhnev claimed that Amin had invited the Soviets to protect Afghanistan from an external threat, Carter called the Russian a liar and asked why Amin was "murdered or assassinated after the Soviets pulled their coup."[91]

Brzezinski hardened his boss's backbone in a flurry of memorandums. The United States should not be too hopeful that Afghanistan would become "a Soviet Vietnam." The mujahideen were neither well organized nor well led. The rebels lacked sanctuaries, an organized army, or a central government, all of which North Vietnam had possessed. They received only "limited foreign support," and the Soviets would probably move more "decisively" to crush the resistance than Americans had against the North Vietnamese. The United States had to send more money, arms, and advisers to the rebels; encourage China, Pakistan, and Islamic countries to do the same; and let the Soviets know that they had jeopardized SALT II. Otherwise the Chinese would "certainly note" that the United States had not kept the Soviet Union in check, and Soviet influence would spread from Afghanistan to Pakistan and Iran all through Southwest Asia down to the Arabian Gulf and the Gulf of Oman. Afghanistan was "the seventh state since 1975 in which communist parties have come to power with Soviet guns and tanks, with Soviet military power and assistance (Vietnam, Angola, Laos, South Yemen, Cambodia, Ethiopia, and now probably Afghanistan"). Four of these takeovers had happened on Carter's watch. It was time to turn the tide for "domestic and international reasons."[92]

As he had done with respect to the Soviet brigade, Carter went rhetorically overboard. On January 20, 1980, he characterized the invasion as "the most serious threat to world peace since the Second World War." He also told reporters that the invasion had done more to change his opinion of Soviet goals than anything else that had happened since he had taken office, a remark the press branded "strikingly naive." Dobrynin, the Soviet ambassador to the United States since Kennedy was president, had never witnessed such intense American anti-Soviet feeling. "What particularly caught my attention was the president's personal obsession with Afghanistan."[93]

American aid to the mujahideen rebels skyrocketed, though it remained well under the levels at which Moscow funded the rebels' Afghan Communist antagonists. The White House mistrusted President Muhammad Zia-ul-Haq of Pakistan, a repressive dictator. Yet at the same time that the American government protested the unresponsiveness of the Libyan government to the takeover of the American Embassy in Tripoli, it maintained the fiction that "Zia's government rescued" those incinerated by the Pakistani mob in the American Embassy in Islamabad. And with Carter's approval, the CIA funneled money to the anti-Soviet mujahideen through its Pakistan counterpart, Inter-Services Intelligence. The growth in American support was massive: Where Carter authorized five hundred thousand dollars for the resistance in July 1979, by 1981 the mujahideen were receiving thirty million dollars; by 1984, two hundred million. The United States thereby became indirectly responsible for the growth in power of Osama bin Laden, al Qaeda, and the Taliban.[94]

Carter launched a scattershot array of other reprisals against the Soviet Union. In January 1980 the president announced that he would not seek a Senate vote on SALT II. Against the advice of those who said food should never be used as a weapon and that Carter would hurt himself with Iowa farmers, he imposed an embargo on the sale of grain to the Soviet Union. (Carter lessened the risk of defection in the Iowa caucuses by directing his own government to buy millions of dollars of grain.) He blocked sales of high-grade technology to the Soviets. He took the diplomatically drastic step of recalling the American ambassador to the Soviet Union. He said that the United States might not participate in the summer 1980 Moscow Olympics, as it did not. (The United States tried to pressure other countries into boycotting the Olympic Games as well, although just persuading American athletes to respect the boycott was difficult enough.) The "Carter Doctrine" set out in the president's January 1980 State of the Union address made it "absolutely clear" that the United States would use military force to protect the Persian Gulf and its oil fields from external threat. The president also reactivated draft registration: The Nixon Doctrine of giving regional powers the tools they required to protect American interests was apparently dead. The president increased the defense budget again and drew still closer toward the Chinese, to whom the United States began selling military equipment. "Pique more than prudence dictated Carter's response to the Afghan invasion," historians Burton and Scott Kaufman concluded.[95]

The president's overrreaction to the Soviet invasion that he had not forestalled called into question his patience with respect to the hostage crisis. The double shock of the seizure of the American Embassy in Tehran and the Soviet invasion of Afghanistan left many Americans feeling hawkish, Washington "tense and anxious." The exhilaration about the upset victory of the U.S. hockey team over the Soviet Union at Lake Placid in the Winter Olympics reflected the angry nationalism, yearning for heroes, and frustration. "With all due respect," columnist David Broder asked the president, "we still have 5.8 percent unemployment. Inflation has risen from 4.8 percent to 13 percent. We still don't have a viable energy policy. Russian troops are in Cuba and Afghanistan. Gold is rising. And the hostages, after 78 days, are still in Tehran. Just what have you done, sir, to deserve renomination?"[96]

In January 1980 the Democrats nonetheless seemed inclined to give the nomination to him. Americans rallied around the flag. Carter won a two to one victory over Kennedy in the Iowa caucus on January 21, 1980.[97]

After Iowa, Kennedy attacked Carter's economic and foreign policy. Was the Soviet invasion of Afghanistan "a graver threat than the Berlin blockade, the Korean War, the Soviet march into Hungary and Czechoslovakia, the Berlin Wall, the Cuban Missile Crisis or Vietnam"? Kennedy asked. And was it such a surprise? Dubs had been killed "while Soviet military advisers looked on. We were aware well in advance that the Russians were massing their forces. But the administration said virtually nothing until after the invasion, when they drew a line in the dust that was already rising from the tread of Soviet tanks." During the last week of January, Kennedy also blasted the "Republican economics" of the Carter administration. "The numbers have nearly lost their capacity to shock. Twelve straight months of inflation over 10 percent. Wild gyration in the price of gold. Interest rates at 15 percent. Unemployment at 6 percent. And now recession is just around the corner."[98]

The numbers still shocked. Because of increased defense expenditures and inflation, the deficit for fiscal 1980 "would be almost 50 percent higher than anticipated." When the public heard the news in January 1980, the bond market plunged. Precious metals surged. In one week, gold rose $148 to $660 per ounce before falling to $603. Americans stood in line to sell off jewelry and family heirlooms. They did not bank the proceeds. Though prices continued to soar, and interest rates were the highest in a century, Americans kept right on buying—and borrowing. They had apparently lost hope that prices would drop and were spending money as fast as they could, before it bought even less. The consumer price index rose at an annual rate of 18 percent in January and February. With prices jumping so much more quickly than wages, real purchasing power dropped, and new rounds of "panic-buying" and borrowing followed. By March 1980 the prime interest rate was inching toward a staggering 20 percent.[99]

Stressing that inflation was a global problem and related to the energy crisis, Carter unveiled yet another unpopular anti-inflation program in mid-March. This one featured budget cuts, imposition of credit controls to limit borrowing, an oil import conservation fee that would result in an extra dime in gas taxes on every gallon, and stronger, though still voluntary, wage and price controls. But Congress overwhelmingly defeated the gas tax. When investors realized the combination of tight money and the Carter program would force the economy into recession, silver and gold plunged, the bond market stayed fairly flat, and the Dow Jones fell to its lowest level since 1978.[100]

LIKE KENNEDY, REPUBLICANS highlighted the nation's economic and foreign policy woes. Strangely, Reagan's campaign was struggling. "I firmly believe that there are only two ways your nomination could be endangered: if we give it away ourselves, over our own internal mistakes, or if Gerald Ford, for whatever reasons, should decide to marshal his political strength directly against us," Richard Wirthlin told Reagan in July 1979. In the second half of the year there were internal Reagan campaign mistakes aplenty.[101]

In part, they resulted from the lack of confidence of some Reaganites in their candidate. Consider SALT II, for example. Though Reagan had wanted to declare that the treaty was defective in August, Richard Allen, his chief foreign policy adviser, had counseled him to wait "because every one expected him to be against SALT II, so he would gain nothing by shooting too early; because the mood of the country would harden (we could not have anticipated the Soviet troops in Cuba issue, which accelerated the hardening) and he could ride that wave; and because he, not being a Senator did not have to 'vote' on the Treaty and really didn't owe anybody any specifics on it." With polls showing that some found Reagan too bellicose, the Californian agreed to keep mum on SALT II, "but not with any measurable degree of enthusiasm." In August 1979, Reagan made the case that Soviet aggressiveness and the Iranian Revolution made American defense of Israeli security vital. He did not try to lead the SALT II opposition until mid-September, when he announced that "the Senate should declare that this treaty, fatally flawed as it is, should be shelved and the negotiators should go back to the table and come up with a treaty which fairly and genuinely reduces the number of strategic nuclear weapons." But when Reagan delivered his September speech, no one, save unhappy conservatives, noticed that he had distinguished between rejecting and "shelving" the treaty. The *New York Times* headline bruited that "Reagan Urges Senate to Reject Arms Pact, but His Tone Is Softer." That Reagan had bowed to his advisers' attempts to broaden his appeal became the story and reinforced his image as a right-winger, made him seem his handlers' captive, and strengthened doubts about whether the actor was too extremist, stupid, and old to perform the role of president.[102]

Yet within the Reagan camp, the fear persisted that although allowing Reagan to "be Reagan" would appeal to William Rusher and the other conservatives who read *Human Events* and *National Review* and adored him already, it would backfire because independents and Democrats, to say nothing of moderate Republicans, would never vote for him. Reagan's campaign manager, John Sears, architect of the Schweiker selection in 1976, decreed that Reagan must win the nomination by demonstrating he was both the front-runner and the Republican best able to defeat a Democrat. In the second half of 1979, Sears "neutered" his client (as *Human Events* complained; others protested that Reagan had been "Searscumcised"), refused to allow Reagan to debate his Republican rivals in Iowa or even to campaign much there, ousted several of Reagan's closest policy advisers from the California days, and spent the better part of the primary budget. Muzzled, Reagan disappeared from view.[103]

Despite a debate style campaign accurately characterized by Reagan's campaign staff as "whining" and "strident," George H. W. Bush was coming on strong. Although he lived in Texas, he had grown up in Greenwich, Connecticut, and eastern business interests liked him. In conservative circles, Bush was derided as "the Eastern Establishment candidate." Bush and his campaign manager, James Baker, who had served as Gerald Ford's campaign manager in 1976, had studied Carter's primary record and were trying to replicate it. The Bush forces spent months organizing their supporters in Iowa. Bush won the most delegates in the January 21 caucuses there, though Reagan was a close second. Sounding as if he were at a "preppy pep rally," the Andover and Yale College graduate showed his "goofy side" by saying that he had "Big Mo [momentum]." Perhaps. But Bush lacked a substantive program.[104]

Nevertheless, Reagan and almost everyone else in his campaign—except, perhaps, John Sears and his associates, who remained wedded to their strategy—now agreed that he must campaign vigorously in New Hampshire. A transformed Reagan barnstormed the state: He pushed supply-side economics and Kemp-Roth tax cuts in three commercials, equated Carter's foreign policy with appeasement, and spoke of punishing the Soviets for the Afghanistan invasion by blockading Cuba. He also participated in two Republican debates. Arranged by a local newspaper to feature the two front-runners, the second debate became legendary when the Reagan campaign laid a trap for Bush by inviting the other Republican candidates. Then Reagan made the case to the sponsor and a reluctant Bush that the competitors should be permitted to participate as well. The *Washington Post* recounted that Reagan, who had seemed "passive" during the first debate, "was like a man aroused" and "scored repeated debating points off Bush in the 90-minute confrontation, while the other four, Sens. Howard Baker, Jr. and Bob Dole and Reps. John B. Anderson and Philip M. Crane, had to content themselves with being introduced at the beginning and allowed to make brief statements at the end." In contrast, Bush came across as weak, frozen, and arrogant. He also made enemies. Baker, Dole, Anderson, and Crane pledged to deprive Bush of the Republican nomination, and Reagan now viewed him as "a wimp." Reagan won more than twice as many votes as Bush in the New Hampshire primary on February 26. Even before the results were official, Reagan and his wife fired Sears and his associates. The Reagans now recalled the Californians to the campaign and announced that former SEC chairman William Casey, a wealthy conservative tax lawyer with connections to the intelligence community, would direct it.[105]

Despite Reagan's liberation from moderation in New Hampshire, New Right leaders continued to mistrust him. They had always despised Sears, and even now that Sears had gone, they were still excluded from Reagan's circle. Phyllis Schlafly, the New Right organizer most supportive of Reagan, complained that he lacked "a competent adviser on women's, family, and social issues." Why else would he pledge to oppose the Equal Rights Amendment but work with the members of Carter's Advisory Committee for Women? "Doesn't he know that every single member [of Carter's committee] . . . is pro-ERA, that nearly every one is pro-abortion, that every one is pro-lib [women's liberation] and pro-increased federal spending and control" and wanted to "cut his throat"? Schlafly warned that Republican pragmatists who assumed that in a Reagan-Carter contest, "the pro-family, anti-ERA, pro-life people have no place to go except to Reagan" misunderstood "the dynamics of the grassroots. They do have a place to go—the same place they have been for the rest of their lives: in their churches reading their Bibles." Yet to the New Right, Bush, a former Trilateral Commission member, who supported the Equal Rights Amendment and opposed a constitutional amendment prohibiting abortion, seemed even worse than Reagan.[106]

But the New Right lacked a viable candidate. Some thought John Connally, another choice of some business interests, its best bet. After a disagreement about fund-raising, Richard Viguerie had jumped Crane's ship and approached Connally. "He was interested and we got married" in the summer of 1979, Viguerie recalled. They stayed together even after Connally created a flap by contending that the world's need for Middle Eastern oil compelled Israel to withdraw from the occupied territories, surrender exclusive sovereignty of Jerusalem, and sanction creation of a Palestinian state. In February 1980, *Conservative Digest* devoted most of an issue to touting Connally. Viguerie contended that Carter would "soundly" defeat Reagan in 1980, charged that "John Connally is a leader and that Ronald Reagan is not a leader but a spokesman," and complained that as California's governor Reagan had not built "a conservative power structure that would carry on his conservative principles." But despite the fact that Strom Thurmond had endorsed Connally, he could not even win in South Carolina. Connally never won a primary and dropped out in March, as did Baker. Crane waited until early April to withdraw.[107]

Representative John Anderson, a wry Illinois progressive evangelical who despised Reagan and insisted that Bush was his Ivy League replica, was not winning Republican primaries. But Anderson and Bush tied for first place in the Massachusetts primary on March 4, and Anderson placed ahead of Bush in the Vermont primary, which Reagan won, the same day. Anderson was receiving such wonderful notices that the Americans for Democratic Action felt obligated to remind liberals of "his diehard support for the Vietnam war" and his vote against Humphrey-Hawkins. Nevertheless, Anderson was developing fierce support among college students, educated suburbanites, and reporters who disliked Reagan and Carter—if not among many Republicans. "My, my, how the media love their John Anderson," *Human Events* commented acidly—and with some justification. A centrist, Anderson favored a fifty-cent-per-gallon gas tax Carter had decided was too politically costly, and he joked that Reagan's promise to cut taxes, increase defense spending, and balance the budget would be carried out "with mirrors." In the Illinois primary on March 18, Anderson won 36 percent of the vote, Reagan 49 percent, and Bush, just 11 percent. Reagan liked having Anderson in the race and saw him as a threat to the Carter campaign, which was terrified of Anderson.[108]

Suddenly, as the Republican race narrowed in March, Ford pointed to polls that showed that he would win a general election and Reagan would lose. "I hear more and more often," he told the *New York Times*, "that we don't want, can't afford to have a replay of 1964," with Reagan, a "very conservative Republican," cast as Barry Goldwater. "If there was an honest-to-goodness, bona fide urging by a broad-based group in my party, I would respond." As the *New York Times* headline summed things up, "Ford Declares Reagan Can't Win; Invites G.O.P. to Ask Him to Run." While "[a] visitor from another planet" might have assumed "that here was an extraordinary political gladiator who felt impelled to come out of retirement to rescue his party," *Human Events* incredulously responded, "Ford's credentials as a powerful vote-getter are wafer-thin." Further, one Ford strategist asked rhetorically: If America's situation had become so desperate that it required recalling him from retirement to run against the very individual who had defeated him in 1976, "why has Mr. Ford spent the 3½ years since he left the White House playing golf?" By the time Ford came to his senses and announced at mid-month that he had decided against a run, Reagan had virtually wrapped up the nomination in the Illinois primary.[109]

After Illinois, Anderson began to contemplate a run as an independent. In April he made it official. He would become the candidate of the newly created National Unity Party and work to put his name on the ballot in all the states. Though third party candidacies usually fizzled by fall, political cognoscenti did not dismiss this one. They knew the nomination was Reagan's and guessed that Carter would become his Democratic opponent. Polls reflected voters' antipathy toward both.[110]

Meanwhile, a desperate Bush found his voice after Illinois. He equated Kemp-Roth with "voodoo economics" in Pennsylvania and won the primary there on April 22. Bush's success, like Anderson's popularity, indicated the depth of Republican anxiety about Reagan. Given inflation and deficits, many inside and outside the GOP shared Bush's suspicion of supply-side economics and now advocated what Jack Kemp derisively referred to as the "Eisenhower-Nixon-Ford-Bush" program of putting budget cuts ahead of tax cuts. Reagan "must abandon the idea that cutting tax rates will necessarily increase tax revenues," two Reagan campaign advisers stressed privately. "Though he may well be right, at least over the longer term, the public will not buy it. Moreover, it would be irresponsible to base national budgetary policy on such an uncertain phenomenon." Reagan, however, continued to defend supply-side economics with the same vigor with which he attacked the Soviet Union, and some Republican leaders and most reporters seized upon his unorthodox economics, along with his unrelenting hostility toward the Soviets and his age, as reasons to doubt his viability. But Bush developed his message too late, delivered it poorly, lacked sufficient delegates, and ran out of cash. By Memorial Day he had withdrawn, and the nomination was Reagan's.[111]

Anderson, Baker, Connally, Crane, and Dole had not won a single Republican contest. Bush had triumphed in only seven: Iowa, Puerto Rico, Massachusetts, Connecticut, Pennsylvania, the District of Columbia, and Michigan. Reagan had been victorious in nearly thirty. He had done especially well in states, such as Wisconsin and Indiana, that allowed Democrats to cross over and vote in the Republican primary, and where he had demonstrated "an uncanny ability to appeal to blue-collar, ethnic and Catholic . . . voters who traditionally have voted Democratic."[112]

But that did not mean that Republican leaders had united around him. As Wirthlin said, the primaries had created "tension between Reaganites and the Party," which continued to treat "the Governor himself as an 'outsider.'" The mainstream media had rarely been kind to Reagan. With understated glee, the *New York Times* had once reported that while trying to rally the faithful by reminding them that "Samson slew the Philistines," Reagan told them that "Simpson slew the Philippines." Rusher warned that now the media would hammer home the point that "Reagan is dumb, dumb, dumb." Both Republican elites and reporters seemed doubtful that Americans would choose someone so many viewed as an elderly, out-of-it right-winger. That was the hope to which the Carter camp, which viewed Reagan as the dream adversary, clung.[113]

REAGAN DID HAVE DEMOCRATIC discord going for him. As Carter battled vainly to keep Anderson off the general election ballot in 1980, he engaged in a fight with Kennedy for the nomination reminiscent of the 1976 Reagan-Ford brawl. Except for Kennedy's win in Massachusetts on March 4, Carter at first piled victory on victory. Americans were ready to believe, presidential advisers cheered, that Rose Kennedy "didn't have triplets." Kennedy made a weak start when he could not explain why he wanted to be president to a television interviewer. Thereafter the media played up his every flub. He had an uneven campaign staff. Audiences seemed unmoved by memories of his brothers, he had not cleared up the mysteries of Chappaquiddick and the rumors of philandering, he alienated many when he intervened in the hostage crisis by volunteering that the shah had operated "one of the most violent regimes in the history of mankind" and stolen "umpteen billions" from his countrymen, some voters questioned the liberalism Kennedy personified, and he did not possess the administration's ability to spread around "well-aimed, well-timed grants." Nevertheless, Kennedy triumphed by a large margin in both Connecticut and New York when Democrats went to the polls on March 25, after Carter had announced his anti-inflation program and the administration had voted in favor of a United Nations resolution calling on Israel to dismantle its West Bank and Gaza settlements.[114]

The results augured poorly for Carter in November. "God gave the Arabs a lot of oil, and gave the Jews a lot of clout in the Electoral College," one pundit said. But while many Jews lived in New York City, Kennedy carried rural New York too, and there were relatively few in the Nutmeg State, except in West Hartford, New Haven, and parts of Fairfield County. The economy angered voters of all and no faiths. Carter still possessed more delegates than Kennedy. But Kennedy's victories in New York and Connecticut, followed by wins in Pennsylvania, California, and New Jersey, guaranteed that he would stay in the race until the convention. In addition to dividing the Democrats, Kennedy's quest prevented the Carter campaign from organizing for the general election and pointed up the president's vulnerability.[115]

So did events outside and within the United States. On April 1, six Cubans rammed a bus through the gates in front of the Peruvian Embassy in Havana and were granted asylum there. Some 10,000 more sought and received asylum within the week. In a surprise move designed to rid Cuba of dissident pests, Castro announced on April 19 that anyone could leave Cuba from the port at Mariel. That began the Mariel boatlift, which ultimately brought to Florida 125,000 Cubans, including some criminals and/or mentally ill individuals whom Castro decided to dump. Many Americans disagreed with Carter that the United States should "provide an open heart and open arms" to those who sought freedom from communism and economic want. (Future President Bill Clinton, then the nation's youngest governor, blamed his 1980 failure to win reelection in Arkansas in part on the unpopular administration decision to process 20,000 of "the Marielitos" at Fort Chaffee, Arkansas.) When four Florida policemen were acquitted of violence in the killing of black insurance salesman Arthur McDuffie soon afterward, African Americans in Miami's inner city exploded. The worst and most vicious race riots since the 1960s highlighted hostility to government assistance to Cuban refugees, as well as a revulsion against police brutality.[116]

All the while, negotiations to release the hostages in Iran continued. The administration worked tirelessly to secure their release. On April 1, the day of the Wisconsin primary, Carter called a 7:20 A.M. televised news conference to hail a "positive step" and imply that the hostages would soon be released. He won Wisconsin. But the Iranians refused to set the hostages free. It appeared that the president had used the crisis for political gain, and a diplomatic solution seemed more unlikely than ever.[117]

Just after Carter spent Easter weekend at Camp David musing over his Iranian options, he authorized Operation Eagle Claw, an exceedingly risky military rescue attempt on April 24. He did so over the opposition of Secretary of State Vance, who resigned in protest because of the dangers that the plan presented to the hostages and to American foreign policy. It required six helicopters. Eight were sent to Iran in case one developed problems. When two malfunctioned and a third lost its way, the mission was aborted. As the ninety American servicemen boarded the C-130 whose crew had hoped to fly them and the hostages home, one helicopter crashed into the transport plane. Eight were killed; five, injured.[118]

If the mission had turned out like Entebbe or even the *Mayaguez*, Carter would have been covered in glory. As it was, the Iranians mocked the American government, displayed the charred corpses of the servicemen, threatened the hostages with death, divided them into groups, and transferred them to separate locations to deter future rescue attempts. One analyst thought Americans would say Carter had "botched up another one."[119]

Yet as when the American Embassy in Tehran was seized, the country rallied around the president. Less than a week after an ashen-faced Carter announced the mission's fate in a televised speech from the Oval Office at 7:00 A.M. on April 25, he declared that the challenges of his office were now sufficiently "manageable" to enable him to resume campaigning, "as though somehow the failure of the rescue mission had already lessened his and the country's problems." Then, in his first campaign trip, Carter tactlessly announced that his new secretary of state, Edmund Muskie, would be "a much stronger and more statesmanlike senior figure" than Vance. The president still trounced Kennedy during the first week of May in the Texas, Indiana, North Carolina, and Tennessee primaries. "Carter's very incompetence," Arthur Schlesinger, Jr., mourned, "has been his salvation."[120]

EPILOGUE

IN THE FALL OF 1980, AFTER THE REPUBLICANS MET IN JULY, AND the Democrats in August, four liberal Democrats contemplated the political landscape. My mother was voting for ecologist Barry Commoner. My father and my boyfriend, who is now my husband, decided to protest their choices by not going to the polls at all. I had thrilled to the Kennedy challenge. When "Billygate," the scandal about Billy Carter's acceptance of cash from the Libyan government, erupted on the eve of the Democratic convention and seemed briefly to give legs to the "dump Carter" movement and Kennedy's quest for an open convention, I cheered. I wept at the conclusion of Kennedy's August 12 concession speech urging the party to recommit itself to economic and social justice: "For all those whose cares have been our concern, the work goes on, the cause endures, the hope still lives, and the dream shall never die."[1]

Still, the difference between the Democratic and Republican platforms pushed me toward Carter. Where Democrats pressed for federal financing of all abortions in 1980, Republicans advocated a constitutional amendment banning abortion. Where Democrats supported affirmative action, tax exemptions for private schools that did not racially discriminate, and school desegregation (while characterizing busing to achieve racial balance as a "last resort"), the Republicans called for restoring the right to pray in public schools, pledged to halt "the unconstitutional regulatory vendetta launched by Mr. Carter's IRS Commisisioner against independent schools," and condemned "the forced busing of school children to achieve arbitrary racial quotas." Where Democrats talked of cutting off funding for any candidate who opposed the ERA, Republicans bowed to Phyllis Schlafly and dismayed some longtime GOP activists by abandoning the amendment. Where Democrats condemned inflationary general tax cuts, Republicans promoted Kemp-Roth. Where Democrats advocated a twelve-billion-dollar jobs program, Republicans wanted to promote private enterprise. Where Democrats championed a national health insurance program and federal financing of welfare, Republicans resisted them. Where Democrats focused on energy conservation, Republicans stressed production and decontrol of oil and gas. Where Democrats emphasized the importance of military parity with the Soviet Union, Republicans envisioned military superiority. Where Democrats applauded arms control agreements, Republicans displayed skepticism. Democrats recalled that when Carter became president in 1976, "the most dangerous threat to America's position in the world was the profound disillusionment and mistrust which the American people felt for their own government." According to Republicans, "[t]he only malaise in this country is found in the leadership of the Democratic Party, in the White House and in Congress." Alone among the four of us, I voted for Carter.[2]

He lost anyway. Most expected that outcome, though it would be just the third time in the twentieth century that an elected incumbent had failed to win a second term. But few anticipated the magnitude of Carter's defeat. In those days, networks portrayed Republican states as blue; Democratic ones, as red. Election night, held a year to the day after the seizure of the hostages and while they remained captive in Tehran, revealed a sea of blue. Only 52.6 percent of Americans voted. Reagan won 50.7 percent of the votes cast and 489 votes in the electoral college. Incredibly, the Republicans won a majority in the Senate for the first time since 1954: Conservative bêtes noires Frank Church, George McGovern, Birch Bayh, Gaylord Nelson, John Culver, and Warren Magnuson lost their seats. The GOP also picked up thirty-three places in the House. As they had before the 1974 disaster, Republicans again controlled 44 percent of House seats. They won control of another four state legislatures. Conservative Republicans did especially well. Carter received 41 percent of the popular vote and a pathetic forty-nine electoral votes (Minnesota, West Virginia, Delaware, Maryland, and Georgia). John Anderson garnered 6.6 percent of the popular vote without carrying any states. Libertarian Ed Clark won just 1.1 percent. Some Libertarian Party members had obviously defected to Reagan, despite the fact that their party leaders considered him a hopeless "statist" and winced whenever Reagan said that "small 'l' " libertarianism was "at the heart of conservatism." Commoner received just 0.3 percent. So overwhelming was Carter's defeat that he conceded the election while the polls remained open in California, although Tip O'Neill tried to persuade the White House that the move would prevent late West Coast voters from turning out and would cost some congressional Democrats their seats. The White House refused to wait. "You guys came in like a bunch of pricks," O'Neill told Carter's congressional liaison, Frank Moore. "And you're going out the same way."[3]

Carter ran at least ten points behind his own 1976 performance with many voter groups: Democrats, independents, liberals, men, middle class college graduates, blue-collar workers, union members, suburbanites, southerners (particularly white ones), westerners, Latinos, whites, Protestants (especially evangelicals), Catholics (particularly Irish, Slavs, and Italians), Jews, and people in their thirties and early forties. Only African Americans remained loyal. Carter received 82 percent of their votes in 1976 and 1980.[4]

One theme of this book is that like Ford in 1976, Carter did not deserve to win. As historian Leo Ribuffo has observed, Americans and their presidents have worshiped at the shrine of presidential leadership since the days of Theodore Roosevelt. But to many, presidential leadership from 1974 to 1979 was, quite simply, too often abysmal. Ford should be credited with demonstrating that the phrase "decent politician" is not an oxymoron and for signing the Helsinki Accords. Many also praise his brave decision to pardon Nixon. Carter should be applauded for facing up to the energy crisis, negotiating the Panama Canal treaties, normalizing relations with China, securing peace between Israel and Egypt, and keeping American troops out of harm's way. Yet Gerald Rafshoon's assessment of Carter's situation in 1980 also applied to Ford four years earlier. "Leadership," Rafshoon wrote Carter, "is the single biggest weakness in the public perception of you. You are seen to be weak, providing no sense of direction, unsure yourself about where you want to lead the country and unable to lead if you do discover where you want to go."[5]

The two presidents shared similar fates. In fact, by 1980, Carter was in much the same position as Ford in 1976—except, as Patrick Caddell observed, Americans disliked Carter more. In both cases the incumbent presided over a polarized party and beat off a challenge from a less moderate member. In both instances the challenger won the platform. Because of Reagan, the 1976 Republican platform was substantially more conservative than Ford. So too, thanks to pressure from Kennedy and feminists, the 1980 Democratic platform proved much more liberal than Carter.[6]

AND IN BOTH 1976 and 1980 the moderate incumbent lost the election to an opponent who ran a poor general campaign. Carter blamed his defeat on the schism in the Democratic Party, his own failure to secure the hostages' release, and the putrid economy. Like Ford, Carter did indeed face intractable problems. It is difficult to imagine that Ford, who had almost beaten Carter in 1976, could have done any better, in which case Americans surely would have repudiated the Republicans in 1980 and have deemed Reagan too old to run in 1984, and there would have been no Age of Reagan. Still, as Carter's advisers told him in the summer of 1980, it was "a sign of how bad things have become" that the suggestion that he should base his run on his own record "would be ridiculed if made publicly." Given Carter's presidency, Patrick Caddell said, the theme could not be one of "Why not the best?" as it had been in 1976, but " 'it could be worse.' " Carter and his campaign portrayed Reagan as an elderly, bumbling, simplistic, sexist, racist, and trigger-happy Robin Hood in reverse who would steal from the poor to give to the rich. The GOP tried to be just as negative. "At the outset of the general election campaign, it was agreed that if Governor Reagan became *the issue* it would be very difficult for us to win," one strategist recalled just before November. "Our objective was to make Jimmy Carter *the issue*, to make him defend his failed Presidency, especially his record of economic failure. We are all disappointed that we have not been more successful in realizing that objective."[7]

Reagan's early primary and caucus victories should have left him with plenty of time to unify the Republican Party. Conservatives like Buckley and Schlafly had always rooted for him. Though Senator Jackson reluctantly endorsed Carter after the Democratic convention, most neoconservatives fell behind Reagan. Having repeatedly voted for FDR, Reagan could even claim to be one of them. So, after its fashion, did the New Right. While Paul Weyrich predicted that Reagan as president would "bring many of the tired old Eastern establishment Republicans back to Washington," he reasoned that "at least" Reagan understood that the Soviet Union represented a danger. And Richard Viguerie was extolling Reagan by July 1980, while warning that if the candidate selected a "non-conservative such as Sen. Howard Baker or George Bush" as his running mate, Viguerie "and millions of others" in the New Right and religious right "will sit this election out."[8]

Richard Wirthlin's polling, however, showed that Reagan needed a "non-conservative" who could attract moderates. When he arrived in Detroit for the Republican convention on July 14, Reagan and his advisers clung to the delusion that they might persuade Gerald Ford to take the job. Reagan offered it to the former president, along with an authentic peace pipe. Advisers to Ford and Reagan held serious discussions designed to make the vice presidency more substantive and appealing. Reagan told a horrified Richard Allen that Ford had called for the appointment of Kissinger as secretary of state and Alan Greenspan as secretary of the treasury. Casey thought the ticket would guarantee a win. The moderates "all liked it because they thought they'd have Ford back in and they'd have their share of the gravy, wouldn't be shut out by the . . . crazies that were coming to town with Reagan," Allen recalled. "There was still a very low opinion of Ronald Reagan." So Reagan's men "were running back and forth to Ford's suite, trying to cobble this thing together until the very last minute." But as the media suggested that what Ford sought was a "co-presidency," Reagan developed second thoughts, and Ford became increasingly reluctant. "The important point to emerge, however, was that Ford's instincts always said 'No' and that never were any statutory or Constitutional authorities of the President even considered to be relinquished by Governor Reagan," Reagan's chief of staff, Edwin Meese, stressed to the campaign's executive advisory committee when he laid down the campaign's official version of events afterward. "The notion so popular in the Press of a so-called Co-Presidency wasn't contemplated." All involved had behaved well, including Henry Kissinger, "who had been painted in somewhat self-serving light by the Press" and was now "fully on board with the Reagan efforts." So far, so good. But even given the probability that Ford would turn Reagan down, the campaign had developed no alternative to Bush. Baker's support of the Panama Canal treaties made him anathema to conservatives: According to *Human Events*, at his "core" was "tapioca." And Ford liked Bush. So although Reagan found Bush unimpressive, and New Right chieftains met with Reagan to urge him to choose someone else, Reagan pleased Ford by awarding Bush the vice presidential nomination in Detroit. Although Carter had been ahead of Reagan in the polls since April, Reagan led the president by at least thirty points after the convention.[9]

The Ford and Reagan wings had come together, and veterans of the Ford administration poured into the Reagan campaign. But members of the New Right and the religious right and supply-siders felt left out in the cold. In an about-face after the convention, Viguerie insisted that conservatives must devote themselves to making Reagan president in 1980 and work to deny Bush the vice presidency in 1984. Howard Phillips's Conservative Caucus members embarrassed the GOP with petitions to Bush requesting his wholehearted and enthusiastic support for every plank in the 1980 Republican platform. Phillips complained to Meese that New Right leaders remained outside the corridors of power, a charge Phyllis Schlafly echoed when the campaign announced it was forming an advisory group on women's issues chaired by an ERA proponent. "The anti-ERA women won at the convention (generally they are the strong RR supporters)," one Reagan strategist said, and "we now appear to be giving away the store to the pro-ERA women." In New York, the Right to Life Party refused to endorse Reagan. "The pro-life constituents are furious at a series of perceived antagonistic moves by the campaign," another Reagan insider warned, which also annoyed Catholics. Further, the campaign brought aboard Robert Billings from the Moral Majority as a liaison to evangelicals, then, Billings complained plaintively, "killed" his Christians for Reagan-Bush stationery and his advisory council. And supply-siders grumbled that in its eagerness to satisfy Ford, Alan Greenspan, and other Republicans concerned with inflation and the deficit, the campaign had moved away from the gospel according to Jack Kemp, Arthur Laffer, and Jude Wanniski.[10]

Part of the 1980 Reagan campaign's flat-footedness could be, and was, blamed on William Casey. He was a good financial manager, whom the campaign badly needed, but he mumbled and lacked political expertise. Key supporters complained that calls to Casey went unanswered. Wanniski thought that Meese, Richard Wirthlin, Michael Deaver, Richard Allen, and Reagan's other closest advisers were "almost certainly" aware that Casey was "incompetent" but had decided to protect their own turfs by circling the wagons and pretending that he wasn't. Patrick Caddell told Carter that "John Sears devised a first rate strategy and like Bismarck was dropped," and now there was "no one around Reagan who has the ability to formulate a first class strategy." There was constant sniping between campaign headquarters in Virginia and those campaigning for Reagan on the ground, which was leaked to the press. As one reporter said, Reagan, the former actor, responded well to a good director, and Casey's lack of control jeopardized the candidate.[11]

Partly because of that and partly out of eagerness to reassure those who felt sidelined by his campaign, Reagan made numerous errors. "The strategy from the Convention until mid-September was to appeal to the Republican/conservative political base," Wirthlin recalled, before he tacked toward the middle to win over "soft" Anderson supporters, moderates, and independents and sewed together both groups in a coalition. Reagan overdid the shout-out to conservatives. First, after the *New York Times* reported that the Ku Klux Klan had applauded his platform as one that "could have been written by a Klansman," and despite the fact that he had repudiated the Klan's endorsement, the Republican served red meat to a white crowd at Mississippi's Neshoba County Fair on August 3, 1980, by assuring his audience that he believed in "states' rights" and would return power to the states and local government. Reagan was indeed a longtime supporter of states' rights in many different contexts. "I happen to be one who cheers on and supports the 'Sagebrush Rebellion,'" he said in Salt Lake City of the western states' efforts to win back more than half a billion acres of public land from the federal government. But in Mississippi he seemed to be blending "conservatism, racism, and antigovernment populism." Moreover, Neshoba County Fairground was just five miles from the site of the murder of three civil rights workers by law enforcement officials and Klansmen in 1964. A firestorm ensued.[12]

Next, as Bush and Richard Allen set off to Beijing on a mission designed specifically to reassure the Chinese that Reagan would not destroy the newly created relationship with China, but would not abandon Taiwan, Reagan spoke of his desire to reestablish the official American diplomatic relationship with Taiwan, though the Taiwanese themselves, who were rooting for Reagan, had specifically requested that he avoid the issue. Then Reagan appeared to blame pollution on plants and trees. Then he inserted a reference to the Vietnam War as "a noble cause" in a speech to the Veterans of Foreign Wars. Anthony Dolan, a campaign staffer who specialized in attacks on Carter, urged: "Let's say that after the [e]lection. Reagan's strongest negatives are those who believe he is a war monger." Then, at month's end, Reagan endorsed conservative evangelicals at a conference on Christianity and politics at which a leading Baptist reported that "God Almighty does not hear the prayers of a Jew." Reagan also said that "recent discoveries" had called the theory of evolution into question. Then he announced that Carter had "created a severe Depression," though Reagan's own economists acknowledged that the country was experiencing a "recession." Then, when Reagan went to Detroit in September to rally blue-collar whites, he mentioned that Carter had opened his general election campaign in a city in Alabama that, the Republican said wrongly, "gave birth to and is the parent body of the Ku Klux Klan." Dolan told Casey that the campaign plane was "an unguided missile. Everytime it goes out there is an explosion."[13]

Though the Georgians again responsible for the president's strategy all had agreed "that you must avoid at all costs the temptation to be personal or strident in dealing with Reagan," Carter succumbed. At first he had left the race issue to surrogates like cabinet member Patricia Harris, an African American, who said she saw "the specter" of the "white sheets" of the Ku Klux Klan "behind Ronald Reagan." After Reagan's Neshoba County Fair address, Carter sprang. Speaking in Atlanta to Martin Luther King and other African American leaders on September 16, after Reagan had been forced to retract his remarks about the Klan's birthplace, the president noted "the stirrings of hate and the rebirth of code words like 'States rights'" in the campaign. "Hatred" and "[R]acism" had "no place" in the United States, Carter stressed. The president said slyly—and accurately—that the Reagan campaign had muzzled its candidate to prevent him from speaking out about the Klan, evolution, or China. After suggesting that a Republican victory would turn back the clock on race relations, the president asked his audience to study the Republican platform and to remember Martin Luther King, Jr.'s assassination. "[I]t's going to be hard for the people to understand what this election is about unless you tell them."[14]

As Dolan griped to Meese, Reagan's forces did not even demand an apology, and the networks initially paid little attention to presidential demagoguery. Did the Reagan campaign expect reporters to do its work? (Like the Carter campaign, its Republican counterpart believed itself the victim of media mistreatment.) "We are blowing the opportunity to turn this incredible smear to our advantage. We should be ashamed of ourselves. We're a disgrace."[15]

But even after Dolan and others had stirred the pot and the media had begun to assail Carter for "running mean," the president refused to relent. On September 22, the day that war broke out between Iran and Iraq, Carter pledged the United States to neutrality and said at two campaign stops that the election would help decide "whether we have war or peace." While Democratic and Republican presidents alike historically preferred diplomacy to force, Carter contended, "Governor Reagan, on the other hand, when he's seen trouble spots around the world, is advocating sending in American military forces, in North Korea, in Ecuador, in Cuba, Cyprus, the Middle East, Rhodesia, Angola, Pakistan" and would "start a nuclear arms race as a trump card to be played against the Soviet Union." According to Carter, the election would also determine "whether or not this America will be unified or, if I lose the election, whether Americans might be separated, black from white, Jew from Christian, North from South, rural from urban." Carter insiders acknowledged later that he was damaging his last positive advantage, his reputation as a "nice guy."[16]

But he was narrowing the gap between himself and Reagan. Polls continued to demonstrate the public's disdain for Carter's presidency, but John Anderson's decline in them decided some against spending a vote on him. Beset by misgivings that Reagan was an idiot and ideologue, many seemed to be contemplating a return to the Democratic fold.[17]

Reagan continued to do poorly. Once he and his wife decided to bring Stu Spencer on the campaign plane to keep the candidate under control (despite the fact that Spencer had worked for Ford in 1976 and publicly referred to Reagan as "old foot-in-the-mouth"), the gaffes lessened. But now a muted Reagan talked repeatedly, and apparently vainly, of his California gubernatorial record as proof he could be president of all the people and stressed his abhorrence of war. "We are getting bombed on the 'war monger issue' and all we are doing to counter it, so far as I can see, is use the word 'peace' in ever more improbable contexts in speeches," a staffer grumbled. Wirthlin's polling still indicated that Americans found Reagan "dangerous and uncaring": Voters feared Reagan's finger on the nuclear button and thought he lacked compassion for minorities, women, and the elderly. Even the Soviets seemed to view Carter as preferable. On October 14, Carter moved past Reagan in the polls.[18]

When the race had been going well, the Reagan campaign had insisted that any presidential election debate had to include Anderson. That guaranteed that Reagan and Carter would not confront each other because the Democrats insisted that the independent lacked sufficient support to be viable. Now, however, as Republican strategists recognized, Anderson's campaign was "dying," and Reagan was in trouble. At Reagan campaign headquarters, sentiment built for a debate between Reagan and Carter. Ever doubtful of their candidate, despite Reagan's more than adequate debate performance during primary season, some considered one risky. But increasingly, a debate seemed essential. As Richard Nixon straightforwardly, if tactlessly, informed Reagan on October 22, 1980, "The four principal needs now are: 1) to reassure possible Reagan voters that he is not an ogre, an imbecile, or one who will blunder us into war; 2) to continue the erosion of Carter's 'good guy' and 'trustworthy and true' public image; 3) to remind the voters of what a disaster the Carter presidency has been, for them personally, and for the country; and 4) to give the voters not only a negative reason to vote against Carter."[19]

Reagan satisfied those needs six days later in his debate with Carter six days before the election. (He had the help of notes about the president's debate strategy "provided by a very reliable source who has intimate connections to a Carter debate staffer." Possibly, a Reagan aide was romancing someone in the president's campaign, and given the quantity of material provided, additional moles probably existed.) Carter was unable to cast the Republican as a threat to peace and became a laughingstock when he suggested that he had learned that "nuclear weaponry and the control of nuclear arms" were the most important election issues because his thirteen-year-old daughter, Amy, had told him so. By contrast, Reagan seemed reasonable and commanding as he hammered away at the president's economic policy, defended Kemp-Roth, fended off insinuations that he would endanger Medicare or Social Security, and asked voters whether they were better off than they had been four years earlier. Traditionally, the economy had been a Democratic issue. No longer. Carter's surge dissipated.[20]

Now the Reagan campaign need only worry that the president would dramatically secure the hostages' return. But the Reaganites had laid the groundwork for that contingency by warning voters to expect an "October surprise" with respect to the hostages, and the president could not produce one. (Conspiracy theorists debate to this day whether Casey arranged a "surprise" of his own and secretly promised that the United States would sell weapons to Iran if the hostages' release was delayed until Reagan became president.)[21]

In the end all Carter won was a reputation for nastiness. Like those closest to me, many rejected him by voting for someone else or not voting at all. Turnout in 1980 was the lowest since 1924.

"How sweet it is," crowed *Human Events*. "They said he was too old, that he couldn't match wits with the President, that he was the 'weakest' of all the Republican primary candidates that he was 'too conservative.'" But Reagan had proved them wrong, and the changes in the Senate had dropped liberal Democrats "like flies." From the perspective of conservatives, Carter's 1976 presidential win was aberrant. In exulting that "The Liberal Establishment Has Been Overthrown," a frequent contributor to *National Review* claimed that Goldwater had launched the conservative revolution and that by 1972, when Nixon demolished McGovern, it had spread throughout the country. Only Watergate had enabled Carter to become president. "Essentially an interim figure, he brought the South back into the Democratic Party for one last hurrah—a sort of historical freak." With Reagan as engineer, however, "the anti-liberal revolution got back on the tracks."[22]

Experts today disagree about the extent to which Reagan's victory represented a repudiation of Carter or a triumph of conservatism. As a historian and a liberal I give greater weight to the former than the latter. We do well to remember that before the November 1979 hostage crisis breathed life into Carter's presidency, his political future was bleak. Moreover, as political scientist Andrew Busch pointed out, "Even in the Senate, not all liberal Democrats lost; not all Democrats who lost were liberal; not all Republicans who won were conservative, and at least one Republican (Arlen Specter in Pennsylvania) was not as conservative as the Democrat he defeated." Nonetheless, the congressional results showed that voters were not simply repudiating Carter. While neither Reagan nor the conservative agenda received a mandate, "it would be obtuse to deny that there was a general conservative trend to the congressional results." It would be equally obtuse to deny that during the middle and late 1970s conservatives more effectively used conflicts over race, rights, region, religion, taxes, the market, the family, national security, the Middle East, détente, and American captivity and decline than moderates or liberals.[23]

IT IS EQUALLY CLEAR that the conservative coalition was fragile. Reagan had barely been elected before some in it were grousing that they had been abandoned. According to Richard Viguerie, the transition team had not even returned Jerry Falwell's telephone calls since the election. "Never mind who supported Reagan in 1980," Viguerie said. "Who supported him for fifteen years before 1980?"[24]

This was revisionism. Falwell and the Moral Majority had indeed organized significant registration drives in the churches that, by Falwell's estimate, had "registered four million new voters who voted for the first time in their lives" and "activated another 10 million or so" who had been registered but sat out the past few elections "because of frustration." But the religious right had not settled on Reagan until 1979. The New Right had never done much for Reagan and continued to complain about him, all the while insisting that it had catapulted him to power. Within a month of the inauguration, *Conservative Digest* had denounced the president's appointment of James Baker as chief of staff, Nixon-Ford "retreads," Kissinger protégés, and even veterans of the Carter administration. It complained about the shortage of "Reaganites in the Reagan Administration."[25]

The first year of Reagan's administration brought conservatives other disappointments. Reagan's 1981 tax cut was quite popular with supply-siders, as well as members of the New Right and the religious right, though it was not as large as they had hoped. But then the president fulfilled a campaign promise to appoint a woman to the Supreme Court designed to reassure women of his commitment to gender equality. Conservatives rightly suspected that Sandra Day O'Connor would not prove a secure vote against abortion. Her nomination reflected the White House's "growing attitude of indifference" to New Right and religious right objectives, they complained. Passage of the tax cut had cleared "the way for Congress to take up the 'social issues' but there are those who want our issues to remain on the 'back burner' indefinitely." Jerry Falwell's chief lieutenant told the White House that Moral Majority members were restive and that when he lectured around the country, liberals teased him for falling in behind Reagan's economic program without pressing harder for legislation to end abortion. And Reagan's own Secretary of the Interior, conservative icon James Watt, declared the Sagebrush Rebellion over: "I couldn't afford to have what I'd helped to create eat me." More accurately, in the words of one historian, the Sagebrush Rebellion had "faded quite unspectacularly."[26]

Had Reagan turned into another Nixon? Forty-five conservative leaders gathered in Washington to evaluate the administration's first year and signed a statement drafted by M. Stanton Evans. "Co-signers range across the board spectrum of conservatism—from New Right to neo-conservative to Old Right," a White House aide wrote James Baker. "Their theme is one of deep disappointment with the Administration's recent performance in virtually all areas—economy, foreign affairs, defense, social issues and personnel matters." Although reporters had stressed conservative anger at the administration, participants "had told us that the general mood was actually one of sorrow and disillusionment." Neoconservatives complained that they had positions in the administration but little influence. Everyone else grumbled that he or she did not even have a job.[27]

Nineteen eighty-two brought fresh wounds. Reagan's State Department talked of curtailing arms sales to Taiwan. The president responded to the budgetary deficits that supply-side skeptics had predicted by promoting an enormous tax increase that scaled back his 1981 tax cut. Though Reagan called for overturning *Roe v. Wade* when he was warned that "we are in a critical moment in the relationship between the President and prolife activists," his appeal went nowhere. He also proposed legislation that would deny tax exemptions to private schools that practiced racial discrimination. White House staffers reported that the right's Senate stalwarts Orrin Hatch and Strom Thurmond were "livid" about the school legislation and that the situation fueled "the fires of those who claim that the non-Reaganites have taken control of things." Even *National Review* became uneasy.[28]

"Has Ronald Reagan Deserted Conservatives?" *Conservative Digest* asked an assortment of neoconservative, conservative, New Right, religious right, and supply-sider leaders. Most condemned the president's record on economic policy and his failure to address family issues and wanted him to take a stronger stance against the Soviet Union. Richard Viguerie sent the president a copy of the issue. "He tried to write in sorrow, not anger about my betrayal of the conservative cause," Reagan noted in his diary. "He used crocodile tears for ink."[29]

Many conservatives lost heart. Though Reagan kept Falwell aboard by blandishment, fundamentalist Bob Jones jumped ship after sending the president a blistering 1983 letter alleging that Reagan had "betrayed, deceived and used" Christians. When the president reacted calmly after the Soviets shot down KAL Flight 007, which had been en route from New York to Seoul, and signed into law legislation making Martin Luther King's birthday a federal holiday, the New Right was alarmed.

"You don't run against a sitting president easily," Viguerie told *Newsweek*, "but we're looking."[30]

The search, of course, if ever it was serious, went nowhere. Reagan's antagonist in 1984, former Vice President Walter Mondale, lost in a landslide. The Democratic Party had not recovered from the Carter years, which were to haunt it for decades. In Reagan's second term, both the New Right and the religious right developed financial problems, and the religious right became mired in scandal.

That did not halt conservative complaints about the president. What had Reagan accomplished in his eight years? Viguerie asked. As president "he proclaimed the passing of the 'evil empire' . . . picked supporters of détente for the Cabinet . . . bailed out Soviet agriculture . . . bailed out international banks that lent money to anti-American countries . . . and approved some of the biggest taxes in history." (The White House was just as contemptuous of the New Right: One aide called Viguerie and Paul Weyrich "professional bellyachers" who had given up on Reagan "the day after he was inaugurated.") Neoconservative Irving Kristol professed not to be disappointed because he had never had high expectations in an op-ed entitled "The Reagan Revolution that Never Was."[31]

It turned out that Reagan himself was not "a Reaganite." In this sense, the right's lionization of him at his death was surprising. Perhaps it had learned the valuable lesson taught by the contrast between Reagan's conservative rhetoric and pragmatism. In politics, appearances matter more than reality. Moreover, legends can be useful.

Further, Reagan had inspired many Americans. Just before the election of 1980 a columnist had wrongly predicted that the winner would be "a leader without followers" and that Americans would refuse the new president authority. The day that Congress approved Reagan's 1981 tax cut, a Texas Democrat paid "rueful tribute to Reagan's gifts of political salesmanship by remarking, 'I sure hope he doesn't go on television to promote the elimination of fucking.'" Reasonable people disagree about the directions in which he took the country. But few will dispute that Reagan led it. By assuming command, he ended the seventies.[32]

NOTES

PROLOGUE

1 The translation is from the New Revised Standard Version of the Bible, which Maranatha uses. I have relied on a videotape of Carter's lesson, "Risk Your Routine," July 16, 2000.
2 The translation is from the King James Bible. A portion of "Prayer Explosion in These Last Days," July 23, 2000, is available at http://trbc.org/new/sermons.php?url=20000723.
3 Alonzo Hamby, *Liberalism and Its Challengers: From Roosevelt to Bush*, 2d ed. (New York: Oxford University Press, 1992), 339 ("Roosevelt of the Right").
4 Alan Brinkley, *The End of Reform: New Deal Liberalism in Recession and War* (New York: Alfred A. Knopf, 1995); Jordan Schwartz, *Liberal: Adolf A. Berle and the Vision of an American Era* (New York: Free Press 1987); Laura Kalman, *Abe Fortas: A Biography* (New Haven: Yale University Press, 1990); Tony Freyer, *Hugo L. Black and the Dilemma of American Liberalism* (Glenview, Ill.: Scott, Foresman/Little, Brown, 1990); William Chafe, *Never Stop Running: Allard Lowenstein and the Struggle to Save American Liberalism* (New York: Basic Books, 1993); Bruce Schulman, *Lyndon B. Johnson and American Liberalism: A Brief Biography with Documents* (Boston: Bedford/St. Martin's, 1995); Steven Gillon, *The Democrats' Dilemma: Walter F. Mondale and the Liberal Legacy* (New York: Columbia University Press, 1992); David Farber, *The Age of Great Dreams: America in the 1960s* (New York: Hill and Wang, 1994), 105 ("an understanding"). For these different interepretations, see, e.g., Allen Matusow, *The Unraveling of America: A History of Liberalism in the 1960s* (New York: Harper & Row, 1984); Rick Perlstein, *Nixonland: The Rise of a President and the Fracturing of America* (New York: Scribner, 2008); Thomas Sugrue, *The Origins of the Urban Crisis: Race and Inequality in Postwar Detroit* (Princeton: Princeton University Press, 1996).
5 See, e.g., William Rusher, *The Rise of the Right* (New York: William Morrow, 1984), 161 ("watershed"); Lee Edwards, *The Conservative Revolution: The Movement that Remade America* (New York: Free Press, 1999), 141. Steven Hayward provides a fascinating account of the history of both liberalism and conservatism together from the conservative perspective in *The Age of Reagan: The Fall of the Old Liberal Order, 1964–1980* (Roseville, Calif.: Forum, 2001).
6 Seventies scholarship has become a cottage industry, and as my citations show, I have made grateful use of it, as well as the memoirs of participants, contemporary media coverage, and manuscript collections.
7 Statement of Howard Phillips, Conservatives Should Help Remove Nixon, July 30, 1974, Box 71, File 9, William Rusher Papers, Library of Congress; Robert Mason, *Richard Nixon and the Quest for a New Majority* (Chapel Hill: University of North Car-

olina Press, 2004), 182 ("patriotism"); David Greenberg provides an excellent history of historians' depictions of Nixon as liberal in "Richard the Bleeding Hearted," *Reviews in American History*, 30 (2002): 156–67.

8 See, e.g., Lisa McGirr, *Suburban Warriors: The Origins of the New American Right* (Princeton: Princeton University Press, 2001); Michelle Nickerson, "Domestic Threats: Women, Gender and Conservatism in Cold War Los Angeles, 1945–1966" (Ph.D. Dissertation, Yale, 2003); Darren Dochuk, "From Bible Belt to Sunbelt: Plain Folk Religion, Grassroots Politics, and the Southernization of Southern California, 1939–1969" (Ph.D. Dissertation, Notre Dame, 2005); Kevin Kruse, *White Flight: Atlanta and the Making of Modern Conservatism* (Princeton: Princeton University Press, 2005); Matthew Lassiter, *The Silent Majority: Suburban Politics in the Sunbelt South* (Princeton: Princeton University Press, 2006). And see, e.g., in addition to the sources cited in notes 5 and 6, John Judis, *William F. Buckley, Jr.: Patron Saint of the Conservatives* (New York: Simon & Schuster, 1988); Robert Goldberg, *Barry Goldwater* (New Haven: Yale University Press, 1995); Mary Brennan, *Turning Right in the 1960s: The Conservative Capture of the GOP* (Chapel Hill: University of North Carolina Press, 1995); George Nash, *The Conservative Intellectual Movement in America Since 1945* (Wilmington, Del.: Intercollegiate Studies Institute, 1998); Godfrey Hodgson, *The World Turned Right Side Up: A History of the Conservative Ascendancy in America* (Boston: Houghton Mifflin, 1996); Rick Perlstein, *Before the Storm: Barry Goldwater and the Unmaking of the American Consensus* (New York: Hill and Wang, 2001); David Farber and Jeff Roche, eds., *The Conservative Sixties* (New York: Peter Lang, 2003); Donald Critchlow, *Phyllis Schlafly and Grassroots Conservatism: A Woman's Crusade* (Princeton: Princeton University Press, 2005); Donald Critchlow, *The Conservative Ascendancy: How the GOP Right Made Political History* (Cambridge: Harvard University Press, 2007); Jeff Roche, ed., *The Political Culture of the New West* (Lawrence: University Press of Kansas, 2008); Joseph Lowndes, *From the New Deal to the New Right: Race and the Southern Origins of Modern Conservatism* (New Haven: Yale University Press, 2008); Patrick Allitt, *The Conservatives: Ideas & Personalities Throughout American History* (New Haven: Yale University Press, 2009). Once again, it has become fashionable to proclaim the Republican Party an "endangered species." See e.g., the cover of *Time* (May 18, 2009); Jeffrey Bell, "Kemp Brought America Back from the 1970s," May 3, 2009, http://www.newsmax.com/newsfront/jack_kemp_jeffrey_bell/2009/05/03/210151.html?s=al&promo_code=7F0D-1 ("Think"). Richard Viguerie, for example, exhorted conservatives to oppose the nomination of Justice Souter's replacement, Justice Sotomayor, by reminding them that even if they lost, the confirmation battle could do for them what the Panama Canal treaty fight did for them in the 1970s. "Conservatives Take on Potential Scotus Nominees," *Talk of the Nation*, May 20, 2009, http://www.npr.org/templates/story/story.php?storyId=104349694. For compelling arguments in favor of the "long 1970s" see, e.g., Bruce Schulman, *The Seventies: The Great Shift in American Culture, Society, and Politics* (New York: Free Press, 2001), 1, 254 (1968–84) and Philip Jenkins, *Decade of Nightmares: The End of the Sixties and the Making of Eighties America* (New York: Oxford University Press, 2006), 5, 273 (1975–86).

CHAPTER 1 | THE NIGHTMARE CONTINUES

1 Jordan Miller, "Why Is Everyone Taking the LSAT?," http://economics.stanford.edu/files/Theses/Theses_2004/Miller.pdf, Figure 1; "An Awful Lot of Lawyers Involved," *Time* (July 9, 1973).

2 Robert Dallek, *Nixon and Kissinger: Partners in Power* (New York: HarperCollins, 2007), 609.

3 Barry Werth, *31 Days: Gerald Ford, the Nixon Pardon and a Government in Crisis* (New York: Viking, 2006), 30 ("fucking"); Ken Gormley, *Archibald Cox: Conscience of a Nation* (Reading, Mass.: Perseus, 1997), 360 ("real").

4 Dallek, *Nixon and Kissinger*, at 601–08; *U.S. v. Nixon*, 418 U.S. 683 (1974).

5 Gerald R. Ford, *A Time to Heal: The Autobiography of Gerald R. Ford* (New York: Harper & Row, 1979), 39.

6 Ibid., at 46–48; James Cannon, *Time and Chance: Gerald Ford's Appointment with History* (New York: HarperCollins, 1994), 14 ("Trust").

7 Richard Reeves, *A Ford, Not a Lincoln* (New York: Harcourt, Brace & Jovanovich, 1975), 6.

8 Betty Ford with Chris Chase, *The Times of My Life* (New York: Ballantine Books, 1979), 61, 132.

9 Tip O'Neill, *Man of the House* (New York: St. Martin's Press, 1987), 314 (Ford's plan); Cannon, *Time and Chance*, at 205, 229–31 (choice, investigation); Robert Hartmann, *Palace Politics: An Inside Account of the Ford Years* (New York: McGraw-Hill, 1980), 73 (FBI file); Ford, *A Time to Heal*, at 112.

10 Ford, *A Time to Heal*, at 53, 56 (rank); Hartmann, *Palace Politics*, at 30, 279 (Johnson, Sadat); Tom DeCair to Richard Cheney, January 21, 1975, Box 132, Donald Rumsfeld, 1/75–6/75 (1), Ron Nessen Papers, Gerald R. Ford Library ("judge-uh-ment") (unless otherwise indicated, all archival collections cited in this chapter are in the Ford Library); " 'The Fords from Grand Rapids,' " *Nation* (August 31, 1974) (Mansfield).

11 Arthur Schlesinger, Jr., *The Imperial Presidency* (New York: Popular Library, 1973).

12 Ford, Remarks on Taking the Oath of Office, August 9, 1974, americanpresidency.org, Hartmann, *Palace Politics*, at 159; Elizabeth Drew, *Washington Journal: The Events of 1973–1974* (New York: Random House, 1975), 416.

13 Schlesinger, *The Imperial Presidency*, at 214 (Buckingham Palace); H. R. Haldeman, *The Ends of Power* (New York: Dell, 1978), 110 ("soup"); Ford, *A Time to Heal*, at 127, 140–41; *New Yorker* (September 9, 1974).

14 Address to a Joint Session of the Congress, August 12, 1974, americanpresidency.org.

15 "Gerald Ford: The Man, the Record, the Prospect," *ADA World* (August–September 1974); Reeves, *A Ford, Not a Lincoln*, at 68 (secretary; Meany); "Ford Again Backs Rights Proposal," *New York Times*, August 23, 1974.

16 William Timmons to Robert Hartmann, August 9, 1974, Box 13, August 9–14, 1974, William Timmons Papers (reporting on House Minority Leader John Rhodes and Senate Minority Leader Hugh Scott); William Timmons to Ford, August 14, 1974, ibid. (reporting Scott's views on amnesty).

17 President's News Conference of January 31, 1973, americanpresidency.org.

18 Remarks to the Veterans of Foreign Wars Annual Convention, August 19, 1974, americanpresidency.org; Ford, *A Time to Heal*, at 141–42 ("conditional," "earn"); Geoff Shepard to General Haig, August 21, 1974, Box 1, Kenneth Cole, 8/8/74–8/25/74, Alexander Haig Papers (reporting on reaction to speech).

19 Ford, *A Time to Heal*, at 142–43 ("not yet"); Americans for Democratic Action (ADA), Board Meeting, September 14–16, 1974, Box 1: November 22–24, 1974, ADA Papers, State Historical Society of Wisconsin, and "President Rockefeller," *ADA World* (October 1974) (the ADA objected to Rockefeller's gifts to politicians, such as Henry Kissinger; his response to the 1971 Attica prison uprising; his social service and drug use policies, and his hawkishness on national defense, and it maintained that the Rockefeller family's wealth would create conflicts of interest for him); John Greene, *The Presidency of Gerald R. Ford* (Lawrence: University Press of Kansas, 1995), 30 (slush fund); Cannon, *Time and Chance*, at 423–25 ("weak").

20 Hugh Morrow interview with President Ford, Box 34, James Cannon Papers (Rockefeller's shadow); "Ford Discloses He Expects to Ask Nomination in '76," *New York Times*, August 22, 1974.

21 " 'The Sun Is Shining Again,' " *Newsweek* (August 26, 1974) (quoting Mansfield); "TRB: Postmortem," *New Republic* (August 24, 1974). But see Edward Berkowitz, *Something Happened: A Political and Cultural Overview of the Seventies* (New York: Columbia University Press, 2006), 74 (suggesting that Ford's honeymoon with Congress and the press was not as rosy as I have suggested).

22 James Mann, *Rise of the Vulcans: The History of Bush's War Cabinet* (New York: Viking, 2004), 1–20; Ford, Notes, Box 9, FG Cabinet Meetings, 8/74–1/75, Handwriting File ("Reaffirm"); Ford, *A Time to Heal*, at 147–48 ("grateful," "purge").

23 Hartmann, *Palace Politics*, at 180, 232; Robert Hartmann, "The Loyalists and the Praetorian Guard," *The Ford Presidency: Twenty-two Intimate Perspectives of Gerald R. Ford*, ed. Kennedy Thompson (Lanham, Md.: University Press of America, 1988), 89, 96–98.

24 Ford, *A Time to Heal*, at 164.

25 Don R, n.d. [August 1974], Box 30, Nixon Papers—General (1), Philip Buchen Papers ("Get Nixon"); Philip Areeda to Ford, December 2, 1974, Box 24, Nixon Papers—General (1), John Marsh Papers ("Quite apart").

26 Werth, *31 Days*, at 71–80; Hartmann, *Palace Politics*, at 244–46; "White House Bars Withdrawal Now of Nixon Records," *New York Times*, August 17, 1974.

27 "Presidential Clemency; Ford Says He Will Decide Nixon Case After Legal Process Runs Its Course," *New York Times*, August 29, 1974.

28 Ford, *A Time to Heal*, at 4–13 ("President"); Werth, *31 Days*, at 204–05.

29 "Ford Aides Silent on Link of Pardon and Nixon Health," *New York Times*, September 14, 1974 (reporting that Nixon's son-in-law David Eisenhower had told Ford that Nixon was alternately despairing and euphoric); Henry Kissinger, *Years of Renewal* (New York: Simon & Schuster, 1999), 39; Garment, "Annals of Law: The Hill Case," *New Yorker* (April 17, 1989): 90, 107–08.

30 Leonard Garment to Philip Buchen, August 28, 1974, Box 32, Nixon Pardon—General (2), Buchen Papers; Garment, "Annals of Law," at 108 ("It's all set").

31 "Mr. Ford's Economics . . . ," *New York Times*, August 20, 1974; Ford, *A Time to Heal*, at 157–59; President's News Conference of August 28, 1974, americanpresidency.org.

32 Philip Buchen, "Reflections on a Politician's President," *The Ford Presidency*, at 27, 38–39; see also Ford, *A Time to Heal*, at 159–64; Personal Memorandum of Counsel to President [ca. September 3, 1974], Box 32, Nixon Pardon—General (2), Buchen Papers ("accomplished").

33 Leon Jaworski, *The Right and the Power: The Prosecution of Watergate* (New York: Pocket Books, 1977), 268, 290–92.

34 Ford, *A Time to Heal*, at 159, 173 ("endless," "public"); "Ford, Nixon Sustained Friendship for Decades," *Washington Post*, December 29, 2006 ("I," "And"); Hartmann, "The Loyalists and the Praetorian Guard," *The Ford Presidency*, at 105 ("selfish").

35 Stanley Kutler, *The Wars of Watergate: The Last Crisis of Richard Nixon* (New York: Knopf, 1990), 563, and see Benton Becker, "The History of the Nixon Pardon," *Cumberland Law Review*, 30 (2000): 31–49, and John Greene, *The Limits of Power: The Nixon and Ford Administrations* (Bloomington: Indiana University Press, 1992), 196–200.

36 Ford, *A Time to Heal*, at 166; "For Ford, Pardon Decision Was Always Clear-Cut," *New York Times*, December 29, 2006; *Burdick v. U.S.*, 236 U.S. 79, 94 (1915); "Ford's Long Shadow," *Newsweek* (January 8, 2007) ("loyal," "transmitted").

37 Ford, *The Times of My Life*, at 70.

38 "The Fallout from Ford's Rush to Pardon," *Time* (September 23, 1974); Weekend News Review, September 9, 1974, Box 171, Pardon Statement, Robert Hartmann Papers.

39 President Gerald Ford and Congressman John Lewis Receive 2001 Profile in Courage Award, May 21, 2001, http://www.jfklibrary.org/JFK+Library+and+Museum/News+and+Press/President+Gerald+Ford+and+Congressman+Lewis+Receive+2001+Profile+in+Courage+Award.htm; "For Ford, Pardon Decision Was Always Clear-Cut," *New York Times*, December 29, 2006; "The 38th President," *Newsweek* (January 8, 2007).

40 "Deteriorating Trust in Government—What Was the Impact of Watergate?," Box 32, Nixon Pardon—General (3), Buchen Papers; Cannon, *Time and Chance*, at 386 ("immense shock").

41 Jerald terHorst, *Gerald Ford and the Future of the Presidency* (New York: Joseph Okapu,

1974), 238 (quoting columnist Mary McGrory); Reeves, *A Ford, Not a Lincoln*, at 93 ("muffins").

42 Remarks on Signing a Proclamation Granting Pardon to Richard Nixon, September 8, 1974, americanpresidency.org (quotations); Press Conference, September 16, 1974, ibid. ("heal").

43 "Has Ford Learned Lesson? Outrage over Pardon Shows Liberals Cannot Be Appeased," *Human Events* (September 21, 1974) (call); Carey McWilliams, "But Who Will Pardon Ford?," *Nation* (September 21, 1974) ("no crimes").

44 Jaworski, *The Right and the Power*, at 267–68.

45 "The Theology of Forgiveness," *Time* (September 23, 1974).

46 Statement of the Association of the Bar of the City of New York, Box 32, Nixon Pardon Correspondence (3) 174/09/30, Buchen Papers; Statement on Presidential Clemency and Pardons, September 11, 1974, americanpresidency.org.

47 Press Conference of Philip Buchen, September 8, 1974, Box 35, Nixon Pardon—Press Conference (1) 1974/09/08, Buchen Papers; "Historian Wins Long Battle to Hear More Nixon Tapes," *New York Times*, April 13, 1996.

48 H. Res. 1370, September 17, 1974, 93d Congress, 2d Session; Ken Lazarus to Phil Buchen, October 14, 1974, Box 25, Nixon, Richard—Pardon: House Subcommittee Hearing—General, Marsh Papers ("opportunity," "mischief").

49 "Statements and Responses to Questions from Members of the House Judiciary Committee Concerning the Pardon of Richard Nixon," October 17, 1974, americanpresidency.org; Ken Lazarus to Phil Buchen, October 17, 1974, Box 34, Nixon Pardon, Hungate Subcommittee—General, Buchen Papers.

50 Ford, *A Time to Heal*, at 173, 179 ("bandage;" "salt"); Jerald terHorst, "President Ford and the Media," *The Ford Presidency*, at 209, 214.

51 See, e.g., Hartmann, "The Loyalists and the Praetorian Guard," *The Ford Presidency*, at 100; terHorst, "President Ford and the Media," ibid., at 216; Kenneth Rush, "Ford and the Economy: National and International," ibid., at 41, 143; Charles E. Goodell, "Decision-making in the Ford Presidency," ibid., at 261, 263; "White House Watch: Settling In," *New Republic* (October 5, 1974) (reporting on terHorst column).

52 Remarks Announcing a Program for the Return of Vietnam Era Draft Evaders and Military Deserters, September 16, 1974, americanpresidency.org; "Analysis" (of August 30, 1974, letter from James R. Schlesinger and William B. Saxbe to the President), Box 5, Clemency Program—General (1), Buchen Papers; "Limited Program, Limited Response," *Time* (September 30, 1974) ("gentle"); Lawrence Baskir and William Strauss, *Chance and Circumstance: The Draft, the War, and the Vietnam Generation* (New York: Vintage Books, 1978), 214 ("appeared"); Goodell, "Decision-making in the Ford Presidency," at 264.

53 "Urban League Head Asks U.S. to Grant Total Amnesty to Veterans of Vietnam," *New York Times*, July 28, 1975; Report on the Presidential Clemency Board's Operations, Box 102, Clemency Program—GAO Report, Buchen Papers; Baskir and Strauss, *Chance and Circumstance*, at 222–23 (describing the disappointment of the majority); "Four Members of Clemency Board Send Minority Report to White House," *New York Times*, September 20, 1975.

54 Remarks and a Question-and-Answer Session at the University of New Hampshire in Durham, February 8, 1976, americanpresidency.org (105,000, "tragic"); Baskir and Strauss, *Chance and Circumstance*, at 214–15 (Baskir and Strauss, however, said 350,000 were eligible, meaning that only 6 percent chose to participate, and at a news conference in May 1975, Ford estimated that 120,000 were eligible. President's News Conference of May 6, 1975, americanpresidency.org). And see "By Almost Any Standard, the Amnesty Plan Isn't Working," *New York Times*, October 27, 1974.

55 Ron Nessen, *It Sure Looks Different from the Inside* (Chicago: Playboy, 1978), 148.

56 "Calling Ed Levi," *Washington Post*, August 28, 2007 ("new").

57 "Mr. Dunlop for Labor," *Washington Post*, February 12, 1975.

58 "In 6 Months, Ford's Style Is Set," *New York Times*, February 23, 1975 ("tendency"); Greene, *The Limits of Power*, at 195 (quotation).

59 Nessen, *It Sure Looks Different*, at 29; "Landslide in the Making," *Time* (October 14, 1974) ("sorry").

60 Reeves, *A Ford, Not a Lincoln*, at 180 ("Dummy;" Bozo); "'Pure Prairie,'" *Nation*, December 14, 1974 ("revenge").

61 Julian Zelizer, *On Capitol Hill: The Struggle to Reform Congress and Its Consequences, 1948–2000* (Cambridge, U.K.: Cambridge University Press, 2004), 161; David Broder, *Changing of the Guard: Power and Leadership in America* (New York: Simon & Schuster, 1980), 349 (suburbs); Becky Norton to Clarke Reed, June 30, 1975, Box 49, File 18, American Conservative Union (ACU) Papers, Brigham Young University (reporting that "the Republican Party's fortunes are at an all-time low" and on governorships and state legislatures); "Dems Sweep Congress: Women, Blacks, Browns Make Big Gains," *ADA World* (November–December 1974).

62 "Hardly a Two-Party System," *Nation* (December 7, 1974); "Conservative Lawmakers Suffered Badly," *Human Events* (November 16, 1974); "Reagan Should Make Immediate '76 Bid," ibid.; ("precarious"); "Will the Republican Party Survive?," *National Review* (November 8, 1974); "The Electoral Disaster," ibid. (November 22, 1974); "Commentary: The GOP, Is There Still Hope for Republicans?" *Ripon Forum* (November 14, 1974); "Militant Feminists Find Friend at White House," *Human Events* (September 7, 1974) ("libbers"); "Has Ford Learned Lesson? Outrage over Pardon Shows Liberals Cannot Be Appeased," ibid. (September 21, 1974); ibid. "GOP Survival in Doubt: Is '72 Mandate Finished Under Ford?," *Human Events* (August 31, 1974) ("all smiles," "galling," "virtually").

63 Murray Rothbard, "A Strategy for the Right," *The Irrepressible Rothbard: The Rothbard-Rockwell Report; Essays of Murray N. Rothbard*, ed. Llewellyn Rockwell (Burlingame, Calif.: Center for Libertarian Studies, 2000), 3, 4; Kim Phillips-Fein, *Invisible Hands: The Making of the Conservative Movement from the New Deal to Reagan* (New York: W. W. Norton, 209), 3–15; Leo Ribuffo, *The Old Christian Right: The Protestant Far Right from the Great Depression to the Cold War* (Philadelphia: Temple University Press, 1983); Justus Doenecke, *Not to the Swift: The Old Isolationists in the Cold War Era* (Lewisburg, Pa.: Bucknell University Press, 1979), 25–32; James Patterson, *Congressional Conservatism and the New Deal: The Growth of the Conservative Coalition in Congress, 1933–1939* (Lexington: University Press of Kentucky, 1967).

64 Doenecke, *Not to the Swift*, at 62–69, 181–220; Felix Morley, *For the Record* (South Bend, Ind.: Regnery/Gateway, 1979), 436–37; Nash, *The Conservative Intellectual Movement in America*, at 3–29, 110, 118; John Judis, *William F. Buckley, Jr.: Patron Saint of the Conservatives* (New York: Simon & Schuster, 1988), 113 ("throwbacks").

65 Judis, *William F. Buckley, Jr.*, at 53, 77, 83, 114, 168, 118–19; Phillips-Fein, *Invisible Hands*, at 79–81 (financial support). See William F. Buckley, Jr., *God and Man at Yale* (Washington, D.C.: Regnery, 2002), 162, 175.

66 Judis, *William F. Buckley*, at 137–40, 160–61, 172–78, 197–200; Jonathan Schoenwald, *A Time for Choosing: The Rise of Modern American Conservatism* (New York: Oxford University Press, 2001), 62–99, 176–78 (Birch Society); Patrick Allitt, *The Conservatives: Ideas and Personalities Throughout American History* (New Haven: Yale University Press, 2009), 182 ("characteristic"); Jeffrey Hart, *The Making of the American Conservative Mind: National Review and Its Times* (Wilmington, Del.: ISI Books, 2005), 103 ("retarded"); Joseph Lowndes, *From the New Deal to the New Right: Race and the Origins of Modern Conservatism* (New Haven: Yale University Press, 2008), 48–54 (*National Review* rhetoric in 1950s); Nancy MacLean, *Freedom Is Not Enough: The Opening of the American Workplace* (Cambridge: Harvard University Press, 2005), 231–38 (change in racial rhetoric by the 1970s). For complaints by isolationists and libertarians about their exclusion and that of others from *National Review* circles, see Murray Rothbard, *The Betrayal of the American Right*, ed. Thomas Woods (Auburn, Ala.: Ludwig von Mises Institute, 2007), 147–72; for Buckley's reply, see William F. Buckley, Jr., "Murray Rothbard, RIP—Professor and Libertarian Party Founder," *National Review* (February 6, 1995).

67 Lee Edwards, *The Conservative Revolution: The Movement that Remade America* (New

York: Free Press, 1999), 91–94; Robert Goldberg, *Barry Goldwater* (New Haven: Yale University Press, 1995), 92–96; Robert Goldberg, "The Western Hero in Politics: Barry Goldwater, Ronald Reagan, and the Rise of the American Conservative Movement," *The Political Culture of the New West*, ed. Jeff Roche (Lawrence: University Press of Kansas, 2008), 13; Jeff Roche, "Cowboy Conservatism," *The Conservative Sixties*, ed. David Farber and Jeff Roche (New York: Peter Lang, 2003), 79, 84.

68 John Andrew, *The Other Side of the Sixties: Young Americans for Freedom and the Rise of Conservative Politics* (New Brunswick, N.J.: Rutgers University Press, 1997), 54–60.

69 Ibid., at 90 ("inseparable"); Judis, *William F. Buckley*, at 220–28; Goldberg, *Barry Goldwater*, at 181.

70 Minutes, Board of Directors Meeting, American Conservative Union, September 17, 1965, Box 20, File 18, ACU Papers ("savory"), and see Minutes, Box 20, File 12, December 18–19, 1965, ibid.; Schoenwald, *A Time for Choosing*, at 233–43.

71 Goldberg, *Barry Goldwater*, at 231–32 (quotation). But see Mary Brennan, "Winning the War/Losing the Battle: The Goldwater Presidential Campaign and Its Effects on the Evolution of Modern Conservatism," *The Conservative Sixties*, at 63, 72, for the contention that Goldwater's platform sidelined traditionalists, or social conservatives.

72 Raymond Wolters, "New Right," *American Conservatism: An Encyclopedia*, ed. Bruce Frohnen, Jeremy Beer, and Jeffrey Nelson (Wilmington, Del.: ISI Books, 2006), 624, 625 ("new New"); Alan Lichtman, *White Protestant Nation: The Rise of the American Conservative Movement* (New York: Atlantic Monthly Press, 2008), 308 (seventh); James Patterson, *Grand Expectations: The United States, 1945–1974* (New York: Oxford University Press, 1996), 558 ("first-class"); Richard Viguerie, "Ends and Means," *The New Right Papers*, ed. Robert Whitaker (New York: St. Martin's Press, 1982), 26, 29 ("many"); Paul Weyrich, "Blue Collar or Blue Blood? The New Right Compared with the Old Right," ibid., 49, 51 (ambition); Richard Viguerie and Lee Edwards: "Goldwater: Leader or Legend?," *Conservative Digest* (January 1976).

73 Richard Viguerie, *The New Right: We're Ready to Lead* (Falls Church, Va.: Viguerie Company, 1980), 26–27.

74 Nick Kotz, "King Midas of the New Right," *Atlantic* (November 1978) ("stamps"); Allen Crawford, *Thunder on the Right: The "New Right" and the Politics of Resentment* (New York: Pantheon, 1980), 51 ("Dear Friend," " 'you' ").

75 Viguerie, "Ends and Means," at 31 ("branches," "universities"); Crawford, *Thunder on the Right*, at 66–67.

76 Broder, *Changing of the Guard*, at 180.

77 George Michael, *Willis Carto and the American Far Right* (Gainesville: University Press of Florida, 2008), 62–73 (Liberty Lobby); Broder, *Changing of the Guard*, at 180–81 (Republican Study Committee); Howard Phillips, "A New Political Strategy for Conservatives," *Human Events* (October 19, 1974) ("capital city"); James C. Roberts, "CPAC over 30 Years: Conservatives Have Come a Long Way," February 3, 2003, http://www.humaneventsonline.com/article.php?id=272.

78 Donald Critchlow, "Think Tanks, Antitstatism, and Democracy: The Nonpartisan Ideal and Policy Research in the United States, 1913–1987," *The State and Social Investigation in Britain and the United States*, ed. Michael Lacey and Mary Furner (Cambridge, U.K.: Cambridge University Press, 1993), 279, 292 ("liberal"); Sidney Blumenthal, *The Rise of the Counter-Establishment: The Conservative Ascent to Political Power* (New York: Union Square, 2008), 40–45; Lee Edwards, *The Power of Ideas: The Heritage Foundation at 25 Years* (Ottawa: Jameson Books, 1997), 3–12.

79 "The First Lady of American Conservatism," *Conservative Digest* (September 1975); Phyllis Schlafly, *A Choice Not an Echo* (Alton, Ill.: Pere Marquette Press, 1964); Michelle Nickerson, "Domestic Threats: Women, Gender and Conservatism in Cold War Los Angeles, 1945–1966" (Ph.D. Dissertation, Yale, 2003), 3 ("children").

80 Phyllis Schlafly and Chester Ward, *Strike from Space: How the Russians May Destroy Us* (Alton, Ill.: Pere Marquette Press, 1965); *The Gravediggers* (Alton, Ill.: Pere Marquette Press, 1964); *The Betrayers* (Alton, Ill.: Pere Marquette Press, 1968); Donald

Critchlow, *Phyllis Schlafly and Grassroots Conservatism: A Women's Crusade* (Princeton: Princeton University Press, 2005), 142–61.

81 Lowndes, *From the New Deal to the New Right*, at 106–139 (discussing evolution of Nixon's rhetoric from 1964 to 1972); "A Declaration Pertaining to President Richard Nixon," Minutes, Board of Directors Meeting, American Conservative Union, September 19, 1971, Box 20, File 32, ACU Papers; "John M. Ashbrook" http://www.ashbrook.org ("presentation"); Critchlow, *Phyllis Schlafly and Grassroots Conservatism*, at 217.

82 Goldberg, *Barry Goldwater*, at 284–85, 308, 267; Judis, *William F. Buckley*, at 341.

83 Goldberg, *Barry Goldwater*, at 283 ("Mr. Clean"); Richard Cheney to Ford, November 13, 1975, Box 16, Barry Goldwater, Richard Cheney Papers; Allen Crawford, *Thunder on the Right* (New York: Pantheon, 1980), 114–17; Judis, *William F. Buckley*, at 369; Board of Directors Meeting, Minutes, September 22, 1974, Box 21, File 10, ACU Papers; Viguerie, *The New Right*, at 51; Werth, *31 Days*, at 339.

84 Kevin Phillips, *Post-Conservative America: People, Politics and Ideology in a Time of Crisis* (New York: Random House, 1982), 47.

85 Leo Ribuffo, "Conservatism and American Politics," *Journal of the Historical Society*, 3: 2 (Spring 2003): 163, 169; Ribuffo, Comment on Critchlow, Social Science History Association, October 25, 2008.

86 William F. Buckley, Jr., to M. Stanton Evans, August 12, 1975, Box 135, File 738, William F. Buckley, Jr. Papers, Yale University Archives ("bender"); "A Voice from Philistia," *National Review* (August 15, 1975); Becky Norton to Sarah Sipzer, August 7, 1975, Box 49, File 18, ACU Papers (Conservative Caucus); M. Stanton Evans to Fran Griffin, November 16, 1977, Box 104, File 24, ibid. ("Viguerie"); Phillips-Fein, *Invisible Hands*, at 173 (quoting Baroody); Blumenthal, *The Rise of the Counter-Establishment*, at 2. See also M. Stanton Evans to Members of the Board, n.d., Box 14, File 15, ACU Papers (attaching Phillips, "Notes on the New Right," June 25, 1976, and saying it "is one of a continuous series of negative comments about ACU from this and related sources"); Rolland Heaton, n.d., "To all of you at ACU," n.d., Box 49, File 18, ibid. (complaining that "you use our [supporters'] money to buy and mail duplicate sucker lists from dear honest Dickie boy, . . . the latest millionaire;" Norton's reply of October 23, 1975, ibid., simply denied that Viguerie then did ACU fund-raising). In 1979, Becky Norton Dunlop advised Congressman Robert Bauman to exclude Viguerie and Weyrich from an upcoming program. "Some of our Board members have very negative feelings about them." Dunlop to Bauman, December 5, 1979, Box 8, File 20, ibid.

87 Weyrich, "Blue Collar or Blue Blood," at 53; Larry Sabato, *PAC Power: Inside the World of Political Action Committees* (New York: W. W. Norton, 1984), 150 (quoting Terry Dolan on Republicans as "social club").

88 "From the Publisher," *Conservative Digest* (August 1975); Nick Thimmesch, "The Grass-Roots Dollar Chase—Ready on the Right," *New York* (June 9, 1975) ("In ten years").

89 Kiron Skinner, Annelise Anderson, and Martin Anderson, eds., *Reagan's Path to Victory: The Shaping of Ronald Reagan's Vision: Selected Writings* (New York: Free Press, 2004), iv; Jerry Jones to Donald Rumsfeld and Richard Cheney, September 26, 1975, http://www.ford.utexas.edu/library/exhibits/campaign/2jones.asp ("lightweight"); Ford, *A Time to Heal*, at 294, 346.

90 Gerard De Groot, "'A Goddamned Electable Person': Ronald Reagan and Student Unrest in California, 1966–1970," *Pacific Historical Review*, 65 (February 1996): 107, 111 (Berkeley); Kurt Schuparra, *Triumph of the Right: The Rise of the California Conservative Movement 1945–1966* (Armonk, N.Y.: M. E. Sharpe, 1998), 138 ("extremists"); Matthew Dallek, *The Right Moment: Ronald Reagan's First Victory and the Decisive Turning Point in American Politics* (New York: Oxford University Press, 2000), x, 157 (law and order, Brown-Yorty tensions); Lou Cannon, *Governor Reagan: His Rise to Power* (New York: Public Affairs, 2003), 208–14, 334, 348–61, 388 (record as governor); Lisa McGirr, *Suburban Warriors: The Origins of the New Right* (Princeton: Princeton

University Press, 2001), 201 ("white conservative," quoting Reagan strategist Stu Spencer); Barry Goldwater, "Reagan's Calif. Victory Vindicates 1964 Platform," *Human Events* (June 18, 1966); Robert Shogan, *The Riddle of Power: Presidential Leadership from Truman to Bush* (New York: Dutton, 1991), 241–42; Gil Troy, *Morning in America: How Ronald Reagan Invented the 1980s* (Princeton: Princeton University Press, 2005), 34 ("Goldwater-conservatism"); "Ronald Reagan: Spokesman for Conservatism," *Human Events* (February 2, 1974); "Reagan Should Make Immediate '76 Bid," ibid. (November 16, 1974).

91 Dan Carter, *The Politics of Rage: George Wallace, The Origins of the New Conservatism, and the Transformation of American Politics* (New York: Simon & Schuster, 1998), 344, 220–21, 328–29, 433 ("They all"); Patrick Jones, *The Selma of the North: Civil Rights Insurgency in Milwaukee* (Cambridge: Harvard University Press, 2009); Lowndes, *From the New Deal to the New Right*, at 78, 81, 84, 96 ("both," "nuts"); Jason Sokol, *There Goes My Everything: White Southerners in the Age of Civil Rights, 1945–1975* (New York: Alfred A. Knopf, 2006).

92 "Wallace Rolls," *Newsweek* (April 21, 1975).

93 Viguerie, *The New Right*, at 32–33; ". . . And George Wallace Probably Will Be in It," *New York Times*, September 29, 1974 ("However"); "Wallace's Race for Governor Has Tone of a Presidential Quest," ibid., October 25, 1974 ("best").

94 William Rusher, *The Rise of the Right* (New York: William Morrow, 1984), 265, 268; Minutes, Board of Directors Meetings, American Conservative Union, December 15, 1974, Box 21, File 11, ACU Papers.

95 William Rusher, "Speculation on a New Party . . . Under the Banner of a Conservative Party?" *Human Events* (November 9, 1974).

96 Rusher, *The Rise of the Right*, at 267.

97 Judis, *William F. Buckley*, at 283; Stephan Lesher, *George Wallace: American Populist* (Reading, Mass.: Addison-Wesley, 1994), 428; Steven Gillon, *Politics and Vision: The ADA and American Liberalism* (New York: Oxford University Press, 1987), 202, 208–14.

98 Byron Shaffer, *Quiet Revolution: The Struggle for the Democratic Party and the Shaping of Post-Reform Politics* (New York: Russell Sage Foundation, 1983), 485–93, 531; Bruce Miroff, *The Liberals' Moment: The McGovern Insurgency and the Identity Crisis of the Democratic Party* (Lawrence: University Press of Kansas, 2007), 41–71.

99 Miroff, *The Liberals' Moment*, at 121–39, 239, 202–15, 32, 215–25, 239; "Agnew Depicts McGovern as 'Fraud' on P.O.W. Issue," *New York Times*, July 1, 1972 ("beg").

100 Robert Mason, *Richard Nixon and the Quest for a New Majority* (Chapel Hill: University Press of North Carolina, 2004), 197.

101 William Rusher, *The Making of the New Majority Party* (Ottawa: Green Hill, 1975), 64.

102 William Rusher to Michael Djordjevich, May 18, 1976, Box 26, File 2, William Rusher Papers, Library of Congress; Cannon, *Governor Reagan*, at 401.

103 Lou Cannon, *President Reagan: The Role of a Lifetime* (New York: Simon & Schuster, 1991), 219 ("bad-mouthed"); Hartmann, *Palace Politics*, at 335; Rusher, *The Rise of the Right*, at 271; Kevin Phillips, "A Reagan-Wallace Ticket in 1976?," *Human Events* (November 9, 1974); William Timmons to Donald Rumsfeld, October 25, 1974, Box 20, Conservatives, Timmons Papers. Critchlow speaks of Rumsfeld and Cheney's attitudes toward Reagan in *Phyllis Schlafly and Grass-Roots Conservatism*, at 381, n. 76. Craig Shirley maintains that Cheney alone took Reagan seriously in *Reagan's Revolution: The Untold Story of the Campaign that Started It All* (Nashville: Nelson Current, 2005), 203, 253.

104 Richard Viguerie, "Money, Message, and Marketing," *The New Right at Harvard* (Vienna, Va.: Conservative Caucus, 1983), 109, 116.

105 Shirley, *Reagan's Revolution*, at 29.

CHAPTER II | THE POVERTY OF POWER

1 Barry Commoner, *The Poverty of Power: Energy and the Economic Crisis* (New York: Alfred A. Knopf, 1976), 1; Bruce Schulman, *The Seventies: The Great Shift in American Culture, Society, and Politics* (New York: Free Press, 2001), 125 ("three").

2 Bruce Miroff, *The Liberals' Moment: The McGovern Insurgency and the Identity Crisis of the Democratic Party* (Lawrence: University Press of Kansas, 2007), 286 ("We're not"); Julian Zelizer, *On Capitol Hill: The Struggle to Reform Congress and Its Consequences, 1948–2000* (Cambridge: Cambridge University Press, 2004), 156–76.

3 Richard Cheney, "Forming and Managing an Administration," *The Ford Presidency: Twenty-two Intimate Perspectives of Gerald R. Ford*, ed. Kenneth W. Thompson (Lanham, Md.: University Press of America, 1988), 57, 65 ("no"); "The First Ford Year: Policy Tide Is Turned," *New York Times*, August 8, 1975; "TRB: Mr. Veto," *New Republic* (October 18, 1975).

4 Michael Barone, *Our Country: The Shaping of America from Roosevelt to Reagan* (New York: Free Press, 1990), 540 ("defensive").

5 John Greene, *The Presidency of Gerald R. Ford* (Lawrence: University Press of Kansas, 1995), 54 ("gridlock"); Remarks on Signing the Council on Wage and Price Stability Act, August 24, 1974, americanpresidency.org.

6 Allen Matusow, *The Unraveling of America: A History of Liberalism in the Sixties* (New York: Harper & Row, 1984), 155–75; Allen Matusow, *Nixon's Economy: Booms, Busts, Dollars, and Votes* (Lawrence: University Press of Kansas, 1998), 13.

7 Richard Nixon: A Conversation with the President About Foreign Policy, July 1, 1970, americanpresidency.org; Julian Zelizer, *Arsenal of Democracy: The Politics of National Security—from World War II to the War on Terrorism* (New York: Basic Books, 2009), 235 ("breathing"); Matusow, *Nixon's Economy*, at 154–55, 184–87.

8 Matusow, *Nixon's Economy*, at 220–40.

9 Bennett Harrison and Barry Bluestone, *The Great U-Turn: Corporate Restructuring and the Polarizing of America* (New York: Basic Books, 1988), 5, 12, 23, 29, 51, 109, 137; Daniel Yergin and Joseph Stanislaw, *The Commanding Heights: The Battle Between Government and the Marketplace That Is Remaking the Modern World* (New York: Simon & Schuster, 1998), 64.

10 "Oil Consumers Seem to Learn Little from '74," *New York Times*, May 25, 1979.

11 Lois Gordon and Alan Gordon, *The Columbia Chronicles of American Life* (New York: Columbia University Press), 607 (Matchbox); Matusow, *Nixon's Economy*, at 282–96.

12 "Greenspan—Atlas Jogs," *Newsweek* (February 24, 1975) ("full"); William Greider, *Secrets of the Temple: How the Federal Reserve Runs the Country* (New York: Simon & Schuster, 1987), 67; Arthur Burns, "Ford and the Federal Reserve," *The Ford Presidency*, at 135, 136 ("angelic"); Gerald Ford, *A Time to Heal: The Autobiography of Gerald R. Ford* (New York: Harper & Row, 1979), 153; William Simon, *A Time for Truth* (New York: Berkley, 1979), 116–17.

13 Ford, *A Time to Heal* at 66, 155.

14 Ibid., at 152; Yanek Mieczkowski, *Gerald Ford and the Challenges of the 1970s* (Lexington: University Press of Kentucky, 2005), 105–08; "Liberals Prescribe," *ADA World* (October 1974) (reprinting statement adopted by Americans for Democratic Action Board at its September 1974 meeting).

15 Hobart Rowen, *Self-Inflicted Wounds: From LBJ's Guns and Butter to Reagan's Voodoo Economics* (New York: Times Books, 1994), 112 (Meany); President's News Conference of August 28, 1974, americanpresidency.org.

16 Remarks Concluding the Summit Conference on Inflation, September 28, 1974, americanpresidency.org; Ford, *A Time to Heal*, at 189–92; Matusow, *Nixon's Economy*, at 300–01; Rowen, *Self-Inflicted Wounds*, at 107–11, 119; "Recession Now, Trouble Ahead," *Time* (October 21, 1974).

17 Address to a Joint Session of Congress on the Economy, October 8, 1974, americanpresidency.org.

18 "The Cheerleader," *Nation* (October 19, 1974); "Button, Button," *New Yorker* (October 21, 1974).
19 Arthur Taylor to Gerald Ford, October 17, Box 126, Ron Nessen, Philip Areeda Papers, Ford Library (unless otherwise indicated, all manuscript collections cited in this chapter are in the Ford Library); Remarks to the Annual Convention of the Future Farmers of America, October 15, 1974, americanpresidency.org.
20 Donald Rumsfeld to Ford, February 28, 1975, Box 4, Business and Economics—National Economy, 10/74, Handwriting File (quoting Greenspan); Mieczkowski, *Gerald Ford and the Challenges of the 1970s*, at 164–65 (Simon).
21 Barbara Kellerman, *The Political Presidency: Practice of Leadership* (New York: Oxford University Press, 1984), 160–61; Phone Call from Rep. LaMar Baker, October 7, 1974, Box 12, Whip Inflation Now (1), William Timmons Papers. Baker was defeated in November 1974.
22 Robert Hartmann, *Palace Politics: An Inside Account of the Ford Years* (New York: McGraw-Hill, 1980), 299 (cartoonists); "BURP," *Nation* (November 9, 1974); "The Cheerleader," ibid. (October 19, 1974).
23 Ford, *A Time to Heal*, at 154; "The Outlook: A Deeper Slump Before the Upturn," *Time* (December 23, 1974) (BATH); "TRB: Alice in Blunderland?," *New Republic* (March 22, 1975).
24 Ford, *A Time to Heal*, at 203–04; Alan Greenspan to Ford, November 26, 1974, Box 4, Business and Economics—National Economy (1), Handwriting File; "Detroit on the Brink of Depression," *Washington Post*, November 25, 1974; Remarks at a Meeting of the Business Council, December 11, 1974, americanpresidency.org.
25 "Despite Doomsayers, U.S. Has Abundant Energy Resources," *Human Events* (February 22, 1975).
26 Richard Vietor, *Energy Policy in America Since 1945: A Study of Business-Government Relations* (Cambridge: Cambridge University Press, 1984), 202–10; "Squeeze on Fuel: A Puzzle to Irked Public," *New York Times*, January 14, 1974.
27 Matthew Yeomans, *Oil: Anatomy of an Industry* (New York: New Press, 2004), 53–54; James Burnham, "The Easy Way to Save Lots of Gasoline," *National Review* (November 22, 1974) (gas tax).
28 Peter Carroll, *It Seemed Like Nothing Happened: America in the 1970s* (New Brunswick, N.J.: Rutgers University Press, 1990), 120 (quoting John Ehrlichman).
29 President's News Conference of October 29, 1974, americanpresidency.org; Ford, *A Time to Heal*, at 228–29; "G.M. Would Back Gasoline Tax Rise: New Chairman Shifts Stand of Company—Calls Henry Ford a 'Gloom Prophet,'" *New York Times*, December 3, 1974.
30 http://www.pbs.org/wgbh/pages/frontline/shows/reaction/interact/silkwood.html.
31 Brian Balogh, *Chain Reaction, Expert Debate and Public Participation in American Commercial Nuclear Power, 1945–1975* (Cambridge, U.K.: Cambridge University Press, 1991), 310, 307, 234, 306; "Madison Says 'No,'" *Nation* (August 17, 1974).
32 "Forecast for Forecasting: Cloudy," *New York Times*, December 29, 1974. The sidebar to this Sunday *Times* magazine article by Alan Anderson read: "In the long term, climate is cooling off—or is it warming up? As for tomorrow's weather, even the world's biggest computer can't say for sure what it will be."
33 Russell Train to Ford, December 17, 1974, Box 17, S. 425 (1), Legislative Case Files; Pat Buchanan to Alexander Haig, August 15, 1974, Box 2, Timmons, William E., Alexander Haig Papers; "Buchanan Questions Ford's Leadership," *Human Events* (November 23, 1974); Patrick Buchanan, "'Nuts' Are Sending Ford a Message," ibid., June 5, 1976; "Ford's Rental of a Ski Chalet Involves Him in a Controversy," *New York Times*, December 19, 1974.
34 "Kissinger on Oil, Food, and Trade," *Business Week* (January 13, 1975); "Henry the K: 'Don't Fence Me In,'" *Newsweek* (January 20, 1975); "The Petrodollar: Will Araby Bankrupt the World?," cover, *Saturday Review* (January 25, 1975).
35 Tax Proposals and Options, Box 4, Business and Economics, National Economy,

12/21–31/74, Handwriting File; "Summary of Decisions," Economic Review, December 28, 1974; Ron Nessen, *It Sure Looks Different from the Inside* (Chicago: Playboy, 1978), 79 ("last").

36 Address Before a Joint Session of the Congress Reporting on the State of the Union, January 15, 1975, americanpresidency.org; Nessen, *It Sure Looks Different*, at 77; Kellerman, *The Political Presidency*, at 166–67.

37 Address Before a Joint Session of the Congress Reporting on the State of the Union, January 15, 1975.

38 Remarks at a News Briefing on the Fiscal Year 1976 Budget, February 1, 1975, ameri canpresidency.org.

39 "Ford Makes His Move," *Newsweek* (January 27, 1975) ("The Ford Presidency"); "The Recession: Ford's Risky Plan Against Slumpflation," *Time* (January 27, 1975) ("We know"); "A Race to Prime the Pump," *Newsweek* (January 20, 1975) (Greenspan, Simon, and Burns); "That Sudden Sinking Feeling," *Newsweek* (February 17, 1975).

40 Rowen, *Self-Inflicted Wounds*, at 113 ("Discomfort "); "Bigger Tax Cuts for Faster Recovery," *Time* (February 17, 1975); "Measuring Misery," *Time* (December 22, 1975); Archie Robinson, *George Meany and His Times* (New York: Simon & Schuster, 1981), 338; "President Ford Bites His Bullet," *ADA World* (January 1975); "A Strategy of Misery," ibid. (February–March 1975); "The Conservative Majority Myth," ibid. (January 1976) (the author, John Kenneth Galbraith had made a similar argument when Kennedy and Johnson proposed a tax cut); Recession, Inflation and Equity, Box 1, Americans for Democratic Action (ADA), National Board Meeting, February 1, 1975, January 31–February, 1975, ADA Papers, State Historical Society of Wisconsin.

41 "Demos May Wreck Good Points in Ford's Energy Plan, " *Human Events* (February 1, 1975); "Ford: Facing a Fresh Gusher of Criticism," *Time* (February 3, 1975) (cost estimates); Bipartisan Leadership Breakfast, Box 9, Congress, Jack Marsh Papers; "An Earful from the People," *Newsweek* (February 24, 1975); Vietor, *Energy Policy in America*, at 249–51; Energy Strategy, n.d. [ca. January 1975], Box 13, Economic and Energy Program (4), Marsh Papers.

42 Republican House and Senate Leadership Breakfast, January 21, 1975, Marsh Papers ("nit pick"); "Ford: Facing a Fresh Gusher of Criticism."

43 John Casserly, *The Ford White House: The Diary of a Speechwriter* (Boulder: Colorado Associated University Press, 1977), 36, 43, 47.

44 *Algonquin SNG, Inc. v. Federal Energy Administration*, 518 F. 2d. 1051 (1975); Ford, *A Time to Heal*, at 340.

45 Assessment of Congressmen Involved in Final Agreement, Box 51, Utilities Energy Legislation (5), n.d., Handwriting File; GOP Leadership Meeting, November 13, 1975, ibid. (6); Mieczkowski, *Gerald Ford and the Challenges of the 1970s*, at 252–58.

46 Ford, *A Time to Heal*, at 340–41; Jay Hakes, *A Declaration of Energy Independence: How Freedom from Foreign Oil Can Improve National Security, Our Economy, and the Environment* (Hoboken, N.J.: John Wiley, 2008), 42 ("Given").

47 Vietor, *Energy Policy in America*, at 252; Hakes, *A Declaration of Energy Independence*, at 68–71, 159–65, 148–49; Yeomans, *Oil: Anatomy of an Industry*, at 54–59; Simon, *A Time for Truth*, at 86; "Another Reason to Support Reagan: Ford Collapsing on Oil Deregulation," *Human Events* (November 22, 1975).

48 Jack Marsh to Ford, January 29, 1975, Box 20, Finance, Taxation (1), Handwriting File; Bill, Notes, n.d., ibid. ("disarray"); Kellerman, *The Political Presidency*, at 171.

49 Kellerman, *The Political Presidency*, at 174; "Russell B. Long, 84, Senator Who Influenced Tax Laws," *New York Times*, May 11, 2003 ("cleaned-up"); Dennis Ventry, "The Collision of Tax and Welfare Politics: The Political History of the Earned Income Tax Credit, 1969–99," *National Tax Journal*, 53 (2000): 983–1026.

50 Greene, *The Presidency of Gerald R. Ford*, at 76 ("responsible," "something"); Ford, *A Time to Heal*, at 258.

51 Letters to Ford from Alan Greenspan (March 23, 1975); William Simon (March 28);

Arthur Burns (March 28) (Ford said in his memoirs that Burns was among those who "strenuously" urged him to sign the bill. Either Burns changed his advice, or Ford did not remember correctly. Ford, *A Time to Heal*, at 259); Caspar Weinberger (February 26, 1975); L. William Seidman (March 28, 1975), all in Box 20, Finance—Taxation (1)-(2), Handwriting File; James Cannon to Ford, n.d. (c. March 28, 1975), Box 12, Economy—Meeting on Economy and Energy Matters, James Cannon Papers; Ford, *A Time to Heal*, at 258–59 ("if I").

52 "Highlights of 1975 Political Action Conference," *Human Events* (March 1, 1975) ("gathering's," "nearly 1000"); "Political Action Conference Meets: Reagan Key to Conservative Hopes," ibid. ("What"); Text of Resolution, ibid.

53 "Highlights of 1975 Political Action Conference" ("Is"); Reagan, "Time for a New Second Party," *Time* (March 17, 1975) (Wallace).

54 "Highlights of 1975 Political Action Conference" ("most"); "The Growling on Ford's Right," *Time* (March 17, 1975).

55 Ford, *A Time to Heal*, at 259; Max Friedersdorf to Ford, March 27, 1975 (override); and Memorandums to Ford from Robert Hartmann (March 28) ("You"); R. L. Dunham (March 27); Jack Marsh (March 28); Ron Nessen (March 28); Nelson Rockefeller (March 28); all in Box 20, Finance—Taxation (2), Handwriting File.

56 Address to the Nation upon Signing the Tax Reduction Act of 1975, March 29, 1975, americanpresidency.org.

57 Paul Samuelson, "Bonanzas from Democrats," *Newsweek* (July 26, 1976); Dana Frank, *Buy American: The Untold Story of Economic Nationalism* (Boston: Beacon Press, 1999), 137; "The 'Label Song' Stitches Harmony into Garment Union," *New York Times*, September 30, 1980.

58 http://www.conservationtech.com/x-MILLTOWNS/EXHIBITIONS/75-Currier .htm. Tamara Hareven and Randolph Langenbach, *Amoskeag: Life and Work in an American Factory City* (Hanover, N.H.: University Press of New England, 1978), 381; Governor Jeanne Shaheen, State of the State Speech, February 3, 2000, http:// www.stateline.org/live/details/speech?contentId=16038; Edward Berkowitz, *Something Happened: A Political and Cultural Overview of the Seventies* (New York: Columbia University Press, 2006), 228; David Nye, "Declension and Renewal: New England's Shifting Mood in the 1970s," *The Lost Decade: America in the Seventies*, ed. Elsebeth Hurup (Aarhus: Aarhus University Press, 1996), 41.

59 Thomas Sugrue, *The Origins of the Urban Crisis: Race and Inequality in Postwar Detroit* (Princeton: Princeton University Press, 1996), 127 ("closing"); Jefferson Cowie and Joseph Heathcott, eds., *Beyond the Ruins: The Meanings of Deindustrialization* (Ithaca, N.Y.: Cornell University Press, 2003); Bruce Schulman, *The Seventies: The Great Shift in American Culture, Society, and Politics* (New York: Free Press, 2001), 102–14; Raymond Mohl, ed., *Searchingfor the Sunbelt: Historical Perspectives on a Region* (Athens: University of Georgia Press, 1993); Bethany Moreton, *To Serve God and Wal-Mart: The Making of Christian Free Enterprise* (Cambridge: Harvard University Press, 2009), 80, 41.

60 Mieczkowski, *Gerald Ford and the Challenges of the 1970s*, at 109 ("fast"); Moreton, *To Serve God and Wal-Mart*, at 50, 84 ("Rather"); *Statistical Abstract of the United States* (Washington, D.C.: Government Printing Office, 1976), 361, 362.

61 "Autos: Widening Beachhead," *Time* (April 7, 1975) (Datsun executive); John Rae, *Nissan/Datsun: A History of Nissan Motor Corporation in U.S.A. 1960–1980* (New York: McGraw-Hill, 1980), 144–47; Robert Shook, *Honda: An American Success Story* (New York: Prentice Hall, 1988), 38.

62 Woodcock quoted in "The Growing Specter of Unemployment," *Time* (February 17, 1975); "Perceiving Poverty amid the Plenty," ibid. (March 3, 1975).

63 Talking Points—Economy in State Dinners, n.d., Box 39, Betty Ford—WIN Program, Sheila Weidenfeld Papers; "Perceiving Poverty amid the Plenty."

64 "The Vulnerable Managers," *Time* (February 17, 1975); "Enterprise: Prospering in Hard Times," *Newsweek* (February 3, 1975); "Apocalypse Chic," *Newsweek* (February 17, 1975) ("bleak chic"); Bruce Springsteen, "Born to Run" (1975); "America's New

Jobless: The Frustration of Idleness," *Time* (March 17, 1975) (*Mary Worth*); Richard Zoglin, *Comedy at the Edge: How Stand-up in the 1970s Changed America* (New York: Bloomsbury, 2008).

65 " 'Jaws,' Setting Records, Help Revitalize Movies," *New York Times*, July 8, 1975; William Graebner, "America's Poseidon Adventure: A Nation in Existential Despair," *America in the Seventies*, ed. Beth Bailey and David Farber (Lawrence: University Press of Kansas, 2004), 158, 169.

66 Judith Rossner, *Looking for Mr. Goodbar* (New York: Simon & Schuster, 1975); "The Skid Row Slasher," *Time* (February 10, 1975).

67 Ford, *A Time to Heal*, at 309–12; "Victim or Terrorist?," *Newsweek* (October 6, 1975); William Graebner, *Patty's Got a Gun: Patricia Hearst in 1970s America* (Chicago: University of Chicago Press, 2008), 108–11.

68 "4 Killed, 44 Injured in Fraunces Tavern Blast," *New York Times*, January 25, 1975; "The La Guardia Blast: 'My God It Was Terrible!,' " *Time* (January 12, 1976) (quotation). No one was prosecuted for the Fraunces Tavern bombing.

69 President's News Conference of July 9, 1976, americanpresidency.org (quoting Reagan); Melani McAllister, *Epic Encounters: Culture, Media, and U.S. Interests in the Middle East, 1945–2000* (Berkeley: University of California Press, 2001), 181–87.

70 "Entebbe Derby," *Time* (July 28, 1976) ("reads," "sky"); "6 Film Studios Vie over Entebbe Raid," *New York Times*, July 26, 1976; Thomas Harris, *Black Sunday* (New York: Putnam, 1975); McAllister, *Epic Encounters*, at 187–92.

71 John Snow, "Wild Easterns," *Time* (May 26, 1975); Marvin Albert, *The Gargoyle Conspiracy* (New York: Doubleday, 1975); Edward Pollitz, *The 41st Thief* (New York: Delacorte, 1975); J. E. Vacha, "It Could Happen Here: The Rise of the Political Scenario Novel," *American Quarterly*, 29 (1977): 194–206, http://corky.net/scripts/network.html. Salim Yaqub called attention to the anti-Arab aspect of *Network* in "Some in the Family: The United States and the Arab World in the 1970s," February 7, 2005, UCSB.

72 Greene, *The Presidency of Gerald R. Ford*, at 80–81; Message to the Congress Transmitting Annual Manpower Report of the President, April 24, 1975, americanpresidency.org; Remarks at the Annual Meeting of the Chamber of Commerce of the United States, April 26, 1976, ibid.

73 Jack Kemp to Rogers C. B. Morton, March 17, 1976, Box 130, Council of Economic Advisers, Burton G. Malkiel, Legislation—Jobs Creation Act of 1976, Kemp Bill ("We," "losing"); see also Jack Kemp to Gerald Ford, October 16 and 28, 1975, ibid.; William Gorog to the Economic Policy Board, n.d., Box 109, Unemployment—Esch Kemp Bill, L. William Seidman Papers ("passive").

74 GOP Leadership Meeting, October 7, 1975, Box 9, Congress, Marsh Papers; Rowen, *Self-Inflicted Wounds*, 130 (quotations).

75 Ford, *A Time to Heal*, at 339; Statement on House Action Sustaining Veto of the Tax Reduction Bill, December 18, 1975, americanpresidency.org; Nessen, *It Sure Looks Different*, at 89; "Ford Buckles Again on Tax Issue," *Human Events* (January 3, 1976).

76 Simon, *A Time for Truth*, at 138 (quotation); Ford, *A Time to Heal*, at 315–16.

77 James Cannon to Ford, May 14, 1975, Box 23, New York City Finances: Meeting with the President, Vice President, Beame and Carey, May 13, 1975, Cannon Papers.

78 Letter to Mayor Abraham D. Beame Responding to New York City's Financial Assistance Request, May 14, 1975, americanpresidency.org; George L. Hinman to Nelson Rockefeller, Warren Anderson, Ellmore Patterson, May 30, 1975, Box 23, New York City Finances, May–August 1975, Cannon Papers ("average," "turned"); "New York's Near D Day," *Newsweek* (October 27, 1975); Ford, *A Time to Heal*, at 316 (Burns); William Simon to Ford, September 8, 1975, Box 78, File: New York City, May–October (3), Seidman Papers.

79 Ford, *A Time to Heal*, at 319; "Presidential Piety," *New York Times*, October 30, 1975.

80 President's News Conference of November 26, 1975, americanpresidency.org; Joshua

Freeman, *Working Class New York: Life and Labor Since World War II* (New York: New Press, 2000), 267–81; Martin Shefter, *Political Crisis/Fiscal Crisis: The Collapse and Revival of New York City* (New York: Columbia University Press, 1992), 136 ("all but"); Simon, *A Time for Truth*, at 182, 179–81; "The New York Flip-Flop: Ford's Leadership Called into Question," *Human Events* (December 13, 1975).

CHAPTER III | BETWEEN PUBLIC AND PRIVATE: FAMILY MATTERS

1 Sixty Minutes: A Conversation with Betty Ford with CBS News Correspondent Morley Safer, Box 36, Sheila Weidenfeld Papers, Betty Ford—Abortion (all archival collections cited in this chapter are in the Ford Library); Sheila Weidenfeld, *First Lady's Lady: With the Fords at the White House* (New York: G. P. Putnam's Sons, 1979), 168.

2 Gil Troy, *Affairs of State: The Rise and Rejection of the Presidential Couple Since World War II* (New York: Free Press, 1997), 221–27.

3 Sara Evans, *Personal Politics: The Roots of Women's Liberation in the Civil Rights Movement and the New Left* (New York: Vintage, 1980), 212 (quoting Charlotte Brunch).

4 "Women of the Year: Great Changes, New Chances, Tough Choices," *Time* (January 5, 1976).

5 Alice Echols, *Daring to Be Bad: Radical Feminism in America, 1967–1975* (Minneapolis: University of Minnesota Press, 1990); Evans, *Personal Politics*, at 215. See Winifred Wandersee, *American Women in the 1970s: On the Move* (Boston: Twayne, 1988); Daniel Horowitz, *Betty Friedan and the Making of The Feminist Mystique: The American Left, the Cold War, and Modern Feminism* (Amherst: University of Massachusetts Press, 1998); Kate Weigand, *Red Feminism: American Communism and the Making of Women's Liberation* (Baltimore: Johns Hopkins University Press, 2001); Amy Farrell, *Yours in Sisterhood: Ms. Magazine and the Promise of Popular Feminism* (Chapel Hill: University of North Carolina Press, 1998); Patricia Bradley, *Mass Media and the Shaping of American Feminism 1963–1975* (Jackson: University Press of Mississippi, 2003); Dorothy Cobble, *The Other Women's Movement: Workplace Justice and Social Rights in Modern America* (Princeton: Princeton University Press, 2004); Kimberly Springer, *Living for the Revolution: Black Feminist Organizations, 1968–1980* (Durham, N.C.: Duke University Press, 2005); Winifred Breines, *The Trouble Between Us: An Uneasy History of White and Black Women in the Feminist Movement* (New York: Oxford University Press, 2006); Ruth Rosen, *The World Split Open: How The Modern Women's Movement Changed America* (New York: Penguin, 2000); Estelle Friedman, *No Turning Back: The History of Feminism and the Future of Women* (New York: Ballantine Books, 2002).

6 Susan Brownmiller, *Against Our Will: Men, Women and Rape* (New York: Simon & Schuster, 1975), 183, 15, 309; "Revolt Against Rape," *Time* (October 13, 1975) (2 percent); Deborah Rhode, *Justice and Gender: Sex Discrimination and the Law* (Cambridge: Harvard University Press, 1989), 251 (quoting California Senator Bob Wilson); Erin Pizzey, *Scream Quietly or the Neighbours Will Hear* (London: I. F. Books, 1974); Erin Pizzey, *Scream Quietly or the Neighbors Will Hear* (Short Hills, N.J.: Enslow, 1978); Susan Estrich, "Rape," *Yale Law Journal*, 95 (1986): 1087, 1087–88, 1179; "Joan Little's Story," *Time* (August 25, 1975); Breines, *The Trouble Between Us*, at 156–57.

7 Gloria Steinem, *Outrageous Acts and Everyday Rebellions* (New York: Holt, Rinehart and Winston, 1983), 17–18.

8 "Abortion-Rights' Scorned Prophet; Hated by Both Sides, Bill Baird Raises Hackles, Not Funds," *New York Times*, April 14, 1993; Rickie Sollinger, *The Abortionist: A Woman Against the Law* (California: University of California Press, 1994).

9 David Garrow, *Liberty and Sexuality: The Right to Privacy and the Making of Roe v. Wade* (New York: Macmillan, 1994), 16, 78, 129; *State v. Nelson*, 126 Conn. 412 (1940); *Poe v. Ullman*, 367 U.S. 497, 508 (1961).

10 *Griswold v. Connecticut*, 381 U.S. 479, 484–85, 500 (1965).

11 *Eisenstadt v. Baird*, 405 U.S. 438, 453 (1972); Garrow, *Liberty and Sexuality*, at 541–44.

12 Garrow, *Liberty and Sexuality*, at 270–334; Kristin Luker, *Abortion and the Politics of Motherhood* (Berkeley: University of California Press, 1984), 66–91.
13 Luker, *Abortion and the Politics of Motherhood*, at 92 (emphasis in the original); Garrow, *Liberty and Sexuality*, at 431–32, 561.
14 Wandersee, *On the Move*, at 183.
15 *Roe v. Wade*, 410 U.S. 113, 151–65 (1973); *Doe v. Bolton*, 410 U.S. 179 (1973).
16 Garrow, *Liberty and Sexuality*, at 599; Gerald Rosenberg, *The Hollow Hope: Can Courts Bring About Social Change?* (Chicago: University of Chicago Press, 1993), 178–89.
17 Luker, *Abortion and the Politics of Motherhood*, at 214, 224.
18 Garrow, *Liberty and Sexuality*, at 617.
19 John Hart Ely, "The Wages of Crying Wolf: A Comment on Roe v. Wade," *Yale Law Journal*, 92 (1973): 920, 944; Gary Leedes, "The Supreme Court Mess," *Texas Law Review*, 57 (1979): 1361, 1437 ("classic").
20 Garrow, *Liberty and Sexuality*, at 237; *Yick Wo v. Hopkins*, 118 U.S. 356, 373–74 (1886).
21 Betty Ford, *The Times of My Life*, at 228; John Greene, *Betty Ford: Candor and Courage in the White House* (Lawrence: University Press of Kansas, 2004), 44 (Gerald Ford's opposition to *Roe*).
22 Catherine McKinnon, *Toward a Feminist Theory of the State* (Cambridge: Harvard University Press, 1989), 190–92; Sylvia Law, "Rethinking Sex and the Constitution," *University of Pennsylvania Law Review*, 132 (1984): 955, 1020.
23 See, e.g., *Bigelow v. Virginia*, 421 U.S. 809 (1975) (approving right of abortion providers to advertise their services).
24 Cobble, *The Other Women's Movement*, at 190–95; Jane Mansbridge, *Why We Lost the ERA* (Chicago: University of Chicago Press, 1986).
25 Carol Felsenthal, *Phyllis Schlafly: The Sweetheart of the Silent Majority* (New York: Doubleday, 1981), 240 ("between"); Phyllis Schlafly, *The Power of the Positive Woman* (New Rochelle, N.Y.: Arlington House, 1977), 166 ("remake").
26 Schlafly, *The Power of the Positive Woman*, at 49, 30, 38, 180, 166; Donald Critchlow, *Phyllis Schlafly and Grassroots Conservatives: A Woman's Crusade* (Princeton: Princeton University Press, 2005), 218 (potential to rally conservatives).
27 Felsenthal, *The Sweetheart of the Silent Majority*, at 110, 192.
28 Schlafly, *The Power of the Positive Woman*, at 180 ("perverts"); Felsenthal, *The Sweetheart of the Silent Majority*, at 238.
29 Schlafly, *The Power of the Positive Woman*, at 79, 84 ("basic;" "Extra"); "Should Women Be Drafted?," *Phyllis Schlafly Report* (March 1973) ("get out"); Rhode, *Justice and Gender*, at 68 ("*legal*," "only reason"); Jane DeHart Mathews and Donald Mathews, "The Cultural Politics of ERA's Defeat," *Rights of Passage: The Past and Future of the ERA*, ed. Joan Hoff-Wilson (Bloomington: Indiana University Press, 1986), 44, 48 (sex crimes); Mansbridge, *Why We Lost the ERA*, at 111 ("subject"); Donald Mathews and Jane DeHart, *Sex, Gender, and the Politics of the ERA: A State and a Nation* (New York: Oxford University Press), 172 ("desexegrate").
30 "E.R.A. Means Abortion and Population Shrinkage," *Phyllis Schlafly Report* (December 1974); Mathews and DeHart, *Sex, Gender, and the Politics of the ERA*, at 159; Schlafly, *The Power of the Positive Woman*, at 12, 161–62, emphasis in the original.
31 Reva Siegel, "Constitutional Culture, Social Movement Conflict and Constitutional Change: The Case of the De Facto ERA," *California Law Review*, 94 (2006): 1323, 1395 ("robust"); Mansbridge, *Why We Lost the ERA*, at 45–59, 67–84 (Court and combat); Rhode, *Justice and Gender*, at 68, 66 ("clearly" and bathrooms); Barbara Ehrenreich, *The Hearts of Men: American Dreams and the Flight from Commitment* (New York: Doubleday, 1983), 146.
32 Siegel, "Constitutional Culture, Social Movement Conflict and Constitutional Change," at 1332–49; Joan Hoff, *Law, Gender and Injustice: A Legal History of U.S. Women* (New York: New York University Press, 1991), 328 ("gradually").
33 Rhode, *Justice and Gender*, at 69; Mathews and DeHart, *Sex, Gender, and the Politics of the ERA*, at 154–55, 160–62.

34 Schlafly, *The Power of the Positive Woman*, at 18 ("self-discipline"); Hoff, *Law, Gender and Injustice*, at 325 ("average"); Felsenthal, *The Sweetheart of the Silent Majority*, at xiii, 4, 118–19, 156.

35 "The ERA: What the Hell Happened in New York?," *Ms.* (March 1976) ("troops," "time"); Catherine Rymph, *Republican Women: Feminism and Conservatism from Suffrage Through the Rise of the New Right* (Chapel Hill: University of North Carolina Press, 2006), 205; Remarks at a Reception for Members of the National Commission on the Observance of International Women's Year, 1975, April 14, 1975, americanpresidency .org.

36 Daniel Yankelovich, *The New Morality: A Profile of American Youth in the 70's* (New York: McGraw-Hill, 1974), 4–11, 56; Daniel Yankelovich, *The New Rules: Searching for Self-Fulfillment in a World Turned Upside Down* (New York: Random House, 1981), 57, 7–8, 176; Sam Binkley, *Getting Loose: Lifestyle Consumption in the 1970s* (Durham, N.C.: Duke University Press, 2007).

37 Theodore Caplow, Howard Bahr, John Modell, and Bruce Chadwick, *Recent Social Trends in the United States 1960–1990* (Montreal: McGill Queen's University Press, 1991), 114 (cohabitation); Lenore Weitzman, *The Divorce Revolution: The Unexpected Social and Economic Consequences for Women and Children in America* (New York: Free Press, 1985), x, 37, 51; and see Ehrenrich, *The Hearts of Men*, at 120; Wandersee, *On the Move*, at 131.

38 Weitzman, *The Divorce Revolution*, 51, 350; Diana Pearce and Harriette McAdoo, *Women and Children: Alone and in Poverty* (Washington, D.C.: National Advisory Council on Economic Opportunity, 1981), 1, 9; Diana Pearce, "The Feminization of Poverty: Women, Work and Welfare," *Urban and Social Change Review* 11 (February 1978): 28–36.

39 Ford, *The Times of My Life*, at 231.

40 Andrew Edelstein and Kevin McDonough, Introduction, *The Seventies: From Hot Pants to Hot Tubs* (New York: Dutton, 1990) (the book is not paginated) ("Everybody"); Thomas Hine, *The Great Funk: Falling Apart and Coming Together (on a Shag Rug) in the Seventies* (New York: Farrar, Straus and Giroux, 2007), 174–76; Erica Jong, *Fear of Flying* (New York: Holt, Rinehart and Winston, 1973), 11; Dennis Altman, *The Homosexualization of America* (New York: Beacon, 1982); Rita Mae Brown, *Rubyfruit Jungle* (Plainfield, Vt.: Daughters, Inc., 1973).

41 Leigh Rutledge, *The Gay Decades: From Stonewall to the Present: The People and Events that Shaped Gay Lives* (New York: Plume, 1992), 61, 77–78, 85.

42 Randy Shilts, *The Mayor of Castro Street: The Life and Times of Harvey Milk* (New York: St. Martin's Press, 1982), 119, 109, 123.

43 Echols, *Daring to Be Bad*, at 265–69; Carolyn Heilbrun, *The Education of a Woman: The Life of Gloria Steinem* (New York: Ballantine Books, 1995), 284–300; Loch Johnson, *A Season of Inquiry: Congress and Intelligence* (Chicago: Dorsey, 1988), xi ("intelligence wars").

44 Richard Helms with William Hood, *A Look over My Shoulder: A Life in the Central Intelligence Agency* (New York: Random House, 2003), 409–15; Jefferson Morley, "The Gentlemanly Planner of Assassinations: The Nasty Careeer of CIA Director Richard Helms," *Slate* (November 1, 2002), http://www.slate.com/?id=2073470; "Mr. Energy: Doing the Doable—And More," *Time* (April 4, 1977) ("demythologize"). The CIA's woes were discussed in a cover story, "CIA: Time to Come In from the Cold," *Time* (September 30, 1974).

45 William Colby and Peter Forbath, *Honorable Men: My Life in the CIA* (New York: Simon & Schuster, 1978), 391, 12; "Huge C.I.A. Operation Reported in U.S. Against Antiwar Forces, Other Dissidents in Nixon Years," *New York Times*, December 22, 1974.

46 Kathryn Olmsted, *Challenging the Secret Government: The Post-Watergate Investigations of the CIA and FBI* (Chapel Hill: University of North Carolina Press, 1996), 33–39.

47 Colby, *Honorable Men*, at 389–92, 12; William Colby to Ford, December 24, 1975, Box 30, National Security—Intelligence (1), Handwriting File.

48 Henry Kissinger to Ford, December 25, 1974, Box 5, Intelligence, Richard Cheney Papers; Colby, *Honorable Men*, at 397–98 (quotations).

49 Gerald Ford, *A Time to Heal*, at 229; Colby, *Honorable Men*, at 337–41, 398. The full "family jewels" report, released by the CIA in 2007, is available at http://www.gwu.edu/~nsarchiv/NSAEBB/NSAEBB222/index.htm.

50 Colby, *Honorable Men*, at 341–42; Johnson, *A Season of Inquiry*, xi ("trust," "skepticism").

51 Steven Hayes, *Cheney: The Untold Story of America's Most Powerful and Controversial Vice President* (New York: HarperCollins, 2007), 85; Henry Kissinger, *Years of Renewal* (New York: Simon & Schuster, 1999), 321; "Will CIA Be Wrecked by 'People's Right to Know' Zealots?," *Human Events* (February 8, 1975) ("top"); "Is a Whitewash of the CIA in the Making?," *Economist* (January 11, 1975).

52 Tom Wicker, *On Press* (New York: Berkley, 1979), 209–18.

53 Daniel Schorr, *Clearing the Air* (Boston: Houghton Mifflin, 1978), 144–46; Colby, *Honorable Men*, at 409–10; Olmsted, *Challenging the Secret Government*, at 66.

54 Colby, *Honorable Men*, at 400; John Prados, *Lost Crusader: The Secret Wars of CIA Director William Colby* (New York: Oxford University Press), 303 (White House rewrite); "Leaving Murky Murders to the Senate," *Time* (June 16, 1975) ("There").

55 Family Statement by the Wife and Children of Frank R. Olson, n.d., Box 9, FG CIA (1), Handwriting File; "Family Plans to Sue C.I.A. over Suicide in Drug Test," *New York Times*, July 10, 1975; Richard Cheney to Roderick Hills, July 18, 1975, Box 23, October 1975 (1) (Ford's eagerness for a meeting and a settlement); Statement by the White House Press Secretary, July 21, 1976, Box 117, CIA (2) ("heartened"). When the Justice Department offered the Olsons five hundred thousand dollars, Ford encouraged Congress to enact a private relief bill awarding the family more than twice that to keep the case from going to trial. Edward Levi to Roderick Hills, September 24, 1975, Box 9, FG CIA (2), Handwriting File (settlement value); William Colby to Ford, October 29, 1975, ibid. (recommending private relief bill); James Connor for Edward Schmults, November 6, 1975, ibid. (Ford's approval of bill).

56 David Belin, *Final Disclosure: The Full Truth About the Assassination of President Kennedy* (New York: Scribner, 1988), 162–65.

57 Colby, *Honorable Men*, at 411, 402–03; Minutes, National Security Meeting, May 15, 1975, http://www.ford.utexas.edu/library/document/nscmin/minlist.htm ("prisoner," "All"); Kissinger, *Years of Renewal*, at 326 (salvation or purification); Johnson, *A Season of Inquiry*, at 46–47 (Church Committee reaction to Colby). For a discussion of the agency and White House reaction to Colby's testimony, see Colby, *Honorable Men*, at 406, 18, 436–37, 443–44. Though Helms said he wanted to stand trial, Washington superlawyer Clark Clifford warned it might result in conviction. Instead his lawyers negotiated a deal, and he was convicted of a misdemeanor. His sentence, a two-thousand-dollar fine and two years in prison, was suspended. Richard Helms, *A Look over My Shoulder* (New York: Random House, 2003), at 436–46.

58 Johnson, *A Season of Inquiry*, at 47–53.

59 Ibid.; at 59, 61; John Ranleagh, *The Agency: The Rise and Decline of the CIA* (New York: Simon & Schuster, 1987), 596.

60 Colby, *Honorable Men*, at 366, 434; Wicker, *On Press*, at 224.

61 Executive Order 11905—United States Foreign Intelligence Activities, February 18, 1976, americanpresidency.org; NSC Minutes, May 15, 1975 ("act"); Angus McKenzie, *Secrets: The CIA's War at Home* (Berkeley: University of California Press, 1997), 63 (quoting Bush in 1975); Bob Drogin, "Spy Agencies Fear Some Applicants Are Terrorists," *Los Angeles Times*, March 8, 2005 ("untutored"); Gates, *From the Shadows: The Ultimate Insider's Story of Five Presidents and How They Won the Cold War* (New York: Simon & Schuster, 1996), 155 ("more").

62 "National Security Agency; Biggest Big Brother," *Economist* (October 18, 1975); "Investigations: Project Minaret," *Newsweek* (November 10, 1975); "N.S.A. Chief Tells of Broad Scope of Surveillance: Describes Scanning of Calls and Cables of Foreign and U.S. Citizens and Groups," *New York Times*, October 30, 1975.

63 Diane Piette and Jesselyn Radack, "Piercing the 'Historical Mists': The People and Events Behind the Passage of FISA and the Creation of the 'Wall,'" *Stanford Law and*

Policy Review, 17 (2006): 437–85; Stephen Schulhofer, "The New World of Foreign Intelligence Surveillance," ibid., at 531, 534–35 ("sealed," and noting that after 9/11 civil libertarians came to view FISA more warmly); "Bush Lets U.S. Spy on Callers Without Courts," *New York Times*, December 16, 2005; "For Some, Spying Controversy Recalls a Past Drama," ibid., February 6, 2006 (quoting former Senator Walter Mondale, who had served on the Church Committee).

64 Johnson, *A Season of Inquiry*, at 125–29.

65 Curt Gentry, *J. Edgar Hoover: The Man and His Secrets* (New York: W. W. Norton, 1991), 721, 750, 756–67 (quoting Nixon and Clarence Kelley).

66 Address in Minneapolis Before the Annual Convention of the American Legion, August 19, 1975, americanpresidency.org; President's News Conference of November 14, 1975, ibid.; Johnson, *A Season of Inquiry*, at 169.

67 Memorandum of Conversation, Ford, Kissinger, November 21, 1975, http://www.fordlibrarymuseum.gov/library/document/memcons/1553303.pdf; *A Season of Inquiry*, at 131–37, 189–91; Ranleagh, *The Agency*, at 598–99.

68 See, e.g., "J.F.K. and the Mobsters' Moll," *Time* (December 29, 1975) ("close," "close personal"); "A Shadow over Camelot," *Newsweek* (December 29, 1975); "Memoirs: Lady in Waiting," *Newsweek* (January 26, 1976). See Judith Exner, as told to Ovid Demaris, *My Story* (New York: Grove, 1977), 254: "Love with Sam was not as exciting as it had been with Jack, but it was gentle and tender and emotionally fulfilling." In *My Story*, Exner said nothing about acting as courier between the Mob and Kennedy, though she did admit to the possibility that Giancana was "using me because I was the President's girl." Ibid. at 254, 142. But she seemed skeptical (ibid., at 254–55) and in any event said nothing about what it was Giancana would have used her to do. Compare Seymour Hersh, *The Dark Side of Camelot* (New York: Back Bay, 1997), 295, 303–14 (quoting Exner as admitting she had served as courier).

69 "A Shadow over Camelot," at 14 ("code"); "Jack Kennedy's Other Women," *Time* (December 29, 1975); "Closets of Camelot," *Newsweek* (January 19, 1976): 31; "Exposés Tarnish Knight of Camelot," *Human Events* (January 10, 1976); Johnson, *A Season of Inquiry*, at 159 (Church).

70 Greene, *Betty Ford*, at 32, 29, 68; Troy, *Affairs of State*, at 230 ("politics of personality"); Letters, *Time* (January 19, 1976) (letter of William McGrath). In her own memoir, Mrs. Ford's press secretary seemed astonished that the media had not covered her boss's slurred speech and erratic behavior. Weidenfeld, *First Lady's Lady*, at 273, 304–07, 311–13, 372–74.

71 Gerald Posner, *Case Closed, Lee Harvey Oswald and the Assassination of JFK* (New York: Anchor Books, 1993), 448; "Who Killed J.F.K.? Just One Assassin," *Time* (November 24, 1975) (250,000 copies; Zapruder); Michael Kurtz, *Crime of the Century: The Kennedy Assassination from a Historian's Perspective* (Knoxville: University of Tennessee Press, 1982), 157–60; Robert Sam Anson, *They've Killed the President!: The Search for the Murderers of JFK* (New York: Bantam, 1975), 300, 3 (quoting poll conducted by Cambridge Survey Research).

72 Peter Carroll, *It Seemed like Nothing Happened: America in the Seventies* (New Brunswick, N.J.: Rutgers University Press, 1990), 235 (poll); "Truman Nostalgia," *New Republic* (May 31, 1975).

CHAPTER IV | THE FADING OF AMERICA

1 "Ford's Unquiet Oasis," *Newsweek* (April 14, 1975) ("would"); Ron Nessen, *It Sure Looks Different from the Inside* (Chicago: Playboy, 1979), 96; "The Theater: Scars of the Sixties," *Time* (November 17, 1975) ("hangover").

2 "It's Super K," *Newsweek* (June 10, 1974); Jeremi Suri, *Henry Kissinger and the American Century* (Cambridge: Belknap, 2007), 68–71, 194; Memorandum of Conversation, Ford, Kissinger, Rumsfeld, Cheney, February 5, 1976, http://www.fordlibrarymuseum.gov/library/document/memcons/1553357.pdf ("I").

3 John Gaddis, *Strategies of Containment: A Critical Appraisal of Postwar American National*

Security Policy (New York: Oxford University Press, 1982), 289, 294, 314 (French, linkage); Vladislav Zubok, *A Failed Empire: The Soviet Union in the Cold War from Stalin to Gorbachev* (Chapel Hill: University of North Carolina Press, 2009), 225, 230; Jeremi Suri, *Power and Protest: Global Revolution and the Rise of Détente* (Cambridge: Harvard University Press, 2003). As Mario del Pero observed, "Kissinger's attention to the domestic dimension—the media, public opinion and Congress—was obsessive and almost maniacal." Mario del Pero, *The Eccentric Realist: Henry Kissinger and the Shaping of American Foreign Policy* (Ithaca, N.Y.: Cornell University Press, 2010), 150.

4 Gerald R. Ford, *A Time to Heal: The Autobiography of Gerald R. Ford* (New York: Harper & Row, 1979), 33; Robert Kaufman, *Henry M. Jackson: A Life in Politics* (Seattle: University of Washington Press, 2000), 245, 256–57.

5 Brent Scowcroft to Ford, October 25, 1974, Box A1, Kissinger/Scowcroft, The "O" File, National Security Adviser, Ford Library ("parrot") (unless otherwise indicated, all archival sources cited in this chapter are in the Ford Library); Salim Yaqub, "Henry Kissinger and the Arab-Israeli Conflict," *Nixon in the World: American Foreign Relations 1969–1977*, ed. Fredrik Logevall and Andrew Preston (New York: Oxford University Press, 2008), 227, 228.

6 Daniel Yergin, *The Prize: The Epic Quest for Oil, Money & Power* (New York: Free Press, 1992), 593; Anwar Sadat, *In Search of Identity: An Autobiography* (New York: Harper & Row, 1978), 249, 255.

7 Gershom Gorenberg, *The Accidental Empire: Israel and the Birth of the Settlements 1967–1977* (New York: Henry Holt, 2006), 100–01, 118 (referring to warning of Theodor Meron).

8 "The Palestinians Become a Power," *Time* (November 11, 1974).

9 Raymond Garthoff, *Détente and Confrontation: American-Soviet Relations from Nixon to Reagan* (Washington, D.C.: Brookings Institution, 1985), 406. See Zubok, *A Failed Empire*, at 231–34, for a discussion of Soviet restrictions on Jewish emigration.

10 Norman Podhoretz, *Breaking Ranks: A Political Memoir* (New York: Harper & Row, 1979), 7, 350–51; Mark Gerson, *The Neoconservative Vision: From the Cold War to the Culture Wars* (Lanham, Md.: Madison Books, 1996), 165, 7; Norman Podhoretz, "Neoconservatives: A Eulogy," *Commentary* (March 1996) (origin of the term); John Ehrman, *The Rise of Neoconservatism: Intellectuals and Foreign Affairs* (New York: Yale University Press, 1995), 34 ("shorthand"); John Judis, *William F. Buckley, Jr.: Patron Saint of the Conservatives* (New York: Simon & Schuster, 1988), 326.

11 Irving Kristol, *Neoconservatism: The Autobiography of an Idea* (New York: Free Press, 1995), 32, 350, 346; Podhoretz, *Breaking Ranks*, at 339, 343–44, 165–66, 291 ("upper"); Radio Address About Second Annual Foreign Policy Report to Congress, February 25, 1971, americanpresidency.org ("new isolationism" and definition); J. David Hoeveler, *Watch on the Right: Conservative Intellectuals in the Reagan Era* (Madison: University of Wisconsin Press, 1991), 157 ("old Democrats"); Ehrman, *The Rise of Neoconservatism*, at 60 (quoting Midge Decter on "good old days" of Truman).

12 Podhoretz, *Breaking Ranks*, at 287, 326–28, 346–47. On the *Public Interest*, see Kristol, *Neoconservatism*, at 31; J. David Hoeveler, "Populism, Politics, and Public Policy: 1970s Conservatism," *Journal of Policy History*, 10 (1998): 75, 83–85. See Peter Steinfels, *The Neoconservatives: The Men Who Are Changing America's Politics* (New York: Simon & Schuster, 1979), 68, for a discussion of the neoconservatives' shift from domestic to foreign affairs.

13 Joshua Marshall, "Party Crashers," *American Prospect* (November 30, 2002), http://www.prospect.org/cs ("bow"); Christopher Andrew and Vasili Mitrokhin, *The Sword and the Shield: The Mitrokhin Archive and the Secret History of the KGB* (New York: Basic Books, 1999), 240–41; Kaufman, *Henry M. Jackson*, at 6, 248–51, 263, 244–45.

14 *SALT Hand Book: Key Documents and Issues, 1972–1979*, ed. Roger Labrie (Washington, D.C.: American Enterprise Institute, 1979), 144 ("long run"); Kissinger, *Years of Upheaval*, at 253 "(created"); Kaufman, *Henry Jackson*, at 255.

15 Kissinger, *Years of Renewal*, at 280, 283, 294; Melvin Leffler, *For the Soul of Mankind:*

The United States, the Soviet Union and the Cold War (New York: Hill and Wang, 2007), 245–47.

16 Memorandum of Conversation, November 23, 1974, Box A1, Vladivostok Summit (1) (2), Kissinger/Scowcroft Temporary/Parallel file, National Security Adviser ("Without"); Garthoff, *Détente and Confrontation*, at 464.

17 Nessen, *It Sure Looks Different*, at 50 (describing his comments); Ford, *A Time to Heal*, at 218.

18 Ford, *A Time to Heal*, at 219; Kissinger, *Years of Renewal*, at 300–02; Nessen, *It Sure Looks Different*, at 52 (describing Perle's comments and Ford's reaction). When Ford telephoned Jackson to complain about Perle's remarks, Jackson accused him of oversensitivity. Henry Jackson to Ford, November 30, 1974, Box 40, Name File: Henry Jackson, White House Central Files.

19 Anatoly Dobrynin, *In Confidence: Moscow's Ambassador to America's Six Cold War Presidents* (New York: Times Books, 1995), 339–42 ("Probably"); Address Before a Joint Session of the Congress Reporting on United States Foreign Policy, April 10, 1975, americanpresidency.org ("quiet"); Kaufman, *Henry Jackson*, at 279–81. The number of émigrés is disputed. Ford placed it at fifty-five thousand; Dobrynin at fifty thousand. See Ford, *A Time to Heal*, at 139, and Dobrynin, *In Confidence*, at 339–40.

20 George Meany, "Détente Has Been a Flop," *Conservative Digest* (April 1976); Memorandum of Conversation, November 27, 1974, http://www.fordlibrarymuseum.gov/library/document/memcons/1552865.pdf ("bugged").

21 William Buckley, Jr., to Henry Kissinger, February 24, 1977, Box 178, File 1236, William F. Buckley, Jr., Papers, Yale University Archives (Kissinger declined the offer; Kissinger to Buckley, March 7, 1977, ibid.); "The Menace of Henry Kissinger," *Human Events* (March 30, 1974), 13; "Détente Is Wrecking Ford's Foreign Policy," ibid. (April 19, 1975); "The Fraud Called Détente," *Phyllis Schlafly Report* (July 1974); "Dr. Kissinger's Strange Question," ibid. (November 1974).

22 Brent Scowcroft to Ford, November 27, 1974, Box A1, Kissinger Reports (2), Kissinger/Scowcroft, National Security Adviser (enclosing Kissinger report: "favorite," "turn"); Patrick Tyler, *A Great Wall: Six Presidents and China* (New York: PublicAffairs, 2000), 198–99; National Security Council Minutes, December 2, 1974, http://www.fordlibrarymuseum.gov/library/document/nscmin/741202.pdf ("nothing," "We").

23 Frank Barnett to Bryce Harlow, August 16, 1974 (enclosing August 15 Memorandum on the comments of Soviet Foreign Ministry Officer Vassily V. Averianov, Assistant to the Undersecretary General for Political and General Assembly Affairs), Box 50, CO 158 USSR 9/15/74–9/30/74, White House Central Files; Walter Isaacson, *Kissinger* (New York: Simon & Schuster, 1992), 607–09.

24 Ford, *A Time to Heal*, at 137–38; see, e.g., Kissinger, *Years of Renewal*, at 307.

25 Ford, *A Time to Heal*, at 137–38; Remarks at a Dinner in New York City Honoring Vice President Rockefeller, February 13, 1975, americanpresidency.org; Memorandum of Conversation, Republican Congressional Leadership Meeting, March 18, 1975, Box 10, Ford, Republican Congressional Leadership, 5 Cabinet Members, National Security Adviser.

26 Kissinger, *Years of Renewal*, at 592, Isaacson, *Kissinger*, at 564 ("missionary work"); Steven Hayward, *The Age of Reagan: The Fall of the Old Liberal Order 1964–1980* (Roseville, Calif.: Forum/Prima, 2001), 553 (Khomeini).

27 Ford, *A Time to Heal*, at 247 ("mad"); Steven Spiegel, *The Other Arab-Israeli Conflict: Making America's Middle East Policy from Truman to Reagan* (Chicago: University of Chicago Press, 1985), 294 (tears); Minutes, National Security Council Meeting, March 28, 1975 ("businesslike"), http://www.fordlibrarymuseum.gov/library/document/nscmin/750328.pdf; Part III, May 15, 1975 ("suspension"), http://www.fordlibrarymuseum.gov/library/document/nscmin/750515.pdf.

28 Kissinger, *Years of Renewal*, at 630–31; Garthoff, *Détente and Confrontation*, at 485–86; W. R. Smyser to Henry Kissinger, March 4, 1975, http://www.gwu.edu/~nsarchiv/NSAEBB/NSAEBB174/ ("policy"); Telegram 10244, "Indonesia and Portuguese

Timor," August 21, 1975, http://www.gwu.edu/~nsarchiv/NSAEBB/NSAEBB174/989.pdf.

29 Yanek Mieczkowski, *Gerald Ford and the Challenges of the 1970s* (Lexington: University Press of Kentucky, 2005), 289 (*Economist*); "Kissinger's World of Woes," *Newsweek* (April 7, 1985) ("Gulliver").

30 George Herring, *America's Longest War: The United States and Vietnam, 1950–1975*, 2d ed. (New York: Alfred A. Knopf, 1986).

31 Memorandum of Conversation, Ford, House Select Committee on MIAs, http://www.fordlibrarymuseum.gov/library/document/memcons/1553347.pdf; "P.O.W.'S Were Left, Top Aides Believed," *New York Times*, September 22, 1992; "Vast Aid from U.S. Backs Saigon in Continuing War," ibid., February 25, 1974; Larry Berman, *No Peace, No Honor: Nixon, Kissinger, and Betrayal in Vietnam* (New York: Free Press, 2001), 261.

32 Fredrik Logevall, "The Vietnam War," *The American Congress: The Building of Democracy*, ed. Julian Zelizer (Boston: Houghton Mifflin, 2004), 584, 585, 595. "In 1968 the initial reports of the North Vietnamese successes were greatly exaggerated, yet journalists who had grown disgusted with the optimistic assessments from [General] Westmoreland's staff refused to believe that Tet represented a defeat for the revolutionary forces." Robert Schulzinger, *A Time for War: The United States and Vietnam, 1941–1975* (New York: Oxford University Press, 1997), 262.

33 "President Accepts Aug. 15 Deadline; Some Doves Angry," *Washington Post*, June 30, 1973; LeRoy Ashby and Rod Gramer, *Fighting the Odds: The Life of Senator Frank Church* (Pullman: Washington State University Press, 1994), 406 (Kennedy); Louis Fisher, "War Power," *The American Congress*, at 687, 691–92.

34 Memorandum of Conversation, October 5, 1974, Ford, Kissinger, South Vietnamese Foreign Minister Vuong Van Bac, http://www.fordlibrarymuseum.gov/library/document/memcons/1552815.pdf.

35 Schulzinger, *A Time for War*, at 318–19.

36 Bob Wolthius to Max Friedersdorf and Jack Marsh, January 14, 1975, Box 43, Vietnam—General, Jack Marsh Papers; Special Message to the Congress Requesting Supplemental Assistance for the Republic of Vietnam and Cambodia, January 28, 1975, americanpresidency.org; Kissinger, *Years of Renewal*, at 492 (congressional cold warriors); Frank Snepp, *Decent Interval: An Insider's Account of Saigon's Indecent End Told by the CIA's Chief Strategy Analyst in Vietnam* (Lawrence: University Press of Kansas, 2002), 153; Memorandum of Conversation, Ford, Congressional Vietnam Delegation, March 5, 1975, http://www.fordlibrarymuseum.gov/library/document/memcons/1552980.pdf.

37 "The Siege of Phnom Penh," *Newsweek* (February 10, 1975).

38 "Is This What America Has Left?," *Time* (April 7, 1975); Arnold Isaacs, *Without Honor: Defeat in Vietnam and Cambodia* (Baltimore: Johns Hopkins University Press, 1983), 363–79.

39 President's News Conference of February 26, 1975, americanpresidency.org.

40 See, e.g., President's News Conferences of March 6, 1975 ("bloodbath," "shame," credibility); March 17, 1975, and April 3, 1975 ("domino theory"), all ibid.

41 "Commitment?," *New York Times*, April 6, 1975; "Now, Trying to Pick Up the Pieces," *Time* (April 14, 1975) ("We might").

42 "Blood-Bath Talk," *Nation* (June 14, 1975) (quoting Frances FitzGerald). Compare "Next Round," *National Review* (April 25, 1975).

43 David Reimers, *Still the Golden Door: The Third World Comes to America*, 2d ed. (New York: Columbia University Press, 1992), 180–81; "Emergency," *New Republic* (June 30, 1979); "Reconsidering the Antiwar Movement: Were We Wrong About Vietnam?," ibid. (August 18, 1979); "George McGovern's Heart of Stone," *Conservative Digest* (October 1979); "More Trials for the Boat People," *Time* (August 13, 1979) (estimate).

44 Sydney Schanberg, "Cambodia Reds Are Uprooting Millions as They Impose a

'Peasant Revolution,'" *New York Times*, May 9, 1975; John Barron and Anthony Paul, *Murder of a Gentle Land* (New York: Reader's Digest Press, 1977); William Shawcross, *The Quality of Mercy: Cambodia, Holocaust and Modern Conscience* (New York: Touchstone, 1985), 51–64; "The Cambodia Genocide Controversy File," http://www.radioislam.org/totus/CGCF/index.html; "American Leftists Were Pol Pot's Cheerleaders," *Boston Globe*, April 30, 1998 ("leftists"); Human Rights Violations in Cambodia, Statement by the President, April 21, 1978, americanpresidency.org; Betty Glad, *An Outsider in the White House: Jimmy Carter, His Advisers, and the Making of American Foreign Policy* (Ithaca, N.Y.: Cornell University Press, 2009), 237–39, 246.

45 Minutes, National Security Council Meeting, April 9, 1975, http://www.fordlibrarymuseum.gov/library/document/nscmin/750409.pdf; Christopher Andrew and Vasili Mitrokhin, *The World Was Going Our Way: The KGB and the Battle for the Third World* (New York: Basic Books, 2005), 13, 264–66.

46 John Hersey, *The President* (New York: Alfred A. Knopf, 1975), 9; "Orphans of the Storm," *Newsweek* (April 14, 1975); George Gallup, *The Gallup Poll, Public Opinion 1972–1977*, 2 vols., 1 (Wilmington, Del.: Scholarly Resources, 1978), 440.

47 "The Current Cinema: A Filmmaker's Meditation on America," *New Yorker* (April 28, 1975).

48 John Casserly, *The Ford White House: Diary of a Speechwriter* (Boulder, Colo.: Associated University Press, 1977), 70 (quoting column and describing reaction).

49 "The Politics of Disaster," *Nation* (April 5, 1975); "It's All Your Fault," *National Review* (April 25, 1975).

50 Press Conference, April 3, 1973, americanpresidency.org ("assessing blame"); Minutes, National Security Council Meeting, April 9, 1975, http://www.fordlibrarymuseum.gov/library/document/nscmin/750409.pdf; Memorandum of Conversation, Ford, Kissinger, April 15, 1975, http://www.fordlibrarymuseum.gov/library/document/memcons/1553028.pdf; Jack Marsh to Donald Rumsfeld, April 3, 1975, Box 43, Vietnam—General, Marsh Papers (reporting that Kissinger wanted Ford to blame Congress); Bob Wolthuis to Jack Marsh, Vietnam—Supplemental Military Assistance (2), ibid. ("President," "probably," "record").

51 Address Before a Joint Session of the Congress Reporting on United States Foreign Policy, April 10, 1975, americanpresidency.org; T. Christopher Jespersen, "Kissinger, Ford and Congress: The Very Bitter End in Vietnam," *Pacific Historical Review*, 71 (2002): 439, 458–60.

52 "The Whys Behind Ford's Speech," *New York Times*, April 12, 1975; "The Evacuation Issue: Congress Suspects Saigon Aid Bill Is Meant Only to Get Americans Out," ibid., April 18, 1975; Jespersen, "Kissinger, Ford and Congress," at 460–62.

53 Ford, *A Time to Heal*, at 252; Nessen, *It Sure Looks Different*, at 106–07; Nguyen Tien Hung and Jerrold Schecter, *The Palace File* (New York: Harper & Row, 1986), 306–26, 346–47, 353–60.

54 "Fed Up and Turned Off," *Time* (April 14, 1975) (quoting *Detroit Free Press*); "Operation Self-Deception," *Nation* (April 26, 1975).

55 "Defeat for Ford," *New York Times*, April 18, 1969; "Kissinger Calls Aid Debate Over," ibid.; "The Privileged Exiles," *Time* (May 12, 1975).

56 Address at a Tulane University Convocation, April 23, 1975, americanpresidency.org; Robert Hartmann, *Palace Politics: An Insider Account of the Ford Years* (New York: McGraw-Hill, 1980), 322; Kissinger, *Years of Renewal*, at 535 ("declaration"). Presidential Press Secretary Nessen recalled, however, that he and other Ford staffers shared the students' joy. Nessen, *It Sure Looks Different*, at 108–09.

57 Casserly, *The Ford White House*, at 80–81, 58.

58 Ford, *A Time to Heal*, at 253. See "Fear in Pentagon: Kissinger Opposes Call for an Immediate Pullout by U.S.," *New York Times*, April 22, 1975. Kissinger telephoned Deputy Secretary of Defense William Clements to "congratulate the Defense Department for having put me on the front page of the *Times*" and complained that according to the story, "Defense wishes total evacuation, but that son of a bitch Kissinger,

who is thinking of national honor and dignity of the United States won't permit it." He and Clements blamed Schlesinger. Henry Kissinger, *Crisis: The Anatomy of Two Major Foreign Policy Crises* (New York: Simon & Schuster), 488–89.

59 Graham Martin to Henry Kissinger, April 10, 1975, Box 3, National Security Adviser, Back Channel Messages, Martin Channel, April 1975 (1) (quotation); Graham Martin to Henry Kissinger, April 26, 1975, Box 3, ibid., Martin Channel (3); Cabinet Meeting, April 16, 1975, http://www.fordlibrarymuseum.gov/library/exhibits/cabinet/cm750416.pdf; Martin to Kissinger, April 19, 1975, Box 3, National Security Adviser, Martin Channel (20); Martin to Kissinger, April 15, 1975, Box 12, ibid., East Asian/Vietnam.

60 Snepp, *Decent Interval*, at 297, 295.

61 Martin to Kissinger, April 15, 1975 (quotation); Snepp, *Decent Interval*, at 366; Martin to Kissinger, April 18, 1975, Box 3, National Security Adviser, Martin Channel (2); Martin to Kissinger, April 26, 1975.

62 "Senate Unit Bars Troops as Guard for Vietnamese," *New York Times*, April 15, 1975; Kissinger, *Years of Upheaval*, at 531; Memorandum of Conversation, Ford, Senate Foreign Relations Committee, Kissinger, Schlesinger, Scowcroft, April 14, 1975, http://www.fordlibrarymuseum.gov/library/document/memcons/1553026.pdf; Ford, *A Time to Heal*, at 255 ("cut"); Memorandum of Conversation, Cabinet Meeting, April 16, 1975, http://www.fordlibrarymuseum.gov/library/document/memcons/1553029.pdf.

63 Memorandum of Conversation, President, Kissinger, Schlesinger, Rumsfeld, Marsh, April 17, 1975, http://www.fordlibrarymuseum.gov/library/document/memcons/1553031.pdf ("How"); Ford Interview with Walter Cronkite, Eric Sevareid, and Bob Schieffer of CBS News, April 21, 1975, americanpresidency.org.

64 National Security Council Minutes, April 24, 1975, http://www.fordlibrarymuseum.gov/library/document/nscmin/750424.pdf; Martin to Kissinger, April 26, 1975; Kissinger to Martin, April 17, 1975, Box 3, Back Channel Messages 4/75, Outgoing (1), National Security Adviser; Kissinger to Martin, April 17, 1975, ibid. ("recognizing," "trigger"); Kissinger, *Years of Upheaval*, at 530.

65 Memorandum of Conversation, April 25, 1975, Ford, Kissinger, http://www.fordlibrarymuseum.gov/library/document/memcons/1553046.pdf (Kissinger promised to continue pressuring Martin but reminded Ford that "we are better off having a few Americans with the Vietnamese on each flight"); Kissinger to Martin, April 24, 1975, Box 3, National Security Adviser, Martin Channel—Outgoing (3) ("amazed," "redouble"); Martin to Kissinger, April 25, 1975, Box 3, ibid.

66 "Ford Risked U.S. Lives—and Won," *Los Angeles Times*, May 1, 1975 (reporter); "Turning Off the Last Lights," *Time* (May 4, 1975).

67 Isaacs, *Without Honor*, at 457; Snepp, *Decent Interval*, at 565.

68 "Last Chopper out of Saigon," *Time* (May 12, 1975).

69 Ford, *A Time to Heal*, at 256; Memorandum of Conversation, Ford, Kissinger, Dean Brown, Republican Congressional Leadership, May 6, 1975 ("quarterbacks") http://www.fordlibrarymuseum.gov/library/document/memcons/1553061.pdf; Jack Marsh to Ford, April 29, 1975, Box 64, Vietnam—Evacuation: Saigon (1), Philip Buchen Papers; Bob Tamarkin, "Diary of S. Viet's Last Hours," *Chicago Daily News*, May 6, 1975, *Reporting Vietnam*: Part II, 537, 538 ("big numbers"). The theme of betrayal runs through Snepp's *Decent Interval*.

70 Statement on House Action Rejecting Vietnam Humanitarian Assistance and Evacuation Legislation, May 1, 1975, americanpresidency.org.

71 "Troubled Trips to Safety," *Time* (May 5, 1975) (quoting Chicago Mayor Richard Daley).

72 "TRB: Ten Years After," *New Republic* (February 1, 1975) (quoting Brogan); "War and the American Character," *Nation* (May 3, 1975); James Patterson, *Grand Expectations: The United States, 1945–1974* (New York: Oxford University Press, 1996), 769.

73 Chester Pach, "And That's the Way It Was: The Vietnam War on the Network

Nightly News," *The Sixties: From Memory to History*, ed. David Farber (Chapel Hill: University of North Carolina Press, 1994), 90–118.

74 Kim Willenson with the correspondents of *Newsweek*, *The Bad War: An Oral History of the Vietnam War* (New York: New American Library Books/Plume, 1987), 398 (quoting Richard Holbrooke); Laura Kalman, *Yale Law School and the Sixties: Revolt and Reverberations* (Chapel Hill: University of North Carolina Press, 2005), 76.

75 Proclamation 4647—Vietnam Veterans Week, 1979, americanpresidency.org, March 20, 1979; Vietnam Veterans Week, 1979 Remarks at a White House Reception, May 30, 1979, ibid.; Philip Caputo, *A Rumor of War* (New York: Holt, 1996).

76 "Loss of Southeast Asia: Why Not Recriminations?," *Human Events* (May 10, 1975) ("Then," "That"); "Many Contributed to Vietnam Debacle," ibid. (May 24, 1975) ("orgies," "cheerleaders," "strategists," "we," "masters," "If"); "Hollywood Lost to Liberalism," ibid. (August 16,1976) ("far-flung"); " 'Hearts and Minds:' Academy Award for Pro-Communist Propaganda Film," ibid. (April 19, 1975); "Why U.S. Lost in Vietnam," ibid. (September 20, 1975): 10 ("bound").

77 Richard Viguerie, "No Reason for Friends to Say Goodbye," *Conservative Digest* (November 1985) (quoting from first issue); Minutes, American Conservative Union, Board of Directors, December 15, 1974, Box 21, Folder 11, American Conservative Union Papers, Brigham Young University Archives. See also, e.g., "Ford's Dangerous Softness," *Human Events* (April 26, 1975); Kevin Phillips, "My Turn: A Reagan-Wallace Ticket," *Newsweek* (May 9, 1975); "Reagan and Wallace: Some Scenarios," *Human Events* (May 24, 1975); William Rusher, *The Making of the New Majority Party* (Ottawa, Ill.: Green Hill Publishers, 1975); William Rusher, *The Rise of the Right* (New York: William Morrow, 1984), 274–75.

78 Press conference, May 6, 1975, americanpresidency.org.

CHAPTER V | THE DEATH OF DÉTENTE

1 Thomas Harris, *I'm OK—You're OK* (New York: Avon, 1976). Harris originally published the book in 1967. Coincidentally, it and another iconic book of the early 1970s, Richard Bach's *Jonathan Livingston Seagull: A Story* (New York: Avon, 1970), remained "sleepers" until 1972, when they soared to the top of best seller lists. "$1-Million Paperback Sale Sets Record," *New York Times*, July 27, 1972.

2 Memorandum of Conversation, Ford, Kissinger, May 14, 1975, http://www.fordlibrarymuseum.gov/library/document/memcons/1553076.pdf ("tough," "ferociously"); Minutes, National Security Council Meeting, May 12, 1975, http://www.fordlibrarymuseum.gov/library/document/nscmin/750512.pdf (all archival sources cited in this chapter are in the Ford Library); Henry Kissinger, *Years of Upheaval* (New York: Simon & Schuster, 1999), 551; Gerald Ford, *A Time to Heal: The Autobiography of Gerald R. Ford* (New York: Harper & Row, 1979), 275.

3 Ford, *A Time to Heal*, at 279.

4 Ralph Wetterhahn, *The Last Battle: The Mayaguez Incident and the End of the Vietnam War* (New York: Carroll and Graf, 2001), 263; "Capitol Comment," *ADA World* (June 1975) (noting that most in Congress were falling over themselves to endorse President Ford's action in the *Mayaguez* incident); "Ford's Cambodian Move: A Breath of Fresh Air," *Human Events* (May 24, 1975); Ford, *A Time to Heal*, at 284.

5 Christopher Lamb, *Belief Systems and Decision Making in the Mayaguez Crisis* (Gainesville: University of Florida Press, 1989), 32, 266, 17–18, n. 1 ("If"; *Chicago Tribune*, "over"); Roy Rowan, *The Four Days of the Mayaguez* (New York: W. W. Norton, 1975), 217–18. See also "Why the Backlash Against Handling of 'Mayaguez' Incident?," *Human Events* (July 5, 1975).

6 *Seizure of the Mayaguez*, Reports of the Comptroller General of the United States, Submitted to the Subcommittee on International Political and Military Affairs, Committee on International Relations (94th Congress, 2d Session) (Washington, D.C.: Government Printing Office, 1976), 10–17, iv; "Raid to Free Mayaguez Crewmen

Called Futile," *Detroit Free Press*, October 5, 1976, Box 8, Congressional Relations Staff, GAO Report, NSC Press and Liaison; Remarks and a Question-and-Answer Session at a Public Forum in West Bend, Wisconsin, April 2, 1976, americanpresidency.org; Kissinger, *Years of Upheaval*, at 575; Richard Cheney, "Forming and Managing an Administration," *The Ford Presidency*, ed. Kenneth Thompson (Lanham, Md.: University Press of America, 1988), 57, 72.

7 "Ford Falls but Is Unhurt," *New York Times*, June 2, 1975; Ford, *A Time to Heal*, at 289 ("exclusion"); Nessen, "The Ford Presidency and the Press," *The Ford Presidency*, at 179, 187 (quoting Ford on "those reporters"); Ron Nessen to Eric Rosenburger, February 19, 1975, Box 127, Jim Connor, Ron Nessen Papers; Jim Shuman to Ron Nessen, PL/Ford Exec, White House Central Files ("jock" to "klutz").

8 Interview with European journalists, May 23, 1975, americanpresidency.org (quotations); Robert Kaufman, *Henry M. Jackson: A Life in Politics* (Seattle: University of Washington Press, 2000), 299.

9 Walter Isaacson, *Kissinger: A Biography* (New York: Simon & Schuster, 1992), 657–58.

10 Ford, *A Time to Heal*, at 298; Max Friedersdorf to Ford, Box 7, Countries—USSR, Handwriting File; Nessen, *It Sure Seems Different from the Inside* (Chicago: Playboy, 1978), 345 ("horse's ass"); Craig Shirley, *Reagan's Revolution: The Untold Story of the Campaign that Started It All* (Nashville: Nelson Current, 2005), 43–44 ("snub"); Kaufman, *Henry M. Jackson*, at 292 ("met"); "Ford Refuses to Meet Solzhenitsyn: 'We Will Bury You' Now Called Détente," *Human Events* (July 12, 1975).

11 Ford, *A Time to Heal*, at 298; Isaacson, *Henry Kissinger*, at 658 (quoting Solzhenitsyn).

12 "Détente in Space," *New York Times*, July 16, 1975; Edward Ezell and Linda Ezell, *The Partnership: A History of the Apollo-Soyuz Test Project* (Washington, D.C.: National Aeronautics and Space Administration, 1978).

13 Ford, *A Time to Heal*, at 299; John Gaddis, *The Cold War: A New History* (New York: Penguin, 2005), 190–92; Yanek Mieczkowski, *Gerald Ford and the Challenges of the 1970s* (Lexington: University Press of Kentucky, 2005), 299 ("greatest"); Kissinger, *Years of Renewal*, at 635 ("landmark").

14 Memorandum of Conversation, Ford/Kissinger August 15, 1974, http://www.fordlibrarymuseum.gov/library/document/memcons/1552750.pdf, and see Memorandum of Conversation, Cabinet Meeting, August 8, 1975, http://www.fordlibrarymuseum.gov/library/document/memcons/1553206.pdf; Ford, *A Time to Heal*, at 299–300; "On the Right: The Helsinki Document," *National Review* (August 29, 1975).

15 Ford, *A Time to Heal*, at 301–04.

16 Cabinet Meeting, August 8, 1975.

17 Ford, *A Time to Heal*, at 306–07, 294; "U.S. Gives Praise to City but No Aid," *New York Times*, August 9, 1975 ("don't know"); "Summit in Helsinki," *Newsweek* (August 11, 1975).

18 "Why Laxalt Favors Reagan over Ford," *Human Events* (August 9, 1975), and see Melvin Laird, "Is *This* Détente?," *Reader's Digest* (July 1975); "What Price Détente," *Newsweek* (July 28, 1975).

19 Jussi Hanhimaki, "Ironies and Turning Points: Détente in Perspective," *Reviewing the Cold War: Approaches, Interpretations, Theories*, ed. Odd Arne Westad (London: Frank Cass, 2000), 325, 329–33; Vladislav Zubok, *A Failed Empire: The Soviet Union in the Cold War from Stalin to Gorbachev* (Chapel Hill: University of North Carolina Press, 2009), 205.

20 National Security Council Minutes, December 22, 1975, http://www.fordlibrarymuseum.gov/library/document/nscmin/751222.pdf; John Gaddis, *The Cold War*, at 189.

21 National Security Council Minutes, September 17, 1975, http://www.fordlibrarymuseum.gov/library/document/nscmin/750917.pdf ("morbid"); ibid., August 9, 1975, http://www.fordlibrarymuseum.gov/library/document/nscmin/750809.pdf ("We'll end up"); Steven Hayward, *The Age of Reagan: The Fall of the Old Liberal Order, 1964–1980* (Roseville, Calif.: Forum/Prima, 2001) ("fancy"), 427.

22 Ford, *A Time to Heal*, at 287–88.
23 Notes of Bi-Partisan Leadership Meeting, September 4, 1975, Box 9, Congress, Jack Marsh Papers.
24 William Quandt, *Peace Process: American Diplomacy and the Arab-Israeli Conflict Since 1967* (Washington, D.C.: Brookings Institution, 1993), 239–45.
25 Godfrey Hodgson, *The Gentleman from New York: Daniel Patrick Moynihan: A Biography* (Boston: Houghton Mifflin, 2000), 245–46; Quandt, *Peace Process*, at 244; Memorandum of Conversation, Ford, Kissinger, October 25, 1975, http://www.fordlibrarymuseum.gov/library/document/memcons/1553277.pdf ("going wild"). "He has carried on more violently than the Israeli ambassador," Kissinger subsequently complained. Memorandum of Conversation, Ford, Kissinger, November 11, 1975, http://www.fordlibrarymuseum.gov/library/document/memcons/1553294.pdf.
26 Quandt, *Peace Process*, at 245; "J.D.L. Burns Rocket Model Here in Protesting Détente," *New York Times*, July 15, 1975; Isaacson, *Henry Kissinger*, at 668.
27 National Security Council Minutes, August 9, 1975 ("cynical"); Clarence Robinson, "Backfire Draws Focus in SALT," *Aviation Week and Space Technology* (August 25, 1975); Ford, *A Time to Heal*, at 320 ("we," "That").
28 James Cannon, *Time and Chance: Gerald Ford's Appointment with History* (New York: HarperCollins, 1994), 407 ("cowardly"); Ford, *A Time to Heal*, at 328.
29 Cable, George Bush to Henry Kissinger, November 2, 1975, Box A1, George Bush's CIA Appointment, Kissinger/Scowcroft Temporary Parallel File, NSA Files ("I"); Bush to Brent Scowcroft, November 3, 1975, ibid. ("ugliness," "feel"); Ford, *A Time to Heal*, at 337–38.
30 Lloyd Bentsen, News Release, November 3, 1975, Box 1, Shake-Up, Marsh Papers ("replaces"); "Up from Anonymity," *Newsweek* (November 17, 1975) ("Babycakes"); Robert Schulzinger, *Henry Kissinger: Doctor of Diplomacy* (New York: Columbia University Press, 1989), 217–21; Kissinger, *Years of Renewal*, at 839–40.
31 Ford, *A Time to Heal*, at 330; Kaufman, *Henry M. Jackson*, at 288–99; Raymond Garthoff, *Détente and Confrontation: American-Soviet Relations from Nixon to Reagan* (Washington, D.C.: Brookings Institution, 1985), 441 ("détente without illusions"; "Henry is"); Memorandum of Conversation, Ford, Kissinger, November 3, 1975, http://www.fordlibrarymuseum.gov/library/document/memcons/1553284.pdf; President's News Conference of November 3, 1975, americanpresidency.org.
32 Interview on NBC News' *Meet the Press*, November 9, 1975, americanpresidency.org; "Ford's Big Shuffle," *Newsweek* (November 17, 1975) ("hastily"); "The Sunday Morning Massacre: A Murder Suicide," *New York* (December 22, 1975).
33 "Ford's Big Shuffle"; "King of the Castle," *Newsweek* (November 17, 1975) ("winner"); James Mann, *Rise of the Vulcans: The History of Bush's War Cabinet* (New York: Viking, 2004), 66–67 (reporting and refuting belief in Rumsfeld's responsibility); "Up from Anonymity" ("While"); Phil McCombs, "The Unsettling Calm of Richard Cheney; Defense's Civilian Chief and Seasoned Washington Hand, Playing It Cool," *Washington Post*, April 3, 1991; "White House Shakeup Undermines U.S. Defense," *Human Events* (November 15, 1975).
34 Ford, *A Time to Heal*, at 331; "Ford's Big Shuffle," at 25 ("appeased"); "Reagan Opens '76 Bid, Attacks Ford Policies," *Washington Post*, November 21, 1975 ("Eleventh Commandment"; Soviet Union).
35 Piero Gleijeses, *Conflicting Missions: Havana, Washington, and Africa, 1959–1976* (Chapel Hill: University of North Carolina Press, 2002), 278–93; National Security Council Minutes, June 27, 1975, http://www.fordlibrarymuseum.gov/library/document/nscmin/750627.pdf; ibid., December 22, 1975, http://www.fordlibrarymuseum.gov/library/document/nscmin/751222.pdf; Memorandum of Conversation, Ford, Kissinger, July 27, 1975, http://www.fordlibrarymuseum.gov/library/document/memcons/1553170.pdf (quotation).
36 Gleijeses, *Conflicting Missions*, at 293–99, 389–90; Zubok, *A Failed Empire*, at 251–53; Kissinger, *Years of Upheaval*, at 816–17; Memorandum of Conversation, Ford,

Kissinger, November 13, 1975, http://www.fordlibrarymuseum.gov/library/document/memcons/1553298.pdf; President's News Conference of November 26, 1975, americanpresidency.org.

37 Jussi Hanhimaki, *The Flawed Architect: Henry Kissinger and American Foreign Policy* (New York: Oxford University Press, 2004), 420 ("shit"); Seymour Hersh, "Early Angola Aid by U.S. Reported," *New York Times*, December 19, 1975 ("aggressive"); Seymour Hersh, "Angola-Aid Issue Opening Rifts in State Department," ibid., December 13, 1975 ("losers," "end up"); John Prados, *Safe for Democracy: The Secret Wars of the CIA* (Chicago: Ivan R. Dee, 2006), 452–53; Kissinger, *Years of Upheaval*, at 830–32; Memorandum of Conversation, Ford and Kissinger, December 18, 1975, http://www.fordlibrarymuseum.gov/library/document/memcons/1553319.pdf ("nightmare," "bastards"); ibid., Ford and Moynihan, January 27, 1976, http://www.fordlibrarymuseum.gov/library/document/memcons/1553319.pdf ("guts"); National Security Council Minutes, December 22, 1975.

38 Odd Arne Westad, *The Global Cold War: Third World Interventions and the Making of Our Times* (Cambridge, U.K.: Cambridge University Press, 2005), 237 ("benchmark"), and see Christopher Andrew and Vasili Mitrokhin, *The World Was Going Our Way: The KGB and the Battle for the Third World* (New York: Perseus, 2005), 453.

39 Memorandum of Conversation, Ford, Kissinger, January 25, 1975, http://www.fordlibrarymuseum.gov/library/document/memcons/1553346.pdf ("deeply," "Vietnam"); Kissinger, *Years of Upheaval*, at 851, 894–95 ("geopolitical," "psychological").

40 Kissinger, *Years of Upheaval*, at 840, 848, 860; Ford, *A Time to Heal*, at 357–58.

41 Patrick Tyler, *A Great Wall: Six Presidents and China* (New York: PublicAffairs, 1999), 219, 204, 207–08, 212, 216 ("appeasement"); Memorandum of Conversation, October 25, 1975, http://www.fordlibrarymuseum.gov/library/document/memcons/1553277.pdf; ibid., Ford, Kissinger, October 31, 1975, http://www.fordlibrarymuseum.gov/library/document/memcons/1553283.pdf; ibid., Ford, Kissinger, November 4, 1975, http://www.fordlibrarymuseum.gov/library/document/memcons/1553285.pdf.

42 Tyler, *A Great Wall*, at 205–14; Robert Hartmann to Ford, October 25, 1975, Box 39, President, Hartmann Papers ("main"); Memorandum of Conversation, October 25, 1975 ("leverage"; "screwed"); ibid., October 31, 1975 ("get").

43 Memorandum of Conversation, Ford, Kissinger, November 21, 1975, http://www.fordlibrarymuseum.gov/library/document/memcons/1553298.pdf ("Without"); Tyler, *A Great Wall*, at 215–19; "What Price Détente? Schlesinger and Zumwalt Confirm SALT Violations," *Human Events* (December 20, 1975) ("stand up"); "Ex-Chief of Navy Accuses Kissinger: Zumwalt Says Ford Was Not Given Full Data on Soviet Violations of Arms Pact," *New York Times*, December 3, 1975; "Zumwalt Charges Called Ridiculous," ibid., December 4, 1975; "Schlesinger Backs a Wary Détente," *Washington Post*, December 4, 1975 (SALT I, "clearly," "ambiguities," "swiftly").

44 Memorandum of Conversation, Ford, Kissinger, Rumsfeld, January 8, 1976, http://www.fordlibrarymuseum.gov/library/document/memcons/1553334.pdf ("toady"; "best interests"); ibid., Ford, Kissinger, Scowcroft, January 8, 1976, http://www.fordlibrarymuseum.gov/library/document/memcons/1553335.pdf; Kissinger, *Years of Upheaval*, at 854, 851–53 ("rubbing"). On the postponement of Kissinger's trip, see Memorandum of Conversation, Ford, Kissinger, December 6, 1975, http://www.fordlibrarymuseum.gov/library/document/memcons/1553316.pdf; ibid., December 9, 1975, Ford, Kissinger, Soviet Ambassador Dobrynin, http://www.fordlibrarymuseum.gov/library/document/memcons/1553316.pdf (Kissinger and Ford tried to explain to Dobrynin that Angola complicated prospects for détente and SALT II. Dobrynin insisted: "We are not interested in Angola. It was the process of decolonization. But you know how Africa goes. One day it goes this way; another day that way."); ibid., Ford, Kissinger, December 9, 1975, http://www.fordlibrarymuseum.gov/library/document/memcons/1553319.pdf (reporting that Dobrynin was "upset" about the delay. "He said it is another case of my being over-ruled").

45 Sidney Blumenthal, *The Rise of the Counter-Establishment: The Conservative Ascent to*

Political Power (New York: Union Square Press, 2008), xvi (Cheney and Rumsfeld); "New C.I.A. Estimate Finds Soviet Seeks Superiority in Arms," *New York Times*, December 26, 1976; Minutes, National Security Council Meeting, January 13, 1977, http://www.fordlibrarymuseum.gov/library/document/nscmin/770113.pdf. Ironically, Bush himself had guaranteed maximum publicity for Team B by giving *New York Times* correspondent David Binder an on-the-record interview about its work. Anne Cahn, *Killing Détente: The Right Attacks the CIA* (University Park, Pa.: Pennsylvania State University Press, 1998), 178.

46 See, e.g. Remarks at a Briefing for Representatives of Military Organizations on Defense and Foreign Policy, February 10, 1976; President's News Conference of February 13, 1976; Remarks to President Ford Committee Volunteers in Ft. Lauderdale, February 14, 1976; President's News Conference of February 17, 1976, all in americanpresidency.org; *Alerting America: The Papers of the Committee on the Present Danger*, ed. Charles Tyroler (McLean, Va.: Pergamon-Brassey, 1984), xv; Remarks and a Question-and-Answer Session at the Everett McKinley Dirksen Forum in Peoria, March 5, 1976, americanpresidency.org; Memorandum of Conversation, Ford, Kissinger, Scowcroft, March 18, 1976, http://www.fordlibrarymuseum.gov/library/document/memcons/1553400.pdf; ibid., March 19, 1976, Ford, Kissinger, http://www.fordlibrarymuseum.gov/library/document/memcons/1553403.pdf.

47 *Brown v. Board of Education*, 347 U.S. 483 (1954); *Brown v. Board of Education*, 349 U.S. 294 (1955); Robert Cover, "The Origins of Judicial Activism in the Protection of Minorities," *Yale Law Journal*, 91: 1287, 1316 (1982) ("paradigmatic").

48 "The Lawyers' War Against Democracy," *Commentary* (October 1979); Gerald Rosenberg, *The Hollow Hope: Can Courts Bring About Social Change?* (Chicago: University of Chicago Press, 1991), 4 ("those specific"); Laura Kalman, *The Strange Career of Legal Liberalism* (New Haven: Yale University Press, 1996).

49 See, e.g., Michael Klarman, *From Jim Crow to Civil Rights: The Supreme Court and the Struggle for Racial Equality* (New York: Oxford University Press, 2004); Barry Friedman, *The Will of the People: How Public Opinion Has Influenced the Supreme Court and Shaped the Meaning of the Constitution* (New York: Farrar, Straus and Giroux, 2009).

50 Joseph Lowndes, *From the New Deal to the New Right: Race and the Southern Origins of Modern Conservatism* (New Haven: Yale University Press, 2008), 5, 106–39; Meg Jacobs, *Pocketbook Politics: Economic Citizenship in Twentieth-Century America* (Princeton: Princeton University Press, 2004); Matthew Lassiter, *The Silent Majority: Suburban Politics in the Sunbelt South* (Princeton: Princeton University Press, 2006), 137, 5–6, 8 (*Brown*, "no," "entitlement," "homeowner"); Ira Katznelson, *When Affirmative Action Was White: An Untold History of Racial Inequality in Twentieth-Century America* (New York: W. W. Norton, 2005); Kevin Kruse, *White Flight: Atlanta and the Making of Modern Conservatism* (Princeton: Princeton University Press, 2005), 257 ("sealing").

51 *Green v. County School Board of New Kent County*, 391 U.S. 430 (1968); *Swann v. Charlotte-Mecklenburg Board of Education*, 402 U.S. 1 (1971); Kruse, *White Flight*, at 239; John Egerton, *The Americanization of Dixie: The Southernization of America* (New York: Harper's Magazine Press, 1974), 84–85; James Patterson, *Brown v. Board of Education: A Civil Rights Milestone and Its Troubled Legacy* (New York: Oxford University Press, 2001), 157 (Carter).

52 Lassiter, *The Silent Majority*, at 186.

53 Thomas Sugrue, *Sweet Land of Liberty: The Forgotten Struggle for Civil Rights in the North* (New York: Random House, 2008), 451–52, 460.

54 *Keyes v. School District No. 1*, 413 U.S. 189, 189, 208, 201, 213 (1973).

55 *San Antonio Independent School District v. Rodriguez*, 411 U.S. 1, 71 (1973).

56 *Milliken v. Bradley*, 418 U.S. 717, 759–60 (1974); Kruse, *White Flight*, at 257 ("suburban").

57 "Ford Chooses a Chicagoan for Supreme Court Seat; Nominee Is Appeals Judge: Seen as Centrist," *New York Times*, November 29, 1975; "Good Choice—for a Change," *Nation* (December 13, 1975); Dennis O'Brien, "Filling Justice William O. Douglas's

Seat: President Gerald R. Ford's Appointment of Justice John Paul Stevens," *Yearbook 1989, Supreme Court Historical Society*, 20, 35 (quotations).

58 *Milliken v. Bradley*, at 782, 814.

59 Jeane Theoharis, " 'They Told Us Our Kids Were Stupid': Ruth Batson and the Educational Movement in Boston," *Groundwork: Local Black Freedom Movements in America*, ed. Jeane Theoharis and Komozi Woodard (New York: New York University Press, 2005), 17, 25, 32–33 ("told"); Jeane Theoharis, " 'I'd Rather Go to School in the South': How Boston's School Desegregation Complicates the Civil Rights Paradigm," *Freedom North, Black Freedom Struggles Outside the South, 1950–1980*, ed. Jeane Theoharis and Komozi Woodard (New York: Palgrave, 2003), 125, 132–38; *Morgan v. Hennigan*, 379 F. Supp. 410, 482 (1974).

60 Theoharis, " 'I'd Rather Go to School in the South,' " at 141 (Hyde Park); J. Anthony Lukas, *Common Ground: A Turbulent Decade in the Lives of Three American Families* (New York: Vintage, 1986), 239–43; "4 Boston High Schools Hit by Walkouts," *New York Times*, December 13, 1974; and see Ronald Formisano, *Boston Against Busing: Race, Class, and Ethnicity in the 1960s and 1970s* (Chapel Hill: University of North Carolina Press, 1991).

61 President's News Conference of October 9, 1974, americanpresidency.org ("most," "in my"); Remarks and a Question-and-Answer Session with Members of the Northern Illinois Newspaper Association in Chicago, March 12, 1976, ibid. ("problem"); "425 Extra Policemen," *New York Times*, October 11, 1974 ("fanned").

62 Formisano, *Boston Against Busing*, at 76.

63 "Coleman: Some Second Thoughts," *Time* (September 15, 1975) ("imposed"); Diane Ravitch, "Busing: The Solution that Has Failed to Solve," *New York Times*, December 21, 1975 (quoting Biden and McGovern).

64 See, e.g., Remarks in Dallas at the Biennial Convention of the National Federation of Republican Women, September 13, 1975, americanpresidency.org ("better way"); Dick Parsons to James Cannon and Phil Buchen, October 23, 1975, Box 5, Busing, James Cannon Papers.

65 Derrick Bell, "Serving Two Masters: Integration Ideals and Client Interests in School Desegregation Litigation," *Critical Race Theory: The Key Writings that Formed the Movement*, ed. Kimberle Crenshaw, Neil Gotanda, Gary Peller, and Kendall Thomas (New York: New Press, 1995), 5, 8–9.

66 Ibid., at 6–7; Richard Kluger, *Simple Justice: The History of Brown v. Board of Education and Black America's Struggle for Equality* (New York: Alfred A. Knopf, 1976).

67 Bell, "Serving Two Masters," at 5, 10, 11.

68 Sugrue, *Sweet Land of Liberty*, at 485 (black power groups and Panthers); Emmett Buell with Richard Brisbin, *School Desegregation and Defended Neighborhoods: The Boston Controversy* (Lexington, Mass.: D. C. Heath, 1982), 20 (surveys); Lukas, *Common Ground*, at 282 (quoting mother; emphasis in the original).

69 Andrew Edelstein and Kevin McDonough, *The Seventies: From Hot Pants to Hot Tubs* (New York: Dutton, 1990) (the book is not paginated).

70 William Jones, "Blacks on the Slopes," *Washington Post*, April 10, 1977; Michael Ruby, "Blacks—on a New Plateau," *Newsweek* (October 4, 1976) (31.3 percent); *Statistical Abstract of the United States*, 1980 (Washington, D.C.: Government Printing Office, 1980), 52. By the federal government's estimate, a family of four with an income of $15,318 was middle class, and an urban family of four with an income of $5,500 or less lived in poverty.

71 Evelyn Schlatter, *Aryan Cowboys: White Supremacists and the Search for a New Frontier 1970–2000* (Austin: University of Texas Press, 2006), 37, 60; Peter Carroll, *It Seemed Like Nothing Happened: America in the 1970s* (New Brunswick, N.J.: Rutgers University Press, 1990), 177 ("real issue"; emphasis in the original); "The Busing Dilemma," *Time* (September 22, 1975) ("It's Not"); Theoharis, " 'I'd Rather Go to School in the South,' " at 142 ("linked"); Lukas, *Common Ground*, at 134 ("neighborhood").

72 Michael Novak, *The Rise of the Unmeltable Ethnics: Politics and Culture in the Seven-*

ties (New York: Macmillan, 1972), 53,18; Patrick Jones, *The Selma of the North: Civil Rights Insurgency in Milwaukee* (Cambridge: Harvard University Press, 2009), 107.

73 Jonathan Rieder, *Canarsie: The Jews and Italians of Brooklyn Against Liberalism* (Cambridge: Harvard University Press, 1985), 96, 98, 122; "The Busing Dilemma" ("both"); Carroll, *It Seemed Like Nothing Happened*, at 109 (quoting Rodriguez).

74 Philip Gleason, "American Identity and Americanization," *The Harvard Encyclopedia of American Ethnic Groups*, ed. Stephan Thernstrom, Ann Orlov, and Oscar Handlin (Cambridge: Belknap, 1981), 31, 54–55 (quotations); Matthew Jacobson, *Roots Too: White Ethnic Revival in Post Civil-Rights America* (Cambridge: Harvard University Press, 2006).

CHAPTER VI | INTANGIBLES

1 Tom Wolfe, "The 'Me' Decade and the Third Great Awakening," *New York* (August 23, 1976); Elizabeth Drew, *American Journal: The Events of 1976* (New York: Random House, 1977), 94, 188 ("style," "spirit," "intangibles").

2 "How Sick Is the GOP?," *Newsweek* (August 23, 1976).

3 *Buckley v. Valeo*, 424 U.S. 1 (1976).

4 Larry Sabato, *PAC Power: Inside the World of Political Action Committees* (New York: W. W. Norton, 1984), 10–11, 53.

5 Jerome Himmelstein, *To the Right: The Transformation of Conservatism in America* (Berkeley: University of California Press, 1990), 141; Sabato, *PAC Power*, at 16, 5, 96–105; Paul Taylor, "PACs Proliferate as Debate Rages; Committees Are New Sugar Daddy of Politics," *Washington Post*, March 30, 1982 ("Talking"). On Dart's role in the corporate PAC movement, see Kim Phillips-Fein, *Invisible Hands: The Making of the Conservative Movement from the New Deal to Reagan* (New York; W. W. Norton, 2009), 185–88.

6 Fred Wertheimer and Susan Manes, "Campaign Finance Reform: A Key to Restoring the Health of Our Democracy," *Columbia Law Review*, 94 (1994): 1126, 1142–45.

7 Bruce Miroff, *The Liberals' Moment: The McGovern Insurgency and the Identity Crisis of the Democratic Party* (Lawrence: University Press of Kansas, 2007), 277 ("whipping").

8 Adam Clymer, *Edward M. Kennedy: A Biography* (New York: William Morrow, 1999), 209–10, 225–26, 239; Kandy Stroud, *How Jimmy Won: The Victory Campaign from Plains to the White House* (New York: William Morrow, 1977), 20 ("Birds").

9 Carl Solberg, *Hubert Humphrey: A Biography* (New York: W. W. Norton, 1984), 452.

10 Jules Witcover, *Marathon: The Pursuit of the Presidency 1972–1976* (New York: Viking, 1977), 127, 216, 150, 162 (Mondale, Harris, Shapp, and Bentsen); Drew, *American Journal*, at 38 (Shriver).

11 Drew, *American Journal*, at 75 ("progressive"); Americans for Democratic Action (ADA), National Board Meeting, March 20, 1976, Box 1, ADA Papers, State Historical Society of Wisconsin; Stroud, *How Jimmy Won*, at 256–59 (press); Donald Carson and James Johnson, *Mo: The Life and Times of Morris K. Udall* (Tucson: University of Arizona Press, 2001).

12 Drew, *American Journal*, at 133–34 ("the only"); "ADA Hits Jackson Record; Senator Answers Charges," *ADA World* (January 1976); John Gerring, *Party Ideologies in America 1828–1996* (Cambridge, U.K.: Cambridge University Press, 1998), 284, 249–50 ("running away").

13 Witcover, *Marathon*, at 170 ("fine"); Dan Carter, *The Politics of Rage: George Wallace, the Origins of the New Conservatism, and the Transformation of American Populism* (New York: Simon & Schuster, 1995), 457.

14 Leo Ribuffo, "Writing About Jimmy Carter as If He Was Andrew Jackson: The Carter Presidency in (Deep Historical) Perspective," Conference on the Thirtieth Anniversary of Carter's Inauguration, University of Georgia, January 2007 ("prosperous"); Jimmy Carter, *Why Not the Best?* (New York: Bantam, 1976), 4, 7; James Wooten, *Dasher: The Roots and the Rising of Jimmy Carter* (New York: Summit Books,

1978), 148, 365 ("two wars"); E. Stanly Godbold, *Jimmy and Rosalynn Carter: The Georgia Years* (forthcoming, Oxford University Press, 2010) (Carter wealth).

15 Jimmy Carter, *Turning Point, A Candidate: a State, and a Nation Come of Age* (New York: Three Rivers Press, 1992), 72; Bob Short, *Everything Is Pickrick: The Life of Lester Maddox* (Macon, Ga.: Mercer University Press, 1999), 78, 126–29 ("hard-scrabble"); Peter Bourne, *Jimmy Carter: A Comprehensive Biography from Plains to Post-Presidency* (New York: Scribner, 1997), 167–70, 180–99 (religion, 1970 campaign); Inaugural Address, January 12, 1971, http://www.jimmycarterlibrary.gov/documents/inaugural_address.pdf; "New Governor of Georgia Urges End of Racial Bias," *New York Times*, January 13, 1971; Betty Glad, *Jimmy Carter: In Search of the Great White House* (New York: W. W. Norton, 1980), 141, 205 (camellias, media coverage).

16 "Carter and the God Issue," *Newsweek* (April 5, 1976) ("25 times," Spanish); Carter, *Why Not the Best?*, at 128, 132 (300, "you"; emphasis in the original); Glad, *Jimmy Carter*, at 177 (reorganization), and see Gary Fink, *Prelude to the Presidency: The Political Character and Legislative Leadership Style of Governor Jimmy Carter* (Westport, Conn.: Greenwood Press, 1980) (using Carter's legislative reorganization effort to study his leadership style as governor).

17 Wooten, *Dasher*, at 329, 328 ("charm," "[a]lways"); Glad, *Jimmy Carter*, at 207, 208–09 ("ABM"); Fink, *Prelude to the Presidency*, at 165–75. Carter's mother talked about him in "Sizing Up Carter; The Question of Character," *Newsweek* (September 13, 1976).

18 Bourne, *Jimmy Carter*, at 231–33; Victor Lasky, *Jimmy Carter: The Man and the Myth* (New York: Marek), 139 (quoting Bourne on "asset," "charm"); Martin Schram, *Running for President: A Journal of the Carter Campaign* (New York: Pocket Books, 1977), 59 ("smile," "depth").

19 Witcover, *Marathon*, at 110–15. Though Nixon vowed to campaign in every state, he ran for office in an age of far fewer primaries.

20 Robert Goldberg, *Barry Goldwater* (New Haven: Yale University Press, 1995), 296–97 (Trilateral Commission); Trilateral Commission, Frequently Asked Questions, http://www.trilateral.org/moreinfo/faqs.htm; Schram, *Running*, at 78 ("it might just"); Rosalynn Carter, *First Lady from Plains* (New York: Fawcett, 1984), 115.

21 Bourne, *Jimmy Carter*, at 185–86 (Jordan and Powell); "The Powell Behind Carter," *Newsweek* (June 21, 1976); "Jody Powell, The President's Trusted Aide de Camp," *Washington Post*, January 30, 1979; "Young Lawyer Helped Carter Get Past Many Shoals," *New York Times*, December 7, 1976; "An 'Aw-Shucks' Banker for Jimmy," *Time* (December 6, 1976); "The Atlantans Who Advise Jimmy Carter," *Business Week* (July 19, 1976) (Kirbo).

22 Bourne, *Jimmy Carter*, at 230; Carter, *First Lady from Plains*, at 115.

23 Schram, *Running*, at 19 ("silly"); Witcover, *Marathon*, at 201–02 ("politics").

24 Glad, *Jimmy Carter*, at 235 (Apple); Witcover, *Marathon*, at 213 (quotations).

25 Schram, *Running*, at 22.

26 Glad, *Jimmy Carter*, at 241 ("Peanut Brigade"); Robert Turner, *"I'll Never Lie to You": Jimmy Carter in His Own Words* (New York: Ballantine Books, 1976), 8 (quoting Carter); Schram, *Running*, at 26–27.

27 Lasky, *Jimmy Carter*, at 194 (coverage); Stroud, *How Jimmy Won*, at 266 ("overgrown").

28 Glad, *Jimmy Carter*, at 243, 300 (quoting Reston); Drew, *American Journal*, at 41; "The Boys on the Carter Bus," *National Journal* (May 29, 1976).

29 Andreas Killen, *1973 Nervous Breakdown: Watergate, Warhol, and the Birth of Post-Sixties America* (New York: Bloomsbury, 2006), 177 (nostalgia); Charles Morhr, "A Young Pollster Plays Key Role for Carter," *New York Times*, August 1, 1976; Drew, *American Journal*, at 286 ("major"); Bill Adler, *The Wit and Wisdom of Jimmy Carter* (Secaucus, N.J.: Citadel, 1977), 94 ("So"); Richard Reeves, "Carter's Secret," *New York* (March 22, 1976) ("post").

30 Adler, *Wit and Wisdom*, at 103 (quoting Carter).

31 Turner, *Jimmy Carter in His Own Words*, at 10, 11 ("instant," mannequin); Drew, *American Journal*, at 189 ("'What we'"); Witcover, *Marathon*, at 233 (school).

32 Witcover, *Marathon*, at 330; Robert Fogel, *The Fourth Great Awakening and the Future of Egalitarianism* (Chicago: University of Chicago Press, 2000), 30; "The Awakening We're Awaiting," *Christianity Today* (September 24, 1976) ("we"); David Kucharsky, "The Year of the Evangelical," ibid. (October 22, 1976); Drew, *American Journal*, at 93 ("mushy," "Perhaps").

33 Carter, *Why Not the Best?*, at 112 ("Show me"); Adler, *Wit and Wisdom*, at 103 ("intend"); Hugh Carter, *Cousin Beedie and Cousin Hot: My Life with the Carter Family of Plains, Georgia* (Englewood Cliffs, N.J.: Prentice Hall, 1978), 280 (monster peanut); Drew, *American Journal*, at 145 ("humble").

34 Bruce Schulman, *The Seventies: The Great Shift in American Culture, Society, and Politics* (New York: Free Press, 2001), xiv, 112–14; "Developing Sunbelt Hopes to Avoid North's Mistakes," *New York Times*, February 12, 1976, 1; "Houston, as Energy Capital, Sets Pace in Sunbelt Boom," ibid., February 9, 1976; "Design Notebook," ibid., July 30, 1978; Bethany Moreton, *To Serve God and Wal-Mart: The Making of Christian Free Enterprise* (Cambridge: Harvard University Press, 2009), 38, 46 ("twang"); Shane Hamilton, *Trucking Country: The Road to America's Wal-Mart Economy* (Princeton: Princeton University Press, 2008), 220–23; Scott Von Doviak, *Hick Flicks: The Rise and Fall of Redneck Cinema* (Jefferson, N.C.: McFarland & Company, 2004); C. Vann Woodward, *The Burden of Southern History*, 3d ed. (Baton Rouge: Louisiana State University Press, 1993), 236.

35 "How Southern Is He?," *Time* (September 27, 1976) ("farm boy"); Stroud, *How Jimmy Won*, at 154 ("marine"); Bruce Maizlish and Edwin Diamond, *Jimmy Carter: An Interpretive Biography* (New York: Simon & Schuster, 1979), 104 ("two Jimmy Carters"); Scott Kaufman, *Rosalynn Carter: Equal Partner in the White House* (Lawrence: University Press of Kansas, 2007).

36 Bob Colcello, *Holy Terror: Andy Warhol Close Up* (New York: Cooper Square Press, 2000), 361; Malcolm MacDougall, *We Almost Made It* (New York: Crown Publishers, 1977), 3 (phone call).

37 *Redneck Power: The Wit and Wisdom of Billy Carter*, ed. Jeremy Rifkin and Ted Howard (New York: Bantam, 1977) (the book is not paginated).

38 "Out of a Cocoon," *Time* (September 27, 1976) (Young); Kaye Pullen, Carter and the Solid South, n.d., Box 14, Jimmy Carter, Michael Raoul-Duval Papers, Ford Library ("Carter is playing"); Glad, *Jimmy Carter*, at 323 (three Rs).

39 Schram, *Running*, at 96–98.

40 Ibid., at 219; Glad, *Jimmy Carter*, at 245 (quoting Joel McCleary).

41 Schram, *Running*, at 90 ("grits"); Glad, *Jimmy Carter*, at 247 (absence of media speculation, "was still"); Witcover, *Marathon*, at 285–86, 289.

42 Witcover, *Marathon*, at 302–08.

43 Schram, *Running*, at 133–34, 145–51 (Shrum's hiring and firing, "offend"); Glad, *Jimmy Carter*, at 296, 297 (quoting Shrum on "dichotomy," public compassion"); Witcover, *Marathon*, at 326 (possible later impact); Christopher Lydon, "A Carter Writer Quits in Protest," *New York Times*, May 3, 1976; "Giving Carter the Fish Eye," *Newsweek* (May 17, 1976); Robert Shrum, *No Excuses: Confessions of a Serial Campaigner* (New York: Simon & Schuster, 2007), 62–69. For the rebuttal to Shrum, see Simon Lazarus and Harry Huge, "They Done Him Wrong," *New Republic* (June 5, 1976) ("handed," "questions," "Carter's"; I am grateful to E. Stanly Godbold for sending me this article).

44 Drew, *American Journal*, at 288, 168–70; Schram, *Running*, at 152 ("Anybody").

45 Drew, *American Journal*, at 293, 198–99 ("California hip," "limits"); Schram, *Running*, at 161 ("inner meaning"); Lasky, *Jimmy Carter*, at 231 ("new me"); Witcover, *Marathon*, at 331, 335 ("lowered," "important," "If"); "Jerry Brown, He Thinks He Wants to Be President," *Washington Post*, May 9, 1976.

46 LeRoy Ashby and Rod Gramer, *Fighting the Odds: The Life of Senator Frank Church* (Pullman: Washington State University Press, 1994), 495–515.

47 Stroud, *How Jimmy Won*, at 304–05 (audience); Dudley Buffa, *Union Power and American Democracy: The UAW and the Democratic Party 1972–1983* (Ann Arbor: University

of Michigan Press, 1984), 146–60; Schram, *Running*, at 167–70; Schram, ibid., at 167–69, 185.

48 Witcover, *Marathon*, at 349–50.

49 Schram, *Running*, at 6–7 (jeans); "Nominee-in-Waiting," *Newsweek* (June 21, 1976) (quotations).

50 Drew, *American Journal*, at 281–83.

51 "Buysentennial Sellabration," *New York* (July 5, 1976); Christopher Capozzola, " 'It Makes You Want to Believe in the Country': Celebrating the Bicentennial in an Age of Limits," *America in the Seventies*, ed. Beth Bailey and David Farber (Lawrence: University Press of Kansas, 2004), 29–49; Schram, *Running*, at 239 ("welcomed back," "captured," "also"); Drew, *American Journal*, at 295 (reporting and refuting "love-in" characterization); Patrick Anderson, *Electing Jimmy Carter* (Baton Rouge: Louisiana State University Press, 1992), 56 ("hillbilly"); Richard Reeves, *Convention* (New York: Harcourt Brace Jovanovich, 1977), 69, 79, 92–93 ("their," Carter operatives, New York).

52 Reeves, *Convention*, at 213–15; emphasis in the original.

53 Stroud, *How Jimmy Won*, at 329–30 (plane); Richard Reeves, "There's a Smile on Plains' Face for the Whole Human Race," *New York* (July 26, 1976) ("If," "drink"); Anderson, *Electing Jimmy Carter*, at 87 (pot).

54 Glad, *Jimmy Carter*, at 374–75.

55 Gerald R. Ford, *A Time to Heal: The Autobiography of Gerald R. Ford* (New York: Harper & Row, 1979), 341–43; Richard Viguerie, *The New Right: We're Ready to Lead* (Falls Church, Va.: Viguerie Company, 1980), 122; David Lissy to James Cannon, December 4, 1975, Box 8, White House Central Files/LA6, Ford Library; "Dunlop Ties Picket Bill, Labor Peace," *Washington Post*, December 18, 1975; Statement Announcing Intention to Veto the Common Situs Bill, December 22, 1975, americanpresidency.org; "The Nation: Ford Is Candidly Political on the Situs Veto," *New York Times*, December 28, 1975 ("ran out"); "A Lost Cause that Was Won," *Conservative Digest* (April 1976).

56 Paul Weyrich, "Blue Collar or Blue Blood?," *The New Right Papers*, ed. Robert Whitaker (New York: St. Martin's Press, 1982), 48, 60.

57 Nick Thimmesch, "The Grass-Roots Dollar Chase—Ready on the Right," *New York* (June 9, 1975) ("fund-raiser extraordinaire"); Nick Kotz, "King Midas of 'The New Right,' " *Atlantic Monthly* (November 1978) ("rolls," "encoded"); David Broder, *Changing of the Guard: Power and Leadership in America* (New York: Simon & Schuster, 1980), 184 (two hundred).

58 Grace Lichtenstein, "G.O.P. in Arizona Endorses Reagan," *New York Times*, April 25, 1976 (reporting Goldwater "all but endorsed" Ford and said Reagan misinterpreted Ford's foreign policy); Richard Cheney to Ford, November 13, 1975, Box 16, Cheney/Goldwater, Ford Library; William Rusher, *The Rise of the Right* (New York: William Morrow, 1984), 272, 280–82 (reporting on actual Goldwater endorsement, which did not come until June 30, 1976); "The Ford Record: A Trail of Broken Promises," *Conservative Digest* (May 1976).

59 Witcover, *Marathon*, at 412 (quoting Ford); Drew, *American Journal*, at 53 (quoting Reagan).

60 George Michael, *Willis Carto and the American Far Right* (Gainesville: University Press of Florida, 2008), 177; "Fund Raiser Becomes New Kind of Power Broker," *New York Times*, May 23, 1975; Craig Shirley, *Reagan's Revolution: The Untold Story of the Campaign that Started It All* (Nashville: Nelson Current, 2005), 74 (the contract went to Bruce W. Eberle & Associates); *Allen Crawford, Thunder on the Right: The 'New Right' and the Politics of Resentment* (New York: Pantheon, 1980), 118 (on Viguerie's irritation and quoting Weyrich); Stuart Spencer, Oral History, Miller Center of Public Affairs, November 15, 2001, http://web1.millercenter.org/poh/transcripts/ohp_2001_1115_spencer.pdf, 35–37.

61 "An Explanation of the Reagan Victories in Texas and the Caucus States," n.d. (c. May 1976), http://www.fordlibrarymuseum.gov/library/exhibits/campaign/reagan.asp.

"I, along with most conservatives, want Ronald Reagan to win the Republican nomination and to be elected president this November," Viguerie insisted to *Conservative Digest* readers in the summer of 1976. But if that did not happen, he continued, conservatives should bolt and form a third party to bring conservative Democrats and Republicans together. Even if Reagan became the GOP nominee, conservatives should "divorce" the party and establish their own because the Republicans had taken them for granted. "An Alternative Plan," *Conservative Digest* (August 1976).

62 William Rusher to William F. Buckley, Jr., February 19, 1976, Box 121, File 9, William Rusher Papers, Library of Congress, and see Rusher to Buckley, March 16, 1976, ibid.; John Judis, *William F. Buckley, Jr.: Patron Saint of the Conservatives* (New York: Simon & Schuster, 1988), 387 ("kooks"); "If Ford Wins, Will You Support a Third Party?," *Conservative Digest* (June 1976) (of the twenty-three conservative leaders surveyed, nine said they would, five said they would not, and the rest refused to commit themselves).

63 Rusher, *The Rise of the Right*, at 275–77, 314; Minutes, Board of Directors Meeting, June 7, 1975, Box 21, File 13, American Conservative Union (ACU) Papers, Brigham Young University Archives; Minutes, September 27, 1975, Box 21, File 14, ibid.; "Conservative Plans Drive for Connally in New Hampshire; Loeb Denies Any Role," *New York Times*, February 10, 1976; "Campaign for Connally Yields 42 Write-In Votes," ibid., February 26, 1976; "Connally Favors Ford's Candidacy as 'Better Choice,'" ibid., July 28, 1976.

64 Richard Viguerie and David Franke, *America's Right Turn: How Conservatives Used New and Alternative Media to Take Power* (Chicago: Bonus Books, 2004), 125–26.

65 Witcover, *Marathon*, at 394, 388–89; Steven Hayward, *The Age of Reagan, 1964–1980: The Fall of the Old Liberal Order* (Roseville, Calif.: Forum/Prima, 2001), 453 (media); Drew, *American Journal*, at 49 (handlers).

66 Witcover, *Marathon*, at 376, 386–87, 396, 397 ("They"); Memorandum of Conversation, Ford, Kissinger, Rumsfeld, Cheney, February 5, 1976, http://www.fordlibrarymuseum.gov/library/document/memcons/1553357.pdf ("slips"); "Nixon, in Peking, Says Mere Pacts Don't Bring Peace: Toast in China Is Regarded by Some as Criticism of Ford and Kissinger," *New York Times*, February 23, 1976; Memorandum of Conversation, Ford, Kissinger, February 25, 1976, http://www.fordlibrarymuseum.gov/library/document/memcons/1553382.pdf; ibid., Ford, Clare Boothe Luce, February 25, 1976, http://www.fordlibrarymuseum.gov/library/document/memcons/1553381.pdf (Keene); Remarks and a Question-and-Answer Session at a Public Forum in Keene, February 19, 1976, americanpresidency.org.

67 "Ford Shatters 11th Commandment," *Human Events* (February 28, 1976) ("savage"); "Will Cruise Missile Be Scrapped at Salt II? Reagan Opens Fire on Kissinger's Détente Policy," ibid. (February 21, 1976) ("without"); "Conservatives Angered by Ford Campaign Tactics," ibid. (March 6, 1976); Witcover, *Marathon*, at 398–99 (Sears); Shirley, *Reagan's Revolution*, at 174 ("holy"); Ford, *A Time to Heal*, at 346, 373 ("sole architect"; Number Two); Isaacson, *Henry Kissinger*, at 696 ("we built it"); Witcover, *Marathon*, at 402–03 (quoting Reagan adviser David Keene); Peter Hannaford to M. Stanton Evans, November 9, 1977, Box 11, File 8, Peter Hannaford Papers, Hoover Institution (stressing importance of canal issue to Florida).

68 Drew, *American Journal*, at 28 ("more"); "'Santa Claus' Ford on the Campaign Trail," *Human Events* (April 3, 1976); James Burnham to William F. Buckley, Jr., Box 105, File 395, William F. Buckley, Jr., Papers, Yale University Archives.

69 William Rusher to Mary Louise Self, March 18, 1976, Box 81, File 6, Rusher Papers ("better way," "fussy"); Rusher to Ted Robertson, June 10, 1975, Box 77, Folder 1, ibid. ("primitive"); Rusher to Buckley, February 19, 1976 ("since").

70 Shirley, *Reagan's Revolution*, at 158–67; William Link, *Righteous Warrior: Jesse Helms and the Rise of Modern Conservatism* (New York: St. Martin's Press, 2008), 150–59.

71 Peter Hannaford to Ronald Reagan, Texas Events, April 13, 1976, Box 6, File 4, Hannaford Papers; Hayward, *The Age of Reagan*, at 471 (liquor); "Reagan Wins in Nebraska and Church Is Leading Carter; Ford West Virginia Victor," *New York*

Times, May 12, 1976 ("viable"); Ron Nessen, *It Sure Looks Different from the Inside* (Chicago: Playboy, 1978), 214.

72 "Reagan and Credibility: The Faith Conservatives Had in Him Suffers from His Choice of a Liberal," *New York Times*, July 30, 1976.

73 "High Noon," *Newsweek* (August 23, 1976) ("more"); "The Plight of the GOP," *Time* (August 23, 1976.)

74 Steven Hayes, *Cheney* (New York: HarperCollins, 2007), 107; Nessen, *It Sure Looks Different*, at 222–23 (joke); Robert Novak, *The Prince of Darkness: 50 Years Reporting in Washington* (New York: Three Rivers, 2007), 294 ("handsome"); James Baker III with Steve Fiffer, *"Work Hard, Study . . . and Keep out of Politics!"* (New York: Putnam, 2006), 41–48; "RNC Stacks the Deck for Ford," *Human Events* (July 10, 1976); Max Friedersdorf to Richard Cheney, July 2, 1976, Box 3, Campaign: May–July, 1976, Congressional Relations Office: Max Friedersdorf, Ford Library (reporting on Reagan and delegates).

75 Witcover, *Marathon*, at 477; David Keene, "Why Reagan Chose Schweiker for VP," *Human Events*, 36:58 (November 27, 1976): 8 (Mississippi); Link, *Righteous Warrior*, at 164 (Helms); Becky Norton to Polly Lindskog, November 23, 1976, Box 49, File 18, ACU Papers (explaining that though the ACU did not always agree with Reagan and had opposed the Schweiker selection, it believed he would have been "a very fine, conservative President"); Shirley, *Reagan's Revolution*, at 278 (quoting Viguerie and contending that Sears had made a smart move); Hayward, *The Age of Reagan*, at 476 (quoting Phillips); "Reaction to the Schweiker Bombshell," *Human Events* (August 7, 1976).

76 "Instant Replay: How Ford Won It," *Time* (August 30, 1976) ("misery").

77 Ford, *A Time to Heal*, at 397–400; Isaacson, *Henry Kissinger*, at 699 ("I could"); Catherine Rymph, *Republican Women: Feminism and Conservatism from Suffrage Through the New Right* (Chapel Hill: University of North Carolina Press, 2006), 223–24.

78 Craig Shirley, *Rendezvous with Destiny: Ronald Reagan and the Campaign that Changed America* (Wilmington, Del.: Intercollegiate Studies Institute, 2009), 13 (refusal to choose Reagan); Schram, *Running*, at 259 (Reagan's staff).

79 Shirley, *Reagan's Revolution*, at 330, 332–34 (reprinting Reagan's speech).

80 Ibid., at xxvii (intimates); Murray Kempton, "Born Again Republicans," *Harper's* (November 1976).

81 Rusher, *Rise of the Right*, at 287–89.

82 Crawford, *Thunder on the Right*, at 236–37 ("atheistical"); William Rusher to Joseph Coors, September 9, 1976, Box 21, File 3, Rusher Papers.

83 "Independent Party Picks Maddox to Head '76 Ticket," *New York Times*, August 28, 1976; "Should Conservatives Form a Third Party?," *Human Events* (November 20, 1976) ("we're conservative"); Becky Norton to to Claud Edwards, September 3, 1976, Box 49, File 18, ACU Papers; "A Reluctant Vote for Gerald Ford," *Human Events* (October 30, 1976); "From the Publisher: What Should We Do on November 2d?," *Conservative Digest* (November 1976).

84 The Ford Campaign Plan—Final Copy, n.d., Box 13, Duval Papers, Ford Library.

85 Quoted in Schram, *Running*, at 266.

86 Andrew Edelstein and Kevin McDonough, *The Seventies: From Hot Pants to Hot Tubs* (New York: Dutton, 1990). The book is not paginated.

87 "Leadership: The Biggest Issue," *Time* (November 8, 1976); Robert Teeter, The Present National Political Attitude as Determined by Pre-Election Polls, Box 62, Post Election Analysis—Speeches & Reports (2), Ford Library.

88 Peter Carroll, *It Seemed Like Nothing Happened: America in the 1970s* (New Brunswick: N.J.: Rutgers University Press, 1990), 201 ("hoopskirts"); "A Look at the Ford Record," n.d., Press Office, Jody Powell 1976 Campaign/Transition File, Box 4, Ford/Dole Voting Records, Carter Library ("failed"); John Dumbrell, *The Carter Presidency: A Re-Evaluation* (Manchester, U.K.: Manchester University Press, 1995); Joseph A. Califano, Jr., *Governing America: An Insider's Report from the White House to the Cabinet* (New York: Touchstone, Simon & Schuster, 1985), 51.

89 Drew, *American Journal*, at 441.
90 Witcover, *Marathon*, at 547–48 (Kelley).
91 Schram, *Running*, at 309; Stroud, *How Jimmy Won*, at 401.
92 Drew, *American Journal*, at 512 (Carter as issue).
93 Witcover, *Marathon*, at 577.
94 Stroud, *How Jimmy Won*, at 363, 364.
95 Witcover, *Marathon*, at 577, 562–64.
96 Schram, *Running*, at 337 ("killed"); Anderson, *Electing Jimmy Carter*, at 112 ("straight line"); "Carter Proposes a Unified Agency in the Cabinet for Energy Policy," *New York Times*, September 22, 1976 ("mild"); Witcover, *Marathon*, at 590 (quoting students); Nessen, *It Sure Looks Different*, at 300 (bumper stickers).
97 Anderson, *Electing Jimmy Carter*, at 116 ("who promised"); Schram, *Running*, at 340 ("Everything").
98 Schram, *Running*, at 342 (Cheney); Witcover, *Marathon*, at 530 ("as a").
99 Schram, *Running*, at 377–78 (flubs); Nessen, *It Sure Looks Different*, at 279–94 (Butz).
100 Presidential Campaign Debate, October 6, 1976, americanpresidency.org; Leo Ribuffo, "Is Poland a Soviet Satellite? Gerald Ford, the Sonnenfeldt Doctrine, and the Election of 1976," in Leo Ribuffo, *Right Center Left: Essays in American History* (New Brunswick, N.J.: Rutgers University Press, 1992), 189, 190.
101 Richard Cheney, The 1976 Presidential Debate: A Republican Perspective, October 1977, Box 62, Post Election Analysis—Speeches and Reports (5), Robert Teeter Papers, Ford Library; Frederick Steeper, The Public's Response to Gerald Ford's Statements on Eastern Europe During the Second Debate, ibid.
102 Ribuffo, "Is Poland a Soviet Satellite?," at 210–11; Witcover, *Marathon*, at 604 ("'dumb' issue"); Stroud, *How Jimmy Won*, at 381 ("He's not writing"); "Reporters Gang Up on Ford in Third Debate," *Human Events* (November 6, 1976).
103 Drew, *American Journal*, at 473, 477; Stroud, *How Jimmy Won*, at 350; Gerald Rafshoon to Carter, n.d., Box 34, Campaign Strategy, 1980, Susan Clough Papers, Carter Library ("you"); Stuart Eizenstat and David Rubenstein to Carter, November 30, 1976, Domestic Policy Staff Collection, ibid.; Al Stern, "Promises, Promises," Box 6, ibid.
104 Ford, *A Time to Heal*, at 431 ("Bataan Death March"); Nessen, *It Sure Looks Different*, at 303, 307–08 (quoting Cheney, "Joe").
105 Patrick Caddell, Initial Working Paper on Democratic Strategy, December 10, 1976, Press Office, Powell, Box 4, Memorandums—Patrick Caddell, Carter Library; MacDougall, *We Almost Made It*, at 197, 199.
106 Schram, *Running*, at 389.
107 Hamilton Jordan to Carter, The 1980 General Election: An Overview, n.d., Box 37, Campaign Memoranda, July 1980, Clough Papers; Archie Robinson, *George Meany and His Times* (New York: Simon & Schuster, 1981), 355 ("[e]lder"). Leon Shull to Marvin Rosenberg, September 23, 1976, Box 5, File 32, ADA Papers, and Leon Shull to Thomas Carson, February 8, 1977, ibid., File 33 (reporting liberals' lack of enthusiasm and ADA support).
108 Text of Vice President Richard Cheney's Eulogy for President Gerald Ford, December 30, 2006, http://www.usatoday.com/news/washington/2006-12-30-ford-cheney-text_x.htm; Ronald Reagan to Dear ——, Box 6, File 1, Hannaford Papers; Teeter quoted in MacDougall, *We Almost Made It*, at 43–45. Compare, e.g., "Gerald R. Ford, 93, Dies; Led in Watergate's Wake," *Washington Post*, December 27, 2006 (quoting from 2004 interview in which Ford said pardon had "probably" hurt him) with "Ford's Long Shadow: An Unlikely President, Ford Steadied America, and, in an Unpublished Interview, Mused About Her Fate," *Newsweek* (January 8, 2007) (quoting from 1995 interview in which Ford stressed Reagan's failure to campaign).
109 Hayward, *The Age of Reagan*, at 506–07; Shirley, *Rendezvous with Destiny*, at 13–18; "The Senate's Newest Star: Orrin Hatch," *Conservative Digest* (February 1977); Robert Mason, *Richard Nixon and the Quest for a New Majority* (Chapel Hill: University of North Carolina Press, 2004), 27, 47–56; William Rusher, "The Party Should Be

Scrapped," *Human Events* (November 27, 1976); Richard Viguerie, "GOP Leadership Should Resign," *Conservative Digest* (December 1976); "Politicians Find G.O.P. Fighting for Its Survival," *New York Times*, November 24, 1976 ("extinction"); "Reagan Will Not Bar Another Try in 1980," ibid. (November 3, 1976). For negative assessments of the 1976 campaign by Carter's advisers, see the memorandums to the president from Hamilton Jordan, n.d.; Patrick Caddell, n.d. (c. June 1980); and Gerald Rafshoon, all in Box 34, Susan Clough Papers, Campaign Strategies.

CHAPTER VII | FROM BUSING TO *BAKKE*

1 "The Future of the G.O.P," *New York Times*, November 10, 1976.
2 Patrick Caddell, Initial Working Paper on Political Strategy, December 10, 1976, Box 4, Press Office, Jody Powell 1976 Campaign/Transition File (unless otherwise noted, all archival materials cited in this chapter are in the Carter Library).
3 "Carter's Gray Eminence," *Newsweek* (July 12, 1976); Peter Bourne, *Jimmy Carter: A Comprehensive Biography from Plains to the Post-Presidency* (New York: Scribner, 1997), 361–67; Carter to Griffin Bell, December 22, 1978, White House Central Files, Name File: Griffin Bell ("Southern gentleman"); U.S. Senate, Ninety-fifth Congress, First Session, Committee on the Judiciary, *Hearings on the Nomination of Griffin B. Bell*, January 1977, 32, 36, 135–36, 245.
4 *Pasadena Board of Education v. Spangler*, 427 U.S. 424 (1976); *Dayton Board of Education v. Brinkman*, 433 U.S. 406, 413 (1977); *Columbus Board of Education v. Penick*, 443 U.S. 449, 525 (Pilate) (1979); *Dayton Board of Education v. Brinkman*, 443 U.S. 526 (1979); Drew Days, "School Desegregation Law in the 1980's: Why Isn't Anyone Laughing?," *Yale Law Journal*, 95 (1986): 1737, 1749 ("The *Dayton I* decision, as it has come to be called, appeared to turn *Keyes* on its head: rather than *enjoying* a presumption that a school board's intentional segregative actions created a segregative effect, plaintiffs now would have the burden of *rebutting* a presumption that forces beyond the school board's control were largely responsible for the existing segregation"; emphases in the original); Owen Fiss, "The Supreme Court, 1978 Term, Foreword: The Forms of Justice," *Harvard Law Review*, 93 (1979): 1, 5 (characterizing cases as squeakers).
5 Terry Anderson, *The Pursuit of Fairness: A History of Affirmative Action* (New York: Oxford University Press, 2004), 75–76, 17–25.
6 Lizabeth Cohen, *A Consumers' Republic: The Politics of Mass Consumption in Postwar America* (New York: Alfred A. Knopf, 2003), 137–41, 167–71; Ira Katznelson, *When Affirmative Action Was White: An Untold History of Racial Inequality in Twentieth-Century America* (New York: W. W. Norton, 2005), 115 ("For White Veterans"); Executive Order 10925, March 6, 1961, americanpresidency.org; Anderson, *The Pursuit of Fairness*, at 60–66.
7 Nancy MacLean, *Freedom Is Not Enough: The Opening of the American Workplace* (Cambridge: Harvard University Press, 2006), 54; Commencement Address at Howard University: To Fulfill These Rights, June 4, 1965, americanpresidency.org.
8 Allan Sindler, *Bakke, DeFunis and Minority Admissions: The Quest for Equal Opportunity* (New York: Longman, 1978), 204 ("potato"). In 1971 the Court unanimously held that Title VII prohibited "not only overt discrimination but also practices that are fair in form but discriminatory in operation," unless the employer could justify those practices as "a business necessity." Whether the discrimination was intentional was irrelevant. What mattered was that its effects had a disparate impact on those protected by Title VII. *Griggs v. Duke Power Co.*, 401 U.S. 424, 431 (1971). Five years later, however, the Court gave a nod of approval to a police force entrance exam a disproportionate number of African Americans had failed because its challengers had not demonstrated discriminatory intent. *Washington v. Davis*, 426 U.S. 229 (1976). Congressional amendments in 1972 made federal, state, and local governments and secondary and higher education institutions subject to Title VII. And Title IX of the 1972 amendments forbade discrimination against students on the basis of sex in any educational program or activity receiving federal assistance. For a discussion of

the Nixon administration's use of affirmative action, see John Skrentny, *The Ironies of Affirmative Action* (Chicago: University of Chicago Press, 1996), 177–221; MacLean, *Freedom Is Not Enough*, at 95–103.

9 Anderson, *The Pursuit of Fairness*, at 141–43; MacLean, *Freedom Is Not Enough*, at 189–92.

10 Alexander Bickel, "Watergate and the Legal Order," *Commentary* (January 1974). See also Bickel, *The Morality of Consent* (New Haven: Yale University Press, 1975), 123.

11 Alexander Bickel, Brief of Anti-Defamation League of B'nai B'rith as Amicus Curiae in Support of Jurisdictional Statement or in the Alternative Petition for Certiorari, Supreme Court of the United States, Number 73-235, October Term, 1973, 22–24.

12 *DeFunis v. Odegaard*, 416 U.S. 312, 336, 337 (1974); emphasis added.

13 Sindler, *Bakke, DeFunis and Minority Admissions*, at 204.

14 "White/Caucasian—and Rejected," *New York Times Magazine*, April 3, 1977; "'In Fact, There Is No New Wrong,'" *New York Times*, September 12, 1977 (age).

15 "White/Caucasian—and Rejected." The assistant dean, Peter Storandt, insisted that he had not acted inappropriately. "In admissions it is improper to play favorites, or to grant to any one applicant attention or support that would be denied to any other. Hence when Allan Bakke asked for response to his dilemma he received neither more nor less than would any other candidate." Peter Storandt to Editor, *New York Times*, "Reparation, American Style: A 'Stubbornly Fair-Minded' Admissions Officer," *New York Times*, July 3, 1977.

16 Lincoln Caplan, *Up Against the Law: Affirmative Action and the Supreme Court* (New York: Twentieth Century Fund Press, 1997), 18–19.

17 University of California, Memorandum of Points and Authorities in Opposition to Issuance of Preliminary Injunction or Writ or Mandate, Superior Court of the State of California, *Allan Bakke versus Regents of the University of California*, I:101, n. 1; Joel Dreyfuss and Charles Lawrence, *The Bakke Case: The Politics of Inequality* (New York: Harcourt Brace Jovanovich, 1979), 41–43, 24, 65–66; "Reparation, American Style," July 4, 1977 (dean's program); David White, "Culturally Based Testing and Predictive Invalidity: Putting Them on the Record," *Harvard Civil Rights–Civil Liberties Law Review*, 14 (1979): 89–132.

18 Ralph Smith, "Reflections on a Landmark: Some Preliminary Observations on the Development and Significance of *Regents of the University of California v. Allan Bakke*," *Howard Law Journal*, 21:72 (1978), 77–79 (reporting accusation); Sindler, *Bakke, DeFunis, and Minority Admissions*, at 239 (quoting regent).

19 *Bakke v. Regents of the University of California*, 18 Cal. 3d 34, 48, 54, 59, n. 29; (1976); Kathleen Sullivan, "Comment: Sins of Discrimination: Last Term's Affirmative Actions," *Harvard Law Review* 100 (1986): 78, 80, 91("sin-based paradigm," "penance.")

20 18 Cal. 3d 64, 91, 90.

21 Plaintiff's Stipulation, *Allan Bakke versus Regents of the University of California*, 2: 53–54, *Allan Bakke versus Regents of the University of California*, ed. Alfred A. Slocum (Dobbs Ferry, N.Y.: Oceana, 1978). Though UC defended this change in strategy as necessary to obtain speedy review of the case by the United States Supreme Court, its admission that Bakke might have been admitted had there been no special admissions program seemed to many to be unnecessarily damaging to the cause of affirmative action. According to the National Conference of Black Lawyers, "the University failed to allow the case to be returned to the trial court on an issue on which it could prevail; instead the University ignored the weight of its own evidence, contradicted its earlier position and stipulated the issue away so it could obtain the final order that would invoke this Court's jurisdiction." Brief Amicus Curiae of the National Conference of Black Lawyers, *Allan Bakke versus Regents of the University of California*, Slocum, IV:14.

22 Derrick Bell, "Bakke, Minority Admissions, and the Usual Price of Racial Remedies," *California Law Review*, 67 (1979): 5–6; "Justice Dept. Brief 1 of 58 in Bakke Case," *New York Times*, September 20, 1977.

23 "Reparation, American Style," *New York Times*, July 4, 1977. See also "Reparation,

American Style," ibid., June 19, 1977. For example, if a judge wanted to rule in Bakke's favor, one way he could do so was by declaring that courts had interpreted the Fourteenth Amendment's equal protection clause to make race a "suspect" classification. That would mean that any affirmative program based on classification by race was presumptively unconstitutional unless it advanced a "compelling state interest." The judge might then argue that the University of California had shown no compelling state interest in integrating medical schools and the medical profession through affirmative action programs. Or the judge could contend, as Mosk had done, that while the University of California might have established a compelling state interest, it had not proved that affirmative action programs were the least drastic means of achieving its goals. 18 Cal. 3d. 49.

But if a judge wanted to rule in favor of the University of California, he could say that the University of California had demonstrated a compelling state interest in favor of integrating medical schools and the profession and that affirmative action programs were the only way of achieving these goals. Or he could point to the busing cases as support for the idea that race-conscious remedial programs did not violate the equal protection clause because they injured some whites. Or as Tobriner had done, a judge could cite cases supporting the proposition that race was a "suspect classification" only when it involved "invidious discrimination," as opposed to "benign" treatment designed to remedy past discrimination. Tobriner's argument was more novel. It received support, however, when the U.S. Supreme Court in *United Jewish Organizations v. Carey* upheld a reapportionment plan designed to create a black majority voting district soon after the California Supreme Court decided *Bakke*. Justice Brennan there referred to "the settled principle that not every remedial use of race is constitutionally forbidden." *United Jewish Organizations v. Carey*, 430 U.S. 144, 169, 171 (1977). It is not my purpose to explore the many important doctrinal issues associated with *Bakke* here, which have been examined in great detail elsewhere and have overshadowed the political considerations involved in the case.

24 Jonathan Mahler, *Ladies and Gentlemen, the Bronx Is Burning: 1977, Baseball, Politics, and the Battle for the Soul of a City* (New York: Farrar, Straus and Giroux, 2005), 156, 256 ("summer," drop in disco business); "Rock Album by Hendrix Is Examined for a Clue on 'Son of Sam's' Name," *New York Times*, July 7, 1977; Peter Braunstein, "Adults Only: The Construction of an Erotic City in New York During the 1970s," *America in the 1970s*, ed. Beth Bailey and David Farber (Lawrence: University Press of Kansas, 2004), 129, 149 ("disco backlash" of angry white men); "Discophobia," *New York Times*, July 10, 1979; "Disco vs. Rock and Industry Ills Made the Year Dramatic," ibid., December 30, 1979 ("as much"); Bruce Schulman, *The Seventies: The Great Shift in American Culture, Society, and Politics* (New York: Free Press, 2001), 73–74 (Comiskey Park).

25 McGeorge Bundy, "The Issue Before the Court: Who Gets Ahead in America?," *Atlantic Monthly* (November 1977) (percentages); "The Editor's Page," ibid. Some white men of course did obviously blame their female counterparts for the competition. In the course of talking about the divide created between men and women by the war in Vietnam, for example, Lucian Truscott IV said: "Every woman you ever went out with thought you were going to be completely fucked up if you did go to Vietnam, on the one hand. But then there was always an undercurrent that if you didn't go to Vietnam then there's going to be something wrong with you as a man, because we all know that civilizations have constantly over the course of history called upon people to go and fight wars whenever wars have come along. And I think the fact that women were not confronted with this decision that everybody had to make that was a guy back then, and were left free during those years to pursue the kinds of careers that make 49 percent of these women now part of the work force and to increase the number of their enrollments in law schools and whatever, I think that's an extraordinary result of this war." Quoted in Susan Jeffords, *The Remasculinization of America: Gender and the Vietnam War* (Bloomington: Indiana University Press, 1989), 117.

26 J. David Hoeveler, *Watch on the Right: Conservative Intellectuals in the Reagan Era* (Madison: University of Wisconsin Press, 1991), 85 ("mugged"); James Goodman, *Blackout* (New York: North Point Press, 2003), 25, 133 (World Trade Center, neighborhoods); "Met Fans Sing in Dark," *Washington Post*, July 15, 1977; "City Constructs Statistical Profile In Looting Cases," *New York Times*, August 14, 1977; "Night of Terror," *Time* (July 25, 1977); Midge Decter, "Looting and Liberal Racism," *Commentary* (September, 1977). For a comparison of the 1965 and 1977 blackouts, see Blackout History Project, http://www.blackout.gmu.edu/highlights/blackout77.html.

27 John Skrentny, *The Minority Rights Revolution* (Cambridge: Belknap Press, 2002), 264; *Regents of the University of California v. Bakke*, 438 U.S. 265, 273, n. 2 (1978).

28 Skrentny, *The Minority Rights Revolution*, at 291 (Polish Americans). All of these arguments against affirmative action except the last can be found in the *New Republic* (October 15, 1977). For the argument that affirmative action stigmatized minorities see, for example, Thomas Sowell, "Are Quotas Good for Blacks?," *Commentary* (June 1978).

29 Charlotte Steeh and Maria Krysan, "Trends: Affirmative Action and the Public," *Public Opinion Quarterly*, 60 (Spring 1996): 126, 142–43, and see 135–37.

30 Louis Masur, *The Soiling of Old Glory: The Story of a Photograph that Shocked America* (New York: Bloomsbury, 2008), 4–9, 17–19; James Vaznis, "Elite Private School Vows Free Tuition for Middle-, Low-Income," *Boston Globe*, November 10, 2006 (scholarship).

31 "Trends: Affirmative Action and the Public," at 149–50; "Reparation, American Style," July 4, 1977.

32 See Cheryl Greenberg, *Troubling the Waters: Black-Jewish Relations in the American Century* (Princeton: Princeton University Press, 2006).

33 American Conservative Union/Young Americans for Freedom Steering Committee to Policy Committee, February 15, 1978, Box 5, File 22, American Conservative Union (ACU) Papers, Brigham Young University Archive. Nancy MacLean and Carol Horton have stressed the significance of the neoconservative position on race to conservatism. MacLean, *Freedom Is Not Enough*, at 221–23, 234–35; Carol Horton, *Race and the Making of American Liberalism* (New York: Oxford University Press, 2005), 200–04, 221, 227.

34 David Saperstein to Laura Kalman, October 1, 1991. The decision of the liberal CSA to support affirmative action in *DeFunis* proved controversial. CSA counsel David Saperstein recalled that after the split within the Jewish community over *DeFunis* was leaked to the press, controversy broke out in the UAHC. Some leading members of the UAHC's board claimed that "the existing resolutions of the UAHC were ambiguous," and "the CSA, which is charged with implementing the resolutions taken at the national [UAHC] conventions, should not have acted." Indeed a new mechanism was established consisting of a joint delegation of the CSA and board that could meet quickly "when such situations arose again." There was no need to use the new delegation in *Bakke*, however, because the majority of the CSA decided against filing a brief. Ibid.

35 "The War Inside the Jews," *New Republic* (October 15, 1977).

36 "Why the AFL-CIO Hasn't Filed a Brief," *New Republic* (October 15, 1977); and see Denis Deslippe, " 'Do Whites Have Rights?': White Detroit Policemen and 'Reverse Discrimination' Protests in the 1970s," *Journal of American History*, 91 (2004): 932–60.

37 Hugh Graham, "Civil Rights Policy in the Carter Presidency," *The Carter Presidency: Policy Choices in the Post–New Deal Era*, ed. Gary Fink and Hugh Graham (Lawrence: University Press of Kansas, 1998), 202, 208–09 ("balanced," " 'anti-'," quoting Andrew Young); Archie Robinson, *George Meany and His Times* (New York: Simon & Schuster, 1981), 363; Hamilton Jordan to Carter, n.d., June 1977, Box 34, Foreign Policy/Domestic Politics, Hamilton Jordan Papers ("extraordinary"), Carter Library (unless otherwise indicated, all archival collections cited in this chapter are in the Carter Library). At least Eizenstat reminded the president that he had supported affir-

mative action and opposed quotas. Stuart Eizenstat and Robert Lipshutz to Carter, Box 149, Bakke, 2/77–9/77 (CF 0/A 28 [3]), Domestic Policy Staff (hereafter DPS Eizenstat). But see "White House Watch," *New Republic* (October 15, 1977) (claiming that while Eizenstat and others "often assumed" candidate Carter had said he supported affirmative action and opposed quotas, "[n]owhere in the 'promises book' of Carter campaign commitments compiled by Eizenstat after the election is there a specific mention of affirmative action or quotas").

38 *Hearings Before the Committee on the Judiciary, United States Senate, Ninety-fifth Congress, First Session, Nomination of Griffin B. Bell,* January 11, 1977, 19, 28–29, 74.

39 Annie Guiterrez to Stuart Eizenstat, March 24, 1977, Box 228, Justice—General [0/A 6318] [6], DPS Eizenstat ("We have had problems"). See also Notes of Conversation with Annie Guiterrez, August 12, 1977, Box FG-46, White House Central Files, Exec (indicating that Guiterrez had been "forceful in her denunciation of what is happening in Justice—they are not willing to allow any participation in their policy decisions . . . [and are] very discouraged about any impact on DOJ—Bell's relationship with the P. thwarts every effort"); Margaret McKenna to Robert Lipshutz, June 16, 1977, Box 120, *Bakke v. U.C. Regents*, 4/6/77–7/8/77 [0/A 5329], Staff Offices, Counsel, Office Files of Margaret McKenna ("legal issue," "this is really").

40 Lincoln Caplan, *The Tenth Justice: The Solicitor General and the Rule of Law* (New York: Alfred A. Knopf, 1987), 3, 41; Hugh Heclo and Lester Salamon, *The Illusion of Presidential Government* (Boulder, Colo.: Westview, 1981).

41 Draft Brief, n.d., Box 149, Bakke [3], DPS Eizenstat, 32, 3, 38, 72, 46, 85, 87.

42 Carter made this comment in the margin of a memorandum to the president and vice president written by Stuart Eizenstat, September 10, 1977, Box 149, Bakke [1], DPS Eizenstat; "Justice Dept. Brief Opposes Race Quota at Coast University," *New York Times*, September 8, 1977; Dreyfuss and Lawrence, *The Bakke Case*, at 168 (taxicab); Bunny Mitchell to Tim Kraft, September 12, 1977, Box HU-9. HU 1-1/ST 5, White House Central Files, Exec. ("Anxiety"); Message left by Nathaniel Jones for the President, September 12, 1977, ibid. ("believes").

43 Griffin Bell with Ronald Ostrow, *Taking Care of the Law* (New York: William Morrow, 1982), 29; Joseph Califano to Carter, September 9, 1977, Box 149, Bakke [2], DPS Eizenstat; Califano to Griffin Bell and Wade McCree, September 7, 1977, Bakke [3], ibid.; Patricia Roberts Harris to Carter, Bakke [1], ibid.; Eleanor Holmes Norton to Carter, September 8, 1977, Bakke [2], ibid.; Hamilton Jordan to Carter, n.d., ibid. Eizenstat made those comments on the draft brief cited in note 41; Stuart Eizenstat and Robert Lipshutz to Carter, September 6, 1977, Box 149, Bakke [3], DPS Eizenstat. Others in the DPS echoed Eizenstat's and Jordan's fears. See, e.g., Doug Huron to Robert Lipshutz and Stuart Eizenstat, September 2, 1977, Box 120, *Bakke v. UC Regents*, 9/1–9/8/77, ibid.

44 Stuart Eizenstat to Hamilton Jordan, September 6, 1977, Box 149, Bakke [3], DPS Eizenstat; Eizenstat and Lipshutz to Carter, September 6, 1977; Stuart Eizenstat to Griffin Bell, September 10, 1977, Box 149, Bakke [1], ibid.: "If there is some way, indirectly, that Bakke can get into school without our suggesting that he be admitted, the President would prefer this." Carter made the "jump" comment in the margin of Eizenstat and Lipshutz to Carter, September 6, 1977.

45 Undated memorandum setting out a working outline for the brief following a meeting among Mondale, Bell, and Eizenstat, Box 149, Bakke [2], DPS Eizenstat; Stuart Eizenstat and Robert Lipshutz to Carter and Walter Mondale, September 10, 1977, Box 149, Bakke [1], ibid.: ("For the most part the revised brief is the same document which Justice submitted last week"); Lincoln Caplan, *The Tenth Justice* (New York: Alfred A. Knopf, 1987), 47.

46 Stuart Eizenstat to Carter, October 26, 1977, Box 149, Bakke [1], DPS Eizenstat (reporting McCree had demurred); Brief Amicus Curiae of the United States of America, *The Regents of the University of California v. Allan Bakke, Allan Bakke versus Regents of University of California* VI: 75 (at p. 70 of the government's brief). Sindler, *Bakke, DeFunis, and Minority Admissions*, at 251 (suspicion). For Eizenstat's strained

but credible contention that the record would still justify remand even if the brief were to differentiate goals from quotas, see his September 6 memorandum to Carter. The strongest arguments for remand were made by the National Conference of Black Lawyers in its brief.

47 "Bakke," *ADA World* (September 1977) ("We," quoting civil rights lawyer Joe Rauh); Eizenstat to Carter, October 26, 1977.

48 "White House Watch: Carter's Brief," *The New Republic* (October 15, 1977).

49 See, e.g., Norman Silber, "The Solicitor General's Office, Justice Frankfurter, and Civil Rights Litigation, 1946–1960: An Oral History," *Harvard Law Review*, 100 (1987): 833, 842; Caplan, *The Tenth Justice*, at 40 ("dictate").

50 Bernard Schwartz provides a full account of how the Court reached its decision in *Behind Bakke: Affirmative Action and the Supreme Court* (New York: New York University Press, 1988), 56–150.

51 Lewis Powell to Eugene Snydor, Jr., August 23, 1971, http://www.historyisaweapon.com/defcon1/powellmemo.html; "The Legend of the Powell Memo," *American Prospect* (April 27, 2005), http://www.prospect.org/cs/articles?article=the_legend_of_the_powell_memo ("routinely," "blueprint"). The author of "The Legend of the Powell Memo," Mark Schmitt, suggested that the Powell memo has acquired legendary status "because it helps tell the story of the institutions that support the modern right in a tidy, accessible way, and one that shows how similar institutions of the left could be designed and built." This is not to deny the memo's influence. For example, it helped convince Joseph Coors to commit a substantial amount of money to promoting conservatism in Washington and, ultimately, to the Heritage Foundation. Lee Edwards, *The Power of Ideas: The Heritage Foundation at 25 Years* (Ottawa, Ill.: Jameson Books, 1997), 9.

52 *Regents of the University of California v. Bakke*, 438 U.S. 265, 317, 318, 323.

53 William Bowen and Derek Bok, in collaboration with James Shulman, Thomas Nygren, Stacy Dale, and Lauren Meserve, *The Shape of the River: Long-Term Consequences of Considering Race in College and University Admissions* (Princeton: Princeton University Press, 1998), 283, 285. To be sure, the discussion of diversity has become richer. *Pomona College Magazine* online (Winter 2003), http://www.pomona.edu/Magazine/PCMwin03/contents.shtml.

54 "The Landmark Bakke Ruling," *Newsweek* (July 10, 1978) (quoting Philip Kurland).

55 J. Harvie Wilkinson, *From* Brown *to* Bakke*: The Supreme Court and School Integration: 1954–1978* (New York: Oxford University Press, 1979), 302 (minority enrollments); "Why Bakke Won't End Reverse Discrimination: 2," *Commentary* (September 1978).

56 Vincent Blasi, "Bakke as Precedent: Does Mr. Justice Powell Have a Theory?," *California Law Review*, 67 (1979): 21, n. 1 ("Solomonic"); Wilkinson, *From Brown to Bakke*, at 299 ("comforting," quoting Anthony Lewis); *Hopwood v. Texas*, 78 F. 3d. 932, 945 (1996); *Gratz v. Bollinger*, 539 U.S. 244 (2003); *Grutter v. Bollinger*, 539 U.S. 306, 328–42 (2003); John Jeffries, "Bakke Revisited," *Supreme Court Review, 2003* (2003): 1, 2.

57 Sullivan, "Sins of Discrimination," at 78. For example, although *Bakke* invalidated quotas, a majority of the Court subsequently upheld affirmative action plans setting aside a specific percentage of jobs for minorities. The employer had voluntarily adopted one; Congress had forced the other on federal contractors. In those cases, as in other affirmative action programs it upheld or ordered, the Court adopted Mosk's "sin-based paradigm." *United Steelworkers Union v. Weber*, 443 U.S. 193 (1979); *Fullilove v. Klutznick*, 448 U.S. 448 (1980). Meanwhile, the Domestic Policy Staff continued to nudge the Justice Department in directions that would satisfy civil rights activists, while watching the administration's flank. In *Weber*, Eizenstat and other White House politicos suggested to Carter "that some of the rhetoric [in the Justice Department's draft brief] be toned down and that favorable references to 'quotas' per se . . . be removed." Some groups would correctly contend that *Weber* involved an "outright quota," those advisers warned Carter. "This may create some resentment

in conservative circles and among blue collar workers toward 'the government,' if not toward you." But the administration had to submit the brief because any other course would alienate "civil rights and black groups." Walter Mondale, Hamilton Jordan, Bob Lipshutz, Stuart Eizenstat to Carter, January 13, 1979, Box 50, Weber Case, Counsel's Office, Robert Lipshutz. Hugh Graham discussed the administration's support for civil rights groups on low-profile issues in "Civil Rights in the Carter Presidency," *The Carter Presidency: Policy Choices in the Post–New Deal Era*, at 206–10. The administration seized upon 1977 legislation providing that at a minimum, 10 percent of a four-billion-dollar appropriation for public works contracts must be awarded to minority business enterprises (MBE) "as an opportunity to rally minority loyalty." While the amendment received little attention at the time of its enactment, it provided a crucial opportunity for minority business.

58 Hamilton Jordan, Robert Lipshutz, and Frank Moore to Carter, April 12, 1978, Box 29, Judgeships (Active): Miscellaneous Closed, Counsel Lipshutz ("injustice"); Sheldon Goldman, "Carter's Judicial Appointments: A Lasting Legacy," *Judicature*, 61 (1981): 344–56; Griffin Bell to Robert Lipshutz, July 7, 1978, Box 29, Judgeships (Active): Omnibus Judgeship Bill, Counsel Lipshutz; Doug Huron and Margaret McKenna to Robert Lipshutz, October 12, 1978, Box 29, Judgeships (Active): Miscellaneous Closed, ibid. ("white male Establishment"); Doug Huron to Hamilton Jordan, January 12, 1979, Box 57, Women's Advisory Committee ("the Attorney General"), Hamilton Jordan Subject File; Bell and Ostrow, *Taking Care of the Law*, at 41 ("keepers").

CHAPTER VIII | LIMITS

1 Inaugural Address, January 20, 1977, americanpresidency.org; Jimmy Carter, *Keeping Faith: Memoirs of a President* (New York: Bantam, 1982), 21; Patrick Caddell, Initial Working Paper on Democratic Strategy, December 10, 1976, Press Office, Powell, Box 4, Memorandums—Patrick Caddell, Carter Library (unless otherwise noted, all archival collections cited in this chapter are in the Carter Library); Steven Gillon, *The Democrats' Dilemma* (New York: Columbia University Press, 1992), 192 ("How"); John Dumbrell, *The Carter Presidency: A Re-Evaluation* (Manchester, U.K.: Manchester University Press, 1995), 17–19 ("post"); Leo Ribuffo, "Jimmy Carter and the Ironies of American Liberalism," *Gettysburg Review* (Autumn 1998): 738–49.

2 "Some U.S. Homes May Face Cutoffs of Natural Gas," *Washington Post*, January 29, 1977.

3 Report to the American People—Remarks from the White House Library, February 2, 1977, americanpresidency.org; "Warm Words from Jimmy Cardigan," *Time* (February 14, 1977).

4 Inaugural Address, January 20, 1977; Proclamation 4483—Presidential Proclamation of Pardon, January 21, 1977, americanpresidency.org; "Vietnam Pardons Will Divide, Not Heal U.S.," *Human Events* (February 26, 1977); Myra McPherson, *Long Time Passing: Vietnam and the Haunted Generation*, 2d ed. (Bloomington: Indiana University Press, 2001), 336–37 ("nearly," "tailor"); Hamilton Jordan to Carter, n.d., Hamilton Jordan Confidential File, Box 34, Early Months Performance: HJ memos to President, 1977.

5 Carter, *Keeping Faith*, at 65; see, e.g., Paul Quirk and Joseph Hinchliffe, "The Rising Hegemony of Mass Opinion," *Loss of Confidence: Politics and Policy in the 1970s*, ed. David Robertson (University Park: Pennsylvania State University Press, 1998), 19–50.

6 Carter, *Keeping Faith*, at 78; Kathy Fletcher and Kitty Schirmer to Stuart Eizenstat, March 11, 1977, Box 315, Water Projects (2/77–3/77) [CF 0/A 46 (2)], Domestic Policy Staff Eizenstat (hereafter DPS Eizenstat); James Speer, "Jimmy Carter Was a Baptist President," *The Presidency and the Domestic Policy of Jimmy Carter*, ed. Herbert Rosenbaum and Alexj Ugrinski (Westport, Conn.: Greenwood Press, 1994), 83, 94 (quoting legislative liaison Bill Cable, "most powerful").

7 Bert Lance, with Bill Gilbert, *The Truth of the Matter: My Life in and out of Politics* (New York: Summit Books, 1991), 114; Gillon, *The Democrats' Dilemma*, at 192 ("hang tough").

8 Carter, *Keeping Faith*, at 79.

9 Jeffrey Stine, "Environmental Policy During the Carter Presidency," *The Carter Presidency: Policy Choices in the Post–New Deal Era*, ed. Gary Fink and Hugh Graham (Lawrence: University Press of Kansas, 1998), 179, 182, 188 ("we have," "only known"); "The Big Federal Land Grab," *Conservative Digest* (December 1978). See generally "Environmentalists Praise Carter but Are Critical on Some Issues," *New York Times*, December 21, 1978.

10 "Carter's First Big Test," *Time* (April 25, 1977) ("bushels"); Dan Tate to Carter, April 5, 1977, Box 30, Fifty-Dollar Tax Rebate, March 8, 1977–April 14, 1977, Frank Moore Papers ("concern," "result"); "Proving Ground," *Newsweek* (May 2, 1977) ("stupid").

11 Economic Stimulus Package Remarks and a Question-and-Answer Session on the Tax Rebate and Business Tax Credit Proposals, April 14, 1977, americanpresidency.org; William Greider, *Secrets of the Temple: How the Federal Reserve System Runs the Country* (New York: Simon & Schuster, 1987), 346–47 (theory); W. Carl Biven, *Jimmy Carter's Economy: Policy in an Age of Limits* (Chapel Hill: University of North Carolina Press, 2002), 88–93 (Carter and Burns); "Playing Make-Believe," *Business Week* (November 28, 1977) (feud and impact); "Burns Says He Wants to Be Reappointed; Burns Wants to Keep Fed Chairmanship," *Washington Post*, November 30, 1977; "Arthur Burns; Strong, Outspoken," ibid., December 29, 1977 ("team player"); Charles Jones, *The Trusteeship Presidency: Jimmy Carter and the United States Congress* (Baton Rouge: Louisiana University Press, 1988), 134 (treasury).

12 Carter, *Keeping Faith*, at 78; John Woolley, "Exorcising Inflation-Mindedness," *Loss of Confidence*, 130, 144 ("quick"); Stuart Eizenstat, Charles Schultze, and Gerald Rafshoon to Carter, December 2, 1978, Box 28, Memorandums from Rafshoon, Office of Communications, Rafshoon ("zigged"); Benjamin Stein with Herbert Stein, *On the Brink* (New York: Ballantine Books, 1977), 68, 170, 180.

13 Robert Shogan, *Promises to Keep: Carter's First Hundred Days* (New York: Thomas Crowell, 1977), 230 ("little"); Meeting with the House Ways and Means Committee, June 2, 1977, Box 199, Energy Bill [0/A 6341] [8], Stuart Eizenstat Subject File ("very").

14 Proclamation 4558—Sun Day, 1978, March 27, 1978, americanpresidency.org; Solar Energy Remarks Announcing Administration Proposals, June 20, 1979, ibid.; "Carter Welcomes Solar Power," *New York Times*, June 21, 1979.

15 Stuart Eizenstat, "President Carter, the Democratic Party, and the Making of Domestic Policy," *The Presidency and Domestic Policies of Jimmy Carter*, at 3, 12; "Discussant: Lynn Coleman," ibid., at 595, 597 ("lied to").

16 The Energy Problem: Address to the Nation, April 18, 1977, americanpresidency.org; Barbara Kellerman, *The Political Presidency: Practice of Leadership* (New York: Oxford University Press, 1984), 190 (quoting James Reston's comparison of Carter with Churchill). The reference to Henny Penny draws on a comment by one White House aide, who described Carter's address to the American people as his "the-sky-is-falling" message. Jones, *The Trusteeship Presidency*, at 139.

17 John Farrell, *Tip O'Neill and the Democratic Century* (Boston: Little, Brown, 2001), 381, 5, 423, 235 ("big," "gut," "personal"); Thomas O'Neill, with William Novak, *Man of the House: The Life and Political Memoirs of Speaker Tip O'Neill* (New York: Random House, 1987), 361–62, 383, emphasis in the original.

18 Jones, *Trusteeship Presidency*, at 139, 6–7 ("vintage"); Kellerman, *The Political Presidency*, at 217 (quoting Powell); "The Energy War," *Time* (May 2, 1977) ("rhetorical flourishes," "rushed"); National Energy Plan: Address Delivered Before a Joint Session of Congress, April 20, 1977, americanpresidency.org.

19 "Carter on Oil & Gas: Fudging away from a Hard Line," *Nation* (May 28, 1977); "Carter Plan Mistaken: There Is No Energy Shortage," *Human Events* (May 28, 1977).

20 Jones, *Trusteeship Presidency*, at 142; (statistics); President's News Conference of April 22, 1977, americanpresidency.org; Kellerman, *The Political Presidency*, at 190 (*Post*, Baker).
21 O'Neill, *Man of the House*, at 383–84; Kellerman, *The Political Presidency*, at 193–94 (Carter's silence); "Senate Last Hurdle for Carter's 'Energy' Package," *Human Events* (August 13, 1977).
22 Michael Malbin, "Rhetoric and Leadership: A Look Backward at the Carter National Energy Plan," *Both Ends of the Avenue: The Presidency, the Executive Branch, and Congress in the 1980s*, ed. Anthony King (Washington, D.C.: American Enterprise Institute, 1983), 212, 232; *The Gallup Poll: Public Opinion 1972–77* (Wilmington, Del.: Scholarly Resources, 1978), 2: 995–96, 1183–85.
23 Remarks of the President at a News Conference by Bert Lance Following the Investigation of His Finances, August 18, 1977, americanpresidency.org. For media evaluations of Carter's handling of the Lance affair, see Mark Rozell, *The Press and the Carter Presidency* (Boulder, Colo.: Westview Press, 1989), 56–60.
24 Kellerman, *The Political Presidency*, at 197 (quoting Long); "G.O.P. Energy Reply Features New Faces," *New York Times*, June 3, 1977.
25 "NAACP Hits Carter Energy Plan," *Washington Post*, January 12, 1978; "NAACP Discovers the Enemy," *Human Events*, 38 (February 18, 1978); "N.A.A.C.P. Energy Position Causes Major Dispute Among Supporters," *New York Times*, January 30, 1978.
26 Robert Byrd, *Child of the Appalachian Coalfields* (Morgantown: West Virginia University Press, 2005), 394 ("three"); "Leadership Gap in the Senate," *New York Times*, September 28, 1977.
27 Kellerman, *The Political Presidency*, at 196–201; Remarks at a Campaign Rally for Democratic Candidates for State Office, September 24, 1977, americanpresidency .org ("add"); "President Says He Would Veto Bill to Deregulate Natural Gas," *Washington Post*, September 25, 1977; "Mondale Helps Break Gas Pricing Filibuster," ibid., October 4, 1977; "A Blitz by Fritz," *Newsweek* (October 17, 1977); Natural Gas Deregulation Statement on Senate Action, October 4, 1977, americanpresidency.org; "Energy Follies and Energy Drama," *New York Times*, November 3, 1977.
28 James Schlesinger and Stuart Eizenstat to Carter, October 12, 1977, Box 199, Energy Bill [0/A 6341] Stuart Eizenstat Subject File; Hamilton Jordan to Carter, November 1, 1977, Box 34, 1, Hamilton Jordan Papers; Norman Ornstein, "The Open Congress Meets the President," *Both Ends of the Avenue*, at 185, 208 ("no savvy").
29 David Farber, *Taken Hostage: The Iran Hostage Crisis and America's First Encounter with Radical Islam* (Princeton: Princeton University Press, 2005), 75; Carter, *Keeping Faith*, at 433–34; "What Price OPEC Unity?," *Time* (December 26, 1977) ("price hawk," "grateful"); Gaddis Smith, *Morality, Reason and Power: American Diplomacy in the Carter Years* (New York: Hill and Wang, 1986), 184–86.
30 "Jimmy's Journey: Mostly Pluses," *Time* (January 16, 1978) ("surprising"); Toasts of the President and the Shah at a State Dinner, December 31, 1977, americanpresidency .org; David Harris, *The Crisis: The President, The Prophet, and the Shah—1979 and the Coming of Militant Islam* (New York: Little, Brown, 2004), 72–75.
31 Rozell, *The Press and the Carter Presidency*, at 50, 60–64; Jody Powell to Carter, December 27, 1977, Box 39, Memorandums: President Carter, 9/6/77–12/27/77 Staff Office, Press, Powell; Carter, *Keeping Faith*, at 101.
32 Kellerman, *The Political Presidency*, at 207; Daniel Yergin, *The Prize: The Epic Quest for Oil, Money and Power* (New York: Free Press, 1992) (quoting Schlesinger); "President Takes Yet Another Turn in His View of Gas Deregulation," *Washington Post*, March 10, 1978.
33 Rozell, *The Press and the Carter Presidency*, at 82, 95 (failure, "never come"); Gerald Rafshoon to Carter, June 14, 1977, Box 34, Image, Hamilton Jordan Papers ("boring"); Greg Schneiders to Gerald Rafshoon, Developing Public Support for the President's Energy Plan, n.d., c. June 1978, Box 28, Memorandums from Greg Schneiders, June 1978, Office of Communications, Rafshoon ("significant disagree-

ment"); Gerald Rafshoon, Developing Public Support for the President's Energy Program, Box 2, Energy Strategy, n.d., c. Summer 1978, Rafshoon Papers; Gerald Rafshoon to Carter, July 19, 1978, September 1, 1978, Box 28, Office of Communications, Rafshoon. See, e.g., "Jerry Rafshoon's Ministry of Propaganda," *New Times* (July 10, 1978) (the author of the piece was Robert Shrum, who had resigned from the Carter campaign in 1976) and see generally Gerald Rafshoon, Oral History, April 8, 1983, Miller Center of Public Affairs, http://millercenter.org/scripps/archive/oralhistories/detail/3860.

34 Kellerman, *The Political Presidency*, at 206–09; Kenneth Morris, *Jimmy Carter: American Moralist* (Athens: University of Georgia Press, 1992), 257 (quoting the *New Republic*).

35 Stuart Eizenstat and Frank Moore to Carter, October 16, 1978, Box 36, Legislative Priorities, June 13, 1977–November 1, 1978, Frank Moore Papers ("major legislative"); Jay Hakes, *A Declaration of Energy Independence: How Freedom from Foreign Oil Can Improve National Security, Our Economy, and the Environment* (Hoboken, N.J.: John Wiley, 2008), 53 ("more than"); Barrow, "The Quest for a National Energy Policy," at 175 ("artificially"); Jeffrey Stine, "Environmental Policy During the Carter Presidency," at 179, 191 ("environmentalists").

36 "At Last, the Energy Bill," *Washington Post*, October 16, 1978.

37 Interview with the President: Remarks at a Question-and-Answer Session with Editors and News Directors, September 22, 1978, americanpresidency.org ("massive," "relatively"); Civil Service Reform Act of 1978, Remarks at the Bill Signing Ceremony, October 13, 1978, ibid. See James Pfiffner and Douglas Brook, eds., *The Future of Merit: Twenty Years After the Civil Service Reform Act* (Washington, D.C.: Woodrow Wilson Center Press, 2000).

38 LeRoy Ashby and Rod Gramer, *Fighting the Odds: The Life of Senator Frank Church* (Pullman: Washington State University Press, 1994), 533 ("prostitutes," quoting Dale Bumpers); E. Stanly Godbold, "Jimmy Carter and the Art of Presidential Leadership," Conference on the Thirtieth Anniversary of Carter's Inauguration, University of Georgia, January 2007.

39 "Another Contrary Congress," *Time* (November 3, 1980); "The Swarming Lobbyists," ibid. (August 7, 1978); Frank Moore, Dan Tate, and Bill Cable to Carter, July 29, 1977, Box 34, Hamilton Jordan Confidential File ("many," "perhaps"); James Riddlesberger, Jr., and James King, "Political Constraints, Leadership Style, and Temporal Limits: The Administrative Presidency of Jimmy Carter," *The Presidency and Domestic Policies of Jimmy Carter* ("sign"), 353, 364; O'Neill, *Man of the House*, at 340, 372, 369–70; Farrell, *Tip O'Neill*, at 452 ("horse's").

40 One Hundred Days of the Carter Administration, Draft No. 2, April 26, 1977, Box 4, File 27, Americans for Democratic Action (ADA) Papers, State Historical Society of Wisconsin; "ADA's President Sparks National Debate," *ADA World* (July 1977) ("slashing"); "Carter Faulted on Six Counts," ibid. (September 1977); Carter, *Keeping Faith*, at 102; Kellerman, *The Political Presidency*, at 208 (quoting Metzenbaum); Russell Motter, "Seeking Limits: The Passage of the National Emergency Act as a Microcosm of the Carter Presidency," *The Presidency and Domestic Policy of Jimmy Carter*, at 571, 589 ("symbolic").

41 Hamilton Jordan to Carter, n.d., Box 34, Early Month's Performance: HJ Memos to Pres., 1977, Hamilton Jordan Confidential File.

42 Thomas Sugrue, "Carter's Urban Policy Crisis," *The Carter Presidency: Policy Choices in the Post–New Deal Era*, at 137, 152, 149, 143, 151; Hamilton Jordan to Carter, March 24, 1978, Box 37, Urban Policy, March 24, 1978, Hamilton Jordan Confidential File.

43 Harvey Schantz and Richard Schmidt, "The Evolution of Humphrey Hawkins," *Policy Studies Journal*, 8 (1979): 368–77; President's News Conference of May 3, 1976, americanpresidency.org; Dumbrell, *The Carter Presidency: A Re-Evaluation*, at 100 (economic advisers); Melvyn Dubofsky, "Jimmy Carter and the End of the Politics of Productivity," *The Carter Presidency: Policy Choices in the Post–New Deal Era*, at 95,

103 (quoting Eizenstat, aide); "Was Humphrey-Hawkins Bill Worth It?," *Washington Post*, November 24, 1977; "The Sanitizing of Humphrey-Hawkins," *Business Week* (November 28, 1977).

44 Martin Halpern, *Unions, Radicals and Democratic Presidents: Seeking Social Change in the Twentieth Century* (Westport, Conn.: Praeger, 2003), 123–36, 157–58; Taylor Dark, *The Unions and the Democrats: An Enduring Alliance* (Ithaca, N.Y.: Cornell University Press, 1999), 109–14; "Big Labor Dealt Stunning Defeat," *Human Events* (April 2, 1977): 4; Thomas Byrne Edsall, *The New Politics of Inequality* (New York: W. W. Norton, 1984), 135 (eleven Democrats); Bethany Moreton, *To Serve God and Wal-Mart: The Making of Christian Free Enterprise* (Cambridge, Mass.: Harvard University Press, 2009), 185.

45 Dubofsky, "Jimmy Carter and the End of the Politics of Productivity," at 104 (quoting Eizenstat); Dark, *The Unions and the Democrats*, at 99 (quoting Meany); "Carter Tells Caucus He'll Push Jobs Bill; Carter, Black Caucus Are Reconciled," *Washington Post*, September 30, 1978; Remarks on Signing H.R. 50 and S.R. 2570 into law, October 27, 1978, americanpresidency.org.

46 Bruce Schulman, "Slouching Toward the Supply Side," *The Carter Presidency: Policy and Domestic Choices in the Post–New Deal Era*, at 51, 54; Richard Moe to Walter Mondale, Hamilton Jordan, Jody Powell, and Landon Butler, April 3, 1978, Box 145, Anti-Inflation 4/78, DPS Eizenstat ("we do"); Anti-Inflation Policy: Remarks to Members of the American Society of Newspaper Editors Announcing the Administration's Policy, April 11, 1978, americanpresidency.org.

47 Anti-Inflation Program Address to the Nation, October 24, 1978, americanpresidency.org; White House Fact Sheet on Details of the Program, October 24, 1978, ibid.; Remarks and a Question-and-Answer Session with Editors and News Directors, December 1, 1978 ("Phase II"), ibid.; President's News Conference of April 25, 1978, ibid.; Biven, *Jimmy Carter's Economy*, at 185–91.

48 "Dollar Plunges to Record Lows Around the World," *Washington Post*, October 31, 1978; "The Buying of America," *Newsweek* (November 27, 1978).

49 Value of the Dollar in Domestic and International Markets: Remarks Announcing Measures to Strengthen Dollar, November 1, 1978, americanpresidency.org; Biven, *Jimmy Carter's Economy*, at 169–71.

50 Gillon, *Democratic Dilemma*, at 206 ("killing"); President's News Conference of December 12, 1978, americanpresidency.org ("widening," denial); "Meany's Caustic Critique; Meany Takes a Tough New Stance Against President Carter," *Washington Post*, November 10, 1978 (Coolidge); "George Meany Suggests Mandatory, Not Voluntary, Wage-Price Plan," ibid., October 11, 1978; "Government Controls versus Market Discipline," *Proceedings of the American Academy of Political Science*, 33 (1979): 203, 211 (polls); "Carter's Inflation Proposals Deserve Public Ridicule," *Human Events* (November 4, 1978).

51 "Discussant: Hamilton Jordan," *The Presidency and Domestic Policies of Jimmy Carter*, at 163, 165.

52 Morris, *Jimmy Carter*, at 246; Stephen Skowronek, *The Politics Presidents Make: Leadership from John Adams to George Bush* (Cambridge, Mass.: Belknap, 1993), 365, 371, 377, 393.

CHAPTER IX | THE MARKET AS MAGNET

1 Patrick Caddell, Initial Working Paper on Democratic Strategy, December 10, 1976, Press Office, Powell, Box 4, Memorandums, Patrick Caddell, Carter Library. (All archival collections cited in this chapter are in the Carter Library.)

2 "Is Keynes Dead?," *Newsweek* (June 20, 1977).

3 http://www.fritzholte.com/bilder/fig_ha2000_6_2.gif.

4 http://www.dalefranks.com/images/laffer.gif.

5 See Bruce Bartlett, "Supply-Side Economics: Voodoo Economics or Lasting Con-

tribution?," November 11, 2003, http://web.uconn.edu/cunningham/econ309/lafferpdf.pdf.

6 Jude Wanniski, "Taxes Revenues, and the 'Laffer Curve,'" *The Economics of the Tax Revolt: A Reader*, ed. Arthur Laffer and Jan Seymour (New York: Harcourt Brace Jovanovich, 1979), 7, 10; "Introduction," ibid., at 1, 2 ("free lunch"); "The Tax Revolt's Guru," *Newsweek* (June 26, 1978) (Laffer's politics); John Brooks, "Annals of Finance: The Supply Side," *New Yorker* (April 19, 1982), 96–150, 143 ("immoral," "Social Security").

7 Brooks, "Annals of Finance," at 100 ("It"). At his own drawing board, Laffer called for a monetary policy centered on sound money: the maintenance of quality, as opposed to the regulation of quantity. "You don't care how much money there is if it's worthless," he liked to say. He sometimes advocated a return to the gold standard. Laffer, "Response," *Reaganomics: A Midterm Report*, ed. William Stubblebine and Thomas Willett (San Francisco: Institute for Contemporary Studies, 1983), 71, 75.

8 Gary Dorrien, *The Neoconservative Mind: Politics, Culture, and the War of Ideology* (Philadelphia: Temple University Press, 1993), 103; Irving Kristol, *Neoconservatism: The Autobiography of an Idea* (Chicago: Ivan R. Dee, 1995), 35.

9 Sidney Blumenthal, *The Rise of the Counter-Establishment: The Conservative Ascent to Political Power* (New York: Union Square, 2008), 167, 166. Wanniski came up with both Mundell-Laffer hypothesis and Laffer Curve, ibid.

10 Brooks, "Annals of Finance," at 99, 100 (failure to remember, "bubbly"); "The Tax Revolt's Guru"; Blumenthal, *The Rise of the Counter-Establishment*, at 167, 155–57 ("saved," historical examples).

11 Brooks, "Annals of Finance," at 108.

12 Ibid., at 103.

13 Heller, "The Kemp-Roth-Laffer Free Lunch," *The Economics of the Tax Revolt*, at 46, 47–48; "The Fallacy of Slashing Taxes Without Cutting Spending," *Business Week* (August 7, 1978) (Stigler).

14 Martin Tolchin, "Jack Kemp's Bootleg Run to the Right," *Esquire* (October 24, 1978) ("almost"); "The Tax Revolt's Guru," at 25 ("There's more," "But").

15 Brooks, "Annals of Finance," at 104 ("right wing"); Blumenthal, *The Rise of the Counter-Establishment*, at 170, 169 ("trickle-down," "boats"); David Broder, *Changing of the Guard: Power and Leadership in America* (New York: Simon & Schuster, 1980), 171 ("enemy," "I").

16 Craig Shirley, *Reagan's Revolution: The Untold Story of the Campaign that Started It All* (Nashville: Thomas Current, 2005), 326 (strategist); Kiron Skinner, Annelise Anderson, and Marton Anderson, eds., *Reagan's Path to Victory: The Shaping of Ronald Reagan's Vision: Selected Writings* (New York: Free Press, 2004), 132; Martin Anderson, *Revolution* (San Diego: Harcourt Brace Jovanovich, 1988), 152 ("would not lose") compare Steven Hayward, *The Age of Reagan: The Conservative Counterrevolution 1980–1989* (New York: Crown Forum, 2009), 70 (maintaining that Reagan did claim that the tax cut would pay for itself); Richard Viguerie, *The New Right: We're Ready to Lead* (Falls Church, Va.: Viguerie Company, 1980), 177; "An Incisive View of 'The Way the World Works,'" *Human Events* (October 7, 1978); John Judis, *William F. Buckley, Jr.: Patron Saint of the Conservatives* (New York: Simon & Schuster, 1988), 419 (suggesting that Buckley did not share in the enthusiasm); Blumenthal, *The Rise of the Counter-Establishment*, at 163–66 (*Journal*).

17 "G.O.P. Leaders Ask Carter to Support 30% Tax Cut," *New York Times*, October 6, 1977; Jude Wanniski, *The Way the World Works*, twentieth anniversary ed. (Washington, D.C.: Regnery, 1998). Laffer made that comment in a blurb on the back book jacket.

18 "Is Carter in Trouble? Kemp's Tax Cut Plan Proves Decisive in Louisiana Race," *Human Events* (September 10, 1977), Wanniski, *The Way the World Works*, at 326 ("failure," "renaissance").

19 Wanniski, *The Way The World Works*, at xi ("dramatic").

20 Howard Jarvis, with Robert Pack, *I'm Mad as Hell: The Exclusive Story of the Tax Revolt and Its Leader* (New York: Times Books, 1979), 4 ("Death"); "Mr. Proposition 13," *Newsweek* (June 19, 1978) ("Holy").
21 Robert Kuttner, *Revolt of the Haves: Tax Rebellions and Hard Times* (New York: Simon & Schuster, 1980), 51 (rise in prices); Jarvis, *I'm Mad as Hell*, at 115 (pet food); Clarence Lo, *Small Property Versus Big Government: Social Origins of the Property Tax Revolt* (Berkeley: University of California Press, 1990), 143–76.
22 Kuttner, *Revolt of the Haves*, at 65.
23 Jarvis, *Mad as Hell*, at 53; David Sears and Jack Citrin, *Tax Revolt: Something for Nothing in California* (Cambridge: Harvard University Press, 1985), 22.
24 Terry Schwadron, ed., *California and the American Tax Revolt: Proposition 13 Five Years Later* (Berkeley: University of California Press, 1984), 88 (accountant's $110,000 house).
25 Jarvis, *Mad as Hell*, at 93 ("All); Peter Schrag, *Paradise Lost: California's Experience: America's Future* (New York: New Press, 1998), 151–52 (quarter).
26 Jarvis, *Mad as Hell*, at 95; Kuttner, *Revolt of the Haves*, at 80 ("sugar daddy").
27 "Mr. Proposition 13," at 25 ("liars," "manure"); "Maniac or Messiah?," *Time* (June 18, 1978): 21 ("dummies").
28 Jarvis, *Mad as Hell*, at 88–90, 64, 103, 131, 129; Charles Kadlec and Arthur Laffer, "The Jarvis-Gann Tax Cut Proposal: An Application of the Laffer Curve," *The Economics of the Tax Revolt*, at 118–22; Sears and Citrin, *Tax Revolt*, at 28 ("library").
29 Kuttner, *Revolt*, at 73–79.
30 Jarvis, *Mad as Hell*, at 118, 145 ("put," "big league"); "Maniac or Messiah?," at 21 ("We," "We").
31 Sears and Citrin, *Tax Revolt*, at 47–60; Arthur O'Sullivan, Terri Sexton, and Steven Sheffrin, *Property Taxes and Tax Revolts: The Legacy of Proposition 13* (Cambridge, U.K.: Cambridge University Press, 1995), 94–95 (increased reliance on state government); Kuttner, *Revolt of the Haves*, at 94 (scapegoat).
32 Kuttner, *Revolt of the Haves*, at 93 ("California"); Sears and Citrin, *Tax Revolt*, at 43 ("Taxes, no!").
33 Milton Friedman, "The Message from California," *Newsweek* (June 19, 1978) ("The"); Milton Friedman, *Bright Promises, Dismal Performances: An Economist's Protest* (New York: Harcourt, Brace Jovanovich, 1983), 322–24.
34 Milton Friedman, "Schools at Chicago," *University of Chicago Magazine* (Autumn 1974); George Stigler, *Memoirs of an Unregulated Economist* (New York: Basic Books, 1988), 20.
35 Friedman's 1971 *Newsweek* column, entitled "Roofs or Ceilings," discussing the pamphlet is reprinted in *The Essence of Friedman*, ed. Kurt Leube (Stanford, Calif.: Hoover Press, 1987), 139; F. A. Hayek, *The Road to Serfdom*, fiftieth anniversary ed. (Chicago: University of Chicago Press, 1994).
36 Kim Phillips-Fein, *Invisible Hands: The Making of the Conservative Movement from the New Deal to Reagan* (New York: W. W. Norton, 2009), 207–11; "Jimmy Carter: Four Years of Failure," *Human Events* (July 19, 1980) ("chief"); Woodrow Wilson, "Benevolence, or Justice?," *Progressivism: The Critical Issues*, ed. David Kennedy (Boston: Little, Brown, 1971), 51, 56.
37 Phillips-Fein, *Invisible Hands*, at 3–182 (Weidenbaum is discussed at 176–77); John Kelley, *Bringing the Market Back In: The Political Revitalization of Market Liberalism* (New York: New York University Press, 1997), 31–78; Bethany Moreton, *To Serve God and Wal-Mart: The Making of Christian Free Enterprise* (Cambridge: Harvard University Press, 2009), 148–53, 180–84 (business major, Students in Free Enterprise); Neil Duxbury, *Patterns of American Jurisprudence* (New York: Oxford University Press, 1995), 364 (quoting Stigler).
38 Leube, *Essence of Friedman*, at 13, 17. But Stephen Holmes stressed the compatibility of classical liberalism with welfare politics in *Passions and Constraint: On the Theory of Liberal Democracy* (Chicago: University of Chicago Press, 1995), 236, 240–45, 12.
39 Friedman, *Bright Promises*, at 61 ("era").

40 Ibid., at 62–63, 19, 16; Milton Friedman, with Anna Schwartz, *A Monetary History of the United States, 1867–1960* (Princeton: Princeton University Press, 1971).
41 Friedman, *Bright Promises*, at 91; Kelley, *Bringing the Market Back In*, at 78–79, 204–08; Friedman's Nobel Prize lecture, "Inflation and Unemployment," is reprinted in Leube, *Essence of Friedman*, at 347.
42 Richard Posner, *Economic Analysis of Law* (Boston: Little, Brown, 1972), 1, 4; Gary Minda, *Postmodern Legal Movements: Law and Jurisprudence at Century's End* (New York: New York University Press, 1995), 95 ("law should be efficient" was a favorite slogan of law and economics in the 1970s).
43 Posner, *Economic Analysis of Law*, at 7–8.
44 Steven Teles, *The Rise of the Conservative Legal Movement: The Battle for Control of the Law* (Princeton: Princeton University Press, 2008); Ann Southworth, *Lawyers of the Right: Professionalizing the Conservative Coalition* (Chicago: University of Chicago Press, 2008); Alice O'Connor, "Financing the Counterrevolution," *Rightward Bound: Making America Conservative in the 1970s*, ed. Bruce Schulman and Julian Zelizer (Cambridge: Harvard University Press, 2008), 148–68.
45 Robert Bork, *The Antitrust Paradox: A Policy at War with Itself* (New York: Basic Books, 1978), 61, 418, 7 (see ibid., at ix–x, for Bork's assessment of his deep "intellectual indebtedness" to the University of Chicago Law School and ibid., at 405–07 for a summary of Bork's specific recommendations for antitrust law); James May, "Redirecting the Future: *Law and the Future* and the Seeds of Change in Modern Antitrust Law," *Mississippi College Law Review*, 17 (1996): 43, 74 ("symbol"). For historians' assessment of Bork's history, see the sources cited in Daniel Ernst, "The New Antitrust History," *New York Law School Review*, 35 (1990): 879, 882, n. 23.
46 Richard Posner, *Overcoming Law* (Cambridge: Harvard University Press, 1995), 173 ("Bork called"); Posner, "Utilitarianism, Economics, and Legal Theory," *Journal of Legal Studies*, 8 (1979): 103, 105, 116–17; Richard Posner, *The Economics of Justice* (Cambridge: Harvard University Press, 1981), 84 ("Nazi," "buy").
47 Richard Posner and Elizabeth Landes, "The Economics of the Baby Shortage," *Journal of Legal Studies*, 7 (1978): 323–48.
48 For an overview of criticisms of the wealth maximization criterion, see Duxbury, *Patterns of American Jurisprudence*, at 400–16.
49 Daniel Yergin and Joseph Stanislaw, *The Commanding Heights: The Battle Between Government and the Marketplace that Is Remaking the Modern World* (New York: Simon & Schuster, 1998), 342–43 ("plums"); Remarks in Chicago at the Convention of the American Hardware Manufacturers Association, August 25, 1975, american presidency.org ("federal"); Paul Pierson, "The Rise and Reconfiguration of Activist Government," *The Transformation of American Politics: Activist Government and the Rise of Conservatism*, ed. Paul Pierson and Theda Skocpol (Princeton: Princeton University Press, 2007), 19, 24–26 (explosion of regulatory activity between 1969 and 1974). For example, in the Midwest, the CAB had set the fare in 1974 for the 339-mile trip between Chicago and Minneapolis at $38.89 the previous year ($145.67 in 2005 real dollars). But in California, where competition was welcome and price wars were permitted, one could fly the 338 miles between Los Angeles and San Francisco for $18.75. Thomas McCraw, *Prophets of Regulation: Charles Francis Adams, Louis D. Brandeis, James M. Landis, Alfred E. Kahn* (Cambridge: Belknap Press, 1984), 267.
50 "Carter's Kiddie Corps," *Newsweek* (April 10, 1978): 33 ("Typhoid"); Mary Schuman to Stuart Eizenstat, April 11, 1977, Box 148, Aviation—Airline Regulatory Reform (2) [0/A/ 6232] [2], Domestic Policy Eizenstat (hereafter DPS Eizenstat); W. T. Beebe to Jimmy Carter, August 8, 1977, ibid. (complaining about Schuman).
51 "Jimmy Carter: Four Years of Failure," *Human Events* (July 19, 1980) (Energy and Education); "Discussant: Alfred E. Kahn," *The Presidency and Domestic Policy of Jimmy Carter* ("These"), 667, 669, and see Alfred Kahn, "Deregulation: Looking Backward and Looking Forward," *Yale Journal on Regulation*, 7 (1990): 325–54.
52 Bruce Bartlett, *Reaganomics: Supply-Side Economics in Action* (Westport, Conn.: Arlington House, 1981), 163; Lawrence Lynn and David Whitman, *The President as Policy-*

maker: Jimmy Carter and Welfare Reform (Philadelphia: Temple University Press, 1982), 243.

53 Kuttner, *Revolt of the Haves*, at 242; Tax Reduction and Reform Message to the Congress, January 20, 1978, americanpresidency.org; Burton Kaufman and Scott Kaufman, *The Presidency of James Earl Carter*, 2d ed. (Lawrence: University Press of Kansas, 2006), 91.

54 Agenda, n.d., Box 289, Tax Reform [2], DPS Eizenstat ("little"); "Holes in the Christmas Stocking: Don't Be Fooled by Carter's Tax Cut 'Gift,'" *Human Events* (December 10, 1977); Bartlett, *Reaganomics*, at 161.

55 "About-Face on Capital Gains," *Time* (June 18, 1978) ("baby-faced").

56 Kuttner, *Revolt of the Haves*, at 242–46 (campaign, Mikva); "Tax Cuts on the Hill: Conservatives Celebrate, Liberals Struggle Against Further Slashes," *Washington Post*, July 31, 1978; John Davenport, "Voting for Capitalism," *The Economics of the Tax Revolt*, at 134, 135 ("roar").

57 W. Michael Blumenthal to Carter, April 22, 1978, Box 39, Anti-Inflation Program (CF, 0/A 413) Hamilton Jordan Subject File, "Is There a Constituency for Tax Reform," *Tax Notes* (May 1, 1978).

58 Bob Ginsburg to Stuart Eizenstat, June 14, 1978, Box 289, Tax Reform [6], DPS Eizenstat. Kuttner, *Revolt of the Haves*, at 246 ("tone").

59 "Tussle over a 'Two-Bit' Tax Cut," *Time* (July 10, 1978) ("loud," staff); President's News Conference of June 26, 1978, americanpresidency.org; "Carter Says He'll Veto Capital Gains Tax Cut," *Washington Post*, June 27, 1978 (Steiger).

60 "Money for the Middle Class," *Time* (August 21, 1978).

61 President's News Conference of July 20, 1978, americanpresidency.org; Bob Ginsburg to Stuart Eizenstat, July 21, 1978, DPS Eizenstat, Box 289, Tax Reform [5], DPS Eizenstat.

62 Bob Ginsburg to Stuart Eizenstat, July 21, 1978; Box 143, Anti-Inflation [0/A 6338] [4], DPS Eizenstat; "Carter Losing Control of Tax-Cut Bill," *Washington Post*, July 16, 1978 (Ullman).

63 "The Embattled Businessman," *Newsweek* (February 16, 1976) ("Business feels"); "Carter Ignored During Senate Romp," *Tax Notes* (October 16, 1978).

64 Edward Kennedy to Carter, October 11, 1978, Box 285, Tax Reform [2], DPS Eizenstat; "A Litany of Regression," *ADA World* (November 1978); Bob Ginsburg and Stuart Eizenstat to Carter, October 10, 1978, Box 285, Tax Reform Current (6), DPS Eizenstat; "Current and Quotable: Sen. Kennedy on 'the Worst tax bill,'" *Tax Notes* (October 30, 1978); "Perspectives on the Tax Cut: The Final Bill," ibid. (October 23, 1978) (quoting *Wall Street Journal*).

65 Jimmy Carter, *Keeping Faith: Memoirs of a President* (New York: Bantam, 1982), 84–85.

66 "Bandwagon Issue or Hot Potato?," *Tax Notes* (June 26, 1978); "Kemp-Roth Tax Cut Attacked," ibid. (July 24, 1978).

67 "Bell Rides 'Kemp-Roth' Tax Cut to Victory," *Human Events* (June 17, 1978).

68 "Republicans to Push Kemp-Roth Tax Cuts," *Tax Notes* (July 17, 1978) (quoting Republican National Committee chair Bill Brock).

69 "Kemp-Roth Tax Cut," *Tax Notes* (August 21, 1978); "Money for the Middle Class," *Time* (August 21, 1978) ("offensive"); "Democrats Maneuvering to Derail Kemp-Roth Tax Cuts," *Human Events* (August 12, 1978) ("born again"); "Finance Committee Broadens Tax Cut, Rejects Kemp-Roth, Eyes Big Gains Tax Cut," *Tax Notes* (September 25, 1978). The Senate vote was 10–8.

70 "The Politics of Taxes," *Newsweek* (September 25, 1978) ("Clipper"); "Stumping for Tax Cut; GOP Takes Kemp-Roth Plan to 7 States but Finds Crowds Aren't Turning Out," *Washington Post*, September 23, 1978 ("tax attack," "distinct"); "Ford Plans Active Role in Politics, Suggests 1980 Bid Is a Possibility," *New York Times*, March 26, 1977; "Ford Is Considering Race in 1980 Without Entering State Primaries," ibid., July 10, 1978; Ronald Reagan, "The New Republican Party," February 6, 1977, http://www.conservative.org/pressroom/reagan/reagan1977.asp; "Highlights

of CPAC '77," *Human Events* (February 19, 1977); Mark Smith, *The Right Talk: How Conservatives Transformed the Great Society into the Economic Society* (Princeton: Princeton University Press, 2007), 202, 161 ("revolution," "chumps").

71 Kuttner, *Revolt of the Haves*, at 289 ("The Nunn").

72 "Proposition 13 Had Ragged Coattails," *Tax Notes* (November 13, 1978); "Carter Signs Tax Measures," ibid.; "GOP Gains in Midterm Elections but Democrats Retain Heavy Majorities," *Facts on File* (November 10, 1978); Bartlett, *Reaganomics*, at 133 (quoting *Wall Street Journal*); William Safire, "Dishing the Whigs," *New York Times*, November 9, 1978; Wanniski, *The Way the World Works*, at xii.

73 Wanniski, *The Way the World Works*, at xii.

CHAPTER X | GENDER, GOD, AND GOVERNMENT

1 Randy Shilts, *The Mayor of Castro Street: The Life and Times of Harvey Milk* (New York: St. Martin's Press, 1982), 311, 337; Jerry Strober and Ruth Tomczak, *Jerry Falwell: Aflame for God* (Nashville: Thomas Nelson, 1979), 183.

2 George Marsden, *Understanding Fundamentalism and Evangelicalism* (Grand Rapids, Mich.: Erdmans, 1991), 85; Mark Noll, *God and Race in American Politics: A Short History* (Princeton: Princeton University Press, 2008), 105–35; David Chapelle, *A Stone of Hope: Prophetic Religion and the Death of Jim Crow* (Chapel Hill: University of North Carolina Press, 2004), 5–6, 87–152; Steven Miller, *Billy Graham and the Rise of the Republican South* (Philadelphia: University of Pennsylvania Press, 2009), 21–33, 107–08, 126, 132–54; Daniel Williams, "From the Pews to the Polls: The Formation of a Southern Christian Right" (Ph.D. Dissertation, Brown, 2005), 138, 146–47.

3 Michelle Nickerson, "Domestic Threats: Women, Gender and Conservatism in Cold War Los Angeles, 1945–1966" (Ph.D. dissertation, Yale, 2003), 131–89; Darren Dochuk, "From Bible Belt to Sun Belt: Plain Folk Religion, Grassroots Politics, and the Southernization of Southern California, 1939–1969" (Ph.D. Dissertation, Notre Dame, 2005), 7, 29–38, 97–100, 117, 273–79, 340–53, 391–408, 485–97, 515–29; Clyde Wilcox, *God's Warriors: The Christian Right in Twentieth-Century America* (Baltimore: Johns Hopkins University Press, 1992), 1, 11–12.

4 Alan Lichtman, *White Protestant Nation: The Rise of the American Conservative Movement* (New York: Atlantic Monthly Press, 2008), 346. In 1974, when evangelicals gathered to sign the Lausanne Covenant and launch "a great Christian offensive," they expressed "penitence" that they had "sometimes regarded evangelism and social concern as mutually exclusive." "The Lausanne Covenant," *Christianity Today* (August 16, 1974); "Should Christians Vote for Christians?," ibid. (June 18, 1976).

5 James Moffett, *Storm in the Mountains: A Case Study of Censorship, Conflict, and Consciousness* (Carbondale: Southern Illinois University Press, 1988); William Martin, *With God on Our Side: The Rise of the Religious Right in America* (New York: Broadway Books, 1996), 117–43; "The Battle of Kanawha County Is Not Over," *Conservative Digest* (April 1976).

6 Martin, *With God on Our Side*, at 142 (minister).

7 Donald Tinder, "Sexuality: A New Candor in Evangelical Books," *Christianity Today* (March 18, 1977).

8 Godfrey Hodgson, *The World Turned Right Side Up: A History of the Conservative Ascendancy in America* (Boston: Houghton Mifflin, 1996), 172.

9 Mark Shibley, "The Southernization of American Religion: Testing a Hypothesis," *Sociological Analysis*, 52 (Summer 1991): 159–74; Bethany Moreton, *To Serve God and Wal-Mart: The Making of Christian Free Enterprise* (Cambridge: Harvard University Press, 2009), 89–92, 122.

10 Jeffrey Hadden and Charles Swann, *Primetime Preachers: The Rising Power of Televangelism* (Reading, Mass.: Addison-Wesley, 1981), 101–02; Richard Fox, *Jesus in America: Personal Savior, Cultural Hero, National Obsession* (New York: HarperSanFrancisco, 2004), 318–21; Moreton, *To Serve God and Wal-Mart*, at 5, 44, 126–27, 223, 250.

11 Steve Bruce, *The Rise and Fall of the New Christian Right: Conservative Protestant Politics*

in America 1978–1988 (Oxford, U.K.: Clarendon, 1990), 76–79 (the opinion was *Torcaso v. Watkins*, 361 U.S. 488 [1961]); Phyllis Schlafly, "Parents' Rights in Education," *Phyllis Schlafly Report* (November 1976) ("same").

12 Frances FitzGerald, *Cities on a Hill: A Journey Through Contemporary American Cultures* (New York: Simon & Schuster, 1987), 170, 129; Dinesh D'Souza, *Falwell, Before the Millennium: A Critical Biography* (Chicago: Regnery Gateway, 1984), 81 ("a segregationist").

13 D'Souza, *Falwell Before the Millennium*, at 112, 95 ("biological"); John McGreevy, *Catholicism and American Freedom* (New York: W. W. Norton, 2003), 262–81; Scott Flipse, "Below-the-Belt Politics: Protestant Evangelicals, Abortion, and the Foundation of the New Religious Right, 1960–1975," *The Conservative Sixties*, ed. David Farber and Jeff Roche (New York: Peter Lang, 2003), 127, 134–37; Martin, *With God on Our Side*, at 193 (first sermon).

14 Moreton, *To Serve God and Wal-Mart*, at 4.

15 Alan Crawford, *Thunder on the Right: The "New Right" and the Politics of Resentment* (New York: Pantheon, 1980), 159 ("pacifist," "sissy"); William Goodman and James Price, *Jerry Falwell: An Unauthorized Profile* (Lynchburg, Va.: Paris and Associates, 1981), 128 ("he-man"); Walter Capps, *The New Religious Right: Piety, Patriotism, Politics* (Columbia: University of South Carolina Press, 1994), 31 ("Marines").

16 FitzGerald, *Cities on a Hill*, at 163, 176; "Falwell Warns Jersey Liberals at Capitol Rally," *New York Times*, November 11, 1980 ("Steve"); Bruce, *The Rise and Fall of the New Christian Right*, at 142 ("Edward").

17 Goodman and Price, *Jerry Falwell*, at 91 ("religion and politics"); Jerry Falwell, *Listen, America!* (New York: Bantam, 1980); Jerry Falwell, "Changing the World One Life at a Time," July 14, 1996, http://trbc.org/new/sermons.php?url=071496.html ("across"); Susan Harding, *The Book of Jerry Falwell: Fundamentalist Language and Politics* (Princeton: Princeton University Press, 2001), 120 ("I Love America").

18 "Election '76: Indifference Is No Virtue," *Christianity Today* (October 22, 1976) ("wonders"); Debate Between the President and Former Vice President Walter F. Mondale, October 7, 1984, americanpresidency.org ("In our particular church, we did not use that term, 'born again,' so I don't know whether I would fit that particular term," Reagan said). Ford talked about how his wife's 1974 bout with cancer led us "to a much deeper understanding of our personal relationship with Jesus Christ" in "Lessons from the Presidency," Commencement Address to Gordon-Cornwell Theological Seminary, reprinted in *Christianity Today* (July 29, 1977).

19 Williams, "From the Pews to the Polls," 156, 158, 342; Martin, *With God on Our Side*, at 158 ("disillusioned," "Four").

20 Leo Ribuffo, *Right Center Left: Essays in American History* (New Brunswick, N.J.: Rutgers University Press, 1992), 222.

21 See, e.g., Leo Ribuffo, "Writing About Jimmy Carter as If He Was Andrew Jackson: The Carter Presidency in (Deep) Historical Perspective," Conference on the Thirtieth Anniversary of Carter's Inauguration, University of Georgia (January 2007); Department of Housing and Urban Development: Remarks and Question-and-Answer Session with Department Employees, February 10, 1977, americanpresidency.org; "Mrs. Ford Comments on Carter," *New York Times*, February 21, 1977.

22 Armistead Maupin, *28 Barbary Lane: The Tales of the City Omnibus*, 1 (New York: HarperCollins, 1990), 279–80, 444, 100.

23 Philip Jenkins, *Decade of Nightmares: The End of the Sixties and the Making of Eighties America* (New York: Oxford University Press, 2006), 19, 121, 143–44; "A Dieting Disease Comes out of Hiding," *New York Times*, April 30, 1978; "Alleged Sex Murderer Had His Picture Taken with Rosalynn Carter," *Globe and Mail*, January 22, 1979; "Playboy Interview: Anita Bryant," *Playboy* (May 1978); Crawford, *Thunder on the Right*, at 52 ("Dear Friend").

24 George Chauncey, *Why Marriage? The History Shaping Today's Debate over Gay Equality* (New York: Basic Books, 2004), 38; Timothy Lange, "The New Left Almost Blew It," *Nation* (July 20, 1974).

25 "Playboy Interview: Anita Bryant" (quotations); Dudley Clendinen and Adam Nagourney, *Out for Good: The Struggle to Build a Gay Rights Movement in America* (New York: Touchstone, 1999), 291–311.
26 Clendinen and Nagourney, *Out for Good*, at 319.
27 "Playboy Interview: Anita Bryant" ("wiped"); Anita Bryant, *The Anita Bryant Story: The Survival of Our Nation's Families and the Spirit of Militant Homosexuality* (Old Tappan, N.J.: Fleming H. Revell, 1977), 95, 101–02, 122–24; Clendinen and Nagourney, *Out for Good*, at 319 ("people").
28 Chauncey, *Why Marriage?*, at 39; Clendinen and Nagourney, *Out for Good*, at 377–89.
29 "Playboy Interview: Anita Bryant."
30 Clendinen and Nagourney, *Out for Good*, at 389; "Anita Bryant's Crusade: Where Next?," *Conservative Digest* (August 1977) ("can win").
31 "Anita Bryant's Crusade: Where Next?" (quoting Save Our Children Communications director Mike Thompson).
32 Carol Felsenthal, *The Sweetheart of the Silent Majority: The Biography of Phyllis Schlafly* (New York: Doubleday, 1981), 248–51, 277–81.
33 "The Man Behind the Anti-Abortion Amendment: Henry John Hyde," *New York Times*, July 1, 1980; "New Limits on Abortion," *Time* (December 19, 1977) (Senate liberals); *Planned Parenthood of Central Missouri v. Danforth*, 428 U.S. 52 (1976); *Maher v. Roe*, 432 U.S. 464 (1977); *Harris v. McRae*, 448 U.S. 297 (1980).
34 President's News Conference of July 12, 1977, americanpresidency.org.
35 "New Limits on Abortion."
36 Is There a Pricetag on Fairness? Americans for Democratic Action (ADA), September 17 and 18, 1977, Box 1, National Board Meeting, September 17–18, 1977, ADA Papers, State Historical Society of Wisconsin; Midge Costanza to Carter, July 13, 1977, Box 41, Staff Offices, Press, Powell, Carter Library (unless otherwise noted, all archival collections cited in this chapter are in the Carter Library); Hamilton Jordan to Carter, n.d., Box 34A, Midge Costanza, Hamilton Jordan Confidential File.
37 Jody Powell, *The Other Side of the Story* (New York: William Morrow, 1984), 111–13, 126–34, 177–79; Mark Rozell, *The Press and the Carter Presidency* (Westview, Colo.: Boulder, 1989), 77–79; "Midge Costanza: The View from the Ground Floor," *Washington Post*, July 26, 1978 ("cry"). See Susan Hartmann, "Feminism, Public Policy, and the Carter Administration," *The Carter Administration: Policy Choices in the Post–New Deal Era*, ed. Gary Fink and Hugh Graham (Lawrence: University Press of Kansas, 1998), 224–43, for the argument that the Carter administration's involvement in feminist policy was deeper and more effective than feminists believed at the time.
38 Capps, *The New Religious Right*, at 39 ("abortionist"); "New Limits on Abortion," at 12 ("We lost"); Hartmann, *From Margin to Mainstream*, at 145; Califano, *Governing America*, at 81; "New Limits on Abortion," at 13. See Leo Ribuffo, "Family Policy Past as Prologue: Jimmy Carter, the White House Conference on Families, and the Mobilization of the New Christian Right," *Review of Policy Research*, 23 (March 2006): 311–37; Connie Marshner, "White House Conference on Families Stacked Against Pro-Family Forces," *Conservative Digest* (October 1980) ("We").
39 Beth Abramowitz to Stuart Eizenstat, September 12, 1977, Box 323, Women's Issues 0/A 6348 [5], Domestic Policy Staff Eizenstat (hereafter DPS Eizenstat).
40 Winifred Wandersee, *On the Move: American Women in the 1970s* (Boston: Twayne, 1988), 175 ("high"); "First Ladies out Front," *Time* (December 5, 1977) (Johnson).
41 John Lofton, "IWY Conference (Far) Outside Mainstream," *Human Events* (December 3, 1977).
42 "Women's Conference Approves Planks on Abortion and Homosexuals," *New York Times*, November 21, 1977; "Women's Conference Passes Abortion, Gay Rights Measures," *Washington Post*, November 20, 1977 ("someone").
43 "Pro-Family Rally Attracts 20,000," *Phyllis Schlafly Report* (December 1977); Martin, *With God on Our Side*, at 165 ("that's").
44 Rosalynn Carter, *First Lady from Plains* (New York: Fawcett, 1984), 272 ("appeared"); Bella Abzug and Carmen Votaw to Carter, November 21, 1978, Box 323, Women's

Issues, 0A 6348 [5], DPS Eizenstat; "The Story Behind Bella's Departure; It Was a Matter of Minutes to Decide Bella Had to Go," *Washington Post*, January 17, 1979; "1980 Political Action Conference: Victory in the Air at CPAC," *Human Events* (March 8, 1980) ("same"); "White House Conference Endorses Radical Program," ibid., June 21, 1980 ("revisited").

45 "What Really Happened in Houston," *Phyllis Schlafly Report* (December 1977); Donald Critchlow, *Phyllis Schlafly and Grassroots Conservatism: A Woman's Crusade* (Princeton: Princeton University Press, 2005), 214 ("a party"). See Marjorie Spruill, "Gender and America's Right Turn," *Rightward Bound: Making America Conservative in the 1970s*, ed. Bruce Schulman and Julian Zelizer (Cambridge: Harvard University Press, 2008), 71–89.

46 "Building the Moral Majority," *Conservative Digest* (August 1979); "Why the 'New Right' Isn't Doing Well at the Polls," *Business Week* (October 30, 1978) ("prostitutes," "incumbent"); "How to Cut Your Taxes: Rep. Kemp's Plan Shakes Up Republican Hierarchy," *Conservative Digest* (January 1978); "California's Tax Revolt: June Vote Horrifies Political Establishment," ibid. (May 1978).

47 Moreton, *To Serve God and Wal-Mart*, at 119 ("crimes"); Falwell, *Listen, America!*, at 201; "A Mysterious Drop in the Abortion Rate," *Newsweek* (July 16, 1984); Clendinen and Nagourney, *Out for Good*, at 408 (reporting D.C. police estimate of seventy-five thousand marchers); "The Letters of Mrs. FDR," *Newsweek* (November 5, 1979); "Gays in Washington," ibid. (September 25, 1989).

48 "CD Poll," *Conservative Digest* (November 1977); "Is Prime Time Ready for Sex?," *Time* (July 11, 1977) ("He"); Patrick Allitt, *Religion in America Since 1945: A History* (New York: Columbia University Press, 2003), 119 ("drenched"); "Pornochic; Hard-core Grows Fashionable and Very Profitable," *New York Times*, January 21, 1973; Peter Braunstein, "'Adults Only': The Construction of an Erotic City in New York During the 1970s," *America in the Seventies*, ed. Beth Bailey and David Farber (Lawrence: University Press of Kansas, 2004), 129–56.

49 Raoul Berger, *Government by Judiciary: The Transformation of the Fourteenth Amendment* (Cambridge: Harvard University Press, 1977), 245; Louis Lusky, "'Government by Judiciary': What Price Legitimacy?," *Hastings Constitutional Law Quarterly*, 6 (1979): 403, 404 ("crystallized"). See "Fie on the Fourteenth," *Time* (November 14, 1977).

50 William Greider, "Carter's Unheralded Milestone," *Washington Post*, February 26, 1978; "Settling In at 1600," *Newsweek* (February 7, 1977) ("'Mrs. Carter has said many times that it is better on her budget not to serve hard liquor,' reported Mary Hoyt, the First Lady's new press secretary."); David Kuhn, *The Neglected Voter: White Men and the Democratic Dilemma* (New York: Palgrave Macmillan, 2007), 68, 79.

51 George Moffett, *The Limits of Victory: The Ratification of the Panama Canal Treaties* (Ithaca, N.Y.: Cornell University Press, 1985), 11.

52 Henry Kissinger, *Years of Renewal* (New York: Simon & Schuster, 1999), 761–66; Adam Clymer, *Drawing the Line at the Big Ditch: The Panama Canal Treaties and the Rise of the Right* (Lawrence: University Press of Kansas, 2008), 13–14, 42.

53 Kissinger, *Years of Renewal*, at 716; Moffett, *The Limits of Victory*, at 42.

54 Interview: Jimmy Carter, October 25, 1991, Academy of Achievement, http://www.achievement.org/autodoc/printmember/car0int-1 (Carter there pointed out that Presidents Johnson, Nixon, and Ford all had promised the Panamanians a new treaty. "But it was only when I got into office that I was foolish enough to push it to a conclusion"); Rosalynn Carter, *First Lady from Plains* (New York: Fawcett, 1984), 155–56; Jimmy Carter, *Keeping Faith: Memoirs of a President* (New York: Bantam, 1982), 155–56; Robert Pastor, *Exiting the Whirlpool: U.S. Foreign Policy Toward Latin America and the Caribbean*, 2d ed. (Boulder, Colo.: Westview Press, 2001), 5, 16, n. 8 ("patience machine"); "Torrijos: 'The U.S. Has Lied,'" *Newsweek* (August 25, 1977) ("definitely," "decolonize").

55 Zbigniew Brzezinski, *Power and Principle: Memoirs of the National Security Adviser 1977–1981* (New York: Farrar, Straus and Giroux, 1983), 137.

56 Carter, *Keeping Faith*, at 155 (polls); Moffett, *The Limits of Victory*, at 173 ("vanished," quoting George Will).

57 See, e.g., "From the Publisher: Don't Let Carter Surrender Our Canal," *Conservative Digest* (October 1977); Patrick Buchanan, "Canal Treaty Is Gutless Giveaway," ibid. (November 1977) ("Chablis"); "The Panama Canal: Marxists See Treaty as a Test of Will," *Human Events* (September 3, 1977); "Defeat the Panama Canal Treaty!," *Phyllis Schlafly Report* (October 1977).

58 Buchanan, "Canal Treaty Is Gutless Giveaway" ("Teddy"); Carter, *Keeping Faith*, at 156, 157 (sabotage, "blackmail"); Ronald Reagan, "The Case for Retention of the Panama Canal," *Human Events* (February 11, 1978) ("seen," "top"); Walter La Feber, *The Panama Canal: The Crisis in Historical Perspective*, 2d ed. (New York: Oxford University Press, 1989), 168–69, 216–19; Michael Hogan, *The Panama Canal in American Politics*, at 135–208; Christopher Andrew and Vasili Mitrokhin, *The World Was Going Our Way: The KGB and the Battle for the Third World* (New York: Basic Books, 2005), 110–11 ("Ironically, the KGB believed the charges [of drug trafficking] which Carter and the Intelligence Committee dismissed").

59 ACU Involvement in Panama Canal Issue, n.d., Box 90, File 10, American Conservative Union (ACU) Papers, Brigham Young University; Clymer, *Drawing the Line at the Big Ditch*, at 53–60,158; "Phil Crane: A Conservative Runs Against Reagan," *New York* (March 26, 1979) ("Phil"); John Judis, *William F. Buckley, Jr.: Patron Saint of the Conservatives* (New York: Simon & Schuster, 1998), 397–98; "A Bid for Votes on Panama," *Business Week* (September 12, 1977) (business and AFL-CIO). *Commentary* carried no articles about the Panama Canal treaties during the 1970s. According to his biographer, Senator Jackson "remained uncharacteristically reticent during the acrimonious debate over the Panama Canal Treaty." When Carter dispatched Energy Secretary James Schlesinger to lobby the senator, "Jackson told Schlesinger not to worry. He would vote for the treaty but 'wanted to make Carter sweat.'" Robert Kaufman, *Henry M. Jackson: A Life in Politics* (Seattle: University of Washington Press, 2000), 366.

60 Carter, *Keeping Faith*, at 159 ("nuts"); "Reagan Protests Party Fund Drive," *New York Times*, December 21, 1977 ("used"); Richard Viguerie, *The New Right: We're Ready to Lead* (Falls Church, Va.: Viguerie Company, 1980), 84–85, 83 (quoting Buchanan).

61 Script, Box 91, File 11, ACU Papers; Minutes, Board of Director Meetings, American Conservative Union, March 19, 1978, Box 21, File 24, ibid. (times broadcast and viewed); Philip Crane, *Surrender in Panama: The Case Against the Treaty* (Ottawa, Ill.: Green Hill, 1978); Peter Hannaford to Reagan, October 16, 1978, Box 2, File 7, Deaver and Hannaford Papers, Hoover Institution (advising Reagan on how to position himself for an interview with Kevin Phillips); Clymer, *Drawing the Line at the Big Ditch*, at 70–74, 159 (describing the evolution of Reagan's position on the canal, conservatives' reaction, and importance of New Right to Crane); Lou Cannon, *President Reagan: The Role of a Lifetime* (New York: Simon & Schuster, 1991), 342–43 (pollster).

62 Kenneth Morris, *Jimmy Carter: American Moralist* (Athens: University Press of Georgia, 1986), 266–67 (*Times*, Buckley); "Playboy Interview: Anita Bryant"; "TV Evangelist Snags Reagan, but Not Everyone Down Home," *Washington Post*, October 5, 1980 (Falwell); "Senator Mark Hatfield; He Waves a Mean Olive Branch," *Christian Science Monitor*, June 17, 1972. The Southern Baptist Convention and the Roman Catholic Church officially approved the Panama Canal treaties out of a desire to avoid losing influence in Latin America. Hodgson, *The World Turned Right-Side Up*, at 228. Within a year of the treaties' signature, fundamentalists had wrested leadership of the Southern Baptist Convention from the moderates, and the convention became less supportive of Carter. Oran Smith, *The Rise of Baptist Republicanism* (New York: New York University Press, 1997), 48–52, 75–76, 95–97.

63 Moffett, *The Limits of Victory*, at 112–37.

64 Carter, *Keeping Faith*, at 173.

65 Walter Mondale, "The Perspective of the Vice President," *The Carter Presidency: Fourteen Intimate Perspectives of Jimmy Carter*, ed. Kenneth Thompson (Lanham, Md.: University Press of America, 1990), 239, 245; LeRoy Ashby and Rod Gramer, *Fighting the Odds: The Life of Senator Frank Church* (Pullman: Washington State University Press, 1994), 537–52, 603; Mark Rozell, *The Press and the Carter Presidency* (Boulder, Colo.: Westview, 1989), 80–81; William Jorden, *Panama Odyssey* (Austin: University of Texas Press, 1984) (Byrd and see ibid. at 555, 622).

66 Jorden, *Panama Odyssey*, at 623.

67 Carter to Hamilton Jordan, April 22, 1978, Box 50, Hamilton Jordan Subject File; Viguerie, *The New Right*, at 91, 83, 100; Carter, *Keeping Faith*, at 184 ("Eleven"); Clymer, *Drawing the Line at the Big Ditch*, at 117–96 (suggesting that in 1978 the canal was the most important issue in explaining the defeat of Democrat Senator Tom McIntyre by Republican Gordon Humphrey in New Hampshire, played an important role in explaining the defeat of Democrat Senator Dick Clark by Republican Roger Jepsen in Iowa, and may have helped Republican Bill Armstrong defeat Democrat Senator Floyd Haskell in Colorado, Republican William Cohen defeat Democrat William Hathaway in Maine, and Jeffrey Bell defeat Clifford Case in the New Jersey Republican Primary. Clymer maintains that in the 1980 Senate elections, the canal played a role in the defeat of Senator Robert Morgan by Republican John East in North Carolina, the defeat of Senator Frank Church by the New Right's Steve Symms in Idaho, the defeat of Democrat Herman Talmadge by Republican Mack Mattingly in Georgia, the defeat of George McGovern by Republican James Abdnor in South Dakota, and the defeat of Senator John Culver by Republican Charles Grassley in Iowa).

68 Falwell, *Listen, America!*, at 191; Hodgson, *The World Turned Right Side Up*, at 176; Peter Skerry, "Christian Schools Versus the IRS," *Public Interest*, 61 (Fall 1980): 18–41; Joseph Crespino, *In Search of Another Country: Mississippi and the Conservative Counterrevolution* (Princeton: Princeton University Press, 2007), 240–65.

69 David Niven and Robert Bills, *The Schools that Fear Built: Segregation Academies in the South* (Washington, D.C.: Acropolis Books, 1976), 19, 176.

70 Alan Peshkin, *God's Choice: The Total World of a Christian Fundamentalist School* (Chicago: University of Chicago Press, 1986), 119, 127, 58, 77, 136–41; Eileen Luhr, *Witnessing Suburbia: Conservatives and Christian Youth Culture* (Berkeley: University of California Press, 2009), 30–53, 75 (music).

71 American Conservative Union Legislative Alert, n.d. (c. October 1978), Box 79, File 14, ACU Papers ("IRS Says"); Martin, *With God on Our Side*, at 172–73; "Outsiders No More," http://www.christianitytoday.com/ct/1997/april28/7t5022.html, April 28, 1997 ("Stamp Act").

72 "Inside the Media," reprinted from the Media Report, August 14, 1978, the Committee for the Survival of a Free Congress, Box 16, File 3, Paul Weyrich Papers, American Heritage Center, University of Wyoming ("novelty," "genuine"); Martin, *With God on Our Side*, at 198–99; Williams, "From the Pews to the Polls," at 318 ("nation's").

73 Viguerie, *The New Right*, at 162 ("million"); Martin, *With God on Our Side*, at 204, for a discussion of the difficulty of gaining access to Falwell's mailing list).

74 Falwell, *If I Should Die*, at 98; Falwell, *Strength for the Journey*, at 359–63; D'Souza, *Falwell Before the Millennium*, at 109–11.

75 Sanford Levinson, *Constitutional Faith* (Princeton: Princeton University Press, 1988); "Mobilizing the Moral Majority," *Conservative Digest* (August 1979); "Jimmy Carter's Betrayal of the Christian Voter," ibid.

CHAPTER XI | RETURN TO THE COLD WAR: THE UNITED STATES, THE SOVIET UNION, AND THE MIDDLE EAST

1 "Interview with Author of 'Perjury': Who Is Allen Weinstein and What has He Got on Alger Hiss?," *Human Events* (May 6, 1978); "Hiss Book a Cold War Landmark,"

ibid. (April 15, 1978) ("those"); Allen Weinstein, *Perjury: The Hiss-Chambers Case* (New York: Alfred A. Knopf, 1978).

2 Robert Strong, *Working in the World: Jimmy Carter and the Making of American Foreign Policy* (Baton Rouge: Louisiana State University Press, 2000), 274, 270; Robert Gates, *From the Shadows: The Ultimate Insider's Story of Five Presidents and How They Won the Cold War* (New York: Simon & Schuster, 1997), 178–79. Not all revisionist accounts of Carter's foreign policy defend him. See, e.g., Itai Sneh, *The Future Almost Arrived: How Jimmy Carter Failed to Change Foreign Policy* (New York: Peter Lang, 2008), 159–61, 232–37 (criticizing the Carter administration for practicing a more traditional foreign policy than his human rights rhetoric envisioned), and Scott Kaufman, *Plans Unraveled: The Foreign Policy of the Carter Administration* (De Kalb: Northern Illinois University Press, 2008), 3–4 (classifying the different interpretations of Carter's foreign policy and characterizing Carter's foreign policy record as "confused," "mediocre," and "lackluster"); Betty Glad, *An Outsider in the White House: Jimmy Carter, His Advisors, and the Making of American Foreign Policy* (Ithaca, N.Y.: Cornell University Press, 2009), 40, 279 (intimating that Zbigniew Brzezinski hijacked Carter's foreign policy and did not serve the president well).

3 John Ehrman, *The Rise of Neoconservatism: Intellectuals and Foreign Affairs* (New Haven: Yale University Press, 1995), 100; http://nobelprize.org/nobel_prizes/peace/laureates/1977/amnesty-lecture.html.

4 David Skidmore, *Reversing Course: The Carter Administration's Foreign Policy, Domestic Politics, and the Failure of Reform* (Nashville: Vanderbilt University Press, 1996), 31–33. Carter's definition of human rights varied, but he once said that the most significant was the right "to be free of arbitrary violence." John Dumbrell, *The Carter Presidency: A Re-Evaluation* (Manchester, U.K.: Manchester University Press, 1995), 120.

5 Robert Shogan, *Promises to Keep: Carter's First Hundred Days* (New York: Thomas Crowell, 1977), 83–86 ("new"); "Mr. Outside Opts for 'Ins,'" *Time* (January 3, 1977); "China Policy: A Born-Again Brzezinski; The Carter Presidency," *Washington Post*, February 8, 1979 ("always"); Cyrus Vance, *Hard Choices: Critical Years in America's Foreign Policy* (New York: Simon & Schuster, 1983), 46, 62; Zbigniew Brzezinski, *Power and Principle: Memoirs of the National Security Adviser 1977–1981* (New York: Farrar, Straus and Giroux, 1983), 146–47; Glad, *An Outsider in the White House*, at 279, 28, 34. Robert Strong, who maintains that the media exaggerated differences between Vance and Brzezinski and that Carter made his own foreign policy concedes that "the president did display an apparent indifference, or perhaps an arrogant indifference, towards the public perception of disarray among his senior foreign policy advisers." Strong, *Working in the World*, at 267.

6 Sidney Blumenthal, *The Rise of the Counter-Establishment: The Conservative Ascent to Political Power* (New York: Union Square, 2008), 116 (quoting Jackson aide Elliot Abrams).

7 "Should a Conscientious Objector Be the New CIA Chief?," *Human Events* (January 8, 1977); "Sorensen Defended by Carter," *Washington Post*, January 17, 1977; "Sorensen Story: 'Like Being Blind-Sided by a Truck,'" ibid., January 19, 1977; "The CIA Gauntlet," *Nation* (January 29, 1977).

8 Andrew DeRoche, *Andrew Young: Civil Rights Ambassador* (Wilmington, Del.: Scholarly Resources, 2003), 77 (DeRoche persuasively maintains that Young's remarks were taken out of context, ibid.); "A Muzzle for 'Motor Mouth?,'" *Time* (April 25, 1977) (reporting that State Department officials referred to Young as "Motor Mouth"); "Andrew Young: Apologist for Marxist Repression," *Human Events* (September 2, 1978); "The World According to Andrew Young," *Commentary* (August 1978); Fran to Carter, May 23, 1979, CO 129, PLCarter Exec, 1/11/78–8/31/79 (repeating remarks of Maynard Jackson comparing Africa with Israel), Carter Library (unless otherwise noted, all archival collections cited in this chapter are in the Carter Library); Gregory Jaynes, "Rhodesia's Resolute Leader: Robert Gabriel Mugabe," *New York Times*, March 5, 1980 ("murderer"); Nancy Mitchell, "Tropes of the Cold War: Jimmy Carter and Rhodesia," *Cold War History*, 6 (2007): 263, 275–77;

Gerald Horne, *From the Barrel of a Gun: The United States and the War Against Zimbabwe, 1965–1980* (Chapel Hill: University of North Carolina Press, 2001), 159–65; Andrew DeRoche, *Black, White & Chrome: The United States and Zimbabwe, 1953–1998* (Trenton, N.J.: Africa World Press, 2001), 257, 275–81; Clara Holloway, "'Hasten the Inevitable Day of Freedom': The Carter Administration and Namibian Independence 1977–1981" (History Department Honors Thesis, Vanderbilt University, 1997), http://discoverarchive.vanderbilt.edu/handle/1803/99.

9 "Human Rights Spokeswoman," *New York Times*, June 23, 1977; "Argentine Military Believed U.S. Gave Go-Ahead for Dirty War," National Security Archive, http://www.gwu.edu/~nsarchiv/NSAEBB/NSAEBB73/index3.htm; "Carter Rights Aide, Visitng Argentina, Warns on Violations," *New York Times*, April 3, 1977; Kaufman, *Plans Unraveled*, at 32–35, 212–13; Northern Ireland Statement on U.S. Policy, August 30, 1977, americanpresidency.org ("solution"); Dumbrell, *The Carter Presidency: A Re-Evaluation*, at 131 (quoting the organizer of the Congressional Ad Hoc Committee on Irish Affairs, Representative Mario Biaggi, and see ibid. at 133–41).

10 Paul Warnke, "Apes on a Treadmill," *Foreign Policy* (Spring 1975); "The Lives They Lived: Paul Warnke, b. 1920: A Separate Peacenik," *New York Times*, December 30, 2001; Robert Kaufman, *Henry M. Jackson: A Life in Politics* (Seattle: University of Washington Press, 2000), 358–61; Jerry Sanders, *Peddlers of Crisis: The Committee on the Present Danger and the Politics of Containment* (Cambridge, Mass.: South End Press, 1983), 204–10, 254.

11 See, e.g., "Carter Gets Passing Grade in Foreign Policy," *ADA World* (April–May 1978); "Carter in Asia: McGovernism Without McGovern," *Commentary* (January 1978); "The Rise & Fall of the New Foreign-Policy Establishment," *Commentary* (July 1980) ("new"); "Ford Dies at 93: Helped Reunite Divided Nation After Becoming 38th President," *USA Today*, December 27, 2006 ("incubator").

12 Dan Tate to Frank Moore, November 18, 1977, Box 37, SALT, 1977, Hamilton Jordan Confidential File; "Behind-Scenes Power over Arms Policy," *Washington Post*, June 26, 1977 ("dozen").

13 Raymond Garthoff, *Détente and Confrontation: American-Soviet Relations from Nixon to Reagan* (Washington, D.C.: Brookings Institution, 1985), 585–86.

14 Carter, *Keeping Faith: Memoirs of a President* (New York: Bantam, 1982), 216; Brzezinski, *Power and Principle*, at 153, 158–59; Vance, *Hard Choices*, at 55, 50–53 ("sacrosanct").

15 Leonid Brezhnev to Carter, February 25, 1977, Box 18, Zbigniew Brzezinski, USSR C-B Correspondence, January–May 1977.

16 Frances FitzGerald, *Way Out There in the Blue: Reagan, Star Wars and the End of the Cold War* (New York: Simon & Schuster, 2000), 176–79; Kaufman, *Henry M. Jackson*, at 364.

17 Brzezinski, *Power and Principle*, at 154–56.

18 Vladislav Zubok, "An Offered Hand Rejected? The Carter Administration and the Vance Mission to Moscow in March 1977," *Jimmy Carter: Foreign Policy and Post-Presidential Years*, ed. Herbert Rosenbaum and Alexej Ugrinsky (Westport, Conn.: Greenwood, 1994), 357, 365 ("weaseling" and citing one Russian source who maintained that "the human rights issue did not play a critical role in the diplomatic failure of Vance's visit. If the American approach to SALT had appeared more reasonable to the Kremlin, that irritant would not have prevented a cordial welcome in Moscow"). On the impact of human rights, see Gates, *From the Shadows*, at 90; Garthoff, *Détente and Confrontation*, at 572–73.

19 Dumbrell, *The Carter Presidency: A Re-Evaluation*, at 116–18, 121–22 (quoting Powell); "The President's Meeting with USSR Foreign Minister Gromyko," September 23, 1977, 34–35, Memcon, President 9/19–30/77, Brzezinski Material Subject File.

20 Strobe Talbott, *Endgame: The Inside Story of SALT II* (New York: Harper & Row, 1980), 69–75.

21 Vance, *Hard Choices*, at 55; Kaufman, *Henry M. Jackson*, at 364–65.

22 "Did We Expect a Dancing Bear?," *Nation* (April 16, 1977).

23 Jimmy Carter, University of Notre Dame, Address at Commencement Exercises at the University, May 22, 1977, americanpresidency.org.

24 "The Singlaub Affair," *Washington Post*, May 24, 1977 ("Who," "some"); "Carter Disciplines Gen. Singlaub Who Attacked His Policy on Korea," *New York Times*, May 22, 1977 (citing the "numerous officers" who shared Singlaub's view); Harold Brown, *Thinking About National Security: Defense and Foreign Policy in a Dangerous World* (Boulder, Colo.: Westview, 1983), 123–26 (intelligence and its impact). By this time the Senate had deleted an expression of support of Carter's troop withdrawal policy from a 1977 Foreign Relations Committee bill by a vote of 79–15. "Senate Bars Support for a Korean Pullout; Removes Backing of Carter Policy from Committee Bill," *New York Times*, June 17, 1977.

25 "Ford Unhappy over Move," *New York Times*, April 29, 1978 (reporting on Ford's reaction to Singlaub's subsequent retirement after he had questioned the wisdom of the Panama Canal treaties); "Reagan Is Critical of Carter on Rights," *New York Times*, June 10, 1977; Ronald Reagan, "Free World Idealism Faces Soviet Realities," *Human Events* (July 2, 1977) (quotations). Singlaub became a charter member of the Reagan for President Exploratory Committee. "Reagan for President Committee Formed," ibid. (March 17, 1979).

26 Peter Hannaford to Molly, April 21, 1984, Box 12, File 3, Deaver and Hannaford Papers, Hoover Institution (describing courtship process); Jeane Kirkpatrick, "Dictatorships and Double Standards," *Commentary* (November 1979); James Mann, *The Rise of the Vulcans The History of Bush's War Cabinet* (New York: Viking, 2004), 129–37; Richard Allen, "Jeane Kirkpatrick and the Great Democratic Defection," *New York Times*, December 16, 2006.

27 Nick Kotz, *Wild Blue Yonder: Money, Politics, and the B-1 Bomber* (Princeton: Princeton University Press, 1988), 151–57, 169 (campaign, "We'd"); "ACU Chief Charges: Carter's B-1 Decision 'Dangerously Foolish,'" *Human Events* (July 9, 1977); "Ford Assails President on Defense and Urges Work on Neutron Bomb," *New York Times*, April 2, 1978; David McClellan, *Cyrus Vance* (Totowa, N.J.: Rowman & Allanheld, 1985), 44 ("cancellation").

28 Zbigniew Brzezinski, Memorandum of Conversation with Anatoly Dobrynin, June 23, 1977, Memcon, Brzezinski, National Security Adviser; Press Conference, President's News Conference of June 30, 1977, americanpresidency.org.

29 Kotz, *Wild Blue Yonder*, at 149, 175–76; "Carter's Decision on Bomber Jars Rockwell and Its Workers; but Optimism Is Felt at Boeing over Revised Defense Plans," *New York Times*, July 1, 1977; "Soviet Seems Unsure About Carter's Moves; Ignores Opposition to B-1 While Criticizing Cruise Missile," *New York Times*, July 2, 1977 ("militaristic," "seriously").

30 "Is America Becoming Number 2?: Current Trends in the U.S.-Soviet Military Imbalance," October 2, 1978, *Alerting America: The Papers of the Committee on the Present Danger*, ed. Charles Tyroler (Washington, D.C.: Pergamon, 1984), 39, 88; Phyllis Schlafly, "The Biggest News Story," *Phyllis Schlafly Report* (January 1977); "How Do We Know Who's Ahead?," *Washington Post*, February 5, 1977; Brian Auten, *Carter's Conversion: The Hardening of American Defense Policy* (Columbia: University Press of Missouri, 2008), 142–43; Skidmore, *Reversing Course*, at 55, 60–61; Vladislav Zubok, *A Failed Empire: The Soviet Union in the Cold War from Stalin to Gorbachev* (Chapel Hill: University of North Carolina Press, 2007), 243.

31 Kotz, *Wild Blue Yonder*, at 139–44, 171; "Carter to Announce B-1 Decision Today; Approval Indicated," *New York Times*, June 30, 1977; George Keegan, "How to Keep the Russians Away," ibid., July 6, 1977.

32 Norman Podhoretz, "The Culture of Appeasement," *Harper's* (October 1977).

33 Hamilton Jordan to Carter, n.d., June 1977, Box 34, Foreign Policy/Domestic Politics, Hamilton Jordan Papers.

34 See, e.g., Department of the Interior, Remarks at a Question-and-Answer Session with Department Employees, February 18, 1977, americanpresidency.org.

35 Steven Spiegel, *The Other Arab-Israeli Conflict: Making America's Middle East Policy, from Truman to Reagan* (Chicago: University of Chicago Press, 1985), 334 ("unguided").

36 Ibid., at 331–32 ("defensible," "code," "minor"); Remarks and a Question-and-Answer Session at the Clinton Town Meeting, March 16, 1977, americanpresidency.org; Brzezinski, *Power and Principle*, at 91 ("This").

37 Kenneth Stine, *Heroic Diplomacy: Sadat, Kissinger, Carter, Begin, and the Quest for Arab-Israeli Peace* (New York: Routledge, 1999), 192 ("dead fish"); "Hanafi Muslim Bands Seize Hostages at 3 Sites; 1 Slain, Others Wounded," *Washington Post*, March 10, 1977; Melani McAllister, *Epic Encounters: Culture, Media, and U.S. Interests in the Middle East, 1945–2000* (Berkeley: University of California Press, 2001), 125 ("Tutmania"); Visit of President Sadat of Egypt, Toasts of the President and President Sadat at a Dinner Honoring the Egyptian President, April 4, 1977, americanpresidency.org; Meeting with President Asad [*sic*] of Syria: Toasts of the President and President Asad [*sic*] at a Dinner Hosted by President Carter, May 9, 1977, americanpresidency.org.

38 "Begin: Israel's Ronald Reagan," *Human Events* (July 23, 1977); Stine, *Heroic Diplomacy*, at 198 ("total").

39 President's News Conference of May 26, 1977, americanpresidency.org.

40 "Begin Bars a Return to '67 Borders," *New York Times*, May 23, 1977 (quotations); Carter, *Keeping Faith*, at 288 ("frightening").

41 Carter, *Keeping Faith*, at 288; "Begin's American Bandwagon," *Time* (September 5, 1977).

42 William Quandt, *Camp David: Peacemaking and Politics* (Washington, D.C.: Brookings Institution, 1986), 122–23; United Nations, Address Before the General Assembly, October 4, 1977, americanpresidency.org.

43 Mark Siegel to Hamilton Jordan, October 3, 1977, Box 35, Middle East, 1977 [1], Hamilton Jordan Papers.

44 Stine, *Heroic Diplomacy*, at 218–19 (quoting from Stine's interview with Brzezinski).

45 Quandt, *Camp David*, at 125, n. 38; Anthony Barnett, Interview with Edward Said, "Where I'm Coming From," September 26, 2003, http://www.opendemocracy.net/node/1508; Edward Said, *Orientalism* (New York: Vintage, 1979); "2 Professors Deny They Received Offers to Represent Palestinians," *New York Times*, November 16, 1977 (quotation).

46 Jody Powell, *The Other Side of the Story* (New York: William Morrow, 1984), 58 ("currency"); Quandt, *Camp David*, at 349, 352, 147–48; "Israel Festive for Sadat Arrival Today," *Washington Post*, November 19, 1977; E-mail, Eran Shalev to Laura Kalman, August 7, 2009 (homemade flags).

47 "Goodbye, Arab Solidarity," *Time* (December 12, 1977); "Habash: 'Israel Will Fall,'" ibid. (December 19, 1977); Quandt, *Camp David*, at 158–60.

48 Leonid Brezhnev to Jimmy Carter, December 16, 1977, Box 18, Brzezinski, USSR, C-B-C 6/77–12/77; January 12, 1978, ibid., 1/78–12/78 ("invested," "great," "question"); February 27, 1978, ibid. ("it is"); and see September 14, 1978, and March 19, 1978, ibid.; Christopher Andrew and Vasili Mitrokhin, *The World Was Going Our Way: The KGB and the Battle for the Third World* (New York: Basic Books, 2005), 165 ("treacherously"); and see Garthoff, *Détente and Confrontation*, at 582.

49 President's News Conferences of May 25, 1978 ("surrogate") and June 14, 1978, americanpresidency.org.

50 Vladislav Zubok, *A Failed Empire: The Soviet Union in the Cold War from Stalin to Gorbachev* (Chapel Hill: University of North Carolina Press, 2009), 257 ("One comes to the conclusion that détente would have continued, despite all these problems, had Brezhnev still been willing to make a determined effort to maintain a political partnership with the American leadership"); Odd Arne Westad, *The Global Cold War: Third World Interventions and the Making of Our Times* (Cambridge, U.K.: Cambridge University Press, 2005), 241, 279, 302 (quotations, surprise in Afghanistan); Andrew and Mitrokhin, *The World Was Going Our Way*, at 471 (Andropov); Thomas Odom, "Shaba II: The French and Belgian Intervention in Zaire in 1978" (Fort Leavenworth: U.S. Army Command and General Staff College, 1993), 35, http://cgsc.leavenworth

.army.mil/carl/resources/csi/odom2/odom2.asp; Piero Gleijeses, "Moscow's Proxy? Cuba and Africa 1975–1988," *Journal of Cold War Studies* (Fall 2006): 3, 15–18, 31; Melvin Leffler, *For the Soul of Mankind: The United States, the Soviet Union, and the Cold War* (New York: Hill and Wang, 2007), 314–15 (Carter and CIA director).

51 Brzezinski, *Power and Principle*, at 187.

52 "A Communist Coup in Afghanistan," *New York Times*, May 5, 1978 (describing Carter administration as "so far rightly unruffled" by Afghanistan coup); "The Red Menace," *New York Times*, May 14, 1978 (op-ed by Norman Podhoretz contending that the Carter administration and *New York Times* should be alarmed by events in Afghanistan and Africa); "Cubans March Across Africa," *Conservative Digest* (December 1977); "1978; Conservative Political Action Highlights," *Human Events* (April 1, 1978); Kaufman, *Henry M. Jackson*, at 341 (Jackson's attacks on administration for its "complacency" with respect to African developments); "Africa, Soviet Imperialism and the Retreat of American Power," *Commentary* (October 1977); "Ford Calls for Harder Line," *New York Times*, May 26, 1978.

53 Vance, *Hard Choices*, at 63; Brzezinski, *Power and Principle*, at 183; Glad, *An Outsider in the White House*, at 77–87.

54 Mark Rozell, *The Press and the Carter Presidency* (Boulder, Colo.: Westview, 1989), 93 ("tug"); Garthoff, *Détente and Confrontation*, at 597.

55 Gaddis Smith, *Morality, Reason and Power: American Diplomacy in the Carter Years* (New York: Hill and Wang, 1986), 155; Paul Henze to Zbigniew Brzezinski, March 10, 1978, National Security Affairs, Box 2, Brzezinski Material Country File; Memorandum of Conversation, Anatoly Dobrynin/Zbigniew Brzezinski, September 20, 1978, Box 19, July 1978–March 1980, Brzezinski, USSR US-Soviet Relations; "Brzezinski Calls Democrats Soft Toward Moscow," *New York Times*, November 30, 1980 ("buried"); "Vance, Looking Back, Lauds Pact on Arms and Retorts to Brzezinski," ibid., December 3, 1970. Donna Johnson addresses the conflict between Carter's advisers and challenges Brzezinski's conclusion that détente lay buried in the sands of Ogaden in *Jimmy Carter and the Horn of Africa: Cold War Policy in Ethiopia and Somalia* (Jefferson, N.C.: McFarland, 2007), 96–106, 175, 180.

56 Address at Wake Forest University, March 17, 1978, americanpresidency.org; Garthoff, *Détente and Confrontation*, at 594–95.

57 Brzezinski, *Power and Principle*, at 189; Enhanced Radiation Weapons Statement by the President, April 7, 1978, americanpresidency.org ("influenced").

58 Strong, *Working in the World*, at 127–28, 136 ("capitalist"); Leonid Brezhnev to Jimmy Carter, January 5, 1978, Box 18, Brzezinski Correspondence, 1/78–12/78 ("unhuman"); Carter to Zbig and others, August 2, 1978, Box 22, Brzezinski, Defense ERW 3/78–8/78; Brzezinski, *Power and Principle*, at 304 ("queasy," "introduced").

59 Dr. Brzezinski's Call on Chancellor Schmidt, October 3, 1978, Box 33, Memcons, Brzezinski, September 1978–February 1979, Brzezinski Material Subject File; Helmut Schmidt, *Men and Powers: A Political Retrospective*, trans. Ruth Hein (New York: Random House, 1989), 79, 64–65, 181, 184–85, 166, 170.

60 Vance, *Hard Choices*, at 94.

61 Richard Burt, "Aides Report Carter Bans Neutron Bomb," *New York Times*, April 4, 1978; Richard Burt, "Neutron Bomb Controversy Strained Alliance and Caused Splits in the Administration," ibid., April 9, 1978; Bruce Cummings, "Chinatown: Foreign Police and Elite Realignment," *The Hidden Election: Politics and Economics in the 1980 Presidential Campaign*, ed. Thomas Ferguson and Joel Rogers (New York: Pantheon, 1981), 196, 208 (relationship between Brzezinski and Burt); Garthoff, *Détente and Confrontation*, at 853; *Power and Responsibility*, at 304–06; Schmidt, *Men and Powers*, at 213; Strong, *Working in the World*, at 143 ("widely").

62 Patrick Caddell to Carter and Hamilton Jordan, May 10, 1978, Box 6, SALT [5], Office Files, Rafshoon.

63 Richard Moe to Walter Mondale, Frank Moore, and Zbigniew Brzezinski, April 10, 1978, Box 37, SALT, 1978 ("current," "impression"); "A Republican Manifesto," *New York Times*, May 5, 1978; "Feckless!," *Time* (May 15, 1978) (three-quarters).

64 Talking Points for Deputy Secretary, April 8, 1978, Box 22, Defense—ERW, Brzezinski Donated; Kingman Brewster to Cyrus Vance, April 11, 1978, ibid.
65 North Atlantic Alliance Summit Remarks at the Opening Ceremonies, May 30, 1978, americanpresidency.org; North Atlantic Alliance Summit Text of Remarks on NATO Defense Policy, May 31, 1978, ibid.; Garthoff, *Détente and Confrontation*, at 863 ("from"); Brian Auten, *Carter's Conversion: The Hardening of American Defense Policy* (Columbia: University of Missouri Press, 2008), 226–28 , 257–58.
66 "Teng Reportedly Will Be Named Deputy Party Chairman in China," *New York Times*, January 24, 1977; "The President's Meeting with USSR Foreign Minister Gromyko," September 23, 1977.
67 Brzezinski, *Power and Principle*, at 200–06.
68 Vance, *Hard Choices*, at 114–15; Brian Hilton, "'Maximum Flexibility for Peaceful Change': Jimmy Carter, Taiwan, and the Recognition of the People's Republic of China," *Diplomatic History*, 33 (2009): 595, 602 ("lives"); Adam Clymer, *Edward M. Kennedy: A Biography* (New York: William Morrow, 1999), 263–65; Kaufman, *Henry M. Jackson*, at 378, 382; Zbigniew Brzezinski to Carter, May 4, 1978, Meeting with Senator Jackson on China, Vertical: USSR Related; Zbigniew Brzezinski to Carter, May 5, 1978, Box 9, China, Brzezinski Donated (reporting that Kennedy had told Brzezinski that the national security adviser's trip to China "will be counterproductive if I do not focus in some fashion on normalization"); Brzezinski, *Power and Principle*, at 208 ("You," "a consultative"). For the argument that Vance played a larger role in achieving normalization than Brzezinski's account, which at times almost implies that the secretary of state resisted it, see Breck Walker, "Friends, but Not Allies—Cyrus Vance and the Normalization of Relations with China," *Diplomatic History*, 33 (2009): 579–94. On the relative indifference to China's human rights record, see Hilton, "'Maximum Flexibility for Peaceful Change,'" at 601: "A 1977 study suggested that the number of executions in China that year may have reached 20,000. In comparison, the administration had placed sanctions on Bangladesh for that country having performed just thirty-seven political executions, suggesting that Carter's efforts to improve relations with Beijing constituted a double standard in his human rights policy. American analysts noted confusion among the foreign media about the 'pilgrimages to Peking of political and military notables paying their respects to the leader of a Communist Party which would not know a human right if it saw one.'"
69 Vance, *Hard Choices*, at 116; Brzezinski, *Power and Principle*, at 210, 219–21; "A New Cold War?," *Newsweek* (June 12, 1978); Carter, *Keeping Faith*, at 196 ("seduced").
70 Kaufman, *Plans Unraveled*, at 135 (May consultations); Leonid Brezhnev, Speech to CPSU CC Politburo, June 8, 1978, http://www.wilsoncenter.org/index.cfm?topic_id=1409&fuseaction=va2.document&identifier=5034F5A8-96B6-175C-9DD9D17B9F404E16&sort=Subject&item=Jimmy%20Carter; Thomas McCormick, *America's Half-Century*, 2d ed. (Baltimore: Johns Hopkins University Press, 1995), 206–07.
71 Vance, *Hard Choices*, at 101–02.
72 Ibid., at 102; Brzezinski, *Power and Principle*, at 320; Strong, *Working in the World*, at 99–100; United States Naval Academy Address at the Commencement Exercises, June 7, 1978, americanpresidency.org.
73 Rozell, *The Press and the Carter Presidency*, at 93–94 (*Time*); Garthoff, *Détente and Confrontation*, at 604 (quoting *Pravda*).
74 "The 'Pitiful, Helpless Giant' Returns," *New Republic* (December 16, 1978) (quoting Nixon on "pantywaist").
75 Richard Allen to Reagan, August 25, 1978, Box 3, Folder 3, Deaver and Hannaford Papers, Hoover Institution.
76 Ibid. ("packaging"); Text of Address by Alexander Solzhenitsyn, June 8, 1978, http://www.columbia.edu/cu/augustine/arch/solzhenitsyn/harvard1978.html; "Solzhenitsyn: The West Has Lost Its Courage," *Conservative Digest* (August 1978); "Solzhenitsyn at Harvard: Is the West Declining?," *Human Events* (July 1, 1978);

Norman Podhoretz, "Countering Soviet Imperialism," *New York Times*, May 31, 1978 ("paranoid"); Norman Podhoretz, "The Carter Stalemate," ibid., July 9, 1978 ("irresolute").

77 "Yamani Links F15s, to Oil, Dollar Help," *Washington Post*, May 2, 1978; "Church, Panel Colleagues Seek 2d Postponement of F-15 Sale to Saudis," ibid., June 24, 1978.

78 "Arms Issue Hindering Peace Efforts," *Washington Post*, May 14, 1978 ("only child"); Spiegel, *The Other Arab-Israeli Conflict*, at 347.

79 Mark Siegel to Hamilton Jordan, March 1, 1978, Box 37, Siegel, Mark, Hamilton Jordan Papers; Mark Siegel to Carter, March 8, 1978, ibid.; Marianne Sanua, *Let Us Prove Strong: The American Jewish Committee, 1945–2006* (Waltham, Mass.: Brandeis University Press, 2006), 214–16; http://www.peacenow.org.il/site/en/peace.asp?pi=43; "Group of U.S. Jews Disputes Begin's Line," *New York Times*, June 15, 1980.

80 "Fatah Admits Raid," *New York Times*, March 12, 1978; "U.S. Aides Gloomy on Talks with Begin," ibid., March 13, 1978; Statement to the Press by Prime Minister Begin on the Massacre of Israelis on the Haifa–Tel Aviv Road, March 12, 1978, http://www.mfa.gov.il/MFA/Foreign%20Relations/Israels%20Foreign%20Relations%20since%201947/1977-1979/133%20Statement%20to%20the%20press%20by%20Prime%20Minister%20Begin; Marvine Howe, "Some Palestinians Are Proud of Attacks," *New York Times*, March 14, 1978 (Syrian press, Saudi radio); Patrick Tyler, *A World of Trouble: The White House and the Middle East—from the Cold War to the War on Terror* (New York: Farrar, Straus and Giroux, 2009), 197.

81 George Michael, *Willis Carto and the American Far Right* (Gainesville: University Press of Florida, 2008), 128, 141; "Television and the Holocaust," *Time* (May 1, 1978) ("clothed"); Peter Novick, *The Holocaust in American Life* (New York: Houghton Mifflin, 1999), 156, 209; Robert Hunter to Zbigniew Brzezinski, May 3, 1978, Your Meeting with British Ambassador Jay, April 21, Box 33, Memcons Brzezinski, 10/77–7/78, Brzezinski Material Subject File. For a discussion of the shift from victimization to resistance, see William Greider, *Patty's Got a Gun: Patricia Hearst in 1970s America* (Chicago: University of Chicago Press, 2008), 143–51.

82 Carter, *Keeping Faith*, at 311–13; Quandt, *Camp David*, at 186, n. 15.

83 "A Turning Point for Israel," *Washington Post*, May 17, 1978 ("generated"); "Oil and the 'New Realities,'" ibid., May 16, 1978; Hamilton Jordan to Carter, May 14, 1978, Arms Sale Package (Israel-Egypt-Saudi Arabia) [CF, 0/A 646] ("First," "signs," and attaching wire "to selected"); "Jet Deal: 'Gang that Can't Shoot Straight' Wins One," *Washington Post*, May 18, 1978.

84 Mark Gerson, *The Neoconservative Vision: From the Cold War to the Culture Wars* (Lanham, Md.: Madison Books, 1996), 192 ("bad"); "Is Peace Still Possible in the Middle East?," *Commentary* (July 1978); "Why Bakke Won't End Reverse Discrimination," ibid. (September 1978).

85 Quandt, *Camp David*, at 202, 204.

86 Carter, *Keeping Faith*, at 315–18; Vance, *Hard Choices*, at 217.

87 Quandt, *Camp David*, at 206–12.

88 Brzezinski, *Power and Principle*, at 262 ("psycho"); William Quandt, *Peace Process: American Diplomacy and the Arab-Israeli Conflict Since 1967* (Washington, D.C.: Brookings Institution, 1993), 279 (Sadat); "Discussant: Samuel Lewis," *Jimmy Carter: Foreign Policy and Post-Presidential Years*, 155, 157 (Begin).

89 Carter, *Keeping Faith*, at 322; "Discussant: Hermann Eilts," *Jimmy Carter: Foreign Policy and Post-Presidential Years*, 151, 153 (diplomats); Spiegel, *The Other Arab-Israeli Conflict*, at 325 ("mystical)."

90 Carter, *Keeping Faith*, at 359–60.

91 Quandt, *Camp David*, at 228, 230.

92 Carter, *Keeping Faith*, at 386–93; Brzezinski, *Power and Principle*, at 272; Carter to Anwar Sadat and Prime Minister Begin, September 15, 1978, http://www.jimmycarterlibrary.org/documents/campdavid25/cda11.pdf (planning for failure of summit and its end on September 17, 1978).

93 Brzezinski, *Power and Principle*, at 263 ("right hand"); Carter, *Keeping Faith*, at 396.

94 Quandt, *Peace Process*, at 446–48. The accords are reprinted ibid., at 445–52.
95 Brzezinski, *Power and Principle*, at 274.
96 Carter, *Keeping Faith*, at 403.
97 William Quandt, ed., *The Middle East: Ten Years After Camp David* (Washington, D.C.: Brookings Institution, 1988), 16 ("There," "mistake"); Quandt, *Camp David*, at 244 ("fuzz"); Quandt, *Peace Process*, at 281.
98 Vance, *Hard Choices*, at 223 (concentration camp); Burton Kaufman, *The Arab Middle East and the United States: Inter-Arab Rivalry and Superpower Diplomacy* (New York: Twayne, 1996), 113 (disappointment of Sadat and his advisers); Carter, *Keeping Faith*, at 400. Carter believed that Sadat's advisers strengthened his recalcitrance, while Begin's moderated his recalcitrance. Carter, *Keeping Faith*, at 388–89, 382, 356, 378.
99 Remarks of the President, President Anwar el-Sadat of Egypt, and Prime Minister Menahem Begin of Israel at the Conclusion of the Camp David Meeting on the Middle East, September 17, 1978, americanpresidency.org; Rosalynn Carter, *First Lady from Plains* (New York: Fawcett, 1984), 254; The Nobel Peace Prize 2002, http://nobelprize.org/nobel_prizes/peace/laureates/2002/press.html.
100 "Jimmy Parts the Red Sea," *New Republic* (September 30, 1978) (quotations); "Blubber Lips," ibid. (August 26 and September 2, 1978); Rozell, *The Press and the Carter Presidency*, at 95–101 ("born again").
101 Powell, *The Other Side of the Story*, at 88; Carter, *Keeping Faith*, at 405; Spiegel, *The Other Arab-Israeli Conflict*, at 362 (calling "Carter's failure to pinpoint Begin's commitment on settlements . . . his greatest error of the Camp David conference"); Tyler, *A World of Trouble*, at 208 ("The ambiguity in the record suggests that Carter may have overinterpreted Begin's comments in a late-night session").
102 Quandt, *Camp David*, at 280 ("cowards," "snakes," "harden"); Vance, *Hard Choices*, at 239–40 ("take it"); "Jewish Groups Charge Carter Has Abandoned Role of Mediator," *New York Times*, December 17, 1978 ("advocate"). Actually, the Arab League could have responded more negatively: Its summit meeting ended with "an unexpectedly mild declaration" that urged Egypt not to sign a peace treaty but made no mention of imposing sanctions if it did and did not directly criticize Sadat. One way to interpret that was that the jet sales had worked their magic and the Saudis were acting as a voice of moderation. "Arab League Appeals to Egyptians to Renounce Accord with Israelis," *New York Times*, November 6, 1978. Another was to say that once the sale was approved, the Saudis "doublecrossed the Americans and supported the radical Arabs" in demanding linkage. "Carter Blames the Jews," ibid., December 18, 1978.
103 David Harris, *The Crisis: The President, the Prophet, and the Shah—1979 and the Coming of Militant Islam* (New York: Little, Brown, 2004), 85–86; David Farber, *Taken Hostage: The Iran Hostage Crisis and America's First Encounter with Radical Islam* (Princeton: Princeton University Press, 2005), 92.
104 Gary Sick, *All Fall Down: America's Fateful Encounter with Iran* (London: I. B. Tauris, 1985), 92, 106 ("Iran"); Stansfield Turner, *Burn Before Reading: Presidents, CIA Directors, and Secret Intelligence* (New York: Hyperion, 2005), 180 ("asleep") (contrast this statement with Turner's stronger defense of CIA reporting on Iran in Stansfield Turner, *Secrecy and Democracy: The CIA in Transition* (Boston: Houghton Mifflin, 1985), 113–18, 124–25; Harris, *The Crisis*, at 76 ("Muslims"); Westad, *The Global Cold War*, at 294; Andrew and Mitrohkin, *The World Was Going Our Way*, at 181–82.
105 Sick, *All Fall Down*, at 122, and see 121–23, 70–71; Harris, *The Crisis*, at 95 ("cheerleader"); Vance, *Hard Choices*, at 328; Brzezinski, *Power and Principle*, at 363–66; Smith, *Morality, Reason and Power*, at 188 ("impossible"); Tyler, *A World of Trouble*, at 224 ("what was most remarkable was that Carter chose not to call the shah in these fateful days of decision").
106 Harris, *The Crisis*, at 140, 127, 109, 151 ("vacation," "Gandhi"); "The Shah's Final Days," *Newsweek* (January 29, 1979) ("Where"); Farber, *Taken Hostage*, at 103–04, 108–12 ("cheered"); "Graveside Homage Paid to Martyrs," *Washington Post*, February 2, 1979; Glad, *An Outsider in the White House*, at 174 (Brzezinski).

107 Vance, *Hard Choices*, at 242; Quandt, *Camp David*, at 291 ("needed").
108 Tyler, *A World of Trouble*, at 236 ("grasped"); Quandt, *Camp David*, at 317, 290–91.
109 Hedrick Smith, "Treaty Impact Still Unknown: 'Hopes and Dreams' but 'No Illusions' for Carter," *New York Times*, March 26, 1978 (speeches, gamble); Remarks of President Carter, President Anwar al-Sadat of Egypt, and Prime Minister Menahem Bagin of Israel at the Egyptian-Israeli Peace Treaty Signing Ceremony, March 26, 1979, americanpresidency.org; Quandt, *Camp David*, at 310, n. 18 ("postman").
110 Carter, *Keeping Faith*, at 426–27; Richard Wirthlin, Reagan for President Committee, April 12, 1979, Box 109, Campaign Operations Polls, Edwin Meese Papers, Reagan Library; Richard Whalen to Reagan; April 4, 1979, Box 104, Campaign Planning Research—Policy Issues Papers 4/1979–8/1979, ibid. (1 of 12), ibid. ("President Carter's").
111 Rael Jean Isaac, "The Real Lessons of Camp David," *Commentary* (December 1993); S. Fred Singer, "Who Won at Camp David?," ibid. (October 1986), and see also Robert Tucker, "Behind Camp David," ibid. (November 1978); Theodore Draper, "How Not to Make Peace in the Middle East," ibid. (March 1979); Jimmy Carter, *Palestine: Peace Not Apartheid* (New York: Simon & Schuster, 2006).

CHAPTER XII | TO THE MOUNTAINTOP AND BACK

1 Rosalynn Carter, *First Lady from Plains* (New York: Fawcett, 1984), 286; James Carter, *Keeping Faith: Memoirs of a President* (New York: Bantam, 1982), 115.
2 Steering Committee Meeting, January 13, 1979, Box 105, Campaign Operations: Citizens for the Republic, Edwin Meese III Papers, Reagan Library (remarks of Charles Black); "Elections '78," *National Review* (November 24, 1978); "Democrats Dominate," *New York Times*, November 9, 1978; "Moderation Is the Message for New Right Campaigners," *New York Times*, November 26, 1978 ("Don't worry"); "Dixie's Heart Doesn't Yet Belong to the Republicans," *New York Times*, December 16, 1979; Kenneth Bridges, *Twilight of the Texas Democrats* (College Station: Texas A&M University Press, 2008); Earl Black and Merle Black, *The Rise of Southern Republicans* (Cambridge: Harvard University Press, 2002).
3 "Foreign Relations Committee's Influence at Lowest Point in 20 Years," *New York Times*, November 23, 1977; LeRoy Ashby and Rod Gramer, *Fighting the Odds: The Life of Senator Frank Church* (Pullman: Washington State University Press, 1994), 562–63, 577–78 (Church's chairmanship, relationship with Carter, and Helms's role); Robert Johnson, *Congress and the Cold War* (New York: Cambridge University Press, 2006), 242–43 (Armed Services Committee); "Sweeping Right-to-Life Goals Set as Movement Gains New Power," *New York Times*, November 27, 1978 ("ludicrous"); "Labor's View: Future Is Dim: Leaders Fear Congress Will Shift to the Right," ibid., November 14, 1978; "Social Reforms and Arms Accord Likely to Face Snag on Capitol Hill," ibid., November 9, 1978 (Democratic strategist; the article did not identify the strategist); "Gallup Poll Indicates President Wasn't Helped or Hurt by Voting," ibid., November 26, 1978.
4 American for Democratic Action (ADA), National Board Minutes, January 12–14, 1979, Box 1, National Board Minutes, 1979, ADA Papers, State Historical Society of Wisconsin; "The Human Budget v. the Pentagon," *ADA World* (January–February 1979); Adam Clymer, *Edward M. Kennedy: A Biography* (New York: William Morrow, 1999), 276–77.
5 Raymond Garthoff, *Détente and Confrontation: American-Soviet Relations from Nixon to Reagan* (Washington, D.C.: Brookings Institution, 1985), 619; Cyrus Vance, *Hard Choices: Critical Years in America's Foreign Policy* (New York: Simon & Schuster, 1983), 109–10.
6 Zbigniew Brzezinski, *Power and Principle: Memoirs of the National Security Adviser 1977–1981* (New York: Farrar, Straus and Giroux, 1983), 232.
7 Vance, *Hard Choices*, at 110–13; Strobe Talbott, *Endgame: The Inside Story of SALT II* (New York: Harper, 1980), 226–48.

8 Patrick Tyler, *A Great Wall: Six Presidents and China: An Investigative History* (New York: Public Affairs, 2000), 272; "The China Card," *New Republic* (January 6, 1979) (compare "On the Right: The New Face of America," *National Review* [January 19, 1979] with "The Zbig and Jerry Show," *New Republic* [January 13, 1979] ["flops," "melange"]).

9 Richard Nixon to Jimmy Carter, December 20, 1978, Box 34, File N, Susan Clough Papers, Carter Library. (Unless otherwise noted, all archival references in this chapter are from the Carter Library.) "Very good letter," Carter wrote on the margin.

10 Enrico Fardella, "The Sino-American Normalization: A Reassessment," *Diplomatic History*, 33 (2009): 545, 575 ("small"); Clymer, *Edward M. Kennedy*, at 278; Hal Lindsey, *The Late Great Planet Earth* (Grand Rapids, Mich.: Zondervan, 1970); "A Planet Doomed," *New York Times*, January 18, 1979; "Brother Billy," *New York Times*, January 12, 1979; "Billy Carter, Reporter at Odds over Tarmac Toilet Stop," *Globe*, January 18, 1979; "Billy Out of Control," *Newsweek* (January 22, 1979) ("hell"); Jimmy Carter, State of the Union Address, January 25, 1979, americanpresidency.org; "President's News Conference of January 26, 1979, ibid. (media reaction); "Slogan Power!, Slogan Power!," *Time* (February 12, 1979) ("dud").

11 "The Polar Bear," *New Republic* (February 10, 1979); "Bearbaiting," *Newsweek* (February 12, 1979); Dan Caldwell, *The Dynamics of Domestic Politics and Arms Control: The Salt II Treaty Ratification Debate* (Columbia: University of South Carolina Press, 1991), 49.

12 David Farber, *Taken Hostage: The Iran Hostage Crisis and America's First Encounter with Radical Islam* (Princeton: Princeton University Press, 2005), 113–14; "Yankee, We've Come to Do You In," *Time* (February 26, 1979).

13 "SALT II Threatened by Iranian Revolution," *Human Events* (February 24, 1979) ("essentially"); Tyler, *A Great Wall*, at 278.

14 "Death Behind a Keyhole," *Time* (February 26, 1979); "Soviet Role Alleged in Dubs' Death," *Washington Post*, February 22, 1979; Anatoly Dobrynin, *In Confidence: Moscow's Ambassador to America's Six Cold War Presidents (1962–1986)* (New York: Touchstone, 1995), 441; Christopher Andrew and Vasili Mitrokhin, *The World Was Going Our Way: The KGB and the Battle for the Third World* (New York: Basic Books, 2005), 390–91.

15 Gerald Rafshoon to Carter, February 5, 1979, Box 28, Memorandums from Greg Schneiders, January and February, 1979, Office of Communications, Rafshoon; Toasts at the Luncheon Honoring President Carter, February 14, 1979, americanpresidency .org; "Scolding in Mexico," *Newsweek* (February 26, 1979); Poll Report #2, Box 15, President's Trip to Mexico, June 14, 1979 (2), Rafshoon Papers; Richard Lyon ("literally"). The American ambassador to Mexico, Patrick Lucey, soon resigned to work for Kennedy.

16 National Security Council Meeting, February 16, 1979, 4:30–5:15, Box 10, China: Sino-Vietnamese Conflict, Feburary 17–21, 1979, Brzezinski Donated; Special Coordination Meeting, February 17, 1979, 10:30–12:30, ibid.; Carter, *Keeping Faith*, at 206–09; Gaddis Smith, *Morality, Reason and Power: American Diplomacy in the Carter Years* (New York: Hill & Wang, 1984), 97 ("the first case"); Brzezinski, *Power and Principle*, at 25, 413, 410 ("appreciation," "frozen"); Vance, *Hard Choices*, at 1212 ("'anti-Soviet'"). On the deterioration of the relation between China and Vietnam, see Chen Jian, *Mao's China and the Cold War* (Chapel Hill: University of North Carolina Press, 2001), 229–37.

17 Hamilton Jordan to Carter, February 17, 1979, Box 37, Schedule Matters, Presidential, 1977–1979.

18 "Slain U.S. Diplomat Buried in Virginia," *New York Times*, February 21, 1979; Jimmy Carter, Remarks at a Special Convocation of the Georgia Institute of Technology, February 20, 1979, americanpresidency.org; "The Charge of the Right Brigade," *New York Times*, February 21, 1979 (Baker).

19 Tom Wicker, "Time for a Leader," *New York Times*, February 18, 1979; "America's World of Woes: Feeling Helpless," *Newsweek* (February 26, 1979) ("emotional,"

"strike"); "Where's Papa?" *New Republic* (February 24, 1979); "Small Stick Diplomacy," *Newsweek* (March 6, 1979) (Mayaguez, "monotonic").

20 Gerald Rafshoon to Carter, Leadership, n.d., Box 27, Leadership Memorandums, Office of Communications, Rafshoon ("No," "Yet," "project," "sense," "national," "act"), Gerald Rafshoon to Carter, Style, n.d., Box 28, Memorandums from Rafshoon, June, July, and August 1979, ibid. (remaining quotations).

21 "Beyond 'The China Syndrome,'" *Newsweek* (April 16, 1979): 31; J. Samuel Walker, *Three Mile Island: A Nuclear Crisis in Historical Perspective* (Berkeley: University of California Press, 2004), 162–69 (media); Allan Mazur, *A Hazardous Inquiry: The Rashomon Effect at Love Canal* (Cambridge: Harvard University Press, 1998), 127, 131.

22 Energy Address to the Nation, April 5, 1979, americanpresidency.org; "The Energy Tangle," *Newsweek* (April 16, 1979) ("summons").

23 President's News Conference of April 10, 1979, americanpresidency.org; W. Carl Biven, *Jimmy Carter's Economy: Policy in an Age of Limits* (Chapel Hill: University of North Carolina Press, 2002), 175–77.

24 Energy Address to the Nation, April 5, 1979.

25 "James Schlesinger," Box 1, National Board Meeting Minutes 1979, ADA Papers; "Long-Term 'Vision' Urged by Kennedy," *New York Times*, May 1, 1979 ("intimidated," "transparent"); President's News Conference of April 30, 1979, americanpresidency.org ("baloney"); Stuart Eizenstat to Carter, April 25, 1979, Box 37, Memorandums, April 27–May 31, 1979, Jody Powell Papers.

26 "Nader Coalition Plans Nuclear Policy Protest," *Washington Post*, April 19, 1979; Stuart Eizenstat, Anne Wexler, Gerald Rafshoon, Jack Watson, Hamilton Jordan, and Frank Moore to Carter, May 2, 1979, Box 23, Energy, February 23, 1979–June 12, 1979, Frank Moore Papers ("Secretary"; Carter did meet privately with the leaders of the May event); Gerald Rafshoon to Carter, May 15, 1979, not sent, Rafshoon, Box 28, Memorandums from Jerry Rafshoon: March, April, and May 1979, Office of Communications, Rafshoon (suggesting that you "take the one step that *everyone* seems to agree on: fire Schlesinger. I would not recommend this for political reasons if I did not feel that it is absolutely justified on the merits. Jim has had four major responsibilities: 1) to develop a workable comprehensive energy plan; 2) to help steer that plan through Congress; 3) to set up and run a Department of Energy; 4) to administer U.S. energy policy. In each case the results are, by all objective measures a total disaster"); "The Protesters: 65,000 Protest Dependence on A-Energy," *Washington Post*, May 7, 1979 (Schlesinger); "Nothing Indicates Change in Carter View of A-Power Needs," ibid., May 20, 1979.

27 "House Votes Down White House Plan for Gas Rationing; Stunning Defeat for Carter," *New York Times*, May 11, 1979.

28 "California's Waiting Game," *Newsweek* (May 21, 1979).

29 "Ripping Apart the Guidelines," *Time* (April 16, 1979); National Board Meeting, Americans for Democratic Action, March 23–25, 1979, "Inflation Controls," Box 1, National Board Minutes: 1979, ADA Papers ("Only").

30 "The Fed v. Jimmy's Aides," *Time* (April 30, 1979); Bad Things Come in Threes," *Time* (June 11, 1979) ("price surge").

31 "The Trouble Is Serious," *Time* (April 30, 1979).

32 Steven Gillon, *The Democrats' Dilemma: Walter F. Mondale and the Liberal Legacy* (New York: Columbia University Press, 1992), 256–59; James Fallows, "The Passionless Presidency," *Atlantic* (May 1979); "The Passionless Presidency, Part II," ibid. (June 1979): 75, 78; "'Passionless Presidency' and the Insider's Dilemma; James Fallows Defends His 'Honorable' Criticism," *Washington Post*, April 25, 1979 ("20 years"); President's News Conference of April 30, 1979, americanpresidency.org; "The News Hawk; Editor James Fallows Declares War on Journalism's Status Quo," *Washington Post*, March 5, 1997.

33 "Health Plan Is Challenge to President," *Washington Post*, May 15, 1979; "Carter Aides Showing Toll of Attacks from All Sides," *New York Times*, May 29, 1979 ("suffering").

34 "'I'll Whip His Ass,'" *Newsweek* (June 25, 1979). See Leo Ribuffo, "'I'll Whip His Ass': Jimmy Carter, Edward Kennedy, and the Latest Crisis of American Liberalism," Organization of American Historians, April 15, 1994.

35 Scott Kaufman, *Plans Unraveled: The Foreign Policy of the Carter Administration* (De Kalb: Northern Illinois University Press, 2008), 180 (close relationship of SALT II to Vladivostok); Jimmy Carter, Meeting with Chancellor Schmidt of the Federal Republic of Germany, White House Statement, June 6, 1979, americanpresidency.org ("expeditiously"); "MX Missile Could Mark Big Switch in U.S. Nuclear Policy," *New York Times*, June 16, 1979 ("pinpoint").

36 Brian Auten, *Carter's Conversion: The Hardening of American Defense Policy* (Columbia: University Press of Missouri, 2008), 271–304; "Our Most Important Task—Selling SALT," *ADA World* (May–June 1979); "Nunn Links His Support for Pact to Arms Budget Rise," *New York Times*, July 26, 1979 (Nunn, McGovern, Proxmire); "Search for an Invulnerable Missile," ibid., May 27, 1979 ("cheered"); Garthoff, *Détente and Confrontation*, at 731 (Jackson); "Senator Jackson's 'Slander' About Soviet Involvement in Terrorism," BBC Summary of World Broadcasts, July 9, 1979; "Terror: A Soviet Export," *New York Times Magazine*, November 2, 1980; Robert Byrd, *Child of the Appalachian Coal Fields* (Morgantown: West Virginia University Press, 2005), 403; "New Joint Chiefs Are Not Cigar-Chewing Warriors," *New York Times*, June 24, 1979.

37 "Carter Discloses He Offered Freeze in Atomic Arms to Brezhnev in '79," *New York Times*, May 7, 1982; Garthoff, *Détente and Confrontation*, at 736–38; "MX Missile Could Mark Big Switch in U.S. Nuclear Policy," *New York Times*, June 16, 1979; "Change in Nuclear Target Policy Not a Radical One, Brown Says, Brown: No Big Nuclear Shift," *Washington Post*, August 21, 1980; "Presidential Directive 59; A Barrage of Theories," ibid., August 21, 1980; Tom Wicker, "In the Nation Terror in Disguise," *New York Times*, August 24, 1980.

38 Johnson, *Congress and the Cold War*, at 243 (informed critics); Gerald Rafshoon to Carter, June 8, 1979, Box 28, Memorandums from Gerald Rafshoon—June, July, and August 1979, Office of Communications, Rafshoon; "Leaders Make Signing of Treaty a Warm and Poignant Closing," *New York Times*, June 19, 1979; "Will Senate Buy Carter's Distortions? SALT II Gives Soviets First Strike Capability," *Human Events* (June 30, 1979).

39 Strobe Talbott, *Endgame: The Inside Story of SALT II* (New York: Harper & Row, 1980), 6, 12 ("respectfully," Soviets); Edward Rowny, *It Takes One to Tango* (New York: Brassey's, 1992), 116–22.

40 "Yamani on Oil—and Israel," *Newsweek* (July 9, 1979); Carter, *Keeping Faith*, at 112; "Giscard: Oil Is the Issue," *Newsweek* (July 2, 1979).

41 "OPEC's Painful Squeeze," *Time* (July 9, 1979) (North Sea).

42 The President's Trip to Japan and the Republic of Korea, Remarks During a Background Briefing Given by Administration Officials for Reporters on Board Air Force One, July 1, 1979, americanpresidency.org; "And the Gas Lines Grow," *Time* (July 9, 1979); "Nothing Else Has So Frustrated the American People," *Washington Post*, July 7, 1979 (Vietnam); Hamilton Jordan to Carter, July 3, 1979, Box 37, Speech, President's, July 15, 1979, Hamilton Jordan Papers ("hell").

43 "President Cancels Address on Energy; No Reason Offered," *New York Times*, July 5, 1979; Carter, *Keeping Faith*, at 114–20; "Carter, Aides, Staying at Camp David," *Washington Post*, July 6, 1979; "Aides Fear Country Expects the Impossible from Summit," ibid., July 12, 1979.

44 Carter, *Keeping Faith*, at 118–19.

45 Jordan to Carter, July 3, 1979 ("'hell,'" reporting Caddell's view); Patrick Caddell, "Of Crisis and Opportunity," Box 40, Memorandums: President Carter, 1/10/79–4/23/79, Powell (quotations).

46 Gerald Ford, "Lessons from the Presidency," *Christianity Today* (July 29, 1977); Christopher Lasch, *The Culture of Narcissism: American Life in an Age of Diminishing Expectations* (New York: W. W. Norton, 1979) xiii, 5; Natasha Zaretsky, *No Direc-*

tion Home: The American Family and the Fear of National Decline, 1968–1980 (Chapel Hill: University of North Carolina Press, 2007), 214–221 (Lasch on Carter). Among the interpretations of the "malaise" speech I found most helpful are Robert Strong, "Recapturing Leadership: The Carter Administration and the Crisis of Confidence," *Presidential Studies Quarterly*, 16 (Fall 1986): 636–50; Leo Ribuffo, "'Malaise' Revisited: Jimmy Carter and the Crisis of Confidence," *The Liberal Persuasion*, ed. John Diggins (Princeton: Princeton University Press, 1997), 164–84; Daniel Horowitz, *Jimmy Carter and the Energy Crisis of the 1970s: The 'Crisis of Confidence' Speech of July 15, 1979: A Brief History with Documents* (New York: Bedford, 2005); Kevin Mattson, *"What the Heck Are You Up To, Mr. President?" Jimmy Carter, America's "Malaise," and the Speech that Should Have Changed the Country* (New York: Bloomsbury, 2009).

47 "Winter of Discontent," *New York Times*, April 15, 1974 (report by Anthony Lewis that Caddell saw "a crisis of confidence in institutions"); Patrick Caddell to Carter, December 12, 1978, Box 15, State of the Union Address, January 20, 1979, 1/20/79 (3), Rafshoon (quotations). The undated draft is in Box 32, State of the Union Message, 1979, Notes—Patrick Caddell, ibid.

48 Greg Schneiders to Gerald Rafshoon, n.d., Box 33, State of the Union Message, 1979, Notes—Greg Schneiders, Rafshoon; Democratic National Committee Remarks and a Question-and-Answer Session at the Committee's Spring Meeting, May 25, 1979, americanpresidency.org; Mattson, *"What the Heck Are You Up To, Mr. President?,"* at 81.

49 Oral History, Stuart Eizenstat, Miller Center of Public Affairs, January 29, 1982, 72, http://web1.millercenter.org/poh/transcripts/ohp_1982_0129_eizenstat.pdf; Patrick Caddell, "What Is to Be Done?," July 2, 1979, Box 36, Principles for Leadership, Clough Papers.

50 Caddell, "What Is to Be Done?"

51 Hamilton Jordan, Leading the Country, Box 34, Image Analysis and Changes, July 16, 1979, Jordan Papers.

52 Mattson, *"What the Heck Are You Up To, Mr. President?,"* at 133, 144, 6 ("duked," "scold,"); Charles Jones, *The Trusteeship Presidency: Jimmy Carter and the United States Congress* (Baton Rouge: Louisiana State University Press, 1977), 177 ("mumbly"); Greg Schneiders to Gerald Rafshoon, July 10, 1979, Box 28, Memorandums from Gerald Rafshoon: June, July, and August 1979, Office of Communications, Rafshoon.

53 "Carter at the Crossroads," *Time* (July 23, 1979) (*Moses*); Energy and National Goals Address to the Nation, July 15, 1979, americanpresidency.org.

54 Energy and National Goals Address; "A Crisis of Spirit," *Time* (July 23, 1979); Jones, *The Trusteeship Presidency*, at 177.

55 Horowitz, *Jimmy Carter and the Energy Crisis of the 1970s*, at 155 (Bellah); Zaretsky, *No Direction Home*, at 220 ("played").

56 *Carter, Keeping Faith*, at 121; Mattson, "*What the Heck Are You Up To, Mr. President?,*" at 159–60, 204; Jimmy Carter, Energy Security Act Remarks on Signing S. 952 into Law, June 30, 1980, americanpresidency.org; "Energy—One Year Later," *Washington Post*, July 6, 1980; Rozell, *The Press and the Carter Presidency*, at 131–33.

57 Jordan, Leading the Country (quotations, summarizing criticisms of Carter); Hamilton Jordan to Carter, Thoughts on Cabinet/Staff Meeting, n.d., Box 33, Administration Coordination, April 1978, Jordan Papers; Joseph Califano, *Governing America: An Insider's Report from the White House and the Cabinet* (New York: Simon & Schuster, 1981), 189, 292–93, 406–18, 430–32; "Crusading at HEW," *Newsweek* (May 29, 1978) ("Keep").

58 Hamilton Jordan to Carter, July 1979, Box 33, Cabinet Resignations, Hamilton Jordan Confidential File, Gillon, *Democrats' Dilemma*, at 265 ("sugar").

59 Carter, *First Lady from Plains*, at 288; "Jimmy Carter's Cabinet Purge," *Newsweek* (July 30, 1979).

60 Richard Nixon to Jimmy Carter, July 23, 1979, Box 46, File N, Clough Papers; Richard Moe to Hamilton Jordan, August 8, 1979, Box 57, White House Staff—

Reorganizations, 1979 [CF, 0/A 647], Hamilton Jordan Subject File ("There is a widespread feeling in the press, on the Hill and elsewhere that we have shaken up the Cabinet plenty, but the White House not at all"); "Jimmy Carter's Cabinet Purge," at 27 ("upstaged"); "Califano: A Rumble of Angry Thunder from the Liberals," *Washington Post*, July 20, 1979; "Georgians Have the President on Their Minds; A Down-Home Welcome for Their Man-in-Washington," *Washington Post*, January 23, 1978 ("Washington insider"); "When A Nation Yearns for Action," *New York Times*, February 18, 1979 ("three"); Andrew DeRoche, *Andrew Young: Civil Rights Ambassador* (Wilmington, Del.: Scholarly Resources, 2003), 111–15.

61 "Carter's Balancing Act," *Newsweek* (July 23, 1979) (recession); W. Carl Biven, *Jimmy Carter's Economy: Policy in an Age of Limits* (Chapel Hill: University of North Carolina Press, 2002), 140, 237 (markets); "The Bountiful Bailout Planned for Chrysler," *Business Week* (November 19, 1979); Peter Bourne, *Jimmy Carter: A Comprehensive Biography from Plains to PostPresidency* (New York: Scribner, 1997), 448 ("if"); Naomi Klein, *The Shock Doctrine: The Rise of Disaster Capitalism* (New York: Picador, 2007), 199; "Volcker Asserts U.S. Must Trim Living Standard," *New York Times*, October 18, 1979.

62 "Jimmy Carter's Cabinet Purge," at 22–23, 27; Jordan, Leading the Country (summarizing criticisms); "Now, Ham and Coke?," *Newsweek* (September 10, 1979) ("Washington's most"); Jody Powell, *The Other Side of the Story* (New York: William Morrow, 1984), 110.

63 Katy Harriger, *The Special Prosecutor in American Politics*, 2d ed. (Lawrence: University Press of Kansas, 2000), 56–72; Arthur Christy, "Trials and Tribulations of the First Special Prosecutor Under the Ethics in Government Act of 1978," *Georgetown Law Journal*, 86 (1998): 2287, 2289.

64 "A McGovern-Jackson Candidate?," *Washington Post*, July 29, 1979; "Kennedy to Win 1980 Nomination, Jackson Predicts," ibid., July 25, 1979 ("now;" Jackson covered his bases by telling reporters that "he still is supporting President Carter for the nomination, but he praised Kennedy lavishly for pursuing a course that 'can't split the party' "); ADA Board Meeting, July 28, 1979, Box 1, National Board Minutes, 1979, ADA Papers; "Kennedy Drafted as Grass Roots Take Charge," *ADA World* (November 1979).

65 Richard Wirthlin to Reagan, July 19, 1979, Box 10, File 20, Deaver and Hannaford Papers, Hoover Institution; "Reagan and Ford Hold G.O.P. Lead, Poll Says," *New York Times*, July 29, 1979; "Ford, Warning on U.S. Security, Seems to Encourage G.O.P. Draft," ibid., September 28, 1979 ("Truthfully," "roared").

66 David Newsom, *The Soviet Brigade in Cuba: A Study in Political Diplomacy* (Bloomington: Indiana University Press, 1987), 14.

67 President's News Conference of July 25, 1979, americanpresidency.org (Carter on Nicaragua); "A Red Nicaragua Ready to Expand Northward: Carter Shake-up Covers Disastrous Foreign Policy Defeat," *Human Events* (August 4, 1979); "Communists in the Caribbean," *Conservative Digest* (September 1979); William LeoGrande, *Our Own Backyard: The United States in Central America, 1977–1992* (Chapel Hill: University of North Carolina Press, 1998), 44–45 (quoting Ambassador Robert White). See generally Andrew and Mitrokhin, *The World Was Going Our Way*, at 117–25; John Soares, "Strategy, Ideology, and Human Rights: Jimmy Carter Confronts the Left in Central America, 1979–1981," *Journal of Cold War Studies* (Fall 2006): 57–91; Glad, *An Outsider in the White House*, at 250–60, 282.

68 Newsom, *The Soviet Brigade in Cuba*, at 12–14; Ashby and Gramer, *Fighting the Odds: The Life of Senator Frank Church*, at 594 ("sink," "immediately"); Frank Moore and Bob Russell Memorandum, October 19, 1979, Box 37, Political, May 9, 1978–October 23, 1980, Clough Papers ("anything"); "Church Perceived as Apostate Fearful of Election Disaster," *Washington Post*, October 12, 1979.

69 Powell, *The Other Side of the Story*, at 104–07 (reporting on story and media reaction); "A Tale of Carter and the 'Killer Rabbit'; President Orders Photograph," *New York Times*, August 30, 1979 ("swinging"); Plains, Georgia, Informal Exchange with

Reporters, August 31, 1979, americanpresidency.org; "The Banzai Bunny," *Newsweek* (September 10, 1978); "Banzai Bunny," *Time* (September 10, 1979).

70 "Church Delays Arms Pact Hearings to Study Soviet Troop Use in Cuba," *New York Times*, September 5, 1979; "Vance Tells Soviet Its Troops in Cuba Could Imperil Ties," ibid., September 6, 1979 ("likelihood," "status quo)"; Clymer, *Edward M. Kennedy*, at 284; "For the President, an Afternoon of Gospel; The President, the Pretender and the Crown Prince of Gospel; The Kennedy Question," *Washington Post*, September 10, 1979. ("The predominant question of the day was whether Senator Edward M. Kennedy [D-Mass.] had asked Carter to step down as a candidate for reelection when the two of them had lunch together Friday at the White House." Kennedy, who admitted to being "baffled" by Carter, whom he considered a poor listener, later said that at the luncheon Carter had asked *him* "to make a 'Shermanesque statement'—that under no circumstances would I run for president or accept a draft from my party," which "I declined to do.") Edward Kennedy, *True Compass* (New York: Twelve Books, 2009), 352, 360, 364; Soviet Combat Troops in Cuba: Remarks to Reporters, September 7, 1979, americanpresidency.org.

71 Gloria Duffy, "Crisis Mangling and the Cuban Brigade," *International Security*, 8 (Summer 1983): 67–87; "Soviet Views of Troop Issue Colored by 1962 Debacle," *Washington Post*, October 1, 1979; "Wrangling over SALT Illustrates U.S.-Soviet Gulf," ibid., January 2, 1981 ("concocted," "pretext"); "Soviets; Cuban Issue Clouds U.S. Ties; Doubts Voiced About Carter's Goals," ibid., September 28, 1979 ("anti-Soviet"); Garthoff, *Détente and Confrontation*, at 840, 844–45.

72 "Jackson Says U.S. Seeks Deal with Soviet on Cuba," *New York Times*, September 14, 1979; "Carter's Job Rating at 19%, the Lowest Since the 1950s," *Washington Post*, September 14, 1979.

73 "Carter Drops out of 6.2 Mile Race Near Its Midpoint," *Washington Post*, September 16, 1979 ("rabbit stories," "headline"); "Carter, Exhausted and Pale, Drops out of 6-Mile Race," *New York Times*, September 16, 1979 (a hundred dropouts); "I've Got to Keep Trying," *Time* (October 1, 1979) ("speculation").

74 "Brzezinski Cautions Soviet on Cuba Unit," *New York Times*, September 23, 1979; Brzezinski, *Power and Principle*, at 350, 351.

75 "Gromyko, at U.N., Calls Concern over Soviet Unit in Cuba Artificial," *New York Times*, September 26, 1979; New York Question-and-Answer Session at a Town Meeting with Residents of the Borough of Queens, September 25, 1979, americanpresidency.org; "White House Attacks Kennedy's Questioning of Leadership," *Washington Post*, September 27, 1979 (denial).

76 Leonid Brezhnev to Carter, September 27, 1979, Box 149, Handwriting File; President's Address to the Nation re Soviet Brigade in Cuba, October 1, 1979, american presidency.org; "Castro Denounces Carter, Calls Troop Charge False," *Washington Post*, September 29, 1979.

77 Peace and National Security Address to the Nation on Soviet Combat Troops in Cuba and the Strategic Arms Limitation Treaty, October 1, 1979, americanpresidency.org ("brigade," "danger"); Zbigniew Brzezinski to Carter, September 29, 1979, Box 149, President's Address to the Nation: The Soviet Brigade in Cuba (1), Handwriting File ("Every"); Brzezinski, *Power and Principle*, at 351; "Senate Deeply Split on Carter's Speech," *New York Times*, October 3, 1979; "Soviet Troops in Cuba: The Carter Cave-in," *Human Events* (October 13, 1979).

78 Caldwell, *The Dynamics of Domestic Politics and Arms Control*, at 167–69 (Long, Christopher, delay); Newsom, *The Soviet Brigade in Cuba*, at 51 ("near-fatal").

79 Farber, *Taken Hostage*, at 125.

80 Ibid., at 125–26 ("imagine," "He'll"); Harris, *The Crisis*, at 193, 194 ("guys," "fire"). See "Why Carter Admitted the Shah," *New York Times Magazine*, May 17, 1981. The shah died in Egypt in July 1980.

81 Farber, *Taken Hostage*, at 128–47.

82 "Pakistanis Attack, Burn U.S. Embassy," *Washington Post*, November 22, 1979; "Khomeini's 'Holy War' Call Is Troubling Moslem World," ibid., November 25,

1979 ("stooge"); "You Could Die Here," *Time* (December 3, 1979); Hamilton Jordan to Carter, n.d., Box 34, Iran 11/79, Jordan Papers. See Steve Coll, *Ghost Wars: The Secret History of the CIA, Afghanistan, and Bin Laden, from the Soviet Invasion to September 10, 2001* (New York: Penguin, 2004), 21–37; Yaroslav Trofimov, *The Siege of Mecca: The Forgotten Uprising in Islam's Holiest Shrine and the Birth of Al Qaeda* (New York: Doubleday, 2007).

83 American Hostages in Iran: Statement Requesting Special Prayers for the Hostages During the Thanksgiving Holiday Weekend, November 17, 1979, americanpresidency.org; "Toughing Stance, U.S. Raps Khomeini for Stirring Turmoil," *Washington Post*, November 22, 1979.

84 "The President Employs the Better Part of Valor in Iran," *Washington Post*, November 18, 1979; Virginia Hammill, "Moslems Supporting Iran March Against U.S. Missions in 3 Nations," *Washington Post*, December 1, 1979; "Shah Flown to Texas; Embassy in Libya Hit; Mob Invades U.S. Embassy in Tripoli," ibid., December 3, 1979; "President at Arlington Rites for Marine Killed in Pakistan," ibid., December 1, 1979 ("haggard," "eyes"); President's News Conference of November 28, 1979, americanpresidency.org.

85 Ronald Reagan, Remarks Announcing Candidacy for Political Nomination, November 13, 1979, americanpresidency.org.

86 "The Latest Political Wisdom: Sagacities Etched in Sand," *Washington Post*, December 9, 1979.

87 "Carter Reversal on Arms Budget Meets Skeptical Hill Reception," *Washington Post*, December 14, 1979; "Senate Committee Says SALT Not in America's Best Interest," ibid., December 21, 1979 ("repose").

88 "The CIA's Intervention in Afghanistan," http://www.globalresearch.ca/articles/BRZ110A.html ("knowingly"). Asked in this 1988 interview whether he regretted that the CIA had aided the fundamentalists, who were to blow up the World Trade Center in 2001, Brzezinski said he did not. "What is most important to the history of the world?" he reportedly asked. "Some stirred up Moslems, or the liberation of Central Europe and the end of the Cold War?"; Garthoff, *Détente and Confrontation*, at 923–24; Robert Gates, *From the Shadows: The Ultimate Insider's Story of Five Presidents and How They Won the Cold War* (New York: Touchstone, 1996), 143–49; Andrew and Mitrokhin, *The World Was Going Our Way*, at 397–403. See Mohammad Yousaf and Mark Adkin, *Afghanistan—The Bear Trap: The Defeat of a Superpower* (Havertown, Pa.: Casemate, 1992), 235 for the contention that the Americans sought "a stalemate" in Afghanistan.

89 Gates, *From the Shadows*, at 134; Brzezinski, *Power and Principle*, at 428–29.

90 Dobrynin, *In Confidence*, at 442–43; Matthew Ouimet, *The Rise and Fall of the Brezhnev Doctrine in Foreign Policy* (Chapel Hill: University of North Carolina Press, 2003), 95 ("nothing"); Garthoff, *Détente and Confrontation*, at 937 ("notably").

91 Vladislav Zubok, *A Failed Empire: The Soviet Union in the Cold War from Stalin to Gorbachev* (Chapel Hill: University of North Carolina Press, 2007), 228, 262–64 (miscalculation, KGB role); Andrew and Mitrokhin, *The World Was Going Our Way*, at 399, 412–13 (KGB role); "Soviets Mass Force near Afghan Frontier; Carter Rebukes Brezhnev, Assails 'False' Response," *Washington Post*, January 1, 1980 ("murdered").

92 Zbigniew Brzezinski to Carter, Reflections on Soviet Intervention in Afghanistan, December 26, 1979, Box 17, Southwest Asia, Persian Gulf Afghanistan, 1/5/80–10/1/80, Brzezinski ("Soviet," "limited," "decisively," "certainly"); Brezezinski to Carter, Strategic Reaction to the Afghanistan Problem, January 3, 1980, 12/26/79–1/80, ibid. ("seventh," "domestic"); Brzezinski to Carter, Our Response to Soviet Intervention in Afghanistan, December 29, 1979, ibid.

93 *Meet the Press* Interview with Bill Monroe, David Broder, and Judy Woodruff, January 20, 1980, americanpresidency.org, and see Remarks at a White House Briefing for Congress, January 5, 1980, ibid.; "My Opinion of the Russians Has Changed Most Drastically . . . ," *Time* (January 14, 1980) ("strikingly"); Dobrynin, *In Confidence*, at 451.

94 Coll, *Ghost Wars*, at 65–66; "U.S. Evacuation Was 'Overreaction' to Embassy Attack, Pakistan Aide Says," *Washington Post*, November 27, 1979 ("Zia's").

95 State of the Union Address, January 20, 1980, americanpresidency.org; Burton and Scott Kaufman, *The Presidency of James Earl Carter*, 2d ed. (Lawrence: University of Kansas Press, 2006), 199. See Helmut Schmidt, *Men and Powers: A Political Retrospective*, trans. Ruth Hein (New York: Random House, 1989), 78–79, 206–08.

96 "Finally, Something to Cheer," *Washington Post*, February 26, 1980; "Fiscal '81 Budget a Victim of New Cold War," ibid., January 20, 1980 ("tense"); Jimmy Carter, *Meet the Press* Interview with Bill Monroe, Carl T. Rowan, David Broder, and Judy Woodruff, January 20, 1980, americanpresidency.org.

97 "Carter Stay-at-Home Strategy Seems to Be Helping Him," *Christian Science Monitor*, January 10, 1980.

98 " 'Sometimes a Party Must Sail Against the Wind,' " *Washington Post*, January 29, 1980 (reprinting Kennedy's January 28 address at Georgetown University).

99 Biven, *Jimmy Carter's Economy*, at 8 ("almost," quoting Stuart Eizenstat); "Gold and Silver Go Bonkers," *Time* (January 14, 1980); "Curbing Credit; Restraints Program: Did It Really Work?," *Washington Post*, October 5, 1980 ("panic-buying").

100 "House, by 335–34, Overrides Carter on Oil-Import Fee," *New York Times*, June 6, 1980; Martin Tolchin, "Oil-Import Fee Dies as Senate Overrides Carter by 68 to 10, ibid., June 7, 1980; "Price of Bullion Plummets Below $500 (U.S). Mark," *Globe and Mail*, March 18, 1980; "Stocks Drop Sharply, Bonds Gain Strength," *Washington Post*, March 18, 1980.

101 Wirthlin to Reagan, July 19, 1979.

102 Richard Allen to Bill Gavin, September 21, 1979, Box 3, File 3, Deaver and Hannaford Papers, Hoover Institution ("because," "measurable"); Richard Allen to Peter Hannaford and Martin Anderson, August 24, 1979, Box 3, File 3, ibid. (enclosing Reagan's articles "Why America Needs Israel" and "Israel: A Strategic Bastion of the United States"); Reagan, "SALT and the Search for Peace," September 15, 1979, Box 11, File 22, ibid.; "Reagan Urges Senate to Reject Arms Pact, But His Tone Is Softer," *New York Times*, September 16, 1979.

103 William Rusher, "Will Reagan 'Trim Toward the Center' for 1980?" *Human Events* (October 13, 1979); Deborah Strober and Gerald Strober, *The Reagan Presidency: An Oral History* (Washington, D.C.: Brassey's, 2003), 17 ("be Reagan"); Craig Shirley, *Rendezvous with Destiny: Ronald Reagan and the Campaign that Changed America* (Wilmington, Del.: Intercollegiate Studies Institute, 2009), 37, 66, 96–105; "Top Strategist Sears Under Fire: Reagan Campaign Backfires in Iowa," *Human Events* (February 2, 1980) ("neutered"); Stephen Knott and Jeffrey Chidester, *At Reagan's Side: Insiders' Recollections from Sacramento to the White House* (Lanham, Md.: Rowman & Littlefield), 54 ("Searscumcised," quoting *Manchester Union Leader*).

104 Myles Martel to Bill Carruthers, August 21, 1980 (analyzing Bush's debate style in primaries), Box 245, Debate Strategies (1), James Baker III Papers, Reagan Library; "George Bush: Eastern Establishment Candidate," *Human Events* (February 23, 1980); "The Outlook for Bush," ibid. (February 2, 1980) (Bush on Carter's 1976 campaign); Robert Novak, *The Prince of Darkness: Fifty Years Reporting in Washington* (New York: Three Rivers, 2007), 348 ("goofy"); "George Bush, Running Hard, with Brand New Track Suit," *New York Times*, April 27, 1980 ("preppy").

105 E-mail, Craig Shirley to Laura Kalman, January 2, 2009 (suggesting Sears remained invested in his strategy); but see Lou Cannon, *Governor Reagan: His Rise to Power* (New York: PublicAffairs, 2003), 458 (suggesting that Sears orchestrated the change in strategy); Novak, *The Prince of Darkness*, at 349–51 (commercials); "A Polite Republican Race Takes Turn for the Bitter; A Well-Mannered Republican Race Explodes into Anger," *Washington Post*, February 24, 1980 (quotations); Jack Germond and Jules Witcover, *Blue Smoke and Mirrors: How Reagan Won and Carter Lost the Election of 1980* (New York: Viking, 1981), 169 ("wimp," quoting Reagan adviser on Reagan's views of Bush).

106 Phyllis Schlafly to Edwin Meese, April 2, 1980, Correspondence 4/1980 (1), Meese

Papers; Joanie to Reagan, April 23, 1980, Box 13, Campaign Operations, Volunteers and Special Groups Programs (1), ibid. (noting that Reagan did not have even one "movement conservative" adviser).

107 "Could Be Unstoppable: Reagan Regains Front-Runner Role," *Human Events* (March 8, 1980); "South Carolina: Connally's Last Hurrah," ibid. (March 22, 1980); "Bickering Racks Crane's Presidential Campaign," *Washington Post*, May 5, 1979; Sidney Blumenthal, *The Permanent Campaign* (New York: Touchstone, 1982), 237 ("married"); "John Connally for President," *Conservative Digest* (February 1980); "Connally Gets Tough on Israel," *Newsweek* (October 22, 1979).

108 "ADA Says Anderson's No Liberal," *ADA World* (Spring 1980); "John Anderson: The Media Candidate," *Human Events* (March 15, 1980); "Retreat on the Energy Front," *Time* (January 21, 1980); Germond and Witcover, *Blue Smoke and Mirrors*, at 231, 227 ("mirrors").

109 "Ford Declares Reagan Can't Win; Invites G.O.P. to Ask Him to Run," *New York Times*, March 2, 1980; "Reagan: The Most Electable Republican," *Human Events* (March 22, 1980) ("planet"); "Fresh off the Links, Gerald Ford Reviews His Old Political Ties," *Wall Street Journal*, March 13, 1980 ("why"); "Ford Says He Won't Be a Candidate; Ford Bows out of Race; Unusual Odyssey Ends After Weeks Hoping for Draft," *Washington Post*, March 16, 1980.

110 Germond and Witcover, *Blue Smoke and Mirrors*, at 232–34; John Stacks, *Watershed: The Campaign for the Presidency 1980* (New York: Times Books, 1981), 166–68.

111 "George Bush Running Hard, with Brand New Track Suit"; Kevin Hopkins and Doug Bandow to Richard Wirthlin, May 21, 1980, Box 107, Campaign Operations/ Memos, Meese Papers ("must abandon"); William Casey to Reagan, Martin Anderson, Jack Kemp, Ed Meese, William Simon, April 7, 1980, Box 6, File 15, Deaver and Hannaford Papers, Hoover Institution (reporting concern in media over supply-side economics).

112 "The Devine Memo: A Winning Strategy for Ronald Reagan," *Human Events* (July 5, 1980).

113 Richard Wirthlin, "Some Initial Strategic and Tactical Considerations for the 1980 Presidential Campaign," March 28, 1980, Box 15, Strategic Consideration Report, Richard Wirthlin Papers, Hoover Institution; "Reagan Supporters Convene in Atlanta," *New York Times*, January 23, 1978 (Samson/Simpson); "Brace Yourself for Liberal Media Attack on Reagan," *Human Events* (May 3, 1980).

114 Gerald Pomper, "The Presidential Election," *The Election of 1980*, ed. Gerald Pomper (Chatham, N.J.: Chatham House, 1981), 65, 85 (Anderson); Phil Wise to Carter, December 7, 1979, Box 40, Memoranda: President Carter, October 1, 1979–December 31, 1979, Powell ("triplets"); "Teddy the Underdog Flies into the Maine Event," *Washington Post*, February 10, 1980 (Kennedy's drawbacks); "Kennedy Attack on Shah Brings Critical Barrage," ibid., December 4, 1979 ("violent," "umpteen"); Elizabeth Drew, *Portrait of an Election: The 1980 Campaign* (New York: Simon & Schuster, 1981), 126, 84 ("well-aimed"). The White House said later that it did not think the resolution applied to Jerusalem. When he realized it did, "Carter reaffirmed his administration's support for the resolution, which most of the American Jewish community read as anti-Israeli, whether Jerusalem was included or not." Kaufman and Kaufman, *The Presidency of James Earl Carter*, at 209.

115 "Carter Found Far Behind '76 Pace in Jewish Support," *New York Times*, October 25, 1980 ("God"); "Conn., N.Y. Vote Spells Bad News Ahead for Carter," *Washington Post*, March 27, 1980.

116 League of Women Voters Remarks and a Question-and-Answer Session at the League's Biennial Convention, May 5, 1980, americanpresidency.org ("provide"); David Engstrom, *Presidential Decision Making Adrift: The Carter Administration and the Mariel Boatlift* (Lanham, Md.: Rowman & Littlefield, 1997); "President Moves to Halt Illegal Cuban Boatlift; Carter's Ad Lib Affected Policy," *Washington Post*, May 15, 1980; "Resettling of Cuban Refugees Is Proceeding at a Slow Pace; Criminal Records, Homosexuality, Mental Illness Are Factors," ibid., February 10, 1981 (Clin-

ton); "The Latinization of Miami," *New York Times*, September 21, 1980; "Fire and Fury in Miami," *Time* (June 2, 1980).

117 American Hostages in Iran: Remarks to Reporters, April 1, 1980, americanpresidency.org; "Carter: A Worried Winner," *Newsweek* (April 14, 1980).

118 "Anger and Frustration," *Time* (April 14, 1980); Vance, *Hard Choices*, at 410–11; Kaufman and Kaufman, *The Presidency of James Earl Carter*, at 211–13.

119 "Vance Quits, Opposed Hostage Rescue Try; Iranians Display Bodies of U.S. Servicemen," *Washington Post*, April 27, 1980; "Politics: Fallout; Rivals of Carter Supportive, but Democrats Fear Fallout," ibid., April 26, 1980 ("botched," quoting NBC News public opinion analyst Richard Scammon).

120 Address to the Nation on the Rescue Attempt for American Hostages in Iran, April 25, 1980, americanpresidency.org; White House Briefing for Civic and Community Leaders Remarks and a Question-and-Answer Session, April 30, 1980, ibid. ("manageable"); "The Aftermath; Carter Responds by Returning to the Political Fray," *Washington Post*, May 4, 1980 ("somehow"); Remarks and a Question-and-Answer Session at a Townhall Meeting at Temple University, May 9, 1980, americanpresidency.org ("stronger"). The remark evidently caused Carter some embarrassment. See Department of State Reception for Cyrus Vance: Remarks at the Reception for the Former Secretary of State, November 18, 1980, ibid.; "Fiascos Can Help at the Polls, Carter Discovers," *Globe and Mail*, May 8, 1980 (Schlesinger).

EPILOGUE

1 "Good Intent, Poor Judgment Mark Handling of Billy Affair," *Washington Post*, July 27, 1980; Address, Democratic National Convention, August 12, 1980 http://www.jfklibrary.org/Historical+Resources/Archives/Reference+Desk/Speeches/EMK/Address+to+the+Democratic+National+Convention.htm.

2 Republican Party Platform of 1980, July 15, 1980, americanpresidency.org; Democratic Platform of August 11, 1980, ibid.

3 Walter Dean Burnham, "The 1980 Earthquake: Realignment, Reaction or What?," *The Hidden Election: Politics and Economics in the 1980 Presidential Campaign*, ed. Thomas Ferguson and Joel Rogers (New York: Pantheon, 1981), 98, 99–103; Jeff Greenfield, *The Real Campaign: How the Media Missed the Story of the 1980 Campaign* (New York: Summit, 1982); John Kelley, *Bringing the Market Back In: The Political Revitalization of Market Liberalism* (New York: New York University Press, 1997), 134–35, 141–42 ("statist," "small 'l' "); John Farrell, *Tip O'Neill and the Democratic Century* (Boston: Little, Brown, 2001), 536 ("pricks").

4 Gerald Pomper, "The Presidential Election," *The Election of 1980: Reports and Interpretations*, ed. Gerald Pomper (Chatham, N.J.: Chatham House, 1981), 65, 70–73; Andrew Busch, *Reagan's Victory: The Presidential Election of 1980 and the Rise of the Right* (Lawrence: University Press of Kansas, 2005), 127–28.

5 Leo Ribuffo, "Writing About Jimmy Carter as If He Was Andrew Jackson: The Carter Presidency in (Deep) Historical Perspective," Conference on the Thirtieth Anniversary of Carter's Inauguration, University of Georgia, January 19, 2007; Gerald Rafshoon, Memorandum for the President, "Campaign Themes," n.d., Box 24, Communications, Campaign Themes Memorandum, Rafshoon, Carter Library.

6 Patrick Caddell to Carter, n.d. (c. June 1980), Box 34, Campaign Strategies, 1980, Susan Clough Papers, Carter Library; Stuart Eizenstat to Carter, Platform Compromises, July 31, 1980, Box 38, Political Papers, Memos, ibid.; "Platform Battle on the Economy Is Still Looming," *New York Times*, August 12, 1980; "Rights and Abortion Planks Are Achieved by Feminists," ibid., August 13, 1980.

7 Jimmy Carter, Miller Center of Public Affairs, Oral History, November 29, 1982, http://webstorage3.mcpa.virginia.edu/poh/transcripts/ohp_1982_1129_carter.pdf, 59; Gerald Rafshoon to Carter, July 3, 1980, Box 34, Campaign Strategies, 1980, Clough Papers ("sign"); Patrick Caddell to Carter, n.d., ibid.; Rich Williamson to Paul Laxalt, William Casey, and Edwin Meese, October 21, 1980, Box 51, Staff

Advisers, Williamson, Richard, Edwin Meese III Papers, Reagan Library ("outset," "objective," emphasis in the original).

8 John Judis, *William F. Buckley, Jr.: Patron Saint of the Conservatives* (New York: Simon & Schuster, 1988), 413–14; Robert Kaufman, *Henry M. Jackson* (Seattle: University of Washington Press, 1980), 399–403; "Weyrich from Washington: The Reagan-Do-It-Yourself Administration," *Conservative Digest* (July 1980); "From the Publisher: Reagan's VP Choice Must Share His Own Views," ibid. (July 1980).

9 Craig Shirley, *Rendezvous with Destiny: Ronald Reagan and the Campaign that Changed America* (Wilmington, Del.: Intercollegiate Studies Institute, 2009), 6–7; Jack Germond and Jules Witcover, *Blue Smoke and Mirrors: How Reagan Won and Why Carter Lost the Election of 1980* (New York: Viking, 1981), 166–90; Richard Allen, Oral History, Miller Center of Public Affairs, May 28, 2002, http://web1.millercenter.org/poh/transcripts/ohp_2002_0528_allen.pdf, 42–44 ("liked," "There," "running"); Reagan Executive Advisory Committee Meeting, July 25, 1980, Box 125, Executive Advisory Committee Meeting, July 1980, Meese Papers, Reagan Library ("important," "notion," "who," "fully"); "George Will's Temper Tantrum," *Human Events*, June 28, 1980 ("tapioca"); Howard Phillips to Edwin Meese, July 24, 1980, Box 119, Mail from California (briefcase) (Personal Files), Meese Papers (thanking him for arranging meeting); "The Republicans in Detroit: Ford's Support Boosts Bush as Reagan's Running Mate," *Washington Post*, July 14, 1980. Allen has said that he suggested Bush as vice president when it became clear that the Reagan campaign had no vice presidential candidate ready if Ford declined. Allen, Miller Center Oral History Project, 44; Richard Allen, "George Herbert Walker Bush; The Accidental Vice President," *New York Times Magazine*, July 30, 2000. Michael Deaver, Edwin Meese, and Richard Wirthlin maintain that Reagan had engaged in a long search for a running mate that had yielded three names at the top of the list: Howard Baker, Ford, and Bush. According to Deaver, Meese, and Wirthlin, "we were never close to a 'deal' " with Ford, and Reagan privately told Meese on the afternoon he made Bush's nomination public that "he believed Bush was the best prospect. That night, he went to the convention hall to announce it was Bush and to quell the dream-ticket rumors that were building." Michael Deaver, Edwin Meese, and Richard Wirthlin, "The Accidental Vice President," *New York Times*, October 8, 2000.

10 Phillips to Meese, July 24, 1980 ("My greatest concern is that there does not seem to be any one in the Governor's inner circle who is an advocate for the perspectives of those of us in the New Right/Pro-Family movement"); "From the Publisher: Conservatives Must Work Hard and Vote for Ronald Reagan for President," *Conservative Digest* (September 1980); Petition to Ambassador George Bush, n.d., Box 119, Mail from California (briefcase) (Personal Files), Meese Papers; Draft, News from the Conservative Caucus, "For Immediate Release: Top George Bush Campaign Official Threatens Conservative Lobbying Group," n.d., ibid.; Phyllis Schlafly to Edwin Meese, Telegram, September 18, 1980, Box 136, Women's Issues (1), ibid.; Lyn Nofziger to William Casey, William Timmons, Edwin Meese, and Loreli Kinder, n.d., Box 151, Nofziger, Lyn, ibid. ("anti-ERA women"); "Right to Life Party Won't Slate Reagan," *New York Times*, August 27, 1980; Lorelei Kinder and Shannon Fairbanks to William Casey, Edwin Meese, Robert Garrick, Ed Gray, Bill Galvin, and Stef Halper, September 18, 1980, Box 150, Kinder, Lorelei, ibid. ("pro-life constituents"); Robert Billings to Max Hugel, n.d., Box 255, Christians: Evangelicals (1), William Timmons Papers, Reagan Library ("killed"); Max Hugel to William Timmons and Stan Anderson, September 11, 1980, ibid.; Jude Wanniski, "The Campaign Homestretch," October 1980, Box 117, Incoming September 30–October 2, 1980, Meese Papers.

11 Lou Cannon, *Governor Reagan: His Rise to Power* (New York: Public Affairs, 2003), 483 (Casey); Anna Chennault to Ronald and Nancy Reagan, April 28, 1980, Box 124, Memos 4/1980–6/1980, Meese Papers (calls); Jude Wanniski, FYI: Reagan Campaign, September 8, 1980, Box 6, File 9, Hannaford Papers, Hoover Institution; "With Nomination Won: Reagan Campaign Needs to Gear Up for Fall," *Human Events*

(July 7, 1980); "The Reagan Saboteurs," ibid., October 11, 1980; Patrick Caddell, Memorandum on Campaign Strategy, n.d. (c. June 25, 1980), Box 34, Clough Papers; John Stacks, *Watershed: The Campaign for the Presidency, 1980* (New York: Times Books, 1981), 232 (director).

12 Richard Wirthlin to Ronald Reagan, National Campaign Director, Co-Chairpersons and Deputy Campaign Directors, October 9, 1980, Box 21, Ronald Reagan Personal Letters, Richard Wirthlin Papers, Hoover Institution; "Reagan's Gaffes: If in Doubt, Repeat It," *Economist* (August 30, 1980); Joseph Lowndes, *From the New Deal to the New Right: Race and the Southern Origins of Modern Conservatism* (New Haven: Yale University Press, 2008), 160 ("conservatism"); "Race Issue in Campaign: A Chain Reaction," *New York Times*, September 27, 1980 ("could have been written," Neshoba); " 'States' Rights Move in West Influencing Reagan's Drive," ibid., July 5, 1980; Steven Hayward, *The Age of Reagan: The Fall of the Old Liberal Order: 1964–1980* (Roseville, Calif.: Forum/Prima, 2001), 696 (juxtaposing Reagan's endorsement of Sagebrush Rebellion with his remarks in Neshoba).

13 Richard Allen to Reagan, Taiwan and China Policy, July 1, 1980, Box 6, File 15, Peter Hannaford Papers, Hoover Institution (Taiwanese urging); "Reagan, Conceding Misstatements, Abandons Plan on Taiwan Office," *New York Times*, August 26, 1980; "Reagan Denies Plan to Answer Carter," ibid., August 17, 1980 (plants); Anthony Dolan to Edwin Meese, This Week, n.d., Box 869, Memorandums to Ed Meese: This Week's Activities, Dolan Papers; "Reagan in Union Talk, Says Carter Has Created a Severe Depression," ibid., August 28, 1980; Reagan Statement, September 1, 1980, Detroit, Michigan—Michigan State Fair, Box 560, Press Section, Ronald Reagan Statements to Press (1), Reagan Library ("birth"); Anthony Dolan to William Casey, Our Problem, n.d., Box 867, File: Memos Undated (3), Dolan Papers ("missile").

14 Jody Powell to Carter, n.d., Box 37, Planning Memo Re the Campaign, July 1980, Clough Papers: "Carter Says Reagan Injects Racism," *Washington Post*, September 17, 1980 (noting Harris's remarks and the Carter campaign's prior reliance on surrogates); Anthony Dolan to Edwin Meese, Box 867, Harris Smear/Ku Klux Klan (c. 9/1980), Dolan Papers; "Under Heavy Fire, Reagan Retreats on His Klan Ad Lib," *Washington Post*, September 3, 1980; Atlanta: Remarks at Meeting of Black Leaders, September 16, 1980, americanpresidency.org; Informal Exchange with Reporters, September 16, 1980, ibid.; "Carter Speech: An Extra Edge," *New York Times*, September 19, 1980.

15 Anthony Dolan to Edwin Meese, n.d., Carter smear, Box 867, Dolan Papers: Memos Undated (3/3).

16 See Anthony Dolan to Edwin Meese, Laxalt Letter, n.d., Box 148, Dolan, Tony (1), Meese Papers; see, e.g., "Running Mean," *Washington Post*, September 18, 1980; Torrance, California: Remarks and a Question-and-Answer Session at a Town Meeting, September 22, 1980, americanpresidency.org ("war or peace"); Remarks at the California State AFL-CIO Convention, September 22, 1980, ibid. (this time, "peace or war"); Texarkana, Remarks at a Rally with Local Residents, October 22, 1980, ibid. ("Governor," "trump"); Carter, Remarks at a Democratic National Committee Fundraising Reception, October 6, 1980, ibid. ("whether"); Albert Hunt, "The Campaign and the Issues," *The American Elections of 1980*, ed. Austin Ranney (Washington, D.C.: American Enterprise Institute, 1980), 142, 156 ("nice guy," quoting Greg Schneiders). Caddell had complained that reporters were "fairly easy on Reagan—ever since they proved wrong on Iowa," in part because of "their dislike of the President" in his June 25 memorandum on campaign strategy.

17 Cannon, *Governor Reagan*, at 483 ("old foot").

18 John McClaughry to Edwin Meese, Richard Allen, Martin Anderson, William Casey, Bob Gray, and Richard Wirthlin, Peace, October 15, 1980, Box 868, Memos 10/1980 (2), Dolan Papers ("We"); William Casey to Reagan, Deputy Directors, James Baker, Michael Deaver, Stuart Spencer, and Cliff White, September 26, 1980, Box 148, File: Casey (2/2), Meese Papers (competence); Richard Wirthlin to Reagan, William

Casey, and Deputy Campaign Directors, October 11, 1980, Box 152, Staff—Wirthlin (2), Meese Papers ("dangerous"); "Kremlin Isn't Wild About Carter—But It Likes Reagan Even Less," *Christian Science Monitor*, October 7, 1980.

19 Ed Gray to William Casey, Edwin Meese, Richard Wirthlin, James Baker, and William Timmons, October 13, 1980, Box 140: Debate: Cleveland (2), Meese Papers ("dying"); James Baker to Stuart Spencer, October 14, 1980, ibid. (2) (reporting on sentiment at Reagan Headquarters); Richard Nixon to Reagan, October 22, 1980, ibid.

20 Wayne Valis to James Baker, October 21, 1980, Box 140, Debate: Cleveland (2), Meese Papers ("reliable"); Presidential Debate, October 28, 1980, americanpresidency.org; on the national response to Carter's allusion to his daughter, Amy, see Germond and Witcover, *Blue Smoke and Mirrors*, at 284. Craig Shirley has argued persuasively that it was Paul Corbin, a veteran of the 1980 Ted Kennedy campaign, "who—with a little help from some friends—stole the Carter briefing books and gave them to Ronald Reagan's campaign." Shirley, *Rendezvous with Destiny*, at 420.

21 Stef Halper to Edwin Meese, The Hostage Question, October 19, 1980, Box 130, Subject Files Hostages (1), Meese Papers; Hostages, n.d., Box 140, Debate: Cleveland (3), ibid.

22 "How Sweet It Is: Victory at Last!," *Human Events* (November 15, 1980); Jeffrey Hart, "The Liberal Establishment Has Been Overthrown," ibid. (November 29, 1980).

23 Busch, *Reagan's Victory*, at 157, 159, 137–38. See William Schneider, "The November 5 Vote for President: What Did It Mean?," *The American Elections of 1980*, at 212, 213–14.

24 "The Reverend Jerry Who?," *Newsweek* (December 22, 1980).

25 " 'Christian Right' Groups Welcome Reagan Victory," *Human Events* (November 15, 1980) (Falwell); "New Right Should Give Reagan a Chance," ibid. (November 22, 1980); "Baker, Bell, Regan, Haig, Pierce, Clausen, Weinberger, Carlucci Worry Conservatives," *Conservative Digest* (February 1981); "Shortage of Reaganites in Administration Concerns, Surprises, Supporters of Reagan," ibid.; "Religious Right Urged to Fight Harder on the Issues to Achieve Their Goals: New Right Leaders Stress that Battle Has Just Begun and Now Is the Time for Redoubling of Common Effort," ibid.

26 "O'Connor Choice Breaks Reagan Promise, Made in Haste and Harms His Coalition," *Conservative Digest* (August 1981); "That Sound You Hear Is the Cracking Apart of Reagan's Great Electoral Coalition," ibid.; Richard Viguerie to Dear Friend, August 19, 1981, Box 2, Conservative Groups [OA 2903], Lee Atwater Papers, Reagan Library; Cal Thomas to James Baker, October 9, 1981, Morton Blackwell Papers, Moral Majority (2) [OA 90709], ibid.; "Exclusive Interview with Secretary James Watt: Despite Critics, Interior Dept. Makes Rapid Progress," *Human Events* (July 3, 1982) ("I"); James Turner, " 'The Specter of Environmentalism': Wilderness, Environmental Politics, and the Evolution of the New Right," *Journal of American History*, 96 (June 2009): 123, 134–35; Jedediah Roers, "Land Grabbers, Toadstool Worshippers, and the Sagebrush Rebellion in Utah, 1979–1981" (M.A. Thesis, History, Brigham Young University, 2005), 119 ("faded"), http://contentdm.lib.byu.edu/ETD/image/etd954.pdf.

27 Executive Summary of the Conservative Political Conference, First Year Reagan Review, January 21, 1982, Box 2, Conservative Groups 1982 [OA 2903], Atwater Papers; Statement of Conservative Leaders, Washington, D.C., January 21, 1982, ibid.; Ed Rollins to James Baker, n.d., ibid. (quotations); "Conservative Leaders Denounce Reagan Tax Hike," July 20, 1982, ibid.; Statement of Conservative Leaders, July 8, 1982 (Taiwan), ibid.; "Washington Talk; Neoconservatives and Reagan: Uneasy Coalition," *New York Times*, September 28, 1971; "The Neoconservative Anguish over Reagan's Foreign Policy," ibid., May 2, 1982.

28 Statement of Conservative Leaders, July 8, 1982, Box 2, Conservative Groups [OA 2903], Atwater Papers; Conservative Leaders Denounce Reagan Tax Hike, July 20, 1982, ibid.; Donald Critchlow, "Mobilizing Women: The Social Issue," *The Reagan*

Presidency, ed. W. Elliot Brownlee and Hugh Davis Graham (Lawrence: University Press of Kansas, 2003), 293, 303 ("critical"); Pamela Turner to Kenneth Duberstein, January 19, 1982, Box 1, Memos to Duberstein (5) [OA 1285], Pamela Turner, Reagan Library ("livid"); Gregory Newell, Schedule Proposal, Meeting with Senator Strom Thurmond and Senator Orrin Hatch, January 19, 1982, ibid. ("non-Reaganites"); John Judis, *William F. Buckley, Jr.: Patron Saint of Conservatives* (New York: Simon & Schuster, 1988), 431; Editors of *National Review*, *Tear Down This Wall: The Reagan Revolution—A National Review History* (New York: Continuum, 2004).

29 "Has Reagan Deserted the Conservatives?," *Conservative Digest* (July 1982); Ronald Reagan, *The Reagan Diaries*, ed. Douglas Brinkley (New York: HarperCollins, 2007), 97.

30 Cal Thomas and Ed Dobson, *Blinded by Might: Why the Religious Right Can't Save America* (Grand Rapids: Zondervan, 2000), 82–83 (Falwell); Bob Jones to Ronald Reagan, December 30, 1983, Bob Jones University [OA 90804], Blackwell Papers; "The New Right: Betrayed?," *Newsweek* (February 7, 1983) ("You"); "Shoring Up the Right," ibid. October 10, 1983.

31 Richard Viguerie, "What Reagan Revolution?: A Conservative Laments a Lost Chance to Alter the Political Balance," *Washington Post*, August 21, 1988; Irving Kristol, "The Reagan Revolution that Never Was," *Wall Street Journal*, April 19, 1988. As Steven Hayward writes, "The extent to which conservatives were frustrated with Reagan much of the time, particularly during his second term, is another aspect of the Reagan years that has receded from view." Hayward, *The Age of Reagan: The Conservative Counterrevolution 1980–1989* (New York: Crown Forum, 2009), 6.

32 "Sorry, Folks, We Have to Have A President," *Washington Post*, November 2, 1980; "The Reagan Difference," ibid., December 11, 1981; James Ceaser, "The Theory of Governance of the Reagan Administration," *The Reagan Presidency and the Governing of America*, ed. John Palmer and Isabel Sawhill (Washington, D.C.: Urban Institute, 1984), 57, 67; Haynes Johnson, *Sleepwalking Through History: America in the Reagan Years* (New York: W. W. Norton, 1991), 163 ("rueful").

INDEX

Page numbers beginning with 367 refer to notes.